Governing China in the 21st Century

Series Editor
Yijia Jing
Institute for Global Public Policy
Fudan University
Shanghai, China

Since 1978, China's political and social systems have transformed significantly to accommodate the world's largest population and second largest economy. These changes have grown more complex and challenging as China deals with modernization, globalization, and informatization. The unique path of sociopolitical development of China hardly fits within any existing frame of reference. The number of scientific explorations of China's political and social development, as well as contributions to international literature from Chinese scholars living and researching in Mainland China, has been growing fast. This series publishes research by Chinese and international scholars on China's politics, diplomacy, public affairs, and social and economic issues for the international academic community.

Chang Su

From Two to Three

Motivations and Outcomes in Chinese-initiated Tripartite Cooperation Infrastructure and Construction Projects

palgrave
macmillan

Chang Su
School of Global Affairs
King's College London
London, United Kingdom

ISSN 2730-6968 ISSN 2730-6976 (electronic)
Governing China in the 21st Century
ISBN 978-981-95-8707-0 ISBN 978-981-95-8708-7 (eBook)
https://doi.org/10.1007/978-981-95-8708-7

This Palgrave Macmillan imprint is published by the registered company Springer Nature Singapore Pte Ltd.
The registered company address is: 152 Beach Road, #21-01/04 Gateway East, Singapore 189721, Singapore

Acknowledgements

This monograph is based on my PhD research. The completion of the doctorate was an incredibly rewarding and transformative journey, and I am filled with deep gratitude for those who have supported me throughout. These four years have been marked not only by academic growth but also by the invaluable connections, encouragement, and guidance that have uplifted me during every step of the way.

First and foremost, I want to express my profound gratitude to my supervisor, Dr. Jan Knoerich. His insightful guidance, unwavering support, and thoughtful feedback have been invaluable to me. His mentorship has been a source of both intellectual and personal growth, and I cannot imagine having reached this point without his patience and encouragement.

Then I would like to express my gratitude to all the interviewees who contributed to my research, thank you for your time and insights. Each of you played an important role in bringing this project to completion. I am also grateful to the editors of this book for their professionalism support throughout the publication process. Their thoughtful comments and guidance helped improve the manuscript and bring this work to publication.

Finally, my deepest appreciation goes to my families. Your boundless love and encouragement have been the foundation upon which this entire journey rests. You have always believed in me, even when I struggled to believe in myself.

This book is the product of sustained academic effort, but it is equally indebted to the support and confidence extended to me by those acknowledged here.

Contents

List of Abbreviations

ADB	Asian Development Bank
AFD	Agence Française de Développement
AIIB	Asian Infrastructure Investment Bank
B3W	Build Back Better World
BMZ	Germany's Federal Ministry for Economic Cooperation and Development
BOO	Build, Own, Operate
BOOT	Build, Own, Operate, and Transfer
BOT	Build, Operate, and Transfer
BRI	The Belt and Road Initiative
BRICS	Brazil, Russia, India, China, and South Africa
CADF	China Africa Development Fund
CCCC	China Communications Construction Company
CDB	China Development Bank
CEEC	China Energy Engineering Group Company Limited
CFD	Contract for Difference Model
CGGC	China Gezhouba Group Company Limited
CGN	China General Nuclear Power Corporation
CHEC	China Harbour Engineering Company
CHEXIM	The Export-Import Bank of China
CMHI	China Merchants Holding International
CNOOC	China National Offshore Oil Corporation
CNPC	China National Petroleum Corporation
CRBC	China Road and Bridge Corporation
CRCC	China Railway Construction Corporation Limited
CSCEC	China State Construction Engineering Corporation
CTG	China Three Gorges

DAC	Development Assistance Committee
DBFO	Design Build-Finance Operate
DCMF	Design-Construct-Manage-Finance
EDF	Électricité de France
EDP	Energias de Portugal
EMNEs	Emerging Market Multinational Enterprises
EPC	Engineering, Procurement, and Construction
EPR	European Pressurized Reactor Technology
FDI	Foreign Direct Investment
GCL	Government Concessional Loan
GDA	Generic Design Assessment
HPC	Hinkley Point C Nuclear Station
HPR1000	Hualong One Nuclear Reactor Technology
ICRC	International Committee of the Red Cross
IDSP	Ibom Deep Sea Port
IPP	Independent Power Producer
JBF	Japan Business Federation
JICA	The Japanese International Cooperation
JV	Joint Venture
LAC	Latin America and the Caribbean Region
LFTZ	Lekki Free Trade Zone
LNG	Liquefied Natural Gas
LPLEL	Lekki Port LFTZ Enterprise Limited
M&A	Mergers and Acquisitions
MAF	Ministry of Foreign Affairs of the People's Republic of China
MNEs	Multinational Enterprises
MOC/MOFCOM	The Ministry of Commerce of the People's Republic of China
MOUs	Memoranda of Understanding
NDRC	National Development and Reform Commission of China
NEPAD	New Partnership for Africa's Development
NPA	Nigerian Ports Authority
O&M	Operation and Management
ODA	Official Development Assistance
OECD	The Organisation for Economic Co-Operation and Development
PBC	Preferential Export Buyer's Credit
PGII	Partnership for Global Infrastructure and Investment
PowerChina	Power Construction Corporation of China
QII	Quality Infrastructure Investment

R&D	Research and Development
RAB	Regulated Asset Base
SASAC	State-Owned Assets Supervision and Administration Commission (China)
SEPCO III	Shandong Electric Power Construction Corporation III
SGCC	State Grid Corporation of China
SINOPEC	Sinopec Group
SINOSURE	China Export & Credit Insurance Corporation
SMBC	Sumitomo Mitsui Banking Corporation
SOE	State-Owned Enterprises
SPV	Special Purpose Vehicle
TICT	Tincan Island Container Terminal Limited
TPMC	Third-Partner Market Cooperation
UN	United Nations
UNDP	United Nations Development Programme
UNESCO	United Nations Educational, Scientific and Cultural Organisation
UNHCR	United Nations High Commissioner for Refugees
UNICEF	United Nations International Children's Emergency Fund
USD	United States Dollar
WFP	World Food Programme
WHO	World Health Organisation

List of Figures

List of Tables

CHAPTER 1

Introduction

1.1 Chinese Tripartite Cooperation: Research Problem and Questions

In the field of international development, bilateral cooperation mechanisms, where one country offers financial and other support to another to advance the latter's economic and social development, have been in operation for many years. Many advanced economies have, over the past decades, engaged in various forms of bilateral development cooperation, and China also has for a long time supported the developing world through bilateral means. China has, for example, formulated the 'Angola Model' and the Belt and Road Initiative (BRI) to promote development elsewhere (Samy, 2010; Halper, 2010; Tan-Mullins et al., 2010; Begu et al., 2018; Jepson, 2021). Its approaches to development assistance have differed in many ways from those of traditional donors (i.e., advanced economies), for instance focusing on infrastructure projects through the provision of loans, rather than the traditional donors' preference for aid that is conditioned on the adherence to fiscal, governance, and other conditions. Yet, despite these differences in development approach, China has in more recent years developed a growing interest in engaging traditional donor countries in some of its overseas development projects through collaborative efforts. One important way in which both China and the traditional donor countries work together in international development is the engagement in what this study will refer to as 'tripartite cooperation'.

C. Su, *From Two to Three*, Governing China in the 21st Century,
https://doi.org/10.1007/978-981-95-8708-7_1

Chinese tripartite cooperation emerged in 2015, when the Chinese government proposed 'third-party market cooperation' (第三方市场合作, *dì sān fāng shì chǎng hé zuò*) as a new approach that facilitates "the economic cooperation between Chinese enterprises and enterprises of other countries in third-party markets" (NDRC, 2019, p. 2). This involves Chinese business entities collaborating with companies from advanced economies in areas such as investment, construction, consultation, and operation to promote industrial and infrastructure development in third-party developing countries. Through this new tripartite cooperation initiative, the Chinese government aims to engage more traditional donor countries[1] in jointly undertaking cooperative activities in beneficiary countries, as a way to complement bilateral projects through a formal policy. Chinese government media often present tripartite cooperation as an ideal 'triple win' plan for all participants, involving China, traditional donor countries as collaborators, and beneficiary countries where the projects take place. These reports assert that through the tripartite cooperation mechanism, China and traditional donor countries can synergise their production capacity, resources, and innovative technology to meet the needs of beneficiary countries. In addition, this approach could reduce vicious competition, upgrade the pattern of international division of labour, as well as improve the existing global governance system and international cooperation model (NDRC, 2019; Zheng 2020; Feng, 2019).

[1] To clarify the usage of terms in the theoretical chapters of this research:

Traditional Donor Countries: The term 'traditional donor countries' substitutes terms such as 'North' countries, OECD-DAC donors, developed countries, and Western countries. It will also be used when reviewing the history of tripartite cooperation and the international development regime. This term specifically refers to OECD-DAC countries with a history of providing development aid and established frameworks or standards. The traditional donor countries typically include 32 OECD-DAC members. Sixteen of these countries have participated in Chinese-initiated tripartite cooperation projects in this research: Australia, Austria, Belgium, Canada, France, Germany, Greece, Italy, Japan, Korea, the Netherlands, Portugal, Spain, Switzerland, the United Kingdom, and the United States.

Advanced Economies: The term 'advanced economies' will be used when discussing tripartite cooperation projects in practice. It refers to countries with advanced technology, infrastructure, and high-income levels, leveraging these advantages in tripartite projects. This suggests a complementary relationship between China's engineering and financing abilities and the technological and management skills of advanced economies. For Chinese-initiated tripartite cooperation projects in this research, 'advanced economies' include the 16 OECD-DAC countries plus Singapore.

In this research, tripartite cooperation is defined as economic collaboration involving China, its partner countries, and beneficiary countries. These cooperative activities encompass project financing, construction, operation, and services related to economic infrastructure projects. China's partner countries primarily refer to advanced economies with formal or informal cooperation arrangements with China, including Australia, Austria, Belgium, Canada, France, Germany, Greece, Italy, Japan, South Korea, the Netherlands, Portugal, Singapore, Spain, Switzerland, the United Kingdom, and the United States. While tripartite cooperation intersects with international development and investment, it is classified as economic cooperation because the beneficiary countries encompass both developed and developing countries.

However, the feasibility of such tripartite cooperation can also be put into question. Traditional bilateral partnerships have their own advantages, such as lower transaction costs and tighter partnerships. Moreover, in tripartite cooperation, divergent development scopes and approaches to infrastructure projects and underlying governance of development issues between China and traditional donor countries may generate friction and increased costs. For example, traditional donor countries focus on poverty reduction, the environment, healthcare, education, infrastructure, democracy promotion, and pluralistic civil society (Carbone 2011, 2014; Carothers, 2008; Alesina & Dollar, 2000; Youngs, 2008). International financing groups, such as the IMF and World Bank, typically provide funding with attached standards related to labour, fiscal policies, and macroeconomic management (Mody & Rebucci, 2006; World Bank, 2017). In contrast, China often adopts a no-strings-attached loan approach, focusing on cost efficiency (Tseng & Krog, 2016; Kjøllesdal & Welle-Strand, 2010; Bräutigam, 2011). In addition, with the involvement of more participants, complex processes may generate more transaction costs during the negotiation, bargaining and risk transferring (Motiar Rahman & Kumaraswamy, 2002; Tang et al., 2020; Lam et al., 2007). It is therefore important to explore in greater detail as to why participants opt for a tripartite cooperation model and how collaboration in a group of three lead to different project outcomes.

To address this problem, this research will examine Chinese tripartite cooperation projects in economic infrastructure, particularly in the transportation and energy sectors, seeking insights on the following research questions:

- Why do participants opt for a tripartite cooperation model even though they have to potentially bear the additional transaction costs?
- What are the determinants for countries and/or firms to engage in tripartite cooperation, and how do their actions within the tripartite model reshape project finance activities?
- How does the involvement of a third partner bring additional benefits, complexities, and challenges in infrastructure and construction projects?

This introduction chapter offers a background discussion on Chinese tripartite cooperation projects. It then outlines the research rationales and contributions, methodology, and findings of this research. Finally, it outlines the structure of this research.

1.2 Global Context: Recent Trends in the International Development Regime

In recent years, one important trend in international development is 'the rise of the Global South'. China, as a representative of emerging donor countries, has had an unprecedented impact on the existing international development regime (Mawdsley, 2012). In contrast to the core values of traditional donor countries, such as good governance, fiscal soundness, poverty eradication, anti-corruption, market-oriented reforms, democratic norms, peace and security, and debt relief (OECD, 2016), China's international development policies focus more on infrastructure and trade relations. Its international development packages often include commercial financing arrangements and trade agreements (Severino and Ray, 2009; Apodaca, 2017). China often blends international assistance with commercial loans, investment, trade, and finance, and this development approach has been widely used in China's BRI projects, which offers a newly legitimised approach to development finance that focuses on infrastructure development (Griffiths, 2013; Janus et al. 2014).

In response to China's efforts to build infrastructure projects in a 'better' way, traditional donor countries have recently begun to offer alternatives to developing countries through their own infrastructure assistance plans, adhering to the OECD-DAC standard. For example, at the 2019 Group of 20 (G20) summit, Japan proposed a set of principles for quality infrastructure investment. Then Japan and the EU announced a 'Partnership on Sustainable Connectivity and Quality Infrastructure.' Then Japan, the United States, and Australia created the 'Blue Dot Network' to develop higher criteria on financial transparency and environmental sustainability for certifying worldwide infrastructure projects. In 2021, the European Parliament announced the EU-Asia Connectivity Strategy that aims to "contribute to the enhanced prosperity, safety and resilience of people and societies in Europe and Asia"[2] and the EU Global Gateway strategy that aims to "boost smart, clean and secure links in digital, energy and transport sectors and to strengthen health, education and research systems across the world."[3] In the same year, the Group of Seven (G7) declared the initiative Build Back Better World (B3W) as "an affirmative initiative for meeting the tremendous infrastructure needs of low- and middle-income countries to respond to China's BRI moving back."[4] The US government launched the Partnership for Global Infrastructure and Investment (PGII) in 2022 to support global infrastructure investment.[5] These actions of traditional donor countries suggest that influenced by the Chinese development assistance approach, traditional donor countries and international financing institutions have changed their approach, reallocating a part of supportive funding from good governance principles such as elections, democratic promotion, market-oriented reforms, and legislative institutions, back to hard infrastructure construction such as roads, railways, and power stations (Baumann 2017; Skupien, 2019).

[2] The Diplomatic Service of European Union., "Connecting Europe & Asia: The EU Strategy," EEAS Website, 2019, https://www.eeas.europa.eu/eeas/connecting-europe-asia-eu-strategy_en.

[3] European Commission, "Global Gateway," European Commission, 2023, https://commission.europa.eu/strategy-and-policy/priorities-2019-2024/stronger-europe-world/global-gateway_en.

[4] The White House, "Fact Sheet: President Biden and G7 Leaders Launch Build Back Better World (B3W) Partnership," The White House, June 12, 2021, https://www.whitehouse.gov/briefing-room/statements-releases/2021/06/12/fact-sheet-president-biden-and-g7-leaders-launch-build-back-better-world-b3w-partnership/.

[5] The White House, "FACT SHEET: President Biden and G7 Leaders Formally Launch the Partnership for Global Infrastructure and Investment," The White House, June 26, 2022, https://www.whitehouse.gov/briefing-room/statements-releases/2022/06/26/fact-sheet-president-biden-and-g7-leaders-formally-launch-the-partnership-for-global-infrastructure-and-investment/.

Traditional donor countries have also aimed to address these changes in the international development landscape by collaborating more with emerging nations to minimise paternalistic approaches to development assistance (where traditional donors claim to know the best approaches to development) and enhance the political legitimacy of development projects (Chahoud 2008; Rosseel et al., 2009; Power et al., 2012; Dornan and Brant, 2014). Tripartite development cooperation is therefore viewed by traditional donor countries as an alternative policy tool to existing bilateral development cooperation (Stahl, 2012). There have already been tripartite cooperations between traditional donor countries in areas such as agriculture and food security, education, health, social infrastructure and services, disaster risk management, and environment protection (Pantoja, 2009; Schulz, 2010; OECD, 2012). In contrast to these efforts of traditional donor countries, the Chinese tripartite cooperation projects focus more on hard infrastructure projects and economic activities.

However, such large-scale infrastructure projects often involve multiple stakeholders and complex systems that integrate with national strategies and corporate profitability, leading to increased conflicts, uncertainty, and risks (Dooms, 2010; Osipova and Eriksson, 2013; Guo et al., 2014; Lawer, 2019). These challenges are exacerbated by the scarcity of 'safe' and 'investable' projects due to the saturation of fully developed, low-risk, and high-profit international infrastructure projects in recent years (Ehlers, 2014; Zelikow & Savas, 2022). Chinese enterprises are compelled to venture into riskier regions to develop infrastructure projects because the safe places have already been occupied by traditional donor countries' firms (Cai, 2017; Jones & Hameiri, 2020; Huld, 2022). At the same time, traditional donor countries' firms now seek risk-sharing partnerships rather than undertaking high-risk projects individually to sustain profitability and growth rates while effectively controlling risks (Lool, 2016). Consequently, both Chinese and traditional donor countries' firms aspire to use the tripartite cooperation mechanism to share risks in large-scale infrastructure projects.

1.3 Research Rationales: Why Is this Research Important?

Many previous documents (Kim and Lightfoot, 2011; GPI, 2019; Zhang, 2020) claim that China and traditional donor countries could—at least in theory—use their respective advantages to enhance transparency, improve effectiveness, and ensure the long-term sustainability of development projects through tripartite cooperation. However, previous research has not investigated the detailed process of existing Chinese tripartite cooperation projects, nor how they generate the anticipated synergies and costs. It remains unclear when and why governments and firms opt for tripartite cooperation, how China and traditional donor countries and their firms work together through tripartite cooperation, and how they can do so effectively in theory and practically.

1.3.1 *Theoretical and Practical Gaps in Understanding Tripartite Cooperation*

There are some theoretical gaps in existing studies of tripartite cooperation. Firstly, the literature lacks systematic reviews on tripartite cooperation. Previous global research has documented the impacts of emerging economies on changing the international development system (Chaturvedi et al. 2012; Akinola, 2015; Davies, 2010; Cheru et al. 2013). However, most of this literature focuses on the international policies and practices of bilateral cooperation. While there are a few books on Germany-led (Kaplan et al., 2020) and Japan-led (Stallings & Szkely, 1993) tripartite cooperation projects, this literature remains limited. Kaplan et al. (2020) evaluate the objectives and expectations of Germany-led tripartite cooperation, noting its potential to achieve impacts in beneficiary countries as well as improve relationships between DAC donors and emerging countries. However, their analysis remains at the country level without focusing on specific projects. Stallings and Szkely (1993) discuss Japanese tripartite cooperation since the 1980s, highlighting collaboration with the United States and leveraging experience and social connections in Latin America, but this book is obsolete and does not reflect current practices in tripartite cooperation. China-led tripartite cooperation has not been systematically reviewed.

Secondly, the literature specifically on Chinese tripartite cooperation is also nascent. The majority of research concentrates more on trilateral cooperation from the macro perspective of the country level (e.g., Zhang, 2017a, 2017b, 2018; Zhang & Li, 2020; He and Yan 2021). Studies find that the Chinese government strengthens bilateral partnerships with traditional donor countries by working together in other developing countries' markets. Normally, these researchers only discussed tripartite cooperation from a macro point of view, and they explained tripartite cooperation through vague assumptions such as comparative advantage theory in international economics, or common interests in international cooperation (e.g., Men and Yu, 2020; Wu and Ding, 2020). Furthermore, there is less work reviewing China's tripartite cooperation projects in detail. Most literature only describes the general facts of projects, and it does not thoroughly analyse the financing and operating process of these Chinese tripartite cooperation projects. Additionally, there is a lack of review on the determinants[6] for participants to engage in tripartite cooperation.

Thirdly, there is a theoretical gap when applying economics theories to tripartite cooperation. Previous researchers such as Deng (2013), Zhang (2017a), Kamwengo (2020), and Fordelone (2011) have utilised Ricardo's theory, focusing on comparative advantages and industrial specialisation. However, they assume transaction costs[7] are zero and overlook the costs of coordination and transactions within the intricate tripartite cooperation structure. They do not investigate how the additional partner influences the change of transaction costs and the benefits in practical projects. Therefore, the differences between traditional bilateral cooperative approaches and trilateral cooperation need to be explored further. This research aims to fill this gap by providing a systematic examination of Chinese tripartite cooperation, identifying why participants choose the tripartite cooperation model, and examining transaction costs in the context of infrastructure projects.

There are also practical challenges associated with tripartite cooperation. It is worthwhile to investigate the underlying reasons behind its sluggish development. Tripartite cooperation has a developmental history

[6] In this research, the 'determinants' of tripartite cooperation projects primarily focus on the motivations of governments and firms to engage in such collaboration.

[7] The theory category comprises two components: transaction costs and additional benefits. These two categories prove instrumental in addressing the research question concerning why participants choose the tripartite cooperation model over other types of cooperation, despite incurring additional transaction costs.

Transaction costs involve changes in costs during the risk diversification process and the transfer of technology, knowledge, and experience. In this research, transaction cost is narrowly defined as the cost of facilitating the completion of tripartite cooperation projects. This includes negotiation costs, contract costs, agency costs, and other related expenses that are not directly associated with the construction and operation of projects. Further discussion on the definition of transaction cost is in Chap. 3.

Additional benefits encompass financial advantages and operational benefits, such as the potential for tripartite cooperation to reduce capital costs, provide tax incentives, leverage economies of scale for enhanced efficiency, and facilitate technology upgrades.

spanning over four decades, with Japan's practices in the 1970s, Germany's in the 1980s, and the OECD's promotion of triangular cooperation since the 1990s. However, tripartite cooperation has not yet become mainstream within the international development regime. Compared to bilateral cooperation, the term 'tripartite cooperation' is still rarely mentioned in international development discourse today.

For China-led tripartite cooperation, there are also various challenges such as the stagnation of the cooperative process at the country level, the dilatory process of existing projects, and the standstill of initiating new projects. At the country level, there has been no progress since 2019 after China signed memoranda of understanding (MOUs) with 14 countries. China did not add any new members to its Tripartite Cooperation MOUs list. Under such contexts, the Chinese government needs to consider promoting tripartite cooperation continually or returning to bilateral cooperation that collaborates directly with the beneficiary countries (Scholz, 2020; Derviş, 2020; Banga, 2021).

As of June 2023, there were 68 China-led tripartite cooperation projects, but some projects had/have been suspended because the partner firms quit, or the local community protested.[8] Many potential participants doubt the feasibility and sustainability of tripartite cooperation projects. Additionally, with increasing global competition and conflicts, they hesitate to join Chinese infrastructure projects at the current stage.

Because China has gradually played a critical role in the international development regime, it is important to analyse China's tripartite cooperation model and how its actions influence other players' activities. It is crucial to study Chinese tripartite cooperation when it confronts both theoretical and practical challenges.

1.3.2 *Contributions of this Research*

To address the knowledge gaps mentioned above, this research examines why China, traditional donor countries, and local entities are interested in engaging in tripartite cooperation projects, and how these three parties collaborate to make these large and complex projects work in practice, both at the country level and at the project level. In the context of dynamic power shifts, it is important to understand and analyse China's cooperative behaviours in the international development system. Accordingly, this

[8] According to the author's database, see Appendix B.

research makes several contributions to the existing literature by applying economic and international business theories to tripartite cooperation, analysing the global landscape of Chinese tripartite cooperations and considering specific case studies to understand the motivations and outcomes of such projects.

The first contribution of this research is from a theoretical perspective. This research expands the use of existing theories to the context of project finance and tripartite cooperation. I primarily utilise New Institutional Economics (NIE), drawing insights from transaction cost economics (Coase, 1937, 1960; Williamson, 1971, 1975; North, 1991), international relation theories (Nye & Keohane, 1977; Keohane, 1984; Moravcsik, 1993; Smith & Ikenberry, 2001; Wendt, 1999; Mearsheimer, 2001; Devetak et al., 2011), and internalisation theories (Buckley and Casson, 1976; Teece 1981, 1986; Hennart 1988; Rugman, 1985) to understand tripartite cooperation projects.

This research extends these theoretical frameworks to the realm of tripartite cooperation. Specifically, this research applies transaction cost and internalisation theories to understand tripartite cooperation projects and the concept of transaction costs in the context of infrastructure projects. My main argument is that tripartite cooperation functions as a form of *semi-internalisation*—it is more internalised than transactions in the open market or at arm's length but less internalised than purely bilateral cooperation. Bilateral cooperation can be considerably internalised given the involvement of fewer countries and firms, while tripartite cooperation involves more contracts among firms that can increase transaction costs, even though actors involved employ Special Purpose Vehicles (SPVs) and other internalised structures to reduce these transaction costs.

Additionally, foreign direct investment (FDI) theories, such as the eclectic paradigm (Dunning, 1988, 2001) and the springboard perspective (Luo and Tung, 2007, 2018), are used to explore the determinants for firms to engage in tripartite cooperation. This study expands FDI theories to assess their relevance and applicability to the tripartite cooperation mode of international development. It aims to fill a gap in the literature by providing a systematic examination of Chinese tripartite cooperation. As this research focuses on tripartite cooperation projects in the economic infrastructure sector, theories related to natural monopolies (Waterson, 1987; Baumol et al., 1977, 1982; Sharkey, 1982) are also utilised to analyse the additional reasons for participants to engage in tripartite cooperation.

The special characteristics of economic infrastructure blur the line between international development and international business. Some projects are funded by international donors through concession loans or grants, while others are financed by multinational enterprises (MNEs) through direct investment. By reviewing the literature on international development (Chap. 2) and international business (Chap. 3), this research contributes to opening the 'black boxes' of tripartite cooperation and reviewing its processes. This research investigates the determinants and actions that drive tripartite cooperation projects, revealing the detailed cooperative mechanisms through empirical analysis. By establishing a database of tripartite cooperation projects in the economic infrastructure sector and employing case studies and process tracing methods to analyse the procedure of these projects, this research advances knowledge in tripartite cooperation.

The second contribution of this research is in terms of practical implications. It is valuable to examine changes in transaction costs in tripartite cooperation projects, as this can inform assessments of whether such cooperation deserves continuous investing, including preferential policies, loans, and investments from the Chinese government as well as other international public and private sectors. It is crucial to determine whether Chinese tripartite cooperation offers long-term developmental value, or if it is merely a fleeting trend or a catchy-sounding policy effort aimed, for example, at strengthening diplomatic links. A better understanding of the consequences of moving beyond traditional development arrangements can help inform the strategic choices of governments and enterprises on whether it is preferable to maintain traditional cooperation mechanisms or if there are compelling reasons to embrace the expansion of tripartite cooperation partnerships. This research provides insights that can guide decision-making regarding the allocation of resources and the strategic direction of international cooperation in the international development regime.

1.4 Methodology

This research aims to understand why participants choose tripartite cooperation and to examine how costs and benefits are generated in these projects. The research primarily used qualitative analysis, with limited incorporation of quantitative analysis, to investigate Chinese tripartite cooperation in infrastructure projects. Data were collected through desk research and semi-structured interviews, which were then used to form a database that supported in-depth case studies. Both within-case and cross-case analyses were conducted to explore tripartite cooperation across different contexts.

The data was collected, processed, and analysed in three steps. The first step involved collecting secondary data on all Chinese tripartite cooperation projects in economic infrastructure between 2005 and 2022 from various sources, including government websites, company reports, news articles, and academic journals. Furthermore, first-hand data was obtained through semi-structured interviews conducted between 2021 and 2023 with 25 key stakeholders selected via purposive sampling, including project managers, policymakers, and academics. These interviews gathered insights into various dimensions of tripartite cooperation, covering perspectives, practices, motivations, and outcomes.

The second step involved organising the vast amount of data collected by creating a large database and selecting some in-depth case studies. A significant contribution of this research is the establishment of a database encompassing 68 economic infrastructure projects involving Chinese tripartite cooperation. This database includes over 1600 documents detailing the processes of these projects, providing extensive information such as participating countries, companies, official agencies, project duration, construction costs, financing sources, government support approaches, cooperative methods, capital structures, records of bilateral cooperation, and project introductions. This database reduces case selection bias by supplementing the in-depth case studies. In addition, I conducted in-depth case studies on the Hinkley Point C nuclear power station in the United Kingdom due to its full-range documentation. I followed the entire project process and identified the actions of participants that impact project costs and benefits. I also selected three Nigerian port projects—Tincan Terminal B, Ibom Deep Seaport, and Lekki Deep Seaport—for comparative analysis. These port projects started at different times and have different cooperation performances, yet they share Chinese and French shipping giants as common participants. The selected cases were examined using within-case and cross-case approaches to uncover similar or different determinants, actions, and policies among multiple tripartite cooperation stakeholders. By combining qualitative data from the database with insights from the interviews and case study analysis, I was able to examine the determinants for forming tripartite arrangements, as well as the mechanisms generating transaction costs and benefits.

In the final step, the collected data from the database, interviews and case studies were analysed through descriptive statistics, comparative case studies, stakeholder analysis, and process tracing methods. The descriptive statistics were used to examine the trends in the expansion of tripartite cooperation. The stakeholder analysis was conducted using a stakeholder management framework (Freeman, 2010; Elias 2017) at three levels: the rational level, process level, and transaction level. This approach identified key stakeholders, examined internal stakeholder relationship management, and discovered transaction and bargaining costs among stakeholders. Using process tracing, this research tracked the procedures of the projects to understand the entire process from the rationale for participants to engage in tripartite cooperation to the generation of transaction costs and additional benefits. The various dimensions of the tripartite cooperation mechanism are designated as independent variables, such as the role of governments and firms, and the outcomes of cost and additional benefits are dependent variables. Through these three steps, the examination of both primary and secondary data offers a research framework for a detailed analysis of tripartite cooperation.

1.5 Findings

Through detailed analysis of Chinese tripartite cooperation, this research uncovers several important findings that offer both theoretical and practical insights into such collaborations. The research contributes to the literature on international development and cooperation by providing a nuanced understanding of the mechanisms of tripartite cooperation.

First, by integrating three theoretical perspectives—transaction cost economics, internalisation theory, and natural monopolies in infrastructure—with the context of tripartite cooperation in the economic infrastructure sector, this research advances the theoretical understanding of international infrastructure projects. The findings highlight that tripartite arrangements generate additional transaction costs compared to traditional bilateral arrangements, due to more transactions between various parties involved, as well as the fact that tripartite arrangements are still in the early development phase and have not yet established mature cooperative institutions. Tripartite cooperations are therefore considered to be semi-internalised arrangements, with additional transaction costs but also some notable benefits such as creating the right type of project environment for the cooperators and amalgamating resources from participants in more effective ways. The higher transaction costs due to the semi-internalised nature of tripartite cooperation can be partially overcome by, for example, avoiding consulting costs associated with price discovery in the open market through the use of internal accounting prices, resolving contract disputes internally through prescribed procedures, and mitigating "the costs of legitimate transactions and uncertainty" (Keohane, 1984, p. 220) by addressing information asymmetry. Moreover, participants in existing projects often have a history of bilateral cooperation before engaging in trilateral cooperation, which implies participants know their counterparties' information and behaviour patterns, which reduces transaction costs. In addition, participants use multiple instruments, such as legal contracts, preferential policies, partnership agreements, and so on, to manage risks and bridge their differences during the negotiation and implementation stages to make the projects work, thereby seeking to manage the enhanced transaction costs from the trilateral arrangements.

The second set of findings concerns the comparison between traditional bilateral cooperation and tripartite cooperation. There are few, yet very notable, differences between the motivations for traditional bilateral cooperation and trilateral cooperation. For example, traditional donor countries' firms aim to diversify risks by transferring their knowledge and expertise, while also reinforcing their commercial influence in regions where they have historical ties. For China, involving traditional donor partners can be beneficial in several ways: it allows China to upgrade its industrial value chains, acquire operational knowledge, promote Chinese standards, and mitigate international criticism during the collaborative process of infrastructure projects. Beneficiary countries use tripartite cooperation to bolster their bargaining power and gain greater independence from traditional donors. These benefits are distinct from those sourced via bilateral projects.

Furthermore, tripartite cooperation facilitates Chinese companies' entry into high value-added international markets. Previously, traditional donor countries' firms have leveraged their strengths in advanced technological products and services, playing roles as designers, developers, evaluators, and operators (Pheng & Hou, 2019). Chinese firms have often operated as engineering, procurement, and construction (EPC) contractors, focusing on labour-intensive goods and services (Wang et al., 2016; Chen & Orr, 2009). This contrasts with the assumption that China has accumulated massive experience in the developing world. In fact, China is a relatively new participant engaging in the high value-added market of international infrastructure projects. This is an area in which traditional donor countries and enterprises have accumulated vast, mature, and advanced expertise, both in developed and in developing countries. China's proposed tripartite cooperation particularly aims to secure a share of the interests in beneficiary countries, where markets are dominated by traditional donor countries' firms.

The third set of findings concerns the benefits and transaction costs of tripartite cooperation. The reason firms choose internalisation is that intangible assets, including know-how, management skills, technological innovation, and brand name capital are not easily purchased, imitated, or transferred to outsiders in open markets (Rumelt, 1984; Wernerfelt, 1984). Tripartite cooperation offers a viable alternative, which allows firms to access the desired assets and capabilities without requiring full ownership, thereby circumventing the barriers posed by direct acquisition. Participants in tripartite cooperation can gain additional benefits when specialised goods or services are exchanged internally rather than being purchased from external markets. These specialised goods or services can include raw materials, advanced machinery, technology, local networks, and so on. Other determinants of tripartite cooperations are that firms from China and traditional donor countries engage in vertical and/or horizontal integration to gain additional benefits from economies of scope and scale in project financing, operation, and management in practice.

However, the engagement of an additional partner introduces higher transaction costs, as aligning the interests and practices of multiple stakeholders increases complexity. Differences between Chinese and traditional donor countries' approaches to project finance also cause significant challenges. Chinese financing often involves concessional loans and preferential credit, while traditional donor countries may rely more on private-sector involvement. These divergent approaches can lead to conflicts and misunderstandings. Furthermore, policy instruments employed by recipient governments to influence project implementation can further complicate the process. These policies may be tailored to national interests and regulatory frameworks, which may not always align with the expectations and practices of Chinese and traditional donor countries. Because of the complex mechanisms and higher transaction costs, tripartite cooperation has not yet become mainstream compared to bilateral cooperation.

In conclusion, this research examines the collaborative efforts of China and its traditional donor partners in tripartite cooperation projects. It advances the understanding of tripartite cooperation in infrastructure projects by systematically analysing the transaction costs and benefits. Through an extensive collection of sources and data analysis, the findings reveal the nuanced nature of tripartite projects, showing that these complex processes are influenced by the determinants and actions of China, traditional donor partners, and beneficiary countries. The research provides valuable insights to inform future tripartite cooperation activities in infrastructure projects from both theoretical and practical perspectives.

1.6 Chapter Structure

After the introductory chapter, the next chapter reviews the general background of tripartite cooperation based on secondary sources from previous literature, including journal articles, reports, and data from OECD and development agency websites. The first section of Chap. 2 includes the definitions of tripartite cooperation, its ideal assumptions, the tripartite cooperation framework, and project financing approaches in this research. It is noted that tripartite cooperation is characterised by various terms used by different groups, and its ideal assumptions, such as equal partnership among participants, are often hard to realise in practice. The second section reviews the development of tripartite cooperation in international communities. Originating from 'North-South cooperation' and 'South-South cooperation,' tripartite cooperation has a development history spanning four decades within the context of liberalism. State participants have their own motivations for engaging in tripartite cooperation projects. The third section examines the previous practices of tripartite cooperation in Japan, Germany, and South Africa, alongside an analysis of China's unique characteristics in tripartite cooperation. China draws lessons from previous experiences in tripartite cooperation and places greater emphasis on the development of industry, commerce, and infrastructure through an integrated financing approach including loans, trade, and investment. This chapter finds that, despite decades of evolution, tripartite cooperation has yet to become mainstream within the international development regime. Against this challenging context, the empirical chapters will explore tripartite cooperation through critical, detailed, and empirically grounded analysis.

Chapter 3 moves on to the literature review of Chinese tripartite cooperation. The existing literature on tripartite cooperation primarily emphasises the comparative advantages and the benefits-generation process, while overlooking the transaction cost-generation process. The chapter further introduces several theoretical frameworks that are relevant to tripartite cooperation and are drawn on during the rest of this research. It begins with New Institutional Economics, drawing insights from transaction cost economics and internalisation theories to analyse the formation of tripartite cooperation in international infrastructure projects. In the second section, international relation theories are applied to explain the determinants and changes in transaction costs at the country level. In the third section, FDI theories such as the eclectic paradigm and the springboard perspective are introduced to consider their relevance for examining the determinants for firms to engage in tripartite cooperation. As this research mainly focuses on the economic infrastructure sector, characterised by natural monopolies, this is also drawn to consider why participants engage in tripartite cooperation. These theories are later combined with the empirical findings to explain the determinants behind firms' decisions to engage in tripartite cooperation, despite the potential for higher transaction costs.

Chapter 4 elaborates on the methodological considerations of data collection, processing, and analysis. The research primarily used qualitative analysis, with limited incorporation of quantitative analysis, to investigate Chinese tripartite cooperation in infrastructure projects. The first section of this chapter explains the rationale behind the research design, the second section illustrates the data collection approaches, and the third section clarifies the methods of data analysis. Other considerations, such as research ethics, are also covered. The following three empirical chapters adhere to the research methods outlined in this chapter.

Based on the collected data from 68 Chinese economic infrastructure and construction projects using the tripartite cooperation model between 2005 and 2022, the findings chapters of the empirical research begin with Chap. 5, which provides a broad overview of current Chinese tripartite cooperation projects. Chapter 6 delves into the determinants and actions of participant countries and firms, providing a more detailed exploration of the practices involved in tripartite cooperation. Finally, specific case studies in Chap. 7 illustrate how tripartite cooperation model operates in practice.

Chapter 5 provides an overview of current Chinese tripartite cooperation projects. The first section demonstrates the Chinese tripartite cooperation approaches, the official classification system, and a new two-step system for Chinese tripartite cooperation. This new system shows how tripartite cooperation projects alter traditional project finance activities.

The involvement of an additional partner introduces more complexities, as it creates another cooperative process in tripartite cooperation activities. The second section examines the trends and development of 68 China-led tripartite cooperation projects based on the established database. This section includes the development of projects across different time periods, industrial sectors, and geographical regions. These patterns provide indications of participants' preferences and strategies. The third section examines the roles played by China, China's partner countries, and beneficiary countries in tripartite cooperation projects, and analyses their actions in these projects. This chapter provides an overview and important facts about Chinese tripartite cooperation and relevant trends and developments.

Chapter 6 conducts a more in-depth analysis of the determinants and outcomes of Chinese tripartite cooperation projects. This chapter focuses on the determinants driving participants to engage in tripartite cooperation and the actions they employ in these projects. It draws on an extensive array of sources, including government documents, corporate records, media reports, and interview notes related to tripartite cooperation projects. The first section of this chapter identifies the determinants of governments and firms. Tripartite cooperation emerges as a complementary tool to advance their traditional overseas investment objectives, such as securing strategic assets and markets. Chinese companies' initial motivations in tripartite cooperation mirror those of traditional foreign investment activities, including seeking strategic assets, expanding into new markets, upgrading technology, and acquiring cash liquidity. The second section reviews the actions of governments. Governments employ various methods, including financing, soft law, policy, and relationships, to either promote or impede the progress of tripartite cooperation projects. The third section examines how enterprises form tripartite cooperations, such as by forming partnerships before engaging in tripartite cooperation, and the establishment of consortia/joint ventures/special purpose vehicles. Finally, this chapter examines the intricate competition and cooperation relationships among participants, as well as the influence of sudden changes in the external environment.

Chapter 7 examines the working mechanisms of tripartite cooperation in practical projects and analyses how the actions of participant governments and companies influence costs and benefits in the implementation process. This analysis is conducted through case studies of the Hinkley Point C project and the three Nigerian Port projects, drawing on over 230 documents related to the HPC project and more than 180 documents related to the Nigerian port projects. These documents include government reports, news articles, and interview transcripts. These cases represent two types of tripartite cooperation: the HPC project, located in a developed country, and the three Nigerian port projects, situated in a developing country. The major distinctions between the China-North-North and China-North-South cooperation lie in their different financing approaches. Depending on the financing method, a tripartite cooperation project can be classified as either a business-model project or a development-model project. This chapter uses the stakeholder framework and process tracing method to explore the generation process of transaction costs and benefits. It reveals the complex circumstances and relationships in tripartite cooperation, addressing the research question by drawing on focused case studies.

Finally, this research concludes with the overall findings and extended discussions on theoretical implications and future tripartite cooperation. It is important to further the study of other districts' tripartite cooperation projects. There are a lot of tripartite cooperation projects in South Asia and South America that could be further examined. The comparison among different districts and sectors can display a more comprehensive analysis of tripartite cooperation in global practice.

References

Akinola, O. (2015). The Political Economy of Chinese and Indian Trade, Aid and Investments in Nigeria: A Comparative Analysis. *Journal of Asian and African Studies, 52*(6), 824–837. https://doi.org/10.1177/0021909615622338

Alesina, A., & Dollar, D. (2000). Who Gives Foreign Aid to Whom and Why? *Journal of Economic Growth, 5*(1), 33–63. https://doi.org/10.1023/a:1009874203400

Apodaca, C. (2017). Foreign Aid as Foreign Policy Tool. In *Oxford Research Encyclopedia of Politics*. Oxford University Press. https://doi.org/10.1093/acrefore/9780190228637.013.332

Banga, A. (2021, March 2). Remaking International Cooperation Post-COVID-19: The Role of Private Companies and Countries. *PIIE*. https://www.piie.com/events/remaking-international-cooperation-post-covid-19-role-private-companies-and-countries

Baumann, M.-O. (2017). Forever North–South? The Political Challenges of Reforming the UN Development System. *Third World Quarterly, 39*(4), 626–641. https://doi.org/10.1080/01436597.2017.1408405

Baumol, W. J., Bailey, E. E., & Willig, R. D. (1977). Weak Invisible Hand Theorems on the Sustainability of Multiproduct Natural Monopoly. *The American Economic Review, 67*(3), 350–365. https://www.jstor.org/stable/1831405

Baumol, W. J., Panzar, J. C., & Willig, R. D. (1982). *Contestable Markets and the Theory of Industry Structure.* Harcourt Brace Jovanovich.

Begu, L., Vasilescu, M., Stanila, L., & Clodnitchi, R. (2018). China-Angola Investment Model. *Sustainability, 10*(8), 2936. https://doi.org/10.3390/su10082936

Bräutigam, D. (2011). Aid "With Chinese Characteristics": Chinese Foreign Aid and Development Finance Meet the OECD-DAC Aid Regime. *Journal of International Development, 23*(5), 752–764. https://doi.org/10.1002/jid.1798

Buckley, P. J., & Casson, M. (1976). *Future of the Multinational Enterprise.* Palgrave Macmillan London.

Cai, P. (2017). Understanding China's Belt and Road Initiative. Www.lowyinstitute.org; Lowy Institute. https://www.lowyinstitute.org/publications/understanding-china-s-belt-road-initiative

Carbone, M. (2011). The European Union and China's Rise in Africa: Competing Visions, External Coherence and Trilateral Cooperation. *Journal of Contemporary African Studies, 29*(2), 203–221. https://doi.org/10.1080/02589001.2011.555195

Carbone, M. (2014). Much ado about Nothing? The European Union and the Global Politics of Untying Aid. *Contemporary Politics, 20*(1), 103–117. https://doi.org/10.1080/13569775.2014.882572

Carothers, T. (2008). Democracy Assistance: Political vs. Developmental? *Journal of Democracy, 20*(1), 5–19. https://doi.org/10.1353/jod.0.0047

Chahoud, T. (2008). Financing for Development Series: Southern Non-DAC Actors in Development Cooperation. Www.die-Gdi.de. https://www.die-gdi.de/en/briefing-paper/article/financing-for-development-series-southern-non-dac-actors-in-development-cooperation/

Chaturvedi, S., Sidiropoulos, E., & Fues, T. (2012). *Development Cooperation and Emerging Powers: New Partners or Old Patterns?* Zed Books.

Chen, C., & Orr, R. J. (2009). Chinese Contractors in Africa: Home Government Support, Coordination Mechanisms, and Market Entry Strategies. *Journal of Construction Engineering and Management, 135*(11), 1201–1210. https://doi.org/10.1061/(asce)co.1943-7862.0000082

Cheru, F., Modi, R., & Afrikainstitutet, N. (2013). *Agricultural Development and Food Security in Africa: the Impact of Chinese, Indian & Brazilian Investments.* Zed Books.

Coase, R. H. (1937). The Nature of the Firm. *Economica, 4*(16), 386–405. https://doi.org/10.1111/j.1468-0335.1937.tb00002.x

Coase, R. H. (1960). The Problem of Social Cost. *The Journal of Law & Economics, 3*, 1–44. https://www.jstor.org/stable/724810

Davies, P. (2010). the Roles and Activities of New Development Partners. [Review of the Roles and Activities of New Development Partners]. World Bank. CFP Working Paper Series No. 4.

Deng, P. (2013). Chinese Outward Direct Investment Research: Theoretical Integration and Recommendations. *Management and Organization Review, 9*(03), 513–539. https://doi.org/10.1111/more.12030

Derviş, K. (2020). Multilateralism: What policy options to strengthen international cooperation? Brookings. https://www.brookings.edu/research/multilateralism-what-policy-options-to-strengthen-international-cooperation/

Devetak, R., Burke, A., & George, J. (2011). *An Introduction to International Relations.* Cambridge University Press.

Dooms, M. (2010). *Crafting the Integrative Value Proposition for Large Scale Transport Infrastructure Hubs.* ASP / VUBPRESS / UPA.

Dornan, M., & Brant, P. (2014). Chinese Assistance in the Pacific: Agency, Effectiveness and the Role of Pacific Island Governments. *Asia & the Pacific Policy Studies, 1*(2), 349–363. https://doi.org/10.1002/app5.35

Dunning, J. H. (1988). The Eclectic Paradigm of International Production: A Restatement and Some Possible Extensions. *Journal of International Business Studies, 19*(1), 1–31. JSTOR. https://www.jstor.org/stable/154984

Dunning, J. H. (2001). The Eclectic (OLI) Paradigm of International Production: Past, Present and Future. *International Journal of the Economics of Business, 8*(2), 173–190. Tandfonline. https://doi.org/10.1080/13571510110051441

Ehlers, T. (2014). Understanding the Challenges for Infrastructure Finance Monetary and Economic Department. https://www.bis.org/publ/work454.pdf

Elias, A. A. (2017). Systems Thinking and Modelling for Stakeholder Management. *IIM Kozhikode Society & Management Review, 6*(2), 123–131. https://doi.org/10.1177/2277975216681105

Feng, Q. (2019). Vigorously Expanding Third-Party Market Cooperation. https://www.gov.cn/zhengce/2019-04/03/content_5379223.htm

Fordelone, T. Y. (2011). Triangular Co-operation and Aid Effectiveness. *OECD Journal: General Papers, 2010*(1), 47–67. https://doi.org/10.1787/gen_papers-2010-5kgc6cl31rnx

Freeman, R. E. (2010). *Strategic Management.* Cambridge University Press. https://doi.org/10.1017/cbo9781139192675

GPI. (2019). Triangular Co-operation in the Era of the 2030 Agenda, Global Partnership for Effective Development Co-operation. Www.effectivecooperation.org. https://www.effectivecooperation.org/content/triangular-co-operation-era-2030-agenda

Griffiths, J. (2013). *Global Financial Flows, Aid and Development.* Eurodad for Concord Aid Watch.

Guo, F., Chang-Richards, Y., Wilkinson, S., & Li, T. C. (2014). Effects of Project Governance Structures on the Management of Risks in Major Infrastructure Projects: A Comparative Analysis. *International Journal of Project Management, 32*(5), 815–826. https://doi.org/10.1016/j.ijproman.2013.10.001

Halper, S. A. (2010). *The Beijing Consensus: How China's Authoritarian Model will Dominate the Twenty-First Century*. Basic Books.

He, P., & Yan, Y. (2021). Japan's Third Party Market Cooperation in Africa: Models, Characteristics, and Inspirations. *Fudan Public Administration Review, 02*, 1–25. http://www.jsc.fudan.edu.cn/view.php?id=1596

Hennart, J.-F. (1988). A Transaction Costs Theory of Equity Joint Ventures. *Strategic Management Journal, 9*(4), 361–374. https://doi.org/10.1002/smj.4250090406

Huld, A. (2022, February 11). China Infrastructure Investment in 2022 - Spurring Economic Growth. China Briefing News. https://www.china-briefing.com/news/china-infratsructure-investment-in-2022-spurring-economic-growth/

Janus, H., Klingebiel, S., & Paulo, S. (2014). Beyond Aid: A Conceptual Perspective on the Transformation of Development Cooperation. *Journal of International Development, 27*(2), 155–169. https://doi.org/10.1002/jid.3045

Jepson, N. (2021). Hidden in Plain Sight: Chinese Development Finance in Central and Eastern Europe. *Development and Change, 52*(5), 1222–1250. https://doi.org/10.1111/dech.12686

Jones, L., & Hameiri, S. (2020). Debunking the Myth of "Debt-trap Diplomacy." Chatham House—International Affairs Think Tank. https://www.chathamhouse.org/2020/08/debunking-myth-debt-trap-diplomacy

Kamwengo, C. (2020). Beneficiary Country Ownership and the Politics of Partnership in Trilateral Development Cooperation: A Case Study of Zambia. Etheses.dur.ac.uk. http://etheses.dur.ac.uk/13696/

Kaplan, M., Busemann, D., & Wirtgen, K. (2020). Trilateral Cooperation in German Development Cooperation. German Institute for Development Evaluation (DEval), Bonn. https://www.deval.org/en/publications/trilateral-cooperation-in-german-development-cooperation

Keohane, R. O. (1984). *After Hegemony: Cooperation and Discord in the Political Economy*. Princeton University Press.

Kim, S., & Lightfoot, S. (2011). Does "DAC-Ability" Really Matter? The emergence of non-DAC Donors: Introduction to Policy Arena. *Journal of International Development, 23*(5), 711–721. https://doi.org/10.1002/jid.1795

Kjøllesdal, K. A., & Welle-Strand, A. (2010). Foreign Aid Strategies: China Taking Over? Asian. *Social Science, 6*(10). https://doi.org/10.5539/ass.v6n10p3

Lam, K. C., Wang, D., Lee, P. T. K., & Tsang, Y. T. (2007). Modelling Risk Allocation Decision in Construction Contracts. *International Journal of Project Management, 25*(5), 485–493. https://doi.org/10.1016/j.ijproman.2006.11.005

Lawer, E. T. (2019). Examining Stakeholder Participation and Conflicts Associated with Large Scale Infrastructure Projects: The Case of Tema Port Expansion Project. *Ghana. Maritime Policy & Management, 46*(6), 735–756. https://doi.org/10.1080/03088839.2019.1627013

Lool, H. (2016). How has China Moved-up the Global Value Chains? Blogs. worldbank.org. https://blogs.worldbank.org/developmenttalk/how-has-china-moved-global-value-chains

Luo, Y., & Tung, R. L. (2007). International Expansion of Emerging Market Enterprises: A Springboard Perspective. *Journal of International Business Studies, 38*(4), 481–498. https://doi.org/10.1057/palgrave.jibs.8400275

Luo, Y., & Tung, R. L. (2018). A General Theory of Springboard MNEs. *Journal of International Business Studies, 49*(2), 129–152. https://doi.org/10.1057/s41267-017-0114-8

Mawdsley, E. (2012). The changing geographies of foreign aid and development cooperation: contributions from gift theory. *Transactions of the Institute of British Geographers, 37*(2), 256–272. https://doi.org/10.1111/j.1475-5661.2011.00467.x

Mearsheimer, J. J. (2001). *The Tragedy of Great Power Politics*. W.W. Norton & Company.

Men, H., & Yu, Q. (2020). Third Party Market Cooperation: Theoretical Structure, Historical Evolution and China's Path. *Journal of Contemporary Asia-Pacific Studie, 6*, 4–40. https://spsir.tongji.edu.cn/e6/59/c18787a190041/page.htm

Mody, A., & Rebucci, A. (2006). Overview in: IMF-Supported Programs. https://www.elibrary.imf.org/view/book/9781589063617/pr001.xml

Moravcsik, A. (1993). Preferences and Power in the European Community: A Liberal Intergovernmentalist Approach. *Journal of Common Market Studies, 31*(4), 473–524. https://doi.org/10.1111/j.1468-5965.1993.tb00477.x

Motiar Rahman, M., & Kumaraswamy, M. M. (2002). Risk Management Trends in the Construction Industry: Moving Towards Joint Risk Management. *Engineering, Construction and Architectural Management, 9*(2), 131–151. https://doi.org/10.1108/eb021210

NDRC. (2019). Third-Party Market Cooperation Guidelines and Cases. National Development and Reform Commision, P.R. China. http://images.mofcom.gov.cn/mz/201909/20190912093710956.pdf

North, D. C. (1991). Institutions. *Journal of Economic Perspectives, 5*(1), 97–112. https://doi.org/10.1257/jep.5.1.97

Nye, J. S., & Keohane, R. O. (1977). *Power and Interdependence*. Harpercollins, Cop.

OECD. (2012). OECD Principles for Public Governance of Public-Private Partnerships-OECD.Www.oecd.org.https://www.oecd.org/gov/budgeting/oecd-principles-for-public-governance-of-public-private-partnerships.htm

OECD (2016). Development Co-operation Report 2016: The Sustainable Development Goals as Business Opportunities, OECD Publishing, Paris, https://doi.org/10.1787/dcr-2016-en.

Osipova, E., & Eriksson, P. E. (2013). Balancing Control and Flexibility in Joint Risk Management: Lessons Learned from Two Construction Projects. *International Journal of Project Management, 31*(3), 391–399. https://doi.org/10.1016/j.ijproman.2012.09.007

Pantoja, E. (2009). *Triangular Cooperation: New Paths to Development.* OECD. https://www.oecd.org/dac/dac-global-relations/43705278.pdf

Pheng, L. S., & Hou, L. S. (2019). The Economy and the Construction Industry. In *Construction Quality and the Economy* (pp. 21–54). Ncbi. https://doi.org/10.1007/978-981-13-5847-0_2

Power, M., Mohan, G., & Tan-Mullins, M. (2012). *China's Resource Diplomacy in Africa: Powering Development?* Palgrave Macmillan.

Rosseel, P., De Corte, E., Blommaert, J., & Verniers, E. (2009). Approaches to North-South, South-South and North-South-South collaboration. A policy document.

Rugman, A. M. (1985). Internalisation is Still a General Theory of Foreign Direct Investment. *Weltwirtschaftliches Archiv, 121*(3), 570–575. https://www.jstor.org/stable/40439351

Rumelt, R. P. (1984). Towards a Strategic Theory of the Firm. In R. B. Lamb (Ed.), *Competitive Strategic Management* (pp. 566–570). Englewood Cliffs.

Samy, Y. (2010). China's Aid Policies in Africa: Opportunities and Challenges. *The Round Table, 99*(406), 75–90. https://doi.org/10.1080/00358530903513756

Scholz, I. (2020). Beyond Vested Interests: Reforming International Cooperation Post Covid-19. OECD Development Matters. https://devinit.org/blog/beyond-vested-interests-reforming-international-cooperation-post-covid-19/

Schulz, N-S. (2010). Boosting South-South Cooperation in the Context of Aid Effectiveness Telling the Story of Partners Involved in more than 110 Cases of South-South and Triangular Cooperation. https://www.oecd.org/dac/effectiveness/46080462.pdf

Severino, J.-M., & Ray, O. (2009). The End of ODA: Death and Rebirth of a Global Public Policy. *SSRN Electronic Journal, 19*(1), 5–44. https://doi.org/10.2139/ssrn.1392460

Sharkey, W. W. (1982). *The Theory of Natural Monopoly.* In The Economic Journal. Oxford University Press. https://doi.org/10.1017/cbo9780511571817

Skupien, S. (2019). Searching for Macro-Meso-Micro-Level Links in Studies of North-South Research Collaborations. *Learning and Policy, 57*(3), 391–410. https://doi.org/10.1007/s11024-019-09371-8

Smith, T., & Ikenberry, G. J. (2001). After Victory: Institutions, Strategic Restraint, and the Rebuilding of Order after Major Wars. *Foreign Affairs, 80*(2), 170. https://doi.org/10.2307/20050090

Stahl, A. K. (2012). *Trilateral Development Cooperation Between the European Union, China and Africa: What Prospects for South Africa?* Centre for Chinese Studies, Stellenbosch University. https://scholar.sun.ac.za/handle/10019.1/70766

Stallings, B., & Szkely, G. (1993). *Japan, the United States, and Latin America: Toward a Trilateral Relationship in the Western Hemisphere?* Palgrave Macmillan London.

Tang, Y., Chen, Y., Hua, Y., & Fu, Y. (2020). Impacts of Risk Allocation on Conflict Negotiation Costs in Construction Projects: Does Managerial Control Matter? *International Journal of Project Management, 38*(3), 188–199. https://doi.org/10.1016/j.ijproman.2020.03.002

Tan-Mullins, M., Mohan, G., & Power, M. (2010). Redefining "Aid" in the China-Africa Context. *Development and Change, 41*(5), 857–881. https://doi.org/10.1111/j.1467-7660.2010.01662.x

Teece, D. J. (1981). The Market for Know-How and the Efficient International Transfer of Technology. *The ANNALS of the American Academy of Political and Social Science, 458*(1), 81–96. https://doi.org/10.1177/000271628145800107

Teece, D. J. (1986). Transactions Cost Economics and the Multinational Enterprise An Assessment. *Journal of Economic Behavior & Organization, 7*(1), 21–45. https://doi.org/10.1016/0167-2681(86)90020-x

Tseng, H.-K., & Krog, R. (2016). No Strings Attached: Chinese Foreign Aid and Regime Stability in Resource-Rich Recipient Countries. https://api.semanticscholar.org/CorpusID:53312

Wang, H., Sexton, M., & Lu, S.-L. (2016). Investment by Chinese Construction firms in the UK Infrastructure Sector: Volumes, Patterns and Trends. Centaur. reading.ac.uk. http://centaur.reading.ac.uk/67075/

Waterson, M. (1987). Recent Developments in the Theory of Natural Monopoly. *Journal of Economic Surveys, 1*(1–2), 59–80. https://doi.org/10.1111/j.1467-6419.1987.tb00024.x

Wendt, A. (1999). *Social Theory of International Politics.* Cambridge University Press.

Wernerfelt, B. (1984). A Resource-Based View of the Firm. *Strategic Management Journal, 5*(2), 171–180. https://www.jstor.org/stable/2486175

Williamson, O. E. (1971). The Vertical Integration of Production: Market Failure Considerations. *The American Economic Review, 61*(2), 112–123. https://www.jstor.org/stable/1816983

Williamson, O. E. (1975). *Markets and Hierarchies: Analysis and Antitrust Implications.* Free Press.

World Bank. (2017). Bank Policy Development Policy Financing. https://thedocs.worldbank.org/en/doc/b07a01de330e0775384b66b21e54b103-0290012023/original/Bank-Policy-Development-pol-fin.pdf

Wu, B., & Ding, M. (2020). Third Party Market Cooperation Between China and South Korea: Progress, Resistance, and Countermeasures. *Northeast Asia Forum, 29*(3), 75–89+128. https://doi.org/10.13654/j.cnki.naf.2020.03.006

Youngs, R. (2008). Trends in Democracy Assistance: What Has Europe Been Doing? *Journal of Democracy, 19*(2), 160–169. https://www.journalofdemocracy.org/articles/trends-in-democracy-assistance-what-has-europe-been-doing/

Zelikow, D., & Savas, F. (2022). Mind the Gap: Time to Rethink Infrastructure Finance. Blogs.worldbank.org. https://blogs.worldbank.org/ppps/mind-gap-time-rethink-infrastructure-finance

Zhang, D. (2017a). *A Promising New Trend? Factors Driving Chinas Growing Trilateral Aid Cooperation [Doctoral Dissertation]*. Australian National University (ANU) Press.

Zhang, D. (2017b). Why Cooperate with Others? Demystifying China's Trilateral aid Cooperation. *The Pacific Review, 30*(5), 750–768. https://doi.org/10.1080/09512748.2017.1296886

Zhang, D. (2018). A Tango by two Superpowers: China-US Cooperation in Trilateral Aid and Implications for Their Bilateral Relations. *Asian Journal of Political Science, 26*(2), 181–200. https://doi.org/10.1080/02185377.2018.1462218

Zhang, F., & Li, H. (2020). Third Party Market Cooperation: A new Model of International Cooperation Under the "The Belt and Road" Initiative—based on the Analysis of the Third Party Market Cooperation Between China and France. *International Economic Cooperation, 02*, 26–33.

Zhang, Y. (2020). Third-Party Market Cooperation Under the Belt and Road Initiative: Progress, Challenges, and Recommendations. *China International Strategy Review, 1*, 310–329. https://doi.org/10.1007/s42533-019-00026-7

Zheng, C. (2020). *Zhong Ou Di San Fang Shi Chang He Zuo Mian Lin De Ji Yu He Tiao Zhan (Opportunities and Chanlleages in China-Europe Tripartite Cooperation)*. World Knowledge.

CHAPTER 2

Review of Trends in the International Development of Tripartite Cooperation

This chapter introduces the issue of tripartite cooperation and outlines general trends within the international development context. The first section provides the definitions of tripartite cooperation, ideal assumptions, and the tripartite cooperation framework in this research. The second section reviews the development of tripartite cooperation in international communities and explores the determinants of participation in trilateral cooperation from previous research. The third section examines the practices of tripartite cooperation in both developed and developing countries, alongside an analysis of China's unique characteristics in tripartite cooperation.

Through a comprehensive review of these contents, this chapter aims to identify the diverse forms of tripartite cooperation in international development. By examining various tripartite cooperation practices across different countries and international organisations, the chapter highlights the special characteristics of Chinese tripartite cooperation.

2.1 Definition of Tripartite Cooperation

2.1.1 Trilateral, Triangular, and Tripartite Cooperation

In most documents or reports, terms like 'trilateral,' 'triangular,' and 'trilateral development cooperation' are frequently used as synonyms and are

C. Su, *From Two to Three*, Governing China in the 21st Century,
https://doi.org/10.1007/978-981-95-8708-7_2

often employed interchangeably. The inconsistent terminology is used by different scholars and institutions, such as the Organisation for Economic Co-operation and Development (OECD) and individual countries' aid agencies. (e.g., Hauck, 2011; Langendorf et al., 2012, p. 15; OECD, 2019; GPI, 2019a). Trilateral cooperation and triangular cooperation are more concerned with international relations and countries' behaviour (Grimm, 2008, 2011). In the current academic literature on international cooperation, 'trilateral cooperation' commonly refers to cooperation among three countries in general (e.g., McEwan and Mawdsley, 2012; Stahl, 2012; Mehta and Nanda, 2005; Kamwengo, 2020).

International organisations such as the OECD often use 'triangular cooperation' to denote the cooperation projects among OECD countries, large international organisations, and post-conflict/developing countries (e.g., OECD 2012a, 2013, 2014b, 2017; GPI, 2019a). For instance, Japan and Cambodia collaborated on comprehensive actions in "humanitarian demining, mine risk education, national standards, and comprehensive assistance to victims" in Colombia's post-conflict society (GPI, 2019a, p. 26). Triangular cooperation has effectively addressed global issues such as public health, education, food security, and environmental protection. Through the integration of political negotiation and capacity building, triangular cooperation brings all parties together to participate in projects (Chaturvedi et al. 2012). However, the application of tripartite cooperation in infrastructure was less mentioned in these international organisation documents.

Regarding 'trilateral development cooperation,' the OECD defines it as partnerships between Development Assistance Committee (DAC) donors and emerging countries to implement development cooperation projects in beneficiary countries (OECD 2009). Grimm (2011) elaborates on it as an international collaboration aimed at promoting development, engaging three players. McEwan and Mawdsley (2012) defined it as a development relationship wherein a DAC donor or multilateral agency (e.g., Japan, Germany, or the United Nations Development Programme) partners with an emerging country (e.g., China, Brazil, or South Africa) to work with a beneficiary country (e.g., Ghana, Laos, or Mozambique). As of April 2019, at the 11th Round of the China-European Union Consultation on African Affairs, the participating countries had not yet arrived at a clear and commonly agreed definition of trilateral development cooperation (European Commission, 2019).

Tripartite cooperation is viewed as a process that exploits the comparative advantages of the three parties and integrates resources for international cooperation. In this sense, tripartite cooperation is increasingly attractive as a collaborative instrument (Kamwengo, 2020; GPI, 2019a). Negotiations among the three parties often conclude with a joint tripartite agreement, a memorandum of understanding (MoU), a partnership agreement, or other legal frameworks that clarify the implementation rules (International Labour Organisation, 2019; GPI, 2019a).

Diverging from the focus on international relations and development found in 'trilateral,' 'triangular,' or 'trilateral development cooperation,' this research directs its attention towards costs and benefits at the project level. I use 'tripartite cooperation' to substitute 'trilateral,' 'triangular,' 'trilateral development cooperation,' or 'third-party market cooperation' for clarification in the analysis sections. However, I maintain the original word usage in quoted sections.

As for the participants in tripartite cooperation, similar terms often refer to different actors in different models, leading to confusion. For example, the role of the third party is unclear. In some documents, it refers to the beneficiary countries, while in others it refers to the facilitator or provider partners that offer expertise and experience (Kato, 2012; Shiga, 2016; NDRC, 2019). The complexity of these situations complicates the unification of terms and leads to chaos in academic writing.

In theoretical research, I unified the term 'traditional donor countries' to substitute terms such as 'North countries,' 'OECD-DAC donors,' 'developed countries,' 'advanced economies,' and 'Western countries,' referring to them as the partner countries. Similarly, 'beneficiary countries' is used instead of terms such as 'South countries' and 'developing countries.'

In this research, tripartite cooperation is defined as economic collaboration involving China, its partner countries, and beneficiary countries. These cooperative activities encompass project financing, construction, operation, and services related to economic infrastructure projects. China's partner countries primarily refer to advanced economies with formal or informal cooperation arrangements with China, including Australia, Austria, Belgium, Canada, France, Germany, Greece, Italy, Japan, South Korea, the Netherlands, Portugal, Singapore, Spain, Switzerland, the United Kingdom, and the United States. While tripartite cooperation intersects with international development and investment, it is classified as economic cooperation because the beneficiary countries encompass both developed and developing countries.

2.1.2 *The Ideal Assumptions of Tripartite Cooperation*

Previous researchers such as Deng (2013), Zhang (2017a), and Kamwengo (2020) have utilised Ricardo's theory, focusing on comparative advantages and industrial specialisation to explain the determinants of participants joining in tripartite cooperation. Some studies hypothesise when investing in beneficiary countries with high political risk, low market efficiencies, and weak institutional frameworks, China and partner companies could benefit from each other's experience when both countries already have cooperative records with local entities (e.g., NDRC, 2019; Zheng 2020; Feng, 2019).

On the one hand, the research on entry strategy suggests that early entrants usually earn higher profits than late movers, and traditional donor countries have the advantage of being early entrants in many cases. However, China, as a late mover, may take lower risks in environments with poor governance conditions (Yang et al. 2015; Perkins, 2014). On the other hand, their advantages reverse. The inefficient markets in less-developed countries may impede the transfer of technological and firm-specific resources of companies in advanced economies. Instead, Chinese companies possess knowledge of operating in environments with less-developed institutional mechanisms (Cuervo-Cazurra & Genc, 2008; Luo, Zhang, & Bu, 2019; Rui, 2010). They also expand their cooperative modes of entry. Such modes of entry include joint ventures (JVs), strategic alliances, and short-term contracting, which allow partner countries to reduce investment risks and access local resources (Demirbag et al. 2008; Meyer et al. 2009; Xu & Meyer, 2012). By using these cooperative entry modes, Chinese firms and firms from advanced economies attempt to exploit their comparative advantages in the beneficiary countries and lower the costs of project coordination.

International organisations and scholars (Fordelone, 2011; Mehta and Nanda, 2005; UNDP, 2009; OECD, 2017) have also outlined a series of ideal assumptions regarding tripartite cooperation, which they refer to as the 'principles' of tripartite cooperation. At the country level, Altenburg and Weikert (2007) have identified three assumptions for effective tripartite cooperation: alignment with good international cooperation practices by donors, efficient implementation processes to enhance productivity, and the ability of society to pool fragmented resources at the initial stage of programmes. Fordelone (2009) has also proposed preconditions to maximise the benefits of tripartite cooperation: beneficiary countries should have ownership over projects, and traditional donor countries and emerging providers should prioritise the development of beneficiary countries. These principles underscore that two providers with respective interests should not impose their ideas on the beneficiary partner (Zhang, 2018).

At the project level, the core principles include equal partnership among the three parties, shared responsibility, mutual benefit, multi-stakeholder dialogues, transparency, accountability, reciprocity, knowledge-sharing, and joint learning (GPI, 2019a, 2019b). Participants hope tripartite collaboration can break the cycle of poverty (Power et al., 2012; Dornan and Brant, 2014). They also view it as an innovative policy tool to overcome the limitations of existing bilateral and multilateral development cooperation (Stahl, 2012), aiming to break up traditional aid's vertical relationship to potentially foster triple-win situations.

Participants in tripartite cooperation projects should aim to reduce transaction costs by adhering to these ideal assumptions, which foster strong partnerships and alignment of actions. However, these principles are often overly optimistic and the realisation of such 'triple-wins' in practice is questionable. It is difficult to distribute power equally among the three parties due to the existing asymmetry of information and incomplete contracts (more details in Chap. 3). Provider or donor countries typically exert more control over projects, especially when beneficiary countries are developing countries. When developing countries require capital and technology, they encounter difficulties in negotiating on equal footing with providers. Moreover, these developing countries often lack robust private business actors and entrepreneurial environments, hindering local companies' full engagement in infrastructure projects. Additionally, the institutional structures of their governments to manage projects' procedures and financial allocations are less developed (Li & Bonschab, 2012), further impeding the negotiation power and implementation capacity in tripartite cooperation.

Conversely, when beneficiary countries possess significant power, transaction costs also tend to escalate due to their strong private sectors and entrepreneurial environments. These strengths embolden beneficiary countries to pursue greater interests in projects, thereby prolonging negotiating and bargaining processes with provider countries, leading to increased transaction costs (more details in Chap. 7, the Hinkley Point C case). Furthermore, both traditional donor countries and emerging providers have their own project priorities, which may diverge from the needs of beneficiary countries (Hooijmaaijers, 2018; Bertucci and Locatelli, 2020). Consequently, it is hard to achieve an equal distribution of power in tripartite cooperation.

Therefore, these ideal assumptions may appear as rhetoric with fancy terms that overlook internal contradictions. For example, the assumption that "each party should divide responsibilities based on their expertise and comparative advantages" (Fordelone, 2009, p. 6) implies that advanced economies excel in technology, while developing countries excel in cheap labour force and manufacturing. However, the principles also emphasise "mutual benefit from joint learning and knowledge-sharing" (OECD, 2018, p. 8), which may pose challenges for countries with advanced technology to learn from beneficiary countries.

2.1.3 *The Tripartite Cooperation Framework of this Research*

According to the National Development and Reform Commission of China (NDRC, 2019, p. 2), "Third-party market cooperation refers to the economic cooperation between Chinese enterprises and enterprises of other countries in third-party markets." This involves Chinese business entities collaborating with companies from advanced economies in areas such as investment, construction, consultation, and operation to promote industrial and infrastructure development in third-party developing countries, achieving the effect of '1+1+1>3.'

In effect, tripartite projects can be conceptualised as consisting of double triangular partnerships in this research (see Fig. 2.1). The country-level tripartite cooperation partnership constitutes a large triangular relationship, involving three participants: the Chinese government, a traditional donor country's government, and a beneficiary country's government. The project-level tripartite cooperation partnership forms a small triangular relationship, consisting of three participants: a Chinese firm, a partner firm from advanced economies, and an entity/entities in beneficiary countries.

While participants at the country level are not directly engaged in specific projects, they issue policies to support tripartite cooperation. Typically, the Chinese government and traditional donor countries' governments sign MOUs to motivate private sector participation in tripartite cooperation projects. The Chinese government may also provide financial support

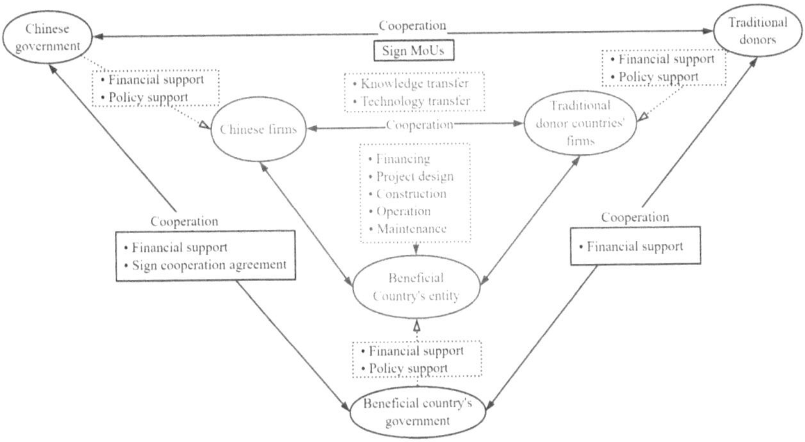

Fig. 2.1 Tripartite cooperation mechanism. (Source: Author)

and/or enter into cross-national cooperation agreements with beneficiary countries (NDRC, 2019; Wu & Ding, 2020). In contrast, the governments of traditional donor countries are rarely directly involved in practical projects and typically provide financial support to the governments of beneficiary countries (Zhang & Li, 2020).

The participants in the small triangular relationships are responsible for the practical implementation of infrastructure projects, providing relevant support to entities in the beneficiary countries. In each project, both the Chinese firms and firms from advanced economies may offer financing, design, construction, operation, and/or maintenance services to the beneficiary country. After the firms in the small triangular partnership establish a cooperative relationship, they usually use special purpose vehicles (SPVs), JVs, or other arrangements to facilitate the tripartite cooperation process. In some cases, the host government in beneficiary countries issues franchises or concessions to the SPV and influences the project's processes through laws, administrative policies, or regulations (detailed in Chap. 5, Sect. 5.1.3). Throughout the cooperation process, there may also be knowledge transfer and/or technology transfer between the Chinese firms and their partner firms from advanced economies. This process may align with principles that emphasise "mutual benefit from joint learning and knowledge-sharing" (OECD, 2018, p. 8), but its practical performance needs further observation.

On the one hand, state power can contribute to global capitalism and promote the process of globalisation. In some strategic sectors, states continue to maintain a dominant position compared to private corporations. On the other hand, the current global structure favours corporations over states from the perspective of transnational capitalism. The transnational space is predominantly occupied by corporate elites, professional corporate services, and transnational patterns of production, trade, and ownership (e.g., Babic et al. 2017; de Graaff & van Apeldoorn, 2017). In the tripartite cooperation framework, the double triangular model represents a balance between these two perspectives. The government, especially the Chinese and beneficiary countries' governments, continue to play important roles in the tripartite cooperation mechanism, while the traditional donor countries' participants tend to prioritise capitalism and market-orientated rules. In the field of project finance, presumably, governments are relatively more involved as it ties in with aid and other forms of development assistance provided by governments.

There are also some shortcomings in the concept of 'tripartite cooperation,' according to the Chinese government's definition. Ideally, participants in such cooperation would only come from three distinct nations. In practice, mega-infrastructure projects often involve multiple stakeholders from more than three countries. However, some Chinese reports (Qu, 2017; Gao, 2018) still classify projects with participants from more than three nations as 'tripartite cooperation,' which diverges from the definition used in this research. Therefore, it raises a question: Is 'tripartite cooperation' a technical term to describe cooperative statements on infrastructure construction, or is it a political narrative invented by the Chinese government to strengthen the partnership with traditional donor countries and justify its economic statecraft in acquiring foreign strategic assets?

Taking the Kuwait Al-Zour refinery project as an example, this project is led by Spain's Técnicas Reunidas in a JV with Sinopec Engineering and South Korea's Hanwha Engineering & Construction. They were awarded a $4.1 billion EPC contract for the main process units of the project. However, in Chinese government reports and some academic research papers (e.g., Zheng, 2020; Wan & Wang, 2020), this project is presented as an example of China–Spain tripartite cooperation in high-level leadership meetings or China–South Korea tripartite cooperation. Which narrative of this project is selected depends on China's desire to enhance its partnership with a particular country. In addition, this project holds significant importance as it is located in the Middle East and serves as a vital component of Kuwait Vision 2035. As the largest eco-friendly oil refinery in Kuwait, it represents a joint effort between Kuwait and China.

2.1.4 *Project Financing Approaches in Tripartite Cooperation*

In theory, tripartite cooperation expands the financing sources for infrastructure projects by attracting investment from multiple parties. This research empirically explores the financing process of infrastructure projects, particularly in developing countries in Africa, Asia, and South America, where infrastructure financing deficits are significant. If infrastructure projects in these countries only rely on their domestic general budget appropriations for financing, meaning that infrastructure is entirely funded by the public sector (Estache et al., 2002), it places considerable financial pressure on governments. Any suspension of government sponsorship can significantly delay project progress. To alleviate these financial burdens, privatisation and seeking funds from international development sponsors have been proposed as viable solutions (Newbery, 1997; Megginson & Mueller, 2022). The following sections discuss how tripartite cooperation can address these challenges in infrastructure project financing.

The international development community has advocated for multi-channel financing approaches (e.g., private sector involvement, financing from other governments via aid or loans) to bridge the infrastructure financing gap in developing countries (Della Croce and Yermo 2013; Mamatzakis and Tsionas, 2018). Since the early 1990s, the Private Finance Initiative (PFI) has introduced private-sector investment and management techniques to the public sector. International private investment has become a driving force in supplying cost-effective infrastructure in developing countries. Project finance arrangements create partnerships between host country governments and international investors.

Due to increasingly restrictive financing conditions imposed by Multilateral Development Banks and the national development agencies of OECD countries, some developing countries have gradually come to rely more on international private investment (Kerr, 1995). Project financing is particularly attractive to cash-strapped governments because it allows infrastructure projects to generate revenue streams for repayment, rather than requiring capital or equity at the outset (Fernandes et al. 2019). This shift enables developing countries to undertake critical infrastructure projects without the immediate financial burden.

In tripartite infrastructure projects, private actors and international entities play important roles. They utilise various financing vehicles or contracts to participate in infrastructure delivery, including long-term contracts, partial ownership agreements, public–private partnerships (PPPs), concessions and franchises, and private equity (details in Table 2.1). Beneficiary country governments employ these financing vehicles or contracts as efficient solutions to tackle complex problems and mitigate adversarial interests in specific assets (Joskow, 1990; Pisano et al., 1988). These financing vehicles or contracts, to some extent, help participants in tripartite cooperation reduce uncertainty in the open international market.

All of these financing methods can be used in tripartite cooperation projects, each offering distinct advantages. For instance, specific-purpose and securitised borrowing utilise public external funding from multilateral agreements (such as long-term loans) and investments from private entities (such as the banking sector) (Allen et al. 2019). Concessions and franchises are effective mechanisms that encourage private sector participation in infrastructure development, operations, and maintenance (World Bank 2012). In developing countries where property rights are weak, local governments often resort to concessions or licensing to attract investors.

Private equity represents an innovative approach to financing long-term infrastructure projects, blending financial and business strategies where debt and equity are repaid from project-generated revenues. Williamson (1995) argues that debt and equity function both as financial instruments and as governance mechanisms, with their ratio tailored to the project's financial requirements. Given that revenue streams are generated during the operations phase, sponsors assume greater risk in the construction phase and company shareholders usually bear liability proportional to their holdings (Sharafi et al., 2021). Participants seek to align interests and enhance cooperation by forming JV/SPVs, thereby deepening collaboration, strengthening linkages among stakeholders, and mitigating contractual risks (Doloi, 2012).

Among these financing vehicles, the PPPs model stands out as a popular method for financing tripartite cooperation projects due to its potential to reduce average construction costs and improve performance in terms of on-time and on-budget delivery (Raisbeck et al., 2010; Hampton et al., 2012). PPPs include various types, including build-operate-transfer (BOT), build-own-operate-transfer (BOOT), build-own-operate (BOO), design-build-lease (DBL), operation and maintenance/management

Table 2.1 Financing vehicles/contracts that use private capital in infrastructure delivery (OECD 2012b; Araújo & Sutherland, 2010)

Long-term contracts	The government signs legal contracts with two or more parties, clarifying terms and conditions for a long-term period. This arrangement allows participants to avoid repeatedly drawing up short-term contracts Participants in tripartite cooperation often enter into long-term contracts for specific projects. For example, a French company signed a long-term lease contract with the Nigerian government for the Tincan Island Container Terminal in the Port of Lagos.
Partial ownership agreements	Partial ownership agreements, also known as fractional ownership, involve the government including several unrelated parties who share ownership of high-value tangible assets, thereby mitigating risks. Participants often utilise this approach to collectively own luxury goods, land and agricultural infrastructure, or to establish community ownership in local energy initiatives (Pasimeni, 2021). In tripartite cooperation, local governments or authorities in beneficiary countries often join projects with minority equity. For example, the local assembly of Lüderitz holds a 5% equity stake in the China-France-Namibia Ombepo wind farm project.
Public–private partnerships (PPPs)	The government and private partners sign long-term agreements to provide public services. Under these agreements, the private partner delivers and finances public services using a capital asset, thereby sharing the associated risks. There are many forms of PPPs, as detailed in footnote 1. In tripartite cooperation, participants frequently use PPPs approaches to collaboratively develop infrastructure projects.
Concessions and franchises	The government uses concessions or franchises to transfer risk and attract investment from private partners. At the same time, private partners seek projects that can generate new revenue and provide a reasonable return, with the understanding that the state bears some of the risks involved. In tripartite cooperation, Chinese or Western firms often obtain long-term concession or franchise agreements from the beneficiary country's government to develop local transportation or energy projects.
Private equity	The government permits private equity to invest in public projects. In tripartite cooperation, for beneficiary countries, besides their official authorities directly involved in projects, external parties—Including Chinese SOEs, Western firms, and local private companies—may act as private equity stakeholders.

contract (O&M/MC), design-build-finance-operate-maintain (DBFOM), stand-alone concessions, and subsidised concessions.[1]

Participants in tripartite cooperation often adopt the PPP model to structure the development of complex infrastructure projects. PPPs are contractual arrangements that involve diverse roles for the private sector (Ferrari et al. 2016). Traditionally, PPPs involved bilateral contracts between the government and a single private concessionaire. In recent years, the PPP model has been reframed, with partnerships extending to three or more partners (Arezki, et al., 2017).

When a country's government embarks on a new infrastructure project but prefers not to shoulder the entire liability of repaying a multilateral loan, PPP transactions offer a straightforward and commonly adopted solution. The PPP model offers numerous advantages when applied in tripartite cooperation projects. In PPP projects, each participant contributes design, financial, management, and technical resources throughout the execution and operation phases. Many tripartite cooperation initiatives utilise the PPP model to tailor projects according to each partner's competitive strengths. Usually, investors establish a SPV to handle the design,

[1] The PPP project models (ADB, EBRD, IDB, ISDB, and WBG, 2016)

1. Build-operate-transfer (BOT): During the agreed contract period, the private partner designs, finances, constructs, operates, and maintains project assets, collecting fees and charges. Assets are transferred back to the government after contract expiry.
2. Build-own-operate-transfer (BOOT): Private partner designs, finances, constructs, operates, and maintains project assets. Different from the BOT, the private partners own the project assets during the contract period. Assets are transferred back to the implementing agency after the contract period.
3. Build-own-operate (BOO): Private partner designs, finances, constructs, owns, and operates project assets for an indefinite period. Commercial use of assets, including fee collection, is permitted.
4. Management agreement (O&M): Private partner provides daily operations and maintenance services for project assets owned by the implementing agency, with payment based on service charges. No ownership rights are granted to the private partner.
5. Design-build-finance-operate-maintain (DBFOM): A private partner is responsible for designing, building, financing, operating, and maintaining project assets. Revenue collection is permitted, and assets are transferred back to the implementing agency after the contract period.
6. Design-build-lease (DBL): A private partner designs, builds, and leases project assets from the implementing agency, providing operation and maintenance services.

engineering, construction, financing, operation, and maintenance of infrastructure projects. At the end of a specified ownership period, investors transfer ownership of the facility to the host country (Car-Pušić, 2014; Zhang et al., 2016; Cui et al., 2018).

In tripartite cooperation projects, all three participants share both risks and benefits. The PPP model facilitates the transfer of a portion of project financing risks and costs from the host country's government to international investors, although the government retains some liability (Pessoa, 2008). Similarly, in tripartite cooperation, beneficiary countries distribute risks and costs among the two other investment partners. This approach allows beneficiary countries to alleviate budgetary pressures while accessing higher-quality services, while investors stand to gain attractive returns if the projects prove profitable (Xu et al., 2010).

2.2 Trilateral Cooperation[2] in the International Community

This part traces the developmental trajectory of tripartite cooperation within the international community. Firstly, it reviews the shift from bilateral North-South cooperation and South-South cooperation to trilateral development cooperation. Additionally, it examines what the existing literature has found about the determinants of advanced economies, beneficiary countries, and China to participate in trilateral cooperation.

2.2.1 From 'North-South Cooperation' and 'South-South Cooperation' to 'Trilateral Development Cooperation'

Tripartite cooperation is not a new modality in the international cooperation system. Pioneering tripartite cooperation projects date back to the 1970s, primarily in the fields of international trade and manufacturing. For example, the United States and Japan collaborated to invest in the texture and semiconductor products industries of South Korea and Taiwan in the 1970s (Schroder, 1977; Ichiro et al., 2021). Japan officially proposed trilateral cooperation in its 1974 Foreign Affairs Bluebook. Similarly, Germany has participated in over 150 triangular cooperation projects as

[2] In the current literature on international cooperation, most research uses the term 'trilateral cooperation' to refer to cooperation among three countries. Therefore, this section use 'trilateral cooperation' instead of 'tripartite cooperation at the country-level.'

an aid modality in Latin America and the Caribbean, Southeast Asia, and sub-Saharan Africa from the 1980s to 2021 (BMZ, 2022). In addition, the OECD triangular cooperation database[3] reveals that development projects prior to the 2000s were relatively scarce, with only two initiatives: one in Colombia and multiple countries focusing on kangaroo care in 1993 and another involving Japan, Kenya, and Africa in forestry protection in 1996. However, since the 2000s, tripartite cooperation has expanded into a broader range of sectors, including banking and financial services, agriculture and food security, social infrastructure and services, health, and environmental protection, with rapid growth observed within the first five years of the new millennium.

In the international community, the first meeting on tripartite cooperation was the 1978 United Nations Conference on Technical Co-operation among Developing Countries in Buenos Aires, Argentina. For the next 30 years, no UN meetings promoted tripartite cooperation. The documents of tripartite cooperation practices, both internationally and within individual countries, are largely missing and blank from this three-decade period. This interruption ended in 2008 with the Third High-Level Forum on Aid Effectiveness in Accra, Ghana, which marked the resumption of collective actions in the tripartite cooperation process. Since 2008, with the evolution of North-South and South-South cooperation, tripartite cooperation in international development has gradually developed.[4]

The concept of trilateral development cooperation is linked between North-South Cooperation and South-South Cooperation (Li & Bonschab, 2012). The 'North-South-South partnership' represents a shift from traditional development forms to new development forms (Grimm, 2011; Stahl, 2018). The development of tripartite cooperation has been a gradual process marked by an increasing number of international and regional conferences on trilateral cooperation in recent years (Heiligendamm Process, 2009; Pantoja, 2009; Schulz, 2010; OECD, 2012a), alongside more publications and the promotion of more cooperation projects by both traditional donors and emerging countries (see Fig. 2.2a, b).

[3] "Triangular Co-Operation Repository of Projects," OECD (n.d.). https://www.oecd.org/dac/triangular-co-operation/triangular-co-operation-repository.htm.

[4] Summarised from the OECD website on "Triangular Co-Operation in the International Development Agenda," OECD, accessed June 22, 2024, https://www.oecd.org/dac/dac-global-relations/triangular-cooperation.htm.

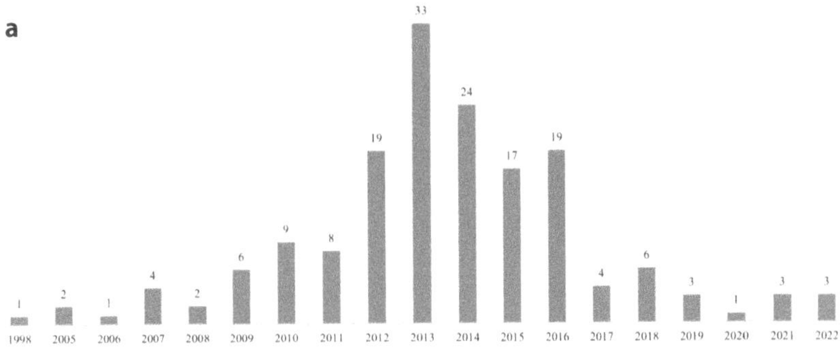

(Source: Data compiled by the author from the OECD Publications.
https://www.oecd.org/dac/dac-global-relations/oecdpublicationsontriangularco-operation.htm)

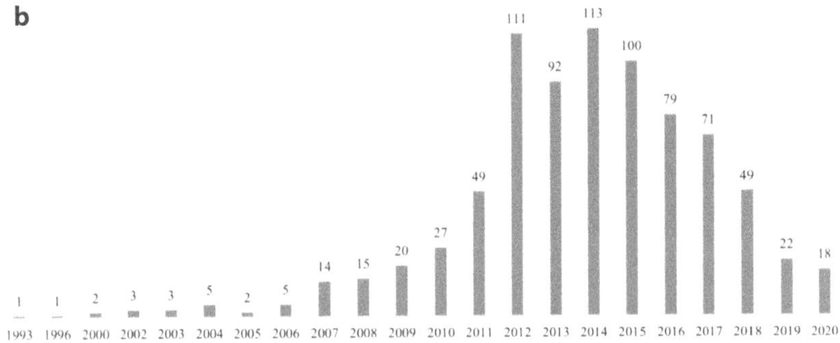

(Source: Data compiled by the author from the OECD Database.
https://www.oecd.org/dac/dac-global-relations/triangular-co-operation-repository.htm)

Fig. 2.2 (**a**) Number of OECD triangular cooperation documents (1998–2022). (**b**) Number of OECD triangular cooperation projects (1993–2020)

As of 2022, there are 168 documents related to triangular cooperation. Despite infrastructure being frequently mentioned in OECD documents, it has not been more extensively covered in academic and theoretical literature. The number of OECD documents on triangular cooperation peaked between 2012 and 2016, aligning with a period of increased project activity observed from 2011 to 2018. This surge was likely influenced by several key international meetings, such as the 2011 Fourth High-Level Forum on Aid Effectiveness in Busan, South Korea, and the First and Second High-Level Meetings of the Global Partnership for Effective

Development Cooperation in 2014 and 2016. However, the decline in the number of documents since 2017 remains unexplained, a trend that began before the onset of the COVID-19 pandemic.

By 2020, a total of 807 projects had been recorded, with a primary focus on areas such as agriculture, food security, health, environmental protection, disaster risk management, education, and training. Nevertheless, there is a noticeable lack of projects cantered on economic infrastructure. The OECD database listed only 83 projects on infrastructure (46 energy projects and 37 water management and sanitiser projects). This gap may be attributed to the differing priorities of traditional donor countries, which have focused on other areas of development assistance, in contrast to China's consistent emphasis on infrastructure. The relatively limited number of infrastructure projects in recent years may also help explain the scarcity of academic and theoretical literature on this topic.

Regarding North-South Cooperation and triangular cooperation, the initial dialogue between the DAC countries and emerging countries began in 2005, echoing the development trends shown in Fig. 2.2a, b. In DAC chair Richard Manning's speech titled 'Will Emerging Donors Change the Face of International Cooperation,' he asserted that the rise of emerging countries has altered the multilateral development architecture, prompting the DAC to adapt to the reality, and he emphasised fostering cooperation and synergy between the traditional international development agenda and the new forms represented by emerging countries (Stahl, 2012). Subsequently, in the 2008 Accra and 2011 Busan High-Level Forum on Aid Effectiveness, OECD-DAC donors acknowledged the contributions made by all development actors, particularly middle-income countries, as both providers and recipients of aid, which greatly contributed to international cooperation (Davies, 2010; OECD, 2008; Mawdsley et al., 2013). In 2016, the OECD established the Global Partnership Initiative on Effective Triangular Cooperation with the aim of uniting various development stakeholders to integrate triangular cooperation into the current development landscape, particularly considering the increasing significance of South-South and triangular cooperation (GPI, 2019a).

In South-South Cooperation and triangular cooperation, the United Nations initially mentioned 'South-South and triangular cooperation' in the 2003 High-Level Committee on the Review of Technical Cooperation among Developing Countries, aiming to support technology and economic development by "mobilising resources from developing-country governments and donors under triangular arrangements" (United

Nations, 2003, p. 18). The document of 2019 United Nations Conference on South-South Cooperation held in Buenos Aires (BAPA+40) acknowledged that triangular cooperation complements and adds value to South-South cooperation. It claimed that through triangular cooperation, beneficiary countries can access a broader range of resources, expertise, and capacities, facilitating the achievement of their national development goals as well as global sustainable development goals (UN, 2019).

These meetings illustrated the efforts of North countries to incorporate emerging countries into the international development regime, which established the foundation of North-South-South tripartite cooperation. Trilateral development cooperation combines South-South Cooperation and North-South Cooperation, and this transformative modality aims at finding adaptable, cost-effective, flexible, and context-specific solutions to address development challenges (Kharas et al., 2011).

However, it remains unclear whether the complementary advantages are being effectively utilised in tripartite cooperation, whether there are downsides to such trilateral arrangements, and whether it truly constitutes an 'equal' partnership. Additionally, the engagement of an additional stakeholder complicates the process of reaching agreements on development projects. Tripartite cooperation has not yet become mainstream in the development regime.

2.2.2 *Determinants of Country Participation in Trilateral Cooperation: Insights from Previous Research*

Traditional donor countries, emerging donor countries, and beneficiary countries all have their own motivations for facilitating tripartite cooperation. This section outlines the determinants of their participation based on existing knowledge from previous research, and gaps in the existing literature. The empirical chapters will examine these determinants and empirically identify further determinants.

2.2.2.1 Traditional Donor Countries

According to Fordelone (2009), traditional donor countries employ tripartite development cooperation as a strategy to manage the 're-Westernisation of international development.' This is because Chinese foreign aid agencies adhere to a non-interference policy and provide no-strings-attached loans to developing countries.[5] Traditional donor countries perceive that China uses development cooperation to advance its interests in foreign policy and trade, which impacts existing DAC principles (Tseng & Krog, 2016; Kjøllesdal & Welle-Strand, 2010). The aim of traditional donor countries' efforts to engage with Chinese tripartite cooperation is to shift policy priorities from development to diplomatic strategy in response to China's rise (Bräutigam, 2011). There are 14 traditional donor countries that have signed MOUs with China. Several countries have therefore engaged in Chinese tripartite cooperation projects.

Through tripartite cooperation, traditional donor countries aim to strengthen their relationship with China in less-developed regions (OECD, 2014a). They believe that such cooperation can enhance intra-regional relations and promote global responsibilities towards developing countries. For instance, the EU-China-Africa trilateral dialogue, initiated in 2008, aimed to address topics such as poverty reduction and pro-poor growth. This dialogue brought together high-ranking representatives from the DAC countries and China, enabling them to identify key development sectors in Africa and offer complementary expertise. The European Commission proposed the initiative of 'EU, China, and Africa: Towards Trilateral Dialogue and Cooperation,' with a focus on areas such as peace and security, infrastructure support, environmental management, and agriculture and food security in Africa (European Commission, 2008; Stahl, 2016). In addition, when traditional donors cooperate with China, China's fund and technology can alleviate financial and technological pressure on the DAC donor's development tasks (Kaplan et al., 2020).

As China used to be a recipient country, its development institutions were initially set up to manage inward development funds. In recent years, however, China has established new agencies, such as the Silk Road Fund and the China International Development Cooperation Agency, to manage outward development funds and relevant projects, particularly after the proposal of the BRI. Through tripartite cooperation, traditional donor countries aim to introduce institutionalised practices to China and

[5] China has distinct international development standards, primarily guided by its Five Principles of Peaceful Coexistence (Stahl, 2012). The Five Principles of Peaceful Coexistence includes: mutual respect for sovereignty and territorial integrity, mutual non-aggression, non-interference in each other's internal affairs, equality and mutual benefit, and peaceful coexistence.

influence the development of China to align with OECD-DAC frameworks and norms (Zhang, 2017b).

2.2.2.2 China

There are several explanations for China's motivation to engage in tripartite cooperation. First, China faces challenges regarding its international reputation. Western media and political circles have often portrayed China negatively, citing concerns such as the so-called debt-trap diplomacy to describe China's lending policies in international development finance (Carmody, 2020; Brautigam, 2019; Singh, 2020). The Hambantota Port project, for example, is frequently cited as a 'notorious' case in this narrative (The Morning, 2020; Economic Times, 2023). Additionally, Chinese state-owned enterprises (SOEs) have been accused of engaging in strategic corruption that undermines the international order (McFarland et al., 2022).

In this context, tripartite development cooperation serves as a means for China to improve its international reputation (Abdenur, 2007). China views tripartite cooperation as another approach that can enhance its external image as a responsible stakeholder, as well as reduce political tension through cooperating with both traditional donors and beneficiary countries. China's rapid economic growth has prompted it to further pursue a positive international image. China has used foreign aid and investment as a tool to promote the image of a peaceful and responsible developer (Knodt & Piefer, 2012). The Chinese government has proposed the concept of a 'harmonious world' to counter criticisms such as 'China threat,' 'new imperialism,' or 'neo-colonialism' (Li, 2007). Through tripartite cooperation, China aims to convey the message to traditional donor countries that it has no intention to challenge the current international regime. Instead, China expects to cooperate with traditional donors and integrate into the existing development regime (Zhang, 2020). These claims are made by Chinese officials and represent the government's stance that Chinese foreign development projects are harmless (Jia et al., 2019; MFA, 2024).

Secondly, tripartite cooperation can facilitate China's closer engagement with traditional donor partners and beneficiary countries. Despite the divergent approaches between traditional donor countries and China in international development, they share some common interests in development projects, such as district security and stability, energy and environmental security, economic growth, and sustainable development (Zhang

& Smith, 2017). As participants aim to minimise costs and maximise benefits during the cooperative process, the core issue lies in how provider countries reconcile their interests with the demands of beneficiary countries (Prashad, 2007).

2.2.2.3 *Beneficiary Countries*

For beneficiary countries, tripartite cooperation represents an approach to diminish the influence of a single foreign power. While traditional donor countries offer human and financial resources, technology, and expertise, beneficiary countries aim to formulate their own development strategies. They are often reluctant to invest time in traditional donors' long-term development approaches, such as democratisation, rule of law, and good governance (Kurlantzick, 2006; Gilpin, 2021). To get around such requirements, they are sometimes inclined to accept non-conditional loans offered by emerging developing countries rather than stringent loans from traditional donor countries. For instance, they prefer the short-term progress associated with China's development policy based on non-interference (Bräutigam, 2011). However, they also do not want to totally lose the support of traditional donors, and tripartite cooperation offers a compromise option for them to collaborate with both traditional donor countries and China.

Overall, tripartite cooperation establishes a communicative approach for traditional donor countries, China, and beneficiary countries. A successful tripartite development cooperation project can achieve multiple objectives, such as building institutional capacity and fostering collaborative practices, when it effectively aligns with the diverse interests of all parties involved (McEwan & Mawdsley, 2012). For traditional donor countries, tripartite cooperation facilitates an understanding of Chinese foreign aid and investment, while also increasing their influence over China's relevant foreign policies. For China, tripartite cooperation serves to enhance its global image and strengthen its international partnerships. For beneficiary countries, tripartite cooperation provides additional options, and the involvement of two providers can offer more financial and technological guarantees that stabilise the implemented projects in beneficiary countries (Jin, 2018). While these determinants of tripartite cooperation are well discussed at the country level, there remains a lack of clarity at the firm level. My empirical chapter will address this gap by exploring the determinants that influence firms' decisions to participate in tripartite cooperation.

2.3 Tripartite Cooperation Practices in Different Countries

This section outlines tripartite cooperation practices in different countries, including both traditional donor countries such as Japan and Germany, as well as emerging donors like South Africa. These countries have explicitly stipulated tripartite cooperation policies[6] (Lengfelder, 2015). Subsequently, this section delineates the unique features of the Chinese tripartite cooperation approach.

2.3.1 *Tripartite Cooperation Practices in Japan, Germany, and South Africa*

2.3.1.1 *Japan*[7]

Japan's trilateral cooperation has a long history, dating back to 1974. In the 1974 Foreign Affairs Bluebook (Ministry of Foreign Affairs of Japan, chapter 3, section 1.4), Japan proposed to "promote concrete cooperation in wide-ranging areas, such as science and technology, energy, and development cooperation in third countries," particularly with European countries. Since then, Japan has steadily increased its trilateral cooperation activities (Honda, 2014).

The situation Japan faced in the 1990s is analogous to China's current position. Japan emerged as an important player in the international economic arena during that period, ranked as the world's second-largest economic power with remarkable productive capacity. Accordingly, Japan's Official Development Assistance (ODA) consistently ranked high among the DAC countries from 1991 to 2021 (OECD, 2023). Japan actively engages in cooperation with the United States and the EU. Japan sought collaboration with the United States, leveraging its experience and social connections in Latin America since the 1980s (Stallings & Szkely, 1993). Moreover, Japan and the EU established the Center for International Economic Collaboration in 1987, aimed at supporting business cooperation between the EU and Japanese companies in ASEAN, Africa, and Latin America. In recent years, Prime Minister Shinzo Abe and President

[6] These countries use the terms 'trilateral cooperation' and/or 'triangular cooperation' to refer to 'tripartite cooperation.'

[7] Japan often uses the term 'trilateral cooperation' interchangeably with 'tripartite cooperation.'

of the European Commission Jean-Claude Juncker signed the Partnership on Sustainable Connectivity and Quality Infrastructure in 2019, marking a significant advancement in EU-Japan cooperation with partner third countries (European Commission, 2019).

The Japan International Cooperation Agency (JICA) has developed various patterns and aid instruments for trilateral cooperation, primarily comprising two types. The first type involves Japan transferring knowledge or technology to one Southern country (S1), which then disseminates these practices to other Southern countries (S2, S3...). The second type requires Japan and another Southern country (S1) to collaborate as equal partners to support other Southern countries (S2, S3...). These trilateral cooperation activities typically focus on training programmes, expert dispatch, and technical cooperation in traditional international aid fields such as health and education (Honda et al., 2013). These Japanese institutions' reports reflect Japan's trilateral cooperation practices. They also highlight the complexity of tripartite cooperation with an additional partner in projects, which complicates institutional arrangements and the medium of knowledge sharing.

Japan regards trilateral cooperation as a diplomatic tool to sustain economic and political ties with developing countries (Leheny & Warren, 2009). Japan has a long-standing tradition as a donor and has actively participated in international aid and loan activities within the Asian region. In 2020, approximately 61.2% (US$10.3 billion) of Japan's ODA fund was allocated to Asian countries, with Bangladesh, India, Indonesia, the Philippines, and Myanmar being the principal beneficiaries. Leveraging its development banking arm, the JICA, and the Asian Development Bank (ADB), Japan has maintained a dominant position in Asian infrastructure development projects. However, China's BRI and the establishment of the Asian Infrastructure Investment Bank (AIIB) offer new alternatives for Asian countries, potentially challenging Japan's dominance in this region.

Then, Japan proposed the Free and Open Indo-Pacific strategy to counter China's BRI in 2016. This zero-sum competition significantly hindered the progress of both China and Japan in development projects, leading to a lack of effective coordination and integration. These two development plans were engaged in fierce competition, particularly in the infrastructure sector, with a focus on projects such as ports, railways, and industrial parks (Ministry of Foreign Affairs of Japan, 2023). The Japan Business Federation (JBF) later criticised the Japanese government's zero-sum competition policy, arguing that it had inflicted severe damage on both the Japanese and Chinese economies (Hui & Han, 2021).

Therefore, Umirdinov (2019) suggests that through initiatives like the Japan-China Memorandum on Business Cooperation in Third Countries, the Japanese government can use trilateral cooperation to promote its 'Quality Infrastructure Investment' (QII) principles and curb potentially detrimental economic activities of Chinese companies in Asian markets.

2.3.1.2 Germany[8]

According to a document by Germany's Federal Ministry for Economic Cooperation and Development (BMZ), triangular cooperation is defined as follows: "Germany works together with partners in emerging countries and builds on their efforts in the field of South-South cooperation" (BMZ, 2022, p. 4). In this document, the BMZ demonstrates that triangular cooperation in German development cooperation aligns with Germany's domestic development targets, particularly within the framework of the 'BMZ 2030' reform process. Moreover, it contributes to international development goals by strengthening partnerships with other donor countries to achieve global sustainability objectives.

Similar to the Chinese government's approach, the BMZ views triangular cooperation as a 'triple-win' opportunity for all partners, fostering synergies through joint efforts. It serves as an approach to positively impact beneficiary countries and enhance cooperation partnerships on a strategic level, particularly between DAC donors and emerging country partners. Germany's triangular cooperation encompasses two primary dimensions: the programmatic-thematic dimension and the political-strategic effects dimension. The programmatic-thematic dimension involves traditional development interventions aimed at enhancing the well-being of target groups in beneficiary countries. The political-strategic effects dimension aims to foster cooperation and partnership among all participants within the overall development cooperation framework. Germany strategically employs triangular cooperation to sustain and bolster collaboration with emerging economies (Kaplan et al., 2020).

Triangular cooperation is not a new approach for Germany's development cooperation. According to the BMZ official website on triangular development, from the 1980s to 2021, Germany has participated in over 150 triangular cooperation projects. These projects have covered various

[8] Germany often uses the term 'triangular cooperation' to denote 'tripartite cooperation.'

areas such as preventive healthcare, food security, environmental protection, climate action, and support for sustainable economic activities. They have been implemented in regions including Latin America and the Caribbean, Southeast Asia, and sub-Saharan Africa. Among these projects, approximately 73% of Germany's triangular cooperation portfolio is concentrated in the Latin America and the Caribbean (LAC) region. To facilitate this cooperation, the German government established the special Regional Fund for Triangular Cooperation in the LAC region. Triangular cooperation projects, as an aid modality, have taken on a pronounced political and strategic dimension (BMZ, 2022).

However, many existing projects adopt a short-term approach, lacking sustainability once the project term concludes. Kaplan et al. (2020, p. 68) argue that coordination and communication among the three participants often incur higher transaction costs compared to bilateral cooperation. These costs are difficult to lower due to the one-off projects' duration and budget constraints, which are not sufficient to permit such reductions.

Germany and China have exploited triangular cooperation to enhance synergies in North-South development cooperation, particularly focusing on medium and small businesses. In 2017, they established the Sino-German Center for Sustainable Development (CSD) and financed various triangular cooperation initiatives in Africa and Asia. For instance, projects such as Sustainable Textile Investment and Operation in Ethiopia, Sino-German technical vocational education and training (TVET) for rural jobs in Laos, and Global Low Carbon Tea Triangular Cooperation in Kenya's Tea Value Chain have been implemented. These endeavours aim to bridge knowledge gaps in business and development programmes between China and Germany.[9]

From the practices of Japan and Germany, it is evident that although tripartite cooperation is not a new modality, it has not yet emerged as the mainstream approach in international development compared to direct bilateral cooperation. There is not only a scarcity of relevant documents and systematic theories addressing tripartite cooperation, but the funding process for tripartite cooperation is also slow in practical projects. Therefore, it is worthwhile to investigate whether because of more transaction costs, tripartite cooperation has this sluggish progress. Furthermore, it is notable that, despite the existence of numerous projects, there has been little academic writing on the subject.

[9] https://sg-csd.org/projects/.

2.3.1.3 *South Africa*[10]

South Africa, traditionally classified as a recipient country in the donor–recipient aid hierarchy, has transitioned to a role as a provider or facilitator in peacekeeping and peacebuilding efforts on the African continent in recent years. This transition reflects South Africa's foreign policy direction towards fostering trilateral cooperation (Masters, 2014). In 2011, the White Paper on South African Foreign Policy—Building a Better World—marked the first instance of trilateral development cooperation being mentioned in government policy (South African Government, 2011).

However, South Africa has limitations in both political and financial capacities. Trilateral development cooperation provides an avenue for accessing supplementary resources from developed countries (Masters, 2014). These projects, particularly focusing on security assistance, are often led by traditional donors (Stahl, 2012). For example, police training and capacity building with Japan in the Democratic Republic of Congo (UNECOSOC, 2008). In addition, traditional donor countries view South Africa as a crucial intermediary partner for enhanced engagement in the African region. This enables South Africa to benefit from trade, technology transfer, investment, and remittances from traditional donors (Sidiropoulos, 2012; Besharati, 2013). In 2007, South Africa and Germany established the TriCo Fund, with Germany committing €5 million to support vocational training projects, combat corruption, prevent violence, and enhance vaccine production and logistics (German Foreign Office, 2023). Through trilateral development cooperation projects, Germany aims to support South Africa's reputation as a donor and eventually decrease its aid in the African region (OECD 2014a).

Through trilateral development cooperation, South Africa aims to maintain bilateral ties with traditional donor countries while also bridging the gap between developed and developing countries. South Africa often acts as a facilitator country, helping implement projects initiated by traditional donors in other African countries. Additionally, South Africa seeks a leading position on the African continent, expanding its socio-economic influence through initiatives such as the New Partnership for Africa's Development (NEPAD) and programmes like NEPAD's Presidential Infrastructure Champion Initiative (Masters, 2014).

[10] South Africa often uses the term 'trilateral development cooperation' to refer to 'tripartite cooperation' in their policy paper.

South Africa is willing to participate in trilateral development as it allows the country to expand its influence on the continent while simultaneously reducing the costs associated with participation. Due to its advantageous geographic location and historical ties, South African companies can identify business opportunities that foreign capital may overlook in other African countries (Smith et al., 2006).

However, South Africa's pursuit of national interests during trilateral cooperation has occasionally drawn criticism from other African nations, who perceive its actions as displaying 'neo-colonial' behaviour, particularly in business dealings (McEwan & Mawdsley, 2012). Therefore, based on South Africa's experience, China should enhance engagement processes and promote recipient countries' ownership in trilateral development cooperation projects. This approach would facilitate the transfer of relevant knowledge that is applicable, assimilable, and affordable (Rui et al. 2017), rather than merely replicating traditional donor–recipient hierarchies.

2.3.2 China's Unique Approach to Tripartite Cooperation

The international community and traditional donors have initiated numerous trilateral cooperation development projects involving China as the partner country. China has actively participated in international forums promoting traditional trilateral cooperation, such as the UN Conference on South-South Cooperation and the International Meeting on Triangular Cooperation. Through pragmatic cooperation with over ten international organisations, including UNDP, WFP, UNHCR, UNICEF, WHO, and ICRC, China participates in triangular development programmes in various areas such as food assistance, post-disaster reconstruction, refugee relief, and women and children's health across approximately 50 countries. For example, the UNESCO-China Funds-in-Trust Project supported over 10,000 teachers in more than ten African countries since 2011 (UNDP 2017). The United Kingdom collaborated with China on the Accelerate Agricultural Technology Transfer to Low-Income Countries (AgriTT) project in Malawi and Uganda from 2012 to 2016.[11]

[11] There are 54 projects involved in China from the OECD triangular cooperation project database. "Triangular Co-Operation Repository of Projects," OECD (n.d.). https://www.oecd.org/dac/triangular-co-operation/triangular-co-operation-repository.htm.

These earlier international tripartite development practices laid the foundation for China to develop its own model of tripartite cooperation. Zhang (2020) traced China's historical cooperation with traditional donor countries since 2000 and found that tripartite cooperation often begins with small-scale technical projects, such as those related to health or agriculture, before expanding into other fields such as education, energy, water, and transportation.

The Chinese-initiated tripartite cooperation model emerged prior to its formal proposal by the Chinese government in 2015. From 2008 to 2015, joint bidding projects involving Sino-Japan and Sino-France could be seen as early instances of 'third-party market cooperation.' As early as 2008, the Japanese and Chinese governments signed MOUs to promote cooperation between their enterprises in other markets. In 2010, China and France first mentioned 'third-party market cooperation' in their 'Joint Statement on Strengthening a Comprehensive Strategic Partnership.' Subsequently, Beijing and several EU member states have elevated their relations to strategic comprehensive partnerships under the Third-Partner Market Cooperation (TPMC) framework since 2015 (Zhang, 2020; Bertucci and Locatelli, 2020).

Distinct from traditional donor-led tripartite cooperation projects, China-led tripartite cooperation exhibits unique characteristics. Firstly, China simplifies the classification system of tripartite cooperation projects. Within the framework of traditional donors-led tripartite cooperation, there typically exist three partner roles: the pivotal partner, usually an emerging country with relevant domestic experience and a socio-economic context similar to the beneficiary country, acts as an intermediary between traditional donors and the beneficiary. The facilitating partner, whether developed or developing, offers financial and technical expertise, contributing resources and knowledge to the tripartite cooperation. The beneficiary partner, as the third role, receives support and resources from facilitating partners (OECD, 2022; BMZ, 2022). However, this categorical system generates various combination possibilities, and the roles of each player can be confusing, making it challenging for participants to adhere to existing patterns. In Chinese tripartite cooperation projects, the distinction between the pivotal partner and facilitating partner is not made, as both China and traditional donor countries offer resources to beneficiary countries. China merely clarifies its role in different project types, such as a provider of products and services, an Engineering,

Procurement, and Construction (EPC) contractor, an investor, or a sponsor (as detailed in Chap. 5).

In China-led tripartite cooperation, SOEs play key roles in executing projects, with the government and development agencies taking on more supportive or oversight functions. The private sector, however, is rarely involved in such collaborations and infrequently signs agreements with traditional donor countries. The 2019 China's Report on the Work of the Government emphasised the need for the government to "adhere to the principle of pursuing shared growth through discussion and collaboration and observe market principles and international rules, and regard enterprises as the main actors in advancing third-party market cooperation" (Li, 2021, p. 46). Both Chinese and companies from traditional donor countries are perceived as providers in tripartite cooperation projects, with their roles determined based on their functions within the projects. While the Chinese government asserts that this approach enhances communication and negotiation effectiveness among participants, its practical efficacy requires further investigation.

Secondly, unlike traditional donors' ODA approach, which directly provides grants and loans to less-developed countries, China frequently employs a 'loan-trade-investment' approach to infrastructure projects, whereby foreign aid is tied to investment rather than being purely charitable (Bräutigam, 2011). Termed as 'economic cooperation' rather than 'aid,' this approach views aid or loans as "an element of a broader strategy for synergistic economic development with the partner country that encompasses private investment and trade" (Shiga, 2016, p. 15). China places a greater emphasis on loans rather than aid, resulting in a less-charitable approach to international development. One notable financing model employed by the Chinese government is the 'Angola mode,' involving resource-backed infrastructure financing in development projects. Chinese firms involved in these projects not only benefit from state-backed loans and export credits offered at preferential terms but may also gain access to natural resources or other strategic benefits (Bertucci and Locatelli, 2020; Horn et al., 2021; Mattlin & Nojonen, 2015).

Chinese tripartite cooperation has made significant progress, with China demonstrating a commitment to further expanding such collaboration. This strategic direction was outlined in the 2021 White Paper on China's International Development Cooperation in a New Era. The document emphasises China's aspiration to engage in tripartite cooperation with developed countries and international organisations to maximise benefits for beneficiary countries.[12]

2.4 Conclusion

This chapter introduced the issue of tripartite cooperation and outlined general trends in its development within the international context. Firstly, it is noted that tripartite cooperation is characterised by various terms used by different groups, and its ideal assumptions not only are challenging to realise in practice but also contain internal contradictions. Secondly, it is observed that tripartite cooperation does not represent a recent innovation in developmental paradigms. Originating from 'North-South cooperation' and 'South-South cooperation,' it has a development history spanning four decades within the context of liberalism. State participants have their own motivations to engage in tripartite cooperation projects.

From the 1980s to the 2000s, both academic research and practical experience in tripartite cooperation developed slowly. It was not until the 2008 Third High-Level Forum on Aid Effectiveness in Accra that tripartite cooperation re-emerged and thrived in the international development community. Subsequently, it boomed for about a decade, from 2008 to 2019, as evidenced by the number of projects in the OECD's triangular cooperation database and the relevant documents from these years. This indicates that donor countries were exploring more approaches within the international development regime during this period, particularly in the aftermath of the 2008 economic crisis.

In contrast to traditional cooperation paradigms, Chinese tripartite cooperation exhibits distinctive features. It places greater emphasis on the development of industry, commerce, and infrastructure through an integrated financing approach including loan, trade, and investment. For instance, Japan and Germany, as pioneering initiators, have already initiated trilateral cooperation practices since the 1980s, and have established robust cooperative frameworks. However, their focus was more on issues such as health, democratisation and so on. South Africa, an emerging economy, has engaged in trilateral cooperation within the African continent. Their efforts continue to concentrate on international development

[12] The State Council Information Office of the People's Republic of China, "China's International Development Cooperation in the New Era," www.scio.gov.cn, January 2021, http://www.scio.gov.cn/zfbps/ndhf/2021n_2242/202207/t20220704_130668.html.

domains, including human rights, peacekeeping, health, agriculture, and technology transfer, facilitated by official development funds.

Despite its growth, trilateral cooperation, as a subtype of multilateral cooperation, has not garnered as much academic focus or mainstream status in the international development field compared to bilateral cooperation and larger multilateral cooperation frameworks like BRICS, AIIB, OECD-DAC, and MDB. It still confronts challenges due to the lack of critical, detailed, and empirical-based analyses, especially in the infrastructure development field. Although tripartite cooperation shows the potential to challenge the traditional donor system theoretically by leveraging the expertise of emerging donor countries to enhance effectiveness (Hauck, 2011), empirical evidence to support these assertions remains insufficient. Furthermore, existing tripartite cooperation projects have relied on 'tailor-made' agreements due to the absence of unified international cooperation standards (Zhang, 2020). The absence of clear policy guidelines and operational procedures increases the potential transaction costs. This leads to the proposition that potential transaction costs may play a significant role in tripartite cooperation.

This research further investigated why, despite decades of evolution, 'tripartite cooperation' has not yet become mainstream, and this term has been rarely mentioned in international development discourse. Moreover, although extensive literature exists on South-South cooperation and emerging donors in general, there is an absence of perspectives from the private sector in the implementation processes of tripartite cooperation (Jin, 2018). It seems surprising that both academic and theoretical literature have not extensively covered tripartite cooperation. Therefore, this research aims to explore the reasons behind this phenomenon and fill the research gaps regarding the theoretical foundations of tripartite cooperation. In the empirical chapters, this study aims to further investigate Chinese tripartite cooperation within mega-infrastructure projects. It seeks to analyse why both China and advanced economies occasionally exhibit a preference for the tripartite cooperation model over other types of cooperation, despite the more potential transaction costs in these projects.

References

Abdenur, A. (2007). The Strategic Triad: Form and Content in Brazil's Triangular Cooperation Practices. https://www.files.ethz.ch/isn/46819/2007-06.pdf

ADB, EBRD, IDB, IsDB, and WBG. (2016). The APMG Public-Private Partnership (PPP) Certification Guide. Washington, DC: World Bank Group. https://ppp-certification.com/ppp-certification-guide/31-types-and-variations-ppps

Allen, F., Qian, M., & Xie, J. (2019). Understanding Informal Financing. *Journal of Financial Intermediation, 39*(7), 19–33. https://doi.org/10.1016/j.jfi.2018.06.004

Altenburg, T., & Weikert, J. (2007). A Service of ZBW Trilateral Development Cooperation with "New Donors." https://www.econstor.eu/bitstream/10419/199612/1/die-bp-2007-05.pdf

Araújo, S., & Sutherland, D. (2010). Public-Private Partnerships and Investment in Infrastructure. OECD Economics Department Working Papers. https://doi.org/10.1787/5km7jf6q8f0t-en

Arezki, R., Bolton, P., Peters, S., Samama, F., & Stiglitz, J. (2017). From Global Savings Glut to Financing Infrastructure. *Economic Policy, 32*(90), 221–261. https://doi.org/10.1093/epolic/eix005

Babic, M., Fichtner, J., & Heemskerk, E. M. (2017). States Versus Corporations: Rethinking the Power of Business in International Politics. *The International Spectator, 52*(4), 20–43. https://doi.org/10.1080/03932729.2017.1389151

Bertucci, S., & Locatelli, M. (2020, February 4). Advancing EU-China-Africa Trilateral Partnerships: The Role of Joint Business Ventures in Promoting Sustainability, Innovation and Institutional Synergies. *EIAS*. https://eias.org/briefing-paper/advancing-eu-china-africa-trilateral-partnerships-the-role-of-joint-business-ventures-in-promoting-sustainability-innovation-and-institutional-synergies/

Besharati, N. A. (2013). South African Development Partnership Agency (SADPA): Strategic Aid or Development Packages for Africa? SAIIA. https://saiia.org.za/research/south-african-development-partnership-agency-sadpa-strategic-aid-or-development-packages-for-africa/

BMZ. (2022). Triangular Cooperation in German Development Cooperation. Federal Ministry for Economic Cooperation and Development; BMZ Strategy Paper 1. https://www.bmz.de/en/news/publications/triangular-cooperation-105782

Bräutigam, D. (2011). Aid "With Chinese Characteristics": Chinese Foreign Aid and Development Finance Meet the OECD-DAC Aid Regime. *Journal of International Development, 23*(5), 752–764. https://doi.org/10.1002/jid.1798

Brautigam, D. (2019). A critical Look at Chinese "Debt Trap Diplomacy": The Rise of a Meme. *Area Development and Policy, 5*(1), 1–14. https://doi.org/10.1080/23792949.2019.1689828

Carmody, P. (2020). Dependence not Debt-Trap Diplomacy. *Area Development and Policy, 5*(1), 23–31. https://doi.org/10.1080/23792949.2019.1702471

Car-Pušić, D. (2014). PPP Model Opportunities, Limitations and Risks in Croatian Public Project Financing. *Procedia - Social and Behavioral Sciences, 119*, 663–671. https://doi.org/10.1016/j.sbspro.2014.03.074

Chaturvedi, S., Sidiropoulos, E., & Fues, T. (2012). *Development Cooperation and Emerging Powers: New Partners or Old Patterns?* Zed Books.

Cuervo-Cazurra, A., & Genc, M. (2008). Transforming Disadvantages into Advantages: Developing-Country MNEs in the Least Developed Countries. *Journal of International Business Studies, 39*(6), 957–979. https://doi.org/10.1057/palgrave.jibs.8400390

Cui, C., Liu, Y., Hope, A., & Wang, J. (2018). Review of Studies on the Public–private Partnerships (PPP) for Infrastructure Projects. *International Journal of Project Management, 36*(5), 773–794. https://doi.org/10.1016/j.ijproman.2018.03.004

Davies, P. (2010). the Roles and Activities of New Development Partners. [Review of the Roles and Activities of New Development Partners]. World Bank. CFP Working Paper Series No. 4.

de Graaff, N., & van Apeldoorn, B. (2017). US Elite Power and the Rise of "Statist" Chinese Elites in Global Markets. *International Politics, 54*(3), 338–355. https://doi.org/10.1057/s41311-017-0031-2

Demirbag, M., Tatoglu, E., & Glaister, K. W. (2008). Factors Affecting Perceptions of the Choice Between Acquisition and Greenfield Entry: The Case of Western FDI in an Emerging Market. *Management International Review, 48*(1), 5–38. https://doi.org/10.1007/s11575-008-0002-3

Deng, P. (2013). Chinese Outward Direct Investment Research: Theoretical Integration and Recommendations. *Management and Organization Review, 9*(03), 513–539. https://doi.org/10.1111/more.12030

Doloi, H. (2012). Understanding Impacts of Time and Cost Related Construction Risks On Operational Performance Of PPP Projects. *International Journal of Strategic Property Management, 16*(3), 316–337. https://doi.org/10.3846/1648715x.2012.688774

Dornan, M., & Brant, P. (2014). Chinese Assistance in the Pacific: Agency, Effectiveness and the Role of Pacific Island Governments. *Asia & the Pacific Policy Studies, 1*(2), 349–363. https://doi.org/10.1002/app5.35

Economic Times. (2023, May 19). Like its Apps in India, China has Turned World's Loan Mafia. *The Economic Times.* https://economictimes.indiatimes.com/news/international/world-news/like-its-apps-in-india-china-has-turned-worlds-loan-mafia/articleshow/100361672.cms?from=mdr

Estache, A., Foster, V., & Wodon, Q. (2002). *Accounting for Poverty in Infrastructure Reform: Learning from Latin America's Experience*. World Bank.
European Commission. (2008). Report on the Public Consultation on the Communication of the European Commission on The EU, Africa and China: Towards Trilateral Dialogue and Cooperation on Peace, Stability and Sustainable Development. http://ec.europa.eu/development/icenter/repository/afrique_chine_UE_public_consultation_report_final.pdf%2036
European Commission. (2019). EU-China—A Strategic Outlook. https://ec.europa.eu/info/sites/default/files/communication-eu-china-a-strategic-outlook.pdf
Feng, Q. (2019). Vigorously Expanding Third-Party Market Cooperation. https://www.gov.cn/zhengce/2019-04/03/content_5379223.htm
Fernandes, C., Oliveira Cruz, C., & Moura, F. (2019). Ex Post Evaluation of PPP Government-led Renegotiations: Impacts on the Financing of Road Infrastructure. *The Engineering Economist, 64*(2), 116–141. https://doi.org/10.1080/0013791x.2018.1559384
Ferrari, M., Giovannini, A., & Pompei, M. (2016). The Challenge of Infrastructure Financing. *Oxford Review of Economic Policy, 32*(3), 446–474. https://doi.org/10.1093/oxrep/grw017
Fordelone, T. Y. (2009). Triangular Co-operation and Aid Effectiveness, Paper prepared for the Policy Dialogue on Development Co-operation. http://www.oecd.org/dac/46387212.pdf
Fordelone, T. Y. (2011). Triangular Co-operation and Aid Effectiveness. *OECD Journal: General Papers, 2010*(1), 47–67. https://doi.org/10.1787/gen_papers-2010-5kgc6cl31rnx
Gao, X. (2018). New Model: The "Winning Alliance" of the Three Nations and Four Parties (新样板：三国四方的"赢联盟"). http://www.rmhb.com.cn/zt/ydyl/201808/t20180831_800139852.html
German Foreign Office. (2023, September 22). German development cooperation with South Africa. *Auswärtiges Amt*. https://southafrica.diplo.de/sa-en/04_News/-/2220644
Gilpin, S. I. (2021). China, Africa and the International Aid System: A Challenge to (the Norms Underpinning) the Neoliberal World Order? *Journal of Asian and African Studies, 58*(3), 277–297. https://doi.org/10.1177/00219096211063804
GPI. (2019a). Triangular Co-operation in the Era of the 2030 Agenda, Global Partnership for Effective Development Co-operation. Www.effectivecooperation.org. https://www.effectivecooperation.org/content/triangular-co-operation-era-2030-agenda
GPI. (2019b). Voluntary Guidelines for Effective Triangular Co-Operation, Global Partnership for Effective Development Co-operation.

https://www.effectivecooperation.org/content/voluntary-guidelines-effective-triangular-co-operation
Grimm, S. (2008). Africa-China-Europe trilateral co-operation: is Europe naïve? Www.die-Gdi.de. https://www.die-gdi.de/en/others-publications/article/africa-china-europe-trilateral-co-operation-is-europe-naive/
Grimm, S. (2011). Engaging with China in Africa—Trilateral Cooperation as an Option? EDC2020. https://www.asienhaus.de/upload/pdf/materialien/grimm_2011_engaging_with_china_in_africa.pdf
Hampton, G., Baldwin, A. N., & Holt, G. (2012). Project Delays and Cost: Stakeholder Perceptions of Traditional v. PPP Procurement. *Journal of Financial Management of Property and Construction, 17*(1), 73–91. https://doi.org/10.1108/13664381211211055
Hauck, V. (2011). Triangular Cooperation: Towards Horizontal Partnerships, But How? Bali Workshop Report, 27 February–1 March. Paris: OECD Task Team on South–South Cooperation. https://europa.eu/capacity4dev/public-cd-tc/discussions/triangular-cooperation-towards-horizontal-partnerships-how
Honda, S. (2014). Japan's Triangular Cooperation Mechanism: With a Focus on JICA's Activities. JICA Ogata Research Institute. https://www.jica.go.jp/english/jica_ri/publication/booksandreports/pans_triangular_cooperation_mechanism_with_a_focus_on_jicas_activities.html
Honda, S., Kato, H., & Shimoda, Y. (2013). South-South and Triangular Cooperation for Sub-Saharan Africa's Development—With Special Emphasis on Knowledge Exchange and Co-creation. In *For Inclusive and Dynamic Development in Sub-Saharan*. JICA Research Institute.
Hooijmaaijers, B. (2018). China's Rise in Africa and the Response of the EU: A Theoretical Analysis of the EU-China-Africa Trilateral Cooperation Policy Initiative. *Journal of European Integration, 40*(4), 443–460. https://doi.org/10.1080/07036337.2018.1465418
Horn, S., Reinhart, C. M., & Trebesch, C. (2021). China's Overseas Lending. *Journal of International Economics, 133*, 103539. https://doi.org/10.1016/j.jinteco.2021.103539
Hui, X., & Han, W. (2021). Third Party Market Cooperation Between China and Japan: Opportunities, Challenges, and Response Strategies. *India Ocean Economic and Political Review, 45*(3), 38–58, 152–153.
Ichiro, F., Joo, H. S., Steinberg, J., & Friedhoff, K. (2021). *Cooperating, Competing, Confronting: US-Japan-South Korea Trilateral Cooperation as China Rises*. JSTOR. https://www.jstor.org/stable/resrep33467
International Labour Organisation. (2019). How-to-Guide on South-South and Triangular Cooperation design for Decent Work. South-South Galaxy. https://www.southsouth-galaxy.org/publications/how-to-guide-on-south-south-and-triangular-cooperation-design-for-decent-work-ilo-2019/

Jia, W., Chen, S., & Wu, S. (2019, November 20). Why is China's Insistence on Foreign Aid not Pretent Generous? http://politics.people.com.cn/n1/2019/1120/c429373-31465280.html

Jin, S. (2018). Triangular Cooperation in East Asia: Challenges and Opportunities for Japanese Official Development Assistance. *IDS Bulletin, 49*(3), 1–20. https://doi.org/10.19088/1968-2018.151

Joskow, P. L. (1990). The Performance of Long-Term Contracts: Further Evidence from Coal Markets. *The RAND Journal of Economics, 21*(2), 251. https://doi.org/10.2307/2555423

Kamwengo, C. (2020). Beneficiary Country Ownership and the Politics of Partnership in Trilateral Development Cooperation: A Case Study of Zambia. Etheses.dur.ac.uk. http://etheses.dur.ac.uk/13696/

Kaplan, M., Busemann, D., & Wirtgen, K. (2020). Trilateral Cooperation in German Development Cooperation. German Institute for Development Evaluation (DEval), Bonn. https://www.deval.org/en/publications/trilateral-cooperation-in-german-development-cooperation

Kato, H. (2012). *Scaling Up South-South and Triangular Cooperation.* JICA Research Institute.

Kerr, T. M. (1995). Supplying Water Infrastructure to Developing Countries Via Private Sector Project Financing. *Georgetown International Environmental Law Review, 8*(1), 91–108.

Kharas, H. J., Jung, W., & Makino, K. (2011). *Catalyzing Development: A New Vision for Aid.* Brookings Institution Press.

Kjøllesdal, K. A., & Welle-Strand, A. (2010). Foreign Aid Strategies: China Taking Over? Asian. *Social Science, 6*(10). https://doi.org/10.5539/ass.v6n10p3

Knodt, M., & Piefer, N. (2012). Why Not Cooperate in a Triangle? Explaining Different Motivations in Triangular Cooperatio. In J. Langendorf et al. (Eds.), *Triangular Cooperation: A Guideline for Working in Practice.* Baden-Baden.

Kurlantzick, J. (2006). Beijing's Safari: China's Move into Africa and its Implications for Aid, Development, and Governance. CARNEGIE ENDOWMENT for INTERNATIONAL PEACE. https://carnegieendowment.org/files/kurlantzick_outlook_africa.pdf

Langendorf, J., Piefer, N., Knodt, M., Müller, U., & Lázaro, L. (2012). *Triangular Cooperation A Guideline for Working in Practice. Deutsche Gesellschaft für Internationale Zusammenarbeit.* Nomos Verlagsgesellschaft Mbh & Co. Kg.

Leheny, D., & Warren, K. (2009). *Japanese Aid and the Construction of Global Development.* Routledge.

Lengfelder, C. S. (2015). Why Triangular Development Cooperation? Germany and the Emerging Powers. *German Politics, 25*(1), 1–24. https://doi.org/10.1080/09644008.2015.1024239

Li, R. (2007). Correct Understanding of Debt Sustainability of Developing Countries. *World Economics and Politics, 4*, 7–13.

Li, T. G. (2021). The Third-party Market Cooperation Between China and Japan in Vietnam Under the Belt and Road Framework——A Comparative Study Based on Trade Relations. *Contemporary Economic Management, 43*(2), 40–47.

Li, X., & Bonschab, T. (2012). Nine Challenges of Triangular Cooperation. In J. Langendorf et al. (Eds.), *Triangular Cooperation: A Guideline for Working in Practice*. Nomos.

Luo, Y., Zhang, H., & Bu, J. (2019). Developed Country MNEs Investing in Developing Economies: Progress and Prospect. *Journal of International Business Studies, 50*(4), 633–667. https://doi.org/10.1057/s41267-019-00230-y

Mamatzakis, E., & Tsionas, M. (2018). Revisiting the Returns of Public Infrastructure in Mexico: A Limited Information Local Likelihood Estimation. *Economic Modelling, 75*, 132–141. https://doi.org/10.1016/j.econmod.2018.06.013

Masters, L. (2014). Building Bridges? South African Foreign Policy and Trilateral Development Cooperation. *South African Journal of International Affairs, 21*(2), 177–191. https://doi.org/10.1080/10220461.2014.942206

Mattlin, M., & Nojonen, M. (2015). Conditionality and Path Dependence in Chinese Lending. *Journal of Contemporary China, 24*(94), 701–720. https://doi.org/10.1080/10670564.2014.978154

Mawdsley, E., Savage, L., & Kim, S.-M. (2013). A "Post-Aid World"? Paradigm Shift in Foreign Aid and Development Cooperation at the 2011 Busan High Level Forum. *The Geographical Journal, 180*(1), 27–38. https://doi.org/10.1111/j.1475-4959.2012.00490.x

McEwan, C., & Mawdsley, E. (2012). Trilateral Development Cooperation: Power and Politics in Emerging Aid Relationships. *Development and Change, 43*(6), 1185–1209. https://doi.org/10.1111/j.1467-7660.2012.01805.x

McFarland, K., Linn, E. C., & Hughes, E. S. (2022, May 17). Strategic Corruption Exemplified (Part 2): China, the New Kid on the Block. Medium; The Diplomatic Pouch. https://medium.com/the-diplomatic-pouch/analysis-strategic-corruption-exemplified-part-2-china-the-new-kid-on-the-block-afa566d65305

Megginson, W. L., & Mueller, P. C. (2022). Natural Monopoly Privatization: Minimizing Regulatory Trade-Offs Between Rent Extraction and Innovation. *Academy of Management Perspectives, 36*(1), 111–124. https://doi.org/10.5465/amp.2019.0170

Mehta, P. S., & Nanda, N. (2005). Trilateral Development Cooperation: An Emerging Trend Background. In Briefing Paper No. 1/2005, Centre for International Trade, Economics and Environment (CUTS). http://www.cuts-international.org/pdf/BP1-2005.pdf

Meyer, K. E., Estrin, S., Bhaumik, S. K., & Peng, M. W. (2009). Institutions, Resources, and Entry Strategies in Emerging Economies. *Strategic Management Journal, 30*(1), 61–80. https://doi.org/10.1002/smj.720

MFA. (2024). The Hypocritical Nature and Factual Truth of US Foreign Aid. https://www.mfa.gov.cn/wjbxw_new/202404/t20240419_11284707.shtml

Ministry of Foreign Affairs of Japan. (2023, April 23). Free and Open Indo-Pacific. *Ministry of Foreign Affairs of Japan*. https://www.mofa.go.jp/policy/page25e_000278.html

NDRC. (2019). Third-Party Market Cooperation Guidelines and Cases. National Development and Reform Commision, P.R. China. http://images.mofcom.gov.cn/mz/201909/20190912093710956.pdf

Newbery, D. M. (1997). Privatisation and Liberalisation of Network Utilities. *European Economic Review, 41*(3–5), 357–383. https://doi.org/10.1016/s0014-2921(97)00010-x

OECD. (2008). *Accra Agenda for Action*. OECD Publishing, Paris. https://doi.org/10.1787/9789264098107-en

OECD. (2009). The Paris Declaration on Aid Effectiveness and the Accra Agenda for Action. https://www.oecd.org/dac/effectiveness/34428351.pdf

OECD. (2012a). OECD Principles for Public Governance of Public-Private Partnerships-OECD.Www.oecd.org.https://www.oecd.org/gov/budgeting/oecd-principles-for-public-governance-of-public-private-partnerships.htm

OECD. (2012b). Triangular Co-operation: Emerging Policy Messages and Interim Findings from Analytical Work. https://www.oecd.org/dac/dac-global-relations/DAC%20HLM%20Technical%20document%20Triangular%20Co-operation.pdf

OECD. (2013). TRIANGULAR CO-OPERATION: What's the Literature Telling us? DAC Global Relations The Development Assistance Committee: Enabling Effective Development. https://www.oecd.org/dac/dac-global-relations/OECD%20Triangluar%20Co-operation%20Literature%20Review%20June%202013.pdf

OECD. (2014a). Active with the Peoples Republic of China. https://www.oecd.org/china/active-with-china.pdf

OECD. (2014b). Task Team on South-South Co-operation. https://www.oecd.org/dac/effectiveness/taskteamonsouth-southco-operation.htm

OECD. (2017). Dispelling the Myths of Triangular Co-operation—Evidence from the 2015 OECD survey. https://www.oecd.org/dac/dac-global-relations/2015-oecd-survey-report-on-triangular-co-operation.htm

OECD. (2018). International Workshop: Perspectives on triangular cooperation in the G20. https://www.adelante-i.eu/en/international-workshop-perspectives-triangular-cooperation-g20

OECD. (2019). Toolkit for Identifying, Monitoring and Evaluating the Value Added of Triangular Co-operation. https://www.oecd.org/dac/triangular-co-operation/TOOLKIT%20-%20version%20August%202018.pdf

OECD. (2022). Triangular co-operation with Africa. https://triangular-cooperation.org/wp-content/uploads/2022/10/OECD_Triangular-co-operation-with-Africa.pdf

OECD. (2023, August 31). Development Co-operation Profiles—Japan. *OECD ILibrary*. https://www.oecd-ilibrary.org/sites/b8cf3944-en/index.html?itemId=/content/component/b8cf3944-en

OECD. (n.d.). Official Development Assistance—Definition and Coverage. OECD Development Assistance Committee. Retrieved February 8, 2024, from https://www.oecd.org/dac/financing-sustainable-development/development-finance-standards/officialdevelopmentassistancedefinitionandcoverage.htm

Pantoja, E. (2009). *Triangular Cooperation: New Paths to Development*. OECD. https://www.oecd.org/dac/dac-global-relations/43705278.pdf

Pasimeni, F. (2021). The Origin of the Sharing Economy Meets the Legacy of Fractional Ownership. *Journal of Cleaner Production, 319*, 128614. https://doi.org/10.1016/j.jclepro.2021.128614

Perkins, S. E. (2014). When Does Prior Experience Pay? Institutional Experience and the Multinational Corporation. *Administrative Science Quarterly, 59*(1), 145–181. https://doi.org/10.1177/0001839214523603

Pessoa, A. (2008). Public–Private Partnerships in Developing Countries: Are Infrastructures Responding to the new ODA Strategy? *Journal of International Development, 20*(3), 311–325. https://doi.org/10.1002/jid.1416

Pisano, G. P., Russo, M., & Teece, D. (1988). Joint Ventures and Collaborative Arrangements in the Telecommunications Equipment Industry. In D. Mowery (Ed.), *International Collaborative Ventures in U.S. Manufacturing*. Ballinger Publishing Company.

Power, M., Mohan, G., & Tan-Mullins, M. (2012). *China's Resource Diplomacy in Africa: Powering Development?* Palgrave Macmillan.

Prashad, V. (2007). *The Darker Nations: A People's History of the Third World*. New York The New Press.

Qu, J. (2017, May 3). The China Myanmar Oil and Gas Pipeline Benefits "Four Countries and Six Parties". *Sciencenet*. https://news.sciencenet.cn/htmlnews/2017/5/375219.shtm

Raisbeck, P., Duffield, C., & Xu, M. (2010). Comparative Performance of PPPs and Traditional Procurement in Australia. *Construction Management and Economics, 28*(4), 345–359. https://doi.org/10.1080/01446190903582731

Rui, H. (2010). Developing Country FDI and Development: The Case of Chinese FDI in the Sudan. *Transnational Corporations, 19*(3), 49–80. https://doi.org/10.18356/08e89398-en

Rui, H., Zhang, M., & Shipman, A. (2017). Chinese Expatriate Management in Emerging Markets: A Competitive Advantage Perspective. *Journal of*

International Management, 23(2), 124–138. https://doi.org/10.1016/j.intman.2017.01.002

Schroder, N. (1977). America's Economic Stake in Taiwan. *The International Trade Law Journal, 3*(1) https://digitalcommons.law.umaryland.edu/cgi/viewcontent.cgi?article=1372&context=mjil

Schulz, N-S. (2010). Boosting South-South Cooperation in the Context of Aid Effectiveness Telling the Story of Partners Involved in more than 110 Cases of South-South and Triangular Cooperation. https://www.oecd.org/dac/effectiveness/46080462.pdf

Sharafi, A., Sadegh Amalnick, M., & Allah Taleizadeh, A. (2021). Outcome of Financial Conflicts in the Operation Phase of Public–Private Partnership Contracts. Journal of Construction Engineering and Management, 147(6). https://doi.org/10.1061/(asce)co.1943-7862.0002011

Shiga, H. (2016). No.130 Normative Framing of Development Cooperation: Japanese Bilateral Aid between the DAC and Southern Donors. https://www.jica.go.jp/jica-ri/publication/workingpaper/wp_130.html

Sidiropoulos, E. (2012). Rising Powers, South–South Co-operation and Africa. Policy Brief 47, Global Powers and Africa Programme, SAIIA. https://saiia.org.za/research/rising-powers-south-south-co-operation-and-africa/

Singh, A. (2020). The Myth of "Debt-Trap Diplomacy" and Realities of Chinese Development Finance. *Third World Quarterly, 42*(2), 239–253.

Smith, M., Browne, P., & Dube, N. (2006). High Level Forum on the Harmonization for Aid Effectiveness in South Africa Final Report. https://citeseerx.ist.psu.edu/document?repid=rep1&type=pdf&doi=4d8583eee1d088b4d75c3fd2c1041d47d4225457

South African Government. (2011). White Paper on South African Foreign Policy—Building a Better World: The Diplomacy of Ubuntu. https://www.gov.za/documents/white-papers/white-paper-south-african-foreign-policy-building-better-world-diplomacy

Stahl, A. (2016). Chinas Relations with Sub-Saharan Africa. (IAI Working Paper No. 16). Rome: Istituto Affairi Internazionali. https://www.iai.it/sites/default/files/iaiwp1622.pdf

Stahl, A. K. (2012). *Trilateral Development Cooperation Between the European Union, China and Africa: What Prospects for South Africa?* Centre for Chinese Studies, Stellenbosch University. https://scholar.sun.ac.za/handle/10019.1/70766

Stahl, A. K. (2018). *EU-China-Africa Trilateral Relations in a Multipolar World: Hic sunt dracones*. Palgrave Macmillan.

Stallings, B., & Szkely, G. (1993). *Japan, the United States, and Latin America: Toward a Trilateral Relationship in the Western Hemisphere?* Palgrave Macmillan London.

The Morning. (2020, October 25). Debt Trap: Made in China or Made in Sri Lanka? Latest in the News Sphere; Liberty Publishers. https://www.themorning.lk/articles/102539

Tseng, H.-K., & Krog, R. (2016). No Strings Attached: Chinese Foreign Aid and Regime Stability in Resource-Rich Recipient Countries. https://api.semanticscholar.org/CorpusID:53312

Umirdinov, A. (2019). Generating a Reform of the BRI from the Inside: Japan's Contribution via Soft Law Diplomacy. Discussion Papers, Research Institute of Economy, Trade and Industry, 19076. https://ideas.repec.org/p/eti/dpaper/19076.html

UN. (2019, April 8). Buenos Aires Outcome Document of the 2nd High-Level United Nations Conference on South-South Cooperation. https://digitallibrary.un.org/record/3799433

UNDP. (2009). Enhancing South–South and Triangular Cooperation. Study of the Current Situation and Existing Good Practices in Policy, Institutions, and Operation of South–South and Triangular Cooperation. https://www.cbd.int/financial/southsouth/undp-casebook.pdf

UNDP. (2017). South-South Cooperation in Sub-Saharan Africa: Strategies for UNDP Engagement. UNDP. https://www.africa.undp.org/content/rba/en/home/library/reports/south-south-cooperation-in-sub-saharan-africa0.html

UNECOSOC. (2008). Background Study for the Development Cooperation Forum: Trends in South-South and Triangular Development Cooperation. United Nations Economic and Social Council. https://www.iukdpf.com/background-study-for-the-development-cooperation-forum-trends-in-south-south-and-triangular-development-cooperation/

United Nations. (2003, March 17). Revised Guidelines for the Review of Policies and Procedures Concerning Technical Cooperation Among Developing Countries. *United Nations Office of South-South and Triangular Cooperation*. https://documents.un.org/doc/undoc/gen/n03/285/18/pdf/n0328518.pdf?token=ZUgSPGo5xkYDD8mNkc&fe=true

Wan, J., & Wang, Y. (2020). *Tripartite Cooperation and Triple Win*. Chinese Foreign Currency.

Williamson, O. E. (1995). Hierarchies, Markets and Power in the Economy: An Economic Perspective. *Industrial and Corporate Change, 4*(1), 21–49. https://doi.org/10.1093/icc/4.1.21

Workshop on triangular cooperation: Opportunity for shared responsibility in Africa. (2009). Heiligendamm Process. https://paperzz.com/doc/7128750/winwin-win-situation

World Bank. (2012). Public-Private Partnerships: Reference Guide Version 1.0. https://openknowledge.worldbank.org/handle/10986/16055

Wu, B., & Ding, M. (2020). Third Party Market Cooperation Between China and South Korea: Progress, Resistance, and Countermeasures. *Northeast Asia Forum, 29*(3), 75–89+128. https://doi.org/10.13654/j.cnki.naf.2020.03.006

Xu, D., & Meyer, K. E. (2012). Linking Theory and Context: "Strategy Research in Emerging Economies" after Wright et al. (2005). *Journal of Management Studies, 50*(7), 1322–1346. https://doi.org/10.1111/j.1467-6486.2012.01051.x

Xu, Y., Yeung, J. F. Y., Chan, A. P. C., Chan, D. W. M., Wang, S. Q., & Ke, Y. (2010). Developing a Risk Assessment Model for PPP Projects in China—A Fuzzy Synthetic Evaluation Approach. *Automation in Construction, 19*(7), 929–943. https://doi.org/10.1016/j.autcon.2010.06.006

Yang, J. Y., Li, J., & Delios, A. (2015). Will a Second Mouse Get the Cheese? Learning from Early Entrants' Failures in a Foreign Market. *Organization Science, 26*(3), 908–922. https://doi.org/10.1287/orsc.2015.0967

Zhang, D. (2017a). *A Promising New Trend? Factors Driving Chinas Growing Trilateral Aid Cooperation [Doctoral Dissertation]*. Australian National University (ANU) Press.

Zhang, D. (2017b). Why Cooperate with Others? Demystifying China's Trilateral aid Cooperation. *The Pacific Review, 30*(5), 750–768. https://doi.org/10.1080/09512748.2017.1296886

Zhang, D. (2018). A Tango by two Superpowers: China-US Cooperation in Trilateral Aid and Implications for Their Bilateral Relations. *Asian Journal of Political Science, 26*(2), 181–200. https://doi.org/10.1080/02185377.2018.1462218

Zhang, D., & Smith, G. (2017). China's Foreign Aid System: Structure, Agencies, and Identities. *Third World Quarterly, 38*(10), 2330–2346. https://doi.org/10.1080/01436597.2017.1333419

Zhang, F., & Li, H. (2020). Third Party Market Cooperation: A new Model of International Cooperation Under the "The Belt and Road" Initiative—based on the Analysis of the Third Party Market Cooperation Between China and France. *International Economic Cooperation, 02*, 26–33.

Zhang, S., Chan, A. P. C., Feng, Y., Duan, H., & Ke, Y. (2016). Critical Review on PPP Research—A Search from the Chinese and International Journals. *International Journal of Project Management, 34*(4), 597–612. https://doi.org/10.1016/j.ijproman.2016.02.008

Zhang, Y. (2020). Third-Party Market Cooperation Under the Belt and Road Initiative: Progress, Challenges, and Recommendations. *China International Strategy Review, 1*, 310–329. https://doi.org/10.1007/s42533-019-00026-7

Zheng, C. (2020). *Zhong Ou Di San Fang Shi Chang He Zuo Mian Lin De Ji Yu He Tiao Zhan (Opportunities and Chanlleages in China-Europe Tripartite Cooperation)*. World Knowledge.

CHAPTER 3

Navigating the Tripartite Cooperation Realm: Insights from the Literature

The previous chapter, Chap. 2, primarily focused on the country-level dynamics of tripartite cooperation. This chapter shifts the focus to introduce theoretical frameworks that explore the actions and determinants influencing firms' participation in tripartite cooperation. Both Chinese and Western multinational enterprises (MNEs) possess advanced technology and greater financing abilities, enabling them to engage in cross-border, large-scale economic infrastructure projects, such as power stations, roads, railways, and ports. This chapter retrospectively reviews the previous literature and aims to identify what is already known and where there are still gaps about the central research question of this study: Why do participants opt for a tripartite cooperation model, despite potentially bearing additional transaction costs?

Many academic papers, as well as reports and Chinese government documents (e.g., NDRC, 2019; Meng & Yu, 2020; Deng, 2013; Zhang 2017; Kamwengo, 2020; Fordelone, 2011), employ traditional economic theories to elucidate the benefits of tripartite cooperation. They use Ricardo's comparative advantage theory to argue that the tripartite cooperation mechanism can leverage advanced technology and management skills from traditional donors, along with China's financing capacity and rich construction experience, to expedite the development of beneficiary countries. However, these discussions predominantly focus on industrial specialisation, assuming zero transaction costs and overlooking the costs

C. Su, *From Two to Three*, Governing China in the 21st Century,
https://doi.org/10.1007/978-981-95-8708-7_3

of coordination and transactions within the intricate tripartite cooperation structure. They do not look into how the tripartite cooperation mechanism, by adding a partner, influences the dynamics of transaction costs and the additional benefits in practical projects.

This chapter primarily utilises theories in New Institutional Economics (NIE), drawing on insights from transaction cost economics and internalisation theories to explore tripartite cooperation in international infrastructure projects at both the country and firm levels. In the first section, transaction cost theory (Coase, 1937, 1960; Alchian & Demsetz, 1972; Williamson 1983, 1986) is used to analyse the transaction costs and potential gains of this cooperative structure, which involves an additional actor compared to traditional bilateral cooperation. In the second section, international relation theories are applied to explain the determinants and changes in transaction costs at the country level. Liberalism provides a partial theoretical foundation for understanding tripartite cooperation, where participant countries seek common ground based on shared interests (Nye & Keohane, 1977; Keohane, 1984; Hitchcock & Moravcsik, 1999; Moravcsik, 1993; Smith & Ikenberry, 2001). Realism, which emphasises that states prioritise national interests and security (Wendt, 1999; Mearsheimer, 2001; Waltz, 1979; Reus-Smit & Snidal, 2010; Devetak et al., 2011), is used to explain unsuccessful or underperforming cases of tripartite cooperation with higher transaction cost. In the third section, derived from transaction cost economics, the internalisation school (Buckley & Casson, 1976; Teece 1981, 1986; Hennart 1988; Rugman, 1985) applies transaction cost theory to the context of foreign direct investment (FDI) and international investment at the firm level. The eclectic (ownership, location, and internalisation (OLI)) paradigm (Dunning, 1988, 2001; Dunning & Lundan, 2008) and the springboard perspective (Luo & Tung, 2007, 2018) are used to explore the determinants for participants to engage in tripartite cooperation. The final section specifically discusses the economic infrastructure sector, highlighting its characteristic of natural monopolies, which partially explains why participants engage in tripartite cooperation.

This research extends transaction cost theory, international relation theories, and FDI theories to the realm of tripartite cooperation. Specifically, this research uses transaction cost and internalisation theories as analytical tools to differentiate tripartite cooperation from bilateral projects, which typically incur lower transaction costs, and from arm's-length approaches, which tend to have higher transaction costs.

Additionally, it expands FDI theories to assess their relevance to tripartite cooperation by investigating whether these arrangements enable the exploitation of ownership advantages or facilitate springboarding strategy. This study aims to fill a gap in the literature by providing a systematic examination of Chinese tripartite cooperation and identifying the reasons why participants choose the tripartite cooperation model, even when tripartite cooperation incurs higher transaction costs, and how participants create additional benefits in such arrangements.

3.1 Transaction Cost Theories in Tripartite Cooperation

3.1.1 New Institutional Economics

The core concepts of NIE originated from Coase's (1937) article on the 'Theory of the Firm,' marking a significant shift from these early expansive theories. However, this article remained 'little used' for the next 35 years (Coase, 1972, p. 67). Since the 1970s, new theories about the firm and organisation, such as agency theory, resource-based theory, and property rights theory, have gradually boomed (Williamson, 2008). The emergence of NIE since the 1970s has had a profound impact on the economics over the subsequent 20 years. This impact is particularly evident in the evolution of transaction cost economics, shaped by the work of Oliver Williamson and the institutional analysis of Douglass North. The golden triangle of NIE comprises three key concepts: transaction cost, property rights, and contracts (Menard & Shirley, 2014).

This research explores the tripartite cooperation mechanism as a type of cooperative institution, examining its influence on transaction costs and potential gains in tripartite projects. Based on the premise of positive transaction cost,[1] where information is costly and contracts are inherently incomplete in the 'real world' (Williamson, 1995, p. 27), the presence of effective institutions[2] is crucial for reducing costs and making potential

[1] According to Coase (1992), in our real world transaction costs are positive, which means that engaging in exchange procedures is extremely costly. This often involves a significant amount of legal contracting, which can make the exchange unprofitable.

[2] Institutions are a set of principles, norms, rules, expected patterns of behaviour, and decision-making procedures which include organisations, bureaucratic agencies, treaties, and agreements as well as informal practices that states accept as binding (e.g., North, 1991;

gains achievable (North, 1991). Barzel (1985) agrees that participants can gain at each other's expense in a well-functioning institution. Krasner (1982a) suggests that well-established international regimes can reduce conflicts and foster a stable cooperative environment. These development regimes and institutions promote cooperation among traditional donors by providing information about each party's intentions and addressing issues of non-compliance (Milner, 1992). By facilitating difficult negotiations, reducing mistrust, enhancing the ability to monitor compliance, and making commitments credible, the development regimes play a crucial role in reducing transaction costs. Therefore, tripartite cooperation can be regarded as an institutional arrangement that can "organise economic units, provide a structure within its participant members, and offer a mechanism that can effect a change in laws or property rights" (Davis & North, 1971, pp. 6–7).

3.1.2 The Definitions of Transaction Costs in this Research

Transaction cost is initially defined as "the cost to provide goods or services through the market rather than providing them within the firm" within the framework of the 'Theory of the Firm' by Coase (1937, p. 394). Coase also pointed out that transaction costs between organisations are inevitable. A trader needs to "find another trader, get information on price and quality, strike a bargain, draw up contracts, supervise the performance of contracts and settle disputations" (Coase, 1960, p. 15). Because searching for potential partners with suitable qualifications is particularly costly (Coase, 1960, 1992), the continuity of cooperation is often important (Williamson, 2008). In tripartite cooperation, these operations are typically more expensive due to more interactions, transactions, and contractual relationships among participants. Additionally, finding potential cooperators can be more challenging. For example, a tripartite project needs 6 to 24 months from the initial stage to the implementation stage even if provider countries have rich experience, because of "the distinct management systems, the diversity of stakeholders, the geographic and cultural distances, and the indecision on the rules of the game" (Schulz, 2010, p. 29), and all these factors are the sources of transaction costs.

Duffield, 2013). Institution means tripartite cooperation mechanism in the context of this chapter.

Later, the concept of transaction cost has gradually adopted into other subjects, including development studies, law, and property rights, as discussed further below (Paul & Vandeninden, 2012). Williamson (1986) defined transaction costs as the costs of operating normal activities of companies. It includes the cost of designing, deciding, changing plans, resolving disputes, and after-sales, but it is unlike production costs. When a company decides its business strategies, operation, and management, it measures both transaction costs and production costs. From a contractual perspective, transaction cost encompasses the ex-ante cost of negotiating and drafting contracts, as well as the ex-post costs of execution, monitoring, and, when disputes arise, remedying the contract (Williamson, 1986). Demsetz (1968, p. 35) defined transaction cost as "the cost of exchanging ownership titles." This includes the expenses associated with producing assets necessary for the exchange of assets, including the cost of being informed about the general nature of the market.

Transaction costs are generated during the information-gathering process, pricing and quality negotiation, contract drafting, contract performance supervision, and dispute resolution (Coase, 1960, 1992; Hart & Moore, 1990; Teece, 1986). According to Lawson (2009), different phases of a project generate different types of transaction costs. Transaction costs in projects include search and information costs, bargaining and decision costs, as well as policing and enforcement costs. Search and information costs in tripartite cooperation projects occur in the identification phase. The two providers need to identify their complementary contributions, political backing, and resources for the tripartite cooperation projects. Bargaining and decision costs occur in the negotiation and partnership development phase, and they appear as the costs of cultural understanding and bureaucracy. The three parties need to establish a clear agreement on the 'what' and 'how' of project design and implementation through extensive negotiations. Participants need to coordinate their practices and cultures of project implementation. There are some differences in terms of the costs in the formulation and implementation phases between tripartite cooperation and other cooperative modalities. In traditional bilateral investment activities, logistical arrangements and internal management typically involve companies from the home country and the host country. However, tripartite cooperation requires higher transaction costs than bilateral arrangements in the different phases, as it involves more logistical arrangements and additional layers of reporting from three countries and their respective companies.

As for the application of transaction costs to international development, there has been no consensual definition of 'transaction costs' in development cooperation till now (Jobin, 2008; Paul & Vandeninden, 2012; OECD, 2019a). After the Paris Declaration for Aid Effectiveness proposed "using a pragmatic approach to the division of labour and burden sharing can increase complementarity and reduce transaction costs" (OECD, 2009, p. 6), the researchers began to explore the definition of transaction costs in development cooperation since 2005 (OECD, 2019b). Lawson (2009) defined transaction costs in development cooperation as "the costs which allow an economic transaction to take place, but which add nothing to the value of the transaction" (p. 8). Transaction costs are related to the compliance of each party to abide by their established agreements, such as taking timely action and deploying resources according to the terms and conditions. In the fifth international meeting on triangular cooperation in Lisbon, participants proposed that transaction costs are an investment in the long-term development of the tripartite cooperation projects, so they are a part of the value-added process of the partnership. The 'cost' is the essence of tripartite cooperation, but the participants rephrased it as 'investments' (OECD, 2019a).

In the context of this research, transaction cost is narrowly defined as the cost of facilitating the completion of tripartite cooperation projects. This includes search and information costs, negotiation costs, contract costs, agency costs, and other related expenses that are not directly associated with the construction and operation of projects.

3.1.3 *A New Perspective on Applying Internalisation Theory to Tripartite Cooperation*

According to Coase's theory, transaction cost is defined as "the cost to provide goods or services through the market rather than providing them within the firm" (Coase, 1937, p. 394). This concept is highly relevant to the theories of internalisation in MNEs that explain why MNEs exist (Rugman, 1985). Companies typically incur 'costs of doing business abroad,' such as political and commercial risks, due to their unfamiliarity with foreign environments (Hymer, 1976; Tsurumis, 1976). When the transaction costs that provide goods or services through the international market are higher, companies may decide to invest abroad in order to shift such transactions to within the internal organisational hierarchy, a process known as 'internalising' (Denekamp, 1995; Dunning, 1980).

Internalisation theory suggests that MNEs seek to avoid these high transaction costs in the global market by completing projects internally at lower costs (Buckley & Casson, 1976; Rugman, 1981).

In MNE theories, internalisation is seen as a response to market failure, with profit-seeking enterprises aiming to lower the cost of organising and transacting business through internalised operations. Transactions face disadvantages in highly uncertain markets, particularly when involving long-term complex exchanges of heterogeneous products among traders (Teece, 1986). Additionally, in the real business world, where contracts are often incomplete and the environment is uncertain, firms face hazards when investing in or purchasing specific assets such as natural resource assets or strategic assets. Due to these contracting problems and associated high transaction costs, the market becomes inefficient, prompting firms to consider internal transaction strategies as a substitute for arm's-length market transactions (Williamson, 1986).

North (1991) proposed that individuals who pursue wealth maximisation are more likely to cooperate when they have complete information about the past performance of other players, including actions, intentions, preferences, beliefs, relevant behaviours, and causal knowledge. This information allows them to continuously maintain the exchange relation, adding productive value (Williamson, 1992, 1995). In tripartite arrangements, the past performance of other players is better understood (albeit not completely) than in open market transactions, and the interactions among participants are more likely to be repeated, fostering a more stable and predictable environment.

However, I argue that this internalising arrangement still incurs more transaction costs than bilateral project finance, because the tripartite arrangement is not fully internalised within a single entity but is a combination of three distinct entities working together. Therefore, the context of tripartite cooperation differs from that of bilateral project finance, positioning tripartite cooperation as a '*semi-internalised*' arrangement.

This research therefore conceptualises tripartite cooperation as a form of semi-internalisation. As illustrated in Fig. 3.1, the spectrum of internalisation ranges from open-market arrangements, which are associated with high transaction costs, to full internalisation, as seen in MNEs or bilateral projects that effectively reduce transaction costs. Tripartite arrangements, as a semi-internalised form of cooperation, reduce transaction costs compared to repeated one-time open-market transactions but still incur higher transaction costs relative to fully internalised arrangements.

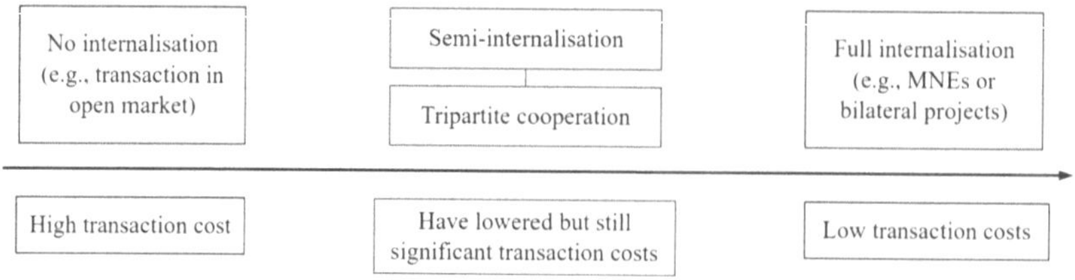

Fig. 3.1 The spectrum of internalisation. (Source: Author)

3.1.3.1 Less Transaction Costs and More Benefits than Open Market

With the development of labour division and specialisation, the firm emerges, and the industrial chain becomes divided on a global scale (Coase, 1937). Internalisation can generate additional benefits through economies of scale, making it advantageous for a firm to internalise production rather than relying on open market transactions (Coase, 1960). One advantage of internal production is that the firm can avoid consulting costs associated with price discovery in the open market by using internal accounting prices for transfers between different stages of production (Williamson, 2008). Therefore, when the administrative costs of the firm are less than the costs of market transactions, internalisation actions occur. Conversely, if the transaction costs exceed the gains, the exchange will not take place (Coase, 1992).

The second reason firms choose internalisation is that intangible assets, including know-how, management skills, technological innovation, and brand-name capital are not easily purchased, imitated, or transferred to outsiders in open markets (Rumelt, 1984; Wernerfelt, 1984). If a firm is unable to acquire the necessary assets through the internalisation of another large firm due to financial limitations or legal restrictions, such as the target firms being SOEs that cannot be sold to foreign entities, tripartite cooperation offers a viable alternative, which allows firms to access the desired assets and capabilities without requiring full ownership, thereby circumventing the barriers posed by direct acquisition.

The third reason firms choose internalisation is its capability to transform interfirm disputes into intrafirm disputes. Transactions between different firms involve different decision-making processes and different hierarchical structures. For small-scale or simple projects, participants typically opt for market contracts, such as purchasing or service agreements. In these cases, suppliers can be readily replaced, allowing participants to choose court resolutions without incurring higher costs. For large-scale projects, participants would choose internalisation by using SPVs. Courts typically decline to hear intrafirm disputes that arise within internal divisions. Disputing parties are therefore compelled to resolve their issues internally through the firm's contracting hierarchy system. In other words, technical disputes within firms are exempted from court-ordered enforcement (Williamson, 1986, 1995). This internal dispute resolution not only avoids the high costs associated with court proceedings but also enhances the efficacy and integrity of organisations, especially in complex infrastructure projects. In addition, internal parties can resolve disputes efficiently due to their in-depth knowledge of the dispute's context and their ability to generate effective alternative solutions (Macneil, 1974).

Finally, in open-market transactions, host countries often employ an asset-specificity strategy to mitigate risks and safeguard investments. This strategy involves several types of specificity: site specificity, physical asset specificity, human asset specificity, and dedicated assets. These specialised assets are tailored to the project, making them costly and difficult to redeploy or repurpose for alternative uses or locations (Joskow, 1985, 1988; Williamson, 1975, 1983, 1986). The host countries often impose investment safeguards in sectors like utilities, such as penalties for early withdrawal, delays, and specific governance regulations to resolve disputes (Thompson, 1991).

The non-redeployable nature of these assets is particularly advantageous for host countries, as it ensures that investors remain committed to the project's success. For MNEs, redeploying or withdrawing specialised assets can be highly challenging due to the significant sunk costs involved in purely market-based arrangements. Additionally, as sunk investments in international foreign investment activities increase, the host country may seek to renegotiate terms, because the local government realises it has a stronger bargaining position. In some instances, particularly in concession agreements in developing countries, foreign investors have been compelled to undergo "renegotiation, adjustment, surtaxes, back taxes, recomputations, and recontracting" with local governments (Teece, 1986, p. 40; Moran, 1975).

In the context of tripartite cooperation, it is crucial for investors to align their interests with local governments and actively involve them in the projects to manage these risks effectively. This alignment not only mitigates risks but also helps explain why bilateral and trilateral arrangements tend to incur lower transaction costs compared to purely market-based transactions.

3.1.3.2 More Transaction Costs than Bilateral Arrangements

Based on the previous illustration, tripartite cooperation, as a semi-internalised arrangement, incurs lower costs than purely market-based alternatives by effectively reducing transaction costs through integration activities and economies of scale. However, tripartite cooperation often leads to increased transaction costs, which is particularly evident when compared to bilateral arrangements. Bilateral arrangements are presumed to be more internalised than tripartite cooperation, thus achieving greater reductions in transaction costs through full internalisation. The involvement of more partners in tripartite cooperation complicates the process, leading to greater complexity and higher costs in areas such as information gathering, negotiation, contracting, supervision, and dispute resolution (OECD, 2019b; Tjønneland, 2008; UNECOSOC, 2008).

Firstly, compared to bilateral arrangements, tripartite cooperation involves larger cooperative groups, which results in higher transaction costs. In conventional firm theories, production costs are determined by the firm's size and product range, specifically in relation to economies of scale and economies of scope (Spulber, 1989; Klein, 1999). Coase (1937) established a correlation between operational efficiency and firm size, suggesting that as a firm expands, its returns decrease. Coase argues that the costs of organising additional transactions within the firm may increase, leading to suboptimal use of factors of production. This principle applies to general business enterprises and can be extended to infrastructure projects. Large-scale projects involving numerous firms that form larger JVs/SPVs in tripartite cooperation projects often require more investment and exhibit lower operational efficiency (Dhingra & Sharma, 2022; Kapsali et al., 2019).

Secondly, each party in tripartite cooperation brings its own set of rules, including legal frameworks, budgeting practices, procurement standards, sectoral priorities, reporting criteria, management structures, monitoring processes, and staff training protocols (Fordelone, 2009). These varying systems complicate the coordination of different business operations, often resulting in redundant organisational structures and further complicating the management of project procedures and funding. In addition, the unclear division of roles and responsibilities in tripartite cooperation leads to inefficiencies. The project-based approaches of tripartite cooperation often result in duplicated efforts, wasted resources, and incoherence among participating firms. These above-mentioned problems are amplified in tripartite cooperation projects because the involvement of more participants introduces additional complexities and redundancies. As a result, project efficiency may tend to be lower and transaction costs higher.

Thirdly, there are more bargaining costs in tripartite cooperation projects. Bargaining is a selection process from various feasible solutions, with each participant aiming to maximise its benefits. This process becomes particularly challenging when all participants wield power from different perspectives, leading to higher transaction costs for the project. Powerful states or firms often control more bargaining information and decision-making power (Martin, 1999). Contrary to the Coase theorem of market failure, Keohane (1984, 1986) proposes that international institutions can assist participants in overcoming collective action dilemmas through bargaining and mutually beneficial agreements with clearly defined property rights. If tripartite cooperation can establish a well-rounded international cooperation institution, the bargaining dilemma can be resolved through complete information, equitable distribution of benefits, and effective contract compliance monitoring. However, achieving this remains challenging in current tripartite cooperation practices.

3.1.3.3 *Trade-off Considerations: Overall Benefits of Participating in Tripartite Cooperation*

Despite potentially higher transaction costs than bilateral arrangements in some tripartite cooperation projects, participants do not view these costs as a barrier to cooperation. This perspective suggests that the anticipated benefits and developmental outcomes of tripartite cooperation outweigh the costs, with these costs considered worthwhile investments in cooperative projects. The generation of benefits aligns with concepts such as 'win-win,' 'integrative,' or 'variable-sum' outcomes (Sebenius, 1992, p. 28; Vetschera, 2009).

In tripartite cooperation, generating benefits involves pursuing mutual gains, improving outcomes, and upholding agreement commitments among participants. During the cooperation process of tripartite arrangements, each participant tries to lower transaction costs and get access to internalisation advantages when they aim to complete one mission together and maximise individual benefits (Sim and Ali, 1998). Participants seek to mitigate "the costs of legitimate transactions and uncertainty" (Keohane, 1984, p. 220) by addressing information asymmetry, efficient transfer, enforcement, and post-contractual monitoring costs (Luo and Park, 2004; Hennart, 1988). Policing and enforcement costs are expected to decrease with closer participant relationships. As projects unfold, participants can foster more trustful interactions, potentially reducing transaction costs at the end of the tripartite cooperation project (Lawson, 2009; OECD 2019a).

In addition, the success of tripartite cooperation projects hinges on the efficient transfer of knowledge amongst others across borders and organisational boundaries. According to Williamson (1992, 1995), the internalisation process allows firms to replicate successful experiences, selectively adopting activities that promise net gains while avoiding those likely to lead to losses. The growth of MNEs is related to their ability to replicate their domestic market advantages in new markets (Kogut & Zander, 1993; Rui & Bruyaka, 2021). This principle also applies to the efficiency of tripartite cooperation projects. During the implementation phase of tripartite cooperation, the process of adding benefits occurs through shared knowledge, exchange of social and geographic contexts, and collaborative development solutions among partners.

In summary, tripartite cooperation can be considered semi-internalised, falling between purely market-based and fully internalised models. As long as the benefits gained from cooperation outweigh the efficiency losses due to transaction costs, MNEs have the incentive to collaborate with other partners. If a tripartite cooperation project generates significant benefits, this cooperative mechanism has the potential to be applied. This underscores the importance of assessing the balance between benefits and overall costs to determine the feasibility and sustainability of tripartite cooperation initiatives.

3.1.4 *Firm Theories and Contract Problem in Tripartite Cooperation*

Following the discussion of why firms choose internalisation in the last section, this section then explores firm theories and contract problems.

In the internal organisation of firms, Coase introduced the famous 'make or buy' trade-off. When the cost of integration is prohibitive, firms may opt for a hybrid form of governance—"long-term contractual relations that preserve autonomy but provide added transaction-specific safeguards, compared with the market" (Williamson, 1996, p. 378). This choice is made instead of pursuing full integration or reverting to standard market contracts, aptly describing the semi-internalised arrangement in tripartite cooperations.

Tripartite cooperations in infrastructure projects integrate diverse modes to organise activities, including long-term contracting, franchising, trading regulation, and establishing JVs/SPVs. The varying degrees of engagement and corresponding cooperative models in these projects reflect participants' inclinations towards market transactions and internalisation in the context of a semi-internalised arrangement. By using multiple contracts, participants seek to transform market transactions into more closely internal transactions, shifting contracts from those signed in the open market to agreements made within the organisation (Kreps, 1990).

A contract is defined as a written or unwritten agreement between a buyer and a supplier, with the terms of exchange of 'price, assets specificity, and safeguards' (Williamson, 1996, p. 377). Within the transaction cost framework, contracts are 'never perfectly enforced and complete' (Menard & Shirley, 2014). The inherent incompleteness of contracts introduces opportunism and influences the cooperation process (Williamson, 1971), resulting in higher transaction costs in tripartite cooperation. As different firms collaborate in such arrangements, the (final consortium) firm can be viewed as a nexus of contracts (Alchian & Demsetz, 1972; Klein, 1999). In tripartite cooperation, the pre-existing contracts in the open market between sellers and buyers can be restructured within the internal administrative operations of the consortium. The entity formed by the participating firms can also be regarded as a nexus of contracts.

In tripartite cooperation, some participants initially enter into informal agreements like MOUs or strategic partnerships that lack legal enforceability. Because the activities and responsibilities of the involved parties are not fully integrated, this represents partial internalisation. Therefore, this approach leaves room for issues such as mistrust, lack of commitment, and accountability problems that are typically associated with open-market transactions to emerge to a greater extent than in bilateral cooperation. Nevertheless, in infrastructure construction projects, despite the presence of moral hazards and risks associated with formal or informal contracts, these agreements play a vital role in enhancing the efficiency of exchanges. They also pave the way for the transition to formal agreement stages.

Furthermore, contract issues in negotiation and enforcement, along with agency problems, are significant transaction cost concerns in long-distance trade and investment in the open market (Coase, 1992;

Williamson, 2008; Martin, 1999). Instituting fixed rules, such as formal economic constraints, and property rights can lower information costs and develop a mature market by spreading risk and uncertainty (North, 1991) for tripartite cooperation. Due to the vagueness and difficulty in enforcing agency contracts, participants in tripartite cooperation often establish JVs or SPVs. These internalising approaches help avoid repeated negotiations, contract specifications, monitoring, and enforcement in tripartite cooperation.

To tackle the uncertain and risky environment, participants have three options. They may choose to abstain from engaging in transactions to address ex-post risks. Another option for participants is to adjust the original price to a higher value that reflects the added risks. The third option involves implementing ex-ante safeguards, such as credible commitments, to mitigate risks through carefully crafted contract terms (Williamson, 1995). These three solutions to manage risks also reflect the varying behaviours of participants in tripartite cooperation projects. Some participants may choose to leave or withdraw from a project, although they did engage in transactions initially, as exemplified by Japan in the Thailand high-speed railway project.[3] On the other hand, more participants might choose to increase their construction and operation prices or develop more comprehensive contracts, as exemplified by French company EDF and the UK government in the UK Hinkley Point C project.

3.2 International Relation Theories and Tripartite Cooperation at Country Level

3.2.1 Liberalism Theories

In international relations theories, liberalism comprises two important assumptions regarding whether individual countries are willing to participate in international cooperation: firstly, that participant countries pursue mutual targets, and secondly, that they can benefit from cooperation

[3] Despite the cooperation agreement between the Chinese and Japanese governments, Japanese firms chose to withdraw after conducting feasibility and cost assessments due to "the inevitable severe loss" (Gao, 2018). Although the Chinese government and firms continued to invest in and develop the Thailand high-speed railway projects, the project faced significant delays after years of sluggish progress. The fate of the railway remained uncertain until 2023 (Gill, 2023).

(Milner, 1992). According to liberalism, states are rational actors that prioritise absolute gains, but they prefer cooperation rather than conflict. Even if liberalism holds negative views about states' characteristics, as in realist theories, it still believes that states have the potential to work together because self-interested states can enhance their gains through cooperation with others (Tarzi, 2003). Therefore, liberalism provides a partial theoretical foundation for understanding tripartite cooperation, wherein participant countries seek common ground based on shared interests (Nye & Keohane, 1977; Keohane, 1984; Hitchcock & Moravcsik, 1999; Moravcsik, 1993; Smith & Ikenberry, 2001).

However, liberalists also argue that there are two obstacles that might impede cooperation. The first is information asymmetry regarding cooperative partners' aims and strategies. The second is non-compliance or cheating, wherein one party fails to fulfil the agreement (Keohane, 1990). To address these obstacles, traditional donors have established international development regimes[4] and institutions, such as the Paris Declaration and the Accra Agenda for Action, the Development Assistance Committee, and national agencies for international multilateral development.

Any issue in international cooperation involves a combination of sanctioning, monitoring, distribution, coordination, and bargaining (Krasner, 1982a, 1985; Fearon, 1998), and these five issues can be addressed through negotiation and policy coordination among states (Keohane, 1984). Krasner (1982a) suggests that a well-established international regime can reduce conflicts, lower transaction costs, and foster a stable cooperative environment. These development regimes and institutions promote cooperation among traditional donors, providing information about the intentions of each party and addressing non-compliance (Milner, 1992). For China, the Chinese government has also tried to establish collaborative institutions such as Strategic Economic Dialogues, Working Groups, Forums, and so on (details in Chap. 5, Sect. 5.1) to promote tripartite cooperation with traditional donor partners and beneficiary

[4] Stephen D. Krasner defines international regimes as "principles, norms, rules, and decision-making procedures around which actor expectations converge in a given issue-area" (Krasner, 1982b, p. 185).

In the context of international development, the terms 'development aid regime,' 'ODA (Official Development Assistance) regime,' and 'DAC regime' are often used interchangeably. The international development regime has a formal governance structure and emphasises performance standards over policy outcomes. Individuals within this regime have self-interested motivations but also consider collective benefits (Hook & Rumsey, 2016).

countries. Still, it is questionable whether these regimes can effectively work in practical projects.

For instance, following the signing of several documents on tripartite cooperation between the Chinese and French governments in 2015, establishing a regime for the governance of such arrangements, the cooperation process between them accelerated. They established the Sino-French Fund for Third Country Cooperation and signed more than ten cooperation projects the following year (Zhang, 2020). By institutionalising the procedures of tripartite cooperation, pre-established institutions can reduce the costs of subsequent cooperation processes in tripartite cooperation, as there is no need to negotiate clauses on which consensus has already been achieved. Additionally, the Chinese government has also accelerated the signing of MOUs with other traditional donor countries' governments, and these MOUs are based on the template of previous agreements.

3.2.2 *Realism Theories*

Contrary to liberalism, which posits that states are willing to cooperate, realism emphasises the competitive and conflictual nature of global politics (Wendt, 1999; Mearsheimer, 2001; Waltz, 1979; Reus-Smit & Snidal, 2010). Tripartite cooperation occasionally is influenced by national security concerns and the international political environment. In the context of realism theory, states operate within the complex dynamics of the security dilemma and often take actions based on security and national interest considerations (Devetak et al., 2011). Walt (1987) argues that states form alliances in response to the distribution of power as well as perceived threats. States form rival alliances, increasing the likelihood of conflict as they seek to mitigate threats from adversaries.

For instance, the China-France-UK Hinkley Point C nuclear power station resulted from the France-UK alliance and the 'golden era' of Anglo-Chinese relations. As discussed in a later chapter, due to its extended construction period and several China-Western tension incidents (such as the removal of Huawei from UK telecommunications infrastructure), the UK government developed reservations about Chinese participation. Consequently, Chinese enterprises were excluded from subsequent nuclear power station projects.

One proposition of realism is self-interest, suggesting that states act in their rational self-interest within the international system (Donnelly,

2000). Morgenthau (2006) argues that the primary target of states is the pursuit of power, which leads to a competitive and conflictual international system. He posits that the struggle for power among states is inevitable because it is driven by inherent tendencies towards domination and self-interest. States are the principal actors in the international system, and other international institutions such as non-governmental organisations, and other sub-state or trans-state actors exert little independent influence (Cai, 2011). Following this logic, in tripartite cooperation, participating governments and enterprises act as rational self-interested players and do not prioritise the tripartite alliance, especially when the MOUs and the alliance lack legally binding force. Traditional donor countries typically do not formally withdraw from these MOUs; instead, they have often been lukewarm about pursuing further actions with China. For instance, Canada signed a Joint Statement on third-party market cooperation with China in 2016, followed by Australia in 2017, Belgium in 2018, and the Netherlands in 2018, but no significant cooperative actions have taken place since these MOUs were signed.

Therefore, when faced with escalating tensions in the international political environment and divergent goals among participants, liberalism theory falls short of fully explaining why some tripartite cooperation projects fail or underperform, even if it helps explain the actual existence of such arrangements. Instead, realism theory, which emphasises that states prioritise national interests and security (Devetak et al., 2011), is more appropriate for explaining these unsuccessful or underperforming cases of tripartite cooperation. However, it is important to note that only a small portion of these projects fail or underperform due to state actions. Since tripartite cooperation projects are primarily business activities, where firms play a major role, their withdrawal is often driven by concerns over business reasons.

3.3 Foreign Direct Investment Theories and Tripartite Cooperation at Firm Level

This section provides a review of the eclectic (OLI) paradigm, the four main motives of OFDI, and the Springboard paradigm. It explores their alignment with tripartite cooperation in the infrastructure sector and identifies areas of divergence. Despite their primary association with MNEs, FDI theories are relevant to tripartite cooperation projects, even though they are seldom applied in project finance activities. The objective is to explore the applicability of FDI theory to the context of tripartite cooperation, aiming to advance theoretical insights in this field.

3.3.1 *The Eclectic Paradigm*

The eclectic (OLI) paradigm, developed by John Dunning in the 1980s, explains FDI decisions. It suggests that a company undertakes FDI when it possesses ownership (O) advantages, such as intangible assets in its home country that can be transferred to other countries with location (L) advantages, such as favourable economic conditions or access to resources. By internalising (I) these activities, the company can produce goods in-house, thereby maximising its competitive advantage. The 'I' in OLI aligns with the concept of semi-internalisation discussed in the context of transaction cost economics in the previous section, so it will not be elaborated on further here.

The OLI paradigm analysed the value-added activities of MNEs in the manufacturing industry initially (Dunning, 2001). Some of these advantages also appear in tripartite cooperation. Only when a company excels in infrastructure projects, possessing O advantages such as unique technological capabilities and proprietary information, counterparts will choose this company as a partner, and local authorities will be willing to cooperate. Otherwise, a different firm will be selected for the project.

Unlike the L advantages assumed in the OLI theory, provider countries and their respective companies find it challenging to apply L advantages because firms cannot necessarily choose which beneficiary country to engage with on a project. However, beneficiary countries may entice donor and partner countries to engage in tripartite cooperation in their territories by offering L advantages, such as low-cost labour, marketplace, raw materials, and favourable policies (Dunning, 2003, 2016; Bartlett & Ghoshal, 1987; Hitt et al., 2006).

Firms do not engage in projects in all beneficiary countries; these countries must also possess certain L advantages to make project finance viable. In other words, beneficiary countries must meet specific criteria, such as political and economic stability, to attract companies for project finance. Additionally, factors like the availability of potential infrastructure projects and accessible financing in host countries are also relevant considerations. When beneficiary countries lack strong L advantages, companies may opt for tripartite arrangements to spread the risks associated with project finance, thereby mitigating the uncertainties of operating in less-favourable environments.

3.3.2 Four Main Motives of OFDI

Based on Dunning's eclectic paradigm, the determinants for MNEs' internationalisation can be categorised into four types: resource-seeking, aimed at securing natural resources; efficiency-seeking, aimed at enhancing economies of scale and scope; market-seeking, aimed at sustaining existing markets or developing new ones; and strategic asset-seeking, aimed at acquiring intangible assets (Dunning & Lundan, 2008; Cui et al., 2014). These four determinants from traditional OFDI theories can serve as complementary theoretical explanations for the infrastructure sector as well.

As a development or expansion of the eclectic paradigm, these determinants can also explain why participants engage in tripartite cooperation projects. Chinese SOEs, for example, primarily adopt a resource-seeking strategy to secure natural resources like minerals, oil, and gas, ensuring a stable, low-cost, and high-quality supply chain (Kamal et al., 2019). This strategy is particularly relevant in certain tripartite cooperation energy projects. For instance, the Chinese government has entered into natural gas supply contracts with the Russian government in projects such as the China-France-Russia YAMAL LNG project. Occasionally, energy giants also participate in energy projects, but their main aim tends to be profit-seeking from the markets of beneficiary countries rather than securing energy supplies for their domestic needs (Hong et al., 2019; Meyer, 2015; Morschett et al., 2015).

In traditional asset-seeking theory, strategic assets encompass brands, human capital, and distribution networks. According to Dunning (1980), firms typically invest in a host country when the combined value of their own assets and local assets surpasses that of local competitors. This is referred to as 'asset-exploitation.' However, in the context of tripartite cooperation, investors adopt a more flexible cooperative approach when they seek and exploit ownership (O) advantages. Through agreements among the three parties involved, participants can create O advantages by pooling resources without the necessity of pursuing mergers and acquisitions for specific assets (Luo et al., 2013). This collaborative strategy enables them to aggregate resources that exceed those available to local rivals, helping them overcome competitive disadvantages (Amit & Schoemaker, 1993; Rui & Yip, 2008). For example, a consortium led by

Portugal's Mota-Engil, China Communications Construction Company (CCCC), and three Mexican partners ultimately secured the contract for the Mexico Mayan Railway Project. They ultimately won the contract and were awarded the project by offering the most competitive price.[5]

Kuemmerle (1997, 1999) argues that when MNEs pursue strategic assets, their primary focus is not on reducing production costs, overcoming trade barriers, or exploiting economies of scale. Instead, they prioritise factors such as "the presence of high-quality physical and human infrastructure and a favourable political and commercial environment towards M&As and cooperative alliances" (Dunning, 2001, p. 183).

While Dunning's traditional OFDI theories can explain the determinants of Chinese and Western MNEs in internationalising and investing in beneficiary countries, they do not fully disclose why these MNEs choose to partner with each other. Specifically, they do not sufficiently explain why Chinese and Western firms prefer to cooperate together rather than directly invest in beneficiary countries alone. Tripartite cooperation involves higher transaction costs due to the inclusion of an additional partner, leading to increased complexities and potential challenges arising from differences in the approaches of Chinese and Western firms. In the empirical chapters, it is worth assessing whether firms leverage their Ownership (O) advantages in tripartite cooperation, exploit Internalisation (I) advantages, and seek the Location (L) advantages of beneficiary countries. Additionally, further exploration is needed to determine whether participant companies pursue strategic assets alongside the three traditional goals of seeking markets, resources, and efficiency in tripartite cooperation projects.

3.3.3 *Springboard Perspective*

The springboard perspective, introduced in 2007 by Luo and Tung, explains that emerging market multinational enterprises (EMNEs) engage in asset-seeking strategies to accelerate their catch-up process (Luo & Tung, 2018). These EMNEs use international expansion as a springboard to acquire strategic resources and overcome institutional and market constraints in their home countries. They often aim to acquire technology,

[5] GCR, "Chinese, Spanish, Portuguese Giants Join Mexican Companies Bidding for Mayan Rail Contract," Global Construction Review, April 20, 2020, https://www.globalconstructionreview.com/chinese-spanish-and-portuguese-giants-join-slew-me/.

know-how, R&D facilities, human capital, brands, consumer bases, distribution channels, managerial expertise, and natural resources. This approach is particularly effective when foreign firms are willing to sell or share these assets due to financial difficulties or restructuring needs (Child & Rodrigues, 2005).

Through springboard strategy, EMNEs overcome their latecomer disadvantage on the global stage via aggressive, risk-taking measures, acquiring or buying critical assets from mature MNEs. This allows them to compensate for competitive weaknesses (Luo & Rui, 2009; Rui & Yip, 2008). MNEs use outward investment as a springboard to bypass stringent trade barriers in beneficiary countries. Without cooperation with Western and local firms, Chinese firms might struggle to tap niche opportunities in Western or beneficiary countries' markets, especially in sensitive energy industries, such as nuclear power. Furthermore, Rui and Bruyaka (2021) develop the springboard perspective and integrate network orchestration mechanisms in analysing how MNEs catch up in production and innovation. Their research suggests that both Chinese and Western firms can leverage their home-country advantages as strengths through strategic network orchestration when collaborating with foreign partners. Therefore, tripartite cooperation, as a closer cooperative network, can be seen as an effective means for exchanging internally developed knowledge among participants.

When MNEs use the springboard strategy, they need to overcome four key challenges to successfully implement this strategy: poor corporate governance, post-spring integration and organisational difficulties, lack of global experience and managerial competence, and weak product/process innovation (Luo & Tung, 2007). However, tripartite cooperation can help address these challenges more effectively. For example, Western firms, with their well-established corporate governance practices, can assist Chinese and beneficiary country firms in improving their post-spring integration and organisational systems. Through tripartite cooperation, participant firms can directly learn from their partners' experience and managerial competence, as well as gain access to product and process innovations during the cooperation stages.

In conclusion, transaction cost and internalisation theories can partly explain why firms are willing to engage in tripartite cooperation despite the higher transaction costs. The OLI paradigm and the springboard perspective further elucidate why firms might opt for tripartite cooperation, highlighting motivations such as exploiting ownership (O) and location

(L) advantages, as well as seeking markets, resources, efficiency, and strategic assets. According to the springboard perspective, tripartite cooperation offers firms an opportunity to access intangible assets and overcome market entry barriers. However, the existing literature does not explicitly address the applicability of these FDI theories to tripartite cooperation. There are gaps in understanding which specific motivations apply uniquely to tripartite arrangements, as opposed to bilateral or other forms of cooperation. Given these gaps, this study will further investigate the applicability of FDI theories to tripartite cooperation projects in the empirical chapters. By examining specific case studies and empirical data, the research aims to assess how these theoretical frameworks manifest in real-world contexts and to clarify the particular benefits and challenges of tripartite cooperation.

3.4 Infrastructure's Special Characteristics: Natural Monopoly

Another significant reason for engaging in tripartite cooperation is that participants use it as a strategic approach to enter the infrastructure industry, which is often viewed as providing public goods with natural monopoly characteristics. Such industries are typically controlled or closely monitored by local public authorities in beneficiary countries. The high barriers to entry in the infrastructure market make it difficult for new entrants to compete independently. As a result, these entrants often find it necessary to collaborate with existing dominant players through tripartite cooperation.

This research focuses on tripartite cooperation in economic infrastructure projects, such as power stations, roads and railways, and ports. When researchers refer to a natural monopoly, they mean an industry where a single firm can achieve greater production efficiency than multiple firms combined. Natural monopoly industries typically have higher barriers to entry for new firms, such as stringent government regulations and higher startup costs, making it difficult for competitors to enter the market. Because of these unique characteristics in infrastructure, participants still choose to engage in tripartite cooperation projects despite higher transaction costs than in bilateral arrangements. Infrastructure industries are normally owned by the government and identified as natural monopolies, not exposed to competitive markets. These projects typically have a long life cycle, characterised by high sunk fixed costs, low variable costs, and low residual value (Megginson & Mueller, 2022). The unique characteristics of infrastructure projects and the advantages offered by tripartite cooperation help explain why participants prefer this model over other types of cooperation, despite the potential for additional transaction costs.

According to Baumol et al. (1977, 1982) and Sharkey (1982), this situation is termed the 'subadditivity' of the cost function. When participant firms collaborate to form a single 'firm' for a specific tripartite cooperation project, they effectively create a form of internalisation that achieves subadditivity, thereby generating additional benefits from the cooperation. Conversely, when participants in certain projects do not form a single 'firm' and instead act individually, conflicting with the principle of subadditivity, it might lead to higher costs.

Participants in tripartite cooperation projects within infrastructure industries are willing to bear potential transaction costs due to the characteristics of natural monopoly industries. In such industries, the pursuit of profit maximisation becomes a less-important goal (Baumol et al., 1977, 1982). This contrasts with industries that have low barriers to entry, such as manufacturing, where the expectation of profit maximisation is more explicit (Koopmans & Beckmann, 1957; Williamson, 1995).

There is ongoing debate about whether natural monopolies are beneficial or detrimental. On the one hand, North and Thomas (1973) argue that monopolies impede development by blocking the adoption of new technologies and more productive working arrangements. In natural monopolies, existing firms accumulate substantial advantages with fixed costs, leading to lower average variable costs compared to potential entrants (Waterson, 1987). Consequently, meeting increased demand often relies on existing firms expanding their production rather than new firms entering the market. New entrants are often reluctant to join due to the challenges of surviving with high initial investment (Waterson, 1987; Dixit, 1979).

On the other hand, a natural monopoly can offer an efficient means of providing public goods or services. Some researchers, such as Sánchez (2000), conducted subadditivity tests[6] on the cost function in the European railways and found that two duopolistic firms, with smaller size and specialised production, yield greater efficiency gains than a single

[6] He used the Evans-Heckman test. This is a statistical method to test for subadditivity on a local scale rather than a global one.

giant firm, suggesting that excessive monopoly can be detrimental. Shaked and Sutton (1983, 1987) shift their focus to the vertical integration of differentiated products and natural oligopoly. They observe that in markets with only two or three entrants, these oligopolies can offer distinct products and generate profits. Even with reductions in fixed costs and increases in market size, new entrants may not emerge. Waterson (1987) further identifies economies of scope[7] in potentially natural monopoly industries, such as railways and electricity generation. He finds that economies of scope occur in railways, where both passenger and freight transport share the same tracks, and in electricity generation when electronic infrastructure and equipment can be used more efficiently throughout both peak and off-peak periods.

Tripartite cooperation seems to offer a compromise between these debates. When new entrant companies aim to enter natural monopoly industries for specific projects, they frequently collaborate with established firms in the sector (Sánchez, 2000). Initially, these cooperative ventures operate as separate subsidiary firms but often consolidate or form alliances over time to establish a larger, unified entity. This consolidation enhances internal coordination (Evans & Heckman, 1984; Adhikari & Guru-Gharana, 2014). Moreover, new entrants bring innovative technology and management expertise, which they leverage in tripartite cooperation projects. For instance, the French container shipping giant CMA CGM has nearly monopolised shipping services in West Africa, resulting in economic inefficiencies such as higher prices and diminished service quality (The World Bank, 2017). Chinese shipping companies adopt a tripartite cooperation approach to penetrate the African market, utilising more efficient equipment and labour forces while sidestepping prohibitive entry costs (Theys et al., 2010; Notteboom et al., 2022; Onyenucheya, 2024). The tripartite cooperation approach not only allows participants to share risks and benefits with established partners but also to introduce competitive practices that can improve overall service quality and reduce costs.

Because infrastructure facilities are considered public goods, it is important to involve the beneficiary country's government in tripartite cooperation. In the process of realigning resources, government intervention plays a vital role in achieving economic efficiency in the market, addressing externalities, and resolving monopoly issues (Demsetz, 1968). However,

[7] Economies of scope are "efficiencies formed by variety, not volume" (Goldhar & Jelinek, 1983).

balancing the interests of monopolies and efficiency poses challenges for governments. While a single firm handling infrastructure construction can be efficient, monopoly pricing can lead to deadweight loss[8] due to information asymmetry and unregulated monopolistic power. To mitigate these issues, governments regulate various aspects such as prices, production costs, output, investment, and quality, while curbing monopoly profits and rent extraction (Joskow, 2007; Saglam, 2016). Governments possess capabilities beyond those of firms, including using policy or law enforcement to ensure the implementation of regulations at a lower cost. Additionally, establishing a well-rounded regime is critical for mitigating conflicts and realising mutual gains (Williamson, 2008; Simon, 1984). Therefore, it is essential to involve government entities in tripartite cooperation and establish transparent mechanisms to ensure fair outcomes.

3.5 Conclusion

This literature review chapter has explored various theoretical frameworks to address the research question: Why do participants opt for a tripartite cooperation model, even though they have to potentially bear the additional transaction costs? The key findings are summarised as follows:

First, transaction cost theory provides a partial explanation for why participants opt for tripartite cooperation. This form of cooperation can be regarded as semi-internalisation activities, where participants internalise transactions that would otherwise be conducted in the market, but not as fully as in bilateral arrangements. By collaborating in a tripartite model, participants can mitigate some of the uncertainties and inefficiencies associated with market transactions, thus reducing transaction costs. In addition, when deciding whether to participate in tripartite cooperation projects, firms weigh the opportunities for receiving additional benefits against the potential additional transaction costs compared to bilateral options. This trade-off is crucial in their decision-making process, and they would consider whether the potential for enhanced efficiency, resource amalgamation, and risk diversification outweigh the added costs.

Second, international relations theories can be used to explain the determinants and changes in transaction costs at the country level. Liberalism provides a partial theoretical foundation for understanding

[8] A deadweight loss is a cost incurred due to market inefficiency, resulting in a loss for the entire society.

tripartite cooperation, wherein participant countries seek common ground based on shared interests. It explains why participants are willing to engage in tripartite cooperation to seek greater benefits. In contrast, realism, which emphasises that states prioritise national interests and security, can be used to explain why tripartite cooperation projects might generate higher transaction costs due to the influence of domestic or foreign government policies.

Thirdly, the international business theories, such as OLI paradigm and the springboard perspective, further elucidate why firms might choose tripartite cooperation despite higher transaction costs. These theories highlight that firms have mixed motivations, such as seeking markets, resources, efficiency, and strategic assets, yet it is less clear which of these apply to tripartite cooperations in particular. According to the springboard perspective, tripartite cooperation provides an opportunity for firms to access intangible assets and overcome market entry barriers. In the empirical chapters, this study will further investigate the applicability of FDI theories to tripartite cooperation projects. By examining specific case studies and empirical data, the research aims to confirm the applicability of these theoretical frameworks.

Finally, the unique characteristics of infrastructure projects also explain the preference for tripartite cooperation. Infrastructure facilities, viewed as public goods with natural monopoly characteristics, are often controlled or closely monitored by local public authorities in beneficiary countries. The high barriers to entry in the infrastructure market make it difficult for new entrants to compete independently. Consequently, these entrants often find it necessary to collaborate with existing dominant players through tripartite cooperation. This collaboration allows participants to navigate complex regulatory environments, secure essential resources such as funding and expertise, and leverage established networks. By pooling resources and expertise, participants can mitigate risks, share costs, and achieve economies of scale that would be difficult to attain individually in the infrastructure sector.

In conclusion, theories suggest that tripartite cooperation is chosen due to a combination of factors explained by transaction cost theory, international relations theories, FDI theories, and the unique characteristics of infrastructure projects. These four main theories form the foundational pillars of tripartite cooperation in economic infrastructure. However, the determinants and applications of tripartite cooperation during the implementation phases remain to be further explored and clarified, in order to confirm these theoretical reasonings. The following empirical chapters (Chaps. 5, 6, and 7) will analyse the transaction costs and benefits generation processes associated with in this cooperative model.

References

Adhikari, D., & Guru-Gharana, K. K. (2014). Econometric Test of Cost Subadditivity in U.S. Electric Industry. https://www.alliedacademies.org/articles/econometric-test-of-cost-subadditivity-in-us-electric-industry.pdf

Alchian, A. A., & Demsetz, H. (1972). Production, Information Costs, and Economic Organization. *The American Economic Review, 62*(5), 777–795. https://www.jstor.org/stable/1815199

Amit, R., & Schoemaker, P. J. H. (1993). Strategic Assets and Organizational Rent. *Strategic Management Journal, 14*(1), 33–46.

Bartlett, C. A., & Ghoshal, S. G. (1987). Managing Across Borders: New Strategic Requirements. *MIT Sloan Management Review, 28*(4), 7–17. https://sloanreview.mit.edu/article/managing-across-borders-new-strategic-requirements/

Barzel, Y. (1985). Transaction Costs: Are They Just Costs? *Zeitschrift Für Die Gesamte Staatswissenschaft / Journal of Institutional and Theoretical Economics, 141*(1), 4–16. https://www.jstor.org/stable/40750776

Baumol, W. J., Bailey, E. E., & Willig, R. D. (1977). Weak Invisible Hand Theorems on the Sustainability of Multiproduct Natural Monopoly. *The American Economic Review, 67*(3), 350–365. https://www.jstor.org/stable/1831405

Baumol, W. J., Panzar, J. C., & Willig, R. D. (1982). *Contestable Markets and the Theory of Industry Structure*. Harcourt Brace Jovanovich.

Buckley, P. J., & Casson, M. (1976). *Future of the Multinational Enterprise*. Palgrave Macmillan London.

Cai, F. (2011, April 28). Absolute and Relative Gains in the Real World. *E-International Relations*. https://www.e-ir.info/2011/04/28/absolute-and-relative-gains-in-the-real-world/

Child, J., & Rodrigues, S. B. (2005). The Internationalisation of Chinese Firms: A Case for Theoretical Extension? *Management and Organization Review, 1*(3), 381–410. https://doi.org/10.1111/j.1740-8784.2005.0020a.x

Coase, R. H. (1937). The Nature of the Firm. *Economica, 4*(16), 386–405. https://doi.org/10.1111/j.1468-0335.1937.tb00002.x

Coase, R. H. (1960). The Problem of Social Cost. *The Journal of Law & Economics, 3*, 1–44. https://www.jstor.org/stable/724810

Coase, R. H. (1972). Industrial Organization: A Proposal for Research. In V. R. Fuchs (Ed.), *Policy Issues and Research Opportunities in Industrial*

Organization (pp. 59–73). National Bureau of Economic Research. https://chicagounbound.uchicago.edu/book_chapters/633/

Coase, R. H. (1992). The Institutional Structure of Production. *The American Economic Review, 82*(4), 713–719. https://www.jstor.org/stable/2117340

Cui, L., Meyer, K. E., & Hu, H. W. (2014). What Drives Firms' Intent to Seek Strategic Assets by Foreign Direct Investment? A Study of Emerging Economy Firms. *Journal of World Business, 49*(4), 488–501. https://doi.org/10.1016/j.jwb.2013.12.003

Davis, L. E., & North, D. C. (1971). *Institutional Change and American Economic Growth.* Cambridge University Press. https://doi.org/10.1017/cbo9780511561078

Demsetz, H. (1968). The Cost of Transacting. *The Quarterly Journal of Economics, 82*(1), 33. https://doi.org/10.2307/1882244

Denekamp, J. G. (1995). Intangible Assets, Internalisation and Foreign Direct Investment in Manufacturing. *Journal of International Business Studies, 26*(3), 493–504. https://www.jstor.org/stable/155558

Deng, P. (2013). Chinese Outward Direct Investment Research: Theoretical Integration and Recommendations. *Management and Organization Review, 9*(03), 513–539. https://doi.org/10.1111/more.12030

Devetak, R., Burke, A., & George, J. (2011). *An Introduction to International Relations.* Cambridge University Press.

Dhingra, T., & Sharma, S. (2022). Rail Infrastructure—Journey Since Indian Independence and Beyond. In *Studies in Infrastructure and Control* (pp. 53–87). Springer Nature. https://doi.org/10.1007/978-981-16-8837-9_4

Dixit, A. (1979). A Model of Duopoly Suggesting a Theory of Entry Barriers. *The Bell Journal of Economics, 10*(1), 20. https://doi.org/10.2307/3003317

Donnelly, J. (2000). *Realism and International Relations.* Cambridge University Press.

Duffield, M. (2013). *Development, Security and Unending War Governing the World of Peoples.* Cambridge Polity Press.

Dunning, J. H. (1980). Toward an Eclectic Theory of International Production: Some Empirical Tests. *Journal of International Business Studies, 11*(1), 9–31. https://www.jstor.org/stable/154142

Dunning, J. H. (1988). The Eclectic Paradigm of International Production: A Restatement and Some Possible Extensions. *Journal of International Business Studies, 19*(1), 1–31. JSTOR. https://www.jstor.org/stable/154984

Dunning, J. H. (2001). The Eclectic (OLI) Paradigm of International Production: Past, Present and Future. *International Journal of the Economics of Business, 8*(2), 173–190. Tandfonline. https://doi.org/10.1080/13571510110051441

Dunning, J. H. (2003). Location and the Multinational Enterprise: A Neglected Factor? In S. Young & S. E. Guisinger (Eds.), *The New Economic Analysis of*

Multinationals. Edward Elgar Publishing Limited. https://doi.org/10.4337/9781843766995.00011
Dunning, J. H. (2016). *Explaining International Production*. Routledge.
Dunning, J. H., & Lundan, S. M. (2008). *Multinational Enterprises and the Global Economy* (2nd Ed.). Edward Elgar.
Evans, D. S., & Heckman, J. J. (1984). A Test for Subadditivity of the Cost Function with an Application to the Bell System. *The American Economic Review, 74*(4), 615–623. https://www.jstor.org/stable/1805127
Fearon, J. D. (1998). Bargaining, Enforcement, and International Cooperation. *International Organization, 52*(2), 269–305. https://doi.org/10.1162/002081898753162820
Fordelone, T. Y. (2009). Triangular Co-operation and Aid Effectiveness, Paper prepared for the Policy Dialogue on Development Co-operation. http://www.oecd.org/dac/46387212.pdf
Fordelone, T. Y. (2011). Triangular Co-operation and Aid Effectiveness. *OECD Journal: General Papers, 2010*(1), 47–67. https://doi.org/10.1787/gen_papers-2010-5kgc6cl31rnx
Gao, Q. (2018, December 14). The Disappearance of Thailand's High-Speed Rail Project in China Japan Third Country Cooperation (中日第三国合作中消失的泰国高铁项目). NIKKEI. https://cn.nikkei.com/columnviewpoint/column/33518-2018-12-14-02-54-16.html
Gill, P. S. (2023, November 23). Thailand's High-Speed Railway: On the Fast Track to Ties with China, But at What Cost? Thediplomat.com. https://thediplomat.com/2023/11/thailands-high-speed-railway-on-the-fast-track-to-ties-with-china-but-at-what-cost/
Goldhar, J. D., & Jelinek, M. (1983, November 1). Plan for Economies of Scope. *Harvard Business Review*. https://hbr.org/1983/11/plan-for-economies-of-scope
Hart, O., & Moore, J. (1990). Property Rights and the Nature of the Firm. *Journal of Political Economy, 98*(6), 1119–1158. https://doi.org/10.1086/261729
Hennart, J.-F. (1988). A Transaction Costs Theory of Equity Joint Ventures. *Strategic Management Journal, 9*(4), 361–374. https://doi.org/10.1002/smj.4250090406
Hitchcock, W. I., & Moravcsik, A. (1999). The Choice for Europe: Social Purpose and State Power from Messina to Maastricht. *The American Historical Review, 104*(5), 1742. https://doi.org/10.2307/2649481
Hitt, M. A., Bierman, L., Uhlenbruck, K., & Shimizu, K. (2006). The Importance of Resources in the Internationalisation of Professional Service Firms: The Good, the Bad, and the Ugly. *Academy of Management Journal, 49*(6), 1137–1157. https://doi.org/10.5465/amj.2006.23478217

Hong, E., Lee, I. H. (Ian), & Makino, S. (2019). Outbound Foreign Direct Investment (FDI) Motivation and Domestic Employment by Multinational Enterprises (MNEs). Journal of International Management, 25(2), 100657. https://doi.org/10.1016/j.intman.2018.11.003

Hook, S. W., & Rumsey, J. G. (2016). The Development Aid Regime at Fifty: Policy Challenges Inside and Out. *International Studies Perspectives, 17*(1), 55–74. https://www.jstor.org/stable/44218891?sid=primo%3Fsid%3Dprimo&seq=4

Hymer, S. (1976). *The International Operations of National Firms: A Study of Direct Foreign Investment.* Mit Press.

Jobin, D. (2008). A Transaction Cost-Based Approach to Partnership Performance Evaluation. *Evaluation, 14*(4), 437–465. https://doi.org/10.1177/1356389008095487

Joskow, P. (2007). Regulation of Natural Monopoly. In *Handbook of Law and Economics* (pp. 1227–1348). Elsevier. https://econpapers.repec.org/bookchap/eeelawchp/2-16.htm

Joskow, P. L. (1985). Vertical Integration and Long-term Contracts: The Case of Coal-burning Electric Generating Plants. *The Journal of Law, Economics, and Organization, 1*(1), 33–81. https://doi.org/10.1093/oxfordjournals.jleo.a036889

Joskow, P. L. (1988). Asset Specificity and the Structure of Vertical Relationships: Empirical Evidence. *Journal of Law, Economics, & Organization, 4*(1), 95–117. https://www.jstor.org/stable/765016

Kamal, M. A., Ullah, A., Zheng, J., Zheng, B., & Xia, H. (2019). Natural Resource or Market Seeking Motive of China's FDI in Asia? New Evidence at Income and Sub-regional Level. *Economic Research-Ekonomska Istraživanja, 32*(1), 3869–3894. https://doi.org/10.1080/1331677x.2019.1674679

Kamwengo, C. (2020). Beneficiary Country Ownership and the Politics of Partnership in Trilateral Development Cooperation: A Case Study of Zambia. Etheses.dur.ac.uk. http://etheses.dur.ac.uk/13696/

Kapsali, M., Roehrich, J. K., & Akhtar, P. (2019). Effective Contracting for High Operational Performance in Projects. *International Journal of Operations & Production Management, 39*(2), 294–325. https://doi.org/10.1108/ijopm-10-2017-0604

Keohane, R. O. (1984). *After Hegemony: Cooperation and Discord in the Political Economy.* Princeton University Press.

Keohane, R. O. (1986). Reciprocity in International Relations. *International Organization, 40*(1), 1–27. https://doi.org/10.1017/s0020818300004458

Keohane, R. O. (1990). Multilateralism: An Agenda for Research. *International Journal, 45*(4), 731–764. https://doi.org/10.2307/40202705

Klein, P. G. (1999). New Institutional Economics. Mospace.umsystem.edu; Edward Elgar. https://mospace.umsystem.edu/xmlui/handle/10355/161

Kogut, B., & Zander, U. (1993). Knowledge of the Firm and the Evolutionary Theory of the Multinational Corporation. *Journal of International Business Studies, 24*(4), 625–645. https://doi.org/10.1057/palgrave.jibs.8490248

Koopmans, T. C., & Beckmann, M. (1957). Assignment Problems and the Location of Economic Activities. *Econometrica, 25*(1), 53. https://doi.org/10.2307/1907742

Krasner, S. D. (1982a). Regimes and the Limits of Realism: Regimes as Autonomous Variables. *International Organization, 36*(2), 497–510. https://doi.org/10.1017/s0020818300019032

Krasner, S. D. (1982b). Structural Causes and Regime Consequences: Regimes as Intervening Variables. *International Organization, 36*(2), 185–205. https://doi.org/10.1017/s0020818300018920

Krasner, S. D. (1985). *International Regimes.* Cornell University Press.

Kreps, D. M. (1990). Corporate Culture and Economic Theory. In E. J. Alt & K. A. Shepsle (Eds.), *Perspectives on Positive Political Economy.* Cambridge University Press.

Kuemmerle, W. (1997). Building Effective R&D Capabilities Abroad. Harvard Business Review, March–April 1997. https://hbr.org/1997/03/building-effective-rd-capabilities-abroad

Kuemmerle, W. (1999). The Drivers of Foreign Direct Investment into Research and Development: An Empirical Investigation. *Journal of International Business Studies, 30*(1), 1–24. https://doi.org/10.1057/palgrave.jibs.8490058

Lawson, A. (2009). *Evaluating the Transaction Costs of Implementing the Paris Declaration.* OECD. https://www.oecd.org/dac/evaluation/dcdndep/44135805.pdf

Luo, Y., & Park, S. H. (2004). Multiparty Cooperation and Performance in International Equity Joint Ventures. *Journal of International Business Studies, 35*(2), 142–160. https://doi.org/10.1057/palgrave.jibs.8400072

Luo, Y., & Rui, H. (2009). An Ambidexterity Perspective Toward Multinational Enterprises From Emerging Economies. *Academy of Management Perspectives, 23*(4), 49–70. https://doi.org/10.5465/amp.23.4.49

Luo, Y., Rui, H., & Maksimov, V. (2013). Tales of Rivals: Inter-Chinese Attacks in International Competition. *Organizational Dynamics, 42*(2), 156–166. https://doi.org/10.1016/j.orgdyn.2013.03.009

Luo, Y., & Tung, R. L. (2007). International Expansion of Emerging Market Enterprises: A Springboard Perspective. *Journal of International Business Studies, 38*(4), 481–498. https://doi.org/10.1057/palgrave.jibs.8400275

Luo, Y., & Tung, R. L. (2018). A General Theory of Springboard MNEs. *Journal of International Business Studies, 49*(2), 129–152. https://doi.org/10.1057/s41267-017-0114-8

Macneil, I. R. (1974). *The Many Futures of Contracts*. Gould School of Law, the Law Center University of Southern California.

Martin, L. L. (1999). The Political Economy of International Cooperation. In I. Kaul (Ed.), *Global Public Goods: International Cooperation in the 21st Century Global Public Goods: International Cooperation in the 21st Century* (pp. 51–64). Oxford University Press. https://doi.org/10.1093/0195130529.003.0003

Mearsheimer, J. J. (2001). *The Tragedy of Great Power Politics*. W.W. Norton & Company.

Megginson, W. L., & Mueller, P. C. (2022). Natural Monopoly Privatization: Minimizing Regulatory Trade-Offs Between Rent Extraction and Innovation. *Academy of Management Perspectives, 36*(1), 111–124. https://doi.org/10.5465/amp.2019.0170

Meng, H., & Yu, Q. (2020). Third Party Market Cooperation: Theoretical Construction, Historical Evolution, and China's Path. *Contemporary Asia Pacific, 6*(4–40), 153–154. 门洪华, 俞钦文. 第三方市场合作:理论建构、历史演进与中国路径[J].当代亚太, 2020(06):4-40+153-154.

Menard, C., & Shirley, M. M. (2014). The Future of New Institutional Economics: From Early Intuitions to a New Paradigm? *Journal of Institutional Economics, 10*(4), 541–565. https://doi.org/10.1017/s174413741400006x

Meyer, K. E. (2015). What is "Strategic Asset Seeking FDI"? *Multinational Business Review, 23*(1), 57–66. https://doi.org/10.1108/mbr-02-2015-0007

Milner, H. (1992). International Theories of Cooperation Among Nations: Strengths and Weaknesses. *World Politics, 44*(3), 466–496. https://doi.org/10.2307/2010546

Moran, T. H. (1975). *Multinational Corporations and the Politics of Dependence: Copper in Chile*. Princeton University Press.

Moravcsik, A. (1993). Preferences and Power in the European Community: A Liberal Intergovernmentalist Approach. *Journal of Common Market Studies, 31*(4), 473–524. https://doi.org/10.1111/j.1468-5965.1993.tb00477.x

Morgenthau, H. J. (2006). *Politics Among Nations: The Struggle for Power and Peace* (7th ed.). Random House.

Morschett, D., Schramm-Klein, H., & Zentes, J. (2015). Motives for Internationalisation. In *Strategic International Management* (pp. 75–98). Springer. https://doi.org/10.1007/978-3-658-07884-3_4

NDRC. (2019). Third-Party Market Cooperation Guidelines and Cases. National Development and Reform Commision, P.R. China. http://images.mofcom.gov.cn/mz/201909/20190912093710956.pdf

North, D. C. (1991). Institutions. *Journal of Economic Perspectives, 5*(1), 97–112. https://doi.org/10.1257/jep.5.1.97

North, D. C., & Thomas, R. P. (1973). *The Rise of the Western World: A New Economic History*. Cambridge University Press.

Notteboom, T., Pallis, A., & Rodrigue, J.-P. (2022). *Port Economics, Management and Policy* (1st ed.). Routledge. https://doi.org/10.4324/9780429318184

Nye, J. S., & Keohane, R. O. (1977). *Power and Interdependence*. Harpercollins, Cop.

OECD. (2009). The Paris Declaration on Aid Effectiveness and the Accra Agenda for Action. https://www.oecd.org/dac/effectiveness/34428351.pdf

OECD. (2019a). Enabling Effective Triangular Co-operation. OECD Development Policy Papers. https://doi.org/10.1787/5fc4501e-en

OECD. (2019b). Toolkit for Identifying, Monitoring and Evaluating the Value Added of Triangular Co-operation. https://www.oecd.org/dac/triangular-co-operation/TOOLKIT%20-%20version%20August%202018.pdf

Onyenucheya, A. (2024, May 2). Tin Can Port Access Gate Automated to Enhance Efficiency. *The Guardian Nigeria News—Nigeria and World News*. https://guardian.ng/business-services/tin-can-port-access-gate-automated-to-enhance-efficiency/

Paul, E., & Vandeninden, F. (2012). Foreign Aid Transaction Costs: What Are They and When Are They Minimised? *Development Policy Review, 30*(3), 283–304. https://doi.org/10.1111/j.1467-7679.2012.00577.x

Reus-Smit, C., & Snidal, D. (2010). *The Oxford Handbook of International Relations*. OUP Oxford.

Rugman, A. M. (1981). *Inside the Multinationals*. Croom Helm.

Rugman, A. M. (1985). Internalisation is Still a General Theory of Foreign Direct Investment. *Weltwirtschaftliches Archiv, 121*(3), 570–575. https://www.jstor.org/stable/40439351

Rui, H., & Bruyaka, O. (2021). Strategic Network Orchestration in Emerging Markets: China's Catch-up in the High-Speed Train Industry. *British Journal of Management, 32*(1), 97–123. https://doi.org/10.1111/1467-8551.12457

Rui, H., & Yip, G. S. (2008). Foreign Acquisitions by Chinese firms: A Strategic Intent Perspective. *Journal of World Business, 43*(2), 213–226.

Rumelt, R. P. (1984). Towards a Strategic Theory of the Firm. In R. B. Lamb (Ed.), *Competitive Strategic Management* (pp. 566–570). Englewood Cliffs.

Saglam, I. (2016). Regulating a Manager-Controlled Natural Monopoly with Unknown Costs. *Managerial and Decision Economics, 38*(6), 792–805. https://doi.org/10.1002/mde.2817

Sánchez, P. C. (2000). A Subadditivity Test for the Cost Function of the Principal European Railways. *Transport Reviews, 20*(3), 275–290. https://doi.org/10.1080/014416400412814

Schulz, N-S. (2010). Boosting South-South Cooperation in the Context of Aid Effectiveness Telling the Story of Partners Involved in more than 110 Cases of South-South and Triangular Cooperation. https://www.oecd.org/dac/effectiveness/46080462.pdf

Sebenius, J. K. (1992). Challenging Conventional Explanations of International Cooperation: Negotiation Analysis and the Case of Epistemic Communities. *International Organization, 46*(1), 323–365. https://doi.org/10.1017/s0020818300001521

Shaked, A., & Sutton, J. (1983). Natural Oligopolies. *Econometrica, 51*(5), 1469–1483. https://www.tcd.ie/Economics/staff/ppwalsh/papers/sutton.pdf

Shaked, A., & Sutton, J. (1987). Product Differentiation and Industrial Structure. *The Journal of Industrial Economics, 36*(2), 131. https://doi.org/10.2307/2098408

Sharkey, W. W. (1982). *The Theory of Natural Monopoly*. In The Economic Journal. Oxford University Press. https://doi.org/10.1017/cbo9780511571817

Sim, A. B., & Ali, Y. (1998). Performance of International Joint Ventures from Developing and Developed Countries: An Empirical Study in a Developing Country Context. *Journal of World Business, 33*(4), 357–377. https://doi.org/10.1016/s1090-9516(99)80080-7

Simon, H. A. (1984). On the Behavioral and Rational Foundations of Economic Dynamics. *Journal of Economic Behavior & Organization, 5*(1), 35–55. https://doi.org/10.1016/0167-2681(84)90025-8

Smith, T., & Ikenberry, G. J. (2001). After Victory: Institutions, Strategic Restraint, and the Rebuilding of Order after Major Wars. *Foreign Affairs, 80*(2), 170. https://doi.org/10.2307/20050090

Spulber, D. F. (1989). *Regulation and Markets*. MIT Press.

Tarzi, S. M. (2003). International Regimes and International Relations Theory: Search for Synthesis. *International Studies, 40*(1), 23–39. https://doi.org/10.1177/002088170304000102

Teece, D. J. (1981). The Market for Know-How and the Efficient International Transfer of Technology. *The ANNALS of the American Academy of Political and Social Science, 458*(1), 81–96. https://doi.org/10.1177/000271628145800107

Teece, D. J. (1986). Transactions Cost Economics and the Multinational Enterprise An Assessment. *Journal of Economic Behavior & Organization, 7*(1), 21–45. https://doi.org/10.1016/0167-2681(86)90020-x

The World Bank. (2017, June 16). Container Terminals Concessions—Making the Most of Ports in West Africa. https://documents1.worldbank.org/curated/en/919071469608006706/pdf/Container-Terminals-Concessions-Making-the-Most-of-Ports-in-West-Africa.pdf

Theys, C., Notteboom, T. E., Pallis, A. A., & De Langen, P. W. (2010). The Economics Behind the Awarding of Terminals in Seaports: Towards a Research Agenda. *Research in Transportation Economics, 27*(1), 37–50. https://doi.org/10.1016/j.retrec.2009.12.006

Thompson, G. (Ed.). (1991). *Markets, Hierarchies, and Networks: The Coordination of Social Life*. Sage Publications.

Tjønneland, E. (2008). Norwegian Aid and Triangular South-South Cooperation—Mapping, analysis and implications for Norwegian knowledge transfer. Oslo: Norad (Discussion Paper, Norad Report). https://www.norad.no/en/toolspublications/publications/2019/norwegian-aid-and-triangular-south-south-cooperation/

Tsurumi, Y. (1976). *The Japanese are Coming*. Ballinger Publishing Company.

UNECOSOC. (2008). Background Study for the Development Cooperation Forum: Trends in South-South and Triangular Development Cooperation. United Nations Economic and Social Council. https://www.iukdpf.com/background-study-for-the-development-cooperation-forum-trends-in-south-south-and-triangular-development-cooperation/

Vetschera, R. (2009). Learning about Preferences in Electronic Negotiations—A Volume-Based Measurement Method. *European Journal of Operational Research, 194*(2), 452–463. https://doi.org/10.1016/j.ejor.2007.12.016

Walt, S. M. (1987). *The Origins of Alliances*. Cornell University Press.

Waltz, K. (1979). *Theory of International Politics*. Addison-Wesley Publishing Company.

Waterson, M. (1987). Recent Developments in the Theory of Natural Monopoly. *Journal of Economic Surveys, 1*(1–2), 59–80. https://doi.org/10.1111/j.1467-6419.1987.tb00024.x

Wendt, A. (1999). *Social Theory of International Politics*. Cambridge University Press.

Wernerfelt, B. (1984). A Resource-Based View of the Firm. *Strategic Management Journal, 5*(2), 171–180. https://www.jstor.org/stable/2486175

Williamson, O. E. (1971). The Vertical Integration of Production: Market Failure Considerations. *The American Economic Review, 61*(2), 112–123. https://www.jstor.org/stable/1816983

Williamson, O. E. (1975). *Markets and Hierarchies: Analysis and Antitrust Implications*. Free Press.

Williamson, O. E. (1983). Credible Commitments: Using Hostages to Support Exchange. *The American Economic Review, 73*(4), 519–540. https://www.jstor.org/stable/1816557

Williamson, O. E. (1986). *Economic Organization*. New York University Press.

Williamson, O. E. (1992). Markets, Hierarchies, and the Modern Corporation. *Journal of Economic Behavior & Organization, 17*(3), 335–352. https://doi.org/10.1016/s0167-2681(95)90012-8

Williamson, O. E. (1995). Hierarchies, Markets and Power in the Economy: An Economic Perspective. *Industrial and Corporate Change, 4*(1), 21–49. https://doi.org/10.1093/icc/4.1.21

Williamson, O. E. (1996). *The Mechanisms of governance*. Oxford University Press.

Williamson, O. E. (2008). Transaction Cost Economics: The Precursors. *Economic Affairs, 28*(3), 7–14. https://doi.org/10.1111/j.1468-0270.2008.00838.x

Zhang, D. (2017). *A Promising New Trend? Factors Driving Chinas Growing Trilateral Aid Cooperation [Doctoral Dissertation]*. Australian National University (ANU) Press.

Zhang, Y. (2020). Third-Party Market Cooperation Under the Belt and Road Initiative: Progress, Challenges, and Recommendations. *China International Strategy Review, 1*, 310–329. https://doi.org/10.1007/s42533-019-00026-7

CHAPTER 4

Research Design and Methodology

The research primarily used qualitative analysis, with limited incorporation of quantitative analysis, to investigate Chinese tripartite cooperation in infrastructure projects. The aims of this research included understanding why participants opt for tripartite cooperation and examining the processes of cost and benefits generation associated with tripartite collaborations. Second-hand data were gathered through desk research, while first-hand data were obtained via semi-structured interviews. Based on the collected data, a comprehensive database was developed, and in-depth case studies were conducted. This study employed both within-case and cross-case approaches to explore tripartite cooperation across different contexts.

4.1 Research Design

This research primarily utilised qualitative analysis, with limited use of quantitative analysis. Quantitative analysis was specifically applied in Chap. 5, which employed descriptive statistics to identify trends and patterns in global tripartite cooperation involving China. In Chap. 6, extensive qualitative analysis was employed to examine the determinants and actions that drive participants to engage in tripartite cooperation projects. I systematically coded similar content, continuously moving between the data and emerging themes by using NVivo software. In Chap. 7, in-depth case

C. Su, *From Two to Three*, Governing China in the 21st Century,
https://doi.org/10.1007/978-981-95-8708-7_4

studies were conducted. Process tracing methodology was utilised to scrutinise the project development process, while stakeholder analysis methodology was employed to compare transaction costs and project efficiency.

Qualitative methods and case studies provide more depth and contextual details, but the generalisation is problematic (Ritchie et al. 2014). The findings and conclusions of this research may not universally apply to all tripartite cooperation projects and may need modification based on different situations. The scientific generalisation of findings and conclusions is an important issue of case studies, and this research focuses on 'analytic generalisation' instead of 'statistical generalisation.' There are four tests that can improve the effectiveness of the result of the case study: external validity (generalising the findings of a study to other situations), construct validity (generalising from the program or measures to the concept), internal validity (a cause-and-effect relationship established in a study), and reliability (the consistency of results across time and different observers) (Judd et al., 1991).

The replication logic in multiple-case studies enhances external validity, and this research established a case database to collect all Chinese tripartite cooperation projects in the economic infrastructure sector. To strengthen construct validity, a wide range of documents about these 68 tripartite cooperation projects were collected, establishing a chain of evidence to examine the transaction cost theory and benefits-generation process. To ensure internal validity, the process tracing method was used to establish a cause-and-effect relationship between the tripartite cooperation mechanism and the changes in cost and value within four in-depth case studies. To enhance reliability, this research gathered both first-hand and second-hand information for selected cases to form a more complete picture of each project.

4.1.1 *Establish a Large Case Database*

Although tripartite cooperation was proposed by the Chinese government in 2015, only 14 countries had signed MOUs with the Chinese government by the end of 2023. The detailed list of countries' MOUs for tripartite cooperation and their corresponding cooperation platforms can be found in Appendix 1. However, there has been currently no official list of tripartite cooperation projects from any institution or authority. Therefore, this research systematically gathered information on all Chinese tripartite cooperation projects within the economic infrastructure sector, as confirmed by the Chinese government through its official platforms such as government Web sites and official news reports. Subsequently, this information was organised into a comprehensive case database.

In the empirical research, I use the term 'partner countries' to refer to the other provider nations (i.e., Western countries or traditional donor countries) involved in China-led tripartite cooperation projects. Specifically, these 'partner countries' include 14 nations that signed Memoranda of Understanding with the Chinese government: France, the Republic of Korea, Canada, Portugal, Australia, Japan, Italy, Belgium, the Netherlands, Spain, Austria, Singapore, Switzerland, and the UK. When discussing 'partner firms/companies/enterprises,' I am specifically referring to business entities headquartered in France, Italy, Spain, Portugal, Germany, the UK, the USA, Japan, South Korea, and Singapore. This distinction is intended to provide clarity regarding the precise countries and entities involved in the context of this research. Sometimes, I use 'Western countries/firms' when these partner countries exert colonial influence, and firms monopolise the infrastructure sector of beneficiary countries.

The list of tripartite cooperation projects was presented in a simplified format in Appendix 2. This large case database included the basic information about tripartite cooperation projects, such as time, partner countries, beneficiary countries, project name, Chinese institutions, partner countries' institutions, local actors, project duration, budget, and other brief descriptions. One limitation concerned the number of cases in the economic infrastructure sector, with the possibility that it may not cover all tripartite cooperation projects involving China. The cases were collected based on information that I found from Chinese government reports and documents by 2022.

Based on the established database, I analysed the collected data from various perspectives in Chap. 5. For example (refer to Sect. 5.2), I created combo charts to explore the correlation among year, investment scale, and project number, aiming to identify development trends in tripartite cooperation. The following figures illustrate the distribution of projects and their investment scale across different industries and geographical locations. These figures revealed patterns of tripartite cooperation and suggest participants' preferences and strategies. These analytical processes involved using Microsoft Excel to record and analyse statistics and to generate the figures.

Furthermore, the documentary data were systematically arranged based on publishing dates, facilitating a chronological understanding of project processes. The processing of qualitative data primarily relied on NVivo, a software capable of coding, categorising, analysing, and extracting insights from interviews, social media, and Web content (Schreier, 2012). Through content analysis, over 1600 documents were processed in NVivo. Relevant contents in each document were highlighted and then categorised into different key coding categories (See Appendix E). Thematic structuring involved four overarching themes: actions, outcomes, motivation, and theory. Similar contents were identified and sub-categorised under these themes, forming the basis for Chap. 6.

In the first category, termed 'actions,' relevant information was subdivided into background details, companies' actions, governmental interventions, and project participants' actions. Within the scope of company actions, categories included bilateral partnership initiatives, co-contractor arrangements, and financial collaborations. Governmental interventions comprised involvement from the Chinese governments and partner countries governments, as well as those of beneficiary countries, alongside the creation of Tripartite Joint Statements and MOUs. In terms of participants' actions within the project, considerations extended to cooperation domains, the distribution of interests, and the allocation of responsibilities.

Following the section on actions, the subsequent category addressed cooperation outcomes, problems, and challenges. These encompassed issues such as disputes during the implementation process, financial constraints, and associated risks. These categories of actions and outcomes facilitated to explore of the research question about how participants alter the dynamics of project financing activities and how the engagement of an additional partner causes more complexities in tripartite cooperation projects.

The motivation category encompassed the cooperation background, which involved competitions and shared interests. Firms and governments from China, partner countries, and beneficiary nations each had distinct reasons for participating in tripartite cooperation endeavours. Data on motivations was collected from interviews and various secondary sources. The written records of the interviews and all second-hand documents related to motivations were reviewed. Relevant content was highlighted in the text documents using NVivo, and the motivations were categorised. These categories included firms aiming for industrial upgrading, knowledge transfer, market seeking, and commercial interests, as well as governments aiming to enable firms to acquire strategic assets and integrate tripartite cooperation with their national development plans. Each category was carefully examined to identify common motivations among participants and to distinguish their differences. These findings were then linked to the theoretical frameworks discussed in Chap. 3, including FDI theories and the concept of natural monopoly, which were integrated into this category.

The theory category mainly comprised two components: additional benefits and transaction costs. Additional benefits included financial advantages and operational efficiencies, while transaction costs involve changes in search and information costs, negotiation costs, contract costs, agency costs, and other related expenses that are not directly associated with the construction and operation of projects. Together, these components were crucial in addressing the research question of why participants chose the tripartite cooperation model, despite the additional transaction costs.

These methodical steps provided a foundation for subsequent analyses in understanding the complexities of tripartite cooperation projects. The determinants and actions of governments and firms were summarised and analysed in Chap. 6. The determinants and actions influenced the costs and benefits of tripartite cooperation projects. The in-depth case studies examined the cause-effect relationship in Chap. 7.

4.1.2 In-Depth Case Studies

The case study approach has unique strengths in synthesising diverse sources of evidence, including direct observation, interviews, documentary analysis, and archival study (Yin, 2018). Moreover, this method could incorporate a model that employs rigorous deductive reasoning to formulate hypotheses regarding causal mechanisms, as demonstrated by the process tracing method (King et al., 1994). To address the research questions, specific tripartite cooperation cases were examined from an in-depth perspective.

This research used the multiple-case studies method to investigate specific tripartite cooperation projects. The multiple-case studies are based on the principle of replication, which enables the development of a more comprehensive theoretical framework and the representation of a broader spectrum of values (Seawright & Gerring, 2008). Specifically, this research focused on two beneficiary countries (the UK and Nigeria) and their corresponding projects (the China-France-UK Hinkley Point C Nuclear Power Station Project and three China-France-Nigeria Seaport Projects).

The selected cases were analysed employing both within-case and cross-case approaches. A challenge arose in identifying all elements of tripartite cooperation mechanisms, including actions and determinants of firms and governments involved in the projects. Therefore, process tracing emerged as a methodology for scrutinising various determinants (King et al., 1994; Ayres et al., 2003) that influence participants to engage in tripartite cooperation projects. By tracing the development process of each project, the complex and dynamic motivations and actions of each participant could be observed over different time periods, within their respective domestic and international contexts. This approach involved tracking the evolution of projects over time, with a particular focus on how the tripartite cooperation mechanism was framed and how costs and additional benefits change within the Hinkley Point C project and the three port projects.

The comparative method involved a limited number of cases. All selected cases were from China-France tripartite cooperation projects, driven by the observation that China and France have engaged in more tripartite cooperation projects than with any other countries, thereby yielding cooperative cases with maturity in project outcomes. This choice facilitated control over variables about partner countries. The selection of China-France-UK Hinkley Point C Nuclear Power Station Project was chosen due to its extensive documentation, rendering it conducive to employing the process tracing method to examine the change of project costs and additional benefits. The UK government has made all government contracts, including operational and financing contracts, fully accessible online. In addition, comprehensive coverage by the UK media further supported the study of this project.

To manage variables associated with beneficiary countries, this study selected three China-France-Nigeria Seaport Projects (Tincan Island Container Terminal B, Ibom Deep Seaport, and Lekki Deep Seaport) for cross-case comparison. Despite their geographic proximity within Nigeria, these projects presented distinct operational processes and outcomes, facilitating an effective comparative analysis among them.

Furthermore, the UK and Nigeria, as two distinct beneficiary countries, one from an advanced economy and one from a developing country, demonstrated different levels of infrastructure development and business environments. It is worthwhile to compare the roles of beneficiary countries in tripartite cooperation and explore the behaviour of firms and the outcomes of projects under different national circumstances, such as economic and political policies, financing approaches, social environments, legal systems, and technical support. Focusing on an advanced beneficiary economy was particularly meaningful, as it provides insights into how tripartite cooperation could be utilised in well-established institutional countries, thereby offering guidance for the future development of other less-developed beneficiary countries.

The brief introductions of each case are the following:

China-France-UK Hinkley Point C Nuclear Power Station: The Hinkley Point C nuclear power station project received approval from the UK government in September 2016. State-owned enterprises, EDF of France and CGN of China, invested in construction costs and took responsibility for the project's development (EDF, 2024). However, after years of delays and escalating costs, this project, initially symbolising the golden era of China-UK and China-France relations, has transformed into one that is now unattractive (White, 2024). By tracing the chronicle of how this project unfolded and examining transaction costs and additional benefits, this case could be used to explore how participants' actions influence the outcome of tripartite cooperation projects.

China-France-Nigeria Port Projects: The Tincan Island Container Terminal B was acquired by the China Merchant Group in 2010. China Merchant Group took over a 47.5% stake in TICT shares, becoming shareholders alongside the French company Bolloré and the local port authority (CMPG, 2024). The Ibom Deep Sea Port, with a \$4.2 billion public-private partnership investment, was approved by the Nigerian government in 2015. The consortium, comprising the French company Bolloré and PowerChina International Group, was awarded the port building contract and a 50-year franchise in 2018. Bolloré assumed responsibility for operating all container activities, while PowerChina took charge of constructing port infrastructure. However, both Bolloré and PowerChina withdrew from the project in 2021 (LUA, 2018). The Lekki Deep Sea Port, operated by Lekki Port LFTZ Enterprise Limited (LPLEL) under a Build, Own, Operate, and Transfer (BOOT) arrangement, secured a 45-year concession from the Nigerian Ports Authority in 2011. The construction and development of the Lekki Port were overseen by Singapore Tolaram and China CHEC.[1] Meanwhile, the

[1] China Harbour Engineering Company, "About Us," accessed February 9, 2024, https://www.cccme.cn/shop/cccme12721/introduction.aspx.

French company CMA CGM was responsible for marketing, operations, and maintenance of the container terminal. This project represented a unique form of tripartite cooperation with a dual triangular structure—one in project financing involving China, Singapore, and Nigeria and another in project operation involving China, France, and Nigeria (Joshi, 2018).[2]

The three Nigerian port projects exhibited distinct differences in their project processes and transaction effectiveness. Both the Tincan and Lekki projects successfully achieved their objectives within designated timeframes and budgets. Conversely, the consortium formed by Bolloré Ports and PowerChina withdrew from the Ibom project. These three projects, located in near geographical positions in Southwest Nigeria, demonstrated different outcomes in port infrastructure projects. Through tracing and comparing these cases, this research illustrated how participants alter the dynamics of project finance activities and cost-benefit generation processes in tripartite cooperation.

Finally, while I conducted a comparative analysis of tripartite cooperation projects involving France, it is worth exploring China's projects with other countries in diverse regions. For instance, partnering with Germany in African countries, Spain in South America, or Japan in Asia could provide valuable insights. Future research could undertake a more comprehensive comparison of partner countries to further enrich our understanding of tripartite cooperation dynamics.

4.2 Data Collection

Data collection involved two steps. First, information on all tripartite cooperation projects in economic infrastructure involving China from 2005 to 2022 was gathered from documents. This collected data was then used to establish a database (see Appendices A and B). Second, first-hand data was collected through semi-structured interviews conducted from October 2021 to May 2023.

[2] Raghavi Joshi, "Lekki Deep Sea Port, Lagos, Nigeria," Ship Technology, 2018, https://www.ship-technology.com/projects/lekki-deep-sea-port-lagos-nigeria/.

4.2.1 *Collecting Second-Hand Data*

The second-hand data were collected from various existing documents, including company reports, government reports, newspaper articles, and academic literature. The selection of these documents adhered to specific criteria:

1. Documents originated from credible sources, such as academia, government reports and statistics, and reputable media organisations.
2. Documents explicitly addressed cooperation projects and offered reliable evidence to support the analysis.

The research on government actions in tripartite cooperation relied extensively on government documents and academic literature. Government documents can provide the most recent and authoritative information about tripartite cooperation at the country level. The government resources were gathered by accessing Web sites such as China International Development Cooperation Agency, Belt and Road Portal, National Development and Reform Commission of China, French Development Agency, UK GOV, Nigerian Ports Authority, Akwa Ibom State Government, Lagos State Government, etc. However, these government announcements often emphasise positive outcomes while overlooking setbacks or failures in programmes. To address this limitation, the research also gathered insights from academic literature and media reports.

The academic literature was gathered by conducting searches in the King's College London's library databases (including ScienceDirect, EbscoHost, and JStor), Google Scholar, and the China National Knowledge Infrastructure (CNKI) database, using combinations of terms such as 'Chinese infrastructure investment,' 'Chinese State-Owned Enterprises (SOEs),' 'trilateral cooperation,' 'tripartite cooperation,' 'triangular cooperation,' 'North-South Cooperation,' 'South-South Cooperation,' etc. While these resources offered a theoretical foundation and valuable insights into cases, their data may be somewhat outdated due to the publishing process. To overcome this limitation and ensure the incorporation of the latest information, the research also integrated insights from the most recent media and government reports, which served as supplementary sources.

Drawing on government and media documents, as well as publications from international organisations like the World Bank, and academic literature, this research seeks to explore pivotal questions about why participants opt for tripartite cooperation instead of bilateral alternatives. Furthermore, it aims to examine the roles of participant governments in either promoting or hindering the progress of practical tripartite cooperation initiatives. The project-level research primarily relied on companies' reports and news reports, which provided timely insights into the processes and performance of each project. These sources were directly collected from each company's Web site. Media coverage, including newspaper articles and blog pieces, also contributed information on tripartite cooperation at the project level. Mainstream media may have access to insights from insiders and professional experts.

For the database encompassing information on tripartite cooperation projects, all relevant documents about these 68 projects were collected and organised chronologically to offer a comprehensive understanding of their development.

The in-depth case study research on projects, specifically the Hinkley Point C Nuclear Power Station and three Nigerian Port projects, gathered information from the government information, companies' reports, and news reports[3] before conducting interviews. Companies' resources were directly collected from their respective Web sites. Additionally, news reports were sourced from authoritative media outlets.[4]

The stability and reliability of findings in tripartite cooperation projects were enhanced through the combination of various documents. To enhance data quality, I gathered as much relevant data as possible, and I collected over 1600 documents by October 2023. Then I established a case database for these 68 tripartite cooperation projects. Through a meticulous review and coding of these documents, this research thoroughly explored the determinants and actions of participants to engage in tripartite cooperation, as well as their influence on the generation of costs and benefits at the project level.

[3] Électricité de France (EDF energy), China General Nuclear Power Group (CGN), Tincan Island Container Terminal Ltd., Bolloré Transport & Logistics Group, China Merchant Group, PowerChina International Group Ltd., China Harbour Engineering Company, CMA CGM, etc.

[4] *The Guardian*, *The Telegraph*, *The Independent*, *Financial Times*, Xinhua News, *China Daily*, *People's Daily*, *Le Monde*, France 24, *Le Figaro*, *Daily Post Nigeria*, etc.

4.2.2 *Collecting First-Hand Material: Semi-Structured Interviews*

In this research, purposive sampling was utilised to select interviewees who could provide valuable insights into tripartite cooperation projects. Interviewees were carefully chosen based on their expertise and ability to share relevant information. Snowball sampling was employed when respondents were willing to introduce other potential interviewees, thereby broadening the scope of insights gathered in the research.

According to Bryson (2004), stakeholders are individuals or institutions with relevant interests in a project. Collecting information from diverse stakeholder groups is essential to gather multiple perspectives on the project, as one respondent may only represent their own group. For instance, government officers or project managers may only emphasise positive outcomes and direct the research findings towards successful businesses, potentially distorting the representativeness of the sample. To mitigate bias, I interviewed individuals from various stakeholder groups, including government, enterprises, and other assisting organisations involved in tripartite cooperation projects. Through interviewing various stakeholder groups, I obtained comprehensive perspectives about tripartite cooperation from interviewees. Interview respondents were selected based on one of the following criteria:

1. The interviewees were knowledgeable about government policies related to international cooperation, enabling them to provide insights from a national perspective.
2. The interviewees included project managers or ordinary staff involved in relevant tripartite cooperation projects, allowing them to address research questions at the project level.
3. Some participants, such as academics and experts, while not directly involved, possessed knowledge about tripartite projects and could offer professional or academic insights into tripartite cooperation.

I attempted to establish connections with potential interviewees from each stakeholder group. Initially, I utilised LinkedIn, a social networking Web site, and open connection channels through online research. I applied search filters to identify key individuals with direct association with the projects and relevant experience. Subsequently, I reached out to them via email. Although I faced challenges accessing interviewees in certain stakeholder groups, I extended my outreach to several interviewees beyond the in-depth cases to capture broader perspectives from other tripartite cooperation projects. In total, I engaged with 25 interviewees, and the list is provided in Appendix D.

I obtained ethics clearance from the ethics office of King's College London (Reference number, LRS/DP-20/21-25361). According to the general rules for ethical research, it is crucial for the interviewer to be honest with the participants about the research goals, purpose, structure, and procedures to build trust (Punch, 2014). The interviewees were informed that there were no foreseeable risks in this study and that they would not place themselves at risk of reprisal by participating.

This research used semi-structured interviews as a primary method to collect first-hand information on tripartite cooperation projects. Semi-structured interviews provide a middle ground between structured and unstructured interviews. Structured interviews may limit respondents' ability to express their opinions, while unstructured interviews can lead to time being spent on irrelevant issues (Hammersley, 2013). Semi-structured interviews allow respondents to share their experiences and guide the research agenda within the scope of the research framework.

Due to COVID-19 travel restrictions, most interviews were conducted online, with only a few conducted face to face in the UK. Additionally, some interviewees preferred online communication tools to avoid in-person meetings with strangers during the pandemic. Conducting interviews online proved to be an effective and cost-efficient approach, particularly since this project involved interviewing stakeholders across multiple countries. The interviews, conducted via online video calls, typically lasted approximately 30–60 min each with individuals based in China, France, Nigeria, the UK, and other locations.

In conducting interviews for the research, I employed general question lists (see Appendix C) as guiding frameworks. Although practical interviews often followed diverse question sequences, I adhered to four overarching categories that covered a comprehensive spectrum of aspects related to tripartite cooperation.

Firstly, the exploration of the overall perspective of tripartite cooperation involved inviting respondents to share their personal opinions on the matter, drawing upon their relevant knowledge and experience. Interviewees often discussed this aspect through comparisons with other cooperative approaches, such as bilateral or multilateral cooperation. This category established a holistic view of tripartite cooperation.

The second category delved into the practices of tripartite cooperation within the respondents' organisations. For government authorities, questions centred around actions related to tripartite cooperation policies, examining how government actions either promoted or hindered project progress. On the interviewees in the enterprise, detailed inquiries were made regarding financing, operation, and construction actions, particularly those relevant to cost or value generation. In addition, the functions of additional actors in these projects were a crucial point, addressing questions about how China and its partner countries influence project finance dynamics, and the introduction of complexities due to the engagement of an additional partner.

The third question category was about the motivations of their organisations. The hypothesis underlying this research is that tripartite cooperation generates higher transaction costs than bilateral cooperation. I inquired about the motivations of respondents—why their organisations continued to use the tripartite cooperation model, even in the face of bearing additional transaction costs.

Finally, the fourth category focused on the outcomes of tripartite cooperation projects. This section sought opinions on the success or failure of such projects, including the criteria used for project evaluation. Furthermore, I inquired about whether interviewees think the tripartite projects aligned more closely with the Chinese approach or traditional donors' approach.

There were some strengths of the interview approach. The interviews were categorised by themes and patterns which could gain a deeper understanding of social contexts and participants' perceptions (Mason, 2002). The semi-structured questions were designed to systematically gather insights into various dimensions of tripartite cooperation from interviewees, covering general perspectives, practices, motivations, and outcomes. The diverse range of interviewees' opinions ensured a comprehensive understanding of the subject matter, contributing to a nuanced analysis of tripartite cooperation in both national and project contexts.

There were also some weaknesses associated with this approach. Firstly, interviews may be influenced by personal biases stemming from factors such as educational background, job position, and political opinions (Spencer et al., 2021). To address this, comprehensive triangulation was employed analysing all interviewees' responses and comparing them with each other and with second-hand sources.

Secondly, there may be issues with distrust and poor response quality from project stakeholders, as they may feel uncomfortable discussing personal feelings openly with a stranger. To mitigate this, it is crucial to establish rapport and gain the trust of interviewees (DeJonckheere & Vaughn, 2019). Before the interviews, the aims and background of the research were briefly introduced, and respondents were informed of their right to anonymity. Informal topics were discussed to break the ice and build trust at the beginning of the interview (Mikecz, 2012).

Data collection, storage, and analysis were maintained confidential and integral, following the UK General Data Protection Regulation (UK GDPR) and the Data Protection Act 2018 in terms of dealing with research subjects and storing data. If the interviewees wanted to remain anonymous, their personal information was kept confidential. After the interview, they were offered to withdraw within three months, and any information they had provided would then not be retained.

There were some limitations about the collected first-hand data. The primary challenge was related to data collection from interviewees and the possibility to undertake on-site fieldwork during the COVID-19 pandemic. The COVID-19 pandemic impeded face-to-face interviews and on-site fieldwork, making it necessary to develop an alternative research design based on online interviews. However, some interviewees, particularly government officials, exhibited reluctance to participate in online interviews. Some potential interviewees rejected my interview request due to a lack of trust in online communications and concerns about information leakage. Online interviews also hindered the establishment of rapport and diminished the nuances, such as body language and potential meanings, that could be observed in face-to-face interviews, although this was not seen to be a major hindrance.

Overall, semi-structured interviews could collect first-hand information, but it is difficult to replicate or check the findings of interview research (Irvine et al., 2013). Based on these problems, the study used second-hand sources to cross-check the results of interviews. Although interviewees have their own opinions, the media reports and statistics could show more wide-ranging evidence.

4.3 Data Analysis

Following data collection, an analysis was conducted to explore the roles of participants, the determinants for forming tripartite arrangements, the mechanisms generating transaction costs, and the processes generating benefits within tripartite cooperation projects.

4.3.1 *Stakeholder Analysis*

Stakeholders, as defined by Bourne (2019), encompass individuals or entities whose efforts and support are vital to the success of a project and whose withdrawal could lead to project failure. In corporate contexts, stakeholders are described as members of "groups without whose support the organisation would cease to exist" (Friedman & Miles, 2006, p. 5). Infrastructure projects and their financing processes typically involve numerous stakeholders, including sponsors, lenders, government agencies, special purpose vehicles, suppliers, EPC contractors, sub-contractors, operators, insurers, off-taker purchasers, and consultants.

In tripartite cooperation projects, key stakeholders are identified and classified according to Freeman's (1984) stakeholder framework. Freeman's framework comprises three analytical levels of stakeholder analysis: rational, process, and transactional. At the rational level, the objective was to identify stakeholders and their interests (see Fig. 4.1a). At the process and transactional levels, Freeman utilised a two-dimensional approach based on stakeholders' level of interest and influence, as depicted in the classical stakeholder grid (see Fig. 4.1b). The following section explains the two figures.

At the rational level, stakeholders were categorised based on their power and stake. For example, owners possess equity stakes and voting power, influencing the company through formal decision-making processes. Governments wield political power and influence, regulating and shaping the operating environment for businesses. Freeman proposes that stakeholder categories do not accurately reflect the complexities of modern stakeholder dynamics. Instead, the boundaries between different types

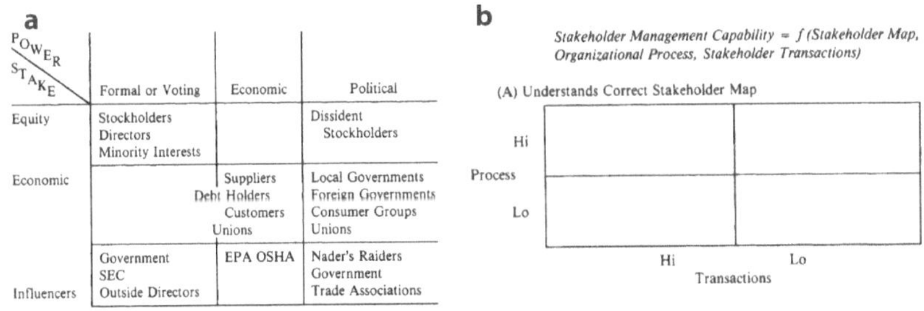

Fig. 4.1 (**a**) Freeman's 'real world' stakeholder grid (Freeman, 1984). (**b**) Freeman's stakeholder framework (Freeman, 1984)

of power—equity, economic, and political—are blurred. Stakeholders may fall into multiple categories, and their influence is more interconnected and complex. Elias (2017) similarly notes that not all stakeholders carry the same level of importance. Clarkson (1995) distinguishes between primary stakeholders, who are essential for a company's survival, and secondary stakeholders, who influence or are influenced by the company but are not vital to its existence. Clarkson argues that effectively managing primary stakeholders is crucial for success. These characteristics were particularly applicable to tripartite cooperation projects, where stakeholder roles were often mixed. For instance, government agencies may wield economic power (e.g., through tax policy and financing supports). Non-traditional directors, such as academics or minority group representatives, may lack equity stakes but still hold formal power to influence tripartite cooperation projects. In addition, this research focused on identifying the key stakeholders in these tripartite cooperation projects from multiple participants in infrastructure projects.

The process level was represented on the vertical axis of Fig. 4.1b. It measures stakeholder management capacity. In large, complex infrastructure projects, project managers typically establish standard operating procedures to efficiently manage these intricate tasks and align with the other participants. To manage stakeholders effectively, an organisation must clearly understand who its stakeholders are and ensure that stakeholders understand the organisation's daily operations (Freeman, 1984). Misalignment in any of these areas could lead to conflict, inefficiency, and failure in stakeholder relationships. The empirical chapters would specifically identify both internal and external trends and events that could impact the organisation. By measuring stakeholder management capacity at the process level, this investigation aimed to understand how the actions of governments and firms influence transaction costs and additional benefits in tripartite cooperation projects. Furthermore, it examined whether resources were effectively allocated to manage these relationships (Freeman et al., 2004).

The transaction level was depicted on the horizontal axis of Fig. 4.1b. It represents the measurement of stakeholder management capacity, a key factor in analysing the transaction costs associated with tripartite cooperation projects. In large-scale projects, numerous routine transactions occur among participants, including procuring supplies from vendors, paying dividends to shareholders, and negotiating various contracts. While these interactions typically follow predictable patterns, transactional capacity could diminish when participants face sudden changes or disruptions. Successful transactions are grounded in recognising the legitimacy of stakeholders' concerns (Mitchell et al., 1997; Friedman & Miles, 2006), which indicates that the organisation is committed to achieving mutually beneficial outcomes. Therefore, it is crucial to identify the determinants that influence participants and to assess how each transaction could generate benefits for both individual stakeholders and the organisation in empirical chapters.

In summary, Freeman's stakeholder analytical approach provided a framework for examining the roles of multiple players and their relationships in tripartite cooperation projects. By employing the stakeholder identification grid (Fig. 4.1a), the study elucidated how participants fulfil their duties within these projects. Utilising the transaction-process grid (Fig. 4.1b) allowed for comparisons of stakeholder management effectiveness across different projects, revealing the change of transaction costs and additional benefits in tripartite cooperation.

4.3.2 *Process Tracing*[5]

Process tracing is a qualitative method aimed at establishing causal-effect relationships, demonstrating how and why a change occurred and its subsequent effects (Punton & Welle, 2015; Beach & Pedersen, 2019). The process-tracing method can utilise a wide range of sources. It involves using multiple sources of evidence, such as stakeholders, experts, and news reporters, to test hypotheses and consider alternative explanations (Bennett & Checkel, 2015). This approach also facilitated data triangulation to compare and complement the first-hand and second-hand data. The cases in this research were traced from their initial proposal stages, highlighting key milestones, and the tracing of cases ceased by the end of 2023.

Beach and Pedersen (2016) distinguish between different types of process tracing (theory testing, theory building, and explaining outcome) and discuss how to select cases, gather evidence, and evaluate causal claims. This research employed the explaining-outcome method, which considered political background and unique social processes to analyse changes in transaction costs and additional benefits in practical tripartite

[5] This study only uses traditional process tracing and doesn't use formal Bayesian process tracing, because in this study, we don't assign 'prior' probabilities to different possible explanations to show how the level of confidence in their correctness (Fairfield & Charman, 2015).

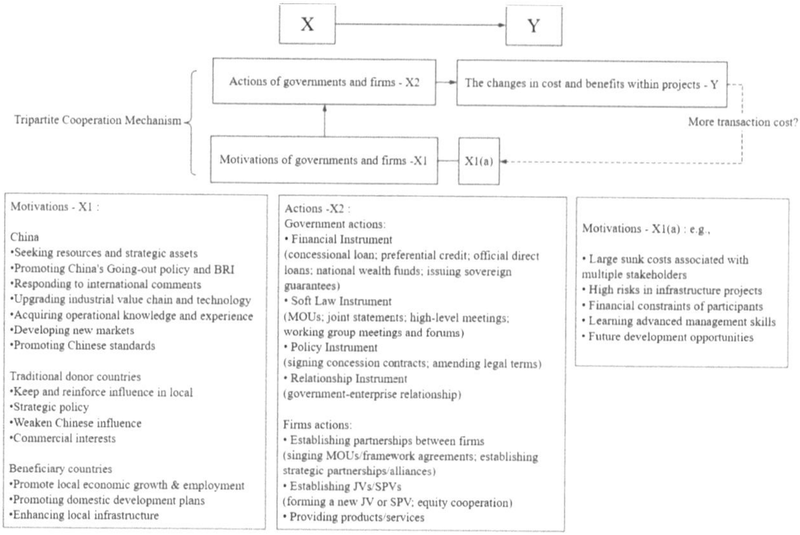

Fig. 4.2 Process tracing framework of tripartite cooperation (source: Author)

cooperation cases. Ruben and Little (1993) emphasise that process tracing is crucial for understanding how individual actions and events aggregate to produce social outcomes, linking micro-level processes to macro-level results. By tracing the processes in the case studies, this research also connected the actions of firms and states, identifying how individual participants influence the outcomes of tripartite cooperation projects. Schmitter (2008) explores the strengths and limitations of process tracing in complex social and political contexts by analysing the sequences of events or decisions within particular cases.

Given these insights, this research utilised the process tracing method to follow the development of each project in the case studies, examining the determinants influencing the actions of participant governments and firms. However, one limitation of this method was that it may not easily lend itself to generalisation across cases. It required a significant amount of data and could be time-consuming due to the detailed nature of the process tracing involved (Beach & Pedersen, 2019).

The analytical process outlined in this study offered a framework for addressing the research questions depicted in Fig. 4.2. Given the focus on tripartite cooperation, process tracing emerged as an appropriate method for exploring the following inquiries: how do participants influence the dynamics of project finance activities? More specifically, how do participants generate additional benefits? And how does the involvement of an additional partner in tripartite cooperation projects impact costs and value? In addressing these key questions about the process of tripartite cooperation projects, I designated the various dimensions of the tripartite cooperation mechanism as independent variables (X), with the outcomes of cost and additional benefits in tripartite cooperation projects as dependent variables (Y).

Mahoney (2012) emphasises that developing strong, theory-driven hypotheses should precede the process tracing. Some determinants were identified through a review of the literature. In the empirical chapters, I examined which determinants and motivations are most relevant to tripartite cooperation and identified additional determinants specific to these arrangements. X1 represented the determinants influencing governments and firms, while X2 represented their respective actions. Together, X1 and X2 influenced Y—the changes in costs and benefits observed in tripartite cooperation projects. Some points in the blue boxes had supporting evidence, while others did not, and these determinants would be examined through empirical research and summarised in the conclusion chapter.

Some elements in X1 were akin to determinants found in traditional FDI or bilateral cooperation, such as seeking markets, resources, efficiencies, and strategic assets, which align with motivations in FDI theories. Yet, to what extent these apply to tripartite cooperations needed further empirical examination, conducted in empirical chapters. Moreover, other elements in X1 differed from those in traditional bilateral cooperation. Examples included objectives such as Western firms aiming to weaken Chinese influence or Chinese firms aiming to acquire operational knowledge and experience from advanced economies, which appeared more specific to tripartite projects. Detailed discussions on these elements can be found in the finding sections of individual chapters and the conclusion chapter.

Fairfield and Charman (2017) emphasise the importance of considering alternative explanations and propose methods for evaluating the likelihood of different causal pathways. In this context, it is necessary to explore further the distinct determinants that drive participants to engage in tripartite cooperation. X1 and X2 had already explored the determinants that motivate participants to join tripartite cooperation projects. However, when outcome Y revealed higher transaction costs, it became crucial to investigate why participants choose to remain involved in the project rather than withdraw. These additional determinants, labelled as X1(a), included factors such as large sunk costs binding multiple stakeholders, high risks, significant financial demands for constructing infrastructure projects, and participants' aims for future opportunities in expanding markets. These insights were inductively generated from the case studies, and the evidence presented in Chap. 7 may either support or challenge the existing theoretical frameworks.

4.4 Conclusion

Based on collected first-hand and second-hand data, this research employed qualitative analysis, with limited quantitative analysis, to investigate Chinese tripartite cooperation in infrastructure projects. A comprehensive database, including both numerical and textual data from various sources, was created to explore the research questions. Employing a stakeholder analysis framework enabled the examination of roles among multiple players and their relationships in tripartite cooperation projects. The transaction-process grid was utilised to compare effectiveness across different projects and to reveal stakeholder management capacity. Additionally, the process tracing method was applied to follow in-depth case studies from their initial proposal stages, highlighting key project milestones. This analytical process offered a framework for exploring the generation of transaction costs and additional benefits in tripartite cooperation projects. It also addressed the key research question of why participants choose a tripartite cooperation model over other types of cooperation, despite the potential for additional transaction costs.

References

Ayres, L., Kavanaugh, K., & Knafl, K. A. (2003). Within-Case and Across-Case Approaches to Qualitative Data Analysis. *Qualitative Health Research, 13*(6), 871–883. https://doi.org/10.1177/1049732303013006008

Beach, D., & Pedersen, R. B. (2016). *Causal Case Study Methods: Foundations and Guidelines for Comparing, Matching and Tracing.* University Of Michigan Press.

Beach, D., & Pedersen, R. B. (2019). *Process-Tracing Methods: Foundations and Guidelines.* University Of Michigan Press.

Bennett, A., & Checkel, J. T. (2015). *Process Tracing: From Metaphor to Analytic Tool.* Cambridge University Press.

Bourne, L. (2019). *Stakeholder Relationship Management: A Maturity Model for Organisational Implementation.* London Routledge Ann Arbor, Michigan Proquest.

Bryson, J. M. (2004). What to do when Stakeholders Matter. *Public Management Review, 6*(1), 21–53. https://doi.org/10.1080/14719030410001675722

Clarkson, M. B. E. (1995). A Stakeholder Framework for Analyzing and Evaluating Corporate Social Performance. *The Academy of Management Review, 20*(1), 92–117. https://doi.org/10.2307/258888

CMPG. (2024). China Merchants Port Group Co., Ltd. Annual Report 2023. https://file.finance.sina.com.cn/211.154.219.97:9494/MRGG/CNSESZ_STOCK/2024/2024-4/2024-04-02/9936539.PDF

DeJonckheere, M., & Vaughn, L. M. (2019). Semistructured Interviewing in Primary Care Research: A Balance of Relationship and Rigour. *Family Medicine and Community Health, 7*(2), e000057. https://doi.org/10.1136/fmch-2018-000057

EDF. (2024, March 15). Presentation Powering China's Low-Carbon Energy Transition and High-Quality Development. *EDF in China.* https://china.edf.com/en/presentation

Elias, A. A. (2017). Systems Thinking and Modelling for Stakeholder Management. *IIM Kozhikode Society & Management Review, 6*(2), 123–131. https://doi.org/10.1177/2277975216681105

Fairfield, T., & Charman, A. (2015, June 5). Formal Bayesian Process Tracing: Guidelines, Opportunities, and Caveats. Www.lse.ac.uk. http://eprints.lse.ac.uk/62368/

Fairfield, T., & Charman, A. (2017). Explicit Bayesian Analysis for Process Tracing: Guidelines, Opportunities, and Caveats. *Political Analysis, 25*(3), 363–380. https://doi.org/10.1017/pan.2017.14

Freeman, R. E. (1984). *Strategic Management: A Stakeholder Approach.* Pitman.

Freeman, R. E., Wicks, A. C., & Parmar, B. (2004). Stakeholder Theory and "The Corporate Objective Revisited". *Organization Science, 15*(3), 364–369. https://doi.org/10.1287/orsc.1040.0066

Friedman, A. L., & Miles, S. (2006). *Stakeholders: Theory and Practice.* Oxford University Press.

Hammersley, M. (2013). *The Myth of Research-Based Policy and Practice.* SAGE.

Irvine, A., Drew, P., & Sainsbury, R. (2013). "Am I not Answering your Questions Properly?" Clarification, Adequacy and Responsiveness in Semi-Structured Telephone and Face-to-Face Interviews. *Qualitative Research, 13*(1), 87–106.

Joshi, Raghavi. (2018). Lekki Deep Sea Port, Lagos, Nigeria. *Ship Technology.* https://www.ship-technology.com/projects/lekki-deep-sea-port-lagosnigeria/.

Judd, C. M., Smith, E. R., & Kidder, L. H. (1991). *Research Methods in Social Relations*. Holt, Rinehart, and Winston.
King, G., Keohane, R. O., & Verba, S. (1994). *Designing Social Inquiry: Scientific Inference in Qualitative Research*. Princeton University Press.
LUA. (2018, November 30). Bollore Ports, PowerChina win Deep-sea Port Contract in Nigeria. *Logistics Update Africa*. https://www.logupdateafrica.com/bollore-ports-powerchina-win-deepsea-port-contract-in-nigeria-logistics-shipping
Mahoney, J. (2012). The Logic of Process Tracing Tests in the Social Sciences. *Sociological Methods & Research, 41*(4), 570–597. https://doi.org/10.1177/0049124112437709
Mason, J. (2002). *Qualitative researching*. Sage.
Mikecz, R. (2012). Interviewing Elites: Addressing Methodological Issues. *Qualitative Inquiry, 18*(6), 482–493. https://doi.org/10.1177/1077800412442818
Mitchell, R. K., Agle, B. R., & Wood, D. J. (1997). Toward a Theory of Stakeholder Identification and salience: Defining the Principle of who and what Really Counts. *The Academy of Management Review, 22*(4), 853–886. https://doi.org/10.2307/259247
Punch, K. F. (2014). *Introduction to Social Research: Quantitative and Qualitative Approaches* (3rd ed.). Sage.
Punton, M., & Welle, K. (2015). Straws-in-the-wind, Hoops and Smoking Guns: What can Process Tracing Offer to Impact Evaluation? Institute of Development Studies. https://www.ids.ac.uk/publications/straws-in-the-wind-hoops-and-smoking-guns-what-can-process-tracing-offer-to-impact-evaluation/
Ritchie, J., Lewis, J., McNaughton Nicholls, C., & Ormston, R. (2014). *Qualitative Research Practice: a Guide for Social Science Students and Researchers*. SAGE.
Ruben, D.-H., & Little, D. (1993). Varieties of Social Explanation: An Introduction to the Philosophy of Social Science. *The Philosophical Review, 102*(1), 120. https://doi.org/10.2307/2185667
Schmitter, P. C. (2008). The Design of Social and Political Research. In *Approaches and Methodologies in the Social Sciences* (pp. 263–295). Cambridge University Press. https://doi.org/10.1017/cbo9780511801938.015
Schreier, M. (2012). *Qualitative Content Analysis in Practice*. Sage.
Seawright, J., & Gerring, J. (2008). Options Case Selection Techniques in Case Study Research: A Menu of Qualitative and Quantitative. *Political Research Quarterly, 61*(294), 294–308.

Spencer, R., McCormack, M. J., Drew, A. L., Gowdy, G., & Keller, T. E. (2021). (Not) Minding the Gap: A Qualitative Interview Study of how Social Class Bias can Influence Youth Mentoring Relationships. *Journal of Community Psychology.*, *50*(3), 1579–1596. https://doi.org/10.1002/jcop.22737

White, S. (2024, February 16). EDF Confident of UK Compromise as it Reveals €12.9bn Hinkley Point Hit. *Financial Times*. https://www.ft.com/content/ca24da3e-6db8-40ca-b99a-a1e7f190cc1a

Yin, R. K. (2018). *Case Study Research and Applications: Design and Methods* (6th ed.). Sage Publications.

CHAPTER 5

Tripartite Panorama: Navigating Chinese Global Tripartite Cooperation Projects

This chapter provides an overview of Chinese tripartite cooperation projects, focusing on their current working mechanisms and development trends. The first section demonstrates the cooperation mechanism, the original classification system, and a new process system for Chinese tripartite cooperation projects. The second section illustrates the development of China-led tripartite cooperation projects, including their development across different time periods, industrial sectors, and geographical distribution. The third section examines the roles played by China, partner countries,[1] and beneficiary countries in tripartite cooperation projects and analyses their actions to participate in these projects. The findings of the second and third sections are based on the established database of 68

[1] In the three empirical chapters (Chaps. 5, 6, and 7), I use the term '(China's) partner countries' to refer to the other provider nations involved in China-led tripartite cooperation projects. Specifically, these 'partner countries' include 14 nations that have signed Memoranda of Understanding with the Chinese government: France, the Republic of Korea, Canada, Portugal, Australia, Japan, Italy, Belgium, the Netherlands, Spain, Austria, Singapore, Switzerland, and the UK.

When discussing 'partner firms/companies/enterprises,' I am specifically referring to business entities headquartered in France, Italy, Spain, Portugal, Germany, the UK, the USA, Japan, South Korea, and Singapore. This distinction is intended to provide clarity regarding the precise countries and entities involved in the context of this research.

Sometimes, I also use 'Western countries/firms' when these partner countries exert colonial influence and firms monopolise the infrastructure sector of beneficiary countries.

C. Su, *From Two to Three*, Governing China in the 21st Century,
https://doi.org/10.1007/978-981-95-8708-7_5

tripartite cooperation projects (see Appendix B). I used descriptive statistics to identify trends and patterns in global tripartite cooperation involving China.

5.1 Chinese Tripartite Cooperation: Mechanism, Classification, and Relevant Activities

5.1.1 Chinese Tripartite Cooperation Mechanism

In 2019, the Chinese National Development and Reform Commission (NDRC) published the *Third-party Market Cooperation Guidelines and Cases*, which aimed to define tripartite cooperation, provide vision and principles of tripartite, clarify Chinese tripartite cooperation mechanisms, and classify cooperation project cases. This document provides a general overview of China-led tripartite cooperation.

By the end of 2022, the Chinese government had signed documents of tripartite cooperation with 14 advanced economies. Table 5.1 lists signed cooperative agreements and relevant information concerning China-led tripartite cooperation. This includes details on the participating countries, the documents signed, the dates and occasions of signing, the involved departments, and the key Chinese officials who signed these documents. These documents are typically in the form of MOUs and are usually signed during high-level leadership meetings between China and partner countries. In some cases, joint statements on tripartite cooperation are also included.

An MOU is regarded as the starting point for international negotiations or high-risk business dealings between two or more parties. When participants have distinct formal governance institutions or competing interests, an MOU can dissolve misunderstandings. By signing an MOU, participants show their willingness to move towards a binding contract and their desire to achieve mutually beneficial goals, ultimately reaching a consensus and aligning their targets (Trivedi, 1990; Alam et al., 2022). Consequently, the signing of the MOU by the Chinese and partner countries' governments establishes a framework for the governance of tripartite arrangements, thereby accelerating the cooperation process. As mentioned in Chap. 2, Sect. 2.3, the signing of several documents on tripartite cooperation between the Chinese and French governments in 2015 serves as an example. They established the Sino-French Fund for Third Country

Table 5.1 Signed documents and relevant information of tripartite cooperation (source: NDRC and updated by author)

Countries	*Signed documents*	*Signing time*	*Occasion*	*Departments of partner countries*	*China's departments*	*Key people*
France	Joint statement on China–France third-party market cooperation	06/2015	State visit by China's Prime Minister Li Keqiang	/	/	Li Keqiang
South Korea	MOU on third-party market cooperation	11/2015	State visit by China's Prime Minister Li Keqiang	South Korea's Ministry of Strategy and Finance and Ministry of Trade, Industry, and Energy on Cooperation	NDRCC; Ministry of Commerce	Li Keqiang
Canada	Joint statement on third-party market cooperation	09/2016	Canada-China Economic and Trade Cooperation ForumState visit by China's Prime Minister Li Keqiang	/	/	Li Keqiang
Portugal	MOU on strengthening third-party market cooperation	10/2016	State visit by Prime Minister of Portugal António Luís Santos da Costa	Ministry of Foreign Affairs of Portugal	Ministry of Commerce	/
Australia	MOU on third-party market cooperation	09/2017	China-Australia Strategic Economic Dialogue	Department of Trade, Tourism and Investment of Australia	NDRCC	He Lifeng

(*continued*)

Table 5.1 (continued)

Countries	*Signed documents*	*Signing time*	*Occasion*	*Departments of partner countries*	*China's departments*	*Key people*
Japan	MOU on third-party market cooperation between Chinese and Japanese businesses	05/2018	The China-Japan-South Korea trilateral summit	Ministry of Foreign Affairs of Japan and Ministry of Economy, Trade, and Industry of Japan	NDRCC; Ministry of Commerce	Li Keqiang; Zhong Shan
Italy	MOU on third-party market cooperation	09/2018	State visit by Italy's Deputy Prime Minister Luigi Di Maio	Italian Ministry of Economic Development	NDRCC	He Lifeng
Belgium	MOU on developing partnerships and cooperation in third-party markets	10/2018	State visit by China's Prime Minister Li Keqiang	Belgian Federal Public Service Foreign Affairs, Foreign Trade and Development Cooperation	Ministry of Commerce	Li Keqiang; Zhong Shan
Netherlands	MOU on strengthening third-party market cooperation	10/2018	State visit by China's Prime Minister Li Keqiang	Ministry of Foreign Affairs of the Netherlands	Ministry of Commerce	Li Keqiang; Zhong Shan
Spain	MOU on strengthening third-party market cooperation	11/2018	State visit by China's President Xi Jinping	/	/	Xi Jinping
Austria	MOU on third-party market cooperation	04/2019	The Second Belt and Road Forum for International CooperationState visit by Chancellor of Austria Sebastian Kurz	Austrian Federal Ministry for Digital and Economic Affairs	NDRCC	Li Keqiang

Singapore	MOU on the implementation of framework for strengthening China–Singapore third-party market cooperation	04/2019	The Second Belt and Road Forum for International CooperationState visit by Singapore's Prime Minister Lee Hsien Loong	Ministry of Trade & Industry of Singapore	NDRCC	Li Keqiang
Switzerland	MOU on third-party market cooperation	04/2019	The Second Belt and Road Forum for International Cooperation	Swiss Federal Department of Finance and Federal Department of Economic Affairs, Education, and Research	NDRCC	Xi Jinping; He Lifeng
UK	MCU on third-party market cooperation	06/2019	Tenth Economic and Financial Dialogue held between the UK and China State visit by Chinese Vice Premier Hu Chunhua	Minister for Investment at the Department for International Trade of the UK	NDRCC	Hu Chunhua; Ning Jizhe

Cooperation and signed over ten cooperation projects the following year (Zhang, 2020). By institutionalising the procedures of tripartite cooperation through MOUs, transaction costs of subsequent cooperation processes can be reduced. This is achieved by reducing the need to re-negotiate clauses on which consensus has already been reached.

China and partner countries often use the MOU as the primary cooperative format to initiate tripartite cooperation at both the firm and project levels. Several MOU documents on tripartite cooperation were signed by government agencies responsible for industrial policy-making. For example, China and Belgium formalised their MOU through the business departments of both nations—the Ministry of Commerce of China and Belgium's Federal Public Service Foreign Affairs, Foreign Trade, and Development Cooperation. A similar approach was taken by China and Japan, with MOU documents signed between the NDRCC, the Ministry of Commerce of China, and the Ministries of Foreign Affairs and Economy, Trade, and Industry in Japan.

As MOU documents lack legal binding, they can be efficiently drafted within a short time. Particularly during high-level leadership meetings, they often serve as symbolic outcomes. Among the 14 signed MOU documents, the majority were formalised during state visits led by top-level leadership. Some MOU documents were signed within the context of economic and/or trade cooperation forums. During the Second Belt and Road Forum for International Cooperation in April 2019, many high-level officers from different countries participated in this forum. China strategically utilised this forum to sign tripartite cooperation MOUs with participating nations, such as Austria, Singapore, and Switzerland. However, the lack of enforceability in these agreements implies that participants can alter their intentions and withdraw from cooperation, potentially resulting in wasted resources and increased transaction costs from previous negotiations. For instance, countries like Belgium, Canada, and the Netherlands did not take any further action to promote tripartite cooperation after signing MOUs with China.

After signing the MoU, China and partner countries usually start to establish stable cooperative mechanisms to consistently advance tripartite cooperation and relevant projects. Typically, these 14 countries engage in regular working group meetings, forums, and/or roundtables to promote progress in tripartite cooperation. Such meetings are usually hosted by the business or industrial policy departments. During these meetings, participants go beyond governmental representatives, including those from industries and companies. This broader participation involves entities such as development agencies, public or business financial institutions, banks, insurance companies, and private businesses (Wan & Wang, 2021).

The objectives of these meetings include reviewing the outcomes of existing projects, identifying potential fields for cooperation (such as infrastructure, industrial parks, digital economy, and shipping logistics), discussing pilot projects, and exploring government financing support. According to the authors' collected resource (see Appendix F), some countries, particularly France and Italy, hold regular working group meetings on tripartite cooperation, typically every 6 months to a year. These regular communications facilitate the exchange of knowledge and experience, ultimately reducing the negotiation costs associated with transactions. Following these working group meetings, Chinese authorities such as the NDRC and the Ministry of Commerce often sign new tripartite cooperation project lists with their counterparts in France and Italy (NDRC, 2024; Shang, 2024).

The contents of these MoU documents are largely similar, emphasising mutually beneficial cooperation in trade and investment. They typically outline the overarching goals of collaboration between the involved parties, specify key sectors for cooperation, and establish working groups or platforms to oversee the MoU's implementation. Additionally, these documents clarify that they are not legally binding agreements but rather expressions of mutual understanding. They also include procedures for modification, renewal, and termination, ensuring flexibility while maintaining a structured framework for ongoing cooperation.

However, some nuances exist. MOU documents with European countries in tripartite cooperation, such as Switzerland and Italy, align more with OECD-DAC standards. For instance, in the MoU with Switzerland,[2]

[2] "The Participants recognize that the cooperation should be enterprise-led, market-based, in compliance with international practices and norms, as well as the laws and policies of the countries benefitting from such cooperation. This cooperation should be based on economic viability and long-term sustainable growth, social and environmental sustainability, mutual benefits, consensus, inclusiveness, open and non-discriminatory procurement processes and a level playing field, in line with national development priorities as devised by the countries concerned and with the common pursuit of the UN Sustainable Development Goals." In "Memorandum of Understanding on Developing Third-Party Market Cooperation between the Federal Department of Finance and the Federal Department of Economic Affairs, Education and Research of the Swiss Confederation and the National Development and Reform Commission of the People's Republic of China," April 29, 2019, https://www.newsd.admin.ch/newsd/message/attachments/56685.pdf.

China commits to principles like 'enterprise-led, market-based cooperation, compliant with international norms and national laws,' focusing on 'economic viability, sustainability, mutual benefit, and non-discriminatory procurement.' Similarly, the MoU with Italy[3] highlights commitment to 'free and open trade and investment,' respect for intellectual property rights, and supporting the development priorities of third countries.

In contrast, the MoU with South Korea[4] places a stronger emphasis on the BRI target in infrastructure connectivity. It outlines collaboration on

[3] "Unimpeded trade and investment. The Parties will work towards expanding two-way investment and trade flow, industrial cooperation as well as cooperation in third country markets, exploring ways to promote substantive mutually beneficial cooperation. The Parties reaffirm their shared commitment to free and open trade and investment, to counter excessive macroeconomic imbalances and to oppose unilateralism and protectionism. In the framework of the Belt and Road Initiative, they will promote transparent, non-discriminatory, free and open trade and industrial cooperation, an open procurement, level playing field and respect for intellectual property rights. They will explore closer and mutually beneficial collaboration and partnerships, which include advancing North-South, South-South and triangular cooperation." in "Memorandum of Understanding between the Government of the Italian Republic and the Government of the People's Republic of China on Cooperation within the Framework of the Silk Road Economic Belt and the 21st Century Maritime Silk Road Initiative," March 2019, https://www.governo.it/sites/governo.it/files/Memorandum_Italia-Cina_EN.pdf.

[4] "Combining each other's competitive advantages together, the two sides jointly seek to explore a third-party market based on the connection of the Belt and the Road and the Eurasia Initiative; seek ways to strengthen cooperation in the areas of a third-party market including infrastructure and urban construction, energy and petrochemical industry, finance and insurance, information technology and communications and environment industry through consortium bidding by Korean and Chinese companies, joint production and investment and others." In "Memorandum of Understanding on Cooperation Concerning the Eurasia Initiative and the Silk Road Economic Belt and the 21st Century Maritime Silk Road between Ministry of Strategy and Finance of Korea and National Development and Reform Commission of China," October 31, 2015, https://president.globalwindow.org/common.FileDownload.do;jsessionid=RxP_elcnraadtV8dudWkP0l6IOffiL8uXx52Q1oq.PD?file_id=FILE_000000000011725&doc_id=DOC_000000000008132.

mutually beneficial projects in highways, railways, civil aviation, ports, oil and gas pipelines, power grids, and telecommunication networks. Additionally, there is a focus on establishing cooperation projects like industrial parks, agriculture clusters, logistics complexes, and renewable energy complexes. The MOU documents with South Korea do not explicitly mention free trade aspects in the context of tripartite cooperation.

5.1.2 Official Classification of Project Cases

The NDRC has classified Chinese tripartite cooperation projects into five categories (See Table 5.2). The first category is *Type I: Cases of Cooperation in Products and Services.* Chinese firms and their partner companies cooperate in equipment procurement, certification and licensing, and law consulting to provide final products, services, and solutions to customers in beneficiary countries.

The second category is *Type II: Cases of Cooperation in Engineering.* Chinese firms and their partner companies cooperate through EPC contracting, sub-contracting, joint bidding, bidding, and other forms of engineering.

The third category is *Type III: Cases of Cooperation in Investment.* Chinese firms and their partner companies co-invest in beneficiary countries through M&A activities, establishment of joint ventures, and shareholding, with the aim of sharing risks and benefits.

The fourth category is *Type IV: Cases of Cooperation in Industry and Finance Combination.* Chinese financial institutions and their partners use

Table 5.2 Tripartite cooperation case type (source: NDRC, 2019)

Category	*Type name*	*Examples*
Type I	Cooperation in Products and Services	Equipment procurement, certification and licensing, law consulting
Type II	Cooperation in Engineering	EPC contracting, sub-contracting, joint bidding, bidding
Type III	Cooperation in Investment	M&A activities, establishment of joint ventures, shareholding
Type IV	Cooperation in Industry and Finance Combination	Syndicated loans, co-finance, on-lending, and equity investment
Type V	Strategic Cooperation among Businesses	Multiple fields, including R&D, manufacturing, engineering, logistics, funding, and human resources

various financing methods, such as syndicated loans, co-finance, on-lending, and equity investment, to absorb more capital and reduce financing risks.

The final category is *Type V: Cases of Strategic Cooperation among Businesses.* Chinese firms and their partner companies cooperate in multiple fields, including R&D, manufacturing, engineering, logistics, funding, and human resources, by signing strategic cooperation agreements and establishing alliances.

This classification method was proposed by the Chinese government, and many Chinese researchers have used it to analyse tripartite cooperation projects (e.g., Pang, 2021; Luo & Chen, 2021; Chen & Wu, 2020). Normally, it works well to classify tripartite cooperation projects in this way. However, this classification method has some problems. The most significant issue with this classification method is that it takes a Chinese-centred perspective, mixing the roles of China, China's partner countries, and beneficiary countries and overlooking the roles and contributions of beneficiary countries in tripartite cooperation. Secondly, when China and its partners engage in both engineering and financing activities, a project can be classified into more than one category since *Types II, III, IV*, and *V* have unclear boundaries and overlapping classification standards. The NDRCC classified these cases randomly into a single category in its Guideline booklet.

For example, *Types III* and *V* activities are intertwined in tripartite cooperation in some cases. In addition to signing a strategic cooperation agreement in *Type V*, some Chinese companies establish alliances with their partner companies by forming JVs or engaging in M&A activities in *Type III*. It is difficult to identify the source of synergy effects and additional benefits from investing activities or companies' strategic cooperation activities.

The China-France-Cameroon Kribi Deep Sea Port Project is an example that illustrates the shortcomings of this classification method. In this project, CHEC, Bolloré, and CMA CGM formed a joint venture (*Type III*) and acted as EPC contractors (*Type II*). The project also utilised a syndicated loan[5] involving the European Union, the World Bank, the

[5]A syndicated loan is a financial arrangement that involves multiple lenders collectively providing a borrower, and the administration is typically undertaken by an agent, often a bank, a large corporation, or a government. Syndicated loans are often used for large-scale projects or acquisitions (Lee et al., 2017).

Japan International Cooperation Agency, the Development Bank of Central African States, the French Development Agency, and China Exim Bank (*Type IV*). Furthermore, CHEC and CMA CGM established a partnership for container terminal operations (*Type V*). As a result, it is challenging to categorise the mega-infrastructure tripartite cooperation projects according to the classification method in the Chinese government Guideline Booklet. This classification method also does not facilitate to solve the research questions in this study.

In addition, the structure of a traditional project financing deal is illustrated in Fig. 5.1. Pinto (2017) identifies the key players in project financing:

1. Project sponsors, who typically hold a controlling equity stake in the project company, either individually or as a group
2. The host government and often SOEs, from whom the project company usually needs to obtain a concession
3. Constructing and engineering firms
4. Legal specialists
5. Accounting, financial, and risk assessment professionals
6. Lead arranging banks

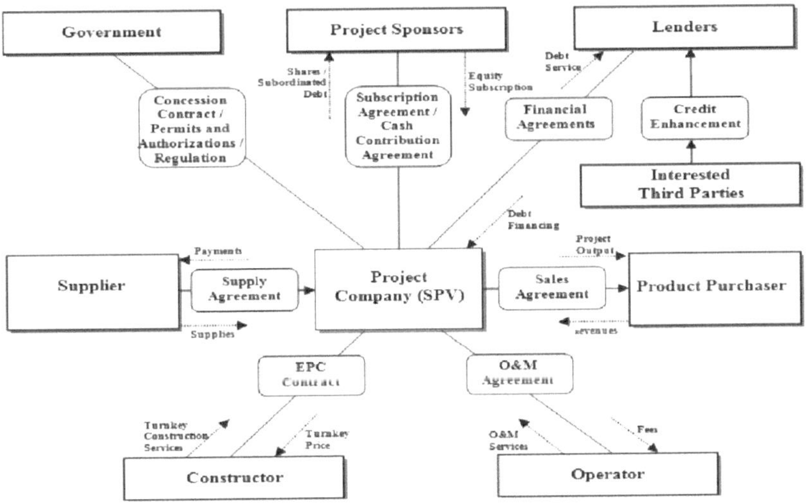

Fig. 5.1 Typical structure of a project finance deal (source: Pinto, 2017)

7. Participating banks
8. Suppliers and customers

Therefore, infrastructure projects involve multiple players in general project financing activities.

Based on this stakeholder analysis framework, I have identified and classified these eight types of players into five categories in tripartite cooperation projects.

1. Host Government (the beneficiary countries' governments): In most cases, the host government issues the concession to SPVs. The host government influences the project's processes through amending laws, administrative policies, or regulations.
2. Suppliers and Operators: They supply materials or services to SPVs, relevant to Type I projects that involve cooperation in products and services.
3. Constructing and Engineering Firms: These entities are involved in the physical execution of the project, relevant to Type II projects that involve cooperation in engineering.
4. Project Sponsors: They typically hold a controlling stake in the equity of a special company established for the project (or SPV). This role is particularly relevant to Type III projects that involve cooperation in investment.
5. Lenders: Financial institutions that play a crucial role in structuring and arranging the financing, relevant to Type IV projects that involve cooperation in finance.

5.1.3 The New Process System for Chinese Tripartite Cooperation Projects

The engagement of an additional partner introduces more complexities to projects. To elaborate on this argument, I have devised a new process system for Chinese tripartite cooperation projects in economic infrastructure and identified that the engagement of an additional partner causes more complexities (see Fig. 5.2).

5.1.3.1 The First Step: Beneficiary Countries' Contracts with SPVs

Because the infrastructure projects are public assets originally owned by the beneficiary countries, the host government is responsible for issuing

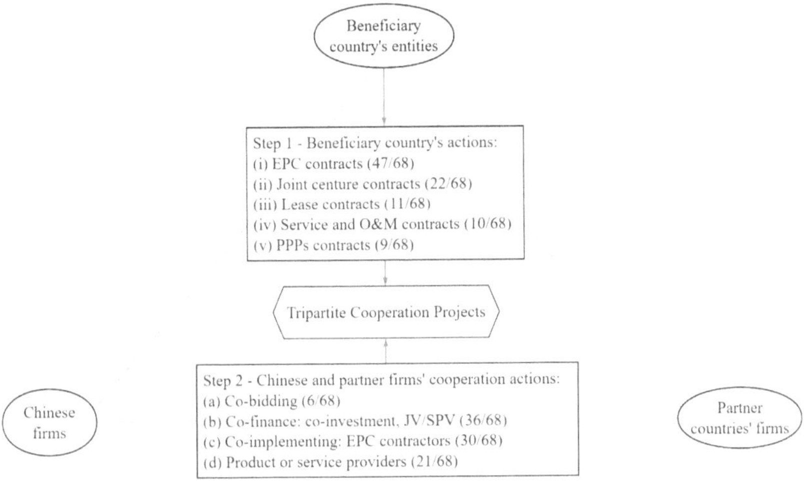

Fig. 5.2 Two-step process system for Chinese tripartite cooperation projects (source: Author)

concessions. The beneficiary countries' governments often use multiple types of contracts, which they sign with SPVs (formed by Chinese and its partner firms). Once these contracts are in place, Chinese and its partner firms can then participate in the projects. The five types of contracts are:

1. EPC Contracts (Engineering, Procurement, and Construction): Beneficiary countries outsource engineering, procurement, and construction activities to Chinese and/or partner contractors. According to the statistics from 68 projects, beneficiary governments used EPC Contracts or basic construction contracts in 47 tripartite cooperation projects. EPC projects involve infrastructure design, procurement, and construction, with Chinese and/or partner contractors assuming complete project management responsibilities and technical risks. This method is the most popular choice for beneficiary countries in tripartite cooperation. The straightfor ward cooperation relationship makes this contract type suitable for complex infrastructure projects, suggesting significant potential for beneficiary countries to participate in multiple project activities within tripartite cooperation frameworks.
2. JV (Joint Venture) Contracts: Beneficiary countries' agencies act as shareholders in tripartite cooperation projects within JV contracts.

The governments of beneficiary countries joined in SPVs with JV Contracts for 22 projects. This contracting approach is the second most frequently utilised method for beneficiary countries participating in tripartite cooperation. Beneficiary countries use JV contracts to align partners' interests in tripartite cooperation, thereby improving the efficiency of resource utilisation. These projects were combined with the sale agreement sometimes. For instance, in projects like the China-France-United Arab Emirates Al Dhafra PV2 solar power plant, the UAE entered into JV contracts along with 30-year power-purchase agreements to ensure that the energy would be sold locally in lower price (PT, 2020a).

3. Lease Contracts, Franchising Contracts, and Concession Agreements: These contracts entail the transfer of land-use rights from beneficiary countries to Chinese and/or partner contractors.
   The governments of the beneficiary countries signed Lease Contracts, Franchising Contracts, and Concession Agreements in 11 out of the 68 projects. When these governments aim to develop local infrastructure projects, such as port development or expansions, road upgrades, and resource exploitation, but face constraints in terms of capital, technology, resources, and skills (Gaitán, 2021), they enter into concessions with Chinese, partner countries' firms, and/or local authorities. For instance, in the China-France-Nigeria Port Projects, which will be further analysed in Chap. 7, the Nigerian government initially signed concession agreements with the Nigerian Ports Authority (NPA) or other local port authorities. Subsequently, these port authorities in the beneficiary countries collaborated with Chinese and French firms (The Guardian, 2019; LUA, 2018).
4. Service Contracts and O&M (Operation and Management) Contracts: In both contracts, beneficiary countries procure services from Chinese firms and/or partner firms.
   Beneficiary countries made Service and O&M (Operation and Management) Contracts when local governments lack expertise or resources for infrastructure operation and/or management. The O&M contracts were signed in 10 out of the 68 projects. These contracts aim to enhance project performance and cost-effectiveness in complex infrastructure projects, reflecting a proactive effort to address skill and resource gaps at the local level (Huang et al., 2019; Che-Ghani et al., 2023). In this strategic collaboration, beneficiary countries engage private companies from both China and/or part-

ner countries through Service and O&M Contracts. Half of the contracts in this category (five out of ten cases) involved a combination of O&M contracts and EPC contracts, indicating that beneficiary countries require ongoing operation and management services from their EPC partners. For example, in the China-Germany-Brazil Jupia and Ilha Solteira Hydroelectric Power Plant Project, the Brazilian government signed an EPC Contract along with a 30-year Operation Deal (EFE, 2015; CGGT, 2016).

5. PPPs Contracts (Public-Private-Partnerships, including BOT, BOOT, DBFO, DCMF, IPP, BOO, etc.[6]): In these arrangements, the public sectors of beneficiary countries also participate in financing, building, and operating projects. However, the projects are predominantly developed by Chinese and/or partner contractors.
   Within these 68 projects, 9 PPP contracts were signed. PPP contracts encompass diverse forms such as BOT, BOOT, DBFO, DCMF, and BOO. These contracts offer distinct advantages. For instance, BOT and BOO arrangements are employed when private sectors finance, design, construct, own, and operate infrastructure, with the local government retaining ownership after the contract period. This approach is particularly favoured in projects with substantial initial capital requirements, enabling the local government to avoid long-term debt (Kumaraswamy & Zhang, 2001; Delmon, 2010). The private sector assumes financial and technical risks, while the government contributes land, permits, and regulatory support. One possible reason for the less frequent employment of PPPs by local governments is the hesitancy of Chinese and partner firms to enter PPP contracts due to the potential risk of debt issues for the individual firm[7] (UNECE, 2012; Wang et al., 2017; Datti et al., 2022).

5.1.3.2 The Second Step: Cooperation Between Chinese and Its Partner Firms in SPVs

The second phase of this new system is the collaboration between the providers (i.e., Chinese firms and their partner firms). This cooperative step is not relevant to the beneficiary countries; it occurs solely between the Chinese firms and their partner firms. Once the governments of

[6] See details in Chap. 2, Sect. 2.1.4.

[7] Interview O-20221201 and O-20230117.

beneficiary countries decide the contracting types of projects, Chinese and partner firms use different cooperation methods to participate in these projects.

Some projects also fall under more than one cooperative type, as Chinese and partner firms cooperate with flexible methods. For instance, an EPC contractor may serve as a sponsor, builder, and operator simultaneously (Pinto, 2017). Within the tripartite cooperation mechanism, the project financing process adds more complexity because both Chinese firms and their partner firms might serve in the capacities of bidder, investor, operator, and service provider at the same time. In the cooperative methods used between Chinese and partner firms, four cooperative approaches are employed:

a. Co-bidder cooperation: The co-bidder cooperative method was employed in 6 out of 68 projects. This approach fosters synergy and coordination among Chinese and partner firms during the initial planning stages, allowing them to pool resources and enhance their ability to secure project tenders from beneficiary countries. Co-bidder activities often precede with other three cooperative activities in tripartite cooperation projects. Once co-bidders secure contracts from beneficiary countries, subsequent financing and resources are injected into the projects. For instance, in the China-Japan-UAE Sweihan Photovoltaic Independent Power Project, Chinese firm JinkoSolar and Japanese firm Marubeni collaborated to submit a bid at a tariff of $2.94 cents/kWh. This bid marked the lowest cost of electricity for solar power in 2016. Following the consortium's successful bid, Jinko Solar and Marubeni established a JV to carry out the construction activities (PT, 2020b).
b. Co-financing: The most widely adopted cooperative method is Co-finance, Co-investment, and Form JV/SPV, employed by Chinese and partner firms in 36 projects. It involves the creation of a new legal entity, usually a SPV, where each partner jointly owns, shares risks, and participates in profits associated with a specific project. This method is favoured for its ability to improve the efficiency of project capital financing and reduce risks associated with capital investment. The establishment of a firm aligns with the actions of beneficiary countries' agencies when entering into JV Contracts. Beneficiary countries may join an existing JV established between a partner and a Chinese firm.

c. Co-implementing: After the beneficiary countries sign EPC contracts with Chinese and/or partner firms, the Chinese and its partner firms cooperate through EPC contractor and subcontractor, designer-contractor, and developer-contractor. In some cases, Chinese and partner firms form co-bidder consortia or JVs/SPVs, leading beneficiary countries to sign EPC contracts with both Chinese and partner firms simultaneously. Alternatively, a beneficiary country might sign an EPC contract exclusively with a Chinese firm, which then acts as the top contractor, and this Chinese firm may subsequently subcontract to partner firms during project execution. Chinese and partner firms collaborated as EPC contractors or developer-contractors in 30 projects. This cooperative method is particularly advantageous when each contractor possesses comparative advantages, particularly when partner firms possess advanced technical expertise and specialised knowledge, while Chinese firms are more skilled in construction (Wan & Wang, 2020; Xiong, 2022) as well as managerial and operational expatriates (Rui et al., 2017).
d. Product or Service providers: Chinese and its partner firms act as product or service suppliers to meet the requirements of tripartite cooperation projects, with this method being employed in 21 projects. For example, consulting firms in partner countries provide more specialised services to Chinese firms. Chinese entities, in turn, gain the advantage of learning advanced technology, better standards, and local management skills from their counterparts. For instance, certain Chinese SOEs, such as the China Gezhouba Group Company and PowerChina, collaborate with the German company GAUFF Engineering in African countries. GAUFF provides supervision and engineering consulting services to these Chinese companies (PowerChina, 2013; GAUFF Engineering, n.d.; EXPO, 2016).

In summary, compared to the official classification method in the NDRC's Guideline Booklet, which adopts a Chinese-centred perspective and often blends the roles and responsibilities of all participants in tripartite cooperation projects, this two-step process system emphasises the complexities introduced by involving three players. Additionally, this system identifies the more frequently used cooperative approaches by each participant and outlines how they collaborate within tripartite cooperation projects. China and its partner countries alter the dynamics of traditional project finance activities, as the engagement of an additional partner in infrastructure projects initiates more transactional activities among the contractors. It is observed that beneficiary countries predominantly depend on EPC contracts in many tripartite cooperation projects, which restricts their engagement and influence in these projects. This approach is similar to traditional project financing projects. However, beneficiary countries have begun to increase their involvement by adopting JV contracts and PPP contracts in tripartite cooperation. These new strategies enable beneficiary countries to deepen their engagement in tripartite cooperation projects by binding more significant financial and stake interests with Chinese and partner companies. Chinese and partner companies frequently employ financial cooperation methods to strengthen their ties in tripartite cooperation. They also collaborate extensively in EPC activities and service provider activities to exchange resources, advanced technology, and management skills.

5.2 Trends and Development of China-Led Tripartite Cooperation Projects

This section displays the trends and development of tripartite cooperation based on the database of the 68 tripartite cooperation projects using the tripartite cooperation model between 2005 and 2022, including the overview of Chinese tripartite cooperation projects in terms of their development over time, industry, geographic location, and estimated investment scale.[8] Figure 5.3 shows the distribution of these projects.

5.2.1 *Development Timeline of Tripartite Cooperation Projects*

These datasets[9] illustrate the number of tripartite cooperation projects involving Chinese, partner countries, and beneficiary countries from 2005 to 2022 (Fig. 5.4a–c).

The development of tripartite cooperation can be divided into three stages. The first stage, from 2006 to 2013, is referred to as the infancy stage, with an average of 1.71 projects per year carried out with a total investment scale of $15.26 billion. Although the number of projects was

[8] It should be noted that the investment scale represents the estimated total investment in a project by 2022, encompassing funds from China, partner countries, and other international agencies.

[9] Based on the database (see Appendix B).

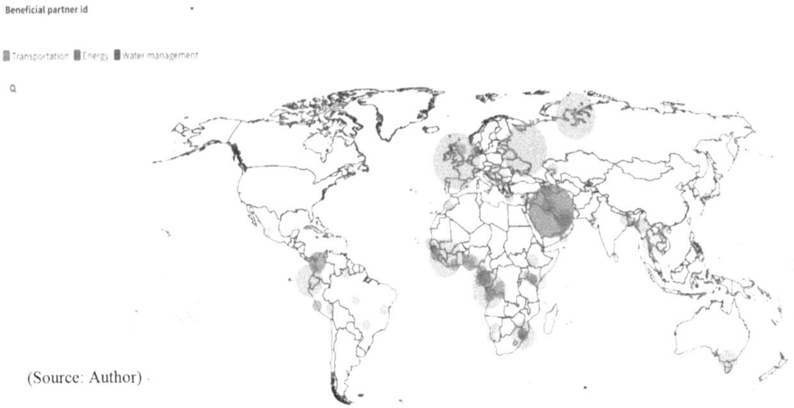

Fig. 5.3 The distribution of 68 Chinese tripartite cooperation projects. (Source: Author)

low, it indicates that tripartite cooperation had been in practice. As the number of projects increases, the average investment scale also rises (Fig. 5.4c). Participants gain more confidence as they undertake more projects, leading to increased investment each year in tripartite cooperation projects. This confidence notably increased, particularly after the proposal of the BRI policy in 2013.

From 2014 to 2019, the second stage can be classified as the development stage, as the number of tripartite cooperation projects showed a significant increase, averaging 8.33 projects per year with a total estimated investment scale of USD 196,861 million. The increasing trend is attributed to the Chinese government's promotion of tripartite cooperation, high-level leadership meetings, and agreements made between countries. The years 2015 and 2019 were the most active years, with 12 and 10 projects, respectively. As a result, more beneficiary countries have attempted to use the tripartite cooperation model in their infrastructure projects.

The third stage, from 2020 to 2022, is recognised as the COVID-19-influenced stage, with an average of 3.67 projects per year and a total estimated investment scale of USD 16.3 billion. Due to the COVID-19 pandemic, many international cooperation activities were suspended. The slow progress in the number of projects during this period suggests that the trend of tripartite cooperation has faltered. This slowdown is also

a

b

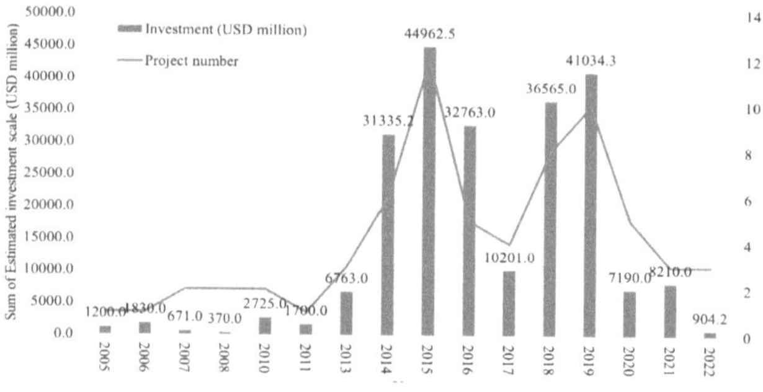

Year	Investment (USD million)	Project Number
2005	1200	1
2006	1830	1
2007	670.97	2
2008	370	2
2010	2725	2
2011	1700	1
2013	6763	3
2014	31335.2	6
2015	44962.5	12
2016	32763	5
2017	10201	4
2018	36565	8
2019	41034.3	10
2020	7190	5
2021	8210	3
2022	904.2	3
Total	228424.17	68

c

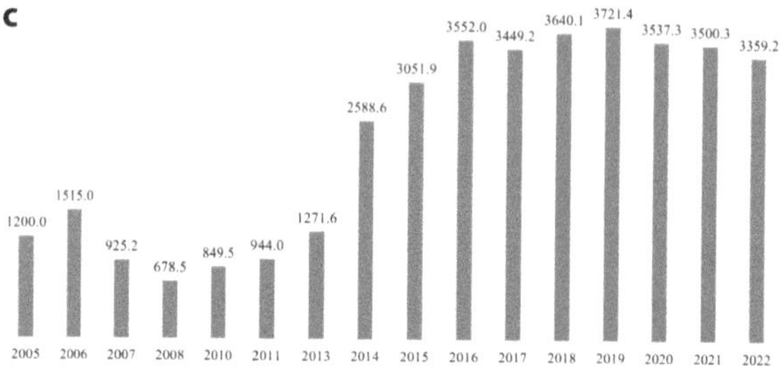

Year	Averaged Investment (USD million)	Project number
2005	1200.0	1
2006	1515.0	2
2007	925.2	4
2008	678.5	6
2010	849.5	8
2011	944.0	9
2013	1271.6	12
2014	2588.6	18
2015	3051.9	30
2016	3552.0	35
2017	3449.2	39
2018	3640.1	47
2019	3721.4	57
2020	3537.3	62
2021	3500.3	65
2022	3359.2	68

Fig. 5.4 (**a**) Number of Chinese tripartite cooperation projects (2005–2022) (Source: Author). (**b**) Project estimated investment scales (Flow) and project number (2005–2022). (Source: Author). (**c**) Average investment on each project per year (2005–2022). (Source: Author)

likely due to governments facing more immediate challenges and prioritising other urgent needs over funding and engaging in large-scale infrastructure projects, compounded by the geopolitical shifts during that period. In this stage, the average investment was USD 5.43 billion per year, significantly lower than the investment during the development stage but still higher than that of the infancy stage.

5.2.2 *Industrial Distribution*

Babic's (2021) research is aligned with the focus of my study, which examines economic infrastructure, particularly in the energy and transportation sectors. Babic identifies three global industries—the oil and energy industry, transportation and logistics, and high-tech manufacturing—as critical for understanding state-led foreign investment. These sectors are important for both China and partner countries. The energy sector is important in foreign state investment because national energy security relies on a dependable energy supply and ownership of energy production. Transportation and logistics are key areas of both cooperation and competition between China and partner countries within global value chains, where governments deploy state capital to acquire global assets and enhance their economic influence (Haberly & Wójcik, 2016). This approach is evident in countries such as Norway, France, and Singapore (Babic et al., 2019). As such, there is great potential for China to engage with partner countries in tripartite cooperation on energy and transportation infrastructure projects. Notably, the tripartite cooperation projects database in my study predominantly covers the energy, transportation, and water management sectors. While my research primarily concentrates on economic infrastructure, it is worth noting that tripartite cooperation also extends to other sectors, including social infrastructure such as schools, hospitals, and stadiums.

According to statistics from 68 projects (Fig. 5.5a, b), the energy sector is the largest category, comprising a total of 40 out of the 68 projects. It is further classified into two subcategories: clean energy (e.g., hydropower, wind, solar, nuclear, gas), with 28 projects, and traditional energy (e.g., oil and coal), with 12 projects. The transportation sector is the second-largest category, comprising 25 projects, which is further divided into two subcategories, ports and roads with 8 and 17 projects, respectively. The water management category (e.g., wastewater treatment, water supply expansion), being a specialised area, comprises only three projects, suggesting that it is not a major focus of the tripartite cooperation projects.

The investment dataset reveals that the clean energy sector has received the largest investment, with a total of USD 125.16 billion, indicating a focus on energy transition strategies in the Chinese overseas investment

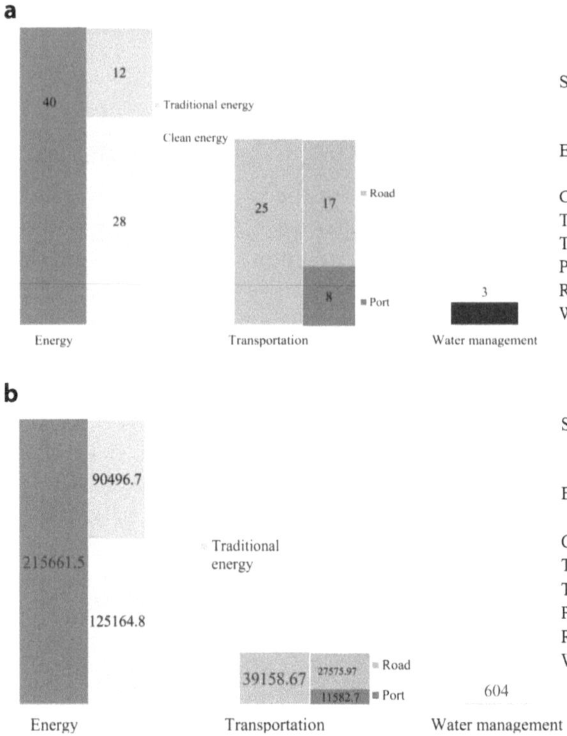

Sector	Project Number
Energy	40
Clean energy	28
Traditional energy	12
Transportation	25
Port	8
Road	17
Water management	3

Sector	Investment (USD million)
Energy	215661.5
Clean energy	125164.8
Traditional energy	90496.7
Transportation	39158.7
Port	11582.7
Road	27576.0
Water management	604.0

Fig. 5.5 (**a**) Sector distribution of 68 Chinese tripartite cooperation projects (Source: Author). (**b**) Estimated investment scale in each sector (USD million) (Source: Author)

plan. The traditional energy sector received a total of USD 90.5 billion. The transportation sector received a total investment of USD 39.16 billion, with the majority of the investment allocated to the road sector (USD 27.58 billion) and the port sector receiving USD 11.58 billion. The investment in the transportation sector aligns with the Chinese BRI's aim of enhancing connectivity and promoting trade (Pang, 2021). The water management sector received the lowest investment, with a total investment of USD 604 million.

5.2.3 Geographical Distribution

The presented datasets (Fig. 5.6a–c) provide information on project numbers and investment scales of tripartite cooperation projects conducted in different regions of beneficiary countries. The projects are categorised by region, including Africa, Asia, Central and South America, Europe, and Oceania.

The data reveals that Europe has the highest total investment of USD 84.68 billion across only eight projects, indicating higher investment in some individual cases. Africa follows with a total investment of USD 59.73 billion and the highest number of tripartite cooperation projects (32 projects), making it the most active region for such collaboration. The Asian region has a total investment of USD 53.04 billion, allocated to 15 projects. Central and South America also contribute significantly to tripartite cooperation, with a total investment of USD 26.05 billion spread over 12 projects. Oceania, however, has only one project with an investment of USD 4.93 billion. Overall, the data indicates that tripartite cooperation investments are predominantly concentrated in Europe, which attracts the highest total investment. In contrast, Africa, despite having the greatest number of tripartite cooperation projects, exhibits lower investment scales compared to Europe.

Figure 5.6c (Average investment per project by region) provides a more detailed analysis. This dataset includes 11 regions by average investment per project: Central Africa, East Africa, North Africa, South Africa, West Africa, Central Asia, Southeast Asia, West Asia, Central America, South America, Europe, and Oceania

According to the collected data by the author (see Appendix B), the dataset reveals significant disparities in the average investment per project across different regions, with a total average investment per project of USD 3.36 billion. In the African region, West Africa received the highest average investment per project at USD 2.64 billion, primarily focusing on port infrastructure projects. In the Asian region, West Asia has the highest average investment per project at USD 7.93 billion, largely due to three solar park projects in the United Arab Emirates and a large-scale oil project, Kuwait's Al-Zour refinery, with an estimated investment of USD 27 billion. The dataset indicates that Southeast Asia has more tripartite cooperation projects and higher investment than Central Asia, reflecting a more favourable economic and investment environment. Southeast Asia and Central Asia have an average investment per project of USD 2.74 billion and USD 1.41 billion, respectively. In the European region, the average

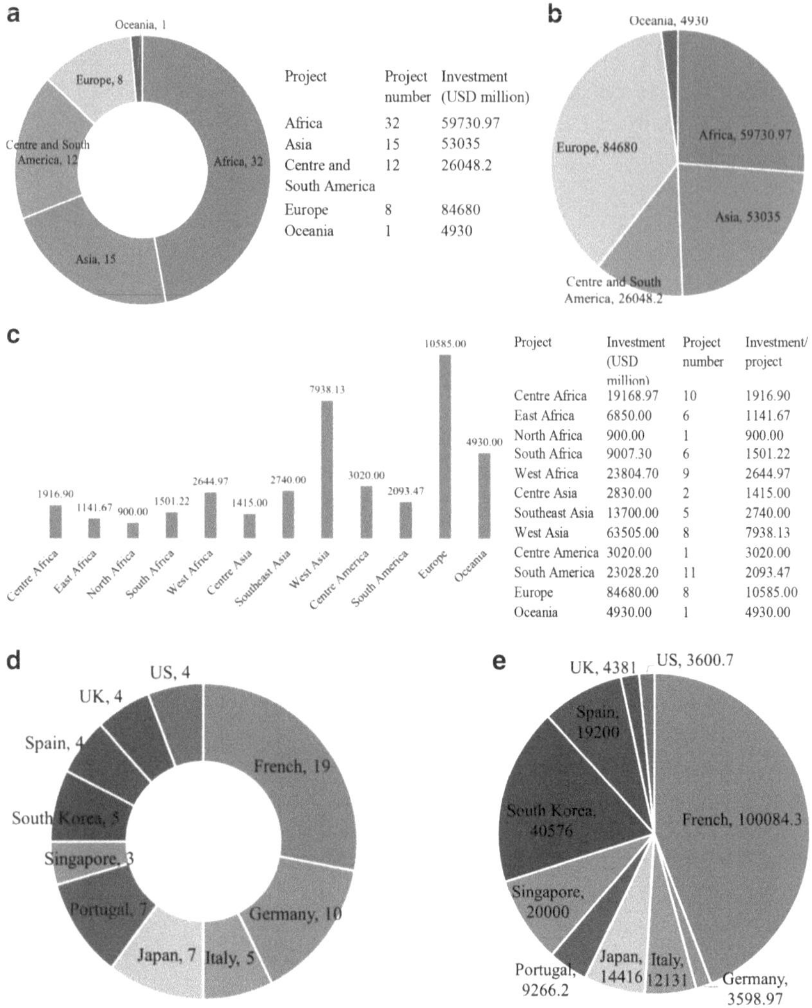

Project	Project number	Investment (USD million)
Africa	32	59730.97
Asia	15	53035
Centre and South America	12	26048.2
Europe	8	84680
Oceania	1	4930

Project	Investment (USD million)	Project number	Investment/project
Centre Africa	19168.97	10	1916.90
East Africa	6850.00	6	1141.67
North Africa	900.00	1	900.00
South Africa	9007.30	6	1501.22
West Africa	23804.70	9	2644.97
Centre Asia	2830.00	2	1415.00
Southeast Asia	13700.00	5	2740.00
West Asia	63505.00	8	7938.13
Centre America	3020.00	1	3020.00
South America	23028.20	11	2093.47
Europe	84680.00	8	10585.00
Oceania	4930.00	1	4930.00

Fig. 5.6 (**a**) Number of Chinese tripartite cooperation projects in each continent (Source: Author). (**b**) Estimated investment scale in each continent (USD million) (Source: Author). (**c**) Average investment per project in different areas (Source: Author). (**d**) Number of involved projects of partner countries (Source: Author). (**e**) Estimated investment scale of involved projects of partner countries (Source: Author)

investment per project is the highest among all 11 regions, at USD 10.58 billion. This high-average investment suggests a superior investment environment, potentially due to factors such as good governance, a strong legal system, a stable political environment, and market-friendly policies (Jensen, 2008). These elements may enhance the attractiveness of Europe to investors, resulting in a higher-average investment per project compared to other regions. Conversely, lower investments in other regions may be due to poor economic conditions, political challenges, and low local infrastructure demands.

As for the distribution of partner countries, ten countries (France, Germany, Italy, Japan, Portugal, Singapore, South Korea, Spain, the UK, and the USA) have engaged in tripartite cooperation projects with China by 2023. Among these, nine countries are OECD-DAC members, excluding Singapore. Figure 5.6d, e illustrates the project numbers and investment scales of tripartite cooperation projects in which they were involved.[10]

To identify patterns in tripartite cooperation among partner countries, I examined the number of projects each country participated in and their respective estimated investment scales (see Table 5.3).

Table 5.3 Investment situation of partner countries (Source: Author)

Country	*Total of estimated investment scale (USD million)*	*Project number*	*Averaged estimated investment scale in each project*	*MoU signed date*
France	100,084.3	19	5267.59	06/2015
South Korea	40,576	5	8115.20	11/2015
Singapore	20,000	3	6666.67	04/2018
Spain	19,200	4	4800.00	11/2018
Japan	14,416	7	2059.43	05/2018
Italy	12,131	5	2426.20	09/2018
Portugal	9266.2	7	1323.74	10/2016
UK	4381	4	1095.25	06/2019
USA	3600.7	4	900.18	Not signed yet
Germany	3598.97	10	359.90	Not signed yet

[10] It needs to be stressed that the investment scale number does not represent the outward investment from the partner countries; rather, it signifies the estimated investment scale for the entire project. The investment might come from multiple sponsors.

France leads with 19 tripartite cooperation projects, whose estimated investment scale exceeds USD 100 billion. This significant performance can be attributed to the early signing of tripartite cooperation MOU documents between the French and Chinese governments in 2015, establishing a foundation for bilateral trust. Their continued efforts, such as regular working group meetings and discussions on potential tripartite cooperation projects, have further solidified this collaborative relationship, attracting more investment and accumulating a greater number of projects (Yang & An, 2019).

However, there are some counterfactual observations. For instance, Germany has ten tripartite cooperation projects with China, but the investment scale in these projects is relatively small. Conversely, South Korea and Singapore have fewer cooperative projects, yet the investment scales in these projects are substantial. For example, the China-South Korea-Kuwait Al-Zour refinery project involves an investment of USD 27 billion, and the China-Singapore-Guinea Simandou iron ore project entails an investment of USD 15 billion.

To explore the reasons behind these phenomena, I delved into the projects of each country. Due to the limited number of tripartite cooperation projects, especially in countries with three to five projects, the average investment values are highly influenced by extreme figures, particularly in sectors such as oil and mining, which often involve high investment scales. These extreme figures may distort the observed trends and development patterns of tripartite cooperation projects.

Additionally, I integrated the investment scale with the function of MOU documents, as discussed in Section 5.1.3, and found that MOU documents function as endorsements to some degree for national support to their firms. Examining specific countries provides further insights.

For example, South Korea signed MOU documents with China in 2015 and engaged in three significant tripartite cooperation projects in the same year. These projects include the China-South Korea-Ecuador Refineria del Pacifico project (USD 10.5 billion), the China-South Korea-Kuwait Al-Zour refinery project (USD 27 billion), and the China-South Korea-Peru supervision service for Lima Metro Line 2 (USD 111 million).

Singapore signed an MOU on third-party market cooperation in 2018 and another 'MOU on the implementation of the framework for strengthening China-Singapore third-party market cooperation' in 2019. In the same year, Singapore participated in the China-Singapore-Guinea Simandou iron ore project with an estimated investment of USD 15 billion in 2019.

Portugal signed MOU documents in 2016, also very early. The main reason for this early engagement is the long-standing cooperation history between China and Portugal in Portuguese-speaking countries. Building on their historical ties, dating back to Portugal's colonial presence in Macao, the two nations established The Forum for Economic and Trade Cooperation between China and Portuguese-speaking Countries in 2003. Portugal participated in projects with a relatively lower-average investment scale. China-Portugal tripartite cooperation projects are mainly in Latin and South America. I assumed the reason for the lower-average investment might be influenced by the unstable social and economic context in beneficiary countries in Latin and South America. However, the actual reason that influences the lower-average investment scale of Portugal is the Moray East Wind Farm project in the UK with a small investment scale of 33 million USD.

The USA and Germany have not signed MOU documents with China to date and are involved in tripartite cooperation projects with lower investment scales. In China-US tripartite cooperation, the sole player is General Electric Company, which cooperated with China Machinery Engineering Corporation in South Asia and Africa. In China-Germany tripartite cooperation, the main player is GAUFF Engineering, which has nine projects with China Communications Construction Company, China Energy Engineering Corporation Limited, and China Three Gorges Corporation in African countries. However, GAUFF only offers supervision and consulting services in these projects and does not engage in further cooperation activities.

5.3 Official Actions in Tripartite Cooperation

This section aims to explore how participants work together in tripartite cooperation projects, despite initially having different aims and actions. Data on tripartite cooperation projects are collected and analysed using four dimensions to measure the official actions of China, partner countries, and beneficiary countries.[11] After processing the 68 projects' data, the detailed statistics are presented in the following sections.

5.3.1 *Chinese and Partner Countries' Actions: SOEs vs. Private Enterprises*

Table 5.4 underscores the disparity in involvement between China and its partner countries' entities in tripartite cooperation projects.

In general, China places significant emphasis on the engagement of its public sector, participating in 67 out of 68 projects (98.53%). In contrast,

Table 5.4 Involvement of China and its partner countries' entities

China	*Overall engagement*	*Chinese government direct financing*	*Chinese high-level government officials' meetings*	*Chinese policy support*	*Chinese SOE involvement*
Project	67	33	15	8	66
Ratio	98.53%	48.53%	22.06%	11.76%	97.06%
Partner countries	Overall engagement	Partner countries' government direct financing	Partner countries' high-level government officials' meetings	Partner countries' policy support	Partner countries' SOE involvement
Project	24	14	12	1	4
Ratio	35.29%	20.59%	17.65%	1.47%	5.88%

[11] A counting system is used to assess four dimensions of tripartite cooperation projects.

For government direct financing, a score of 1 (Yes = 1) is assigned if Chinese policy banks directly finance the project; otherwise, it's 0 (No = 0). In the second dimension, if a tripartite cooperation project is proposed or mentioned in high-level government leadership meetings involving China, partner countries, and/or beneficiary countries' governments, it is included in the count. For the third dimension, policy support, a score of one is counted if the project receives supportive policies from relevant government departments or ambassadors. In the fourth dimension, SOEs' involvement awards a score if SOEs are in the tripartite cooperation project as stakeholders, including both Chinese and partner countries' SOEs. The data does not cover all cases of government support; I only included the cases that I have found.

These scoring rules are consistently applied to partner countries and beneficiary countries, as well as the remaining dimensions.

the involvement of public sector in partner countries is lower, with participation in only 24 out of 68 projects (35.29%).

Chinese SOEs play a dominant role in tripartite cooperation projects, with involvement in 66 out of 68 projects, accounting for 97.06% of the total. Direct financing by the Chinese government is also prevalent, involved in 33 out of 68 projects (48.53%). In contrast, the other two dimensions of involvement, high-level leadership meetings and policy support, are less frequently used. High-level leadership meetings occurred in 15 projects (22.06%), and policy support was observed in only 8 projects (11.76%). This lower frequency may be due to the possibility that evidence for these meetings or policy support was not found in all cases where they actually occurred.

In comparison, partner countries involvement across the four dimensions is significantly lower. Partner countries' government direct financing was involved in 14 out of 68 projects (20.59%), and high-level leadership meetings occurred in 12 projects (17.65%). Partner countries' SOEs participated in only four projects,[12] and partner countries' policy support was evident in just one project (1.47%), specifically the China-France-Serbia Belgrade Metro project. Generally, the partner countries' public sector shows limited involvement in tripartite cooperation projects across all four dimensions.

Chinese SOEs benefit from substantial state-backed capital and generally maintain better cash liquidity, enabling them to undertake and sustain large-scale projects. This financial strength is complemented by China's strategic deployment of government financing, which facilitates the initiation and continuation of projects that align with its geopolitical and industrial interests (García-Herrero & Ng, 2021; Jin et al., 2022; Wu et al., 2023).

Partner firms, instead, leverage their management expertise and extensive foreign experience to participate in tripartite projects. Their strategy often involves divesting shares in existing assets to Chinese SOEs in exchange for cash, enhancing their liquidity to acquire other assets that align more closely with their strategic goals. This approach suggests a

[12] Électricité de France in China-France-Namibia 500 MW Clean Energy Power Station project;

Électricité de France in China-France-UK Hinkley Point C Nuclear Power Station project;

Eni S.p.A. in China-Italy- Mozambique Coral South Floating Liquefied Natural Gas project;

SP Group in China-Singapore-Australia Ausnet Acquisition project.

preference for optimising asset portfolios and focusing on high-return investments (Amihud et al., 2005; Purnamasari, 2015).

The dataset illustrates a clear dichotomy in the strategies and levels of involvement of China and its partner countries' entities in tripartite cooperation projects. China's official extensive engagement and financial commitment underscore its strategic use of these projects to expand its global influence. In contrast, the partner countries' approach, characterised by selective involvement and leveraging management expertise, reflects different strategic priorities and resource allocations.

5.3.2 *Beneficiary Countries' Action: Local Policy Support*

Due to the distinct context experienced by beneficiary countries, this dataset is separately compared to the information on China and its partner countries' approaches. Table 5.5 reveals that official participation of beneficiary countries is crucial in tripartite cooperation projects, with involvement in 67 out of 68 projects.

These beneficiary countries' authorities include the central government, local government, transportation or energy authorities, and SOEs. Both Chinese and beneficiary countries exhibit a high overall official participation rate of 98.53%. However, while China emphasises the engagement of its SOEs, beneficiary countries predominantly use policy support to contribute to tripartite cooperation projects, with an involvement ratio of 88.24% (60 out of 68 projects).

Policy support in beneficiary countries includes laws and administrative policies related to five cooperative approaches discussed in Section 5.1.3: (1) Service Contracts and O&M Contracts; (2) Lease Contracts, Franchising Contracts, and Concession Agreements; (3) EPC Contracts; (4) PPPs Contracts; and (5) JV Contracts. These cooperative approaches require the support of the government. Direct financing by beneficiary

Table 5.5 Involvement of beneficiary countries' entities

Beneficiary countries	*Overall engagement*	*Local government direct financing*	*Local high-level government officials' meetings*	*Local policy support*	*Local SOE involvement*
Project	67	38	23	60	34
Ratio	98.53%	55.88%	33.82%	88.24%	50.00%

countries' governments and the participation of SOEs are used in approximately half of the projects, with ratios of 55.88% and 50.00%, respectively. In contrast, high-level leadership meetings have a lower involvement ratio of 33.82%. Overall, the engagement approaches of beneficiary countries reflect a strategic focus on leveraging local resources and policy frameworks to facilitate these collaborations.

5.3.3 *Past Actions: Bilateral Cooperation Records*

Table 5.6 presented indicates whether there are existing cooperative records between entities of any two parties. In this study of 68 projects, I analysed how often Chinese firms and their partner firms had previously collaborated or engaged in substantial business activities in the counterpart country before entering into tripartite cooperation. I conducted this analysis by tracing the historical interactions of participant firms and gathering information from their Web sites and news reports. Any previous cooperation activities or reports were counted as existing cooperation records. This scoring method was consistently applied to evaluate relationships between partner firms and beneficiary countries, as well as between Chinese firms and beneficiary countries.

The dataset shows that most of the participants in tripartite cooperation projects have bilateral cooperative records. The highest ratio of cooperative records is observed between firms of partner countries and beneficiary countries' entities, with a ratio of 91.18%, while the ratio of cooperative records between Chinese firms and beneficiary countries is 75%. This finding suggests that in contrast with the assumptions that China has accumulated massive experience in the developing world, these Western companies have more extensive experience in bilateral cooperative activities with the beneficiary countries' entities in international infrastructure projects. The high ratio of cooperative records between Western

Table 5.6 The cooperative records between entities of any two participants

Cooperation records	*Chinese firms and their partner firms*	*Partner firms and beneficiary countries' entities*	*Chinese firms and beneficiary countries' entities*
Sum	59	62	51
Ratio	86.76%	91.18%	75.00%

firms and beneficiary countries' entities can be attributed to their colonial history and subsequent post-colonial relationships. Western firms have established a longer presence compared to China in many regions, fostering deeper business connections and collaborations with beneficiary countries' entities over time. These historical connections empower them to navigate complex institutional environments in less developed countries. This historical context may also explain why partner countries (e.g., France, Spain, and Portugal) increased engagement in Africa and South America today (Rangan & Drummond, 2004; Cuervo-Cazurra & Genc, 2008).

Prior to commencing tripartite cooperation projects, the participants were involved in bilateral collaborative activities. The familiarity of the participants with each other's commercial behaviour, management style, cultural background, and other relevant factors (Williamson, 1992, 1995) facilitates the implementation of tripartite cooperation projects. For example, before the initiation of the China-France-UK Hinkley Point C nuclear power station projects, the French company EDF had undertaken many nuclear power projects in both China (e.g., Daya Bay nuclear power station; Taishan EPR project) (EDF, 2024) and the UK (e.g., Hartlepool, Heysham, Torness, and Sizewell B nuclear power stations).[13] Similarly, ahead of the China-Italy-Mozambique Coral South Floating Liquefied Natural Gas project in 2017, the Italian firm Eni had collaborated with various Chinese oil research institutions and companies since the 1980s.[14] Eni also had previously executed the first natural gas project in the Rovuma Basin in Mozambique.[15] More importantly, in 2013, Chinese company PetroChina acquired a 20% stake from ENI in another Mozambique gas project, the Mamba Complex offshore (Eni, 2013). Overall, this dataset provides insight into the level of cooperation between China, partner countries' entities, and beneficiary countries' entities, highlighting the relatively high degree of bilateral collaboration.

In conclusion, the descriptive statistics generate several preliminary observations regarding the dynamics of tripartite cooperation projects. The national capital and SOEs' investment models play major roles when

[13] EDF, "Nuclear Power Stations in the UK," accessed July 24, 2024, https://www.edfenergy.com/about/nuclear/power-stations.

[14] Eni, "Eni in China: Operations," accessed July 24, 2024, https://www.eni.com/en-CN/operations.html.

[15] Eni, "Our Activity in Mozambique," accessed July 24, 2024, https://www.eni.com/en-IT/actions/global-activities/mozambique.html.

China is involved in tripartite cooperation projects, whereas China's partner countries, driven primarily by commercial interests, have less direct government involvement in these projects. Large private firms in partner countries provide advanced design, management, and supervision skills, as well as extensive experience in supporting tripartite cooperation projects. Beneficiary countries often use preferential policies to support these projects. These four dimensions will be analysed further in Chap. 6, Sect. 6.2.

5.3.4 *From Marriage to Divorce: How to Balance Divergence and Convergence?*

In these 68 tripartite cooperation projects, most of the projects have made satisfactory progress and outcomes. However, there were five projects that failed due to one or more parties withdrawing from the projects, resulting in the breakdown of the tripartite partnership. Three projects (China-Japan-Thailand High-Speed Rail Linked 3 Airport Project, China-France-Namibia 500 MW clean energy power station project, and China-South Korea-Ecuador Refineria del Pacifico project) failed at the initial early project stage. The firms merely expressed interest in investing or joining these projects. In contrast, two projects (the China-Spain-DR Congo Grand Inga Dam III project and the Ibom Deep Seaport Project) encountered failure after Chinese and partner firms successfully won the tender and were awarded development contracts by the beneficiary countries' governments.

The failures of tripartite cooperation projects can be attributed to three reasons. Firstly, some projects are proposed during high-level leadership meetings for symbolic purposes, with China and its partners often involved as contractors in these projects, making it easier for them to withdraw. In addition, when bilateral high-level leaders discuss tripartite cooperation, government staff collect information about potential cooperative projects, but often with limited knowledge of specific details. As a result, many projects remain in the initial phase without feasibility tests or return-on-asset analysis. After conducting a cost-return analysis, companies would decline to continue such projects when there is negative revenue, leading to the termination of tripartite cooperation activities with China and/or beneficiary countries' entities.

For example, during the first Sino-Japan Tripartite Cooperation Forum, it was reported that they had a fruitful list of outcomes, with the Lists of Key Projects for 52 tripartite cooperation projects signed. However, most of these tripartite cooperation projects were strategic cooperation agreements, cooperation framework agreements, memoranda of cooperation, etc. between Chinese companies and Japanese companies. Only a small portion of practical projects were included in this list, and these projects had already been initiated before the meeting. This list of outcomes for the Sino-Japan tripartite cooperation is more likely just a decoration for this high-level leadership meeting. After this meeting, the Japanese Itochu Corporation withdrew from the China-Japan-Thailand High-Speed Rail Linked 3 Airport Project because of "the inevitable severe loss" (Gao, 2018).

Another project was proposed in response to COP21. The China-France-Namibia 500 MW clean-energy power station project was proposed during the UN Climate Change Conference (COP21) in Paris, and the China General Nuclear Power Corporation (CGN), EDF Energies Nouvelles, and InnoSun signed an MOU for tripartite cooperation. The signing ceremony was attended by the Namibian Minister of Environment and diplomats from China and France (Xinhua News, 2015). However, no further information was released about the project after the meeting, indicating its failure and the limitations of MOU documents. Signing an MOU also does not guarantee the process of tripartite cooperation projects.

The second reason is the lack of coordination among participants. Chinese and partner firms often form co-bid consortia to develop tripartite cooperation projects, and cooperation often breaks down due to unequal distribution of shares and interests. In the case of the China-Spain-DR Congo Grand Inga Dam III project, tensions arose between a Chinese firm and its partner company, particularly regarding project execution and distribution of shares within the final consortia (M'Bida & Maussion, 2020). Another case is the China-France-Nigeria Ibom Deep Seaport Project. Although the Bolloré-ChinaPower consortium was initially selected as the preferred bidder for the project, the consortium ultimately decided to withdraw (Oritse, 2021). This withdrawal was attributed to concerns about the controversy surrounding the project's location and the lack of coordination among Bolloré, ChinaPower, and local port authorities.

The third reason is geopolitical tensions between the countries involved in the tripartite cooperation. Due to foreign policy considerations, China and its partner countries may cease cooperation. For instance, the China-South Korea-Ecuador Refineria del Pacifico project was terminated due to geopolitical issues between China and South Korea and the establishment of a new US military base in South Korea. This led to the termination of the transaction with Ecuador (Visión 360, 2017). As a result, the cooperation between China and South Korea failed in 2017, and no further tripartite cooperation projects have been initiated between the two countries since 2018.

After a tripartite cooperation project fails, there are generally two solutions. The first is beneficiary countries' entities find other investors/partners to continue developing the project. For example, after the tripartite cooperation broke down in the Ibom Deep Seaport Project and the Grand Inga Dam III project, the beneficiary countries' entities sought new investors. Grand Inga Dam III project will be developed by Spanish company AEE Power, Australian company Fortescue Future Industries, China Three Gorges, and Sinohydro in 2026 (Rogers, 2016). However, the Ibom Deep Seaport Project was still in the process of seeking potential investors by December 2023, causing additional transaction costs in the search for new partners (Anthony, 2021). The second solution is the tripartite cooperation project revert to a bilateral cooperation project, and the project is developed by beneficiary countries' entities and a party willing to take risks. In the case of the China-Japan-Thailand High-Speed Rail Linked 3 Airport Project, after the Japanese Itochu Corporation withdrew, China and Thailand continued to carry forward the project (RT, 2019).

5.4 Concluding Remarks

This chapter provides a general overview of Chinese tripartite cooperation in economic infrastructure and presents three key findings.

The first is the development of a new two-step system that demonstrates how participants from three countries collaborate in economic infrastructure projects. In this system, the first step involves the cooperation types of the beneficiary country, in which beneficiary countries' government entities use five approaches to cooperate with Chinese firms and their partner firms. The second step involves the cooperation between Chinese firms and their partner firms, utilising four flexible ways to cooperate in different phases. This new system reflects how China and its partner are altering the dynamics of project finance activities, and the involvement of an additional partner creates both opportunities and additional complexities.

The second finding of this chapter is the trends and development of Chinese tripartite cooperation projects across different time phases, industrial sectors, and geographical locations. Three stages of tripartite cooperation are identified: the infancy stage (2006–2013), development stage (2014–2019), and COVID-influence stage (2020–2022). During these stages, China focused on the energy sector, particularly clean energy projects, receiving the most investment. Road projects received more investment than port projects in the transportation sector. Geographically, Africa and Asia attracted more investments and hosted the largest number of projects. However, the average investment per project indicates that the highest investments were directed towards European regions with favourable economic conditions, stable political environments, and effective legal systems. Regarding the distribution of partner countries, the number of projects and investment scales have a connection with the signing of MOUs between the Chinese government and partner countries' governments. These MOUs can be seen, to some extent, as endorsements that provide national support to their firms.

The third key finding of this chapter is the actions taken by China, China's partner countries, and beneficiary countries' entities to participate in tripartite cooperation. China depends on national capital and investment from SOEs in tripartite cooperation projects, while Western countries typically rely more on the participation of private sector giants. Beneficiary countries usually provide policy support to tripartite cooperation activities. Before initiating a project, participants typically establish broad bilateral partnerships based on past cooperative experiences.

This chapter provides an overview and important facts about tripartite cooperation, but it is challenging to analyse the determinants of each party to participate in projects based on this analysis alone. More detailed analysis regarding 'the determinants of participants to engage in tripartite cooperation' and 'the actions that influence the transaction cost and benefits in practical projects' will be discussed in the following two empirical chapters.

References

Alam, M., Getchius, T. S., Schünemann, H., Amer, Y. S., Bak, A., Fatheree, L. A., Ginex, P., Jakhmola, P., Marsden, G. L., McFarlane, E., Meremikwu, M., Taske, N., Temple-Smolkin, R. L., Ventura, C., Burgers, J., Bradfield, L., O'Brien, M. D., Einhaus, K., Kopp, I. B., & Munn, Z. (2022). A Memorandum of Understanding has Facilitated Guideline Development Involving Collaborating Groups. *Journal of Clinical Epidemiology, 144*, 8–15. https://doi.org/10.1016/j.jclinepi.2021.12.022

Amihud, Y., Mendelson, H., & Pedersen, L. (2005). Liquidity and Asset Prices. *Foundations and Trends R in Finance, 1*(4), 269–364. https://pages.stern.nyu.edu/~lpederse/papers/LiquidityAssetPricing.pdf

Anthony, L. (2021, October 1). NEWSTell Our People Real Reason Investors Withdrew from Ibom Deep Seaport Project—NKpubre to Gov Emmanuel. *Daily Post*. https://dailypost.ng/2021/10/01/tell-our-people-real-reason-investors-withdrew-from-ibom-deep-seaport-project-nkpubre-to-gov-emmanuel/

Babic, M. (2021). State Capital in a Geoeconomic World: Mapping state-Led Foreign Investment in the Global Political Economy. *Review of International Political Economy, 30*(1), 1–28. https://doi.org/10.1080/09692290.2021.1993301

Babic, M., Garcia-Bernardo, J., & Heemskerk, E. M. (2019). The Rise of Transnational State Capital: State-Led Foreign Investment in the 21st Century. *Review of International Political Economy, 27*(3), 433–475. https://doi.org/10.1080/09692290.2019.1665084

CGGT. (2016). CTG Seals the 30-year Operation Deal of Jupiá and Ilha Solteira Hydroelectric Power Plants in Brazil. *CGGT*. http://www.cggthinktank.com/2016-01-14/100075060.html

Che-Ghani, N. Z., Myeda, N. E., & Ali, A. S. (2023). Efficient Operation and Maintenance (O&M) Framework in Managing Stratified Residential Properties. *Journal of Facilities Management, 21*(4), 609–634. https://doi.org/10.1108/jfm-10-2021-0124

Chen, H., & Wu, B. (2020). Basic Conditions, Challenges and Countermeasures of China-Germany Third-Party Market Cooperation in Africa. *Intertrade, 11*, 45–53. https://doi.org/10.14114/j.cnki.itrade.2020.11.007

Cuervo-Cazurra, A., & Genc, M. (2008). Transforming Disadvantages into Advantages: Developing-Country MNEs in the Least Developed Countries. *Journal of International Business Studies, 39*(6), 957–979. https://doi.org/10.1057/palgrave.jibs.8400390

Datti, Y. U., Zawawi, N. A. W. A., Umar, A. A., Sutanto, M. H., & Danyaro, K. U. (2022). Challenges of Maturity Models in Public-Private Partnerships (PPPs) in the Post-COVID-19 Era. *Journal of Engineering, Project, and Production Management, 12*(2), 149–165. https://doi.org/10.32738/jeppm-2022-0014

Delmon, J. (2010). Understanding Options for Public-Private Partnerships in Infrastructure: Sorting Out the Forest from the Trees: Bot, Dbfo, Dcmf, Concession, Lease...World Bank Policy Research Working Paper, 5173. https://ssrn.com/abstract=1536986

EDF. (2024, March 15). Presentation Powering China's Low-Carbon Energy Transition and High-Quality Development. *EDF in China*. https://china.edf.com/en/presentation

EDF. (n.d.). Nuclear Power Stations in the UK. Accessed July 24, 2024, https://www.edfenergy.com/about/nuclear/power-stations

EFE. (2015, November 25). Brazil Awards Rights to Operate 29 Hydro Plants, Raises $4.6 bn. *ElEconomista.es; elEconomista*. https://www.eleconomista.es/energia-eAm/noticias/7175046/11/15/Brazil-awards-rights-to-operate-29-hydro-plants-raises-46-bn.html

Eni. (2013, March 14). Eni Sells a 20% Share of Area 4 in Mozambique to CNPC and Signs a Joint Study Agreement for Cooperation for the Development of the Rongchang Shale Gas Block in China. https://www.eni.com/en-IT/media/press-release/2013/03/eni-sells-a-20-share-of-area-4-in-mozambique-to-cnpc-and-signs-a-joint-study-agreement-for-cooperation-for-the-development-of-the-rongchang-shale-gas-block-in-china.html

EXPO. (2016, March 1). Construction of Hydroelectric Power Stations to Begin in GABON. *EXPO Group*. https://www.expogr.com/tanzania/powerenergy/detail_news.php?newsid=2770&pageid=2

Gaitán, M. G. (2021). Licensing as a Central Structure of Technology Transfer Agreements. Joint Venture and Franchising Agreements. *GRUR International, 70*(5), 427–439. https://doi.org/10.1093/grurint/ikab032

Gao, Q. (2018, December 14). The Disappearance of Thailand's High-Speed Rail Project in China Japan Third Country Cooperation (中日第三国合作中消失的泰国高铁项目). NIKKEI. https://cn.nikkei.com/columnviewpoint/column/33518-2018-12-14-02-54-16.html

García-Herrero, A., & Ng, G. (2021). China's State-Owned Enterprises and Competitive Neutrality. Policy Contribution. https://www.bruegel.org/sites/default/files/wp-content/uploads/2021/02/PC-05-2021.pdf

Haberly, D., & Wójcik, D. (2016). Earth Incorporated: Centralisation and Variegation in the Global Company Network. *Economic Geography, 93*(3), 241–266. https://doi.org/10.1080/00130095.2016.1267561

Huang, F., Chen, J., Sun, L., Zhang, Y., & Yao, S. (2019). Value-Based Contract for Smart Operation and Maintenance Service Based on Equitable Entropy. *International Journal of Production Research, 58*(4), 1271–1284. https://doi.org/10.1080/00207543.2019.1617450

Jensen, N. M. (2008). *Nation-States and the Multinational Corporation: A Political Economy of Foreign Direct Investment*. Princeton University Press.. https://doi.org/10.1515/9781400837373

Jin, X., Xu, L., Xin, Y., & Adhikari, A. (2022). Political Governance in China's State-Owned Enterprises. *China Journal of Accounting Research, 15*(2), 100236. https://doi.org/10.1016/j.cjar.2022.100236

Kumaraswamy, M. M., & Zhang, X. Q. (2001). Governmental Role in BOT-led Infrastructure Development. *International Journal of Project Management, 19*(4), 195–205. https://doi.org/10.1016/s0263-7863(99)00069-1

Lee, S. J., Liu, L. Q., & Stebunovs, V. (2017). Risk Taking and Interest Rates: Evidence from Decades in the Global Syndicated Loan Market. IMF. https://www.imf.org/en/Publications/WP/Issues/2017/01/27/Risk-Taking-and-Interest-Rates-Evidence-from-Decades-in-the-Global-Syndicated-Loan-Market-44595

LUA. (2018, November 30). Bollore Ports, PowerChina win Deep-sea Port Contract in Nigeria. *Logistics Update Africa*. https://www.logupdateafrica.com/bollore-ports-powerchina-win-deepsea-port-contract-in-nigeria-logistics-shipping

Luo, Y., & Chen, Z. (2021). Challenges and Countermeasures of Chinese Engineering Contracting Enterprises Participating in Third-party Market Cooperation. *International Project Contracting & Labour, 12*, 54–56.

M'Bida, A., & Maussion, E. (2020, January 24). DRC's Giant Inga III Dam: Spanish firm ACS Throws in the Towel. *The Africa Report*. https://www.theafricareport.com/22572/drcs-giant-inga-iii-dam-spanish-firm-acs-throws-in-the-towel/

NDRC. (2019). Third-Party Market Cooperation Guidelines and Cases. National Development and Reform Commision, P.R. China. http://images.mofcom.gov.cn/mz/201909/20190912093710956.pdf

NDRC. (2024). The National Development and Reform Commission Holds a Roundtable on Third Party Market Cooperation between China and France in Beijing. Ndrc.gov.cn. https://www.ndrc.gov.cn/fzggw/jgsj/wzs/sjjdt/202405/t20240501_1366304.html

Oritse, G. (2021, October 13). Controversy Hits Ibaka Deep Seaport Project. *Vanguard*. https://www.vanguardngr.com/2021/10/controversy-hits-ibaka-deep-seaport-project/

Pang, J. (2021). "Yi Dai Yi Lu" shiyu xia si san fang shichang hezuo de jizhixing jianshe yanjiu (Research on the mechanism construction of third-party market cooperation under the vision of the "the Belt and Road"). *Study and Exprolation, 12*, 43–47. https://www.cnki.com.cn/Article/CJFDTotal-GJGC202104002.htm

Pinto, M. J. (2017). What is Project Finance? *Investment Management and Financial Innovations, 14*(1), 200–210. https://doi.org/10.21511/imfi.14(1-1).2017.06

PowerChina. (2013). Gabonese Hydropower Project Began Operation. PowerChina. https://www.chinadaily.com.cn/m/powerchina/2013-08/28/content_16925790.htm

PT. (2020a). Al Dhafra Solar Project, Abu Dhabi, UAE. Power Technology. https://www.power-technology.com/projects/al-dhafra-solar-project-abu-dhabi/

PT. (2020b, May 1). Sweihan Photovoltaic Independent Power Project, Abu Dhabi. Power Technology | Energy News and Market Analysis. https://www.power-technology.com/projects/sweihan-photovoltaic-independent-power-project-abu-dhabi/

Purnamasari, D. (2015). The Effect of Changes in Return on Assets, Return on Equity, and Economic Value Added to the Stock Price Changes and Its Impact on Earnings Per Share. *Research Journal of Finance and Accounting Www.iiste.org ISSN, 6*(6), 2222–2847. https://core.ac.uk/download/pdf/234630582.pdf

Rangan, S., & Drummond, A. (2004). Explaining Outcomes in Competition Among Foreign Multinationals in a Focal Host Market. *Strategic Management Journal, 25*(3), 285–293. https://doi.org/10.1002/smj.375

Rogers, D. (2016, May 9). Chinese Bidder Praised for Speed in DR Congo's Massive Dam Contest. *Global Construction Review*. https://www.globalconstructionreview.com/chinese-bidder-praised-speed-d7r-co7ngos-mas7sive/

RT. (2019). High-Speed Rail Linked 3 Airport Project, Thailand. Railway Technology. https://www.railway-technology.com/projects/high-speed-rail-linked-3-airport-project-thailand/

Rui, H., Zhang, M., & Shipman, A. (2017). Chinese Expatriate Management in Emerging Markets: A Competitive Advantage Perspective. *Journal of International Management, 23*(2), 124–138. https://doi.org/10.1016/j.intman.2017.01.002

Shang, K. (2024). Sino French Economic and Trade Cooperation for Mutual Benefit and Win-Win Results. Paper.people.com.cn. http://paper.people.com.cn/rmrb/html/2024-01/29/nw.D110000renmrb_20240129_1-03.htm

The Guardian. (2019). TICT Invests N70bn in Ports Infrastructure. The Guardian Nigeria News. https://guardian.ng/business-services/maritime/tict-invests-n70bn-in-ports-infrastructure/

Trivedi, P. (1990). Lack of Understanding on Memorandum of Understanding. *Economic and Political Weekly, 25*(47), M175–M182. https://www.jstor.org/stable/4397025

UNECE. (2012). Can public-private Partnerships Improve Infrastructure and Deliver Better Public Services? United Nations Economic Commission for Europe. https://unece.org/DAM/ceci/images/ICoE/Introductionpp.pdf

Visión 360. (2017, September 4). Refinería en polvo [Video]. YouTube. https://www.youtube.com/watch?v=I15PLiHJ28c&ab_channel=Vision360

Wan, J., & Wang, Y. (2020). *Tripartite Cooperation and Triple Win*. Chinese Foreign Currency.

Wan, J., & Wang, Y. (2021). Progress, Challenges, and Countermeasures of Third Party Market Cooperation. HKTDC Research. https://research.hktdc.com/sc/article/NzMyNzE1NjAw

Wang, H., Xiong, W., Wu, G., & Zhu, D. (2017). Public–Private Partnership in Public Administration Discipline: A Literature Review. *Public Management Review, 20*(2), 293–316. https://doi.org/10.1080/14719037.2017.1313445

Williamson, O. E. (1992). Markets, Hierarchies, and the Modern Corporation. *Journal of Economic Behavior & Organization, 17*(3), 335–352. https://doi.org/10.1016/s0167-2681(95)90012-8

Williamson, O. E. (1995). Hierarchies, Markets and Power in the Economy: An Economic Perspective. *Industrial and Corporate Change, 4*(1), 21–49. https://doi.org/10.1093/icc/4.1.21

Wu, C., Xu, L., & Xin, Y. (2023). The State Capital Investing and Operating Company Pilot Reform and SOE Bailouts. *China Journal of Accounting Research, 16*(2), 100302. https://doi.org/10.1016/j.cjar.2023.100302

Xinhua News. (2015, December 11). Coopération sino-française sur l'exploitation de l'énergie propre en Afrique_French.news.cn. http://french.xinhuanet.com/2015-12/11/c_134906950.htm

Xiong, L. (2022). Third Party Market Cooperation Under the "the Belt and Road" Initiative. *Frontiers, 21*, 56–65+75. https://doi.org/10.16619/j.cnki.rmltxsqy.2022.21.007

Yang, Y., & An, R. (2019, March 26). Deepening third-Party Market Cooperation and Opening up New Space for Sino French Cooperation. *China Development Institution*. http://www.cdi.com.cn/Article/Detail?Id=13249

Zhang, Y. (2020). Third-Party Market Cooperation Under the Belt and Road Initiative: Progress, Challenges, and Recommendations. *China International Strategy Review, 1*, 310–329. https://doi.org/10.1007/s42533-019-00026-7

CHAPTER 6

Tripartite Tango: Unravelling Determinants and Actions in Cooperative Projects

China, partner countries, and beneficiary countries together form the triangular framework of tripartite cooperation. The determinants driving these participants to engage in projects significantly influence their actions, subsequently shaping the change of transaction costs and additional benefits within tripartite cooperation projects. However, differences in project financing approaches between Chinese and traditional donors can lead to higher potential transaction costs for certain projects. Consequently, participants may respond differently: most will choose to continue and accept the potential additional transaction costs, while some opt to withdraw from projects, leading to cooperation failure or suspension. Therefore, it is crucial to investigate the determinants that influence transaction costs and benefits and to understand the rationale behind the decisions of participants who choose to remain involved in these projects.

This chapter examines the determinants driving participants to engage in tripartite cooperation, as well as the actions they employ to influence these projects. Using diverse sources, including government documents, corporate records, media reports, and interview notes, the chapter provides a thorough analysis of tripartite cooperation projects. The analysis involved processing over 950 documents using NVivo software, ensuring a comprehensive examination of the determinants and strategies adopted by governments and companies.

C. Su, *From Two to Three*, Governing China in the 21st Century,
https://doi.org/10.1007/978-981-95-8708-7_6

Firstly, the research identifies that the initial determinants influencing participants in tripartite cooperation often resemble those found in bilateral cooperation. For governments, motivations typically align with geopolitical or national development goals, similar to traditional bilateral arrangements. Chinese firms aim to acquire strategic assets by partnering with advanced economy firms to enhance their technological capabilities and gain experience from their partners, reflecting objectives seen in traditional outward FDI. However, there are notable determinants specific to tripartite cooperation projects. The Chinese government, in particular, seeks to mitigate international criticism while advancing its 'Going Out' policy and the BRI. Chinese SOEs aim to develop new markets, specifically targeting industries or strategic assets that are held or monopolised by Western countries while also avoiding the high costs associated with mergers and acquisitions (M&A). Traditional donor partners are motivated by the desire to maintain and reinforce their influence in regions where they have historical ties, as well as to weaken Chinese influence in beneficiary countries. Partner firms in traditional donor countries, on the other hand, are primarily driven by commercial interests, seeking to share costs and risks with their Chinese partners.

The second and third sections examine the actions of governments and firms within tripartite cooperation projects. Government actions involve various mechanisms, including financing instruments, soft law instruments, policy instruments, and relationship instruments, which can either promote or impede the progress of tripartite cooperation projects. For firms, the establishment of a partnership and a new JV/SPV represents a vital strategy. Chinese firms and their partner firms sometimes formalise their collaboration through EPC contracts or service/product agreements.

Finally, this chapter discusses the trade-offs in tripartite cooperation projects by examining the intertwined competition and cooperation in practical projects. Additionally, as more participants are involved in tripartite cooperation projects, the likelihood increases that one participant may encounter significant risks from external international contexts, such as war or sanctions. Such risks could lead to the withdrawal of that party or other participants, potentially transforming a successful project with additional benefits into one burdened with increased transaction costs due to the need for renegotiation or the search for new partners. By examining the intricate interplay of competition and cooperation among firms, this research seeks to uncover the reasons why participants prefer the tripartite cooperation model over traditional bilateral approaches for implementing infrastructure projects.

6.1 Initial Determinants for Joining Tripartite Cooperation

6.1.1 Determinants of Participant Governments

According to many Chinese researchers, such as Men and Yu (2020), Chen and Wu (2020), and Jin (2021), the foundation of tripartite cooperation is rooted in participants sharing national interests and development strategies. Despite China, partner countries, and beneficiary countries maintaining distinct national interests and development plans, they choose to engage in tripartite cooperation with the aim of integrating their respective strategies. The question then arises: given the different national interests and development plans, which lead to more competition rather than cooperation among countries, why do participants still engage in tripartite cooperation?

6.1.1.1 China

Some Chinese tripartite cooperation activities continue to align with its traditional bilateral cooperation model, characterised by the promotion of China's 'Going Out' policy and BRI, while also aiming to mitigate international criticisms.

China has indicated its interest in tripartite cooperation within the BRI with certain countries since 2015. For instance, in the 2015 BRI document with South Korea,[1] besides the standard bilateral cooperation within BRI's targets, both countries specifically highlighted tripartite collaboration in the 'Ways of Cooperation' section. The document emphasises the joint exploration of third-party markets based on the connection of the Belt and the Road and the Eurasia Initiative. It highlights the intention to strengthen cooperation in areas such as infrastructure, urban construction,

[1] "Memorandum of Understanding on Cooperation Concerning the Eurasia Initiative and the Silk Road Economic Belt and the 21st Century Maritime Silk Road between Ministry of Strategy and Finance of Korea and National Development and Reform Commission of China," October 31, 2015, https://president.globalwindow.org/common.FileDownload.do;jsessionid=RxP_elcnraadtV8dudWkP0l6IOffiL8uXx52Q1oq.PD?file_id=FILE_000000000011725&doc_id=DOC_000000000008132.

energy, petrochemical industry, finance, insurance, information technology, communications, and the environment through consortium bidding, joint production, and co-investment by Korean and Chinese companies. Similarly, the 2017 BRI MoU with Italy[2] outlined a commitment from both China and Italy to 'explore closer and mutually beneficial collaboration and partnerships.' This commitment encompasses the promotion of North-South, South-South, and triangular cooperation. Importantly, these targets remain in alignment with China's 'Going Out' policy and the objectives of the BRI.

In addition to determinants aligning with traditional bilateral cooperation activities, another rationale for China promoting tripartite cooperation projects lies in its response to international criticisms. Since the launch of the BRI in 2013, some Western countries have expressed suspicions regarding China's opaque project financing and perceived unsustainable operational approaches, resulting in widespread discussions surrounding the 'debt trap' theory (Mureithi, 2022). To address a part of these concerns, China has sought to involve more stakeholders through tripartite cooperation mechanisms. This approach not only enhances the transparency of the BRI but also aims to mitigate international criticisms[3] (Zhu, 2020).

From an ideological perspective, tripartite cooperation provides Western countries with an opportunity to gain a better understanding of China's overseas actions, potentially alleviating the concerns of Western countries (Chen & Wu, 2020; Luo & Chen, 2021). Tripartite cooperation serves as an effective strategy for China to deflect criticism, as exemplified by the Myanmar Gas Pipelines Project. When China and Myanmar's military government planned to develop the Gas Pipelines Project in 2004, they faced opposition from local and international communities due to perceived human rights and environmental concerns (Li, 2010). Subsequently, China and South Korea formed an upstream consortium in 2009, negotiating with the Myanmar government for preferential policies such as taxation and road franchising. The multi-shareholder structure of the project, involving China, South Korea, and Myanmar's capital,

[2] "Memorandum of Understanding between the Government of the Italian Republic and the Government of the People's Republic of China on Cooperation within the Framework of the Silk Road Economic Belt and the 21st Century Maritime Silk Road Initiative," March 2019, https://www.governo.it/sites/governo.it/files/Memorandum_Italia-Cina_EN.pdf.

[3] Interview A-20220523, A-20220527.

effectively defused political risks and international criticisms that targeted China (Qi & Yang, 2017; An & Zhang, 2019). Anti-government NGOs' propaganda, which accused Chinese SOEs of violating labour rights and alleging geopolitical, encountered challenges when it hindered project progress, as it also affected the interests of South Korean companies. In such cases, South Korean companies acted as mediators to address anti-activities, regulating Chinese SOEs' actions and framing project aims as business oriented rather than political (Chen, 2017).

Through tripartite cooperation, Western companies help Chinese SOEs demonstrate better practices in infrastructure projects. They regularly updated the project's progress for the public, engaged in local social initiatives, donated to local schools and hospitals, and involved local suppliers to mitigate conflicts with the local community[4] (Qu, 2017; Ma, 2017). While these activities may incur additional transaction costs for internal compliance and regulatory measures, they help save costs associated with addressing potential local and international criticisms.

In conclusion, China utilises tripartite cooperation to advance its strategic interests and development objectives, particularly in alignment with its 'Going Out' policy and the BRI. Apart from mitigating international criticism, there is no substantial departure from China's traditional investment approach.

6.1.1.2 China's Partner Countries

For partner countries, tripartite cooperation represents an opportunity to uphold or reinforce their influence in regions where they have historical ties.

For instance, Germany's 'Marshall Plan with Africa' and Japan's 'Free and Open Indo-Pacific' initiative are efforts aimed at asserting their influence in their respective regions. In 2017, the German government introduced its 'Marshall Plan with Africa,' focusing on enhancing trade, stimulating private investment, promoting bottom-up economic development, and fostering job creation across Africa. Federal Minister for Economic Cooperation and Development Gerd Müller remarked, "We cannot leave Africa to the Chinese, Russians, and Turks" (Pham, 2017). Japan's rivalry with China intensified after Indonesia awarded the $5 billion Jakarta-Bandung high-speed railway project to China over Japan in 2015. In response, Japan has used its infrastructure program to counter

[4] Interview O-20220615.

China's economic influence in Southeast Asia. The 'Free and Open Indo-Pacific' initiative targets regions from Southeast Asia to Southeast Africa through Southwest Asia and the Middle East (Tomotaka, 2020; Sinkkonen, 2019; Wallace, 2019), which overlaps with Chinese BRI.

This motivation is more explicit for France. In recent years, France has faced an economic downturn and a decline in its influence in Africa. Its recent donor policy towards the Africa has been largely ineffective and underfunded, making it difficult for France to maintain its influence (Tull, 2023). At the same time, Chinese influence has surged, driven by substantial capital investments. When France is confronted with beneficiary countries seeking to build infrastructure at a lower cost and opting for alternative Chinese investment and construction, France sees tripartite cooperation as a strategy that "cannot allow China to go it alone in Africa" (Harper, 2022). On March 13, 2018, during a visit to eastern Africa, French President Emmanuel Macron asserted that "France does not want emerging international investors to infringe on the sovereignty of France's historical partners (former French colonies) or weaken their economies." He emphasised that BRI construction should adhere to Western 'rules and standards' (Yang & An, 2019). According to Marc Julienne, head of China studies at the Centre for Asian Studies at the Institut français des relations internationales, France's policy towards China combines "dialogue and cooperation where possible" and "systematic competition and opposition where necessary" (Harper, 2022).

With China rapidly expanding its influence in the developing world, Western countries risk missing out on new projects if they do not engage in cooperation with China. Therefore, tripartite cooperation represents their pilot attempts to shift from zero-sum competition to non-zero-sum cooperative activities (Jing, 2022).

6.1.1.3 Beneficiary Countries

Beneficiary countries participating in tripartite cooperation projects generally have two key motivations. They strive to promote local economic growth and employment like the traditional bilateral investment cooperation. As most developing countries face with insufficient transport and energy infrastructure and require foreign capital and technology support, beneficiary countries have higher demands than before to develop domestic infrastructure. One provider may not meet their requirement in both capital and technology, so they try to align with more providers and use tripartite cooperation. For instance, Colombia initiated the

China-Japan-Colombia Concesión Autopista al Mar 2 project in 2015, aligning it with the Colombia's Fourth Generation (4G) road infrastructure program proposed in 2014. This plan aims to bridge the infrastructure investment gap and renew the country's aging road system. The 4G program intends to utilise the public-private-partnership model. Chinese and Japanese invested the initial construction phase and Columbian government loans for the second phase (Dowsett, 2019; Harrar, 2019).

In addition, tripartite cooperation serves as a strategic approach for beneficiary countries to enhance their bargaining power and gain more independence. The China-Italy-Ethiopia Gibe III Dam project exemplifies this strategy. Despite facing international criticism for environmental damage, Ethiopian Prime Minister Meles Zenawi emphasised the completion of the dam 'at any cost' as part of a new 5-year development plan. Zenawi criticised detractors, stating "they don't want to see a developed Africa; they want us to remain undeveloped and backward to serve their tourists as a museum… These people talk about the hazard of building dams after they have already completed building dams in their country" (Moszynski, 2011). Subsequently, the local government sought assistance from China, which provided a loan for construction costs, while the Italian firm Salini Costruttori S.p.A. continued handling the project construction. The Chinese Dongfang Electric Corporation managed the hydro-mechanical and electro-mechanical components of the project (Hydro Review, 2010). This case underscores the determination of beneficiary countries to advance their development plans independently through tripartite cooperation projects.

In beneficiary countries with a colonial history, tripartite cooperation reshapes long-standing investment patterns and commercial ties with former colonial powers. Taking China and France in the African region as an example, in recent years, Chinese SOEs have been awarded many infrastructure and energy projects in a region where French companies historically held stronger roots and connections. The entry of Chinese firms into these markets disrupted the monopoly that many French firms held, creating competitive pressures. China's cost advantages led to a decline in the competitiveness of French firms in the African market. For African countries, on the one hand, they continue to depend on the French legacy in their key economic sectors; on the other hand, they seek to exploit Chinese investment as an alternative. Chinese financial support, often provided without conditions such as requirements for good governance or democratic reforms typically imposed by traditional donor countries, offers an attractive option (Carothers, 2008; Tseng & Krog, 2016; Bräutigam, 2011). Through the tripartite cooperation mechanism, African countries aim to gain more independence by balancing the influence of traditional donor countries with that of China.

However, the determinants for firms in beneficiary countries to engage in tripartite cooperation are often overlooked. Based on the data from Chap. 5, SOEs in beneficiary countries participate in about half of the tripartite cooperation projects. These SOEs typically receive franchises from local governments. Many of the remaining local participants possess both business and official authority characteristics. For example, the Nigerian Ports Authority (NPA) is a government agency that governs ports in Nigeria and is also responsible for operating the Lagos Port Complex and Tin Can Island Port Complex (NPA, 2016). The motivations for these participants to engage in tripartite cooperation include upgrading their technology and production, expanding their employment scale, and aligning with their government's development strategy. Few of them pursue purely private interests.

6.1.2 Determinants of Participant Firms

6.1.2.1 China

Chinese firms actively participate in tripartite cooperation projects and use this cooperative mechanism as a complementary tool to extend their traditional China-only investments. Chinese firms continue to target the upgrading of their industrial value chain and technological capabilities through tripartite cooperation, aiming to acquire valuable know-how and operational experience from their partner firms. This encompasses a broad range of factors, including local networking, social relations, management expertise, business resources, logistical networks, legal systems, human resource management, security issues, negotiation skills, etc. (Chen & Wu, 2020; Hui & Han, 2021). Through learning by doing, Chinese firms incorporate external knowledge and expertise from their partner firms to effectively undertake activities (Rui et al. 2017).

In numerous African projects, Chinese companies collaborate with experienced French counterparts. In the China-France-Cameroon Kribi Deep Seaport Project, the project manager[5] from China Harbour

[5] Interview NPP-20220925.

Engineering Company (CHEC) outlined three reasons for this collaboration. Firstly, CHEC, transitioning from industrial manufacturing to commercial operations, sought to gain port management experience. By cooperating and learning know-how from French companies, the Kribi project marked CHEC's transition from a traditional engineering contractor to a comprehensive construction enterprise. Secondly, it is crucial to ensure cargo volume for the port. CMA-CGM, chosen as a consortium member, offered significant cargo volume as the third-largest global container carrier. CMA-CGM also provided CHEC with valuable logistics networks. The third reason behind CHEC's partnership with French partners involved the logistics assurance provided by Bolloré Logistics. Bolloré, generating revenue mainly from franchises rather than construction services, presented a business model CHEC aimed to learn and implement, particularly in port business running.

At times, Chinese companies secure project participation by acquiring equity from their partner companies. China views "a minority stake as a learning phase, with the idea that they can ramp up in the future" (Clercq, 2015), aligning with the aims of MNEs to proactively advance in other emerging and developing countries as proposed by the springboard perspective (Luo & Tung, 2018). For example, CTG became the largest shareholder of Energias de Portugal (EDP) by acquiring a 21.35% stake, subsequently gaining the rights to develop seven Brazilian hydropower stations (Coalición Regional, 2016). In their Framework Agreement, it stated that the equity partnership aims to "adapt it to the current context of the sector, making it more flexible to maximise value and promote the sharing of best practices for both company and their shareholders while ensuring compliance with the most rigorous corporate governance standards" (EDP, 2022).

In addition to seeking knowledge from partner firms in advanced economies, Chinese firms concurrently aim to access new markets through tripartite cooperation projects. Despite the significant inflow of Chinese investment in recent years, Africa and South America still maintain closer political and economic ties with European countries due to historical colonial connections (EU, 2023; Mills & Nwokolo, 2022). Infrastructure with natural monopoly characteristics, such as ports and railways, remains predominantly monopolised by European firms in these regions (Jedwab & Moradi, 2016). These firms were awarded long-term franchising contracts or concessions from the governments of beneficiary countries. Western companies also establish deep social networks with local authorities and communities, possessing a thorough understanding of the local context[6] (Austin, 2010).

To access these markets or secure control over strategic assets, Chinese SOEs often find it necessary to collaborate with these European firms. For instance, the French company Bollore holds a dominant position in Africa's logistics, with ownership of 16 port concessions, 35 dry ports, 280 logistic warehouses, 250 subsidiaries, and 3 rail concessions.[7] As Chinese shipping SOEs seek to expand their operations in Africa, they often collaborate with both Western partners and local partners. This strategy allows them to acquire business know-how, adapt to the local context, and mitigate risks, thereby reducing costs (Lin, 2011; Fan et al., 2016; Suri, 2016). Tripartite cooperation serves as a springboard or an effective approach for Chinese SOEs to enter African markets.

Aligning with their traditional investment objectives of exploring new markets, Chinese companies aim to promote their standards to beneficiary countries, and tripartite cooperation serves as a platform for Chinese enterprises to encourage European partner companies to familiarise themselves with Chinese construction standards, such as those for road or port building quality[8] (Liang & Cao, 2019; Zhou, 2020). The promotion of Chinese standards is a significant emblem of China's soft power and a vital national interest. In the Kribi Deep Sea Port project, equipment procurement exceeding 100 million US dollars was carried out according to Chinese standards, yielding extensive commercial benefits for China (Wang, 2019).

6.1.2.2 China's Partner Firms

In contrast to Chinese SOEs, their partner firms that participate in tripartite cooperation often aim to seek commercial interests first. The partner companies often demonstrate a willingness to sell minor equity stakes to Chinese firms in exchange for cash. Consequently, tripartite cooperation decisions are primarily driven by commercial considerations and/or the desire to optimise financial statements, with no substantial difference from

[6] Interview A-20230510, NPP-20220922.

[7] Bollore, "Bollore Transport Logistics in Africa Press Kit," accessed February 7, 2024, https://www.bollore-transport-logistics.com/fileadmin/user_upload/Dossier_Presse_Afrique_EN.pdf

[8] Interview NPP-20220925.

when Chinese firms engage in M&A with firms of advanced economies (Joubin-Bret & Knoerich, 2010).

In the tripartite cooperation scenario, partner firms sell minor equity stakes in lower-revenue business sectors to Chinese firms, receiving cash in return. These partner firms utilise the flowing cash to invest in other higher-revenue businesses. For example, the Portuguese company EDP established the equity cooperation by selling 21.35% stakes to CTG, reinforcing EDP's credit profile and financial liquidity. This partnership facilitated EDP's diversification of its business model and the development of new markets with CTG (EDP, 2011). According to EDP's CEO Antonio Mexia, this strategy of 'asset rotation' involves selling minority stakes to investors and using the funds to develop new projects, thereby broadening its portfolio (Clercq, 2015). Similarly, the Italian company Enel offloaded its solar power plant assets to CGN, enabling it to finance other renewable projects in Brazil[9] (RENEWS, 2019). For the same reason, partner firms in developed countries, lacking national financing backup, may encounter limitations in cash capacity for investments in large-scale infrastructure projects in beneficiary countries. Therefore, both Chinese firms and their partner firms seek cooperators with sufficient financing capacity to co-invest or co-develop new projects.

Beyond pursuing commercial interests, partner companies strategically aim to strengthen their presence in the markets of beneficiary countries, especially where they have occupied main market shares. Through tripartite cooperation, partner companies can leverage Chinese funding to expand their business network in Africa, strategically reinforcing their presence in the markets of beneficiary countries. For example, the CMA CGM Group participated in the China-France-Nigeria-Lekki Deep Seaport Project. Farid T. Salem, Executive Officer of CMA CGM Group, emphasised that the Lekki Port would assist CMA CGM in expanding services in the entire region, leveraging their logistics expertise and inland services for the entire Nigerian supply chain and market, from existing to new markets (Adeleye, 2018).

In conclusion, the initial determinants for governments to participate in tripartite cooperation projects often resemble those driving bilateral

[9] However, as mentioned in Chap. 2, in these cases, the role of beneficiary countries diminishes, and the local authorities have limited influence when partner countries' firms decide to sell minor equity to Chinese firms, especially when beneficiary countries lack strong legal and regulatory frameworks.

cooperation. For instance, the Chinese government seeks to advance its 'Going Out' policy and the BRI, and beneficiary countries focus on stimulating local economic growth and employment. However, tripartite cooperation introduces distinct motivations that are not present in bilateral cooperation. China aims to mitigate international criticism, Western partner countries seek to maintain or strengthen their influence in historically connected regions, and beneficiary countries use tripartite cooperation to enhance their bargaining power and achieve greater independence.

For firms involved, Chinese firms, especially SOEs, aim to improve technological capabilities, acquire valuable know-how and operational experience from their partner firms, and promote Chinese standards to their partners. These motivations are distinct in trilateral cooperation and cannot be found in bilateral cooperation. A key reason Chinese firms utilise the tripartite cooperation approach is to acquire know-how and strategic assets by cooperating with their partner firms. China's partner enterprises are primarily driven by commercial interests, including optimising financial statements and enhancing cash liquidity. Some Western firms also adopt strategic approaches to strengthen their dominance and consolidate their presence in existing markets.

6.1.3 Government Actions that Influence the Costs and Benefits of Tripartite Cooperation

In Chap. 5, government actions in tripartite cooperation were examined through four dimensions: direct government financing, high-level meetings with government officials, policy support, and state-owned enterprise (SOE) engagement. These dimensions were abstracted into four instrumental tactics employed by governments in tripartite cooperation (Fig. 6.1). Through these instruments, participating governments exert direct and/or indirect influence on tripartite cooperation projects, thereby affecting the transaction costs and additional benefits. The following sections provide more details on each of these instruments.

6.1.4 Financial Instrument

Every participating government in tripartite cooperation has the opportunity to finance the projects. Focusing on mega-infrastructure projects, it is observed from Table 6.1 that Chinese official finance authorities fund

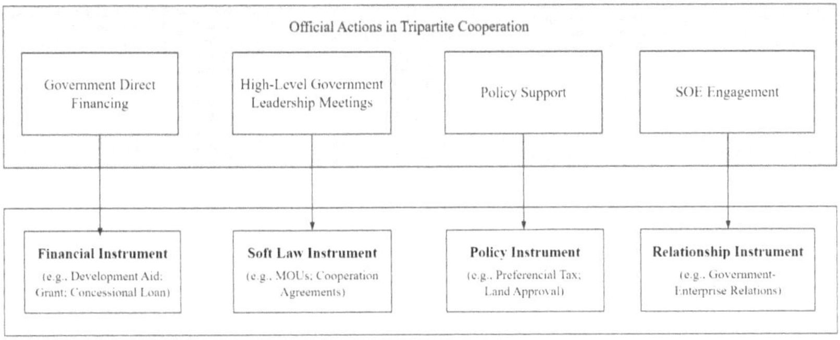

Fig. 6.1 Toolbox for Government in Tripartite Cooperation Projects (Source: Author)

more projects than their counterparts in traditional donor and beneficiary countries.

In the tripartite cooperation projects examined in this research, Chinese development policy financial institutions China Development Bank (CDB) and Export-Import Bank of China (CEXIM) and China Export & Credit Insurance Corporation (Sinosure) play central roles. The Chinese policy banks CDB and CEXIM introduced Government Concessional Loan (GCL) and Preferential Export Buyer's Credit (PBC) to support foreign cooperation.[10] At times, other Chinese state-owned commercial banks, such as the Industrial and Commercial Bank of China, Bank of China, and China Construction Bank, also participate in tripartite cooperation projects. Through GCL and PBC, which feature preferential interest rates (2–3%), generous maturity periods (15–20 years), and grace periods (5–7 years), the Chinese official flow "helps recipient countries undertake manufacturing projects and large and medium-sized infrastructure projects with economic and social benefits, or for the supply of complete plants, machinery and electronic products" (China International Development Cooperation Agency, 2011). These financial institutions align with the Chinese government's 'Going Out' policy and BRI by providing financing facilitates that support Chinese SOEs in their overseas activities. Among the 68 projects examined in this study, the Chinese

[10] The Export-Import Bank of China, "Supporting Foreign Cooperation," The Export-Import Bank of China, accessed February 8, 2024, http://english.eximbank.gov.cn/Business/CreditB/SupportingFC/201810/t20181016_6972.html.

Table 6.1 A part of tripartite projects financing records list (Source: AIDDATA database, https://china.aiddata.org/)

Project	*Finance institutions*	*Project financing*
China-France-Cameroon Kribi deep seaport	China Eximbank	$675.5 million 'mixed credit'—RMB 1 billion government concessional loan (GCL) with 20-year maturity, 7-year grace period, and 2% interest rate; $524.6 million preferential buyer's credit (PBC) with flexible maturity and grace period and 2.7% interest rate, at least 35% is grant[a]
China-France-cote d'lvoire Abidjan port expansion	China Eximbank	US$793.4 million (396.965 billion CFA) preferential buyer's credit (PBC) agreement with 20-year maturity, 7-year grace period, and 2% interest rate[b]
China-Italy-Ethiopia Gilgel gibe III dam	ICBC	US$420.75 million with 14.5-year maturity, 3-year grace period, and 3.067% interest rate[c]
China-Japan-Vietnam Hai Phong thermal power	China Eximbank; JBIC	In 2005 China Eximbank buyer's credit loan US$278 million[d] JBIC loan US$38.7 million; NEXI insurance US$26 million In 2007 JBIC loan US$38 million; Mizuho corporate Bank and Société Générale provided US$21 million in loans, NEXI insurance US$25 million[e]
China-Japan-Kazakhstan Atyrau refinery modernisation project phase 3	China Eximbank; Sinosure; JBIC	China Eximbank provided a US$1.13 billion buyer's credit interest with 13-year maturity, at a rate of 6-month LIBOR plus 4.1% per annum China Eximbank provides a US$199.5 million preferential buyer's credit loan with 13-year maturity and 3% interest rate; Sinosure provided US$1.7 billion of buyer's credit insurance (covering the loan principal and interest)[f] JBIC provides a US$178 million buyer's credit agreement[g]

(*continued*)

Table 6.1 (continued)

Project	*Finance institutions*	*Project financing*
China-Germany-Mozambique Maputo Bay bridge	China Eximbank	China Eximbank provided Mozambique $681.6 million buyer's credit loan with 20-year maturity, 5-year grace period, and 4% interest rate; China Eximbank provided $72.58 million buyer's credit loan to provide supplemental funding[h]
China-Japan-Colombia Concesión Autopista al mar 2	China development Bank; Sumitomo Mitsui banking corporation (SMBC); Financiera de Desarrollo Nacional	CDB and SMBC provided a US$501.7 million senior dollar credit; the complex financing structure also involved currency hedges and approximately COP132.5 billion of EPC performance insurance Colombian state development bank FDN provided COP500.0 billion senior Colombian peso
China-South Korea-Peru Lima metro line 2	China co-financing Fund for Latin America and the Caribbean (CHC)	People's Bank of China via the CHC provided US$50 million loan
China-UK-Bangladesh Karnaphuli tunnel project	China Eximbank	China Eximbank provides RMB 1.95 billion government concessional loan (GCL) with 2% interest rate, 20-year maturity, grace period of 5 years, a 0.2% commitment fee; And a $405.8 million preferential buyer's credit (PBC)[i] Bangladesh government is providing Tk4,461.23 crore
China-Italy-Brazil Ituverava solar plant project	Bank of China; Santander bank	Bank of China and Santander provided a loan to Enel green power Brasil Participações Ltda. ('EGPB'). Sinosure and Enel provided guarantee[j]
China-Portugal-Peru san Gabán III hydro-power project	China development bank	CDB provided $365 million loan with 19-year maturity[k]

(*continued*)

Table 6.1 (continued)

Project	*Finance institutions*	*Project financing*
China-France-cote d'Ivoire-Abidjan port expansion project	China Eximbank	China Eximbank provided US$793.4 million (396.965 billion CFA) preferential buyer's credit (PBC) agreement with 20-year maturity, 7-year grace period, and 2% interest rate
China-France-Russia Yamal LNG	China development Bank; China Eximbank; Sinosure	CDB provided $5.72 billion loans in total. China Eximbank provided $6.537 billion. All interest rates were EURIBOR (EUR −0.141%, RMB -0.138%, April 2016) plus 330 basis points during the pre-completion stage and EURIBOR plus 355 basis points during the post-completion stage, with a 15-year maturity Sinosure provided €730 million loan guarantee
China-France-Senegal wastewater treatment in Dakar Hann Bay	China development Bank; French development agency	CDB and AFD launched tripartite cooperation financing at the first time CDB provided €14.4 million euro (about $14.9 million) AFD provided €83.1 million in grants and loans
China-France-Nigeria Lekki deep seaport	China development bank	CDB provided $630 million loan[l]
China-Germany GAUFF engineering infrastructure projects (160 MW grand Poubara hydroelectric dam construction project)	China Eximbank	China Eximbank provided US$300 million preferential buyer's credit (PBC) with unknown borrowing terms and US$70 million government concessional loan (GCL) agreement with 20-year maturity, 7-year grace period, and 2% interest rate[m] The proceeds from the GCL and the PBC were used to finance approximately $370 million of a $398 million engineering, procurement, and construction (EPC) contract with Sinohydro

(*continued*)

Table 6.1 (continued)

Project	*Finance institutions*	*Project financing*
China-Germany GAUFF engineering infrastructure projects (port Gentil-Omboue road and Booué bridge construction project)	China Eximbank	China Eximbank provided 254.4 billion CFA francs (about US$535 million) preferential buyer's credit (PBC) with unknown borrowing terms and RMB 810 million (or approximately $121 million) government concessional loan (GCL) agreement with 20-year maturity, 7-year grace period, and 2% interest rate[n] The proceeds from the GCL and the PBC were used to finance a $663 million EPC contract with China road and bridge corporation (CRBC)
China-Germany GAUFF engineering infrastructure projects (Caxito-Nzeto highway rehabilitation project)	China Eximbank	China Eximbank provided $429,710,921.10 preferential buyer's credit (PBC) The project was financed through a $2 billion master loan facility agreement (MLFA) that China Eximbank and the Government of Angola signed in September 2007 All subsidiary loans approved through this MLFA carried the same borrowing terms: An interest rate of 7.008% (3-month Libor + a 1.5% margin), a 22 year maturity, and a 5 year grace period The proceeds of the subsidiary loan were used to partially finance $477,456,579 commercial contract with China road and bridge corporation (CRBC)[o]

[a] Export-Import Bank of China, "Preferential Buyer Credit Loan Agreement on Cameroon Kribi Deep Sea Port Project," January 12, 2011, https://www.documentcloud.org/documents/20485594-cmr_2011_171.3

[b] "China Eximbank Provides $793.3 Million Preferential Buyer's Credit for Abidjan Autonomous Port Expansion and Modernization Project," AIDDATA, accessed February 8, 2024, https://china.aiddata.org/projects/30857/

[c] "ICBC Provides $420.75 Million Buyer's Credit Loan for 1870MW Gilgel Gibe III Hydropower Project," AIDDATA, accessed February 8, 2024, https://china.aiddata.org/projects/34447/

[d] "China Eximbank Provides $278 Million Buyer's Credit Loan for 600MW Hai Phong 1 Coal-Fired

(*continued*)

Table 6.1 (continued)

Power Plant Construction Project," AIDDATA, accessed February 8, 2024, https://china.aiddata.org/projects/65736/

[e] "List of Coal Power Plants Funded by JBIC, NEXI and JICA (2003-2019)," Japan Bank for International Cooperation, accessed February 8, 2024, https://sekitan.jp/jbic/wp-content/uploads/2019/07/List-of-Coal-Power-Investments-by-JBIC-NEXI-JICA_0718.pdf

[f] "China Eximbank Provides $199.5 Million Preferential Buyer's Credit for the KazMunayGas Atyrau Refinery Project," AIDDATA, accessed February 8, 2024, https://china.aiddata.org/projects/54798/

[g] "2013 Annual Report of Japan Bank for International Cooperation," *Japan Bank for International Cooperation*, accessed February 8, 2024, https://www.jbic.go.jp/en/ir/image/2013E_00_full.pdf

[h] "China Eximbank Provides $681.6 Million Buyer's Credit Loan for Maputo-Katembe Bridge Construction Project," AIDDATA, accessed February 8, 2024, https://china.aiddata.org/projects/1240/

[i] "China Eximbank Provides RMB 1.95 Billion Government Concessional Loan for Multi Lane Road Tunnel under River Karnaphuli Project," AIDDATA, accessed February 8, 2024, https://china.aiddata.org/projects/55046/

[j] "Bank of China Participates in $111 Million Syndicated Buyer's Credit Loan for 254 MW Ituverava Solar Plant Project," AIDDATA, accessed February 8, 2024, https://china.aiddata.org/projects/64587/

[k] "China Development Bank Provides $365 Million Loan for 209.3 MW San Gabán III Hydroelectric Power Plant Construction Project," AIDDATA, accessed February 8, 2024, https://china.aiddata.org/projects/53087/

[l] CDB, "CDB Assisted the Opening and Operation of Lekki Port in Nigeria," China Development Bank, February 10, 2023, https://www.cdb.com.cn/English/xwzx_715/khdt/202304/t20230410_10744.html

[m] "China Eximbank Provides $70 Million Government Concessional Loan for 160MW Grand Poubara Hydroelectric Dam Construction Project," AIDDATA, accessed February 8, 2024, https://china.aiddata.org/projects/85/

[n] "China Eximbank Provides $534.5 Million Preferential Buyer's Credit for Port Gentil-Omboue Road and Bridge Construction Project," AIDDATA, accessed February 8, 2024, https://china.aiddata.org/projects/73174/

[o] "China Eximbank Provides $429.71 Million Buyer's Credit Loan for Caxito-Nzeto Highway Rehabilitation Project," AIDDATA, accessed February 8, 2024, https://china.aiddata.org/projects/34873/

government frequently finances economic infrastructure projects through concessional loans rather than grants.

In contrast to bilateral cooperation, where financing is offered by the Chinese government but the entire project is not assigned to a Chinese SOE, tripartite cooperation allows China's partner enterprises to share decision-making power regarding equipment procurement, thereby offering more options and optimising project outcomes. For example, Bollore, a French firm, holds shares in this terminal but did not participate in the concession contract signing due to profit motives. Bollore prefers high-tech equipment like the Konecranes Gottwald Model 7 cranes, manufactured in the USA, which feature an electric power system that reduces CO_2 emissions and complies with environmental regulations (Bollore, 2021). This collaborative approach in tripartite cooperation enhances project efficiency and environmental compliance.

Financing instruments yield additional benefits for tripartite cooperation projects. Governments' financial institutions typically use development loans to finance infrastructure projects, reflecting their preference for less risky ventures as debt liability is generally more secure than equity liability. However, some Chinese financing institutions also participate as shareholders in tripartite cooperation projects, which distinguishes this from traditional bilateral project financing activities. In the China-France-Russia Yamal LNG project, for instance, the Chinese Silk Road Fund made a substantial equity investment of €1.087 billion (around 10% share) in the project, alongside the French company Total holding a 20% equity stake. The involvement of firms from advanced economies in equity investments implies more rigorous business due diligence and financial compliance, thereby reducing investment risks. Consequently, Chinese financing institutions are more willing to fund projects as shareholders in tripartite cooperation when additional partners are involved in the financing activities (Tian, 2016; Chu & Zhuang, 2018),[11] indicating tripartite projects can bring about new opportunities that are not available in bilateral cooperation.

Moreover, tripartite cooperation facilitates the collection of more capital due to the endorsement from the three participating governments. In the China-France-Serbia Belgrade Metro project, the project received an €80 million direct loan from the French Treasury and a guarantee of up to €374 million from the French Export Credit Agency. This funding supports the purchase of French equipment, similar to Chinese preferential loans (Ekapija, 2020). Under commercial contracts, Alstom is responsible for 30% of the project, covering electromechanics, trains, rail cars, tracks, and the power system, with financing secured by the French government (Stojkovic, 2021). "I've never seen such favourable conditions as the French have done for Alstom. The Chinese government will secure

[11] Interviewee YP-20211210: "The Yamal LNG project has been financed from multiple sources, and there's been strong interest from both French and Chinese banks. I think that really shows the high quality of the project, and it also sends a very positive signal to other foreign banks about its credibility."

financing with POWERCHINA for the remaining 70% of construction," stated Goran Vesic, the deputy mayor of Belgrade (Rakic, 2020).

In recent years, China has undertaken reforms to its funding structure, collaborating with traditional donors and international development banks to finance some projects through the tripartite cooperation approach. Financial institutions from France and Japan, such as the French development bank, Agence Française de Développement (AFD), and the Japan Bank for International Cooperation (JBIC), employ a comprehensive array of financial tools, including loans, guarantee funds, credit, insurance, and equity capital investments, to stimulate private-sector growth in developing nations within tripartite cooperation projects. For instance, in the China-France-Senegal Wastewater Treatment project in Dakar's Hann Bay, the CDB and AFD co-fund in Senegal to improve local sewage treatment (Zhang, 2022). In the China-Japan-Colombia Concesión Autopista al Mar 2 project, due to the high interest withholding tax on Chinese loans in Colombia, the syndicate of lenders[12] decided to utilise US dollar loans alongside the local Colombian peso to lower financing costs. Given the considerable fluctuation of the Colombian peso at the time, China proposed a locked-in exchange rate to repay the principal and interests, using the local currency to offset the remaining loan. This approach aimed to hedge the risks associated with currency fluctuation and financing costs. Both Japanese Sumitomo Mitsui Banking Corporation (SMBC) and the CDB issued a letter of commitment to finance the project, providing a substantial senior dollar credit of US$501.7 million, along with approximately COP132.5 billion in EPC performance insurance (Paul Hastings LLP, 2019). Japanese economist Hidetoshi Tashiro suggests that financial sector cooperation between Japan and China, combining China's advanced mobile payment technology with Japan's robust financial system, could yield mutual benefits for all parties involved (Qian, 2021; SASAC, 2005).

Beneficiary countries' governments often act as sovereign guarantees/borrowers to secure direct loans from international sponsors, a practice similar to their traditional bilateral cooperation projects. Sometimes, beneficiary countries' governments contribute a minor portion of loans, ranging from 5% to 25%, to fund a project or invest this portion as equity. For instance, in the China-France-Namibia Ombepo Wind Farm project, the

[12] The syndicate of lenders consisting of the Japanese Sumitomo Mitsui Banking Corporation (SMBC), the Colombian development institution Financiera de Desarrollo Nacional, and the Chinese development bank.

Lüderitz Town Council contributed land in exchange for a 5% equity stake in Ombepo Energy, the company undertaking the project. The remaining 95% of equity belonged to the French company InnoSun. The involvement of the beneficiary countries' governments in equity aimed to "diversify the revenue base and benefit from the capital to be generated from [the shareholding] in terms of funding for future developmental or capital projects" (New Era Live, 2018).

In conclusion, China, China's partner countries, and beneficiary countries have their respective financial instruments to support the development of tripartite cooperation projects. Chinese official development banks use concessional loans and preferential credit to finance projects and sometimes fund projects as equity shareholders. While official development banks of partner countries have been less directly involved in tripartite cooperation projects, they are beginning to collaborate with their Chinese counterparts. Beneficiary countries facilitate projects by utilising official direct loans or national wealth funds or issuing sovereign guarantees to support the loans. These collaborative financing approaches enhance the implementation of tripartite projects by sharing costs and increasing financing capacity, thus facilitating the realisation of projects that might have otherwise been challenging to accomplish.

6.1.5 *Soft Law Instrument*

Governments engaged in tripartite cooperation projects, especially between the Chinese government and traditional donor governments, typically foster collaboration through three main methods: signing MOUs or joint statements to express cooperative intentions, confirming tripartite cooperation projects in high-level economic and financial dialogue meetings, and utilising working group meetings and forums to boost the following execution of tripartite cooperation projects. However, these three methods do not involve the signing of legally binding contracts, and they are regarded as soft law instruments, resulting in a lack of enforceability for tripartite cooperation projects.

In Chap. 5, Table 5.1 presents documents signed between the Chinese government and partner countries, predominantly in the form of MOUs. Alam (2022) suggests essential elements for an MOU, encompassing scope and purpose, leadership and team, methods, and commitment. For example, in the MoU between China and Switzerland,[13] the intended scope and purpose of the cooperation are explicitly outlined. The MoU primarily aims to "further deepen the innovative strategic partnership between Switzerland and China, within the field of trade, investment, and finance for projects in third countries along the Belt and Road Initiative." Both governments pledge to support their respective companies in "jointly exploring opportunities and exchanging project information in third-party markets." Regarding official financing cooperation, the MoU expresses a commitment to "encourage commercial and policy banks, insurers, and other financial institutions for infrastructure and trade financing in both countries." A similar statement is reflected in Singapore's MoU, stating that "Singapore and China will work with commercial and policy banks, insurers, and financial institutions to support the financing and project structuring needs of third-party market ventures by companies from both sides."

MOUs, because they lack legal enforceability, do not constitute international agreements that would create obligations under international law. Instead, they often act as preliminary steps towards more formal, binding agreements (Zimmermann & Jauer, 2021). In this context, MOUs can be viewed as a type of 'soft law,' referring to quasi-legal instruments without legally binding force (Druzin, 2016). These elements provide an analytical framework for examining Chinese tripartite MOUs.

High-level leadership meetings and forums constitute another form of soft law instrument. According to Table 5.1, these high-level government meetings witness the endorsement of numerous cooperative agreements on specific projects. Tripartite cooperation often appears to be more of a diplomatic discourse between China and traditional donors. For example, following the introduction of this concept by the Chinese government, reports from the Chinese Ministry of Foreign Affairs and government

[13] "Memorandum of Understanding on Developing Third-Party Market Cooperation between the Federal Department of Finance and the Federal Department of Economic Affairs, Education and Research of the Swiss Confederation and the National Development and Reform Commission of the People's Republic of China," April 29, 2019, https://www.newsd.admin.ch/newsd/message/attachments/56685.pdf

"MOU to Promote Greater Collaboration between Singapore and Chinese Companies in Third-Party Markets along Belt & Road," Ministry of Trade and Industry, Singapore, April 8, 2018, https://www.mti.gov.sg/Newsroom/Press-Releases/2018/04/MOU-to-Promote-Greater-Collaboration-Between-Singapore-and-Chinese-Companies-in-Third-Party-Markets-.

documents consistently mention the continuous promotion of tripartite cooperation after high-level leadership meetings between China and traditional donors.[14] Although these agreements reflect participants' willingness to collaborate in potential tripartite cooperation fields without legal enforcement, these soft law instruments significantly facilitate the progression of tripartite cooperation.

The third soft law instrument facilitating tripartite cooperation involves organising working group meetings and forums, promoting the following process of tripartite cooperation. Following top-level leaders' meetings that finalise MOUs and affirm intentions for tripartite cooperation, lower-level administrative departments begin operationalising these projects. To achieve this, relevant authorities and companies convene working group meetings and forums to advance tripartite cooperation. These meetings and forums are held more frequently to keep tripartite cooperation on track and updated. Based on data collected from reports by the NDRC and the MOC (see Appendix F), after the signing of the MoU for tripartite cooperation between China and Italy in 2018, the Chinese National Development and Reform Commission (NDRC) and the Italian Ministry of Economic Development have hosted bi-annual working group meetings on Sino-Italian tripartite cooperation from September 2018 to January 2023. Typically, these meetings allow participants to review progress; establish consensus on future areas of cooperation, such as oil, chemicals, and finance; and release new lists of key tripartite cooperation projects.

[14] For example, "France and China welcome the results obtained by the 2015 intergovernmental agreement on partnerships in third markets. They are working on monitoring and implementing cooperation projects in third markets that have already been identified. The two governments encourage companies, financial institutions and other players to explore new structural economic cooperation projects in third markets, on the basis of applicable high international standards" in "Joint Statement of the People's Republic of China and the French Republic (中华人民共和国和法兰西共和国联合声明)," The State Council of China, April 7, 2023, https://www.gov.cn/yaowen/2023-04/07/content_5750444.htm.

For example, "Belgium stands ready to become an important gateway for Chinese enterprises to invest in Europe and to work with China to vigorously advance the trilateral cooperation between Belgium, China and Africa and between Europe, China and Africa by making use of their respective advantages, so as to realize mutual benefit and multi-win results" in "Li Keqiang and Prime Minister Charles Michel of Belgium Jointly Meet the Press," Ministry of Foreign Affairs of China, June 29, 2015, https://www.fmprc.gov.cn/mfa_eng/topics_665678/2015zt/lkqcxdsqczgomldrhwbsfblsdfgjxzsfwbfwjjhzyfzzzzb/201507/t20150701_705047.html.

Similarly, France and the UK routinely hold working group meetings with China.

Both the Chinese government and its partner countries' governments employ three soft law instruments to promote tripartite cooperation: signing MOUs or joint statements to express cooperative intentions, confirming tripartite cooperation projects during high-level leadership meetings, and utilising working group meetings and forums to drive the execution of these projects. Through these collaborative approaches, governments aim to enhance tripartite cooperation by fostering more effective communication, coordination, and implementation of tripartite initiatives.

However, due to the lack of enforceability in tripartite cooperation projects, participants may change their intentions and withdraw from cooperation, potentially leading to wasted resources and increased transaction costs from previous negotiations. The existence of these non-binding institutions may also be a distinctive feature of tripartite arrangements, as opposed to bilateral ones, reflecting their role in facilitating initial cooperation without imposing formal legal obligations. It is also important to note that these soft law institutions do not initially involve beneficiary governments.

6.1.6 Policy Instrument

According to the statistics from Chap. 5, Sect. 5.3.2, in tripartite cooperation projects, beneficiary countries' governments employ policy instruments such as signing concession contracts, amending legal terms, and publishing administrative policies to bolster these initiatives. These policy instruments play a crucial role in influencing the transaction costs of tripartite cooperation projects, particularly when beneficiary countries use legal and administrative measures to either facilitate or impede the projects.

Beneficiary countries' authorities often employ the public-private-partnership model to initiate large-scale infrastructure developments, particularly due to their limitations in capital and technology. Since the 1990s, developing countries have extensively used concession contracts to attract private investors for public infrastructure projects (Guasch et al., 2008; Clive, 2003; Grosse, 2005). The concession agreement[15] provides an

[15] As defined by the EU, a concession contract or concession agreement is the agreement signed between public authorities and a private operator for the construction of infrastructure (European Commission, 2016).

outsourcing approach, allowing beneficiary countries to utilise external resources, knowledge, and technologies from foreign partners. In this arrangement, foreign enterprises take on responsibilities for financing, designing, constructing, operating, and maintaining an infrastructure project for a specified period. This approach enables beneficiary countries' authorities to mitigate high risks during the construction and initial operation phases (Sudžuka & Osmanović, 2021). In return, beneficiary countries' governments provide policy support to foreign firms.

This approach, widely used in traditional bilateral cooperation projects, is also extended to tripartite cooperation projects. For example, in the agreement for the China-Myanmar Gas Pipelines Project, Article 5 stipulates that the Myanmar government should provide support to the project. This includes securing pipeline equipment, issuing labour visas, ensuring rights of way, granting land use permits and approvals, providing telecommunication services, offering preferential tax treatment, and addressing other related issues.[16]

While beneficiary countries' governments commonly sign concession contracts with both Chinese participants and their partners in traditional bilateral cooperation projects, they seldom make necessary amendments to their laws. In some cases, beneficiary countries' authorities have modified their laws to facilitate project implementation or, to put it another way, accommodate investor requirements. These amendments typically involve changes in tax incentives and export restrictions. For example, in the China-France-Russia YAMAL LNG project, the Russian government's policy support focused on two critical aspects: tax breaks and the liberalisation of LNG exports. The project benefited from an incentive tax regime, including a zero Mineral Extraction Tax rate for natural gas and gas condensate, zero export duties for LNG and stable gas condensate, and a value-added tax exemption for imported equipment without domestic equivalents in Russia (Yamal LNG, 2014). These tax breaks allowed Novatek to save over $4 billion, promoting the company's growth (Bros & Mitrova, 2016). Regarding LNG export certification, the Russian government amended its export law at the end of 2013, granting the Yamal LNG project independent export rights. Rosneft and Novatek lobbied the

[16] "Cooperation Agreement between the Government of the People's Republic of China and the Government of the Union of Myanmar on the Myanmar-China Oil and Gas Pipelines," March 26, 2009, http://treaty.mfa.gov.cn/tykfiles/20180718/1531876927334.pdf.

Russian government together, aiming to end Gazprom's export monopoly. In mid-2014, Novatek officially acquired the qualification to export natural gas (Tian, 2016). These legislative amendments demonstrate the influential domestic lobbying power in beneficiary countries that can persuade local authorities. In tripartite cooperation involving powerful local partners, they often secure more favourable local conditions for projects.

However, beneficiary countries' governments do not always facilitate tripartite cooperation projects. They also hinder the project process occasionally, leading to increased transaction costs. This hindrance is evident in the China-France-UK Hinkley Point C project, where the UK government suspended construction through official reviews and security processes after the 2016 Brexit government shuffle (Stefanini, 2016). In 2022, CGN also halted contributions to the overruns of the HPC after the UK government excluded the Chinese company from the Sizewell C and Bradwell B nuclear station projects (Pickard et al. 2024). This process will be detailed further in the next chapter.

6.1.7 *Relationship Instrument*

While some tripartite cooperation projects may appear as purely commercial activities, governments often exert influence behind the scenes and manage relationships with enterprises. Nie (2022) identifies four basic types of government-enterprise relations:

1. Government-Enterprise Cooperation, where the government deeply intervenes in the production or commercial activities of enterprises
2. Separation of Government and Enterprise, where the government barely meddles in the business or production activities of companies
3. Government-Enterprise Toxic Relationship, where the government harms enterprises, violating the law
4. Government-Business Collusion, in which the government deeply interferes in the enterprise's production or commercial activities, with both parties benefiting through illegal or illicit means

The different types of relationships between the governments and companies of participant countries can have varying impacts on the outcomes of tripartite cooperation projects.

Although some participant governments do offer supportive policies for enterprises and can influence their activities, the impact on the practical implementation of tripartite cooperation projects remains uncertain. The close cooperation relationship between the government and enterprises can be a double-edged sword. On one hand, state-backed resources can enhance the firm's financing, technological, and risk-resistant capacity in its overseas activities. As evident in the overseas bidding activities of Chinese SOEs, they can secure projects with lower costs in host countries due to support from the Chinese government, which provides benefits such as lower financing costs and reduced resource costs in their home country (Wei et al., 2015; Jin et al., 2022). On the other hand, the close relationship might compromise the independence of the enterprise. Some SOEs, for instance, may have to undertake projects with negative revenues according to government demands, which may align with countries' geopolitical interests (Stone et al., 2021; Lubin, 2023; Fitzgerald & Rui, 2016).

The relationship between governments and enterprises in tripartite cooperation projects often falls between types (1) and (2)—with a level of governmental influence present, but its impact is limited. This dynamic is exemplified in the Japanese context, where the Japan Business Federation (JBF), the largest of three major private-sector-led business associations,[17] plays a pivotal role in fostering collaboration to enhance Japan's and the world's economy. The JBF maintains a close relationship with the Japanese government, evidenced by substantial political donations to the Japanese Liberal Democratic Party. This relationship facilitates a robust exchange of interests, primarily centred around policy and information[18] (Solís, 2021; Yoshimatsu, 1998). For instance, in the first China-Japan tripartite cooperation forum in 2018, over 50 tripartite cooperation projects were signed by the two governments. Before signing tripartite cooperation MOUs and outcome lists, the JBF serves as a liaison between the Japanese government and enterprises. It compiles a list of potential tripartite cooperation projects in collaboration with Chinese enterprises, presenting it to the Japanese government for consideration (He & Yan, 2021).

Nevertheless, the Japanese government cannot compel enterprises to proceed with projects if they choose to withdraw, as Japanese firms possess significant autonomy in their commercial decisions (Fitzgerald & Rui,

[17] The Japan Business Federation (日本経済団体連合会), the Japan Chamber of Commerce and Industry (日本商工会議所), and the Japan Association of Corporate Executives (経済同友会).

[18] Interview A-20220523.

2016). This autonomy is exemplified by the Thailand High-Speed Rail project, which was initially intended as a showcase of China-Japan tripartite cooperation. Although the Japanese company was initially willing to cooperate with China, it eventually withdrew due to commercial considerations, deeming the project unviable (Gao, 2018). Despite potential diplomatic repercussions and costs, Japanese companies carefully evaluated their options and chose to withdraw. This instance underscores not only the considerable autonomy Japanese enterprises have in their business decision-making processes but also the healthy relationship between Japanese enterprises and the Japanese government, which respects their commercial independence.

In some instances, inappropriate government-enterprise relationships, falling under type (3) toxic relationship and potentially intertwining with type (4) collusion relationship, can disrupt project progress and escalate transaction costs. This is exemplified in the China-Italy-Ethiopia Gilgel Gibe III Dam project. Construction contracts were awarded without environmental approval as the Ethiopian government sought loans from Italian financial institutions (BankTrack, 2010). The government proceeded with the project before securing financing, awarding the contract to the Italian company Salini without a tender process. Due to illegal procurement, environmental non-compliance, and negative project impacts, international financing agencies such as The European Investment Bank, JPMorgan Chase, and the Italian export credit agency SACE refused to finance the Gibe III Dam (Gleick, 2012).

Through these four approaches, the government can shape dynamics by fostering collaboration or exerting control as needed. It is important to note that these approaches are not unique to tripartite cooperation projects; they are present in any project where participant companies receive state-backed resources. However, there are typically distinct differences in state-enterprise relations among the three participants in tripartite arrangements, which can influence the nature and outcomes of these collaborations. China, partner countries, and beneficiary countries may each exhibit different forms of government-enterprise relations, which can influence the transaction cost and benefits of these cooperation initiatives.

In summary, this section analyses four instruments employed by participant governments—financial, soft law, policy, and relationship—to influence tripartite cooperation. These instruments, derived from traditional bilateral cooperation activities, are also used in tripartite cooperation for project development. Financial instruments include state development aid, concession loans, and various fiscal support forms from government finance agencies. Soft law instruments entail MOU endorsement during high-level government meetings or working group sessions. Policy instruments involve signing concession contracts, law amendments, and administrative changes. Relationship instruments focus on government-business relations, where the government influences enterprises' activities in tripartite cooperation. Through these instruments, participating governments could influence the transaction costs and additional benefits of tripartite cooperation projects.

6.2 Firm Actions in Tripartite Cooperation Projects

This section predominantly focuses on the roles played by Chinese firms and their partner firms, as the main players in beneficiary countries are local authorities falling under government actions, such as port authorities, highways authorities, and other national departments. The direct participation of enterprises from beneficiary countries in tripartite cooperation projects is often limited. The actions of Chinese firms and their partner firms are classified into three categories: establishing enterprise partnerships before tripartite cooperation, establishing JVs/SPVs in tripartite cooperation, and providing products/services in tripartite cooperation projects. By exploring these roles and actions, this section aims to identify the differences and similarities between tripartite and bilateral cooperation, as well as how these actions influence transaction costs and generate additional benefits in tripartite cooperation projects.

6.2.1 Establishing Partnerships Among Firms

Chinese firms and their partner firms typically employ three approaches to develop partnerships before initiating a tripartite cooperation project. First, similar to the government's use of soft-law instruments, companies sign MOUs to demonstrate their shared aspiration for collaboration. Second, firms sign framework agreements, which outline more detailed terms and conditions for the specific tripartite project, clarifying the specific responsibilities and roles of each participating company and representing a closer partnership. Third, to further reinforce collaborative ties, firms that have already signed a framework agreement may establish a strategic alliance for future project development, enabling them to pool resources and align common interests more effectively.

The first method employed by firms to establish partnerships in tripartite cooperation projects is the signing of a MOU. Chinese firms and their partner firms use MOUs to lay the groundwork for future cooperation. For instance, in the China-Portugal-Brazil São Manoel Hydroelectric Plant Project, the CWE Investment Corporation and EDP Brasil solidified their partnership through an MOU, which served as a guideline for future co-investments (EDP, 2014). Similarly, Shanghai Electric Group and the Spanish energy company Abengoa established an MOU with the Saudi Arabian Power Engineering Company, ACWA Power. With ACWA Power's cooperative willingness, the Chinese and Spanish companies aimed to strengthen their collaborative approach in the Middle East (Shanghai Electric, 2018). These instances underscore how MOUs can effectively foster collaborative initiatives, with companies actively promoting projects and aligning their interests with partners through MOUs. However, the effectiveness of MOUs is often limited, leading to potential resource wastage. For example, while some Chinese companies have mentioned tripartite cooperation plans and signed MOUs with German companies such as Siemens (Siemens, 2019), no confirmed tripartite cooperation projects have materialised by the end of 2023.

Similar to the function of signing MOUs, framework agreements play a crucial role in stipulating the objectives of cooperation. They extend beyond MOUs by further clarifying the responsibilities of participating firms and incorporating specific legal conditions related to construction, equity distribution, obligations, and rights. These agreements establish a structured framework for collaboration, ensuring alignment among all participants. For instance, the framework agreement between NOVATEK and CNPC for the Yamal LNG project stipulated that CNPC would secure a 20% stake in the project and commit to actively support external financing from Chinese financial institutions (NOVATEK, 2013).

The third method companies employ to establish partnerships is the formation of strategic partnerships or alliances. This approach facilitates the sharing of resources and capacities, encouraging the exploration of mature and beneficial opportunities (Gulati, 1995; Wei, 2007). Companies with a successful collaboration history are more inclined to seek additional opportunities in resource sharing and market expansion through strategic partnerships or alliances. Firms often involve other financing mechanisms such as equity exchanges or M&A as a part of strategic partnerships. China

Three Gorges (CTG) exemplifies a company utilising strategic partnerships to facilitate tripartite cooperation with its partner firm. After EDP sold a 21.35% stake to CTG, the executive board of directors at EDP sought to establish a strategic partnership with CTG in global renewable generation projects. This partnership, solidified with a €2bn equity commitment to operating and ready-to-build renewable energy generation projects in 2014 (EDP, 2014), underwent renewal in 2021 through a strategic cooperation agreement. The renewed agreement expanded the cooperation in renewable energy, power grids, downstream business, and technologies (Bai, 2021).

However, merely entering into a strategic partnership agreement may not suffice in establishing a solid relationship and cannot ensure solid projects. CTG and the German company Voith also embarked on a strategic cooperation agreement in the hydropower sector in 2017, with Chinese and German Prime Ministers Li Keqiang and Angela Merkel present. The two firms, having enjoyed a long-standing relationship, previously cooperated on Brazilian hydropower station projects. The strategic cooperation agreement they signed signalled a willingness to extend their collaboration to other hydropower businesses in South America and Africa (SASAC, 2017). However, after these two companies signed a cooperative agreement in 2017, no further steps were taken, and no concrete projects were confirmed.

In summary, enterprises establish partnerships in tripartite cooperation projects through three key approaches. Tripartite cooperation requires additional MOUs and agreements to reduce transaction costs, and these documents would not be necessary for bilateral arrangements. However, since these types of partnerships lack legal enforceability, they primarily serve as preparatory steps for the subsequent implementation of tripartite cooperation. Furthermore, as these agreements are signed between two firms, they focus on developing bilateral partnerships while laying the groundwork for cooperation in the third, beneficiary country's market. This process highlights the additional transaction costs involved in a third partner, which need to be mitigated through these agreements.

6.2.2 *Establishing JVs/SPVs for Tripartite Cooperation Projects*

Enterprises establish JVs or SPVs to reinforce their partnership in tripartite cooperation projects. Out of the 68 tripartite cooperation projects, Chinese firms and their partner firms formed JV/SPVs in 27 instances, with local authorities or firms from beneficiary countries participating in 17 of these 27 projects. This semi-internalised organisational structure is commonly employed by participant enterprises. The JV/SPV, functioning as an independent legal entity, provides a convenient framework for participant companies to arrange their joint bidding and financing activities.

When beneficiary governments issue open tenders, they prefer bidders comprising reputable companies with advanced technology, extensive construction experience, and competitive pricing. In addition, Chinese construction companies may be highly competitive when bidding for a single project, particularly when they possess similar resources and ownership advantages in shared markets (Luo et al., 2013). Therefore, it is a common strategy for bidders to form a consortium/JV/SPV to secure the contracts from beneficiary governments. Through these collaborative structures, participant members can maintain their independence while working together on tripartite cooperation projects. These arrangements serve as short-term collaborative platforms with the common goal of winning bids or securing government contracts (Kenton, 2021; Gordon, 2023). The bidding process can be highly competitive, and on occasions, competing consortiums might be requested to merge to optimise bids by beneficiary governments (GCR, 2017).

Through tripartite cooperation, companies from China, partner countries, and beneficiary nations can pool their resources to jointly bid for such projects. For instance, The Agency for the Development and Promotion of Grand Inga (ADPI) in the beneficiary country asked Spanish and Chinese firms to stop competing and merge to 'optimise' their bids. Subsequently, the Spanish and Chinese companies created a single consortium, worked together, and submitted a joint bid in 2018, securing the financing as the single candidate (GCR, 2018). Similarly, in the case of the China-France-UAE Al Dhafra PV2 solar power plant project, France's EDF and China's Jinko Power formed a consortium and submitted the world's lowest tariff bid for the solar power project (SaudiGulf Projects, 2020). In the Mexico Mayan Railway Project, 15 consortiums competed, including five involving Chinese companies partnering with various firms. Despite the intense competition, a consortium led by Portugal's Mota-Engil, China Communications Construction Company (CCCC), and three Mexican partners ultimately won the contract by offering the most competitive price and was awarded the project.[19]

Equity cooperation is closely tied to the establishment of new JVs or SPVs, where Chinese firms and their partner firms typically distribute shares based on their capital investments in equity. This also ensures an equitable allocation of shareholders' rights and obligations. With each company's voting power directly proportional to its shareholdings, conflicts are mitigated through internal board voting. In cases where consensus cannot be reached, the project may face potential failure (Yan & Warner, 2001; Schuman & Shullman, 2022). A case is the Grand Inga 3 project, where the collaboration between CTG and the Spanish company ACS fell through. In January 2020, ACS announced its withdrawal from the project, as "disagreements over the distribution of shares in the project as the reason for the fall out" (Hollands, 2020). Some infrastructure projects, due to high competition among entities seeking participation, exhibit intricate equity structures. The adoption of a multi-shareholder structure can transform competition into collaboration and, importantly, help mitigate political risks by easing pressure from both international and domestic society (Bergsen et al., 2022).

There are three key additional benefits in establishing JV/SPVs in tripartite cooperation. This strategy is primarily adopted by participant firms to manage risk. Mega-infrastructure projects inherently carry a high degree of risk, and establishing a separate legal entity like a JV or SPV can create a 'firewall' to separate parent companies from potential fluctuations or failures in the project (Tinsley, 2014). Chinese firms and their partner firms are more likely to choose the JV model as their entry strategy when

[19](1) China Railway Construction Corporation cooperated with Constructora Y Edificadora Gia of Mexico City with bid price of $740 m.

(2) China Communications Construction Company cooperated with Portugal's Mota Engil and other three Mexican partners with a bid price of $760 m. Finally, the consortium lowered its price with a price of 15.538 billion pesos (US$630.2 m).

(3) PowerChina cooperated with MM-Mex and GH Maquinaria of Mexico with bid price of $760 m.

(4) China Railway International cooperated with Consorcio De Ingenieros Constructores y Consultores and Grupo Industrial Rubio of Mexico with a bid price of $760 m.

(5) China Gezhouba cooperated with ten Mexican construction and engineering companies with a bid price of $810 m.

GCR, "Chinese, Spanish, Portuguese Giants Join Mexican Companies Bidding for Mayan Rail Contract," Global Construction Review, April 20, 2020, https://www.globalconstructionreview.com/chinese-spanish-and-portuguese-giants-join-slew-me/.

beneficiary countries have a higher degree of uncertainty in their investment environment (Zhang & Wang, 2021). Additionally, tripartite projects, by their nature, involve the sharing of risks as an additional partner joins the project. This additional actor contributes more funding and/or technological support as a stakeholder (Mangano, 2014). For instance, the UK's oil giant BP partnered with Sinopec to establish an SPV in Iraq. This SPV can independently access external financing, thus isolating it from parent firms, which mitigates both BP and Sinopec's exposure to potential geopolitical risks (BP, 2015).

Moreover, this cooperative approach allows participant firms to optimise resource utilisation by improving efficiency, enlarging the economic scale, and leading to potential cost reductions when necessary. By establishing JVs or SPVs, companies have opportunities to pursue greater profits or commercial benefits, despite the higher potential risks involved. In recent years, Chinese companies have increasingly favoured the 'integrated investment, construction, and operation (IICO)' model in their overseas infrastructure investments. This preference stems from the IICO model allowing companies to utilise self-funded equity investments, ensuring decision-making power in a project. This new model finds widespread application in tripartite cooperation projects. The co-invest approach is well received by companies involved in these projects as it facilitates the distribution of risks and benefits in proportion to their shareholding through the establishment of a JV/SPV or engaging in equity cooperation (Nyabiage, 2023). In contrast, the traditional Engineering-Procurement-Construction Plus Financing (EPC+F) approach relies on government funding or debt investment, providing companies with less motivation to utilise this method to influence the project's progress[20] (Zhang, 2023).

Finally, as an independent legal entity, the newly established JV/SPV has the capacity to issue project bonds in the international market, increasing the financing capacity. It can potentially attract capital from both local and international markets to provide financing for tripartite cooperation projects. An example of this is Hydro Global, formed by CTG and EDP

[20] Interviewee O-20230310: "…so when we talk about this sort of project funding, we often refer to something called 'EPC plus,' or sometimes 'EPC+F.' But personally, I think that's a misunderstanding—I've seen this happen for years under the wrong concept. The 'F' stands for finance, which usually comes from banks or the government, so the contractor remains just the EPC contractor and doesn't get to sit in on those early financing discussions. What you really need up front is a solid business plan before moving forward with the project."

to manage hydroelectric projects in South America. In the context of the China-Portugal-Brazil São Manoel Hydroelectric Plant Project, this newly formed firm effectively utilised long-term debt leverage by issuing local bonds (EDP, 2014). Another example is the China-Japan-UAE Sweihan Photovoltaic Independent Power Project, where Japan's Marubeni Corporation and China's JinkoSolar Holding Co., Ltd. issued a $700.8 million green project bond, marking the first such issuance in the MENA region. This bond, listed on Euronext Dublin, refinanced the original senior loan, optimising the capital structure of the project (Marubeni, 2022). In addition, participant firms negotiated with banks for lower interest rates by emphasising that multilateral cooperation with more participants can generate greater benefits. For instance, CHEC, through close cooperation with a French company, demonstrated the project's potential for higher returns and persuaded CEXIM to issue 'mixed credit loans' with the lowest interest rate of 2% for an African project (Atalawei, 2016).

In summary, the establishment of new JVs or SPVs in tripartite cooperation projects serves to mitigate risks, optimise resource utilisation, and enhance financial flexibility. The semi-internalised nature of JVs/SPVs helps limit transaction costs. Typically, enterprises allocate shares in proportion to their capital investments, exemplifying the financial structuring mechanisms used within tripartite projects. These strategies facilitate the effective mobilisation of resources and risk management for participants. However, disagreements over equity distribution can indeed jeopardise projects, leading to increased transaction costs in renegotiation and the search for new potential partners.

6.2.3 *Providing Products/Services in Tripartite Cooperation Projects*

Some firms typically sign legal contracts before assuming roles as co-contractors for EPC projects and offering services and products for the tripartite cooperation projects. Consequently, if participants decide to withdraw from the tripartite cooperation project after entering a legal contract, it may lead to increased transaction costs associated with legal proceedings.

The provision of products and services in tripartite cooperation projects often extends beyond simple outsourcing to involve more complex activities, such as establishing reliable supply chains and providing relevant technical support. For instance, the China Communications Construction Corporation (CCCC) and France's Hima Cement executed a MOU for tripartite cooperation in cement provision. Hima Cement has established a reliable supply chain for Chinese infrastructure construction in African projects (Lafarge, 2017). In another example, within the China-Italy-Lebanon Great Beirut Water Supply Tunnel project, Chinese companies supplied two gripper tunnel boring machines. Paolo Mauri, the Area Manager of the Middle East for CMC di Ravenna, commended the quality and technical assistance provided by CREG, highlighting the value brought by Chinese engineers' involvement (CREG, 2017).

Occasionally, authorities in beneficiary countries may mandate a partner to supervise the project's quality. Partner companies from advanced economies often provide supervision services to assess the quality of Chinese engineering projects. For example, in the China-Germany-Mozambique Maputo Bay Bridge project, the China Roads and Bridges Corporation (CRBC) served as the project's EPC contractor, while the German consultancy firm GAUFF Engineering was responsible for design evaluation, construction supervision, and quality control. Wang Lijun, deputy general manager of CRBC, indicated that "during the negotiation of the contract, CRBC insisted on using Chinese standards for design and construction" (Chen, 2019). However, due to strong European technical influences, the Mozambican government deemed it essential to employ an international supervision team for such an extensive and complex project. As a result, while the bridge was designed according to Chinese standards, it was subjected to examination based on European standards (Yang, 2020). GAUFF Engineering supervised the project's quality and actively contributed to expediting the design, verification, approval, and engineering negotiation processes. They standardised procedures for safety and quality inspections, progress reports, accident investigation reports, and risk management, ensuring the traceability of all project tasks (ENR, 2019).

Overall, enterprises employ three approaches in tripartite cooperation: forming partnerships before engaging in tripartite cooperation, the establishment of consortia/JV/SPV, and providing services and products to the projects. These varied strategies underscore the multifaceted nature of enterprises' involvement and their diverse roles in tripartite cooperation projects, which in turn shape the associated costs and benefits.

6.3 Discussions: Trade-Offs in Tripartite Cooperation

6.3.1 Competition-Cooperation Relationships Between Chinese Firms and their Partner Firms

Chinese and their partner firms may experience significant competition before cooperation. In African countries where Western firms hold a significant advantage in the infrastructure sector, specifically in railways and waterways dominated by European enterprises like Bollore, MSC, and APM, Western companies are reluctant to give up existing interests and revenue. However, in certain regions like South America, Chinese and Western firms tend to cooperate more than compete, driven by their aligned shareholder interests.

The pursuit of business interests is the most important common goal among enterprises participating in tripartite cooperation, as illustrated by the China-Singapore-Guinea Simandou iron ore project. The project manager expressed, "Everyone has their own interests in this project, but everyone is a beneficiary. The success of this project is because of the multiple-win partnership" (Gao, 2018). In this project, Weiqiao Group requires a reliable supply of bauxite resources; Yantai Port Group aims to expand its port cargo sources and construct port terminals abroad; Singapore's Winning International Group, as an integrated shipping group, seeks stable transport cargo to build its brand; UMS, a local motor transport business in Guinea, aims to increase its inland cargo volume (Samb et al., 2023). In this project, the participant companies aim to expand into different business sectors, and they do not have conflicts of interest. Instead, cooperation aligns their interests more closely, benefiting their potential management and operational activities[21] (Winning International Group, 2018).

However, successful and smoothly executed projects like these are rare. In practice, Chinese and Western enterprises often face more competition before cooperation, particularly in African regions. A relevant example can be seen in the China-France-Cameroon Kribi Deep Seaport Project. Cameroon, a country traditionally under French influence, has seen China's influence gradually rising. The Cameroonian government expressed dissatisfaction with the monopoly control exerted by the French

[21] Interview O-20230117.

company Bollore over Cameroon's port terminals (Divine, 2015) and sought to assert authority over its former colonial powers. The entry of Chinese companies into this market disrupted the existing monopoly held by French firms and led to the redistribution of interests.

When the CHEC was awarded a concession contract, French companies attempted to exert pressure on the beneficiary country's government through consultancies and the media. They challenged CHEC's technical and operational capabilities, claiming that the Cameroonian government should not "give such a large project to an incompetent company" (Bone, 2021). Neither Chinese nor French companies were willing to relinquish this profitable opportunity, leading to the formation of a consortium comprising Chinese and French companies to undertake this project jointly.

After a series of negotiations among the Cameroonian government, Chinese, and French enterprises, they reached a cooperation agreement that allocated different project responsibilities for operation and distributed the interests accordingly. CHEC's involvement in the Kribi port project resulted in an alteration of the equity structure, fostering increased local participation (Mbodiam, 2018). As a compromise to secure a stake in the Kribi terminal, the Cameroonian government appointed the French group Catram/Socotec/Grand Port Maritime du Havre as advisors during the development phases of the Kribi project[22] (Nkot & Amougou, 2021).

In some cases, Chinese and Western enterprises tend to cooperate more than compete. For example, in South America, Portuguese and Spanish companies had a significant presence in this market. However, the 2008 economic crisis severely impacted these two countries, prompting them to seek cooperative partners for their existing projects. A common approach was to sell minority stakes to other enterprises, such as Chinese enterprises, in exchange for cash liquidity (Seaman et al., 2017). From the reports, there are no significant challenges that have emerged from these partnerships to date, mainly because of the consistency of shareholder interests. However, potential risks and conflicts may arise in the future (Kratz et al., 2021). Even with the establishment of strong alliances between Chinese firms and their partner firms, and the discussion of all opportunities in JV's Partnership Committees, divergent investment criteria and financial capabilities may induce tensions. Chinese enterprises, pursuing aggressive investment opportunities independently, might inadvertently foster a competitive relationship with their partner

[22] Interview O-20230508.

enterprises in the future (García-Herrero & Xu, 2017), reflecting the dynamic relationship between enterprises in tripartite cooperation.

In addition, the dynamics in tripartite cooperation projects are intricate. In many situations, Chinese firms do not consistently play roles in the low-end value chain, limiting their participation in construction activities within projects. Through tripartite cooperation, China aims to acquire advanced management skills and know-how from partner firms in advanced economies and eventually transition to value chains with higher profits. Disputes often arise between Chinese firms and their partner firms regarding the selection of construction standards for projects, as this decision influences the revenue generated through equipment procurement from either China or its partner countries (Rotberg, 2008; Woods, 2008).

While competition between Chinese firms and their partner firms is prominent in some contexts, such as in African countries, tripartite cooperation emerges as a compromise solution as firms can achieve a balance between competition and cooperation. This approach is obvious when African countries can obtain 'unconditional' loans from China. Consequently, French companies, among others, have been compelled to relinquish their share and renegotiate with African countries and China.

6.3.2 *Good Performance and Sudden External Risks*

While aligned objectives and active engagement of participants can sometimes mitigate transaction costs, tripartite cooperation may still result in higher transaction costs due to exposure to risky international contexts. In extreme external situations, such as war and sanctions, such scenarios may turn a successful project with additional benefits into one burdened with increased costs. The status of one party can cause the suspension or cessation of cooperation, forcing the other two parties to renegotiate or search for a new partner, thereby increasing transaction costs.

The Yamal project serves as an example of how external risks can impact a well-performing tripartite cooperation project. Initially, there were limited direct conflicts among China, France, and Russia, allowing the participants to integrate their respective targets through tripartite cooperation. Their targets were not inherently contradictory: China and France aimed to secure gas resources, with France also seeking commercial interests, while Russia required capital, equipment, and technology for developing the gas field, as well as opportunities to export gas resources to the international market. The participants also viewed this project as a chance to develop their national plan and enhance international relationships.

From the Chinese perspective, Zhou Jiping, Chairman of the Board of Directors of CNPC, highlighted that the Yamal LNG project agreement with NOVATEK ensures a reliable, long-term LNG supply for China. Wang Yanzhi, President of the Silk Road Fund (SRF), expressed SRF's interest in becoming a shareholder to expedite the project's external financing and facilitate the development of Chinese-Russian cooperation in the energy sector (NOVATEK, 2015).

From the French perspective, French energy corporations have established a significant footprint in the Russian energy sector since the early 1990s. Through investing in Russia, Total strengthened its ability to operate within Europe (Bros & Mitrova, 2016). France's motivation was to counterbalance the Russian-German energy alliance, particularly regarding the Nord Stream gas pipeline projects, which were destroyed in 2022 (Adomaitis & Ahlander, 2024). To some extent, both France and China aimed to enhance their energy security through cooperation with Russia.

From the Russian perspective, Leonid V. Mikhelson, Chairman of the Management Board of OAO NOVATEK, conveyed that long-term gas supply agreements from the Yamal Peninsula to China would foster mutually beneficial cooperation and enhance the overall Russia-China relationship. This project aligned with the Russian government's 'The Long-term Programme for the Development of Liquefied Natural Gas Production' (Kardaś, 2021; The Russian Government, 2021), trying to expand Russia's presence in the global LNG market and attract capital from emerging economies with rising LNG demand, such as China and India, as well as from major global LNG companies such as Total and Shell. Through LNG projects, Russia could also develop industrial bases, the Sabetta seaport, the Sabetta International Airport, and the Arctic route (NOVATEK, 2013). By engaging in tripartite cooperation with China and France, Russia could use the resources from both Sinopec and Total, acquiring foreign capital and technological support to accelerate its development goals and improve its overall infrastructure capabilities.

During the construction and operation phases, participants actively engaged in the Yamal project. As previously discussed, tripartite cooperation generated additional benefits. As more parties were involved, Chinese state policy banks funded the project with more financial supportive tools, including concessional loans, loan guarantees, and equity investments. The Russian government amended tax policies and export laws to facilitate project development. Participant companies signed framework agreements to clarify equity distribution, obligations, and rights, ensuring a clear understanding among all parties involved.

The YAMAL project was operating smoothly until the Russian invasion of Ukraine in 2022. Subsequently, the French company Total found itself in a dilemma. If it chose to remain in the YAMAL project, it would face international criticism for providing financial support to Russia. Conversely, if Total decided to divest its share in the YAMAL project, it would imply that Russia retained Total's previous investments without repayment, conflicting with EU sanctions. Therefore, TotalEnergies still holds a 19.4% stake in the company Novatek but recorded an impairment of $3.7 billion in the company's accounts for the 4th quarter of 2022 (TotalEnergies, 2022b). In 2024, it faced a lawsuit from the French senate for the company still keep the share in the Russian gas project (Hernandez, 2024a, 2024b).

Therefore, a well-performing project with additional benefits can become burdened with increased transaction costs due to the impact of risky external factors. Under these circumstances, tripartite cooperation has two sides. For China and Russia, the absence of two directors representing Total on the board of directors led to operational and financial challenges that could not be promptly addressed (TotalEnergies, 2022a), resulting in increased transaction costs for the YAMAL project and Arctic II project. On the other hand, if Russia did not cooperate with China, it might confront even more severe problems in these projects after the disinvestment of the French company. China could still purchase gas and make cash payments to Russia. Participants need to balance the additional benefits brought by the synergised resources in tripartite cooperation with the potential risks associated with the withdrawal of one party.

6.4 Concluding Remarks

I identified various determinants from previous literature, primarily based on theories and practices of bilateral cooperation. For example, determinants include China's promotion of its 'Going Out' policy and the BRI and beneficiary countries' focus on stimulating local economic growth and employment, similar to traditional bilateral investment cooperation. From my empirical research in this chapter, I found that different participants in tripartite cooperation projects exhibit distinct motivations (See Fig. 6.2).

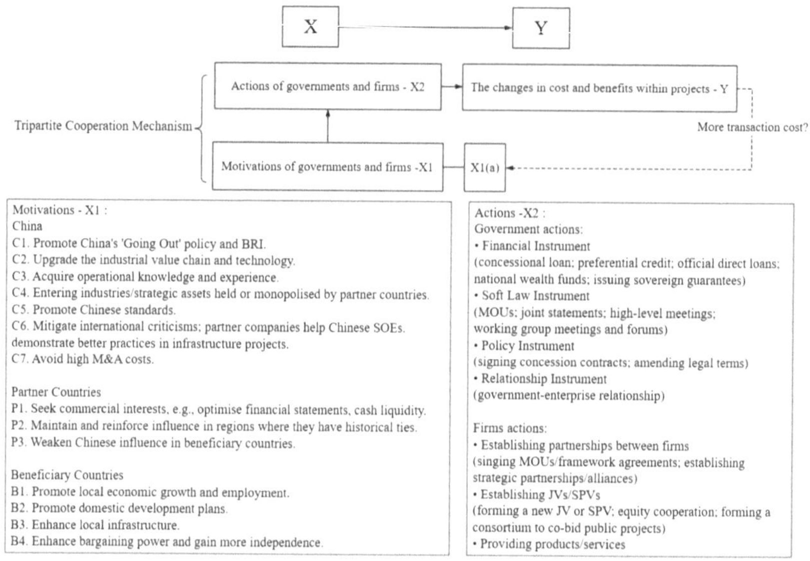

Fig. 6.2 Summary of motivations and actions in tripartite cooperation from empirical research (Source: Author)

For China, tripartite cooperation enhances its global reputation and strengthens international relationships. China's partner countries leverage tripartite cooperation to gain insights into Chinese foreign aid and investment strategies, reinforce their influence in previously colonised regions, and increase their sway over China's foreign policies. Beneficiary countries view tripartite cooperation as an opportunity to diversify their options, benefiting from the involvement of two providers, which offers additional financial and technological guarantees that stabilise project implementation. While specific determinants may differ, the desire to align national strategies and seize opportunities for increased power and influence through tripartite cooperation is a common view among participating countries.

As for the participant firms, empirical studies in this chapter reveal that Chinese companies can access new markets and secure control over strategic assets held by Western firms through tripartite cooperation. Furthermore, tripartite cooperation is another avenue through which Chinese companies can upgrade their industrial value chain and technological capabilities and acquire valuable know-how and operational experience, helping them overcome their latecomer disadvantages. In turn, China's partner companies seek commercial interests, such as optimising financial statements and enhancing cash liquidity. Additionally, Western firms aim to sustain or protect their dominant markets in the beneficiary countries at a lower cost.

Countries and firms continue to prefer the tripartite cooperation model over other types of cooperation, when they see it as an opportunity to redistribute interests, especially for China and beneficiary countries. Some partner countries, such as France, often form intricate cooperative-competitive relationships with China during the cooperation process. They regard tripartite cooperation as an opportunity to slow down this restructuring. Despite additional transaction costs arising from complex relationships and differing approaches to project implementation, participant countries still use tripartite cooperation to expand their influence within this new cooperative framework. Additionally, tripartite cooperation provides beneficiary countries with an opportunity to gain more control and bargaining power over their domestic projects, further enhancing their influence and decision-making authority. This cooperation model can optimise project outcomes by exploiting multiple sources of funding and expertise.

Notably, most interviewees perceived increased transaction costs associated with negotiating and coordinating tripartite cooperation actions. The following chapter explores the practical implementation of tripartite cooperation through case studies.

References

Adeleye, A. (2018, April 16). The CMA CGM Group and Lekki Port LFTZ Enterprise sign a Memorandum of Agreement to operate Lekki Port's future container terminal (Nigeria). *Lekkiport*. https://lekkiport.com/cma-cgm-group-lekki-port-lftz-enterprise-sign-memorandum-agreement-operate-lekki-ports-future-container-terminal-nigeria/

Adomaitis, N., & Ahlander, J. (2024, February 7). Nord Stream: What's Known about the Mystery Pipeline Explosions? *Reuters*. https://www.reuters.com/world/europe/qa-what-is-known-about-nord-stream-gas-pipeline-explosions-2023-09-26/

Alam, M., Getchius, T. S., Schünemann, H., Amer, Y. S., Bak, A., Fatheree, L. A., Ginex, P., Jakhmola, P., Marsden, G. L., McFarlane, E., Meremikwu, M.,

Taske, N., Temple-Smolkin, R. L., Ventura, C., Burgers, J., Bradfield, L., O'Brien, M. D., Einhaus, K., Kopp, I. B., & Munn, Z. (2022). A Memorandum of Understanding has Facilitated Guideline Development Involving Collaborating Groups. *Journal of Clinical Epidemiology, 144*, 8–15. https://doi.org/10.1016/j.jclinepi.2021.12.022

An, B., & Zhang, Y. (2019). PetroChina and Myanmar Ministry of Energy Sign Rights and Obligations Agreement for China Myanmar Crude Oil Pipeline. https://www.gov.cn/jrzg/2009-12/21/content_1492737.htm

Atalawei, M. (2016, February). Kribi Deepwater Port in Cameroon. *Constructionreview*. https://constructionreviewonline.com/news/phase-2-construction-of-deep-sea-port-in-cameroon-approved/

Austin, G. (2010). African Economic Development and Colonial Legacies. *Revue Internationale de Politique de Développement, 1*(1), 11–32. https://doi.org/10.4000/poldev.78

Bai, B. (2021, December 15). Three Gorges Group and Portuguese Electric Power Company Sign a New Strategic Agreement: Launching Renewable Energy Cooperation. *Beijing Daily*. https://ie.bjd.com.cn/a/202112/15/AP61b9b618e4b0d5b7f3634cd0.html

BankTrack. (2010, September 17). Chinese Loan Underwrites Gibe 3 dam Destruction. https://www.banktrack.org/news/chinese_loan_underwrites_gibe_3_dam_destruction

Bergsen, P., Froggatt, A., Nouwens, V., & Pantucci, R. (2022). Briefing Paper Europe Programme Environment and Society Programme China and the Transatlantic Relationship Obstacles to Deeper European-US cooperation. https://www.chathamhouse.org/sites/default/files/2022-06/2022-06-16-china-transatlantic-relationship-bergsen-et-al_0.pdf

Bollore. (2021). Two Mobile Port Cranes for the Port of Tincan in Nigeria. https://www.bollore-ports.com/en/media/press-releases/pour-cacher-les-ccp/two-mobile-port-cranes-for-the-port-of-tincan-in-nigeria

Bone, R. M. (2021). China's Role in Cameroon's Risk of Debt Distress. Thediplomat.com. https://thediplomat.com/2021/06/chinas-role-in-cameroons-risk-of-debt-distress/

BP. (2015). BP and Sinopec Set Up Joint Venture Marine Bunkering Business. BP Global. https://www.bp.com/en/global/corporate/news-and-insights/press-releases/bp-and-sinopec-set-up-joint-venture-marine-bunkering-business.html

Bräutigam, D. (2011). Aid "With Chinese Characteristics": Chinese Foreign Aid and Development Finance Meet the OECD-DAC Aid Regime. *Journal of International Development, 23*(5), 752–764. https://doi.org/10.1002/jid.1798

Bros, A., & Mitrova, T. A. (2016). *Yamal LNG: an Economic Project Under Political Pressure*. Foundation for Strategic Research. https://www.frstrategie.

org/en/publications/notes/yamal-lng-economic-project-under-political-pressure-2016

Carothers, T. (2008). Democracy Assistance: Political vs. Developmental? *Journal of Democracy, 20*(1), 5–19. https://doi.org/10.1353/jod.0.0047

Chen, H., & Wu, B. (2020). Basic Conditions, Challenges and Countermeasures of China-Germany Third-Party Market Cooperation in Africa. *Intertrade, 11*, 45–53. https://doi.org/10.14114/j.cnki.itrade.2020.11.007

Chen, X. (2017, June 30). Exploring the Mystery of Restarting the China Myanmar Pipeline that has been on Hold for 2 years. https://www.china5e.com/news/news-993536-1.html

Chen, Y. (2019, April 28). Bridge of Dreams Brings Two Halves Together. Www.chinadaily.com.cn. https://www.chinadaily.com.cn/a/201904/28/WS5cc4ec06a3104842260b8cd8.html

China International Development Cooperation Agency. (2011, April). China's Foreign Aid White Paper. *Information Office of the State Council the People's Republic of China*. http://www.scio.gov.cn/zfbps/ndhf/2011n/202207/t20220704_130061.html

Chu, Z., & Zhuang, H. (Eds.). (2018). Analyzing the New Model of International Oil and Gas Cooperation from the Successful Operation of the Yamal Project. http://energy.people.com.cn/n1/2018/0227/c71661-29836790.html

Clercq, G. D. (2015, June 18). Portugal's EDP Springboard for China Three Gorges Investment Abroad. Reuters. https://www.reuters.com/article/us-edp-china-three-gorges-idUSKBN0OY1HU20150618

Clive, H. (2003). Private Participation in Infrastructure in Developing Countries. In World Bank Working Papers. The World Bank. https://doi.org/10.1596/0-8213-5512-0

Coalición Regional. (2016, March 1). Chinese Dam Builder Eyeing Major Amazon Mega-Dam Contract. https://www.coalicionregional.net/chinese-dam-builder-eyeing-major-amazon-mega-dam-contract/

CREG. (2017, May 5). China Railway Engineering Equipment Group Co—CREG Gripper TBM LEA First Breakthrough in Lebanon. *China Railway Engineering Equipment Group*. http://en.crectbm.com/detail/6238.html

Divine, N. (2015, July 31). Kribi port's promises on hold. *African Business*. https://african.business/2015/07/trade-investment/kribi-ports-promises-on-hold/

Dowsett, K. (2019). Clifford Chance Advises on Colombia's First Private Investment Made by a Chinese Construction Company in a 4G Toll Road Project. Clifford Chance. https://www.cliffordchance.com/news/news/2019/08/clifford-chance-advises-on-colombia-s-first-private-investment-m.html

Druzin, B. H. (2016). Why does Soft Law have any Power Anyway? *Asian Journal of International Law, 7*, 1–18. https://doi.org/10.1017/S2044251316000229

EDP. (2011, December 22). EDP and China Three Gorges Establish Strategic Partnership | EDP Renováveis. Energias de Portugal, S.A. https://www.edpr.com/es/edp-and-china-three-gorges-establish-strategic-partnership
EDP. (2014, February 7). CTG Group Enters Partnership with EDP Brasil for Construction of Hydro Power Plant São Manoel. *Energias de Portugal, S.A.* https://www.edp.com/en/ctg-group-enters-partnership-edp-brasil-construction-hydro-power-plant-sao-manoel
EDP. (2022, July 29). Sell of 50% Stake in Hydro Global to CTG. Energias de Portugal, S.A. https://www.edp.com/en/news/2022/07/29/sell-50-stake-hydro-global-ctg
Ekapija. (2020, October 5). BG Subway to be Jointly Built by Alstom and POWERCHINA—French Company in Charge of Electromechanics, *Chinese Company to do Construction Works.* https://www.ekapija.com/en/news/3027706/bg-subway-to-be-jointly-built-by-alstom-and-powerchina-french-company
ENR. (2019, September 25). Award of Merit, Airport/Port: Maputo Bridge and Link Roads Project. *Engineering News-Record.* https://www.enr.com/articles/47608-award-of-merit-airportport-maputo-bridge-and-link-roads-project
EU. (2023). African Union: The African Political Integration Process and its Impact on EU-AU Relations in the Field of Foreign and Security Policy. STUDY Requested by the AFET Committee. https://www.europarl.europa.eu/RegData/etudes/STUD/2023/702587/EXPO_STU(2023)702587_EN.pdf
European Commission. (2016). Concession Contracts. Single-Market-Economy. ec.europa.eu. https://single-market-economy.ec.europa.eu/single-market/public-procurement/legal-rules-and-implementation/concession-contracts_en
Fan, J., Zhao, J., Hu, H., & Zhang, P. (2016). Research on Strategic Shipping Development in China. *Journal of Shipping and Ocean Engineering, 6*(4), 255–260. https://doi.org/10.17265/2159-5879/2016.04.007
Fitzgerald, R., & Rui, H. (2016). Whose Fall and Whose Rise? Lessons of Japanese MNCs for Chinese and Emerging Economy MNCs. *Asia Pacific Business Review, 22*(4), 534–566. https://doi.org/10.1080/13602381.2016.1168624
Gao, Q. (2018, December 14). The Disappearance of Thailand's High-Speed Rail Project in China Japan Third Country Cooperation.(中日第三国合作中消失的泰国高铁项目). NIKKEI. https://cn.nikkei.com/columnviewpoint/column/33518-2018-12-14-02-54-16.html
García-Herrero, A., & Xu, J. (2017). How to Handle State-Owned Enterprises in EU-China Investment Talks. https://www.bruegel.org/sites/default/files/wp-content/uploads/2017/06/PC-18-2017_2.pdf

GCR. (2017, June 14). Consortiums Bidding for Huge Inga 3 dam Asked to Merge. *Global Construction Review*. https://www.globalconstructionreview.com/consortiums-bidding-huge-i7ga-3-da7m-as7ked/

GCR. (2018, June 14). Work on Congo's $14bn Inga 3 Dam "to Start this year." *Global Construction Review*. https://www.globalconstructionreview.com/work-congos-14bn-inga-3-dam-start-year/

Gleick, P. H. (2012). China Dams. In *The World's Water Volume 7 the Biennial Report on Freshwater Resources* (pp. 127–142). Island Press. https://doi.org/10.5822/978-1-59726-228-6_6

Gordon, J. (2023, September 10). What is a Consortium? The Business Professor, LLC. https://thebusinessprofessor.com/en_US/business-management-amp-operations-strategy-entrepreneurship-amp-innovation/consortium-definition

Grosse, R. (Ed.). (2005). *International Business and Government Relations in the 21stCentury*. Cambridge University Press. https://doi.org/10.1017/cbo9780511488597

Guasch, J. L., Laffont, J.-J., & Straub, S. (2008). Renegotiation of Concession Contracts in Latin America. *International Journal of Industrial Organization, 26*(2), 421–442. https://doi.org/10.1016/j.ijindorg.2007.05.003

Gulati, R. (1995). Social Structure and Alliance Formation Patterns: A Longitudinal Analysis. *Administrative Science Quarterly, 40*(4), 619–652. https://doi.org/10.2307/2393756

Harper, J. (2022, February 7). China France Cooperation Promotes Infrastructure Projects in Asia, Africa, and Eastern Europe. *Deutsche Welle*. https://p.dw.com/p/47bRZ

Harrar, J. (2019, November 5). Autopista al Mar 2's $658 Million Financing - Lawyer Monthly. *Lawyer-Monthly*. https://www.lawyer-monthly.com/2019/11/autopista-al-mar-2s-658-million-financing/

He, P., & Yan, Y. (2021). Japan's Third Party Market Cooperation in Africa: Models, Characteristics, and Inspirations. *Fudan Public Administration Review, 02*, 1–25. http://www.jsc.fudan.edu.cn/view.php?id=1596

Hernandez, A. (2024a, April 26). TotalEnergies Chief Calls Potential EU Sanctions on Russian LNG a Financial Boon. Reuters. https://www.reuters.com/business/energy/totalenergies-chief-calls-potential-eu-sanctions-russian-lng-financial-boon-2024-04-26/

Hernandez, A. (2024b, June 19). French Senate Urges Government to Buy "Golden Share" in TotalEnergies. Reuters. https://www.reuters.com/world/europe/french-senate-urges-government-buy-golden-share-totalenergies-2024-06-19/

Hollands, C. (2020, August 14). German Investors Interested in Funding DRC's Inga III Dam. *Energy Capital Power*. https://energycapitalpower.com/german-investors-interested-in-funding-drcs-inga-iii-dam/

Hui, X., & Han, W. (2021). Third Party Market Cooperation Between China and Japan: Opportunities, Challenges, and Response Strategies. *India Ocean Economic and Political Review, 45*(3), 38–58, 152–153.

Hydro Review. (2010, May 17). Ethiopia, China Sign Agreement for Gibe III Hydro Project Construction. https://www.hydroreview.com/world-regions/ethiopia-china-sign/#gref

Jedwab, R., & Moradi, A. (2016). The Permanent Effects of Transportation Revolutions in Poor Countries: Evidence from Africa. *Review of Economics and Statistics, 98*(2), 268–284. https://doi.org/10.1162/rest_a_00540

Jin, R. (2021). Research on the Superposition Effect of China-Japan Third-Party Market Cooperation in the New Era. *Japanese Studies, 06*, 67–88.

Jin, X., Xu, L., Xin, Y., & Adhikari, A. (2022). Political Governance in China's State-Owned Enterprises. *China Journal of Accounting Research, 15*(2), 100236. https://doi.org/10.1016/j.cjar.2022.100236

Jing, T. (2022). Third Party Market Cooperation: A Win-Win Model of 1+1+1>3. China Pictorial. http://www.rmhb.com.cn/zt/ydyl/202209/t20220920_800307171.html

Joubin-Bret, A., & Knoerich, J. (2010). Investor-State Disputes: Prevention and Alternatives to Arbitration. UNCTAD Series on International Investment Policies for Development. https://unctad.org/system/files/official-document/diaeia200911_en.pdf

Kardaś, S. (2021, May 17). Great Ambitions: Russia Expands on the LNG Market. OSW Centre for Eastern Studies. https://www.osw.waw.pl/en/publikacje/osw-commentary/2021-05-17/great-ambitions-russia-expands-lng-market

Kenton, W. (2021). Why Consortiums Matter. Investopedia. https://www.investopedia.com/terms/c/consortium.asp

Kratz, A., Zenglein, M., & Sebastian, G. (2021). Chinese FDI in Europe 2020 Update Investment Falls to 10-Year Low in an Economically and Politically Challenging Year. https://rhg.com/wp-content/uploads/2021/06/MERICSRhodium-GroupCOFDIUpdate2021.pdf

Lafarge. (2017, June 12). Hima Cement and CCCC sign MOU for Supply of Cement. https://www.lafarge.co.ug/hima_cement_and_cccc_sign_mou_for_supply_of_cement

Li, Y. (2010). China Myanmar Oil and Gas Energy Cooperation Still Needs to be Deepened. Chinanews. https://www.chinanews.com.cn/ny/news/2010/06-23/2357550.shtml

Liang, H., & Cao, X. (2019, April 19). Third Party Market Cooperation is a "Timely Rain". People.com. http://opinion.people.com.cn/n1/2019/0409/c1003-31018678.html

Lin, C. (2011). China's New Silk Road to the Mediterranean: The Eurasian Land Bridge and Return of Admiral Zheng He. ISPSW Strategy Series. https://www.files.ethz.ch/isn/133405/165_Lin.pdf

Lubin, D. (2023). Collapsing Foreign Direct Investment Might not be all Bad for China's Economy. Chathamhouse. https://www.chathamhouse.org/2023/12/collapsing-foreign-direct-investment-might-not-be-all-bad-chinas-economy

Luo, Y., & Chen, Z. (2021). Challenges and Countermeasures of Chinese Engineering Contracting Enterprises Participating in Third-party Market Cooperation. *International Project Contracting & Labour, 12*, 54–56.

Luo, Y., Rui, H., & Maksimov, V. (2013). Tales of Rivals: Inter-Chinese Attacks in International Competition. *Organizational Dynamics, 42*(2), 156–166. https://doi.org/10.1016/j.orgdyn.2013.03.009

Luo, Y., & Tung, R. L. (2018). A General Theory of Springboard MNEs. *Journal of International Business Studies, 49*(2), 129–152. https://doi.org/10.1057/s41267-017-0114-8

Ma, X. (2017, August 7). China Myanmar Oil and Gas Pipeline (Part 2) a "Going Global" Project that Combines Strategic and Exemplary Significance. *China Pictorial.* http://www.rmhb.com.cn/zt/ydyl/201708/t20170807_800101870.html

Mangano, G. (2014). Risks in Project Finance Initiatives: Current Trends and Future Directions. PhD Thesis. https://doi.org/10.6092/polito/porto/2572574

Marubeni. (2022, January 24). Issuance of Green Project Bond for Sweihan Photovoltaic Independent Power Project. https://www.marubeni.com/en/news/2022/release/00010.html

Mbodiam, B. R. (2018). Cameroon: Kribi deepwater Port has Finally Been Commissioned. Business in Cameroon. https://www.businessincameroon.com/transport/0503-7843-cameroon-kribi-deepwater-port-has-finally-been-commissioned

Men, H., & Yu, Q. (2020). Third Party Market Cooperation: Theoretical Structure, Historical Evolution and China's Path. *Journal of Contemporary Asia-Pacific Studie, 6*, 4–40. https://spsir.tongji.edu.cn/e6/59/c18787a190041/page.htm

Mills, G., & Nwokolo, M.-N. (2022). Africa's External Relations: Reinventing and Pursuing New Partnerships. Brookings. https://www.brookings.edu/articles/africas-external-relations-reinventing-and-pursuing-new-partnerships/

Moszynski, P. (2011, March 7). Ethiopia's Controversial Dam Project. *The Guardian.* https://www.theguardian.com/global-development/poverty-matters/2011/mar/07/ethiopia-controversial-dam-criticism-communities

Mureithi, C. (2022, March 3). Is Uganda's Entebbe airport at risk of seizure by China? *QUARTZ.* https://qz.com/africa/2136934/will-china-take-over-ugandas-entebbe-airport/

New Era Live. (2018, May 2). N$180 Million Wind Farm Commissioned at Lüderitz. https://neweralive.na/posts/n180-million-wind-farm-commissioned-at-luderitz

Nie, Z. (2022, August 8). Multi-Party Cooperation Supports the "Bridge of Dreams". *Xinhua Agency.* http://lw.news.cn/2022-08/08/c_1310650563.htm

Nkot, F., & Amougou, G. (2021, June 3). Cameroon's Kribi Deep Seaport Construction Project: Between State Ownership and Tendencies of Extraversion. *Brill.com; Brill.* https://brill.com/downloadpdf/book/9789004465275/BP000017.xml

NOVATEK. (2013, June 21). NOVATEK Concludes Framework Agreement on CNPC's Entrance into Yamal LNG. https://www.novatek.ru/en/investors/events/?id_4=756

NOVATEK. (2015, September 3). NOVATEK and the Silk Road Fund Conclude Framework Agreement on Acquisition of Stake in Yamal LNG. https://www.novatek.ru/en/investors/events/?id_4=984

NPA. (2016). Home. Nigerian Ports Authority. https://nigerianports.gov.ng/

Nyabiage, J. (2023, March 3). Why Chinese Players are Taking Private Stakes in Africa's New Megaprojects. *South China Morning Post.* https://www.scmp.com/news/china/diplomacy/article/3212071/new-megaprojects-africa-show-chinese-finance-skews-commercial-market-amid-beijings-lending-slowdown

Paul Hastings LLP. (2019, August 1). Autopista al Mar 2 Secures $652 Million, Dual-Tranche, Dual Currency Project Financing. https://www.paulhastings.com/news/news-autopista-al-mar-2-secures-652-million-dual-tranche-dual-currency-project-financing

Pham, J. P. (2017). Germany's "Marshall Plan" for Africa. New Atlanticist. https://www.atlanticcouncil.org/blogs/new-atlanticist/germany-s-marshall-plan-for-africa/

Pickard, J., Parker, G., & White, S. (2024, January 31). Paris seeks UK loan guarantee after Hinkley Point nuclear plant costs soar. Financail Times. https://www.ft.com/content/c1e3bd19-763b-4ea1-b188-d2872cc36bb8?emailId=2866caaf-e0ad-4386-994f-f0fc5bbebdf1&segmentId=22011ee7-8%E2%80%A6

Qi, H., & Yang, M. (2017). Record of PetroChina's Participation in the Construction of the China Myanmar Oil and Gas Pipeline Project. http://www.ce.cn/xwzx/gnsz/gdxw/201706/06/t20170606_23445750.shtml

Qian, Z. (2021, December 3). The Prospect of Cooperation in the Third-Party Market Between China and Japan is Broad. *China Internet Information Center.* http://home.china.com.cn/txt/2021-12/03/content_41811360.htm

Qu, J. (2017, May 3). The China Myanmar Oil and Gas Pipeline Benefits "Four Countries and Six Parties". *Sciencenet.* https://news.sciencenet.cn/htmlnews/2017/5/375219.shtm

Rakic, S. (2020, October 6). Chinese and French Companies to Build Belgrade Subway. *Serbian Monitor*. https://www.serbianmonitor.com/en/chinese-and-french-companies-to-build-belgrade-subway/

RENEWS. (2019, January 17). CGN Acquires 540MW Brazil Bounty from Enel. *RENEWS.BIZ*. https://renews.biz/51026/cgn-acquires-540mw-brazil-bounty-from-enel/

Rotberg, R. I. (2008). *China into Africa Trade, Aid, and Influence*. Dc Brookings Institution Press.

Rui, H., Zhang, M., & Shipman, A. (2017). Chinese Expatriate Management in Emerging Markets: A Competitive Advantage Perspective. *Journal of International Management, 23*(2), 124–138. https://doi.org/10.1016/j.intman.2017.01.002

Samb, S., Miridzhanian, A., & Christensen, S. (2023). Work Set to Resume at Simandou after Guinea, Shareholders Agree on Terms. Reuters. https://www.mining.com/web/work-set-to-resume-at-simandou-project-after-guinea-shareholders-agree-terms/

SASAC. (2005, July 26). Dongfang Electric Group Signed a General Contracting Project for the Vietnam Haiphong Thermal Power Station Project. *State-Owned Assets Supervision and Administration Commission of the State Council*. http://www.sasac.gov.cn/n2588025/n2588124/c3843801/content.html

SASAC. (2017, July 10). China Three Gorges Group and Germany Voith Sign Deepening Cooperation Agreement. *State-Owned Assets Supervision and Administration Commission of the State Council*. http://www.sasac.gov.cn/n2588025/n2588124/c7345892/content.html

SaudiGulf Projects. (2020, April 28). EDF Consortium Submits Lowest bid for 2GW Al-Dhafra Solar PV project. https://www.saudigulfprojects.com/2020/04/edf-consortium-submits-lowest-bid-for-abu-dhabis-2gw-al-dhafra-solar-pv-project/

Schuman, M., & Shullman, D. O. (2022, July 28). Cooperation with China: Challenges and Opportunities. *Atlantic Council*. https://www.atlanticcouncil.org/in-depth-research-reports/report/cooperation-with-china-challenges-and-opportunities/

Seaman, J., Huotari, M., & Otero-Iglesias, M. (2017). Chinese Investment in Europe A Country-Level Approach A Report by the European Think-tank Network on China (ETNC). https://www.ifri.org/sites/default/files/atoms/files/etnc_reports_2017_final_20dec2017.pdf

Shanghai Electric. (2018, November 29). Leaders from Both China and the West Witnessed Shanghai Electric and Abengoa Sign a Cooperation Agreement for the Dubai Solar Thermal Power Project. http://www.cnste.org/html/xiangmu/2018/1129/4143.html

Siemens. (2019, March 26). Siemens and the National Development and Reform Commission of China Strengthen the Cooperation of "the Belt and Road". *Siemens*. https://w1.siemens.com.cn/news/news_articles/7971.aspx

Sinkkonen, E. (2019). The More the Merrier? Sino-Japanese Security Relations in the Context of Complex Interstate Rivalry in the Asia-Pacific Region. *The Pacific Review, 32*(5), 748–777. https://doi.org/10.1080/09512748.2019.1569113

Solís, M. (2021, January 22). Japan's Democratic Renewal and the Survival of the Liberal Order. Brookings. https://www.brookings.edu/articles/japans-democratic-renewal-and-the-survival-of-the-liberal-order/

Stefanini, S. (2016, July 28). Hinkley Nuclear Plant Faces UK Delay. POLITICO. https://www.politico.eu/article/france-approves-hinkley-nuclear-plant-for-the-uk-despite-brexit-worries-edf/

Stojkovic, M. (2021, January 14). Implementation of Belgrade Metro Project. *Stojković Attorneys*. https://statt.rs/implementation-of-belgrade-metro-project/

Stone, R. W., Wang, Y., & Yu, S. (2021). Chinese Power and the State-Owned Enterprise. *International Organization, 76*(1), 1–22. https://doi.org/10.1017/s0020818321000308

Sudžuka, E., & Osmanović, I. (2021). Concession contract in Bosnia and Herzegovina: Introducing the World Commerce & Contracting Principles in the concession contract. *Journal of Strategic Contracting and Negotiation, 5*(4), 235–246. https://doi.org/10.1177/20555636221090207

Suri, G. (2016). China's 21 Century Maritime Silk Road Old String with New Pearls? Vivekananda International Foundation 3, San Martin Marg, Chanakyapuri, New Delhi—110021. https://www.vifindia.org/sites/default/files/china-s-21st-century-maritime-silk-road-old-string-with-new-pearls.pdf

The Russian Government. (2021). The Long-Term Plan for the Development of Liquefied Natural Gas Production in the Russian Federation. http://static.government.ru/media/files/l6DePkb3cDKTgzxbb6sdFc2npEPAd7SE.pdf

Tian, A. (2016, April 29). Visit Yamal LNG Project: The two Heaviest Core Modules of the Project have been Successfully. *China Daily*. http://caijing.chinadaily.com.cn/2016-04/29/content_24965623.htm

Tinsley, R. (2014). *Advanced Project Financing: Structuring Risk*. Euromoney Books.

Tomotaka, S. (2020). "Belt and Road" vs. "Free and Open Indo-Pacific": Competition over Regional Order and ASEAN's Responses*. *NIDS Journal of Defense and Security, 22*(2) https://www.nids.mod.go.jp/english/publication/security/pdf/2021/01/04.pdf

TotalEnergies. (2022a, August 24). No, TotalEnergies Does Not Produce Kerosene for the Russian Army. TotalEnergies.com. https://totalenergies.

com/media/news/press-releases/no-totalenergies-does-not-produce-kerosene-russian-army

TotalEnergies. (2022b, September 12). Russia: TotalEnergies Decides to Withdraw its Directors from Novatek and will no Longer Equity Account for its Stake in Novatek and Record a 3.7 b$ Impairment in Q4. TotalEnergies.com. https://totalenergies.com/media/news/press-releases/russia-totalenergies-decides-withdraw-its-directors-novatek-and-will-no

Tseng, H.-K., & Krog, R. (2016). No Strings Attached: Chinese Foreign Aid and Regime Stability in Resource-Rich Recipient Countries. https://api.semanticscholar.org/CorpusID:53312

Tull, D. (2023). France's Africa policy under president Macron: Good intentions, partial reform and the fiasco in the Sahel. SWP Comments; Stiftung Wissenschaft und Politik (SWP), German Institute for International and Security Affairs. https://ideas.repec.org/p/zbw/swpcom/279945.html

Wallace, C. (2019). Japan's Strategic Contrast: Continuing Influence Despite Relative Power Decline in Southeast Asia. *The Pacific Review, 32*(5), 1–35. https://doi.org/10.1080/09512748.2019.1569115

Wang, Y. (2019, September 20). Port Portal for Sino-African pragmatic cooperation. *China Daily*. https://www.chinadaily.com.cn/global/2019-09/20/content_37511188.htm

Wei, Y. (2007). Factors Influencing the Success of Virtual Cooperation within Dutch-Chinese Strategic Alliances. [PhD Thesis - Research UT, graduation UT, University of Twente]. University of Twente. https://doi.org/10.3990/1.9789036521628

Wei, T., Clegg, J., & Ma, L. (2015). The Conscious and Unconscious Facilitating Role of the Chinese Government in Shaping the Internationalisation of Chinese MNCs. *International Business Review, 24*(2), 331–343. https://doi.org/10.1016/j.ibusrev.2014.08.008

Winning International Group. (2018, June 26). The Messenger of Hope for the "Land of Red Soil"—A Documentary of Winning Alliance's Guinea Bauxite Project Development. https://www.winninggroup.com.sg/cn/1364.html

Woods, N. (2008). Whose Aid? Whose Influence? China, Emerging Donors and the Silent Revolution in Development Assistance. *International Affairs (Royal Institute of International Affairs 1944-), 84*(6), 1205–1221. https://www.jstor.org/stable/25144989

Yamal LNG. (2014, March 6). Intergovernmental Agreement Regarding Cooperation on The Yamal LNG Project Enacted. http://yamallng.ru/en/press/news/207/

Yan, D., & Warner, M. (2001). Research Papers In Management Studies "Sino-Foreign Joint Ventures" Versus "Wholly Foreign Owned Enterprises" In The People's Republic Of China. https://www.jbs.cam.ac.uk/wp-content/uploads/2020/08/wp0111-1.pdf

Yang, H. (2020, February 6). "Three Party Win-win" in Third-party Market Cooperation. *China Investment*. https://m.thepaper.cn/newsDetail_forward_5833859

Yang, Y., & An, R. (2019, March 26). Deepening third-Party Market Cooperation and Opening up New Space for Sino French Cooperation. *China Development Institution*. http://www.cdi.com.cn/Article/Detail?Id=13249

Yoshimatsu, H. (1998). Japan's Keidanren and Political Influence on Market Liberalisation. *Asian Survey, 38*(3), 328–345. https://doi.org/10.2307/2645431

Zhang, D. (2022, November 23). China, France Launches First Third-Party Market Cooperation on Sewage Treatment in Senegal. ECNS. https://www.ecns.cn/cns-wire/2022-11-23/detail-ihchchpu5657009.shtml

Zhang, H. (2023). From Contractors to Investors? Evolving Engagement of Chinese State Capital in Global Infrastructure Development and the case of Lekki Port in Nigeria. https://www.econstor.eu/bitstream/10419/268858/1/1837167907.pdf

Zhang, H., & Wang, J. (2021). Entry Mode Choices and Overseas Business Performance: Evidence from the Chinese Multinational Enterprises. *Strategic Change, 30*(6), 517–525. https://doi.org/10.1002/jsc.2473

Zhou, M. (2020). Third Party Market Cooperation: The Three Optimal Choices after Resource Collaboration and Integration. *International Project Monitor, 16*, 4–10. https://www.chinca.org/CICA/info/20102609570411

Zhu, Y. (2020). Third Party Market Cooperation: Differences in Understanding Between China and Japan and Their Impact. *China International Strategy Review, 2*(1), 110–119. http://www.iiss.pku.edu.cn/fj/PDF/ciss_cn/upload/docs/2020-09-25/doc_7981601047297.pdf

Zimmermann, A. J., & Jauer, N. (2021). Possible Indirect Legal Effects under International Law of Non-Legally Binding Instruments. KFG Working Paper Series, 48. https://papers.ssrn.com/sol3/papers.cfm?abstract_id=3840767

CHAPTER 7

Tripartite Odyssey: Tracing Paths of Cooperation Through In-Depth Case Studies

This chapter explores the practical implementation of tripartite cooperation, using the Hinkley Point C project in the UK and three Nigerian port projects as case studies. The chapter is divided into two sections, each dedicated to one of the case studies. Initially, the chapter provides relevant background information on these cases. It then proceeds to examine the roles of government and firms in influencing project progression, transaction costs, and additional benefits. This examination is pivotal in analysing how China and its partners alter the dynamics of project finance activities. Moreover, the chapter aims to identify how the varied economic and political contexts of the participants impact project outcomes and how beneficiary countries influence transaction costs and benefits within tripartite cooperation frameworks.

Hinkley Point C was selected due to its extensive documentation. The UK government has disclosed relevant documents, including operational and financing contracts, which are fully accessible online. Additionally, the UK media has provided comprehensive coverage throughout the project's timeline. The three Nigerian port projects were chosen for their geographic proximity and differing operational processes, making them ideal for comparative analysis.

The analysis is grounded in more than 230 documents related to the Hinkley Point C project and over 180 documents related to the Nigerian port projects. These documents include government reports and news

C. Su, *From Two to Three*, Governing China in the 21st Century,
https://doi.org/10.1007/978-981-95-8708-7_7

articles. In-depth interviews were conducted with five key individuals involved in the Hinkley Point C project, including project managers, a member of the labour union, and UK government officials. Similarly, interviews were conducted with six individuals from the Nigerian port projects, involving project managers, a vice president, and staff from the Nigeria Ports Authority. By employing a combination of document analysis and interviews, this chapter provides an in-depth examination of these case studies, offering insights into the complexities and dynamics of international infrastructure projects within the tripartite cooperation framework.

7.1 Background of the Hinkley Point C (HPC) Nuclear Power Station Project

In the HPC project, EDF (Frence) and CGN (China) are key investing and construction companies.[1] Before their involvement in the HPC project, CGN and EDF had already cultivated a long-standing and cooperative relationship since the 1980s, laying a solid foundation for their subsequent collaboration (Stewart et al., 2016).

Initially, the Hinkley Point C (HPC) project began as a bilateral cooperation between EDF and the UK. In 2008, EDF acquired eight UK nuclear power plants from the UK government, including the HPC station, for £12.5 billion. The 2008 economic crisis significantly impacted potential sponsors such as E.ON and Centrica, leading them to withdraw from the project (Lynch, 2013). This placed the UK government in a relatively weak bargaining position during negotiations with EDF. As the sole remaining developer willing to proceed, EDF secured a favourable

[1] EDF Energy is a wholly owned subsidiary of the French state-owned company Électricité de France (EDF). In 2004, EDF was partially privatised, with the French government retaining an 85% stake. In 2017, EDF acquired Areva reactor business in a restructuring initiative sponsored by the French government. In 2021, the French government announced 100% renationalisation of EDF, a process that was finalised in 2023 (Rose & Hummel, 2022).China General Nuclear Power Group (CGN) was established in 1994 and operates as a Chinese state-owned energy corporation under the State-owned Assets Supervision and Administration Commission (SASAC) of the State Council. CGN specialises in the development of clean energy sources, including nuclear power, nuclear fuel, wind power, and solar power. CGN's primary nuclear power technology, HPR 1000, aligns with China's Generation-III nuclear power technology, and has emerged as the preferred reactor technology for China's 'going global' strategy in the nuclear power industry (CGN, 2014).

agreement with the UK government. The contract established a strike price of £92.50 per megawatt-hour (MWh) over a 35-year period, ensuring that if the market price of electricity dropped below £92.50 MWh, EDF would receive payments from all electricity consumers (Schneider et al., 2014; BBC, 2013).

However, the process of EDF's final investment decision was slow. The project could only move to the construction phase once the final investment decision was made. In 2015, the UK government announced an initial government guarantee of £2 billion for the HPC to expedite EDF's final investment decision (Watt, 2017). On October 21, 2015, a strategic investment agreement for a new UK nuclear power project was signed in London, with the ceremony attended by Chinese President Xi Jinping and then-UK Prime Minister David Cameron. CGN and EDF established a cooperation framework for the UK nuclear power project. The tripartite cooperation was formalised when EDF, CGN, and the UK government signed the Secretary of State Investor Agreement[2] in 2016. In this arrangement, EDF Energy's share in HPC amounted to 66.5%, with CGN holding the remaining 33.5%. Concurrently, agreements for two additional nuclear power plants, namely Sizewell in Suffolk (the 'Sizewell C' project, based on French EPR technology) and Bradwell in Essex (the 'Bradwell B' project, based on Chinese HPR1000 technology), were linked to the HPC contract, specifying China's involvement in the development of the HPC nuclear power project and the utilisation of the HPR1000 technology for the Bradwell B project (Xie, 2016).

According to Freeman's stakeholder framework (1984), as mentioned in Chap. 4, there are three levels of stakeholder analysis: rational, process, and transactional. At the rational level, he introduced a two-dimensional

[2] "THE SECRETARY of STATE for ENERGY and CLIMATE CHANGE and LOW CARBON CONTRACTS COMPAN Y LTD and NNB HOLDING COMPANY (HPC) LIMITED and NNB GENERATION COMPANY (HPC) LIMITED and NNB FINANCE COMPANY (HPC) LTD and EDF ENERGY PLC and ÉLECTRICITÉ de FRANCE S.A. And CHINA GENERAL NUCLEAR POWER CORPORATION (Each an Ultimate Investor) and EDF ENERGY HOLDINGS LIMITED and INTERNAT IONAL NUCLEAR INVESTMENT LIMITED (Each an Original Investor) and NNB TOP COMPANY HPC (B) LTD and LIBRA INTERNATIONAL LIMITED (Each an Original Investor Super TopCo) and NNB TOP COMPANY HPC (A) LTD and SAGITTARIUS INTERNATIONAL LIMITED (Each an Original Investor TopCo) and NNB FINANCE COMPANY (HPC) LTD (the Original Financing Representative)," 2016, https://assets.publishing.service.gov.uk/media/5a805378ed915d74e622dcef/2_-_Secretary_of_State_Investor_Agreement__redacted_.pdf.

approach for classifying stakeholders based on their level of interest and influence. This conceptualisation is depicted in the classical stakeholder grid. Building upon this framework, I developed the stakeholder grid for the HPC project, classifying the participants in tripartite cooperation.

Although the HPC project is labelled as a 'tripartite' cooperation project among China, France, and the UK, each party has more than one relevant stakeholder, as illustrated in Table 7.1. The most crucial actors are the two major equity and voting stakeholders—EDF and CGN, given their control over the project's financing and construction processes, property assets, and skilled labour resources. The UK government, Chinese government, and French government, have both political and economic impacts on the projects. They utilise financial instruments such as grants, state-backed loans, and insurance to support their respective companies. Additionally, they employ political instruments such as high-level government meetings and administrative orders to either facilitate or hinder the project's progress. Labour unions, especially those from France and the UK, exert influence over the project financing and construction processes. While buyers and suppliers are relevant to the project, they are not directly involved in tripartite cooperation activities.

According to the Secretary of State Investor Agreement (see Footnote 87), Fig. 7.1. maps the specific participants in HPC alongside the multiple stakeholders within the tripartite cooperation framework.

Table 7.1 The stakeholder grid of HPC project (Source: Author)

	Formal or voting	*Economic*	*Political*
Equity	Stockholders (EDF, CGN)		
Economic	French Unions	UK electricity consumers Suppliers (e.g., Areva) French and UK Labour Unions	UK government (Grant) French government (Financial support to EDF) Chinese government (Loan to CGN)
Influencers	UK government		UK government (prime minister, cabinet, energy authorities, nuclear assessment authorities) French government Chinese government

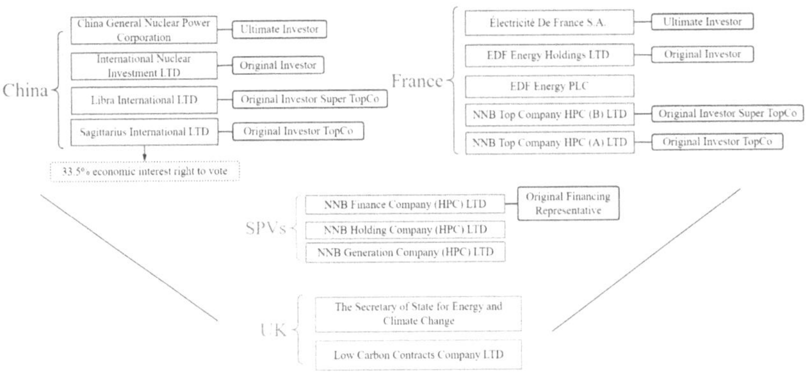

Fig. 7.1 Main participants in the HPC project (Source: Author)

China General Nuclear Power Corporation (CGN) and Électricité De France S.A. (EDF) are the ultimate investors in the HPC project. Due to their diverse business operations, both companies established specialised subsidiaries for international nuclear and energy investments—EDF Energy Holdings Limited and International Nuclear Investment Limited, respectively. For the HPC project specifically, CGN created Libra International Limited and Sagittarius International Limited as original investor super TopCos.[3] EDF Energy PLC manages EDF S.A.'s energy business in the UK. Through EDF Energy PLC, two original investor TopCos were established: NNB Top Company HPC (B) Ltd and NNB Top Company HPC (A) Ltd.

Chinese and French participants established a series of SPVs to facilitate their cooperation in the HPC project: NNB Finance Company (HPC) Ltd as the original financing representative, NNB Holding Company (HPC) Limited, and NNB Generation Company (HPC) Limited. These SPVs signed contracts with the UK government, represented by the Secretary of State for Energy and Climate Change and the Low Carbon Contracts Company Ltd.

[3] The headquarters of CGN and EDF S.A., serving as the Holdco, initiate the process of creating a new parent company, referred to as 'TopCo.' In this process, the headquarters transfers ownership to TopCo.This structure is preferred as it effectively delineates different providers of capital, with TopCo functioning as the company where investors and management hold their ownership interests.

As this arrangement shows, compared with traditional bilateral cooperation projects, which involve two participants and simpler relationships, tripartite cooperation projects exhibit more complex interactions among more participants, resulting in increased transaction costs. This complexity raises several questions: Why do participants choose this cooperative model, and what are their initial motivations? Despite potential transaction costs, why were both EDF and the UK government eager to involve CGN in the HPC project? The following sections aim to answer these questions by analysing the determinants and actions of the key actors involved in the HPC project.

7.1.1 Determinants of Government and Enterprise Engagement in the HPC Project

7.1.1.1 China

The Chinese government actively promoted its BRI across the Eurasia continent, and its diplomatic ties with both the UK and France were in a golden era in 2016. Through collaboration with these two influential countries, China aimed to develop BRI-related projects in other European nations. For CGN, cooperation with EDF was imperative to enter the UK's nuclear market and benefit from EDFs know-how and strategic assets. These determinants align with market-seeking and springboard theories in the FDI literature.

Firstly, CGN faced significant barriers to accessing the UK market due to stringent investment conditions for foreign investors in sensitive infrastructure projects, particularly those related to national security. These restrictions are especially challenging for non-Western investors (Department for Business, Energy and Industrial Strategy, 2017).

Secondly, the UK's nuclear market was predominantly controlled by EDF, so if CGN wanted to enter the UK market, it needed to cooperate with EDF. Moreover, EDF had established a strong brand and an extensive network of local relationships (SMD, 2015). Given the significant investments and risks involved in nuclear power projects, it was challenging for CGN to undertake such projects alone, particularly in overseas markets where it lacked experience. CGN was unfamiliar with the UK's culture, business practices, laws, and regulations. By adopting a tripartite cooperation approach, CGN was able to mitigate risks and gain valuable knowledge and expertise from EDF. This approach allowed CGN to use tripartite cooperation as a learning opportunity to enter the nuclear power market in developed countries (Vaughan & Kuo, 2018), exemplifying classic strategic asset-seeking and springboarding perspectives.

> *The investment is huge, and there's a lot of risk in nuclear power projects... It's really tough for companies to go it alone in overseas markets—especially when you're trying to break into developed countries. That's why the collaboration between Chinese and French companies has been so important.* [4]

Thirdly, CGN aimed to use the UK market as a springboard to expand its presence in other international nuclear markets. By strategically investing in the HPC project, CGN sought to advertise its technology and transition China's nuclear power industry from being an importer to an exporter. By acquiring a 33% stake in the project and sharing one-third of the financial responsibility, China anticipated gaining the opportunity to export its proprietary Generation-III nuclear power technology, HPR 1000. This arrangement was seen as a stepping stone for future approval to construct the Bradwell B nuclear power station (Davies, 2016c; Macalister, 2016a).

> *China's nuclear industry has indeed transitioned from being an importer of technology and expertise to now becoming an exporter. It's not just about exporting technology or capital—though that's certainly part of it—but more importantly, we're also exporting experience and capabilities. Over the years, China has developed a strong foundation in nuclear power construction and operation, and now, that knowledge and know-how are being shared with other countries. This kind of experience is a key part of the industry's growth and global competitiveness.*[5]

The package of three nuclear power station projects exploits the UK and France's reputation, indicating that CGN is not solely a construction partner in the HPC project but, more significantly, is trusted as a technological collaborator (Branigan, 2016). By complying with the UK's rigorous safety regulations, CGN can showcase its design and construction capabilities in nuclear technology to the global market. The UK's Generic Design Assessment (GDA) for nuclear reactors is widely recognised in the nuclear sphere for its great influence (Vaughan & Kuo, 2018). According

[4] Interviewee HPC-20221023.
[5] Interviewee HPC-20221023.

to Antony Froggatt, a nuclear expert at the think tank Chatham House, if the HPR1000 passes the UK's stringent regulatory and licensing process, it would pave the way for CGN to secure more international contracts (Vaughan, 2017a). Robert Davies, the chief operating officer of CGN UK, agreed that "*the UK serves as a springboard for exporting Chinese nuclear technology to other countries*" (Ralston, 2021). Accordingly, the Bradwell B project would have been a pivotal project in the three nuclear projects' package as it symbolises the transition of the Chinese nuclear industry from capital investment to technology export.

7.1.1.2 France

Both the French government and EDF have a strong interest in using tripartite cooperation to deliver the HPC project. First of all, EDF recognised the high risks associated with nuclear power projects when considering the industry's historical delay in delivering power plant projects and over budget (Watt, 2017). More importantly, EDF faced severe financial challenges in 2016. With wholesale power prices dropping by 35% that year, EDF's market value plummeted from €150 billion in 2008 to €30 billion in 2016, falling short of the total investment required for the Hinkley C project (Topping, 2016). Starting in 2016, the French government injected £3.1 billion to strengthen EDF's finances in preparation for the HPC decision (Davies, 2016a). Additionally, the French government agreed to forgo cash dividends for two years, providing an estimated additional capital of €7 billion for EDF. Although these measures helped facilitate EDF's involvement in HPC and eased its financial burdens, EDF's debt ratings were still downgraded by credit rating agencies Moody's and Standard & Poor's (Macalister, 2016a; AFP, 2016). Given these financial constraints, EDF was eager to find a partner willing to share the risks and costs. Collaborating with CGN emerged as a viable solution to bolster EDF's financial capabilities, enhance its financial credibility, and expedite progress on the HPC project.

Secondly, the HPC project was crucial for the EDF's overarching European strategy and the company's reputation, especially considering the longer delays of smaller reactor projects in France and Finland.[6]

[6] Flamanville reactor in France (two times over budget and six years behind schedule) and Olkiluoto reactor in Finland (three times over budget and nearly a decade behind) with European pressurised reactor (EPR) technology.

Without the HPC project, it would undermine EDF's capacity to secure nuclear power contracts in other countries (Macalister, 2016c).

> *...the HPC project is key for our overall strategy and the reputation in Europe—especially since we've seen delays with smaller reactor projects in France and Finland. Without HPC, it would (have) seriously weakened EDF's ability to win nuclear power contracts in other countries.* [7]

Furthermore, the French nuclear industry also faced a decline, confronting the simultaneous decommissioning of its 58 nuclear reactors, most of which were constructed in the 1970s, while no new nuclear power stations were being developed (Krikorian, 2019). The French government, led by President François Hollande at the time, expressed strong support for the controversial HPC project. Hollande emphasised the project's importance, stating, "*I am in favour of this project going ahead. It's very important to understand that we need a high-performance, highly secure nuclear industry in France, and that we cannot let others take over terrain, including on exports, that has been French up to now*" (AFP, 2016). Emmanuel Macron, who served as France's economy minister then, concurred that HPC held strategic significance not only for EDF's presence in the UK but also for the global promotion of French nuclear technology expertise. He warned that if the HPC project were to falter, France would risk ceding its position to American, Chinese, or Russian competitors (Rankin, 2016). Gérard Magnin, a former EDF director, perceives Hinkley as "*a way to make the British fund the renaissance of nuclear in France.*" The HPC project would benefit the entire nuclear industry and smaller enterprises within the sector, contributing to the rejuvenation of the nuclear sector in France (Watt, 2017).

Therefore, despite the HPC project spanning many years from its initial proposal through planning, approval, and fundraising, and facing continually increasing construction costs, France insists on starting this project. To mitigate risks in the financing and construction phases, France seeks to find an additional partner to share these risks.

7.1.1.3 The UK

From the perspective of the UK government, utilising the tripartite cooperation model in the HPC project emerged as a crucial economic and

[7] Interviewee HPC-20221105.

political strategy in the wake of Brexit. EDF, while holding control over the HPC property, faced a slow investment decision process that impeded progress on the UK's 'Great British Nuclear' programme—a key initiative aimed at creating a clean, secure, and affordable energy system (Macalister, 2016c). To mitigate the significant investment risks and accelerate construction, the UK government sought an additional investor to share these risks with EDF. Post-Brexit, the HPC project took on greater significance, becoming more than just an energy initiative. Securing final approval for HPC served as a critical 'litmus test' for the viability of foreign investment in large-scale infrastructure projects, while also signalling the UK's commitment to being open for business and enhancing its credibility (Macalister, 2016d).

The HPC project also plays a pivotal role in the political and economic relations among the UK, China, and France (Stefanini, 2016b). Brexit had put the UK in a difficult position regarding trade and investment, and the UK could not afford to damage relationships with two key trading partners—France and China. Therefore, the HPC project serves as a strategic move to maintain and strengthen ties with European partners. Simultaneously, in the face of Brexit-induced economic uncertainties and the need to replace lost trade within Europe, the UK has grown increasingly reliant on cooperation with China (Stewart & Quinn, 2016).

> *…Now, speaking about civil nuclear projects specifically, the UK has had a bit of a gap in developing new nuclear sites. I remember growing up and seeing places like Sellafield in Cumbria—iconic sites that are part of the UK's nuclear history. But the truth is, since the 1970s or so, there hasn't been much momentum in building new civil nuclear facilities. Over the past 10 or 15 years, though, I think the government has started to realise that nuclear power has to be part of the mix to ensure energy security and meet climate goals. That's where partnerships like the one with China come in—they bring in expertise, technology, and investment to get these kinds of projects off the ground again.*[8]

From a technological perspective, the UK's collaboration with China and France in the nuclear sector is driven by technological reasons, as the UK did not have other technical options at that time. By 2016, only the EPR (French technology) had successfully passed the rigorous assessment conducted by the UK's Office for Nuclear Regulation (ONR). Although

[8] Interviewee HPC-20221121.

the ONR did issue a Design Acceptance Confirmation for the AP1000 design by Westinghouse (U.S. technology) in March 2017 and for the Advanced Boiling Water Reactor by Hitachi-GE (Japan-U.S. technology) in December 2017, both owners encountered financial and operation challenges. Westinghouse, facing bankruptcy, abandoned its project to construct three AP1000 reactors at Moorside, located near the Sellafield nuclear reprocessing site in Cumbria, England (Vaughan, 2018). Likewise, Hitachi suspended plans to build Hitachi-GE ABWRs at Wylfa in Wales and Oldbury in England due to financial constraints and the inability to reach a mutually satisfactory agreement (Hitachi, 2019). Because China's Taishan nuclear power station is the first to use the EPR technology, China holds mature operational experience. About 100 Chinese engineers were involved in the HPC by 2021 (Pickard & Thomas, 2021).

> *China has made remarkable progress in nuclear technologies. It's been a steady development that's really caught the attention of other countries, including the UK. I remember George Osborne, back when he was Chancellor of the Exchequer, around 2015—or it might've even been earlier, maybe 2014 or 2013—visited China. I believe he went to Guangdong to visit a city that's a hub for nuclear technology. It might have been Taishan or somewhere nearby.*
>
> *That visit was a pretty clear signal of recognition from the UK government at the time. They acknowledged that China had made significant strides in nuclear technology and that there was a lot of potential for collaboration. It also tied into the UK's broader strategy of diversifying energy sources. Nuclear power is a key part of that, and China's expertise and capabilities presented an opportunity for the UK to tap into advanced nuclear technology while also securing investment for critical infrastructure projects like Hinkley Point C.*[9]

The determinants of China, France, and the UK to engage in tripartite cooperation are different, and their respective actions impact both the transaction costs and benefits of the projects. The UK government, which does not bear financial responsibility, employs various policy instruments to influence the project's development (UK GOV, 2016). EDF, as the principal investor, assumes the primary financial burden for the construction of the HPC project and aims to alleviate this financial strain while maintaining its reputation in nuclear technology and construction. Meanwhile, CGN, a key shareholder, focuses on promoting its Hualong technology at Bradwell B in the international market and obtaining GDA

[9] Interviewee HPC-20221121.

certifications from the UK government. Due to their divergent primary objectives and partially aligned interests, the complex relationships among the governments and changeable companies' actions influence the project's transaction costs and benefits.

7.2 Tripartite Cooperation in the HPC Project

Before the construction phase of HPC, participants held some idealistic expectations. When the contract for HPC was ultimately signed in September 2016, CGN regarded the HPC project as a 'triple win' for China, Britain, and France, marking the culmination of years of cooperation among the three nations (Mason, 2016). The Chinese Ambassador to Britain expressed confidence that the governments and leaders of the three countries had given great attention to HPC, ensuring the project's progression. HPC represents a venture of commercial and technological collaboration, offering development opportunities for French and Chinese enterprises, and providing employment, tax revenue, and a stable energy supply for the UK (Deng & Gui, 2016). In the China-UK joint statement, both sides stand ready to "work together to ensure the success of Hinkley Point as soon as possible."[10] This section examines whether these ideal objectives can be practically realised in a tripartite cooperation project.

7.2.1 Government Actions

Government actions significantly influence both transaction costs and additional benefits for the HPC project. Initially, participant governments

[10] In the 2014 China-UK joint statement, it said that "The UK welcomed Chinese investment and progressive participation in the construction of new build nuclear energy projects in the UK, and was open to Chinese companies leading the development of other nuclear power station site(s) in the UK and the potential deployment of Chinese reactor technology in the UK, subject to meeting the stringent requirements of the UK's independent regulators. Both countries recognised that companies entering into the UK through partnership would be in the best position later to maximise the growing opportunities that will be on offer in the UK nuclear market. Both sides stand ready to work together to ensure the success of Hinkley Point as soon as possible."Foreign & Commonwealth Office and The Rt Hon Lord Cameron, "Joint Statement from Government of the People's Republic of China & Government of the United Kingdom of Great Britain and Northern Ireland," GOV. UK, June 17, 2014, https://www.gov.uk/government/news/joint-statement-from-government-of-the-peoples-republic-of-china-government-of-the-united-kingdom-of-great-britain-and-northern-ireland.

actively negotiated to lower transaction costs. Although HPC appeared as a business deal, the actual meaningful discussions primarily took place between the governments (Inman, 2018).

In UK-France cooperation, the negotiations between the UK and French governments spanned several years before reaching a conclusion (Goodley, 2016). French President François Hollande and UK Prime Minister David Cameron strongly supported HPC and claimed HPC is 'a pillar of the bilateral relationship' (Carrington, 2016). While the French government did not directly invest in the HPC project, it employed various financial strategies, including asset sales, recapitalisation, and substituting cash for equity dividends (Macalister, 2016d), to facilitate HPC's construction. President Emmanuel Macron affirmed, "*If there is a need to recapitalise EDF, we will do so. If there needs to be a further waiver of dividends from EDF to the government, we will*" (Thomson, 2016). HPC is the French government fully controls EDF's equity and uses state financial instruments to support tripartite cooperation projects. The French government aimed to expedite HPC's progress by endorsing the project and facilitating the collection of more capital.

In UK-China cooperation, the Chinese and UK governments published several documents following their Economic and Financial Dialogue meetings, affirming their collaboration in HPC. Both sides also welcomed proposals for projects at Sizewell C and Bradwell B, with a focus on regulatory approval for HPR1000 technology.[11] In 2019, cooperation remained a priority, emphasising mutual benefit, fostering additional commercial partnerships, and continuing the HPR1000 Generic Design

[11] In 2016 Policy Outcomes of the eighth UK-China Economic and Financial Dialogue "The UK and China welcomed the Final Investment Decision and signing of the contractual documentation for the Hinkley Point C nuclear power station. Both sides welcomed the minority investment from China General Nuclear in the project and recognised the significance of Hinkley Point C as an example of UK-China-France collaboration. *Both sides also welcomed the proposals for projects at Sizewell C and Bradwell B, the latter of which will be led by CGN in partnership with EDF and at which it is intended to deploy HPR1000 technology subject to it meeting regulatory and other requirements. Both countries welcomed the future submission of the HPR1000 reactor technology to the Generic Design Assessment process.* Both sides recognised the independence of the UK's regulators and the robust and transparent nature of the GDA process, and noted that UK and Chinese companies are well placed to support the Requesting Party. *In particular both sides noted the importance of 'win-win' collaboration in supply chain partnerships, making use of each side's respective advantages. Both countries also welcomed opportunities to develop joint projects related to the HPR1000 reactor in the UK, China and third countries.*"

Assessment process. The UK government and Chinese government aim to use their respective advantages and achieve a 'win-win' collaboration in supply chain partnerships.[12]

All things seemed to be going well, and all participants were enthusiastic about promoting the HPC before practical implementation. Governments enhance financing capacity and foster more effective communication and coordination to reduce transaction costs in tripartite cooperation initiatives by using a series of soft-law and financing instruments, such as MOUs, High-Level Economic and Financial Dialogue meetings, and government-backed financing endorsements.

However, the first hindrance for HPC came in the aftermath of the Brexit referendum. HPC was initiated during David Cameron's tenure. Due to the change in leadership within the UK Government, the next Prime Minister, Theresa May, and her government suspended the construction process (Stefanini, 2016a). When EDF made its final decision to proceed with HPC in September 2016, just hours later, the newly formed government of Theresa May announced a delay in the project's approval (Ruddick & Grierson, 2016). The UK government wanted to use negotiation tactics to maximise its interests in a project. This delay was a strategic move by the Theresa May government as it initiated discussions on the Brexit negotiation. Theresa May and Greg Clark, the Secretary of State for Business, Energy and Industrial Strategy, aimed to impose new conditions on EDF and CGN and renegotiate the contract, which specified a generous minimum price for the project's generated electricity (Stewart, 2016). However, many other British political groups criticised May's government action and urged them to push forward the project. Especially considering another participant, the French company's interests, Barry Gardiner, the

[12] In 2019 Policy Outcomes of the ninth UK-China Economic and Financial Dialogue, both government still mention "Both sides attach importance to cooperation in the field of civil nuclear energy, and are willing to ensure the China-UK Civil Nuclear Energy Cooperation Working Group is meaningful and mutually beneficial, in a bid to deepen existing cooperation, including on Hinkley Point C, Sizewell C and Bradwell B and especially welcome the progress being made in construction of Hinkley Point C and recognise the investment and track record of experience China is bringing to support this project. Both sides recognise the potential for further mutual beneficial commercial partnerships in the UK and China. Cooperation in new fields and new projects, including nuclear energy supply chain, nuclear environmental protection will also be sought by both sides. *Both sides welcome the progress on the HPR1000 Generic Design Assessment (GDA) and the continuation of the GDA technical exchange based on the agreement on government to government assurance.*"

shadow energy secretary, said, "*This is not a time to be making enemies, and particularly not of the French*" (Ruddick et al., 2016).

Furthermore, it was the first time that the UK government doubted the engagement of Chinese investors in the HPC project and whether the Chinese investment might influence British national security. This decision postponed the final approval of the HPC project, incurring additional time and negotiation costs (Rawnsley, 2016). Between July 29th, when the UK suspended the HPC project, and September 15th, when it received the green light, numerous reports[13] emerged about Chinese involvement in this tripartite cooperation project.

During this period, various stakeholder groups exerted differing influences over the UK government. China, a crucial participant with a £6 billion investment, actively pushed the project forward. The Chinese Ambassador to the UK emphasised the HPC project's importance for China-UK relations, urging the UK to maintain trust and support (Liu, 2016). Vincent de Rivaz, EDF's UK Chief Executive, endorsed the Chinese participants, stating, "*We know and trust our Chinese partners. There were enormous benefits for the UK from the involvement of China, which has the largest civil nuclear programme in the world.*" He advocated for the UK to put aside security concerns regarding Chinese involvement (Lyons, 2016). Peter Mandelson, the former business secretary and a prominent figure in New Labour, advocated proceeding with the project, asserting that *security concerns about Chinese involvement were unjustified. China is unlikely to jeopardise other countries' national security as it would be 'commercial suicide'. China would suffer considerable losses and deter other nations from doing business with Chinese investors in the future* (Gayle, 2016). He suggested that post-Brexit, the UK cannot be overly selective in its trading partners and should prioritise nurturing a valued trading relationship with China (Quinn, 2016).

In addition, the UK's four trade unions strongly advocated for the progression of Hinkley, highlighting the potential creation of thousands of jobs. They viewed the delay in HPC's progress as devoid of purpose, instead, the delay would lead to potential job losses and further hinder UK economic growth. The GMB, the UK's general trade union, described the

[13] A total of 24 reports from *The Guardian*; six reports from the *BBC*; six reports from *The Sun*; four reports from *Reuters*; two reports from *The Telegraph*; two reports from *The Financial Times*; one report from *The Independent*; one report from *The Times*; one report from *Sky News*.

government's decision as 'bewildering and bonkers' (Macalister, 2016b). Justin Bowden, GMB's National Secretary for Energy, remarked, "*After years of procrastination, what is required is decisive action, not dithering and more delay. This unnecessary hesitation is putting finance for the project in doubt and 25,000 new jobs at risk immediately after Brexit. It is a gross error of judgment and must be reversed*" (Ruddick et al., 2016).

Due to the opposing pressures and the necessary time for scrutiny checks, three months later, Theresa May's government finally granted approval for the project but with conditions giving the UK government more supervision. Theresa May's government asserted that the new agreement would safeguard national security and require state approval for any change in ownership of the nuclear plant. Under these new controls, EDF cannot sell its stake in Hinkley without permission from the UK government (Mason & Goodley, 2016). Nevertheless, the Labour Party and environmental groups said the new security measures were 'window dressing,' with minimal impact on the project, as the price remains unchanged (Stewart, 2016). The special share does not offer additional protection beyond the existing UK's rigorous regulatory regime (Ruddick & Phillips, 2016). This three-month delay did not fundamentally alter the deal from the one previously signed but generated higher transaction costs in negotiation and inspection. The government action is more of a political gesture for the UK public.

> *The financial side of things is obviously critical—these are massive, long-term investments, and they require careful planning. But the political dimension is just as important, and it's actually more complex in a democracy like the UK. The potential for quick changes in government and leadership makes long-term projects like this challenging… After the Brexit vote in 2016, we had a change in government with Theresa May becoming Prime Minister. One of her first major moves was to review Hinkley Point C in August and September of that year, which raised questions about the project's future. Since then, we've had Boris Johnson, and now Rishi Sunak, following Liz Truss's very brief tenure. That constant leadership turnover, combined with broader UK-China diplomatic challenges over the last three years, adds another layer of difficulty.*[14]

Especially, the suspended approval of the HPC project in 2016 seems to be particularly important from the perspective of how tripartite projects involving China can get derailed. It 'buried a bomb' for in China-UK

[14] Interviewee HPC-20220726.

relations related to Chinese investment and national security. Despite eventual approval, May's initial strategic decision fuelled China-phobia sentiments (Phillips, 2016), which continually cast a shadow over the project's following construction. It was uncertain whether the suspension was because of Chinese involvement or the change in the British government. No resource mentioned or indicated whether, if the UK government did not change, CGN would be subjected to tighter rules or not, because Cameron's government held a more friendly attitude towards Chinese investment. In the subsequent years, escalating security concerns led the UK government to exclude CGN from Britain's critical national infrastructure (Ambrose, 2020, 2021). In November 2022, the UK Government directly invested £700 million in Sizewell C, inducing CGN to withdraw from the project (UK GOV, 2022).

> *There's the interaction between politics and security. There's always public concern about security risks when working with foreign partners, especially in sensitive sectors like nuclear power. Personally, I think if the UK's security agencies—who have much deeper insights than the general public or even many politicians—say the risks can be managed, then that should carry significant weight. It's a balance between the political pressures and the actual, expert evaluation of risks. The media, public opinion, and even the democratic process itself can influence decisions in ways that might not always align with the technical or financial realities of a project.*[15]

Despite the initial collaborative efforts of the UK, Chinese, and French governments to advance the development of HPC, political changes in the UK, including shifts in leadership and their respective political ideologies, have had a significant impact on the project's progress and increased transaction costs. Although Chinese and French participants tried to facilitate the cooperation, the practical effectiveness was limited.

7.2.2 *Company Actions*

The history of bilateral cooperation mitigated transaction costs. CGN and EDF have established a close partnership on various projects in China, including the Daya Bay and Taishan nuclear plants in Guangdong Province, China. Their cooperation experience, spanning three decades, has been

[15] Interviewee HPC-20221121.

transferred to projects in the UK (Yang, 2018). As the tacit understanding and mutual trust between EDF and CGN continue to grow, CGN aligns with EDF in resolving significant issues related to the HPC project. Furthermore, CGN and EDF have established a joint venture company, General Nuclear Systems Limited (GNS) for applying the assessment of HP1000 in the UK (EDF Energy, 2022).

In the case of HPC, the involvement of substantial subsidiary companies from CGN and EDF is crucial, and any changes to these branches can increase transaction costs. The inherent complexity of the HPC project (see Fig. 7.1) further heightens these costs, particularly when these entities undergo changes or face challenges. Coordination and negotiation with additional partners add to this complexity, significantly elevating transaction costs. Additionally, CGN's establishment of seven new nuclear-related firms in London demonstrates both their confidence and ambition regarding HPC (Pamilih, 2022), but also leads to higher transaction costs due to the need to negotiate and sign complex legal contracts. The involvement of more participants necessitates a more intricate legal framework and extended time to finalise the terms and conditions.

While both EDF and CGN aim to derive benefits and reduce transaction costs in the HPC project, the practical actions of these companies did not effectively utilise the tripartite cooperation mechanism to achieve these goals. The lack of synergy through tripartite cooperation is partly due to the UK's increasingly stringent policies demanding China withdraw from infrastructure projects (Pickard & Thomas, 2021; Ward et al., 2016). As the relationship between the UK and Chinese governments deteriorated, CGN was asked to withdraw from the Bradwell B and Sizewell C projects. Following this, CGN ceased technological exchanges, refused to fill the financing gaps, and halted further investments in the HPC project (Pickard et al., 2024), further increasing transaction costs.

7.3 Triple-Win or Triple-Loss with Increased Costs in the HPC Project

Projects like Hinkley Point C are designed to meet the UK's renewable energy demand. What's great is that they also benefit from the UK's Guarantees Scheme, which is set up to encourage private investment in infrastructure projects. This project really brings together the best of what CGN and EDF have to offer—their expertise in technology, equipment, and project development, as well as construction. It's a true collaboration. And honestly, at the ideal envi-

sioning stage, this was always a win-win-win situation for all three countries involved. The UK gets clean energy and infrastructure investment, China and France gain through exporting expertise and participating in a major international project. It's a success story for everyone.[16]

Contrary to the initial ideal vision, the cost of building HPC rose from £16 billion in 2012, with an estimated operation cost updated to £46 billion in 2024. The first operation is scheduled for 2025, then to 2029. After EDF began construction, several factors continually led to higher costs, including challenging ground conditions, stringent UK regulatory requirements for nuclear safety, and strike actions related to pay disputes (Vaughan, 2017c; Davies, 2017; White 2024). A question appears with the progress of this tripartite cooperation project: How did a project initially symbolising the golden era of China-France-UK relations transform into one that appears increasingly unattractive with each passing year? Is it still a triple-win project, or have the billions invested rendered it a triple-loss endeavour?

One reason participants insist on tripartite cooperation despite bearing additional transaction costs in the HPC project is its considerable diplomatic and international significance. It intertwines elements of energy, economics, investment, national security, and diplomacy among China, France, and the UK. The huge sunk costs have bound multiple stakeholders, making it challenging to halt the project without erasing decades of work. The comprehensive contractual obligations of HPC increase exit costs for participants, as withdrawal involves paying penalties and the potential humiliation of seeing ten years of effort go to waste (Dudman, 2017). Despite facing criticism for its considerable expenses, HPC is seen by some as a project driven by diplomatic prestige rather than purely economic or energy considerations (Jenkins, 2020).

Another reason that participants insist on tripartite cooperation despite bearing additional transaction costs in the HPC project is that participants benefit from risk sharing and distribution. The HPC project involves various risks, including engineering risks, liability risks, credit risks, and safety risks. To address these, participants have signed extensive legal documentation to distribute these risks. For the UK government, these contracts represent a strategic shift to transfer construction costs and risks to EDF and CGN, aiming to keep these expenses off the government's financial

[16] Interviewee HPC-20221023.

records (Vaughan, 2017b). EDF and CGN can share risks during the construction process and will share revenue upon project completion. While these contracts aim to mitigate potential risks, the extensive documentation, amounting to 'thousands and thousands' of pages (Macalister, 2016a), also increases negotiation and contract costs, thereby increasing overall transaction costs.

7.3.1 The UK

For the UK, it is hard to justify the internal economic return of HPC, given the significant increase in electricity prices for consumers. Although the British government and customers wouldn't bear costs during the construction process, the strike price includes the actual construction costs of the HPC project, as well as all expenses related to decommissioning, nuclear waste management, and potential uncertainties in future operations (Wintour, 2013; Carrington, 2016). In a 2017 report by the UK National Audit Office, it criticised the government's decision for having "locked consumers into a risky and expensive project with uncertain strategic and economic benefits." Government ministers adhered to a conventional model, where the developer assumed construction risks in exchange for a state-guaranteed electricity price. This cost, funded by consumers' bills, extends over a 35-year period (Johnston, 2017).

However, to halt tripartite cooperation with China, the UK government introduced a new financing model for the Sizewell project, known as the Regulated Asset Base (RAB) model (Hands & Kwarteng, 2021). Unlike the CfD model in the HPC project, investors can include costs on household energy bills and collect funds before the plants commence electricity generation. This model transits risks and potential hidden costs from private investors to consumers in the early stage, so nuclear developers can borrow money at cheaper rates, ultimately reducing costs for consumers' bills (Consumer Scotland, 2024). On the other hand, this new model aims to remove CGN from the Sizewell project. Energy Secretary Kwasi Kwarteng introduced legislation aimed at sharing the early construction costs with consumers, with the goal of decreasing the UK's dependency on foreign funding, particularly Chinese investment, for nuclear projects, thus making them more appealing to domestic investors (Ambrose, 2019; Ambrose, 2021).

HPC also incurs the opportunity cost of not investing in other renewable energy sources. The government's decision appears to overlook the ongoing energy revolution occurring beyond the confines of its financial models (Pratley, 2017). Back in 2004, Tony Blair's government launched a nuclear energy review, asserting that nuclear power could significantly contribute to reinforcing Britain's energy security, bridging the energy gap, reducing carbon emissions, and ensuring an uninterrupted energy supply (Torres, 2016; Department of Trade and Industry of the UK, 2006). This perspective was influenced by the then underdeveloped state of solar and wind power and the political vulnerabilities of overseas gas imports, which made them less competitive compared to nuclear electricity production. Despite the participants designing intelligent financial plans and regulatory frameworks for the HPC project, neither the government nor the companies can entirely mitigate the inherent challenges of nuclear power, such as massive upfront investments, complex waste management, and technological risks. Over the last two decades, the cost of renewable energy technologies has decreased, and storage capabilities have significantly improved, making these alternatives more affordable, efficient, and safer. Consequently, nuclear power has become less attractive and not as cost-effective (Ambrose, 2019).

Therefore, the benefits of HPC include fostering include fostering diplomatic relations with France and China, promoting industrial development, and generating employment opportunities for the UK's southwest region (Davies, 2016b). From an economic return perspective, the HPC project does not seem to be a favourable deal for UK customers due to its costly financial model, large sunk cost, and opportunity cost. The actions of the UK government also play a role in influencing transaction costs. While the UK government continues to engage in tripartite cooperation due to foreign pressure, it has introduced a new project financing model and has taken steps to halt further tripartite cooperation with CGN.

7.3.2 EDF

For EDF, this project has become a loss when considering its projected rate of returns. Initially, EDF set the projected rate of returns at 9%, but the rate of returns dropped to 8.5% in 2017 (Vaughan, 2017c). Simone Rossi, the Chief Executive of EDF Energy, maintained that the HPC's cost overruns would not affect energy bills, nor harm EDF's shareholders in 2017. He argued that HPC had a government contract guaranteeing a fixed price of £92.50 per megawatt-hour of electricity, designed to account for the risks associated. This set price was deemed sufficient to ensure healthy shareholder returns for EDF Energy, even with the increasing costs. Nevertheless, when the rate of return fell to 7% in 2019, approaching the company's cost of capital, it posed challenges for EDF to generate profits from the HPC project (Ambrose, 2017). Given the substantial sunk costs already incurred, EDF finds it difficult to withdraw from the project. Additionally, the HPC project is crucial for EDF's reputation and credibility, and the fact that EDF is state-owned may further incentivise the company to remain committed to the project.

However, EDF is also seeking to withdraw investment from further cooperation with the UK's nuclear station project when the UK government stops tripartite cooperation with China. EDF had initially sought to undertake the Sizewell C project with its Chinese partners, replicating strategies from the HPC project in designs, supply chains, feedback, and experience (EDF 2023 Annual Results, 2024). This implicit motivation aimed to enhance schedule and cost predictability, thereby strengthening industrial efficiency through economies of scale.[17] Following CGN being excluded from Sizewell C, EDF planned to reduce its shareholding in the project to no more than 19.99% in the Final Investment Decision, relinquishing project control. Since EDF cannot enjoy the benefits of the tripartite cooperation, the strike price of the HPC will remain at the original £92.50/MWh.

7.3.3 CGN

For CGN, the situation has been disappointing. CGN invested £6 billion in HPC in exchange for opportunities in Sizewell C and the application of their HP1000 reactor in Bradwell B. However, the UK government had persistent concerns regarding the security implications of Chinese participation in the UK's critical infrastructure. The UK government then proceeded with HPC, guided by French EPR technology under EDF's leadership, while delaying the other two reactors that might be under CGN's leadership. The Bradwell B project proposal remains unapproved, and it is unlikely to proceed due to a lack of political support and local

[17] One tripartite contract of HPC stipulated, "The strike price for HPC is set at £92.50/MWh in 2012. The strike price is fully indexed to UK inflation through the Consumer Price Index. The strike price will be reduced to £89.50/MWh if the Sizewell C project reaches a positive Final Investment Decision, with further compensation from Sizewell C to HPC to share the first-of-a-kind cost of EPR across both UK projects" (EDF Energy, 2022).

stakeholder support (EDF Energy, 2022). Ultimately, CGN withdrew from Sizewell C and was denied permission to pursue the Bradwell B project. To avoid antagonising the Chinese, who intended to showcase their nuclear capabilities through the Bradwell B project (Farrell, 2016), the UK government still granted GDA approval, allowing China to leverage this endorsement to promote its nuclear technology in other international markets.[18]

In conclusion, the HPC project represents a complex and intricate scenario with elements of gain and loss for each participant. China, France, and the UK had strong motivations and put forward ideal plans at the initial stage, but their interests were not entirely aligned. Their uncoordinated actions not only increased transaction costs among participants but also hindered the HPC project from realising the potential benefits of the tripartite cooperation mechanism. In this project, China and its partner country, France, did not alter the dynamics of project financing, as the CfD contract is widely employed in national electricity purchasing in the UK. Instead, the UK government introduced a new financing model to exclude China from future tripartite cooperation projects.

Participant firms tried to generate more benefits, but their attempts were interfered with by the beneficiary countries' governments. While none of the parties achieved all their objectives, through negotiations and compromises in this tripartite cooperation, they achieved part of their respective goals. For the UK, it obtained nuclear power without upfront construction costs but committed to higher electricity bills over 35 years for the citizens. EDF, while incurring additional construction expenses, revitalised its nuclear industry and bolstered its SOEs' influence. China, on its part, provided a substantial investment without immediate returns, but received technological endorsement from the UK nuclear authority, which can help China develop other international markets in the future.

[18] In February 2022, the UK HPR1000 reactor technology successfully completed the GDA process, receiving a Design Acceptance Confirmation (DAC) from the ONR and a Statement of Design Acceptability (SoDA) from the Environment Agency.

7.4 Background of Three Nigerian Ports and Key Participants

The Tincan Island Container Terminal B, Ibom Deep Seaport, and Lekki Deep Seaport projects in Nigeria use the tripartite cooperation mechanism during their construction and/or operation processes. These three port projects share commonalities, such as involving firms from China and France and being located in close geographic proximity. However, they exhibit distinct differences in their project processes and transaction effectiveness. The Tincan and Lekki projects achieved their objectives within specified timeframes and budgets. Each participant played a significant role, leading to highly effective bargaining and negotiation processes, as well as reduced transaction costs. In contrast, the Ibom project's development process remains suspended as of March 2024. By tracing and comparing these cases, this research elucidates how participants shape the dynamics of project finance activities and the cost-benefit generation processes in tripartite cooperation.

This section begins by offering background information and introducing each case, along with details about the involved participants. It then outlines the determinants of China, France, and Nigeria for participating in tripartite cooperation, as well as the Public-Private Partnership (PPP) structure employed in these port projects.

7.4.1 Tincan Island Container Terminal B

In 2005, the Nigerian Ports Authority (NPA)[19] adopted the Landlord model and signed concession agreements with five Terminal Operators to enhance port efficiency, reducing turnaround times and increasing berth occupancy. Within the Tincan Island Port Complex, Terminal B is operated by Tincan Island Container Terminal Ltd (TICT),[20] a multinational SPV established in 2004 through a collaboration between Bolloré

[19] Nigerian Ports Authority (NPA) is a government agency supervised by the Federal Ministry of Transportation. The NPA takes responsibility for the governance and operation of these ports, with ownership stakes in the Tin Can Island project and the Lagos project. Nigerian Ports Authority, "Home," accessed February 9, 2024, https://nigerianports.gov.ng/.

[20] Tincan Island Container Terminal, "About Us," n.d., https://www.tict-ng.com/about-us/.

Transport & Logistics Group[21] (France) and ZIM Integrated Shipping Services (Israel). TICT was awarded a 20-year lease agreement by the Federal Government of Nigeria. This project was a tripartite cooperation involving a French company, an Israeli company, and the Nigerian Ports Authority. China later joined the project through an equity acquisition from the Israeli company. In 2010, the China Merchant Group[22] and China Africa Development Fund jointly acquired 47.5% of TICT shares for USD 154 million.[23] According to the CMP company report, after China's involvement in the project, there was a continuous and significant increase in annual throughput and improved financial performance (CMPG, 2024).

7.4.2 *Ibom Deep Sea Port (IDSP)*

The Ibom Deep Seaport (IDSP) is a greenfield project aimed at addressing congestion, delays, and economic losses resulting from the port concentration in Lagos state. As a part of Nigerian domestic development plan, it is strategically designed as an integral part of the proposed Ibom Industrial City, serving as a gateway to Nigeria's East and North-Eastern regions.[24] The Nigerian Federal Ministry of Transport and the Infrastructure Concession Regulatory Commission have designed the IDSP to adopt a government equity and shareholding model through a SPV—the Port Development Management Company (PDMC). The

[21] The Bolloré Group was founded in 1822 in France. The Bolloré Group has started business on Africa since the beginning of the twentieth century. It has established a strong global position in remote transportation, an integrated logistics network, and electricity storage systems. Bolloré Transport & Logistics actively engaged in African operations for over five decades and has also invested significantly in various social infrastructure sectors, including healthcare, education, environmental quality, culture, and sports. Bolloré Ports serves as Africa's leading port concession operator, having expertise in port concession management, and shipping agency services. It manages 21 port concessions globally, with 16 of these situated in Africa.

[22] China Merchants Group (CMG), established in 1872, currently operates as a Chinese state-owned enterprise directly supervised by the State-owned Assets Supervision and Administration Commission of the State Council (SASAC). CMG is engaged in three core industries: transportation, the development and operation of industrial parks, and finance.

[23] China Merchants Port Holdings Company Limited, "Tin-Can Island Container Terminal Limited (TICT)," accessed February 9, 2024, https://www.cmport.com.hk/EN/business/Detail.aspx?id=10005375.

[24] Nigerian Ports Authority, "Nigeria ICRC PPP Platform," accessed February 9, 2024, https://pp.icrc.gov.ng/project/55/ibom-deep-water-portnbsp.

equity participation in the project is structured with Akwa-Ibom state (20%), the private sector (60%), and a 20% floating stake reserved for potential private investors or other state governments (Oritse, 2016). In 2018, the Akwa Ibom State Government initiated the public competing bidding process. After a rigorous evaluation of bids conducted in accordance with international best practices, the co-bidder consortium formed by Bolloré Ports and PowerChina International Group Ltd[25] was awarded the 50-year concession. These two companies, alongside the local authorities, collectively undertake the development, construction, and operation of this tripartite cooperation project (LUA, 2018).

7.4.3 Lekki Port

In 2011, the Nigerian Ports Authority signed a 45-year concession agreement on a Build, Own, Operate, and Transfer (BOOT) basis with Lekki Port LFTZ Enterprise Limited (LPLEL). LPLEL is responsible for the development, financing, construction, and operation of a greenfield port, as well as overseeing the Lagos Free Trade Zone, situated 60 km to the east of Lagos. LPLEL aims to foster synergy between the port and the Free Trade Zone. At the end of the concession term, LPLEL will transfer the port and its infrastructure back to the NPA. The total investment in this project amounts to $1.043 billion USD, making it the most significant private infrastructure investment in Nigeria (Péron, 2019). CHEC[26]

[25] Powerchina International Group, a comprehensive construction conglomerate, provides services including investment, financing, planning and design, equipment manufacturing, and operation management. It operates across diverse market segments, including water environment management, smart cities, rail transit projects, municipal engineering, and residential buildings. It excels more in hydroelectric and electric power projects. Powerchina International Group, "About US," accessed February 9, 2024, http://www.powerchina-intl.com/.

[26] China Harbour Engineering Company Ltd. (CHEC), established in 1980 as a subsidiary of the Chinese Communications Construction Company, with branch offices in over 80 countries. CHEC offers extensive expertise and experience in delivering Engineering, Procurement, and Construction (EPC), Build-Operate-Transfer (BOT), and Public-Private Partnership (PPP) services across a wide range of infrastructure sectors, including marine engineering, dredging, road and bridge construction, railway and airport projects, building construction, power plant development, and energy exploration. China Harbour Engineering Company, "About Us," accessed February 9, 2024, https://www.cccme.cn/shop/cccme12721/introduction.aspx.

was initially only responsible for the design and construction of the marine and landside infrastructure of the Lekki port.

The Lekki port represents a unique example, as there are two pairs of tripartite cooperation relationships. CHEC took over a part of equity from the original shareholder Tolaram Group. LPLEL includes China Harbour Engineering Company Ltd. (52.5%), Singapore Tolaram Group (22.5%), the Lagos State Government (20%), and the Nigerian Ports Authority (5%), formed the first tripartite cooperation relationship in the financing stage.[27] After the port construction was completed, CHEC and NPA cooperated with CMA CGM,[28] and formed the second tripartite cooperation in the port operation stage.[29] Technically, these complex infrastructure projects involve more than three participants, leading some government and media reports to occasionally refer to them as 'quadripartite cooperation.' However, it is important to note that Singapore's Tolaram Group does not have a direct cooperative relationship with France's CMA CGM. Therefore, it is more rigorous to regard this project as comprising two pairs of tripartite cooperation relationships rather than a quadripartite cooperation project with four parties.

7.4.4 *Determinants of Government and Enterprise Engagement in Port Projects*

7.4.4.1 The Determinants of Local Government

The World Bank report (2017) mentions that ports in West Africa are likely to be 'naturally' monopolised by several multinational shipping

[27] The third party in all projects consistently refers to the role of beneficiary countries. The difference lies in the partner countries, sometimes involving more than one partner from advanced economies.

[28] The CMA CGM Group is a global leader in sea, land, and air logistics. The headquarters is in France, with a network comprising 400 offices and 750 warehouses across 160 countries. The company's subsidiary, CMA TERMINAL, is responsible for the port development, design, construction, acquisition, and operation of terminals. It owns and operates 29 terminals worldwide, strategically positioned to complement those managed by CMA TERMINAL LINK. The CMA CGM Group demonstrates a strong commitment to enhancing port infrastructure across the African continent, where it ranks as the second-largest shipping company. The Group maintains a significant position in Sub-Saharan Africa, comprising a network of 75 agencies and employing nearly 1400 experts. In the region, the Group manages 30 services utilising a fleet of 87 vessels calling at 248 ports (CMA CGM, 2018).

[29] "Lekki Deep Sea Port, Lagos, Nigeria," Ship Technology, n.d., https://www.ship-technology.com/projects/lekki-deep-sea-port-lagos-nigeria/.

enterprises. Due to the vast initial investments and unique geographical advantages required for port development, only giant MNEs possess the capacity to invest in and incorporate African ports into their expansive global logistics networks. Then, these industry leaders can reap the benefits of economies of scale derived from their global shipping networks, as well as economies of scope facilitated by their ownership of inland logistic networks and warehouse hubs in Africa. In Africa, port services are predominantly controlled by APM Terminals and Bolloré Africa Logistics, collectively holding an 80% share of the total container market in West Africa in 2013. However, this oligopoly of service providers leads to diseconomies of scale and economic inefficiencies in African countries, resulting in higher prices and reduced service quality (The World Bank, 2017).

Additionally, West African countries often lack governance experience, regulation tools, and legal frameworks for managing and regulating international terminal operation companies (Goss, 1990). These issues exacerbate market power concentration and natural monopolies. The monopoly held by the private company provides them with accumulated advantages (Slack & Fremont, 2005). Even if local governments aim to increase competition among potential market power holders in terminal operating companies, other private firms are unwilling to enter the market (Lieberman & Montgomery, 1998) because they must consider their inter and intra-port networking, as well as their involvement in inland transport and cross-country movement of traffic and goods (Pallis & De, 2006).

> *We had to address significant revenue leakages and manage indebtedness to third parties, which were holding back the financial sustainability of the ports…Another major challenge was dealing with concession agreements. Many of these agreements didn't hold all parties accountable for fulfilling their obligations, creating imbalances and inefficiencies in operations. The port infrastructure we inherited was in a state of decay—it needed substantial renewal to meet modern standards. We need to find someone to upgrade our ports.*[30]

Therefore, governments in Africa want to introduce new entrants into African maritime markets and often resort to competitive bidding for port concessions to break the existing monopolies. However, the oligopoly of service providers has a first-mover advantage, dominating port services and having more competitiveness than new entrants. Furthermore, the

[30] Interview NPP-20220916.

inclusion of new entrants does not guarantee efficiency, as they lack experience in the local market (Kopel & Löffler, 2008).

Because the ultimate objective for local governments and port authorities is to provide high-quality port services at lower prices (Gilpatric & Li, 2020), the adoption of tripartite cooperation emerges as a practical strategy for attaining these goals. This approach effectively challenges the prevailing monopoly without unduly antagonising the existing shipping giants in Africa. It also facilitates new entrants to access established markets and collaborates with dominant firms, thus enhancing operational efficiency.

7.4.4.2 The Determinants of French Enterprises

French companies, in general, have not shown strong motivation to engage in tripartite cooperation, primarily because they have already monopolised the African port market. As discussed in the previous chapter on the interwoven relationship between cooperation and competition in tripartite cooperation projects, French companies are unlikely to give up their high-profit monopolised industry, including port operation services. However, due to the persistent inflow of Chinese investment and local governments' strategies to diversify constructors and operators (Freitas, 2023), tripartite cooperation has emerged as a compromise approach. This allows French companies to secure new projects and reinforce their influence in the port market. For these companies, such cooperation is a strategic business decision involving collaboration with Chinese companies, local authorities, and terminal operators. For example, CMA CGM, when it signed a MOU with LFTZ Enterprises, openly expressed that this tripartite cooperation strategically aligns with the CMA CGM Group's development objectives in the West African region. The MOU stated that the Lekki port's container terminal will enable CMA CGM to extend its footprint into Nigeria, the primary consumer market in West Africa (CMA CGM, 2018).

7.4.4.3 The Determinants of Chinese Enterprises

The determinants of Chinese enterprises align with their market-seeking and strategic asset-seeking objectives, using tripartite cooperation as a springboard to enter monopolised markets. Tripartite cooperation presents more obvious benefits for Chinese companies seeking to enter the African market. If Chinese companies want to participate in the port business, tripartite cooperation is a viable approach for Chinese port companies.

These four figures (Figs. 7.2a, 7.2b, 7.2c, 7.2d) illustrate the landscape of Chinese investments and construction activities, including ports and railways, as well as Bolloré's network in Africa and CMA CGA's land transportation initiatives on the African continent. These figures reveal that French companies exhibit a more comprehensive logistic and business scope in Africa than their Chinese counterparts.

Unlike their French counterparts, Chinese shipping companies lack experience in the port operation business in the international market (Huang et al., 2020). Through tripartite cooperation, Chinese shipping companies can gain not only a better understanding of the local

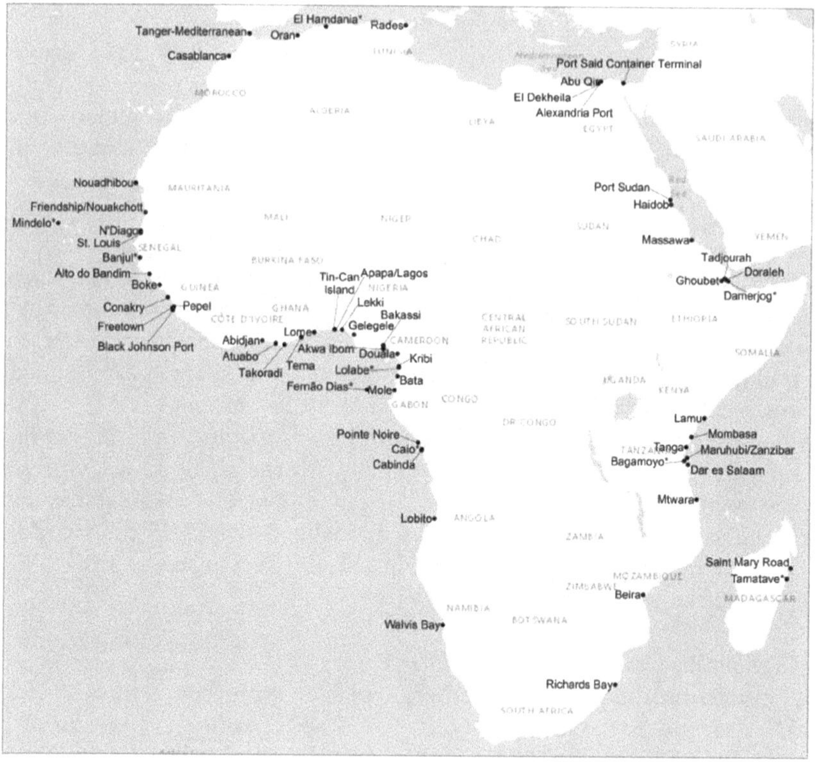

Fig. 7.2a China port projects in Africa in 2022 published document. Source: https://www.nbr.org/publication/inroads-and-outposts-critical-infrastructure-in-chinas-africa-strategy/

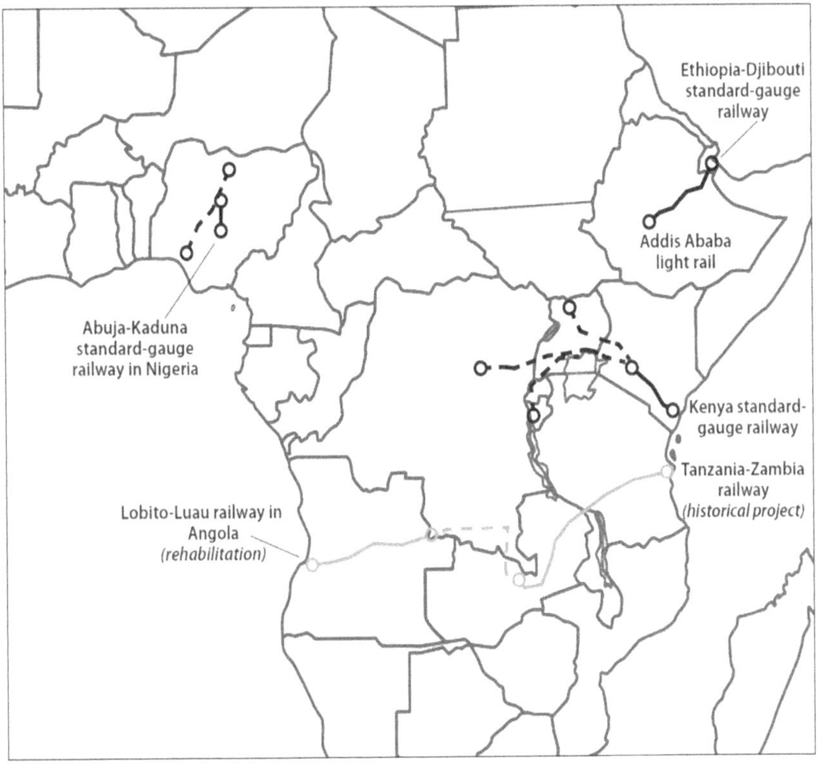

Fig. 7.2b China railway projects in Africa in 2022 published document. Source: https://www.nbr.org/publication/inroads-and-outposts-critical-infrastructure-in-chinas-africa-strategy/

environment but also the know-how from their French partners, enabling them to participate in future concession competitions in other international markets. In the case of the Tincan project, China Merchants regarded this collaboration as an opportunity to establish a partnership with Bolloré, given Bolloré's rich experience and a solid operational network throughout Africa. Following this project, China Merchants Holdings expanded its presence by opening more shipping terminals in the African market, such as terminals in Djibouti, Tanzania, and Togo (Li, 2014). In the Ibom Deep Seaport project, ChinaPower and Bolloré formed a consortium to co-bid for the project. ChinaPower lacked an

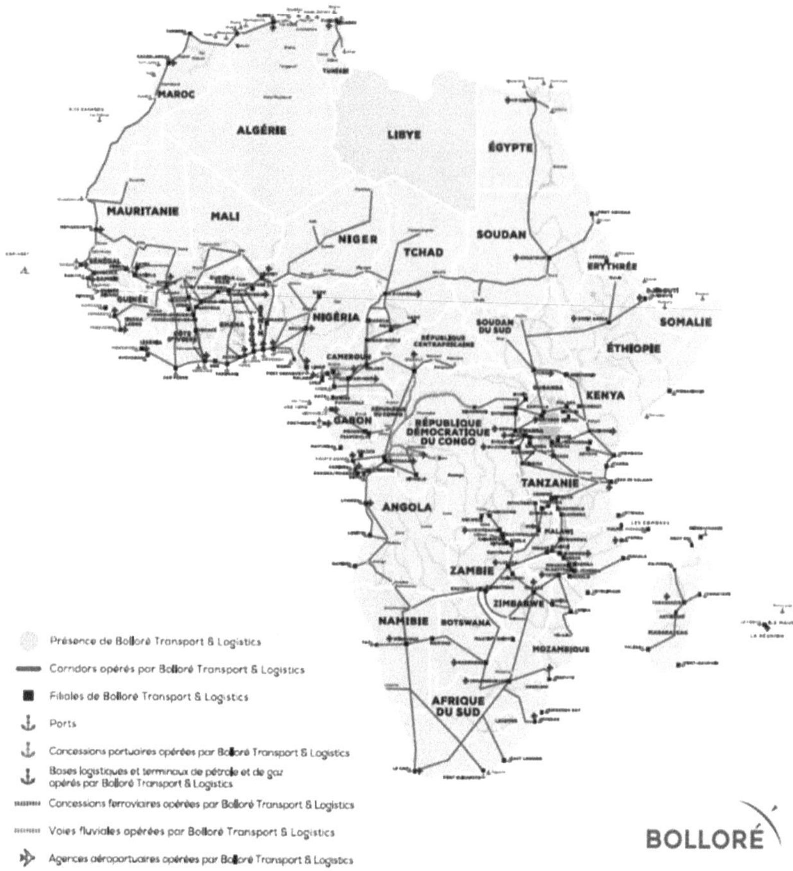

Fig. 7.2c Bollore African network by 2019. Source: https://www.bollore.com/bollo-content/uploads/2020/03/2020-03-12-resultats-bollore-fy-2019_final_uk.pdf

established logistic network in Africa (Shelton & Paruk, 2008) and chose Bolloré as its partner. If ChinaPower had not collaborated with Bolloré with the tripartite cooperation model, its chances of being awarded the bid would have been significantly lower.

For Chinese companies, their expertise lies in engineering project planning, design, and construction, with relatively low-profit margins. In

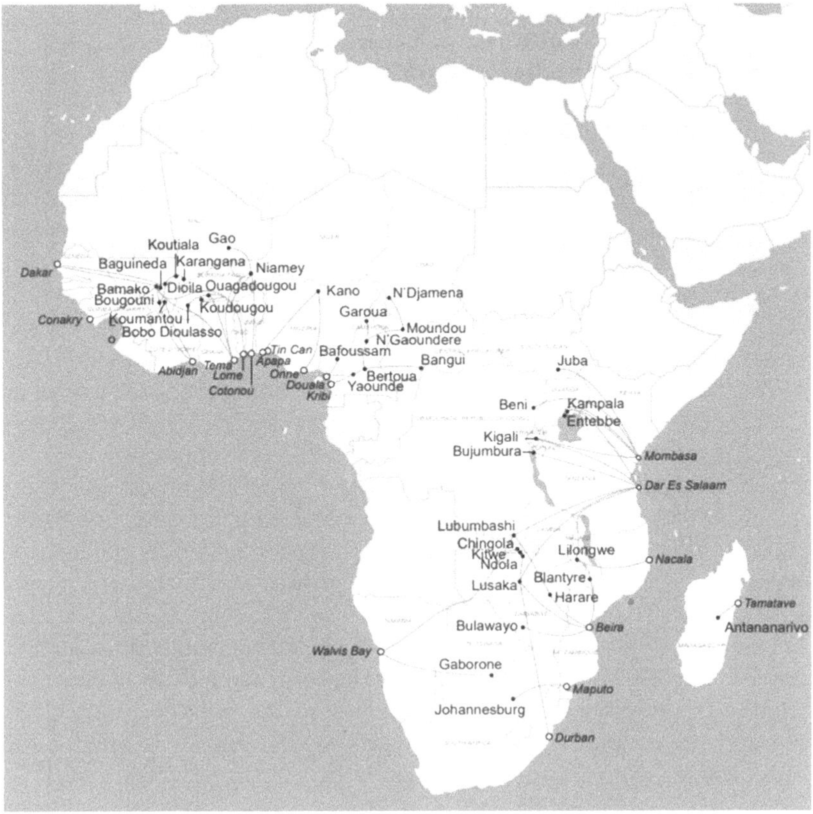

Fig. 7.2d CMA CGA land transportation. (Access on 06 Feb 2024) Source: https://www.cma-cgm.com/intermodal-solutions/africa

recent years, they have proactively ventured into overseas investment and broadened their engagement across the entire spectrum of port-related services. This shift indicates that Chinese companies have embarked on the integration of investment, construction, and asset operations within the port industry (Ghiretti et al., 2023). Tripartite cooperation helped them in this process.

> *China Harbour has built a strong reputation for its capabilities in engineering, especially in planning, design, and construction... Since 2011, China Harbour has made a significant shift by actively expanding into overseas*

investment. This marked a strategic transformation. Instead of just being a contractor, the company started participating in the entire lifecycle of projects—investing, constructing, and even managing operations.[31]

Regarding the Lekki project, this project is the largest deep-water port project in West Africa. CHEC viewed this project as an opportunity to establish its brand image and expand the local market (CCCC, 2012). It was the first time that CHEC utilised the 'build-operation-finance' model in an overseas port project, and then CHEC could apply the experience from the Lekki port to future projects (China Harbour, 2020). At the beginning, CHEC only signed an EPC contract for the Lekki port project. However, when this project encountered financial difficulties in 2015, CHEC decided to invest in the port and transitioned from the role of an EPC contractor to that of a strategic investor (He, 2023). If CHEC were to wait for new investors, there would be additional transaction costs for the construction. Since 2017, CHEC has initiated the process of equity acquisition for the Lekki Port project, encompassing due diligence, equity transaction negotiations, franchise negotiations, operational cooperation negotiations, feasibility studies, decision approvals, and finalising financing arrangements (China Harbour, 2020). In March 2020, CHEC invested 221 million US dollars in LPLEL and concluded the equity infusion process (LPLEL, 2020), thereby becoming the controlling shareholder of the project. In project management, CHEC used the tripartite cooperation approach to streamline management procedures, foster communication, and effectively expedite project progress with their partners (SASAC, 2023).

7.4.5 Public-Private Partnership (PPP) Structure in Port Projects

Large-scale infrastructure projects typically involve longer construction cycles and higher financing requirements, exposing them to significant internal and external risks. Internally, these risks arise during construction and operational phases, while externally, political changes and social influences play a crucial role (Monteiro et al., 2020). To mitigate these risks, beneficiary country governments often employ the PPP model for developing large-scale infrastructure projects. This model involves a concession agreement between the public and private sectors, granting the private

[31] Interview NPP-20221008.

sector authority over activities such as development, design, finance, construction, maintenance, and long-term operation, while the government retains ultimate asset ownership. Consequently, a part of the financial and operational risks is transferred from the government to the private sector (PPIAF, 2007).

The PPP project structure is often complex, involving multiple stakeholders bound by contractual agreements (Demirel et al., 2016). Public sponsors, such as international banks, usually provide loans or equity capital to support these large-scale projects. Given their limited influence and responsibilities during the construction and operation phases, this research does not discuss their roles in tripartite cooperation projects. Instead, the key actors are industrial sponsors, who not only provide equity capital but also contribute the know-how and expertise. They commonly take responsibility for financing, building, and operating the infrastructure (Wang et al., 2023). In these tripartite cooperation case studies, the public authorities in beneficiary countries play important roles, and the international companies are also crucial stakeholders. Although some international participants belong to state-controlled enterprises. They play the role of the private entity in PPPs.

Terminal operating companies have various forms to engage in port operations, including management contracts, strategic equity partnerships, joint ventures, full divestiture, and concessions (Pallis et al., 2008). Management contracts and strategic equity partnerships are less attractive to the private sector due to limited control over performance-enhancing factors like staff retention and investment decisions (Defilippi, 2004). Forming JVs with local authorities is a preferred approach for terminal operating companies, as it allows private investors to exploit their advantages and enhance management efficiency (Notteboom et al., 2022). Chinese port-related companies often form consortia with other international firms, a strategy aimed at sharing benefits and risks. These consortia can pool their collective technical expertise, experience in port construction, operations, and management, along with their extensive network of shipping lines and global alliances (Li et al., 2019). Local port authorities also often use concessions or lease contracts, transferring responsibilities and risks to the private sector while retaining control and ownership of port infrastructure. This landlord port structure is an effective port management approach. The public sector maintains ownership of infrastructure assets and regulatory functions, delegating management activities to the private sector (Guasch, 2004). These methods were also mentioned in Chap. 5, Sect. 5.1.3.

Similar to the general project financing process (see Fig. 7.3), the Nigerian government document detailing the Ibom Deep Sea Port and Free Trade Zone project also suggests using a Public-Private Partnership (PPP) structure in the form of a Port Development & Management Company Model (PDMC). This approach could "combine the interests of the public and private sector, ensure a sufficient level of private capital, expertise and commitment to manage and drive the Ibom DSP Project implementation in a fast and efficient manner."[32]

The original PDMC model, as designed by the Ibom government, comprises several key components:

(1) Concession Agreement: This agreement establishes the terms between the NPA (Grantor) and the Port Development & Management Company (PDMC), with the latter being responsible for the development of the Ibom DSP Project. The PDMC was formed by Bolloré Ports, PowerChina, and Nigerian authorities when the Chinese and French companies were awarded the concession from the Nigerian government.

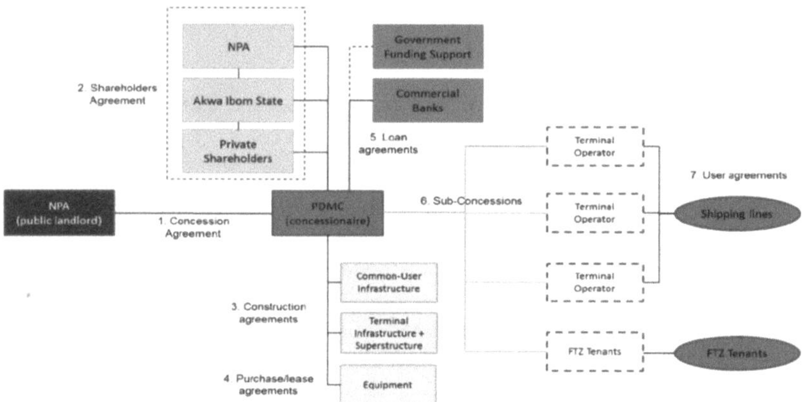

Fig. 7.3 Envisaged PPP structure for Ibom deep sea port and free trade zone project. Source: ICRC, "Ibom deep sea port and free trade zone outline business case final," 2014, https://pp.icrc.gov.ng/media/291

[32] Nigerian Ports Authority, "Nigeria ICRC PPP Platform," accessed February 9, 2024, https://pp.icrc.gov.ng/project/55/ibom-deep-water-portnbsp.

(2) Shareholder Agreement: This agreement involves the Federal Government, represented by the NPA, the Akwa Ibom State Government, and the private sector (Bolloré Ports, PowerChina).

(3–4) Construction Agreement and Purchase/Lease Agreement: These agreements fall under the view of the PDMC, which is responsible for the investment in common-user infrastructure and equipment.

(5) Loan Agreement: The PDMC can arrange debt financing with banks and/or bondholders to secure funding for a portion of its investments.

(6) Sub-Concession Contracts: The PDMC holds the authority to sign sub-concession contracts with separate terminal operators or service providers.

The other two port projects have a similar structure. Although there are more than three entities involved in port projects, this research only focuses on the actions of key stakeholders in the tripartite cooperation dimension, particularly the participants that form the PDMC—they are the pivotal actors in these PPP projects. The stakeholder grid of Nigerian port projects is the following (Table 7.2).

The overall structure of the Nigerian port projects resembles the stakeholder grid of the HPC project. Chinese and French companies with equity stakes are the most crucial stakeholder groups in these port projects. They not only hold the port assets but also bear the responsibility for developing, constructing, and operating these facilities. Additionally, local stakeholders, including the Nigerian Federal Government, the Nigeria Ports Authority (NPA), and the Ibom State Government, also have equity in these projects and exert control over the processes and assets. These parties are pivotal in the Nigerian port projects, and their actions significantly impact transaction costs and additional benefits throughout the cooperation process. They also have economic gains from the projects. Unlike the HPC project, where the UK government wielded substantial political and economic influence that impeded progress, the Nigerian government has been more supportive of these projects. International sponsors, such as the World Bank and Chinese policy banks, have influence on these projects, but their influence is limited to the financing process. While suppliers and shippers are relevant, they are not directly involved in the tripartite cooperation activities.

Table 7.2 The stakeholder grid of Nigerian port projects (Source: Author)

	Formal or voting	*Economic*	*Political*
Equity	Stockholders (Bolloré, CMHI, CHEC, Tolaram, Nigerian Federal government and NPA)	Stockholders (Bolloré, CMHI, CHEC, Tolaram, Nigerian Federal government and NPA)	
Economic		Suppliers Shippers Shipping lines (CMA CGA) Debt holders (International Development Banks; Chinese policy bank)	Government (Federal government, local government)
Influencers	Government (Federal government, transportation authorities, NPA)		Government (Federal government, local government)

7.4.6 Power-Interest Struggles in Nigerian Port Projects

Given that West African port projects operate in naturally monopolistic markets, the Nigerian government introduced port concession and effective contracts. The government can identify more efficient suppliers through a competitive bidding process and regulate company behaviour through contractual terms and conditions (Theys et al., 2010). During concession agreement negotiations between local port authorities and the international private sector, two primary points of contention arise: the duration of the concession and the trade-offs between port performance and investment in port growth.

> *We view port operation rights as strategically critical—not just for economic growth but also for national security reasons. So, we tend to be very selective and involved in the decision-making process.*[33]
>
> *Ports are highly attractive to international investment because of their strong financial returns. This brings another layer of competition, with private investors, multinational corporations, and even state-backed entities all vying for opportunities. It creates a scenario where you're not only competing on tech-*

[33] Interview NPP-20220916.

nical and operational expertise but also navigating complex political, strategic, and financial dynamics to secure and maintain those rights.[34]

In the first wave of port concession in West Africa (2004–2010), most of the concessions focused on the rehabilitation and reuse of existing ports (The World Bank, 2017). The sunk costs in these port projects are relatively lower due to their brownfield nature, and the concession period is shorter (Notteboom et al., 2022, Chapter 3.9). For instance, the Tincan project had an initial contract term of 15 years, with the potential for a five-year extension. In the Tincan project, the government document outlines various risks for the concessionaire, including the provision of utility risk, construction risk, completion risk, technical risk, operational risk, financial risk, and termination risk (NPA, 2006). However, given that the Tincan project is a brownfield project, its overall risk profile is still lower than that of greenfield projects like Ibom and Lekki. The assured throughput and high legacy handling tariffs are more likely to generate high returns on investment for brownfield terminals, allowing them to operate with positive cash flow. In contrast, greenfield infrastructure projects involve larger initial investments, and their throughput is more uncertain.

However, investing the greenfield ports is inevitable as existing ports get closer to capacity. The second wave of port concessions occurred after 2010, there were more large greenfield terminal developments (The World Bank, 2017). In most cases, new ports are in less favourable locations that require higher investment in port construction and in-land transportation connections. Companies involved in these projects needed to be confident about future activity volumes. In greenfield port investments, longer-duration contracts tend to support efficient investments in greenfield assets, as sunk costs are an important component of total costs. This rationale explains why the Nigerian government finally gave the longer concession durations of the Ibom (50 years) and Lekki (45 years) projects.

Another bargaining point exists among different port users. There are three main port users: terminal operation companies, shipping lines (the company carrying shippers' cargo at sea) and shippers (cargo senders, the ultimate clients of the ports). These user groups are exposed to different risks related to operating efficiency and pricing (Notteboom et al., 2022). Therefore, local port authorities must strike a balance among these three key stakeholders. On one hand, they need to prevent terminal operation

[34] Interview NPP-20220830.

companies from extracting monopoly rents and promote transparency of cost information to attract more port users. On the other hand, shipping lines and shippers are highly influenced by the efficiency of terminal operation companies since delays can result in additional costs, whether due to waiting for an available berth or experiencing low productivity while at the berth (Angeldonis, 2010). When there is excess capacity, shipping lines benefit from reduced waiting times, but terminal companies may face issues related to over-investment or overestimation of demand. Therefore, local port authorities have to balance the interests of these three stakeholder groups (Vanelslander, 2005; Haralambides, 2002).

The challenges in these two aspects impact negotiation costs in port projects. Therefore, tripartite cooperation, as a semi-internalisation approach, involves establishing JV/SPVs to strengthen participants' aligned interests in Tincan and Lekki projects. By binding more stakeholders' interests in JV/SPVs, participants in tripartite cooperation aim to reduce negotiation costs and transaction costs for these three port projects.

7.5 Tripartite Cooperation in Nigerian Port Projects

7.5.1 *Benefits from Tripartite Cooperation*

Tripartite cooperation is an approach to upgrade the port technology and infrastructure, while concurrently mitigating competition costs and attracting more international investment. According to the cooperation and coordination in port management (Brooks et al., 2011), some tripartite cooperation projects in the port industry manifest both vertical and horizontal integration. These integration activities generate benefits for tripartite cooperation projects.

> *Historically, our traditional port business was heavily focused on low-profit models like EPC (Engineering, Procurement, and Construction) and DB (Design-Build). While these approaches helped us establish a presence, they offered limited growth potential and struggled with profitability. Over the past three decades, especially in Africa, this traditional EPC model has reached a development ceiling… In response, we started extending the port industry chain both upstream and downstream. By integrating investment and operation into our business model, we've been able to improve the quality of our*

overseas port projects. This approach not only expanded our operational space but also allowed us to achieve higher-quality returns.[35]

Notteboom et al. (2022) presented a figure illustrating cooperation and coordination in strategic port management (see Fig. 7.4). Applying this structure to tripartite cooperation, participants can align processes from the hinterland to the foreland, including port-related logistics, port services, and shipping lines. At the vertical level, it involves a broader range of services, enabling the local port authority and Chinese port companies to integrate the logistical networks of French companies. Participants can expand the port project's reach from maritime to inland services. The additional benefit in this context comes from economies of scope achieved through the expansion of services. On the horizontal level, tripartite cooperation within port terminals includes investments in upgrading facilities, expanding port scale, and implementing modern port management processes, ultimately enhancing port operational efficiency (Juhel, 2001). These activities contribute to economies of scale in tripartite cooperation projects. In contrast, bilateral cooperation aligns with fewer production circles and loses the benefits from the economies of scope and economies of scale.

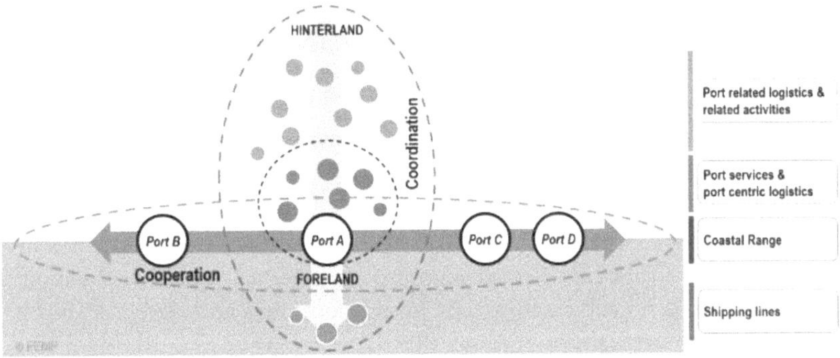

Fig. 7.4 Cooperation and coordination in strategic port management. (Source: Notteboom et al., 2022)

[35] Interview NPP-20221008.

Most tripartite cooperation projects use both vertical and horizontal synergy strategies. For example, when CMHI took control of the Tincan port in 2010, the terminal lacked modern machinery, resulting in severe capacity constraints, low productivity, and severe congestion and penalties for shipping lines and shippers. To address these issues, TICT exploited its resources to modernise the container facilities. CMHI's expertise in handling large-scale loading and equipment, coupled with Bolloré's strong local management experience and logistics network across Africa (NPA, 2006), facilitated equipment upgrades and acquisitions initiated by CMHI, while Bolloré improved organisational and operational efficiency at the terminal level. Through this collaboration, the Tincan terminal significantly improved its efficiency and reduced costs for users (Onyenucheya, 2024).

> *...Our main focus was really on bringing the Chinese and French management teams together for genuine cooperation and a win-win outcome. With the TICP project, we managed to recover our entire investment in just six years after taking it over. And once our French colleagues saw that track record, they couldn't help but voice their admiration. I think the success of the Lagos TICP project has really strengthened our in expanding its port business overseas.*[36]

The participants in the Lekki project also utilised the tripartite cooperation mechanism to generate more benefits from economies of scale and economies of scope. The Managing Director of Lekki Port revealed that the port employs cutting-edge technology and state-of-the-art equipment. In preparation for port operations, CHEC transferred three Super Post Panamax Ships to Shore cranes and ten Rubber Tired Gantries from Shanghai to Nigeria. The NPA also procured the Vessel Tracking System for the Lekki channel, thereby enhancing port efficiency in clearing processes (Onyenucheya, 2022a, 2022b). The Lekki port's competitive advantage lies in its capacity to accommodate larger vessels and expedite ship discharges, thereby minimising vessel port stays and costs for importers and exporters (Gabriel & Ajayi, 2023). The advanced equipment leverages the Lekki port's technology and efficiency, positioning it at the forefront of West African container operations. Upon operation and management, CMA CGA is responsible for the screening and processing of shipments. The CEO of Lekki Freeport Terminal, Mr. Denrick Moos, highlighted CMA CGM's commitment to supporting Lekki's supply

[36] Interviewee NPP-20220922.

chains and enhancing Lekki port as an African hub for trans-shipment, handling cargoes in transit to other destinations (Oladipo, 2023; LPLEL, 2023). Participants align both vertical and horizontal activities to add benefits to the Lekki project.

> *...We've recently rolled out this new Revenue Invoice Management System with provisional and final billing, plus a customer portal module. The idea is to really boost our service quality, strengthen our relationships with partners, streamline payments, and cut down on fraud and revenue leaks...On top of that, we just brought in four new tugboats to make our operations more efficient. And another big step we've taken is starting a review of our concession agreements, so we can work more smoothly with all stakeholders and keep the maritime industry growing. We believe this approach is going to open a whole new chapter for us.*[37]

Another benefit of tripartite cooperation is its potential to mitigate negative international commentary. International rumours or negative reports can sometimes lead to additional costs for projects like the Lekki project. For example, when The Guardian Newspaper published a headline titled 'N595.65b Lekki Deep Seaport Courts Trouble,' participants reacted promptly. Entities like CHEC, Tolaram Group, and local Public Relations Consultants expressed their dissatisfaction with this misleading headline, which mistakenly portrayed the project negatively. Participants actively engaged with the Federal and State Governments, who are shareholders and stakeholders in the project, to reassess the project and reaffirm its standards (Abimbola, 2020).

7.5.2 More Transaction Costs

While the adaptation of tripartite cooperation offers several benefits, participants also incur transaction costs in these port projects. These transaction costs stem from actions taken by both the local government and the private sector.

Firstly, transaction costs arise from the involvement of multiple parties and their lack of coordination. In Nigerian port projects, this process is heavily influenced by various political economy factors. Large-scale port projects involve substantial strategic and financial risks, resulting in a

[37] Interviewee NPP-20220925.

tendering process overseen by a combination of official bodies, such as line ministries, finance ministries, PPP units, and public procurement regulatory agencies, as well as unofficial channels, including direct discussions between bidders and high-level government officials. This intricate process often conveys chaotic signals to the market and escalates costs for local authorities (Bance, 2003; Musso et al., 2006). For example, to secure loans from the China Development Bank, LPLEL and CDB signed numerous agreements, including the Facility Agreement, Sponsor Support Agreement, Completion Guarantee Agreement, and the Tripartite Keepwell Agreement, in addition to seven accompanying security documents (LPLEL, 2021). In cases of project disputes, local governments and container companies can specify dispute resolution mechanisms in their contracts, potentially lowering transaction costs compared to open-market scenarios. However, the multiple agreements generate higher transaction costs than bilateral arrangements.

Secondly, the port authority's role as a shareholder contradicts the landlord principle in theory (UNCTAD, 1998). Port authorities argue that direct participation in commercial operations is necessary to control and regulate the concessionaire (Van Niekerk, 2005). The NPA retained a 5% stake to "give the investors comfort and enable it to perform its oversight technical regulatory functions without being unduly hindered by commercial considerations" (Salau, 2018). Effective monitoring, timely remedies, and alignment shareholder interest on equity can efficiently manage ports (Verhoeven, 2010). Based on these reasons, Mohammed Bello-Koko, the Managing Director of NPA, said that NPA initially planned to hold around 20–25% equity in Lekki Port but later decided to reduce government involvement, lowering its stake while retaining 5% equity. He emphasised that regardless of NPA's equity ownership, it remains the regulator for port activities (ThisDay, 2016). However, if the public sector holds shares but fails to fulfil promised investments, it can hinder the progress of the project. NPA impeded the Lekki project's development by only contributing \$23 million out of the required \$110 million in equity shares in 2018 (Anumihe, 2018). With insufficient development funds for construction and procurement, the development process lagged behind expectations.

Thirdly, the worst situation with more transaction costs arises when tripartite cooperation fails, and the participating companies withdraw from the project. This leads to various losses for both private investors and local authorities. Investors incur sunk costs related to bid preparation, negotiation, etc. For instance, although the Bolloré-ChinaPower consortium initially signed a heads of terms agreement (HTA) with the NPA, the consortium still decided to withdraw from the Ibom project (InfraPPP, 2018). The withdrawal was attributed to concerns about the controversy surrounding the project's location. Okon Nkpubre, who is the Chairman, of Òrò Nation Technical Committee on Ibom Deep Seaport, said the reason is "*concerning the avoidable controversy surrounding the Ibaka Deep Sea Port project, let me categorically say that no investor would want to waste his hard earned money or borrowed funds to go and dig out a dry land equivalent to about 150 football (Soccer) fields to create an artificial ocean for a Deep Sea Port in Ibeno LGA when a natural harbour with undredged draft of 11meters is close by at Ibaka, only 10km away*" (Oritse, 2021). Another reason for withdrawal was the local protests, where the people of Oron submitted a petition against the state government, which deterred Chinese and French investors. The petitioners were irritated over the change in the project's name and the relocation of the project site (Anthony, 2021).

After the Bolloré-ChinaPower consortium's exit in 2020, although some international investors such as Chinese company CHEC, the U.S. Consulate in Nigeria and the South Korea Busan Port Authority expressed interest in the project (Eka, 2021; Odey, 2021) did not yield any practical outcome. More transaction costs arose when the local government sought new potential investors. Local authorities even lost the advantage of negotiating with other potential bidders. The Akwa Ibom government found itself in an unfavourable position, as previous investors had withdrawn, leaving the government with limited financial capacity to develop the Ibom Deep Seaport (Anthony, 2021). This situation diminished their bargaining power in seeking capable and experienced investors for the project.

In conclusion, these three port projects have received vital support from the beneficiary country, with the Nigerian government providing supportive policies, particularly for the Lekki project. While participants in these projects had their own motivations, they made efforts to align their interests, especially through equity cooperation and the establishment of JV/SPVs. Although participants derived benefits from vertical and horizontal cooperation, there were still some transaction costs incurred during the tripartite cooperation process.

7.6 Case Comparison and Conclusion

The cases in this chapter represent two types of tripartite cooperation: the HPC project in a developed country and the three port projects in a developing country. The major distinctions between China-North-North and China-North-South cooperation lie in their different financing approaches. Depending on the financing method, a tripartite cooperation project can be classified as either a business-model project or a development-model project. In developed countries, foreign inflows typically manifest as foreign investments. In the HPC project, the Chinese firm played a major role with a £6 billion investment and acted as a shareholder in the SPV. In developing countries, these inflows often appear as development assistance or concession loans. For instance, in the Lekki port project, although the Chinese company invested $221 million into the JV and became a shareholder, the Chinese policy bank, CDB, still granted medium- and long-term loans amounting to $629 million (CDB, 2023).

Another distinction lies in the domestic environments of developed and developing countries. Differences in economic and political policies, social environments, legal systems, and technical support within beneficiary countries may influence the outcome of a tripartite cooperation project. When beneficiary countries are developed countries, they typically have more well-established political and economic systems compared to developing countries (Coelho et al., 2014). However, their democratic policy procedures for tripartite cooperation projects often take longer, which can influence transaction costs. For example, in the HPC project, the UK government took about three months to review Chinese and French investment and technological documents (Mason & Goodley, 2016). In contrast, the Nigerian federal government fast-tracked approval for the NPA in the Lekki project (Vanguard, 2022). Additionally, the UK government may hold stronger, even antagonistic positions towards Chinese investment in infrastructure projects, as it views China as a competitor (Waitzman, 2023). Conversely, the Nigerian government may adopt a more friendly attitude towards Chinese investment in infrastructure projects, as it regards China as an international donor/developer and an alternative to monopolising French involvement in the country (Bräutigam, 2009; Oshodi, 2022).

In particular, the key difference between the HPC project and the three Nigerian port projects lies in the interests' alignment. In the HPC project, although the UK government aimed to develop nuclear energy, it did not directly invest in the project and did not bear project costs (UK GOV, 2016; Suleiman, 2024). Consequently, the UK government did not prioritise minimising transaction costs, allowing it to implement multiple policies that might hindered project progress. On the contrary, in the Nigerian port projects, the Nigerian government and/or its port authorities are shareholders (Salau, 2018). They invest in these projects and share risks and interests with China and France, thereby having stronger motivations to promote project success.

According to Freeman's (1984) process-level stakeholder analysis of project direction, programmes, and budgets, insights can be gained into the projects' control systems. Additionally, the transactional-level stakeholder analysis can be used to evaluate the stakeholder management capacity of projects. Stakeholder management capacity is defined by both the effectiveness of processes for dealing with stakeholders and the transaction costs incurred in achieving the project's objectives.

In the HPC project, after a thorough examination of the project's delayed progress and budget performance, it has become evident that the project's control system structure was influenced by inherent flaws and external factors. Transaction effectiveness among stakeholders is relatively low, as evidenced by the numerous agreements involved. For instance, participant companies in the HPC project signed a total of 81 agreements, including 56 core agreements, 12 non-core agreements, and 13 government agreements, amounting to over 3000 pages (Xie, 2016). Additionally, as discussed in Sects. 7.2 and 7.3, non-aligned interests among stakeholders have led to increased transaction costs, such as renegotiation costs and contract costs. Financing resources and technological supports are allocated inefficiently for interaction among stakeholders, contributing to low process effectiveness. With continuously increasing construction budgets (from £16 billion to £46 billion) and delays (from 2018 to 2028), the project's progress is significantly hindered.

The analysis of the HPC project reveals the stakeholder management capacity, as depicted in Table 7.3a, with the low process and low transaction effectiveness.

Three Nigerian port projects exhibit distinct differences in their process level and transaction level. The Tincan project and Lekki project stand out for their effective control systems, successfully achieving project targets within stipulated timeframes and budgets. Each participant provided relevant support to these projects. Despite an initial sluggish phase in the Lekki project, after CHEC signed cooperation agreements, the construction process was expedited. The Nigerian authorities used administrative policy and approaches to expedite the delivery of the project. The NPA initiated the process of seeking Presidential approval to designate the port as a Customs Port and Approved Wharf on a fast-track basis (Vanguard, 2022). Additionally, the Minister of Transportation introduced quarterly site visits in August 2020, followed by monthly visits to oversee construction and promptly address any arising issues. Completing the Lekki port in a record time of 45 months shows the effectiveness of diligent ministerial supervision and strict regulatory oversight (Ogunlesi, 2023). At the transactional level, participants displayed prompt responsiveness to each other, fostering high effectiveness in bargaining and negotiation processes, thereby minimising transaction costs in these two projects.

In contrast, the Ibom project's control system appears robust, as both the federal government and local government have clear direction and strategic programmes (ICRC, 2014). Its process has high effectiveness. However, the local government wrongly prioritised the opinions of local protestors over business reasons, a less significant stakeholder group, over the interests of port developers and investors, the more critical stakeholder group. This misplaced prioritisation decision resulted in the withdrawal of Bolloré-PowerChina from the project, making it difficult to attract new investors. Consequently, the transaction effectiveness of the Ibom project is lower than the other two port projects.

The analysis of these three projects depicts their stakeholder management capacities in the following tables (Table 7.3b, 7.3c, 7.3d):

By reviewing these practical tripartite cooperation projects, this research found that China is a relatively new participant engaging in international infrastructure projects. This is an area in which France and its enterprises possess extensive historical experience and advanced expertise, both in developed and developing countries. China's proposed tripartite cooperation aims to secure partial interests in beneficiary countries, where markets are dominated by French enterprises. In these four tripartite cooperation cases, the financing stage combines the Chinese and French approaches, involving the signing of different financial agreements with international policy banks.

Adding a new partner causes more complexities and problems for the projects, leading to increased transaction, negotiation, and bargaining costs (Hass, 2009). In most cases, the actions of participants would generate higher costs in tripartite cooperation projects. However, in some ideal

Table 7.3a Stakeholder management capacity of the HPC project (Source: Author)

Process effectiveness	High		
	Low		√
		High	Low
	Transaction effectiveness		

Table 7.3b Stakeholder management capacity of the Tincan project (Source: Author)

Process effectiveness	High	√	
	Low		
		High	Low
	Transaction effectiveness		

Table 7.3c Stakeholder management capacity of the Ibom project (Source: Author)

Process effectiveness	High		√
	Low		
		High	Low
	Transaction effectiveness		

Table 7.3d Stakeholder management capacity of the Lekki project (Source: Author)

Process effectiveness	High		
	Medium	√	
	Low		
		High	Low
	Transaction effectiveness		

situations, synergy among participants can add value to tripartite cooperation. Through internalisation or semi-internalisation, participants in tripartite cooperation can gain additional benefits when specialised goods or services are exchanged internally rather than being purchased from external markets. These specialised goods or services include raw materials, advanced machinery, technology, local networks, etc. Tripartite cooperation can also broaden economies of scope by aligning the vertical value chain. Companies can drive technological upgrades that improve efficiency and expand economies of scale by aligning the horizontal value chain. For instance, in projects such as the China-France-Nigeria port collaboration, Chinese and French firms directly supplied advanced ship equipment for the Lekki port, thereby enhancing port organisational and operational efficiency and streamlining clearing processes.

This internalisation strategy saved on costs related to equipment sourcing, contract negotiations, and goods delivery. Similarly, French companies provided cargo services and existing networks in Africa, allowing the new ports to directly utilise these services, thus saving transaction costs associated with searching for shipping lines and warehouses (Notteboom et al., 2022; Oladipo, 2023; LPLEL, 2023).

In the final section of Chap. 4, I introduced Fig. 4.2 to illustrate the process tracing framework of tripartite cooperation. In Chap. 6, I revisited this figure, revealing the unique determinants for participants joining infrastructure projects using tripartite cooperation approaches. However, the findings of Chap. 6 did not thoroughly explore X1(a). For the key research question of this study—Why do participants opt for a tripartite cooperation model, even though they potentially bear additional transaction costs?—Chap. 6 and Fig. 6.2 only address the first half of this question. Therefore, this chapter reintroduces and refines this framework, utilising insights from the HPC project and the Nigerian port projects to explore the determinants of X1(a) and answer the second half of the key research question: when participants find they have to potentially bear additional transaction costs, why do they still insist on staying in the project? In Fig. 7.5a, I marked the information for the HPC project in orange, and for the Nigerian port projects in pink in Fig. 7.5b.

In the HPC project, China's initial objectives included promoting Chinese technology in the UK nuclear industry, developing new international markets, and acquiring operational knowledge and experience from its French partner. France aimed to reduce its company's financial burdens and risks while sustaining its reputation in Europe. The UK used tripartite cooperation as a strategic economic and political move post-Brexit. Their overall determinants were to share the high risks and costs of nuclear projects and replicate HPC strategies in the Sizewell C project to lower overall costs. These X1 determinants prompted relevant actions from the participants. The Chinese and French governments employed financial instruments by providing financial support to their respective SOEs and soft law instruments, such as signing MOUs. In contrast, the UK government

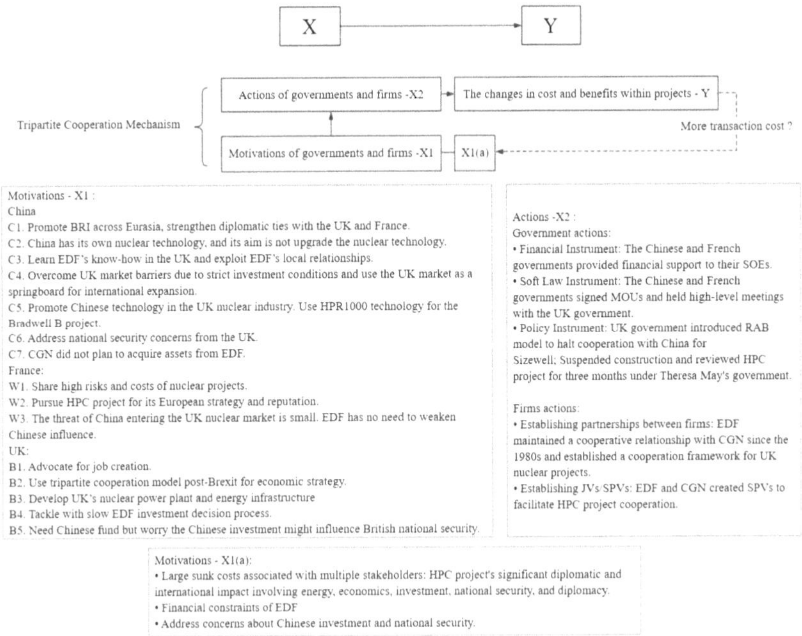

Fig. 7.5a Summary of motivation and actions in tripartite cooperation from the HPC project (Source: Author)

used policy instruments to influence the project's progression and aimed to maximise its interests. Chinese and French firms played crucial roles in the HPC project, forming new SPVs to advance the project. These determinants led to changes in the transaction costs and benefits (Y) in the HPC project.

The critical question for the HPC project is why participants continued despite increased transaction costs—the determinants of X1(a). The reasons include the substantial sunk costs already invested; abandoning the project would result in significant losses for all participants. This project also holds considerable international significance, involving energy, economics, investment, national security, and diplomacy. Additionally, participants also benefit from risk sharing and distribution. France faced severe financial constraints and could not assume the risks alone, and the UK government was also keen to retain Chinese capital in the project. With

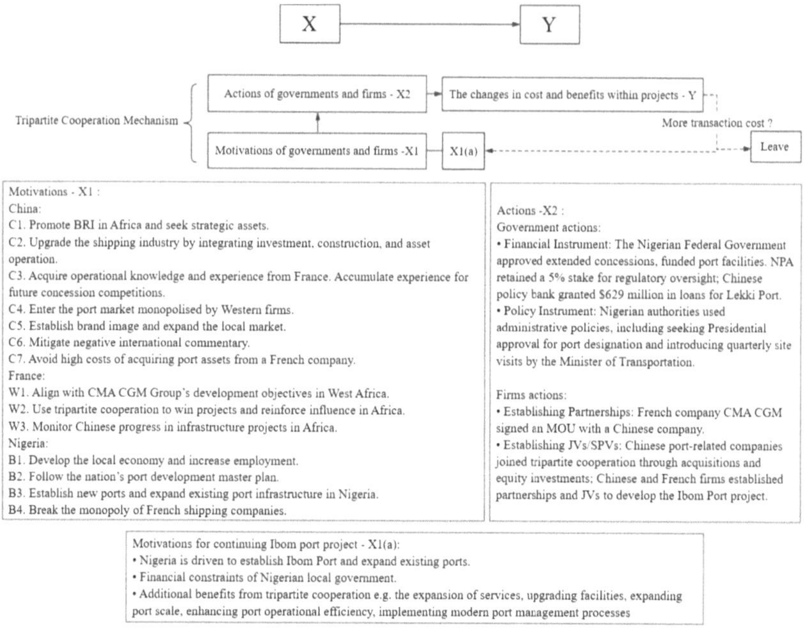

Fig. 7.5b Summary of motivation and actions in tripartite cooperation from Nigerian ports (Source: Author)

French involvement, the UK government could address domestic criticisms and concerns about Chinese investment and national security.

The findings from the three Nigerian port projects reveal distinct differences compared to the HPC project. Determinants relevant to the HPC project do not necessarily apply to these Nigerian projects. Specifically, it was not necessary to consider X1(a) in the Nigerian port projects (see Fig. 7.5b). The Tincan Island Container Terminal B and Lekki Port projects had effective control systems and achieved project targets within stipulated timeframes and budgets, indicating a relative balance between transaction costs and additional benefits. This suggests that the tripartite cooperation framework potentially offers some additional advantages. In contrast, the HPC project has more internal weaknesses (large sunk costs, high risks, and financial constraints) and external threats (economic and political backlash). Therefore, participants easily exited the Ibom Deep Sea Port project due to its early stage and low sunk costs.

In Nigeria, China's goals included seeking strategic assets, entering new markets, and promoting BRI in Africa, while France aimed to maintain and strengthen its influence in Nigeria. Contrary to the assumption that China has accumulated extensive experience in the developing world, the French traditional donor possessed more advantages in Nigeria due to its close historical, political, and economic ties. Therefore, Chinese firms use tripartite cooperation as an approach to enter the markets of beneficiary countries, while French firms use tripartite cooperation as a strategy to control and monitor the progress of Chinese firms.

Similar to the HPC project, Nigeria's motivations for local economic growth, employment, and infrastructure were not the primary reasons for tripartite cooperation, as these objectives could be achieved through cooperation with France alone. Nigeria's primary target was to break the monopoly of French shipping companies and upgrade its local port infrastructure.

These motivations influenced the actions of the participants. Consequently, the Chinese government continued to support its SOEs with financial instruments, and local authorities provided policy support. The French government were reluctant to get involved in these projects. The main actors in these projects were Chinese and French firms, which established partnerships or joint ventures to bid for and develop the projects. Even though potential more transaction costs could arise in the Tincan and Lekki ports, participants were still willing to move forward with these projects due to the additional benefits from tripartite cooperation, such as service expansion, facility upgrades, port scale expansion, enhanced operational efficiency, and the implementation of modern port management processes.

When Chinese and French firms anticipated increased transaction costs and considered the lower commercial returns, they chose to withdraw from the Ibom project. However, the Nigerian government remains eager to find new investors to develop this project, driven by the desire to establish Ibom Port to mitigate congestion, delays, and economic losses resulting from the port concentration in Lagos state. Due to the financial constraints of the Ibom authorities' inability to take on significant risks for developing a greenfield project, the quest for new investment continues.

In conclusion, this chapter uses different cases to illustrate the practice of tripartite cooperation. It presents empirical findings that address the primary research question: Why did participants choose a tripartite cooperation model despite potentially higher transaction costs? Their decisions were influenced by determinants arising from both the internal weaknesses of the projects and external threats to the participants. These factors shaped their actions in tripartite cooperation, as the participants sought to maximise their additional benefits while minimising transaction costs. In the Conclusion chapter, I will provide a comprehensive comparison of the determinants, cooperation instruments, transaction costs, and additional benefits using the information from previous literature and empirical studies.

References

Abimbola, B. (2020, July 30). N595.65b Lekki deep seaport courts trouble. *The Guardian Nigeria News*. https://guardian.ng/opinion/n595-65b-lekki-deep-seaport-courts-trouble-2/

AFP. (2016, May 17). Hollande Renews Support for EDF Nuclear Project in Britain. *Agence France Presse*. https://www.rfi.fr/en/contenu/20160517-hollande-renews-support-edf-nuclear-project-britain

Ambrose, J. (2017, July 3). Cost of Hinkley Point Nuclear Plant Climbs Another £1.5bn to Over £20bn, as Project Faces Further Delay. *The Telegraph*. https://www.telegraph.co.uk/business/2017/07/03/hinkley-nuclear-costs-climb--almost-20bn-start-delayed/

Ambrose, J. (2019, July 27). Despite Hinkley, the New Plan for Nuclear is Hardly Better than the Old One. The Guardian. https://www.theguardian.com/business/2019/jul/27/despite-hinkley-new-plan-nuclear-hardly-better-than-old-one

Ambrose, J. (2020, July 31). Hinkley Point C: French Watchdog Fines EDF €5m for False Claims on Cost. *The Guardian*. https://www.theguardian.com/uk-news/2020/jul/31/hinkley-point-c-french-watchdog-fines-edf-5m-for-false-claims-on-cost

Ambrose, J. (2021, October 27). Government Pledges £1.7bn of Public Money to New Nuclear Plant. *The Guardian*. https://www.theguardian.com/environment/2021/oct/27/government-pledges-17bn-of-public-money-to-new-nuclear-plant

Angeldonis, E. F. D. (2010). Access Regulation for Naturally Monopolistic Port Terminals. https://repub.eur.nl/pub/19881/EPS2010204LIS9789058922458.pdf

Anthony, L. (2021, October 1). NEWSTell Our People Real Reason Investors Withdrew from Ibom Deep Seaport Project—NKpubre to Gov Emmanuel. *Daily Post*. https://dailypost.ng/2021/10/01/tell-our-people-real-reason-investors-withdrew-from-ibom-deep-seaport-project-nkpubre-to-gov-emmanuel/

Anumihe, I. (2018, February 12). Lekki Deep Seaport: NPA Paid Only $23m Out of $110m Equity Share. *The Sun*. https://sunnewsonline.com/lekki-deep-seaport-npa-paid-only-23m-out-of-110m-equity-share/?expand_article=1

Bance, P. (2003). Opening up Public Services to Competition by Putting Them Out to Tender: An Evaluation. *Annals of Public and Cooperative Economics, 74*(1), 33–61. https://doi.org/10.1111/1467-8292.00214

BBC. (2013, February 4). Centrica Pulls Out of New UK Nuclear Projects. *BBC News*. https://www.bbc.com/news/business-21319031

Branigan, T. (2016, August 8). Britain has Struck Out for a Special Relationship with China. If Only we Knew the Way. *The Guardian*. https://www.theguardian.com/commentisfree/2016/aug/08/britain-trading-relationship-china-hinkley-point

Bräutigam, D. (2009). China, Africa and the Global Aid Architecture. SSRN Electronic Journal. https://doi.org/10.2139/ssrn.1525934

Brooks, M., McCalla, R., Palla, A. A., & Lugt, L. V. D. (2011, March 24). Strategic Cooperation in Peripheral Ports: The Case of Atlantic Canada's Ports. *Semantic Scholar*. https://www.semanticscholar.org/paper/Strategic-Cooperation-in-Peripheral-Ports%3A-The-Case-Brooks-McCalla/a6bf8113d-7a313b7d0798575a3c4da02d6acea53

Carrington, D. (2016, March 18). Hinkley Point C Nuclear Deal Contains £22bn "Poison Pill" for Taxpayer. *The Guardian*. https://www.theguardian.com/uk-news/2016/mar/18/hinkley-point-c-nuclear-deal-22bn-poison-pill-taxpayer

CCCC. (2012, May 18). China Communications Group Signed EPC Project for Nigeria's Lekki Deepwater Port. *China Communications Construction Group Corporation Limited*. http://www.sasac.gov.cn/n2588025/n2588124/c3853314/content.html

CDB. (2023, February 10). CDB Assisted the Opening and Operation of Lekki Port in Nigeria. *China Development Bank*. https://www.cdb.com.cn/English/xwzx_715/khdt/202304/t20230410_10744.html

CGN. (2014, August 22). Independent Gen-III Hualong-1 Reactor Technology Passes National Review. *CGN Power Co.* http://en.cgnp.com.cn/encgnp/c100866/2014-08/22/content_551015cef0fc4461a2172b2fc3d11d4d.shtml

China Harbour. (2020, April 3). The Equity Delivery of the China Harbour for Nigeria Lekki Port Project has been Officially Completed. *China Harbour Engineering Company Ltd*. https://www.investgo.cn/article/yw/alfx/202004/482463.html

CMA CGM. (2018, April 16). The CMA CGM Group and Lekki Port LFTZ Enterprise sign a Memorandum of Agreement to Operate Lekki Port's future Container Terminal (Nigeria). https://www.cma-cgm.com/local/nigeria/news/35/the-cma-cgm-group-and-lekki-port-lftz-nterprise-sign-a-memorandum-of-agreement-to-operate-lekki-port-s-uture-container-terminal-nigeria-

CMPG. (2024). China Merchants Port Group Co., Ltd. Annual Report 2023. https://file.finance.sina.com.cn/211.154.219.97:9494/MRGG/CNSESZ_STOCK/2024/2024-4/2024-04-02/9936539.PDF

Coelho, M., Ratnoo, V., & Dellepiane, S. (2014). The Political Economy of Infrastructure in the UK. In ESRC. https://www.instituteforgovernment.org.uk/sites/default/files/publications/Political%20economy%20of%20infrastructure%20in%20the%20UK%20final%20v1.pdf

Consumer Scotland. (2024, March 14). Public Information note on Nuclear RAB and Sizewell C. *Consumer Scotland*. https://consumer.scot/publications/public-information-note-on-nuclear-rab-and-sizewell-c-html/#contents

Davies, R. (2016a, April 24). Hinkley Point C Nuclear Power Plant Decision Delayed again by EDF. The Guardian. https://www.theguardian.com/business/2016/apr/24/hinkley-point-c-nuclear-power-plant-decision-delayed-again-by-edf

Davies, R. (2016b, August 8). EDF Decision on Hinkley Point should be Declared Void, Say French Unions. The Guardian. https://www.theguardian.com/uk-news/2016/aug/08/edf-decision-hinkley-point-should-be-declared-void-french-unions-government-approval-nuclear

Davies, R. (2016c, August 9). China-UK Investment: Key Questions Following Hinkley Point C Delay. The Guardian. https://www.theguardian.com/business/2016/aug/09/china-uk-investment-key-questions-following-hinkley-point-c-delay

Davies, R. (2017, September 21). Hinkley Point C: Fresh Strike Threat Over Pay Dispute. *The Guardian*. https://www.theguardian.com/uk-news/2017/sep/21/hinkley-point-c-fresh-strike-threat-over-pay-dispute-delays

Defilippi, E. (2004). Intra-Port Competition, Regulatory Challenges and the Concession of Callao Port. *Maritime Economics & Logistics, 6*(4), 279–311. https://doi.org/10.1057/palgrave.mel.9100114

Demirel, H. Ç., Leendertse, W., Volker, L., & Hertogh, M. (2016). Flexibility in PPP Contracts—Dealing with Potential Change in the Pre-Contract Phase of a Construction Project. *Construction Management and Economics, 35*(4), 196–206. https://doi.org/10.1080/01446193.2016.1241414

Deng, Q., & Gui, T. (2016, September 30). China, Britain, and France Sign the Final Agreement for the Hinckley Point Nuclear Power Project. *Xinhua News Agency*. https://www.gov.cn/xinwen/2016-09/30/content_5113771.htm

Department for Business, Energy and Industrial Strategy. (2017). The Government's Review of the National Security Implications of Foreign Ownership or Control. https://assets.publishing.service.gov.uk/media/5a82b1f3e5274a2e87dc281b/2017_10_16_NSII_Green_Paper_final.pdf

Department of Trade and Industry of the UK. (2006). The Energy Challenge Energy Review Report 2006. https://assets.publishing.service.gov.uk/government/uploads/system/uploads/attachment_data/file/272376/6887.pdf

Dudman, J. (2017, May 19). Why Size Matters: Measuring Success in the World of Megaprojects. *The Guardian*. https://www.theguardian.com/public-leaders-network/2017/may/19/crossrail-hs2-hinkley-point-infrastructure-measuring-success-megaprojects

EDF 2023 Annual Results. (2024, February 16). Consolidated Financial Statements for 2023 as of December 31, 2023. https://www.edf.fr/sites/groupe/files/2024-02/annual-results-2023-consolidated-financial-statements-2024-02-16.pdf

EDF Energy. (2022). Annual Report and Financial Statements. In EDF ENERGY HOLDINGS LIMITED. https://www.edfenergy.com/sites/default/files/edf_energy_holdings_limited_fy22_signed_complete_set.pdf

Eka, I. (2021, February 9). A'Ibom Govt. Ready to Collaborate with U.S. to Develop Ibom Deep Seaport Project. *News.band*. https://news.band/aibom-govt-seeks-collaboration-with-u-s-to-develop-ibom-deep-seaport-project/

Farrell, S. (2016, September 4). Peers Must Press New Chancellor on Policies. The Guardian. https://www.theguardian.com/business/2016/sep/04/peers-must-press-new-chancellor-on-economic-growth-plans

Freeman, R. E. (1984). *Strategic Management: A Stakeholder Approach*. Pitman.

Freitas, M. (2023, August 2). The Impact of Chinese Investments in Africa: Neocolonialism or Cooperation? *Policy Center*. https://www.policycenter.ma/publications/impact-chinese-investments-africa-neocolonialism-or-cooperation

Gabriel, C. O., & Ajayi, F. (2023, May 15). The Impact of The Lekki Deep Sea Port On The Nigerian Maritime Industry—Marine/ Shipping - Nigeria. https://www.mondaq.com/nigeria/marine-shipping/1315344/the-impact-of-the-lekki-deep-sea-port-on-the-nigerian-maritime-industry

Gayle, D. (2016, August 10). Hinkley Point: Mandelson urges government to support China-backed project. *The Guardian*. https://www.theguardian.com/uk-news/2016/aug/10/hinkley-point-c-mandelson-government-china-backed-project

Ghiretti, F., Gunter, J., & Sebastian, G. (2023). Chinese Investments in European Maritime Infrastructure Policy Department for Structural and Cohesion Policies Directorate-General for Internal Policies PE. https://www.europarl.europa.eu/RegData/etudes/STUD/2023/747278/IPOL_STU(2023)747278_EN.pdf

Gilpatric, S. M., & Li, Y. (2020). Endogenous Price Leadership and Product Positioning. *Review of Industrial Organization*, *58*(2), 287–302. https://doi.org/10.1007/s11151-020-09752-4

Goodley, S. (2016, April 17). France Gives go Ahead to Hinkley Point, French Minister Says. *The Guardian*. https://www.theguardian.com/uk-news/2016/apr/17/france-go-ahead-hinkley-point-macron-andrew-marr-show

Goss, R. O. (1990). Economic Policies and Seaports: Are Port Authorities Necessary? *Maritime Policy & Management, 17*(4), 257–271. https://doi.org/10.1080/03088839000000032

Guasch, J. L. (2004). *Granting and Renegotiating Infrastructure Concessions: Doing it Right.* In openknowledge.worldbank.org. World Bank. http://hdl.handle.net/10986/15024

Hands, G., & Kwarteng, K. (2021, October 26). New Finance Model to Cut Cost of New Nuclear Power Stations. *GOV.UK*. https://www.gov.uk/government/news/new-finance-model-to-cut-cost-of-new-nuclear-power-stations

Haralambides, H. E. (2002). Competition, Excess Capacity, and the Pricing of Port Infrastructure. *International Journal of Maritime Economics, 4*(4), 323–347. https://doi.org/10.1057/palgrave.ijme.9100053

Hass, K. B. (2009). *Managing Complex Projects: A New Model.* Management Concepts.

He, L. (2023, January 23). Lekki Port and the Free Trade Zone Work in Resonance, and China Africa "the Belt and Road" Cooperation has Yielded Fruitful Results. *Southern Finance Omnimedia Group*. https://m.21jingji.com/article/20230113/herald/b553aa96462c1d3c3f8ab378c540616e.html

Hitachi. (2019, January 17). Horizon Suspends UK Nuclear New Build Activities. *Hitachi in Europe*. https://www.hitachi.eu/en/press/horizon-suspends-uk-nuclear-new-build-activities/

Huang, L., Lasserre, F., Pic, P., & Chiu, Y.-Y. (2020). Opening up the Chinese Shipping Market 1988–2018: The Perspective of Chinese Shipping Companies Facing Foreign Competition. *Asian Transport Studies, 6*, 100004. https://doi.org/10.1016/j.eastsj.2020.100004

ICRC. (2014). Ibom Deep Sea Port and Free Trade Zone Outline Business Case Final. https://pp.icrc.gov.ng/media/291

InfraPPP. (2018, November 16). French-Chinese Consortium Selected to Develop US$4.2 Billion Port PPP in Nigeria. *InfraPPP*. https://www.infrapppworld.com/news/megaproject-1365-french-chinese-consortium-selected-to-develop-us-4-2-billion-port-ppp-in-nigeria

Inman, P. (2018, November 9). Toshiba's Failure Shows Business can't Deliver a Nuclear Future. *The Guardian*. https://www.theguardian.com/business/2018/nov/08/toshibas-failure-shows-business-cant-deliver-a-nuclear-future

Jenkins, S. (2020, September 18). Hitachi Failed its Nuclear Test. If only it had the Vanity of HS2. *The Guardian*. https://www.theguardian.com/commentisfree/2020/sep/18/hitachi-nuclear-test-hs2-huge-projects-politicians-wasteful

Johnston, I. (2017, June 22). National Audit Office slams Government's "High Cost and Risky Deal" for Hinkley Point Nuclear Power Station. *The Independent*. https://www.independent.co.uk/climate-change/news/hinkley-point-nuclear-power-national-audit-office-slams-government-high-cost-risky-deal-a7803446.html

Juhel, M. H. (2001). Globalisation, Privatisation and Restructuring of Ports. *International Journal of Maritime Economics, 3*(2), 139–174. https://doi.org/10.1057/palgrave.ijme.9100012

Kopel, M., & Löffler, C. (2008). Commitment, First-mover, and Second-mover Advantage. *Journal of Economics, 94*(2), 143–166. https://doi.org/10.1007/s00712-008-0004-4

Krikorian, S. (2019, September 4). France's Efficiency in the Nuclear Fuel Cycle: What Can "Oui" Learn? Www.iaea.org. https://www.iaea.org/newscenter/news/frances-efficiency-in-the-nuclear-fuel-cycle-what-can-oui-learn

Li, K. X., Zhang, W., Chen, P. S. L., & Huo, W. (2019). International Port Investment of Chinese Port-related Companies. *International Journal of Shipping and Transport Logistics, 11*(5), 430. https://doi.org/10.1504/ijstl.2019.10022864

Li, L. (2014, July 12). Terminal opens doors for Chinese company. China Daily. http://global.chinadaily.com.cn/a/201407/21/WS5a2fd357a3108bc8c672a69f.html

Lieberman, M. B., & Montgomery, D. B. (1998). First-mover (dis)Advantages: Retrospective and Link with the Resource-Based View. *Strategic Management Journal, 19*(12), 1111–1125. https://www.anderson.ucla.edu/faculty/marvin.lieberman/publications/FMA2-SMH1998.pdf

Liu, X. (2016, August 8). Hinkley Point is a Test of Mutual Trust Between UK and China. *Financial Times.* https://www.ft.com/content/b8bc62dc-5d74-11e6-bb77-a121aa8abd95#axzz4GkigtUWR

LPLEL. (2020, April 1). Lekki Port Receives $221 Million China Harbour's Equity Infusion. Lekki Port LFTZ Enterprise Limited. https://lekkiport.com/lekki-port-receives-221-million-china-harbours-equity-infusion/

LPLEL. (2021, March 8). Lekki Port Signs US$629m Facility Agreements with China Development Bank. *Lekki Port LFTZ Enterprise Limited.* https://lekkiport.com/lekki-port-signs-us629m-facility-agreements-with-china-development-bank/

LPLEL. (2023, January 24). Lekki Port and CMA CGM Group to Facilitate Trade Volume Growth, Increase GDP. *Lekki Port LFTZ Enterprise Limited.* https://lekkiport.com/lekki-port-and-cma-cgm-group-to-facilitate-trade-volume-growth-increase-gdp/

LUA. (2018, November 30). Bollore Ports, PowerChina win Deep-sea Port Contract in Nigeria. *Logistics Update Africa.* https://www.logupdateafrica.com/bollore-ports-powerchina-win-deepsea-port-contract-in-nigeria-logistics-shipping

Lynch, D. (2013, February 6). Centrica writes off £200M stake in Hinkley Point C project. *New Civil Engineer*. https://www.newcivilengineer.com/archive/centrica-writes-off-200m-stake-in-hinkley-point-c-project-06-02-2013/
Lyons, K. (2016, August 28). Hinkley Point: EDF boss calls on Government to Look at "Bigger Picture." *The Guardian*. https://www.theguardian.com/uk-news/2016/aug/28/hinkley-point-c-edf-boss-vincent-de-rivaz-government-approve-plans-nuclear
Macalister, T. (2016a, April 3). Hinkley Point: China Incorporates Seven London-Based Firms. The Guardian. https://www.theguardian.com/uk-news/2016/apr/03/hinkley-point-china-incorporates-seven-london-based-firms
Macalister, T. (2016b, July 1). Hinkley Point C critics try to Derail it Amid Brexit Vote Turmoil. The Guardian. https://www.theguardian.com/uk-news/2016/jul/01/hinkley-point-c-critics-try-to-derail-it-amid-brexit-vote-turmoil
Macalister, T. (2016c, July 22). Hinkley Point C Nuclear Project Expected to Get Go-ahead Next Week. The Guardian. https://www.theguardian.com/uk-news/2016/jul/22/hinkley-point-c-nuclear-project
Macalister, T. (2016d, September 3). Hinkley Point C: No Easy Solution to THERESA May's Chinese Puzzle. The Guardian. https://www.theguardian.com/uk-news/2016/sep/03/hinkley-point-c-theresa-may-china-g20-summit
Mason, R. (2016, September 29). Hinkley Point: Ministers Sign Go-ahead for Nuclear Power Plant. *The Guardian*. https://www.theguardian.com/uk-news/2016/sep/29/hinkley-point-ministers-sign-go-ahead-for-nuclear-power-plant
Mason, R., & Goodley, S. (2016, September 15). Hinkley Point C Nuclear Power Station Gets Government Green Light. *The Guardian*. https://www.theguardian.com/uk-news/2016/sep/15/hinkley-point-c-nuclear-power-station-gets-go-ahead
Monteiro, R., Rial, I., & Tandberg, E. (2020). Chapter 11 Fiscal Risks in Infrastructure. In G. Schwartz, M. Fouad, T. S. Hansen, & G. Verdier (Eds.), *Governance can End Waste in Public Investment*. International Monetary Fund. https://www.elibrary.imf.org/display/book/9781513511818/ch011.xml
Musso, E., Ferrari, C., & Benacchio, M. (2006). Port Investment: Profitability, Economic Impact and Financing. *Research in Transportation Economics, 16*, 171–218. https://doi.org/10.1016/s0739-8859(06)16008-4
Notteboom, T., Pallis, A., & Rodrigue, J.-P. (2022). *Port Economics, Management and Policy* (1st ed.). Routledge. https://doi.org/10.4324/9780429318184
NPA. (2006, May). Project Summary of Tincan Island Container Terminal Limited A Public Private Partnership Between Nigerian Ports Authority And Tincan Island Container Terminal Limited. Nigerian Ports Authority. https://pp.icrc.gov.ng/media/146
Odey, P. (2021, November 29). Akwa Ibom Dispatches Delegation to South Korea Over Deep Seaport. *PUNCH*. https://www.vanguardngr.com/2021/12/

ibom-deep-seaport-will-transform-akwa-ibom-to-a-transhipment-city-gov-emmanuel/

Ogunlesi, T. (2023, January 22). Lekki Deep Sea Port: Buhari breaks another jinx. *PM News*. https://pmnewsnigeria.com/2023/01/22/lekki-deep-sea-port-buharibreaks-another-jinx/

Oladipo, O. (2023, November 6). Lekki Port: Innovating Nigeria's Approach to Trade for Modern Future. *Businessday NG*. https://businessday.ng/features/article/lekki-port-innovating-nigerias-approach-to-trade-for-modern-future/

Onyenucheya, A. (2022a, January 26). Amaechi Lauds Work at Lekki Deep Seaport. The Guardian Nigeria News. https://guardian.ng/business-services/maritime/amaechi-lauds-work-at-lekki-deep-seaport/

Onyenucheya, A. (2022b, March 10). Lekki Seaport to Begin Operations this year, Reaches 85 Per Cent Completion. The Guardian Nigeria News. https://guardian.ng/business-services/maritime/lekki-seaport-to-begin-operations-this-year-reaches-85-per-cent-completion/

Onyenucheya, A. (2024, May 2). Tin Can Port Access Gate Automated to Enhance Efficiency. *The Guardian Nigeria News—Nigeria and World News*. https://guardian.ng/business-services/tin-can-port-access-gate-automated-to-enhance-efficiency/

Oritse, G. (2016, December 13). FG Grants 50-year Concessions to Deep Seaport Projects. *Vangard*. https://www.vanguardngr.com/2016/12/fg-grants-50-year-concessions-deep-seaport-projects/

Oritse, G. (2021, October 13). Controversy Hits Ibaka Deep Seaport Project. *Vanguard*. https://www.vanguardngr.com/2021/10/controversy-hits-ibaka-deep-seaport-project/

Oshodi, A.-G. T. (2022, August 18). Nigeria Sees China as a Steady Partner and its Largest Lender. *Merics*. https://merics.org/en/nigeria-sees-china-steady-partner-and-its-largest-lender

Pallis, A. A., & De, P. W. (2006). Analysis of the Benefits of Intra-Port Competition. *International Journal of Transport Economics, 33*(1), 1000–1017. https://doi.org/10.1400/16960

Pallis, A. A., Notteboom, T. E., & De Langen, P. W. (2008). Concession Agreements and Market Entry in the Container Terminal Industry. *Maritime Economics & Logistics, 10*(3), 209–228. https://doi.org/10.1057/mel.2008.1

Pamilih, J. (2022). Briefing: China's Involvement in UK Nuclear. China Research Group. https://chinaresearchgroup.org/research/briefing-chinas-involvement-in-uk-nuclear-power

Péron, A. (2019, November 1). Willkie Advises CMA Terminals in Subconcession of Container Terminal Operations of Lekki Deep Sea Port in Nigeria. Willkie Farr & Gallagher LLP. https://www.willkie.com/news/2019/11/willkie-advises-cma

Phillips, T. (2016, September 16). UK's "China-Phobia" Spells Trouble Despite Hinkley Decision—Chinese Media. *The Guardian*. https://www.theguardian.com/uk-news/2016/sep/16/uks-china-phobia-spells-trouble-despite-hinkley-decision-chinese-media

Pickard, J., & Thomas, N. (2021, July 25). UK Looks to Remove China's CGN from Nuclear Power Projects. *Financial Times*. https://www.ft.com/content/c4a3fe02-8535-45a4-aacf-0c4fbce8409d

Pickard, J., Parker, G., & White, S. (2024, January 31). Paris Seeks UK Loan Guarantee after Hinkley Point Nuclear Plant Costs Soar. *Financial Times*. https://www.ft.com/content/c1e3bd19-763b-4ea1-b188-d2872cc36bb8

PPIAF. (2007). *National program for Public Private Partnership*. https://www.ppiaf.org/sites/default/files/documents/2007-01/Quarterly_Booklet_English.pdf

Pratley, N. (2017, June 23). Hinkley Point C: Watchdog Confirms Fears of Political Vanity Project. *The Guardian*. https://www.theguardian.com/uk-news/nils-pratley-on-finance/2017/jun/23/hinkley-point-c-nuclear-energy-risky-expensive-national-audit-office

Quinn, B. (2016, August 8). China Warns UK Relations are at "Historical Juncture" Over Hinkley Point. *The Guardian*. https://www.theguardian.com/uk-news/2016/aug/08/china-warns-uk-relations-historical-juncture-hinkley-point-liu-xiaoming

Ralston, J. (2021, October 18). China and UK Nuclear Power. *Energy & Climate Intelligence Unit*. https://eciu.net/analysis/briefings/uk-energy-policies-and-prices/china-and-uk-nuclear-power

Rankin, J. (2016, July 27). Flamanville: France's Beleaguered Forerunner to Hinkley Point C. *The Guardian*. https://www.theguardian.com/environment/2016/jul/27/flamanville-france-edf-nuclear-reactor-hinkley-point-c

Rawnsley, A. (2016, July 31). Hinkley Offers a Useful Guide to May's Plans for Cameron's Legacy. *The Observer*. https://www.theguardian.com/commentisfree/2016/jul/31/hinkley-offers-useful-guide-to-mays-plans-cameron-legacy

Rose, M., & Hummel, T. (2022, July 6). France Plans Full Nationalisation of Power Utility EDF. Reuters. https://www.reuters.com/world/europe/frances-edf-be-fully-nationalised-borne-2022-07-06/

Ruddick, G., Asthana, A., & Willsher, K. (2016, July 29). EDF Boss confident Hinkley Point C Nuclear Plant will be Built. *The Guardian*. https://www.theguardian.com/uk-news/2016/jul/29/edf-boss-confident-hinkley-point-c-nuclear-plant-will-be-built

Ruddick, G., & Grierson, J. (2016, July 29). Hinkley Point C in doubt after British government delays approval. *The Guardian*. https://www.theguardian.com/business/2016/jul/28/hinkley-point-c-to-go-ahead-after-edf-board-approves-project

Ruddick, G., & Phillips, T. (2016, September 16). China Must Wait Four Years for Decision on Bradwell Nuclear Plant. *The Guardian*. https://www.theguardian.com/uk-news/2016/sep/16/china-must-wait-four-years-for-decision-on-bradwell-nuclear-plant

Salau, S. (2018, March 30). Government earmarks N90b for special Economic Zones, to earn $200b from Lekki Deep Seaport. *The Guardian* Nigeria News. https://guardian.ng/news/government-earmarks-n90b-for-special-economic-zones-to-earn-200b-from-lekki-deep-seaport/

SASAC. (2023, December 28). The opening and operation of West Africa's largest deep-water port. State Owned Assets Supervision and Administration Commission of the State Council. http://www.sasac.gov.cn/n4470048/n26915116/n29670038/n29670102/c29681289/content.html

Schneider, M., Froggatt, A. P., & Thomas, S. (2014, August 21). The saga of Hinkley Point C: Europe's Key Nuclear Decision. *Energy Post*. https://energypost.eu/saga-hinkley-point-c-europes-key-nuclear-decision/

Shelton, G., & Paruk, F. (2008). The Forum on China- Africa Cooperation A Strategic Opportunity. https://www.files.ethz.ch/isn/103618/mono156full.pdf

Slack, B., & Fremont, A. (2005). Transformation of Port Terminal Operations: From the Local to the Global. *Transport Reviews, 25*(1), 117–130. https://doi.org/10.1080/0144164042000206051

SMD. (2015, October 22). Comment: The Hinkley Point C project is a Great Opportunity for Chinese Nuclear Power Enterprises to Forge Ahead. Southern Metropolis Daily. https://finance.sina.cn/china/cjpl/2015-10-22/detail-ifxizwti6864635.d.html?vt=4&sid=165302

Stefanini, S. (2016a, July 28). Hinkley Nuclear Plant Faces UK Delay. POLITICO. https://www.politico.eu/article/france-approves-hinkley-nuclear-plant-for-the-uk-despite-brexit-worries-edf/

Stefanini, S. (2016b, September 15). Theresa May Gives Hinkley the Green Light. POLITICO. https://www.politico.eu/article/uk-has-approved-hinkley-with-conditions-report/

Stewart, H. (2016, September 14). Theresa May Set to Give Go-Ahead for Hinkley Point C Nuclear Plant. *The Guardian*. https://www.theguardian.com/uk-news/2016/sep/14/theresa-may-conditional-approval-hinkley-point-c-nuclear-power-station

Stewart, H., Mason, R., & Ruddick, G. (2016, September 15). Theresa May Accused of Avoiding Security and Cost Issues of Hinkley. *The Guardian*. https://www.theguardian.com/uk-news/2016/sep/15/theresa-may-accused-backing-down-hinkley-point-c-deal

Stewart, H., & Quinn, B. (2016, August 9). Theresa May Seeks Close Ties with China Despite Hinkley Point delay. *The Guardian*. https://www.theguardian.com/uk-news/2016/aug/09/government-says-links-with-china-are-vital-after-hinkley-point-warning

Suleiman, F. (2024, January 24). British Taxpayers Wont Bear Cost of Hinkley Point C Overruns. *Reuters*. https://www.reuters.com/world/uk/british-taxpayers-wont-bear-cost-hinkley-point-c-overruns-uk-government-2024-01-23/

The World Bank. (2017, June 16). Container Terminals Concessions—Making the Most of Ports in West Africa. https://documents1.worldbank.org/curated/en/919071469608006706/pdf/Container-Terminals-Concessions-Making-the-Most-of-Ports-in-West-Africa.pdf

Theys, C., Notteboom, T. E., Pallis, A. A., & De Langen, P. W. (2010). The Economics Behind the Awarding of Terminals in Seaports: Towards a Research Agenda. *Research in Transportation Economics, 27*(1), 37–50. https://doi.org/10.1016/j.retrec.2009.12.006

ThisDay. (2016). Lekki Deep Seaport Promoters Jittery over FG Disinvestment Plans. THISDAYLIVE. https://www.thisdaylive.com/index.php/2016/12/31/lekki-deep-seaport-promoters-jittery-over-fg-disinvestment-plans/

Thomson, A. (2016, March 17). French Government Pledges Support to EDF "If Needed." *Financial Times*. https://www.ft.com/content/cde46a9f-40c0-3334-92ea-d56cf882e567

Topping, A. (2016, September 15). Your Guide to Hinkley Point C—the UK's First New Nuclear Plant for 20 years. *The Guardian*. https://www.theguardian.com/uk-news/2016/sep/15/hinkley-point-c-guide-uk-first-new-nuclear-plant-for-20-years

Torres, L. (2016, July 28). Hinkley Point C Timeline: All the Key Moments. *The Guardian*. https://www.theguardian.com/environment/2016/jul/28/hinkley-point-c-timeline-all-the-key-moments

UK GOV. (2016). Hinkley Point C: Value for Money Assessment. Department for Energy Security and Net Zero and Department for Business, Energy & Industrial Strategy. https://assets.publishing.service.gov.uk/media/5a8226f8ed915d74e6236106/Detailed_value_for_money_assessment.pdf

UK government. (2022, November 29). UK Government Takes Major Steps Forward to Secure Britain's Energy Independence. *GOV.UK*. https://www.gov.uk/government/news/uk-government-takes-major-steps-forward-to-secure-britains-energy-independence

UNCTAD. (1998). Guidelines for Port Authorities and Governments on the Privatization of Port Facilities. https://unctad.org/system/files/official-document/posdtetibd1.pdf

Van Niekerk, H. C. (2005). Port Reform and Concessioning in Developing Countries. *Maritime Economics & Logistics, 7*(2), 141–155. https://doi.org/10.1057/palgrave.mel.9100129

Vanelslander, T. (2005). The Economics Behind Co-operation and Competition in Sea-port Container Handling. In www.proquest.com. https://www.proquest.com/docview/305351367?pq-origsite=gscholar&fromopenview=true&sourcetype=Dissertations%20&%20Theses

Vanguard. (2022, July 29). Lekki Deep Sea Port: NPA Gets Approval for Designation as Customs Port, approved Wharf. https://www.vanguardngr.com/2022/07/lekki-deep-sea-port-npa-gets-approval-for-designation-as-customs-port-approved-wharf/

Vaughan, A. (2017a, March 25). Foreign Companies Flock to Build Nuclear Plants in the UK. The Observer. https://www.theguardian.com/business/2017/mar/25/foreign-firms-flock-to-build-nuclear-plants-in-uk

Vaughan, A. (2017b, June 22). Spending Watchdog Condemns "Risky and Expensive" Hinkley Point. The Guardian. https://www.theguardian.com/uk-news/2017/jun/23/spending-watchdog-condemns-risky-expensive-hinkley-point-c-nuclear

Vaughan, A. (2017c, July 3). Hinkley Point C is £1.5bn Over Budget and a Year Behind Schedule, EDF Admits. The Guardian. https://www.theguardian.com/uk-news/2017/jul/03/hinkley-point-c-is-22bn-over-budget-and-a-year-behind-schedule-edf-admits

Vaughan, A. (2018, November 8). UK Nuclear Power Station Plans Scrapped as Toshiba Pulls Out. The Guardian. https://www.theguardian.com/environment/2018/nov/08/toshiba-uk-nuclear-power-plant-project-nu-gen-cumbria

Vaughan, A., & Kuo, L. (2018, July 26). China's Long Game to Dominate Nuclear Power Relies on the UK. *The Guardian*. https://www.theguardian.com/environment/2018/jul/26/chinas-long-game-to-dominate-nuclear-power-relies-on-the-uk

Verhoeven, P. (2010). A Review of Port Authority Functions: Towards a Renaissance? *Maritime Policy & Management, 37*(3), 247–270. https://doi.org/10.1080/03088831003700645

Waitzman, E. (2023, October 3). UK: Long-term Strategic Challenges Posed by China. UK Parliament, House of Lords Library. https://lordslibrary.parliament.uk/uk-long-term-strategic-challenges-posed-by-china/

Wang, X., Wang, S., & Gao, Y. (2023). Optimal Equity Structure of PPP Projects when Private-Sector Shareholders' "Investor-Contractor" Dual Roles is Considered. *Construction Management & Economics, 41*(11–12), 910–925. https://doi.org/10.1080/01446193.2023.2216319

Ward, A., Pickard, J., & Stothard, M. (2016, September 15). UK Gives Go-ahead for "Revised" £18bn Hinkley Point Plant. *Financial Times*. https://www.ft.com/content/466704e6-7a4b-11e6-b837-eb4b4333ee43

Watt, H. (2017, December 21). Hinkley Point: the "Dreadful Deal" Behind the World's Most Expensive Power plant. *The Guardian*. https://www.theguardian.com/news/2017/dec/21/hinkley-point-c-dreadful-deal-behind-worlds-most-expensive-power-plant

White, S. (2024, February 16). EDF Confident of UK Compromise as it Reveals €12.9bn Hinkley Point Hit. *Financial Times*. https://www.ft.com/content/ca24da3e-6db8-40ca-b99a-a1e7f190cc1a
Wintour, P. (2013, October 21). David Cameron Hails Nuclear Power Plant Deal as Big Day for Britain. *The Guardian*. https://www.theguardian.com/environment/2013/oct/21/britain-nuclear-power-station-hinkley-edf
Xie, W. (2016, November 1). Revealing the Entire Process of Signing a Nuclear Power Project Agreement Between China, Britain, and France: Over 3000 Pages of Text. *China Economic Weekly*. https://news.sina.cn/gn/2016-11-01/detail-ifxxfuff7411509.d.html?from=wap
Yang, X. (2018, April 14). Exclusive Interview: "The Belt and Road" Cooperation Enables China, France and Britain to Achieve "Three wins"—Interview with Zheng Dongshan, General Manager of CGN UK. *Xinhua News Agency*. http://www.xinhuanet.com/world/2019-04/24/c_1124409411.htm

CHAPTER 8

Conclusion and Discussion About Tripartite Cooperation

This research examined Chinese tripartite cooperation projects within the realm of economic infrastructure, with a specific focus on the transportation and energy sectors. Its primary contribution lies in enhancing the understanding of tripartite cooperation in infrastructure projects by systematically exploring the motivations behind such collaborations and analysing the changes in transaction costs and additional benefits. The research sought to address the following critical questions: Why do participants opt for a tripartite cooperation model even though they have to potentially bear the additional transaction costs? What are the determinants for countries and/or firms to engage in tripartite cooperation, and how do their actions within the tripartite model reshape project finance activities? How does the involvement of a third partner bring additional benefits, complexities, and challenges in infrastructure and construction projects?

This concluding chapter will synthesise the key findings, discuss their theoretical and practical implications, and offer recommendations for future research.

C. Su, *From Two to Three*, Governing China in the 21st Century,
https://doi.org/10.1007/978-981-95-8708-7_8

8.1 Findings on Tripartite Cooperation Across Theory and Practice

In this section, I present three tables to integrate the theoretical framework with the empirical findings discussed in the preceding chapters. Table 8.1 summarises the determinants of participation in tripartite cooperation projects from both theoretical reasoning and empirical findings. The findings reveal that China, China's partner countries,[1] and beneficiary countries have distinct motivations for participating in tripartite cooperation.

Table 8.2 outlines the approaches employed by participants in these collaborations. The research highlights how the actions of participants in tripartite cooperation—ranging from government support to firm-level collaborations—create a complex dynamic that shapes the success of these projects. The combination of financial, soft-law, policy, and relationship instruments employed by China, China's partner countries, and beneficiary countries leads to both coordinated and uncoordinated actions, influencing the overall effectiveness and efficiency of the cooperation.

Finally, Table 8.3 examines how these actions influence transaction costs and benefits within tripartite cooperation. The research identifies that transaction costs and additional benefits in tripartite cooperation projects stem from the interaction of various determinants and actions. While tripartite cooperation offers additional advantages, such as risk-sharing and access to intangible assets, the involvement of more participants and their different approaches to project finance introduces complexities. These complexities can lead to increased transaction costs, particularly in terms of contracts, negotiations, and potential project delays.

[1] To clarify once again, in this research, '***(China's) partner countries***' refers to the other provider nations involved in China-led tripartite cooperation projects. Specifically, these 'partner countries' include 14 nations that have signed MOUs with the Chinese government: France, South Korea, Canada, Portugal, Australia, Japan, Italy, Belgium, the Netherlands, Spain, Austria, Singapore, Switzerland, and the UK. '***Partner firms/companies/enterprises,***' refers to business entities headquartered in France, Italy, Spain, Portugal, Germany, the UK, the USA, Japan, South Korea, and Singapore.

Occasionally, the terms '*Western countries/firms*' are used when these partner countries have colonial influence, and firms monopolise the infrastructure sector of beneficiary countries.

Table 8.1 Summary of determinants for participants joining tripartite cooperation (Source: Author)

Determinants	From the Literature and Previous Research (Chapters 2/3)	From Empirical General Cases (Chapter 6)	From Hinkley Point C (HPC) (Chapter 7)	From Nigerian Ports (NP) (Chapter 7)
China/Chinese firms	• China is motivated by seeking resources, efficiency, market access, and strategic assets (Dunning & Lundan, 2008; Cui et al., 2014). • China uses this as a springboard to acquire strategic resources, market access, and expertise (Luo & Tung, 2007, 2018). • China uses the tripartite cooperation mechanism to reduce friction with other countries (Zhang, 2020). • A means for China to enhance its international reputation (Abdenur, 2007).	C1. Promote China's 'Going Out' policy and Belt and Road Initiative (BRI). C2. Upgrade the industrial value chain and technology (seeking efficiency; springboard). C3. Acquire operational knowledge and experience (seeking intangible assets). C4. Entering industries/strategic assets held or monopolised by partner countries (seeking market: springboard). C5. Promote Chinese standards (springboard). C6. Mitigate international criticisms: partner companies help Chinese SOEs demonstrate better practices in infrastructure projects. C7. Avoid high M&A costs.	C1. Promote BRI across Eurasia, strengthen diplomatic ties with the UK and France. C2. China has its own nuclear technology, and its aim is not to upgrade the nuclear technology. C3. Learn EDF's know-how in the UK and exploit EDF's local relationships. C4. Overcome UK market barriers due to strict investment conditions and use the UK market as a springboard for international expansion. C5. Promote Chinese technology in the UK nuclear industry. Leverage GDA approval to promote nuclear technology globally. Use HPR1000 technology for the Bradwell B project. C6. Address national security concerns from the UK. C7. CGN did not plan to acquire assets from EDF.	C1. Promote BRI in Africa and seek strategic assets. C2. Upgrade the shipping industry by integrating investment, construction, and asset operation. C3. Acquire operational knowledge and experience from France. Accumulate experience for future concession competitions. C4. Enter the port market monopolised by Western firms. C5. Establish brand image and expand the local market. C6. Mitigate negative international commentary. C7. Avoid the high costs of acquiring port assets from a French company.
Partner countries/firms	• Strengthen their relationship with China in less developed regions (OECD, 2014a).	P1. Seek commercial interests, e.g., optimise financial statements, cash liquidity. P2. Maintain and	P1. Share high risks and costs of nuclear projects. EDF had initially sought to undertake the	P1. Align with CMA CGM Group's development objectives in

(continued)

Table 8.1 (continued)

	• Alleviate financial and technological pressure on DAC donors' development tasks (Kaplan et al., 2020). • A strategy to manage the 're-Westernisation of international development' (Fordelone, 2009). • A pilot attempt to shift from zero-sum competition to non-zero-sum cooperative activities (Jing, 2022).	reinforce influence in regions where they have historical ties. P3. Weaken Chinese influence in beneficiary countries.	Sizewell C project with its Chinese partners, replicating strategies from the HPC project in designs, supply chains, feedback, and experience. P2. Pursue HPC project for its European strategy and reputation. P3. The threat of China entering the UK nuclear market is small. EDF has no need to weaken Chinese influence.	West Africa. P2. Use tripartite cooperation to win projects and reinforce influence in Africa. P3. Monitor Chinese progress in infrastructure projects in Africa.
Beneficiary countries	• Beneficiary countries prefer China's short-term progress and non-interference policy (Carothers, 2008; Tseng & Krog, 2016; Bräutigam, 2011). • Beneficiary countries use tripartite cooperation to retain traditional donor support while collaborating with China (McEwan & Mawdsley, 2012).	B1. Promote local economic growth and employment. B2. Promote domestic development plans. B3. Enhance local infrastructure. B4. Enhance bargaining power and gain more independence. They continue to depend on the Western legacy in their key economic sectors; on the other hand, they seek to exploit Chinese investment as an alternative.	B1. Advocate for job creation. B2. Use the tripartite cooperation model post-Brexit for economic strategy. B3. Develop the UK's nuclear power plant and energy infrastructure B4. Tackle with slow EDF investment decision process. The UK government wanted to use negotiation tactics to maximise its interests in a project. This delay was a strategic move by the Theresa May government as it initiated discussions on the Brexit negotiation. B5. Need Chinese funds but worry the Chinese investment might influence British national security.	B1. Develop the local economy and increase employment. B2. Follow the nation's port development master plan. B3. Establish new ports and expand existing port infrastructure in Nigeria. B4. Overcome the oligopoly in port services by APM and Bolloré. Break the monopoly of French shipping companies.

Black: The determinants can also be found in bilateral arrangements.
Blue: The determinants in blue specifically refer to the tripartite cooperation context.
Orange: The determinants in orange are from HPC, differing from those found in the literature, previous research, and general empirical cases.

Table 8.2 Classification of cooperative approaches of participants in tripartite cooperation projects (Source: Author)

Results	From Database Statistics (68 Projects)	From Empirical General Cases	From Specific Case Studies (HPC)	From Specific Case Studies (NP)
China	More frequent use to→ Less frequent use: • Chinese SOEs engagement (66) • Chinese government direct financing (33) • High-level government officer meetings (15) • Policy support (8)	• **Financial Instruments**: Chinese development policy financial institutions, including China Development Bank (CDB), Export-Import Bank of China (CEXIM), and China Export & Credit Insurance Corporation (Sinosure), play central roles. • **Soft Law Instruments**: Chinese government and partner countries, predominantly in the form of MOUs; China and France/Italy hold more working group meetings. • **Relationship Instruments**: In the overseas bidding activities of Chinese SOEs, they can secure projects with lower costs in host countries due to support from the Chinese government.	• **Financial Instruments**: The Chinese and French governments provided financial support to their respective SOEs. • **Soft Law Instruments**: Chinese and French governments signed MOUs and held high-level meetings with the UK government.	• **Financial Instruments**: CDB loaned $629 million to the Lekki project.
China's partner countries	More frequent use to → Less frequent use: • Government direct financing (14) • High-level government officer meetings (12) • Partner countries' SOE engagement (4) • Policy support (1)	• **Financial Instruments**: Sometimes the government loans to their SOEs. • **Soft Law Instruments**: Chinese government and partner countries, predominantly in the form of MOUs; China and France/Italy hold more working group meetings.		\

(*continued*)

Table 8.2 (continued)

Beneficiary countries	More frequent use to ➡ Less frequent use: • Local policy support (60) • Government direct financing (38) • Local SOEs/authorities engagement (34) • High-level government officer meetings (23)	• **Policy Instruments**: Beneficiary countries' authorities have modified their laws to facilitate project implementation or accommodate investor requirements. • **Financial Instruments**: Beneficiary countries' governments often act as sovereign guarantors/borrowers to secure direct loans from international sponsors.	• **Policy Instruments**: Due to a change in leadership within the UK Government, Theresa May, and her government suspended the construction process. • **Financial Instruments**: The UK government announced an initial government guarantee of £2 billion for the HPC to expedite EDF's final investment decision. To halt tripartite cooperation with China, the UK government introduced a new financing model for the Sizewell project, known as the Regulated Asset Base (RAB) model.	• **Policy Instruments**: Nigerian authorities used administrative policies, including seeking Presidential approval for port designation and introducing quarterly site visits by the Minister of Transportation. • **Financial Instruments**: The Nigerian Federal Government approved extended concessions, funded port facilities, and connected the new port to transport infrastructure.
Chinese firms Partner firms	More frequent use to ➡ Less frequent use: • Co-finance, co-investment, and forming JV/SPV (36) • EPC contractor and subcontractor, designer-contractor, and developer-contractor (30) • Product or service providers (21) • Co-bidder cooperation (6)	• **Establishing Partnerships between Firms**: (Signing MOUs/framework agreements, establishing strategic partnerships/alliances) • **Establishing JVs/SPVs**: (Forming a new JV or SPV, equity cooperation, forming a consortium to co-bid public projects) • **Providing Products/Services**	• **Establishing Partnerships between Firms**: CGN and EDF had cultivated a longstanding and cooperative relationship since the 1980s, laying a solid foundation for their subsequent collaboration. CGN and EDF established a cooperation framework for the UK nuclear power project. • **Establishing JVs/SPVs**:	• **Establishing Partnerships**: French company CMA CGM signed an MOU with a Chinese company. • **Establishing JVs/SPVs**: Chinese and French firms established partnerships and JVs to develop the Ibom Port project. Chinese port-related companies joined tripartite cooperation through equity investments.

(continued)

Table 8.2 (continued)

			CGN and EDF established a series of SPVs to facilitate their cooperation in the HPC project.	
Beneficiary countries authorities	More frequent use to ➡ Less frequent use: • Outsource EPC contracts or basic construction contracts (47) • Formalised JV contracts (22) • Lease contracts, franchising contracts, concession agreements (11) • Service and O&M (Operation and Management) contracts (10) • PPP contracts (9)	\	\	• **Formalised JV contracts**: The Nigerian Ports Authority (NPA) retained a 5% stake for regulatory oversight

Black: The actions of participants might also be found in bilateral arrangements.
Blue: The determinants in blue specifically refer to the tripartite cooperation contexts.

8.1.1 *Cross-National Divergence of Determinants in Joining Tripartite Cooperation*

Table 8.1 summarises the determinants that drive participants to engage in tripartite cooperation. This table provides a comparative analysis across both theoretical and empirical chapters, addressing the key research question: Why do participants choose a tripartite cooperation model, despite the potential for increased transaction costs? The findings indicate that China, China's partner countries, and beneficiary countries each have distinct motivations for participating in tripartite cooperation projects.

Drawing from the literature on bilateral cooperation practices, China's objectives in these partnerships include efficiency enhancement, market expansion, and the acquisition of strategic assets (Dunning & Lundan, 2008; Cui et al., 2014) as well as continually promoting the 'Going Out' policy and BRI. Beneficiary countries, for their part, are attracted to China's focus on short-term progress and its non-interference policy.

Table 8.3 Actions that influence transaction costs or additional benefits from empirical cases (Source: Author)

Actions	*Transaction costs*	*Additional benefits*
• Financial instruments: (The government facilitate projects by utilising concessional loans, official direct loans, national wealth funds, or issuing sovereign guarantees, uses state financial instruments to support their SOEs.)	–	Tripartite cooperation facilitates the collection of more capital due to the endorsement from the three participating governments. More rigorous business due diligence and financial compliance lower investment risks in tripartite cooperation.
	For example, the port authority's role as a shareholder contradicts the landlord principle. The public sector holds shares but fails to fulfil promised investments, which can hinder the progress of the project. For example, the Nigerian Ports Authority (NPA) impeded the Lekki project's development by only contributing $23 million out of the required $110 million in equity share in 2018 (Anumihe, 2018). With insufficient development funds for construction and procurement, the development process lagged behind expectations.	By aligning all investors' interests through equity cooperation, participants coordinate their actions in construction and operation.

(*continued*)

Table 8.3 (continued)

Actions	*Transaction costs*	*Additional benefits*
• Soft law instruments (Signing MOUs or joint statements to express cooperative intentions, confirming tripartite cooperation projects in High-Level Economic and Financial Dialogue meetings, and utilising working group meetings and forums to boost the execution of tripartite cooperation projects.)	Lack of enforceability means participants can change their decisions and withdraw from cooperation, potentially resulting in wasted resources and increased transaction costs from previous negotiations.	Through these collaborative approaches, governments foster more effective communication, coordination, and implementation of tripartite cooperation initiatives.
• Policy instruments (Signing concession contracts, amending legal terms and publishing administrative policies to bolster these initiatives.)	Higher transaction costs in negotiation and inspection. For example, the UK government wanted to use negotiation tactics to maximise its interests in a project. However, more negotiation and delays occurred due to opposing pressures and the necessary time for scrutiny checks. The three-month delay generated higher transaction costs in negotiation and inspection. The government's action was more of a political gesture for the UK public. Additionally, trust issues arose, with concerns about Chinese investment and national security, which continually cast a shadow over the project's construction and other investing activities.	The government can identify more efficient suppliers through a competitive bidding process and regulate company behaviour through contractual terms and conditions.

(*continued*)

Table 8.3 (continued)

Actions	*Transaction costs*	*Additional benefits*
• Relationship instruments (Close relationship between the government and firms.)	–	The Chinese Ambassador to the UK emphasised the HPC project's importance for China-UK relations, urging the UK to maintain trust and support.
• Establishing partnerships between firms (Sign MOUs, sign framework agreements, establish a strategic alliance.)	May not suffice in establishing a solid relationship and cannot ensure successful projects.	These agreements demonstrate shared aspirations for collaboration. Strategic alliances allow firms to pool resources, align interests, and enhance efficiency. For example, EDF's endorsed the Chinese participants. It advocated for the UK to put aside security concerns regarding Chinese involvement.
• Establishing JVs/ SPVs	In cases where consensus cannot be reached, the project may face potential failure. Disagreements over equity distribution can jeopardise projects, leading to increased transaction costs in renegotiation and the search for new potential partners. The involvement of more participants necessitates a more intricate legal framework and extended time to finalise the terms and conditions. The worst situation, more transaction costs arises when tripartite cooperation fails, and companies withdraw from the project, leading to various losses for both private investors and local authorities. Investors incur sunk costs related to bid preparation, negotiation, etc.	JV/SPVs help manage risks, optimise resource utilisation, and potentially reduce costs. With each company's voting power proportional to its shareholdings, conflicts are mitigated through internal board voting. As independent legal entities, JVs/SPVs can issue project bonds in international markets, increasing financing capacity.

(*continued*)

Table 8.3 (continued)

Actions	*Transaction costs*	*Additional benefits*
• Providing products/services	If participants decide to withdraw from a tripartite cooperation project after entering a legal contract, it may lead to increased transaction costs associated with legal proceedings.	Establishing reliable supply chains and providing relevant technical support are crucial.

China offers beneficiary countries an attractive option by providing financial support without imposing conditions, such as requirements for democratic reforms, which are typically mandated by traditional donor countries (Carothers, 2008; Tseng & Krog, 2016; Bräutigam, 2011).

Moreover, tripartite cooperation acts as a strategic springboard for China, enabling it to acquire resources, technology, market and expertise, which is only possible through the engagement of a partner firm in an advanced economy (Luo & Tung, 2007, 2018). China's involvement in tripartite cooperation is primarily motivated by a desire to reduce friction in its international projects and bolster its global reputation. China's partner countries, on the other hand, engage in tripartite cooperation as a means of managing the 're-Westernisation of international development' (Fordelone, 2009). This strategy is also designed to strengthen their relationships with China in less developed regions, helping to alleviate the financial and technological burdens on traditional donors' development responsibilities (OECD, 2014; Kaplan et al., 2020). These countries leverage tripartite cooperation to maintain the support of traditional donors while collaborating with China, thereby maximising their benefits from both partnerships (McEwan & Mawdsley, 2012).

Empirical cases demonstrate that, consistent with determinants derived from bilateral cooperation practices, China leverages tripartite cooperation to upgrade its industrial value chains, acquire operational knowledge, promote Chinese standards, mitigate international criticism, and avoid the high costs associated with M&A. For China's partner countries, the strategic objective is to counterbalance Chinese influence in beneficiary countries, thereby preserving their historical dominance and influence in these regions. Beneficiary countries, meanwhile, aim to foster local economic growth, support domestic development plans, and enhance infrastructure. They also use tripartite cooperation to bolster their bargaining power and gain greater independence from traditional donors.

However, in contrast to bilateral cooperation determinants, the empirical cases found participants regard tripartite cooperation as a means to redistribute interests, despite the increased transaction costs associated with more complex relationships. For instance, China may use tripartite cooperation as a strategy to enter markets in beneficiary countries dominated by Western firms and avoid the high costs associated with M&A, while Western firms may cooperate with China to monitor and influence the project's progress. Beneficiary countries seek to collaborate with China to break the Western monopoly. During the cooperation process, participants often renegotiate project interests, such as redistributing equity among investors.

The specific case, the Hinkley Point C project in the UK, illustrates China's strategic use of tripartite cooperation. In this project, China aims to strengthen diplomatic ties, acquire operational expertise from EDF, leverage EDF's established local relationships, and navigate the UK's stringent investment conditions. China strategically avoids acquiring assets from EDF, instead focusing on securing approval for its technology and using HPC as a platform for international expansion. EDF, in turn, partners with Chinese firms to share the substantial risks and costs associated with nuclear projects, a collaboration that aligns with EDF's broader European strategy and reputation. Given the relatively low threat posed by China in the UK's nuclear market, EDF does not find it necessary to actively diminish Chinese influence. Meanwhile, the UK government uses tripartite cooperation as part of its post-Brexit economic strategy, advocating for job creation. The government strategically delayed investment decisions to maximise its leverage in the project while addressing national security concerns related to Chinese investments.

In Nigeria, China's strategy centres on promoting the BRI, integrating its investments, and gaining operational knowledge from French companies to build experience for future concession competitions. China's particular objectives include breaking the French monopoly in the port market, establishing a strong brand presence, and expanding its local influence, all while avoiding the high costs associated with acquiring port assets from French firms through tripartite cooperation. French firms, aligning with their development goals, use tripartite cooperation to secure projects and maintain their influence, while closely monitoring China's infrastructure progress in Africa. For Nigeria, tripartite cooperation serves to boost the local economy, create jobs, and adhere to the national port development plan. By developing new ports and expanding existing infrastructure, Nigeria particularly seeks to dismantle the monopolies held by French firms, thereby enhancing its economic independence.

Using the Hinkley Point C project and Nigerian port projects as case studies to analyse the practical implementation of tripartite cooperation, these examples highlight the complex relationships among participants and stakeholders. In contrast, the Ibom Deep Sea Port project was abandoned during the planning stage due to the French and Chinese companies failing to initiate the project. Although French and Chinese companies had low sunk costs and minimal commitment, the Ibom state government suffered higher transaction costs for seeking new investors and developers.

In the HPC project, several key determinants explain why participants continue to engage in this tripartite cooperation model, despite the potential for additional transaction costs. The first determinant is the diplomatic and international significance. The HPC project holds substantial diplomatic and international importance, intertwining elements of energy, economics, investment, national security, and diplomacy among China, France, and the UK. This convergence of interests at a high geopolitical level makes the continuation of the project strategically valuable for all parties involved. The second is the high sunk costs. The significant capital already invested in the HPC project has created strong ties among multiple stakeholders. These considerable financial commitments and confirmed contracts make it difficult to halt the project without negating decades of work and investment, thus binding the participants to continue despite the challenges. The third is risk sharing and distribution. The HPC project involves various risks, including engineering, liability, credit, and safety risks. To manage these risks, participants have entered into extensive legal agreements that distribute these risks among the parties. This collaborative risk management strategy makes the project more viable and less burdensome for any single participant. The project's continuation, despite the potential for increased transaction costs, can be explained by the complex interplay of diplomatic significance, sunk costs, and risk management.

8.1.2 Combination of Participant Actions in Tripartite Cooperation

This section grounded in Table 8.2, summarised the actions taken by participants in tripartite cooperation projects, particularly how these actions diverge from traditional Chinese or donor country approaches to project finance. The analysis is based on the empirical chapters and seeks to address the central research question: How does the partnership alter the dynamics of project finance activities away from purely Chinese or traditional donor country approaches? The findings indicate that China, China's partner countries, and beneficiary countries each have their respective preferences in their roles and actions within these cooperative projects.

Based on empirical chapters, this table shows the actions and roles of each participant in tripartite cooperation. Government actions in tripartite cooperation projects are classified into four instruments: financial instruments, soft law instruments, policy instruments, and relationship instruments. Financial instruments include concessional loans, preferential credit, official direct loans, national wealth funds, and the issuance of sovereign guarantees. Soft law instruments involve MOUs, joint statements, high-level meetings, working group meetings, and forums. Policy instruments include signing concession contracts and amending legal terms, while relationship instruments focus on the government-enterprise relationship. From the analysis of 68 tripartite cooperation projects in the database, it is observed that the Chinese government frequently utilises SOEs engagement and direct government financing. In contrast, partner countries' governments are less frequently involved in these tripartite cooperation projects. Beneficiary country governments, on the other hand, tend to prefer using policy instruments to participate in the projects.

However, financial instruments, policy instruments, and relationship instruments are also commonly used in bilateral arrangements. Only soft law instruments are specifically employed by participant governments in tripartite cooperation. For instance, the Chinese government and partner countries, such as France and Italy, primarily use MOUs and hold working group meetings to promote their tripartite cooperation process. In the case of the HPC project, the Chinese and French governments signed MOUs and conducted high-level meetings with the UK government to facilitate the collaboration.

There are three primary types of firm actions, mainly involving Chinese and their partner firms: establishing partnerships between firms, establishing JVs/SPVs, and providing products/services. Establishing partnerships includes signing MOUs or framework agreements and establishing strategic partnerships or alliances. Establishing JVs/SPVs involves forming new firms, engaging in equity cooperation, or forming a consortium to co-bid on public projects. Firms also engage in the provision of products and services as part of their involvement in these projects, and these activities are commonly used in bilateral arrangements. The empirical data reveals that the frequent collaboration between Chinese firms and their partner firms in establishing JVs or SPVs and co-investing in projects represents a significant shift from traditional bilateral activities. The governments in beneficiary countries play a crucial role in providing policy support and signing various types of contracts with provider countries, including construction contracts, JV contracts, concession agreements, service contracts, and PPP contracts. These types of contracts are widely used in bilateral arrangements by beneficiary country governments. However, firms in beneficiary countries tend to be less directly involved in the execution of these tripartite cooperation projects.

While participants in tripartite cooperation have their preferred approaches to engagement, they can still synergise these methods, leading to collaborations that not only transform the financial landscape but also introduce new dynamics in project execution. Firms from different countries bring together their expertise and resources in unprecedented ways, fostering innovative solutions. However, the divergent approaches to project finance between China and its partner countries also present significant challenges. Chinese financing often relies on concessional loans and preferential credit, while China's partner countries may favour greater private sector involvement. These differences can lead to conflicts and misunderstandings, complicating the cooperation process. For instance, in the Thailand High-Speed Railway project, Chinese SOEs, supported by state-backed financing, were less concerned about budget overruns. In contrast, the Japanese company, more focused on cost-benefit analysis, chose to withdraw from the project due to concerns over potential overbudgeting. Additionally, the policy instruments employed by beneficiary country governments can further delay project implementation. For example, the UK government suspended the HPC project following a government reshuffle, leading to increased transaction costs.

8.1.3 Origins of Transaction Costs and Additional Benefits in Tripartite Cooperation Projects

Using Table 8.3, I have summarised the actions that influence transaction costs and additional benefits in tripartite cooperation, drawing from the empirical cases presented in previous chapters. This table addresses key research questions, such as how tripartite arrangements yield additional benefits, and how the inclusion of a third partner introduces complexities and challenges, particularly due to the differing approaches of China and its partner countries to project finance. The findings reveal that rather than directly impacting transaction costs, these determinants guide the actions of the participants, whose coordinated or uncoordinated efforts subsequently affect both transaction costs and additional benefits.

From the government's perspective, the synergy of financing instruments among participants plays a crucial role. The collective approach among participants can lead to more rigorous business due diligence and enhanced financial compliance, ultimately lowering investment risks. For example, tripartite cooperation often results in the pooling of greater capital due to the endorsement from the three participating governments. The collaboration between the UK, France, and China in the HPC project illustrates how such partnerships can bolster HPC's financial capabilities, enhance its credibility, and expedite project progress. By aligning all investors' interests through equity cooperation, participants coordinate their actions in construction and operation. However, the involvement of beneficiary country governments in such projects can also introduce complexities. The role of beneficiary countries can also contradict the landlord principle, particularly when the government fails to fulfil its promised investments, thereby hindering project progress. The resulting shortage of development funds for construction and procurement caused the project in Nigeria to fall behind schedule.

Soft law instruments can enhance tripartite cooperation by fostering more effective communication, coordination, and implementation of initiatives. This is particularly needed to make the three partners work together effectively. Governments invest significant time and resources in fostering the signing of MOUs or joint statements to express cooperative intentions. They also hold High-Level Economic and Financial Dialogue meetings to confirm tripartite cooperation projects and utilise working group meetings and forums to facilitate the execution of these initiatives. However, this multiplies the transaction costs needed to bring the projects to fruition, and the lack of enforceability in these agreements means that participants may change their decisions and withdraw from cooperation, leading to wasted resources and increased transaction costs from prior negotiations. The reliance on soft-law instruments illustrates the added complexity of tripartite cooperation, as these kinds of MOUs and similar agreements would be less prevalent in bilateral arrangements.

Policy instruments, on the other hand, generate varied effects depending on the government's objectives. When the goal is to facilitate the project, actions such as signing concession contracts, amending legal terms, and publishing supportive administrative policies can bolster tripartite cooperation. Governments can identify more efficient suppliers through competitive bidding processes and regulate company behaviour through clearly defined contractual terms and conditions, thereby reducing transaction costs. However, when governments use policy instruments as leverage to maximise their own interests, this can lead to higher transaction costs. For instance, the UK government's decision to suspend the HPC project as a negotiation tactic to secure better terms resulted in prolonged negotiations and significant delays. This three-month delay increased transaction costs related to negotiation and inspection. The government's action was largely a political gesture aimed at the UK public. Additionally, trust issues emerged, with concerns about Chinese investment and national security, which continued to overshadow the project's construction and other investment activities.

Finally, relationship instruments tend to have less impact on tripartite cooperation projects compared to the other factors mentioned. The close relationship between government and companies can have positive or negative effects, but these are also observed in bilateral cooperation. For example, in the HPC project, China General Nuclear Power Group (CGN), as the SOE aligned with China's national development strategy, played a significant role. The Chinese Ambassador to the UK highlighted the importance of the HPC project for China-UK relations, urging the UK to maintain trust and support the HPC project.

From the firm's perspective, the establishment of partnerships and cooperation agreements between Chinese and their partner firms demonstrates a shared commitment to collaboration, resource pooling, and efficiency enhancement. For example, EDF's endorsement of Chinese participants and advocacy for their involvement in the UK illustrates how such partnerships can help mitigate security concerns and bolster project viability. Tripartite cooperation also serves as a strategic tool for China to deflect international criticism, though it may incur additional transaction costs due to differing regulations and business practices between companies. However, these costs are often outweighed by the savings achieved from avoiding potential international backlash and fostering smoother collaboration across partners.

When Chinese and their partner firms establish JVs/SPVs, these entities effectively manage risks, optimise resource utilisation, and enhance financing capacity through mechanisms such as issuing project bonds in international markets. In addition, with each company's voting power proportional to its shareholdings, conflicts are mitigated through internal board voting. However, the success of projects is contingent on the ability to reach consensus among partners. Disagreements over equity distribution can jeopardise projects, leading to increased transaction costs in renegotiation and the search for new potential partners. The involvement of multiple participants requires a more complex legal framework and an extended timeline for finalising contracts. The worst-case scenario arises when tripartite cooperation fails, resulting in the withdrawal of companies from the project, leading to significant losses for both private investors and local authorities, including sunk costs related to bid preparation and negotiations.

In terms of cooperation in products and services, firms in tripartite arrangements benefit from the establishment of reliable supply chains and the provision of technical support, which are critical for the success of infrastructure projects. However, once legal contracts are signed, the withdrawal of a participant can trigger increased transaction costs due to potential legal disputes and proceedings.

Overall, the research confirms that tripartite cooperation can yield additional benefits through the combined efforts of governments and firms, which would not be available to the same degree in bilateral arrangements. However, the divergent approaches of China and its partner countries to project finance, introduces complexities that can lead to higher transaction costs, legal challenges, and the potential for project failure. The findings highlight the balance required in tripartite cooperation to harness its benefits while managing the risks and challenges.

8.2 Discussion

8.2.1 *The Mechanism of Tripartite Cooperation*

I previously developed a structured double triangular cooperative framework (Fig. 2.1) to clarify the roles of participants in accordance with the NDRC's guidelines (2019). Based on the findings from the empirical chapters, I have updated the previous figure and presented a new double triangular cooperative framework in Fig. 8.1. The country-level tripartite cooperation is depicted as a large triangular relationship involving three key participants: the Chinese government, the government of a partner country, and the government of a beneficiary country. At the project level, tripartite cooperation forms a smaller triangular relationship, consisting of a Chinese firm, a partner firm, and entities within the beneficiary country.

Prior to conducting the empirical research, previous studies assumed that the Chinese government and partner countries' governments would sign MOUs to incentivise private sector participation in tripartite cooperation projects. The Chinese government was also expected to provide financial support and/or sign cooperation agreements with beneficiary countries (NDRC, 2019; Wu & Ding, 2020). Partner countries'

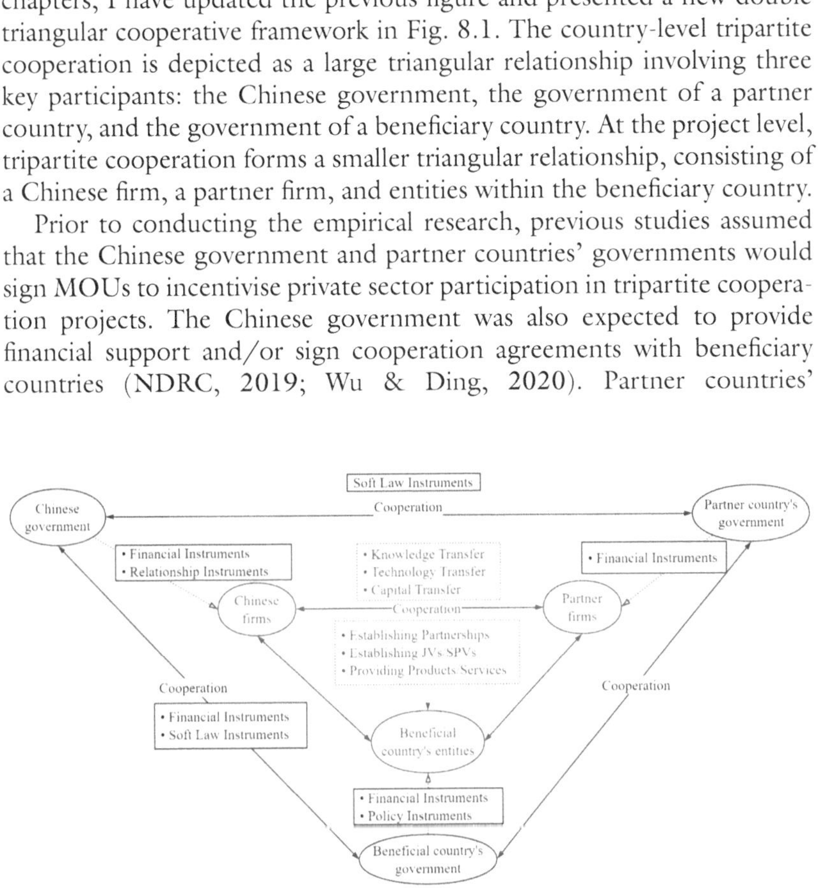

Fig. 8.1 An empirical framework of Tripartite cooperation mechanism. (Source: Author)

governments, were thought to be less directly involved in practical projects, often refraining from providing direct financial support to the beneficiary countries' governments (Zhang & Li, 2020). The participants within the smaller triangular relationship were responsible for the practical implementation of infrastructure projects, offering necessary support to entities in the beneficiary countries. For each project, both Chinese and their partner firms could provide financing, design, construction, operation, and/or maintenance services to the beneficiary country.

Upon completing the empirical research, the findings of this study confirm some assumptions from previous research and update the framework in Fig. 8.1. The actions of participants were systematically revised. Participant governments utilise soft-law instruments to cooperate with each other and employ financial instruments to support their respective firms. In addition to knowledge and technology transfer between Chinese and their partner firms, capital transfer also occurs when they establish partnerships, JVs, or provide services and products for beneficiary countries in tripartite cooperation. Similar to previous research, it was found that partner countries less frequently use policy instruments to support their firms or directly finance beneficiary countries, marking a distinction in how they engage in tripartite projects compared to China.

The interaction between the large and small triangulars merits closer analysis, as these two layers can generate synergistic outcomes. At present, the growing significance of geopolitics at the country level underscores the dynamics within the tripartite cooperation framework. Specifically, power transfer from the national level to the firm level, making the cooperation process inherently a redistribution of power. When governments provide support to firms, projects are more likely to progress smoothly with reduced transaction costs. Such support also enhances firms' confidence in initiating or continuing projects, as evidenced by China's official loans to SOEs engaged in tripartite cooperation projects. This relationship is reciprocal. Successful projects by firms not only bolster their own standing but also enhance their home countries' influence in beneficiary countries or even on a global scale. If firms engage in illegal or unethical practices in beneficiary countries, they risk damaging their home country's international reputation.

8.2.2 Theory Implications of Tripartite Cooperation

8.2.2.1 Revisiting the Theories of International Relations and International Business

This research identifies several knowledge gaps in the existing literature. Systematic reviews on tripartite cooperation are lacking, and the specific literature on Chinese tripartite cooperation is still in its infancy. To bridge these gaps, this study integrates four key theories—transaction cost theory, international relations theories, foreign direct investment theories, and the concept of natural monopolies in infrastructure projects. Together, these frameworks establish the foundational pillars for analysing tripartite cooperation in economic infrastructure development.

According to international relations theories, liberalism provides a cooperative foundation for participant countries, where they seek common ground based on shared interests (Nye & Keohane, 1977; Keohane, 1984). Liberalism assumes that states are rational actors pursuing mutual objectives and that cooperation can yield benefits for all parties involved (Milner, 1992), explaining that participants prefer cooperation over conflict. However, when confronted with escalating international tensions and divergent goals among participants, liberalism falls short in explaining why tripartite cooperation often fails or underperforms. In such cases, realism offers a more suitable explanation, emphasising that the competitive and conflictual nature of states in the international community (Wendt, 1999; Mearsheimer, 2001). National security concerns and the broader international political environment can influence tripartite cooperation. Nonetheless, the empirical research found that since tripartite projects are largely business-driven, firms' decisions are often motivated by commercial concerns rather than purely geopolitical ones.

Therefore, this study applied existing economic theories to the context of tripartite cooperation by integrating three key theoretical perspectives: transaction cost economics, internalisation theory, and the concept of natural monopolies in infrastructure. Through this integration, the research makes a contribution to the theoretical knowledge of international infrastructure projects. Foreign Direct Investment (FDI) theories, particularly the eclectic (OLI) paradigm (Dunning, 1988, 2001) and the springboard perspective (Luo & Tung, 2007, 2018), are used to explore the motivations for firms to engage in tripartite cooperation. This study extends FDI theories to assess their relevance and applicability to the tripartite cooperation model of international development. The empirical findings demonstrate that Chinese firms often seek to enter new markets and engage in projects involving strategic assets, while also aiming to improve efficiency by acquiring management skills through tripartite cooperation projects. In some cases, both Chinese and their partner firms pursue resource acquisition simultaneously, alongside their other strategic objectives.

Similar to the springboard strategy, participants in tripartite cooperation employ accelerated catch-up methods to overcome comparative disadvantages (De Beule et al., 2014; Ramamurti & Williamson, 2019), compensate for latecomer disadvantages (Carpenter & Nakamoto, 1989; Rui & Yip, 2008), and address domestic institutional and market failures (Rottig, 2016). Since this research focuses on tripartite cooperation in the economic infrastructure sector, natural monopolies theories explained that the high barriers to entry in the infrastructure market make it difficult for China, as a new entrant to compete independently. Therefore, China finds it necessary to collaborate with existing dominant Western players in beneficiary countries through tripartite cooperation.

8.2.2.2 Tripartite Cooperation as a Semi-Internalised Arrangement

Based on the four key theories from international relation and international business, the research findings support the argument that tripartite arrangements tend to generate higher transaction costs compared to traditional (fully internalised) bilateral arrangements. This is primarily due to the added complexities of incorporating an additional partner. Empirical evidence from the HPC and Nigeria port projects illustrates that the involvement of additional parties resulted in a greater number of contracts and relationships requiring management, as demonstrated by the intricate company structures involved. For the HPC project, thousands of pages of contracts were initially signed, and numerous issues arose during the construction process, such as political suspensions and the renegotiation of packaged nuclear plant projects, all of which contributed to increased transaction costs.

However, tripartite cooperation, as a semi-internalised arrangement, incurs additional transaction costs but also offers certain benefits meanwhile, such as fostering an environment conducive to effective collaboration and more resource amalgamation among participants. The empirical studies also found that participants employ various instruments, such as legal contracts, preferential policies, and partnership agreements, to manage risks and reconcile differences during the negotiation and implementation phases, thereby aiming to manage the heightened transaction costs associated with trilateral arrangements.

For example, participants in tripartite cooperation typically internalise transactions through newly formed entities. In complex infrastructure projects, JVs/SPVs primarily serve to align the intentions and actions of multiple stakeholders engaged in tripartite cooperation. These alliances facilitate more efficient operations in dynamic environments and improve resource allocation. Participants can transfer their respective advantages to support the project. Although the involvement of additional parties results in an increased number of contracts and relationships that require management, participants benefit from the knowledge and experience gained through the cooperation. Therefore, although tripartite cooperation incurs higher transaction costs compared to bilateral arrangements because the involvement of additional parties, it also generate additional benefits that may offset these transaction costs.

The research also finds that tripartite cooperation, as a cooperative model, potentially reduces transaction costs compared to open market-based arrangements. However, the prerequisite for this proposition is that it only applies to monopolised infrastructure sectors. The semi-internalised nature of tripartite cooperation can mitigate the transaction costs in several ways. For example, when participants form partnerships for the projects, they can avoid consulting costs related to price discovery in the open market by utilising internal accounting prices, resolve contract disputes internally through established procedures, and address information asymmetry to reduce "the costs of legitimate transactions and uncertainty" (Keohane, 1984, p. 220). Through semi-internalisation, participants in tripartite cooperation can reduce transaction costs when specialised goods or services are exchanged internally rather than being purchased from external markets. These specialised goods or services include raw materials, advanced machinery, technology, local networks, etc. For instance, in projects such as the China-France-Nigeria port collaboration, Chinese firms directly provided advanced ship equipment for the projects. This internalisation strategy saved on costs related to equipment sourcing, contract negotiations, and goods delivery. Similarly, French companies provided cargo services and existing networks in Africa, allowing the new ports to directly utilise these services, thus saving transaction costs associated with searching for shipping lines and warehouses (Notteboom et al., 2022; Oladipo, 2023; LPLEL, 2023). The empirical studies proved that, as a cooperative model, tripartite cooperation reduces transaction costs compared to potential open market-based arrangements.

This research offers a novel interpretation of tripartite cooperation as a form of semi-internalisation—more internalised than open market transactions but less so than purely bilateral cooperation. The tripartite model, as a semi-internalised approach, allows firms to mitigate some of the uncertainties and inefficiencies inherent in market transactions, thus reducing transaction costs.

8.2.3 Practical Implication of Tripartite Cooperation

8.2.3.1 Propositions for Effective Tripartite Cooperation

In previous chapters, I reviewed the 'ideal assumptions' for effective tripartite cooperation, such as alignment with best practices and early pooling of resources (Altenburg & Weikert, 2007), the leadership of beneficiary countries in projects (Fordelone, 2009), and principles like equal partnership, shared responsibility, mutual benefit, multi-stakeholder dialogue, transparency, accountability, reciprocity, knowledge-sharing, and joint learning (GPI, 2019a, 2019b).

After the empirical research, this study proposes several conditions under which tripartite cooperation is more likely to be effective. The first condition is cultural affinity. Projects tend to perform better in beneficiary countries where China shares closer cultural ties or historical backgrounds with them (Roy et al., 2018; Li et al., 2020). For example, tripartite cooperation cases have shown success in Southeast Asian countries within the Confucian cultural circle. In cases where such ties are lacking, collaborating with partner countries that share western cultural backgrounds with the beneficiary country can help mitigate challenges and foster smoother cooperation among the three parties.

The second condition is shared development priorities. Aligned development goals can significantly reduce transaction costs. For instance, in the Nigeria port project, both China and Nigeria, as developing countries, prioritised local economic development over national security concerns. This alignment enabled stronger governmental support from both sides, contributing to the project's success. In contrast, the UK's position as a developed country, coupled with its development differences from China, led to heightened national security concerns, complicating collaboration.

The third condition is established relationships or historical ties. Pre-existing relationships and prior cooperation play a crucial role in determining outcomes. For example, in the HPC and Nigeria port projects, France's longstanding presence in the UK nuclear market and its dominance in Africa's shipping infrastructure sectors provided a strong foundation for successful collaboration.

On a practical level, this research provides insights for policymakers and practitioners involved in envisioning and implementing tripartite cooperation projects. These factors—cultural affinity, shared development priorities, and established relationships—emerge as critical determinants of the effectiveness of tripartite cooperation.

8.2.3.2 China-Led Tripartite Cooperation: Aid Policy or Industrial Policy?

Practically, this research distinguished between traditional bilateral cooperative approaches and trilateral cooperation. The preceding discussion has highlighted the significance of tripartite cooperation in the context of international investment and aid, which are the traditional lenses through which such cooperation in infrastructure projects has been understood. However, when considering the practical implications, it is important to recognise that China-led tripartite cooperation can also be viewed as extending China's industrial policies into the realm of project finance, wherein China collaborates with partner countries to enhance the technological capabilities of its firms, similar to the ambitions China held with FDI under its 'Going Out Policy.' Viewing tripartite cooperation through this lens provides a new perspective on China's strategic objectives when promoting project finance, where the focus has been on exporting excess capacity and strengthening China's export links.

Contrary to the assumption that China is an experienced player in international infrastructure projects. In reality, China is a relatively new participant in this arena, where Western countries and their enterprises have established their dominance, having accumulated extensive, mature, and advanced expertise in both developed and developing countries. Firms from partner countries have capitalised on their strengths in advanced technological products and services, taking on roles as designers, developers, evaluators, and operators (Pheng & Hou, 2019). In contrast, Chinese firms have often focused on roles as engineering, procurement, and construction (EPC) contractors, specialising in labour-intensive goods and services (Wang et al., 2016; Chen & Orr, 2009). This research posits that

China is exploiting tripartite cooperation as an industrial policy tool, to further enhance the industrial capabilities and technological innovation of Chinese SOEs (Wang et al., 2021).

In addition, cooperating with partners from advanced economies serves as an endorsement for China, enabling Chinese enterprises to promote their standards in production, technology, and construction in beneficiary countries. Chinese MNEs can obtain financial returns, intangible capabilities, and tangible capacity when pursuing assets and advantages abroad (Knoerich, 2016, 2017). Therefore, China-led tripartite cooperation can be regarded as an industrial policy where China collaborates with advanced economies to acquire cutting-edge technology, facilitating the upgrade of Chinese firms.

8.3 Limitations and Recommendations for Future Research

The first recommendation is the unification of terms related to tripartite cooperation. One of the challenges encountered during this research was navigating the fragmented literature on tripartite cooperation. The varying terminologies and frameworks used by different scholars and institutions added complexity to the analysis. I had unified the terms of tripartite cooperation in my own research. However, Development agencies and international organisations, such as the JICA, MDBs, the OECD, the UN, and platforms for South-South and triangular cooperation, could consider standardising their terminology. Such standardisation would facilitate the promotion and implementation of tripartite cooperation guidelines and practices, making collaboration more efficient and coherent.

The second recommendation is regular updating and expansion of the case database. The study is based on data and 68 projects available up to the end of 2024. However, the dynamic nature of international development and cooperation means that new developments in tripartite cooperation projects may emerge, and previously successful projects might face challenges or even fail due to internal weaknesses or external environmental factors. Furthermore, China's model of tripartite cooperation is still maturing, and that the sample size is relatively small, the findings could be influenced by outliers—such as projects with unusually large investments—skewing the overall distribution. Moreover, the current focus is primarily on the transportation and energy sectors.

Therefore, it is crucial to regularly update and maintain the case database, and monitor the evolution of these projects. Future research should aim to include a larger number and broader range of tripartite cooperation projects, encompassing sectors beyond hard infrastructure, such as transportation, energy, and telecommunications, to include soft infrastructure like education and healthcare. The inclusion of soft infrastructure projects could yield novel insights; for example, educational training programmes typically lack business interests, but when paired with the construction of new school infrastructure, the involvement of building contractors introduces more complex dynamics. Expanding the case database could allow for the application of both quantitative and qualitative methods to deepen the analysis of tripartite cooperation.

The third recommendation is conducting on-site fieldwork and in-depth observation. Fieldwork and direct observation of how tripartite cooperation projects operate in practice, particularly during the negotiation phase, would provide invaluable insights. Unfortunately, due to COVID-19, I was unable to conduct on-site fieldwork. Despite this, I made efforts to conduct online interviews and engage deeply with participants. However, the discussion of failed tripartite cooperation cases remains limited, largely due to the scarcity of publicly available information, as both governments and firms are often reluctant to disclose reasons for failure. In-person interviews could provide access to valuable internal information on both successful and failed cases, enriching the information on tripartite cooperation dynamics.

In Chap. 4, I proposed a process tracing framework for tripartite cooperation cases, highlighting various determinants that influence transaction costs and additional benefits. While some determinants, such as the upgrading of the industrial value chain, reinforcement of influence, and disruption of previous monopolies, are well-supported by evidence, others—such as the relationship instruments between governments and firms—require further investigation. The analysis thus far has primarily focused on internal elements, such as the motivations of firms and governments, while external factors like emerging international issues (e.g., COVID-19, international sanctions) have been overlooked occasionally. Multilateral cooperation involves more complex determinants (see Table 8.1), and the interactions among multiple parties can lead to unpredictable external impacts, such as political shifts or firm withdrawals. By focusing on tripartite cooperation as the simplest form of multilateral cooperation and applying the theoretical framework of semi-internalisation, future research can better analyse and evaluate the complexities of multipartite cooperation.

Additionally, the roles of beneficiary countries have often been overlooked in current tripartite cooperation projects, despite international organisations advocating for equal partnerships. The key consideration in evaluating tripartite cooperation is whether the 'triple win' in these projects is merely an aspirational goal or an actual realisation. For example, the Portuguese company EDP established equity cooperation by selling a 21.35% stake to China Three Gorges (CTG), which enhanced EDP's credit profile and financial liquidity. This collaboration enabled Chinese companies to acquire three hydroelectric power stations and allowed EDP to diversify and develop new markets with CTG's capital support. While both Chinese firms and their partner firms achieved their objectives in this partnership, the role of the beneficiary country remained marginal. It is crucial that future studies place greater emphasis on the role of beneficiary countries to ensure a balanced and comprehensive understanding of tripartite cooperation.

8.4 Final Reflections

The findings of this research have significant implications for both theory and practice, particularly in the context of China's international development and cooperation strategies. Participants choose tripartite cooperation where there are significant internal challenges, such as large sunk costs, high risks, and financial constraints, and external threats, including economic and political backlash. Case studies demonstrate that the considerable sunk costs and the potential for significant losses influence participants' decisions in favour of tripartite cooperation. However, due to its complex mechanisms and higher transaction costs, tripartite and other trilateral cooperation forms have not become mainstream in development studies and practice despite over four decades of development.

By conceptualising tripartite cooperation as a form of semi-internalisation, this study extends existing internalisation theory and provides a deeper analysis of the determinants that drive participation in such cooperative arrangements. This is of both theoretical and practical value. On a practical level, the research offers valuable insights for policymakers and practitioners who are involved in envisioning and implementing tripartite cooperation projects. It provides a framework for why countries and companies engage in these projects. For participants intending to join tripartite cooperation in the future, this research hopes to provide a reference on identifying the crucial determinants for selecting potential partners, how to persuade partners to align interests, and the strategies they can employ during the cooperation process. This research also exposed the internal complexities and higher transaction costs that arise from involving multiple partners, as well as the external factors that can influence the trajectory of these initiatives.

The study primarily focused on China-led tripartite cooperation projects, particularly those involving China, China's partner countries, and beneficiary countries, with a focus on China-France partnerships. Future research should broaden this scope to include more diverse geographic regions and contexts, and to examine tripartite projects where China is not the initiating country, such as Japan-Germany projects in Africa or other South-South-South cooperation models. This broader approach would provide a more wide-ranging understanding of the various practical patterns and outcomes in tripartite cooperation.

Looking ahead, I hope my findings will inspire further research and dialogue on the potential of tripartite cooperation and other multilateral cooperation forms to drive sustainable development. I aspire for this work to inform future policy frameworks and contribute to the development of more effective and equitable cooperation models.

References

Altenburg, T., & Weikert, J. (2007). A Service of ZBW Trilateral Development Cooperation with "New Donors." https://www.econstor.eu/bitstream/10419/199612/1/die-bp-2007-05.pdf

Anumihe, I. (2018, February 12). Lekki Deep Seaport: NPA Paid Only $23m Out of $110m Equity Share. *The Sun*. https://sunnewsonline.com/lekki-deep-seaport-npa-paid-only-23m-out-of-110m-equity-share/?expand_article=1

Bräutigam, D. (2011). Aid "With Chinese Characteristics": Chinese Foreign Aid and Development Finance Meet the OECD-DAC Aid Regime. *Journal of International Development, 23*(5), 752–764. https://doi.org/10.1002/jid.1798

Carothers, T. (2008). Democracy Assistance: Political vs. Developmental? *Journal of Democracy, 20*(1), 5–19. https://doi.org/10.1353/jod.0.0047

Carpenter, G. S., & Nakamoto, K. (1989). Consumer Preference Formation and Pioneering Advantage. *Journal of Marketing Research, 26*(3), 285. https://doi.org/10.2307/3172901

Chen, C., & Orr, R. J. (2009). Chinese Contractors in Africa: Home Government Support, Coordination Mechanisms, and Market Entry Strategies. *Journal of Construction Engineering and Management, 135*(11), 1201–1210. https://doi.org/10.1061/(asce)co.1943-7862.0000082

Cui, L., Meyer, K. E., & Hu, H. W. (2014). What Drives Firms' Intent to Seek Strategic Assets by Foreign Direct Investment? A Study of Emerging Economy Firms. *Journal of World Business, 49*(4), 488–501. https://doi.org/10.1016/j.jwb.2013.12.003

De Beule, F., Elia, S., & Piscitello, L. (2014). Entry and Access to Competencies Abroad: Emerging Market Firms Versus Advanced Market Firms. *Journal of International Management, 20*(2), 137–152. https://doi.org/10.1016/j.intman.2013.05.002

Dunning, J. H. (1988). The Eclectic Paradigm of International Production: A Restatement and Some Possible Extensions. *Journal of International Business Studies, 19*(1), 1–31. JSTOR. https://www.jstor.org/stable/154984

Dunning, J. H. (2001). The Eclectic (OLI) Paradigm of International Production: Past, Present and Future. *International Journal of the Economics of Business, 8*(2), 173–190. Tandfonline. https://doi.org/10.1080/13571510110051441

Dunning, J. H., & Lundan, S. M. (2008). *Multinational Enterprises and the Global Economy* (2nd Ed.). Edward Elgar.

Fordelone, T. Y. (2009). Triangular Co-operation and Aid Effectiveness, Paper prepared for the Policy Dialogue on Development Co-operation. http://www.oecd.org/dac/46387212.pdf

GPI. (2019a). Triangular Co-operation in the Era of the 2030 Agenda, Global Partnership for Effective Development Co-operation. Www.effectivecooperation.org. https://www.effectivecooperation.org/content/triangular-co-operation-era-2030-agenda

GPI. (2019b). Voluntary Guidelines for Effective Triangular Co-Operation, Global Partnership for Effective Development Co-operation. https://www.effectivecooperation.org/content/voluntary-guidelines-effective-triangular-co-operation

Kaplan, M., Busemann, D., & Wirtgen, K. (2020). Trilateral Cooperation in German Development Cooperation. German Institute for Development Evaluation (DEval), Bonn. https://www.deval.org/en/publications/trilateral-cooperation-in-german-development-cooperation

Keohane, R. O. (1984). *After Hegemony: Cooperation and Discord in the Political Economy*. Princeton University Press.

Knoerich, J. (2016). Has Outward Foreign Direct Investment Contributed to the Development of the Chinese Economy? *Transnational Corporations, 23*(2), 1–48. https://doi.org/10.18356/898d556e-en

Knoerich, J. (2017). How does Outward Foreign Direct Investment Contribute to Economic Development in Less Advanced Home Countries? *Oxford*

Development Studies, 45(4), 443–459. https://doi.org/10.1080/13600818.2017.1283009
Li, Q., Han, Y., Li, Z., Wei, D., & Zhang, F. (2020). The Influence of Cultural Exchange on International Trade: An Empirical Test of Confucius Institutes Based on China and the "Belt and Road" Areas. *Economic Research-Ekonomska Istraživanja, 34*(1), 1033–1059. https://doi.org/10.1080/1331677x.2020.1819849
LPLEL. (2023, January 24). Lekki Port and CMA CGM Group to Facilitate Trade Volume Growth, Increase GDP. *Lekki Port LFTZ Enterprise Limited.* https://lekkiport.com/lekki-port-and-cma-cgm-group-to-facilitate-trade-volume-growth-increase-gdp/
Luo, Y., & Tung, R. L. (2007). International Expansion of Emerging Market Enterprises: A Springboard Perspective. *Journal of International Business Studies, 38*(4), 481–498. https://doi.org/10.1057/palgrave.jibs.8400275
Luo, Y., & Tung, R. L. (2018). A General Theory of Springboard MNEs. *Journal of International Business Studies, 49*(2), 129–152. https://doi.org/10.1057/s41267-017-0114-8
McEwan, C., & Mawdsley, E. (2012). Trilateral Development Cooperation: Power and Politics in Emerging Aid Relationships. *Development and Change, 43*(6), 1185–1209. https://doi.org/10.1111/j.1467-7660.2012.01805.x
Mearsheimer, J. J. (2001). *The Tragedy of Great Power Politics.* W.W. Norton & Company.
Milner, H. (1992). International Theories of Cooperation Among Nations: Strengths and Weaknesses. *World Politics, 44*(3), 466–496. https://doi.org/10.2307/2010546
NDRC. (2019). Third-Party Market Cooperation Guidelines and Cases. National Development and Reform Commision, P.R. China. http://images.mofcom.gov.cn/mz/201909/20190912093710956.pdf
Notteboom, T., Pallis, A., & Rodrigue, J.-P. (2022). *Port Economics, Management and Policy* (1st ed.). Routledge. https://doi.org/10.4324/9780429318184
Nye, J. S., & Keohane, R. O. (1977). *Power and Interdependence.* Harpercollins, Cop.
OECD. (2014). Active with the Peoples Republic of China. https://www.oecd.org/china/active-with-china.pdf
Oladipo, O. (2023, November 6). Lekki Port: Innovating Nigeria's Approach to Trade for Modern Future. *Businessday NG.* https://businessday.ng/features/article/lekki-port-innovating-nigerias-approach-to-trade-for-modern-future/
Pheng, L. S., & Hou, L. S. (2019). The Economy and the Construction Industry. In *Construction Quality and the Economy* (pp. 21–54). Ncbi. https://doi.org/10.1007/978-981-13-5847-0_2
Ramamurti, R., & Williamson, P. J. (2019). Rivalry Between Emerging-Market MNEs and Developed-Country MNEs: Capability Holes and the Race

to the Future. *Business Horizons, 62*(2), 157–169. https://doi.org/10.1016/j.bushor.2018.11.001

Rottig, D. (2016). Institutions and Emerging Markets: Effects and Implications for Multinational Corporations. *International Journal of Emerging Markets, 11*(1), 2–17. https://doi.org/10.1108/ijoem-12-2015-0248

Roy, A., Paul, P., Roy, M., & Mukhopadhyay, K. (2018). Mapping Confucian Values in the Context of Ethical Dimensions. *Business and Professional Ethics Journal, 37*(2), 181–212. https://doi.org/10.5840/bpej201841769

Rui, H., & Yip, G. S. (2008). Foreign Acquisitions by Chinese firms: A Strategic Intent Perspective. *Journal of World Business, 43*(2), 213–226.

Tseng, H.-K., & Krog, R. (2016). No Strings Attached: Chinese Foreign Aid and Regime Stability in Resource-Rich Recipient Countries. https://api.semanticscholar.org/CorpusID:53312

Wang, H., Sexton, M., & Lu, S.-L. (2016). Investment by Chinese Construction firms in the UK Infrastructure Sector: Volumes, Patterns and Trends. Centaur.reading.ac.uk. http://centaur.reading.ac.uk/67075/

Wang, J., Mirsardin, I., Sun, Y., & Yang, X. (2021). The Internationalisation of Chinese Multinational Enterprises Under the Belt-and-Road Initiative. *Strategic Change, 30*(6), 509–515. https://doi.org/10.1002/jsc.2467

Wendt, A. (1999). *Social Theory of International Politics.* Cambridge University Press.

Wu, B., & Ding, M. (2020). Third Party Market Cooperation Between China and South Korea: Progress, Resistance, and Countermeasures. *Northeast Asia Forum, 29*(3), 75–89+128. https://doi.org/10.13654/j.cnki.naf.2020.03.006

Zhang, F., & Li, H. (2020). Third Party Market Cooperation: A new Model of International Cooperation Under the "The Belt and Road" Initiative—based on the Analysis of the Third Party Market Cooperation Between China and France. *International Economic Cooperation, 02*, 26–33.

Appendix

Appendix A: Tripartite Cooperation Mechanism and Platforms

C. Su, *From Two to Three*, Governing China in the 21st Century,
https://doi.org/10.1007/978-981-95-8708-7

Countries	*Signed documents*	*Occasion of Signing MOUs*	*Signing time*	*Cooperation platforms*	*Establishing time*	*Partner countries' policy department*	*China's policy department*
Australia	MOU on third-party market cooperation	China–Australia Strategic Economic Dialogue	09/2017	China–Australia strategic economic dialogue	09/2017	Department of Trade, Tourism, and Investment of Australia	NDRCC
Austria	MOU on third-party market cooperation	The Second Belt and Road Forum for International CooperationState visit by Chancellor of Austria Sebastian Kurz	04/2019	China–Austria working group on third-party market cooperation	09/2019	Austrian Federal Ministry for Digital and Economic Affairs	NDRCC
				China–Austria forum on third-party market cooperation	05/2019		
Belgium	MOU on developing partnerships and cooperation in third-party markets	State visit by China's Prime Minister Li Keqiang	10/2018	/		Belgian Federal Public Service Foreign Affairs, Foreign Trade, and Development Cooperation	Ministry of Commerce
Canada	Joint statement on third-party market cooperation	Canada–China Economic and Trade Cooperation ForumState visit by China's Prime Minister Li Keqiang	09/2016	/		/	/
France	Joint statement on China–France third-party market cooperation	State visit by China's Prime Minister Li Keqiang	06/2015	China–France steering committee on third-party market cooperation	11/2016	Agence France Trésor	NDRCC
	MOU on third-party market cooperation	China-France Joint Fact Sheet on the Fourth High Level Economic and Financial Dialogue	11/2016	China–France forum on third-party market cooperation	03/2019		
				China–France fund on third-party market cooperation			

Italy	MOU on third-party market cooperation	State visit by Italy's Deputy Prime Minister Luigi Di Maio	09/2018	China–Italy forum on third-party market cooperation	03/2019	Italian Ministry of Economic Development	NDRCC
				China–Italy working group on third-party market cooperation	09/2018		
Japan	MOU on third-party market cooperation between Chinese and Japanese businesses	The China–Japan–South Korea trilateral summit	05/2018	China–Japan forum on third-party market cooperation	10/2018	Ministry of Foreign Affairs of Japan and Ministry of Economy, Trade, and Industry of Japan	NDRCC; Ministry of Commerce
	List of key projects in China–Japan third-party market cooperation		10/2018	China–Japan working mechanism for third-party market cooperation	09/2018		
Netherlands	MOU on strengthening third-party market cooperation	State visit by China's Prime Minister Li Keqiang	10/2018	/		Ministry of Foreign Affairs of the Netherlands	Ministry of Commerce
Portugal	MOU on strengthening third-party market cooperation	State visit by Prime Minister of Portugal António Luís Santos da Costa	10/2016	China–Portugal working group on third-party market cooperation	11/2021	Ministry of Foreign Affairs of Portugal	Ministry of Commerce
Republic of Korea	MOU on third-party market cooperation	State visit by China's Prime Minister Li Keqiang	11/2015	China–RoK working group on third-party market cooperation	01/2016	South Korea's Ministry of Strategy and Finance and Ministry of Trade, Industry, and Energy on Cooperation	NDRCC; Ministry of Commerce

(*continued*)

(continued)

Countries	*Signed documents*	*Occasion of Signing MOUs*	*Signing time*	*Cooperation platforms*	*Establishing time*	*Partner countries' policy department*	*China's policy department*
Singapore	MOU on third-party market cooperation	State visit by Singapore's Prime Minister Lee Hsien Loong	04/2018	China–Singapore working group on third-party market cooperation	06/2021	Ministry of Trade and Industry of Singapore	NDRCC
	MOU on the implementation of framework for strengthening China–Singapore third-party market cooperation	The Second Belt and Road Forum for International CooperationState visit by Singapore's Prime Minister Lee Hsien Loong	04/2019	China–Singapore Belt and Road Initiative investment forum	10/2018		
Spain	MOU on strengthening third-party market cooperation	State visit by China's President Xi Jinping	11/2018	China–Spain working group on third-party market cooperation	09/2018	The Spanish Institute for Foreign Trade	NDRCC
Switzerland	MOU on third-party market cooperation	The Second Belt and Road Forum for International Cooperation	04/2019	China–Switzerland working group on third-party market cooperation	04/2022	Swiss Federal Department of Finance and Federal Department of Economic Affairs, Education and Research	NDRCC
United Kingdom	MOU on third-party market cooperation	Tenth Economic and Financial Dialogue held between the United Kingdom and China State visit by Chinese Vice Premier Hu Chunhua	06/2019	China– United Kingdom working group on third-party market cooperation	02/2022	Minister for Investment at the Department for International Trade of the United Kingdom	NDRCC

Source: NDRC and updated by author

Appendix B: Tripartite Cooperation Projects in Economic Infrastructure Sector

Time	*Partner countries*	*Project name*	*Beneficial partner*	*Sector*	*Estimated investment scale (USD million)*	*Chinese institutions*	*Partner institutions*	*Beneficiary Country's contract types*	*Chinese role*	*Partner role*
2010	France	Tincan Island Container Terminal in the Port of Lagos	Nigeria	Transportation	225.00	CMHI	Bolloré	long term lease agreement	M&A	operator
2014	France	YAMAL LNG	Russia	Energy	27,000.00	CNPC	Total	construction contract, JV	product provider, shareholder	shareholder
2015	France	Kribi Deep Sea Port Project (Phase 2)	Cameroon	Transportation	675.50	CHEC	Bolloré,CMA-CGM	EPC, 25 years franchise	EPC contractor, lender, concessionary	concessionary
2015	France	500 MW clean energy power station project (Fail)	Namibia	Energy	N, A	CGN	EDF, InnoSun	contract	contractor	contractor
2016	France	Hinkley Point C nuclear power station	United Kingdom	Energy	30,000.00	CGN	EDF	contract	shareholder, contractor	shareholder, contractor
2016	France	Nairobi Western Bypass Highway	Kenya	Transportation	173.00	CCCC	LAFARGE GROUP	EPC	EPC contractor	product provider
2017	France	Infrastructure projects (Mubende–Kakumiro–Kibaale–Kagadi Road construction project, Soroti-Moroto Road upgrade project, Entebbe International Airport Expansion)	Uganda	Transportation	893.00	CCCC	LAFARGE GROUP	construction contract	lender, construction	product provider
2018	France	Ibom Deep Seaport Project (Fail)	Nigeria	Transportation	4600.00	PowerChina	Bolloré	JV, EPC contract	contractor, investor	contractor, investor
2019	France	The National Road No. 1 of the Republic of the Congo Franchising Project	Republic of the Congo	Transportation	2900.00	China State Construction Engineering Corporation	Egis	franchise project, O&M, service contract, JV, TOT(Transfer-Operate-Transfer)	contractor, product and service provider, shareholder	contractor, product and service provider, shareholder
2019	France	Arctic LNG 2 project	Russia	Energy	21,300.00	CNPC, CNOOC	Total	construction contract, JV	investor, product provider, shareholder	investor, product provider, shareholder
2019	France	Ombepo Wind Farm	Namibia	Energy	13.60	Xiangtan Electric Manufacturing Corporation	French Innosun Energy Holdings, BPI	JV, IPP	product provider	product provider, shareholder

2020	France	Lekki Deep Sea Port Project	Nigeria	Transportation	2330.00	CHEC	CMA CGM	JV, BOOT (Build, Own, Operate and Transfer)	investor, contractor, shareholder	investor, contractor, shareholder
2020	France	Kinguélé Aval Hydropower project	Gabon	Energy	210.00	Sinohydro	Meridiam	JV, PPA, EPC contract	EPC contractor	investor
2020	France	Al Dhafra PV2 solar power plant	United Arab Emirates	Energy	1000.00	JinkoSolar, CMEC	EDF	JV,PPA (30-year power-purchase agreement)	shareholder, construction contractor	shareholder, construction contractor
2021	France	Lamu port project	Kenya	Transportation	2860.00	CCCC	LAFARGE GROUP	construction contract	construction	supplier
2021	France	Belgrade metro project	Serbia	Transportation	5000.00	Powerchina	Alstom, Egis	DBF	contractor	investor, construction
2022	France	Wastewater treatment in Dakar Hann Bay	Senegal	Water management	52.00	China Development Bank	French Development Agency	contract	lender	lender
2022	France	Abidjan port expansion project	Côte d'Ivoire	Transportation	472.20	CHEC	Bolloré	construction contract, concession, JV	contractor, lender	shareholder, operator
2022	France	Renovation roads nationale No.1	Guinea	Transportation	380.00	CRBC	Egis	franchising	lender, contractor	supervisor
2006	Italy	Gilgel Gibe III Dam	Ethiopia	Energy	1830.00	PowerChina, Sinohydro, Shanghai Electric Group, Tebian Electric Apparatus	Salini Costruttori, Studio Pietrangeli, ELC Electrocosult and Coyne Et Bellier	JV, EPC	lender, contractors	contractor
2015	Italy	Greater Beirut Water Supply Project	Lebanon	Water management	370.00	CREG	Cooperativa Muratori& Cementisti (CMC)	construction contract	CREC provided hard-rock tunnel boring machines for CMC	contractor

(*continued*)

(continued)

Time	*Partner countries*	*Project name*	*Beneficial partner*	*Sector*	*Estimated investment scale (USD million)*	*Chinese institutions*	*Partner institutions*	*Beneficiary Country's contract types*	*Chinese role*	*Partner role*
2017	Italy	Coral South Floating Liquefied Natural Gas project	Mozambique	Energy	8000.00	PetroChina	ENI	JV, BO	shareholder	shareholder, contractor
2018	Italy	Azerbaijan Integrated Steel Mill Complex	Azerbaijan	Energy	1170.00	CAMCE	Danieli	EPC	EPC contractor	product provider
2019	Italy	Solar Park Projects Ituverava (254 MW) and Nova Olinda (292 MW)	Brazil	Energy	761.00	CGN	Ente nazionale per l'energia elettrica (ENEL)	long-term power purchase agreements (PPAs)	EPC contractor	operator
2015	Spain	Kuwait's Al-Zour refinery	Kuwait	Energy	27,000.00	Sinopec	Tecnicas Reunidas	JV, EPC	contractor	contractor
2018	Spain	Grand Inga Dam, barrage hydroélectrique Inga III	DR Congo	Energy	14,000.00	CTG	Actividades de Construccion y Servicios (ACS Group)	EPC	investor, construction	investor, construction
2015	Spain	Noor III Concentrating Solar Power Projects	Morocco	Energy	900.00	SEPCO III	SENER	PPA-BOOT 25 years, EPC	contractor	contractor, lender
2018	Spain	Mohammed Bin Rashid Al Maktoum Solar Park (DEWA IV)	United Arab Emirates	Energy	4300.00	Shanghai Electric	Abengoa	JV	shareholder, operator	shareholder, operator
2007	Germany	Refurbishment of the Uige—Quinzala—Damba—Maquela do Zombo road	Angola	Transportation	N, A	CRBC	GAUFF Engineering	construction contract	construction	supervision
2007	Germany	Caxito-Nzeto Highway Rehabilitation Project	Angola	Transportation	670.97	CRBC	GAUFF Engineering	construction contract	construction, lender	supervision
2008	Germany	Road Refurbishment "Negage to 31 de Janeiro"	Angola	Transportation	N, A	CRBC	GAUFF Engineering	construction contract	construction	supervision
2008	Germany	Grand Poubara hydropower station	Gabon	Energy	370.00	Sinohydro	GAUFF Engineering	construction contract	construction, lender	supervision
2013	Germany	Port Gentil-Omboue Road and Booué Bridge Construction Project	Gabon	Transportation	663.00	CCCC	GAUFF Engineering	construction contract	construction, lender	supervision

2014	Germany	Empress Eugenie Falls Hydroelectric Power Plant	Gabon	Energy	160.00	CGGC	GAUFF Engineering	construction contract	construction	inspection and assessment
2014	Germany	FE2 hydroelectric power plant	Gabon	Energy	195.00	CGGC, TBEA	GAUFF Engineering	construction contract	construction	inspection and assessment
2014	Germany	Maputo-Katembe Bridge and Linkroad Project	Mozambique	Transportation	785.00	CCCC	GAUFF Engineering	EPC	construction, lender	supervision
2015	Germany	Jupia and Ilha Solteira Hydroelectric Power Plant	Brazil	Energy	573.00	CTG	Voith	30 years Operation Deal	investor	contractor
2019	Germany	Greater Maputo Water Supply Expansion Project	Mozambique	Water management	182.00	CHICO	GAUFF Engineering	management contract construction	construction	supervision
2014	United Kingdom	Rumaila power station	Iraq	Energy	2500.00	CPECC	British Petroleum	JV, EPC	investor, contractor	investor, contractor
2015	United Kingdom	Construction Sheikh Mujibur Rahman Tunnel	Bangladesh	Transportation	1100.00	CCCC	Arup Group	service	lender, consultant	consultant
2019	United Kingdom	Greece MINOS 50 MW Tower Concentrated Solar Power Station	Greece	Energy	31.00	CGGC and Zhejiang Supcon Solar Technology Co., Ltd.	Nur Energie	EPC	EPC contractor, lender	developer
2019	United Kingdom	Kenya A13 Road LOT3 Upgrade project	Kenya	Transportation	750.00	Shandong Hi-speed Company Limited	Guarant Co	10 years franchising, JV, EPC	EPC contractor	guarantee
2005	Japan	Hai Phong Thermal Power Station	Vietnam	Energy	1200.00	Dongfang Electric Corporation	Marubeni Corporation	management contract construction	construction, lender	construction, lender
2011	Japan	Atyrau Refinery Modernization Project Phase 3	Kazakhstan	Energy	1700.00	Sinopec	Marubeni Corporation	EPC	contractor	contractor

(*continued*)

(continued)

Time	*Partner countries*	*Project name*	*Beneficial partner*	*Sector*	*Estimated investment scale (USD million)*	*Chinese institutions*	*Partner institutions*	*Beneficiary Country's contract types*	*Chinese role*	*Partner role*
2013	Japan	Ultra-Deepwater FPSO Chartering Project for Iracema Norte Area of Brazilian Offshore Pre-Salt Oil Field	Brazil	Energy	1170.00	Sinopec	Marubeni Corporation, Mitsui	EPCI + Time Charter Engineering, Procurement, Construction, Mobilisation, Installation, Operation and Maintenance	shareholder	shareholder
2016	Japan	Butendiek Offshore Wind Farm	Germany	Energy	146.00	CITIC Limited	Itochu	O&M	shareholder, operator	shareholder, operator
2017	Japan	Sweihan Photovoltaic Independent Power Project	United Arab Emirates	Energy	870.00	Jinko Solar	Marubeni Corporation	JV,25 years PPA (Power purchase agreement), Build, own and operate (BOO)	shareholder, contractor	shareholder, contractor
2018	Japan	High-Speed Rail Linked 3 Airport Project	Thailand	Transportation	6800.00	CRCC, CITIC	Itochu Corporation	JV	contractor	contractor
2015	Japan	Concesión Autopista al Mar 2	Colombia	Transportation	3700.00	CREC	Sumitomo Mitsui Banking Corporation	EPC	contractor	contractor
2010	South Korea	Sino-Myanmar pipelines	Myanmar	Energy	2500.00	CNPC	Daewoo International	contract, JV	investor, contractor, shareholder	investor, contractor, shareholder
2015	South Korea	Kuwait's Al-Zour refinery	Kuwait	Energy	27,000.00	Sinopec	Hanwha Engineering and Construction	JV, EPC	contractor	contractor, lender
2015	South Korea	The supervision service for Lima Metro Line 2	Peru	Transportation	111.00	CRCC	DOHWA Engineering Company Limited	service	design review, supervision of rolling stock manufacturing, supervision of construction work	design review, supervision of rolling stock manufacturing, supervision of construction work

2015	South Korea	Refineria del Pacifico (fail)	Ecuador	Energy	10,500.00	CSCEC	Hyundai Group		investor	investor
2018	South Korea	Salalah 2 Independent Power Plant (IPP) Greenfield project	Oman	Energy	465.00	SEPCO III	Doosan	EPC service	EPC contractor	supplier
2013	Singapore	SPI Project (the acquisition of SP's Australian assets)	Australia	Energy	4930.00	SGCC	Singapore Power	Co-owned an energy infrastructure group	buyer	seller
2019	Singapore	Simandou iron ore project	Guinea	Resource	15,000.00	China Weiqiao Pineering Group Company Limited, Yantai Port Group	Winning International Group	Formed a consortium	investor, developer	investor, developer
2019	Singapore	Kimbo & Co. Port project	Guinea	Transportation	70.00	Yantai Port Group	Top International Holding	25-year mining concession	shareholder	shareholder
2020	Portugal	The first part of the Mayan railway project	Mexico	Transportation	630.00	CCCC	Mota-Engil	contractor	contractor	contractor, investor
2020	Portugal	Construct Nigeria-Niger rail line between Nigeria and Niger	Nigeria	Transportation	3020.00	CCCC	Mota-Engil	contractor	buyer	seller, contractor
2021	Portugal	Expansion of the Port of Callao	Peru	Transportation	350.00	CCCC	Mota-Engil	contractor	buyer	seller, contractor
2017	Portugal	205.8MW San Gabán III hydro power project	Peru	Energy	438.00	CTG	Energias de Portugal (EDP)	concession, BOT	shareholder, contractor	shareholder, contractor
2015	Portugal	Moray East Wind Farm	United Kingdom	Energy	33.00	CTG	Energias de Portugal (EDP)	O&M, JV	shareholder, developer	shareholder, developer
2014	Portugal	The construction of São Manoel hydroelectric plant	Brazil	Energy	695.20	CTG	Energias de Portugal (EDP)	JV, PPA	shareholder, operator	shareholder, operator

(continued)

(continued)

Time	*Partner countries*	*Project name*	*Beneficial partner*	*Sector*	*Estimated investment scale (USD million)*	*Chinese institutions*	*Partner institutions*	*Beneficiary Country's contract types*	*Chinese role*	*Partner role*
2018	Portugal	Hydroelectric project of Talasa	Colombia	Energy	4100.00	CTG	Energias de Portugal (EDP)	license	shareholder	shareholder
2019	United States	Ncondezi power station project	Mozambique	Energy	26.70	CMEC	General Electric Company	EPC, O&M	shareholder, EPC Contractor	shareholder, equipment subcontractor
2018	United States	Thar Block II Power Plant Thar	Pakistan	Energy	1130.00	CMEC	General Electric Company	JV, 30-year power purchase agreement (PPA)	lender, shareholder	subcontractor
2016	United States	India Adani Godda Coal-fired Power Plant	India	Energy	2100.00	SEPCO III	General Electric Company	EPC, BOO	EPC contractor	supplier
2016	United States	Kipeto Wind Power Station	Kenya	Energy	344.00	CMEC	General Electric Company	EPC, 20-year power purchase agreement	EPC contractor	supplier

Source: Author

Appendix C: Semi-Structured Interview Questions

- Checklist of questions for managers in tripartite cooperation

Personal basic information:

1) What is your role in this tripartite cooperation project?
2) How many years do you work on this project?

Personal experience in project:

3) Did you confront any problems during the design/construction process in this project?

About your company:

4) How did your company distribute the responsibility and interests in the negotiation process with other parties?
5) How did your company deal with the conflicts in the negotiation and operation process with other parties?
6) Why did your company join this project?
7) Do you think tripartite cooperation brings more value or more costs?

Personal opinions:

8) What is your opinion about tripartite cooperation?
9) Do you have any suggestions to improve the performance of this project?
10) Is there anything else you would like to comment or add?

- Checklist of questions for government officers

Personal basic information:

1) What is your role in the government institution?
2) How many years do you work?

About your government:

3) How did your government support (hinder) this project?

4) Does this project connect your country's national strategy?
5) Do you think tripartite cooperation brings more value or more costs?

Personal opinions:

6) What is your opinion about the tripartite cooperation project?
7) What is your opinion about the motivation of your government to sign *MOUs of Third-Party Market Cooperation* with the Chinese government?
8) Is there anything else you would like to comment or add?

- Checklist of questions for academics and experts

Personal basic information:

1) What is your role in this institution?
2) How many years do you work on the topic of tripartite cooperation?

About your publications:

3) Why did you have interests in tripartite cooperation?
4) I tailored various questions regarding their publications, such as their definitions of tripartite cooperation, and their perspectives on its role in international development and international relations.

Personal opinions:

5) What is your opinion about tripartite cooperation?
6) Do you have any suggestions to improve the performance of tripartite cooperation?
7) Is there anything else you would like to comment or add?

Appendix D The List of Interviewees

No.	*Position*	*Organisation*	*Project*	*Interviewed Date*
A-20220523	Professor in Sino-Japanese Relationship	Fudan University	Academic	20220523
A-20220727	Professor in International Relationship	Tongji University	Academic	20220727
A-20230510	Professor in Sino-Japanese Relationship	Sungkyunkwan University	Academic	20230510
A-20230421	Professor in Trilateral Cooperation	Australian National University	Academic	20230421
A-20220527	Reseacher	Chinese Academy of Social Sciences	Academic	20220527
A-20220729	PhD Candidate	Tongji University	Academic	20220729
HPC-20221023	Project Manager	China General Nuclear Power Group	Hinkley Point C Project	20221023
HPC-20221105	Project Manager	Électricité de France	Hinkley Point C Project	20221105
HPC-20221115	Member in Labour Union	Électricité de France	Hinkley Point C Project	20221115
HPC-20220726	Former official in UK government	UK Government	Hinkley Point C Project	20220726
HPC-20221121	UK Parliament Member	UK Parliament	Hinkley Point C Project	20221121
NPP-20220922	Project Manager	China Harbour Engineering Company	Nigeria Port Projects (TICT)	20220922
NPP-20220925	Project Manager	China Merchant	Nigeria Port Projects (Lekki)	20220925
NPP-20220830	Vice President	China Harbour Engineering Company	Nigeria Port Projects (Lekki)	20220830

(*continued*)

(continued)

No.	*Position*	*Organisation*	*Project*	*Interviewed Date*
NPP-20221008	Project Manager	China Harbour Engineering Company	Nigeria Port Projects (Lekki)	20221008
NPP-20220916	Project Manager	Nigerian Ports Authority	Nigeria Port Projects	20220916
NPP-20220920	Staff	Nigerian Ports Authority	Nigeria Port Projects	20220920
YP-20211201	Project Manager	Novatek	Yamal Project	20220811
YP-20211210	Project Manager	China National Petroleum Corporation	Yamal Project	20220823
YP-20211211	Staff	Novatek	Yamal Project	20220824
O-20230310	Project Manager	Beijing Construction Engineering Group	Sofia International Airport	20230310
O-20230508	Project Manager	China Harbour Engineering Company	Kribi Deep Seaport Project	20230508
O-20220615	Project Manager	China National Petroleum Corporation	Myanmar-China Gas Pipeline Project	20220615
O-20221201	Project Manager	China Three Gorges	Hydroelectric Power Plants Project	20221201
O-20230117	Project Manager	Winning Group	Guinea Simandou Iron Ore Project	20230117

Appendix E: The Coding and Categorisation of Tripartite Cooperation Projects

Name	*Files*	*References*
1. Actions		
1.1 Background—bilateral cooperation	32	51
1.2 Company		
1.2.1 Bilateral partnership initiatives	40	78
• Framework agreement	15	25
• MOUs	17	22
• Strategic partnership	17	30
1.2.2 Co-contractor arrangements		
• Co-bidder	7	13
• EPC co-contractor	14	21
• Purchase and service provider	15	33
1.2.3 Financial collaborations		
• Equity acquisition	22	34
• Form new JV or SPV	18	27
1.3 Government		
1.3.1 Chinese government		
• Ambassadors and government officials	9	13
• Financial tools and supports	25	76
1.3.2 Tripartite joint statement and MOUs		
• High-level economic and financial dialogue	33	62
• Tripartite cooperation work group meetings and forums	12	16
1.3.3 Beneficiary countries government		
• Financial supports	15	30
• Government officials	9	11
• Policy supports	30	56
• Concession	22	32
• Legal and tax benefit	8	24

(*continued*)

(continued)

Name	*Files*	*References*
1.3.4 Partner countries' governments	2	5
• Financial support	14	23
1.4 Participants' actions in project		
1.4.1 Cooperation domains	8	16
• Finance and insurance	6	9
• Infrastructure, energy, transportation, and industry	5	6
1.4.2 Interest distribution	5	14
• Loan agreement conditions	2	6
1.4.3 Responsibility allocation	3	3
2. Cooperation outcomes, problems, and challenges		
2.1 Cooperation principles	2	2
2.2 Outcome		
2.2.1 Disputes	7	14
2.2.2 Failure	3	11
2.2.3 Success	6	22
2.3 Problems and challenges		
2.3.1 Arguments in implement process	8	15
• Local ownership	2	3
• Local relationship	7	17
2.3.2 Financing difficulties	12	30
2.3.3 High-level risks	9	27
• Credit default risks	4	7
• Political risks and sanctions	6	14
• Technology difficulties	2	4
2.3.4 Management difficulties	5	6
2.4 Suggestions	4	9
3. Interviews in news reports	10	41
4. Motivations		
4.1 Company	4	4
4.1.1 Chinese company		
• Industrial upgrade and technology transfer	8	15

(*continued*)

(continued)

Name	*Files*	*References*
• Know-how and operation experience	14	18
• New market and going-out policy	33	48
• Promote standards	5	10
4.1.2 Cooperation background		
• Competitions	10	20
• Shared interests	18	23
4.1.3 Local company	5	13
4.1.4 Partner company		
• Commercial interests	11	13
• Reinforce presence and strategic choice	13	17
4.2 Government		
4.2.1 Chinese government		
• Comments from international community	8	21
• Development strategy and BRI	14	22
• Strategic assets	1	1
• Geographic location	4	7
• Resource seeking	6	17
4.2.2 Beneficiary countries government	7	28
• District complex construction plan	13	25
• Economy development and employment	28	68
• Independence	7	16
4.2.3 Shared interests and strategy	31	50
4.2.4 Partner countries' governments	10	18
5. Theory		
5.1 Additional benefits		
5.1.1 Financial benefits	11	15
• Cost of capital	5	15
• Diversification and reduced cost of equity	6	17
• Increased debt capacity and reduce loan cost	7	25

(*continued*)

(continued)

Name	*Files*	*References*
• Return of capital	5	10
• Tax benefits	1	4
5.1.2 Operating benefits	12	17
• Comparative advantages	32	41
• Economies of scale and improved efficiency	9	22
• Strategic similarity	4	4
• Technology and infrastructure upgrade	16	26
• Vertical integration	2	2
5.2 Transaction cost	4	7
5.2.1 Risk diversification	8	13
5.2.2 Technology, knowledge, and experience transfer	6	8

Source: Author

Appendix F: Tripartite Cooperation Mechanism and Platforms

Country	Time	Name	Outcome	Chinese institutions	Partner institutions	Source
France	13/04/2016	China–France–Africa Tripartite Cooperation Seminar	China and France will establish a third-party market cooperation steering committee and accelerate the establishment of a China–France third-party market cooperation fund to provide financial support for third-party cooperation projects.	NDRC	Government official authorities	https://www.ndrc.gov.cn/fzggw/wld/njz/lddt/201604/t20160413_1167275.html
	09/11/2018	The Second Meeting of the China–France Third-Party Market Cooperation Guidance Committee.	Third rounds project lists of tripartite cooperation	NDRC	Agence France Trésor (AFT)	https://www.yidaiyilu.gov.cn/p/71169.html
	28/04/2019	The Second Belt and Road Forum for International Cooperation	Second rounds project lists of tripartite cooperation	NDRC	Agence France Trésor (AFT)	https://www.yidaiyilu.gov.cn/p/71169.html
	02/08/2019	Third-party market cooperation teleconference	\	NDRC	Agence France Trésor (AFT)	https://www.ndrc.gov.cn/fzggw/jgsj/wzs/sjjdt/201908/t20190802_1036967.html
	14/02/2022	Working Group Meeting	Four rounds project lists of tripartite cooperation	NDRC	Agence France Trésor (AFT)	https://www.ndrc.gov.cn/fzggw/jgsj/wzs/sjjdt/202202/t20220214_1315472.html

(*continued*)

Country	*Time*	*Name*	*Outcome*	*Chinese institutions*	*Partner institutions*	*Source*
	01/05/2024	China–France Third-Party Market Cooperation Roundtable	The conference released the "Results Collection of Third Party Market Cooperation Projects between China and France"	NDRC	Financial institutions	https://www.ndrc.gov.cn/fzggw/jgsj/wzs/sjjdt/202405/t20240501_1366304.html
Belgium	27/11/2019	Belgium Third-Party Market Cooperation Seminar	\	MOC	Belgian Federal Public Service Foreign Affairs, Foreign Trade and Development Cooperation	https://www.investgo.cn/article/yw/jmhddt/201911/470189.html
Italy	18/12/2018	The First Meeting of the Sino–Italian Third-Party Market Cooperation Working Group	Both sides had in-depth communication on the implementation of the Memorandum of Understanding on China–Italy Third-Party Market Cooperation, and exchanged views on the next steps of third-party market cooperation, the list of demonstration projects, and the organization of seminars.	NDRC	Ministero dell'Economia e delle Finanze	https://www.ndrc.gov.cn/fzggw/jgsj/wzs/sjjdt/201812/t20181218_1036770.html
	28/09/2020	The Second Meeting of the Sino–Italian Third-Party Market Cooperation Working Group	\	NDRC	Ministero degli Affari Esteri e della Cooperazione Internazionale	https://www.ndrc.gov.cn/fzggw/jgsj/wzs/sjjdt/202009/t20200928_1239795.html

29/10/2020	The Third Meeting of the Sino–Italian Third-Party Market Cooperation Working Group	\	NDRC	Ministero degli Affari Esteri e della Cooperazione Internazionale	https://www.ndrc.gov.cn/fzggw/jgsj/wzs/sjdt/202010/t20201029_1249297.html
04/12/2020	The Fourth Meeting of the Sino–Italian Third-Party Market Cooperation Working Group	\	NDRC	Ministero degli Affari Esteri e della Cooperazione Internazionale	https://www.ndrc.gov.cn/fzggw/jgsj/wzs/sjdt/202012/t20201204_1252260.html
06/05/2021	The Fifth Meeting of the Sino–Italian Third-Party Market Cooperation Working Group	\	NDRC	Ministero degli Affari Esteri e della Cooperazione Internazionale	http://jldrc.jl.gov.cn/fzgz/202105/t20210511_8063108.html
26/10/2021	The Sixth Meeting of the Sino–Italian Third-Party Market Cooperation Working Group	List of Key Projects for the Second Round of Third-Party Market Cooperation	NDRC	Ministero degli Affari Esteri e della Cooperazione Internazionale	https://www.ndrc.gov.cn/fzggw/jgsj/wzs/sjdt/202110/t20211026_1300951.html; https://www.ndrc.gov.cn/fzggw/jgsj/zys/sjdt/202110/t20211029_1302275.html
12/01/2023	The Seventh Meeting of the Sino–Italian Third-Party Market Cooperation Working Group	\	NDRC	Ministero degli Affari Esteri e della Cooperazione Internazionale	https://www.ndrc.gov.cn/fzggw/jgsj/wzs/sjdt/202301/t20230112_1346460.html

(continued)

(continued)

Country	*Time*	*Name*	*Outcome*	*Chinese institutions*	*Partner institutions*	*Source*
	14/09/2023	The Eighth Meeting of the Sino–Italian Third-Party Market Cooperation Working Group	\	NDRC	Ministero degli Affari Esteri e della Cooperazione Internazionale	https://www.ndrc.gov.cn/xwdt/dt/sjdt/202309/t20230914_1360594.html
United Kingdom	22/08/2019	Third-party market cooperation talks	\	NDRC	The United Kingdom's Department for Business and Trade	https://www.ndrc.gov.cn/fzggw/jgsj/wzs/sjdt/201908/t20190822_1036994.html
	23/10/2019	Third-party market cooperation talks	\	NDRC	British Embassy, Beijing	https://www.ndrc.gov.cn/fzggw/jgsj/wzs/sjdt/201910/t20191023_1193548.html
	06/12/2019	China–UK Third-Party Market Cooperation Roundtable (Kenya Session)	China-UK Third-Party Market Cooperation Working Group Goes to Kenya to Promote Cooperation	NDRC	The United Kingdom's Department for Business and Trade	https://www.ndrc.gov.cn/fzggw/jgsj/wzs/sjdt/201912/t20191206_1209924.html
	13/01/2020	Third-party market cooperation talks	\	NDRC	British Embassy, Beijing	https://www.ndrc.gov.cn/fzggw/jgsj/wzs/sjdt/202001/t20200113_1218872.html
	17/04/2020	Third-party market cooperation talks	\	NDRC	British Embassy, Beijing	https://www.ndrc.gov.cn/fzggw/jgsj/wzs/sjdt/202004/t20200417_1225903.html

References

Abbott, K. W., & Snidal, D. (1998). Why States Act Through Formal International Organizations. *The Journal of Conflict Resolution, 42*(1), 3–32. https://www.jstor.org/stable/174551

Abdenur, A. (2007). The Strategic Triad: Form and Content in Brazil's Triangular Cooperation Practices. https://www.files.ethz.ch/isn/46819/2007-06.pdf

Abimbola, B. (2020, July 30). N595.65b Lekki deep seaport courts trouble. *The Guardian Nigeria News.* https://guardian.ng/opinion/n595-65b-lekki-deep-seaport-courts-trouble-2/

ADB, EBRD, IDB, IsDB, and WBG. (2016). The APMG Public-Private Partnership (PPP) Certification Guide. Washington, DC: World Bank Group. https://ppp-certification.com/ppp-certification-guide/31-types-and-variations-ppps

Adeleye, A. (2018, April 16). The CMA CGM Group and Lekki Port LFTZ Enterprise sign a Memorandum of Agreement to operate Lekki Port's future container terminal (Nigeria). *Lekkiport.* https://lekkiport.com/cma-cgm-group-lekki-port-lftz-enterprise-sign-memorandum-agreement-operate-lekki-ports-future-container-terminal-nigeria/

Adesina, F. (2023, January 23). Lekki Deep Sea Port Roars to Life as President Buhari Observes Historic Offloading From Container Ship – The Statehouse, Abuja. *The State House, Abuja.* https://statehouse.gov.ng/news/lekki-deep-sea-port-roars-to-life-as-president-buhari-observes-historic-offloading-from-container-ship/

C. Su, *From Two to Three*, Governing China in the 21st Century, https://doi.org/10.1007/978-981-95-8708-7

Adhikari, D., & Guru-Gharana, K. K. (2014). Econometric Test of Cost Subadditivity in U.S. Electric Industry. https://www.alliedacademies.org/articles/econometric-test-of-cost-subadditivity-in-us-electric-industry.pdf

Adolf, S., Bush, S. R., & Vellema, S. (2016). Reinserting State Agency in Global Value Chains: The Case of MSC Certified Skipjack Tuna. *Fisheries Research, 182*, 79–87. https://doi.org/10.1016/j.fishres.2015.11.020

Adomaitis, N., & Ahlander, J. (2024, February 7). Nord Stream: What's Known about the Mystery Pipeline Explosions? *Reuters*. https://www.reuters.com/world/europe/qa-what-is-known-about-nord-stream-gas-pipeline-explosions-2023-09-26/

AECID. (2010). Triangular Cooperation in the Context of Aid Effectiveness: Experiences and Views of European Donors. https://eldis.org/document/A63056

AFP. (2016, May 17). Hollande Renews Support for EDF Nuclear Project in Britain. *Agence France Presse*. https://www.rfi.fr/en/contenu/20160517-hollande-renews-support-edf-nuclear-project-britain

Akinola, O. (2015). The Political Economy of Chinese and Indian Trade, Aid and Investments in Nigeria: A Comparative Analysis. *Journal of Asian and African Studies, 52*(6), 824–837. https://doi.org/10.1177/0021909615622338

Akomolafe, B. (2022, April 27). Akwa Ibom, Chinese Firm to Partner on $2.03bn Port Construction. *New Telegraph*. https://newtelegraphng.com/akwa-ibom-chinese-firm-to-partner-on-2-03bn-port-construction/

Akpan-Nsoh, I. (2020, December 21). Ibom Deep Seaport to be Built in Phases, Says Commissioner. *The Guardian Nigeria News*. https://guardian.ng/news/ibom-deep-seaport-to-be-built-in-phases-says-commissioner/

Alam, M., Getchius, T. S., Schünemann, H., Amer, Y. S., Bak, A., Fatheree, L. A., Ginex, P., Jakhmola, P., Marsden, G. L., McFarlane, E., Meremikwu, M., Taske, N., Temple-Smolkin, R. L., Ventura, C., Burgers, J., Bradfield, L., O'Brien, M. D., Einhaus, K., Kopp, I. B., & Munn, Z. (2022). A Memorandum of Understanding has Facilitated Guideline Development Involving Collaborating Groups. *Journal of Clinical Epidemiology, 144*, 8–15. https://doi.org/10.1016/j.jclinepi.2021.12.022

Alami, I., Babic, M., Dixon, A. D., & Liu, I. T. (2022). Special Issue Introduction: What is the New State Capitalism? *Contemporary Politics, 28*(3), 1–19. https://doi.org/10.1080/13569775.2021.2022336

Alchian, A. A., & Demsetz, H. (1972). Production, Information Costs, and Economic Organization. *The American Economic Review, 62*(5), 777–795. https://www.jstor.org/stable/1815199

Alden, C., Large, D., Soares, R., & Snow, P. (2009). *China Returns to Africa: A Rising Power and a Continent Embrace*. Hurst.

Alden, C., & Sidiropoulos, E. (2009). Africa-China-EU Cooperation in Africa: Prospects and Pitfalls. Undefined. https://www.semanticscholar.org/paper/Africa-China-EU-Cooperation-in-Africa-%3A-Prospects-Alden-Sidiropoulos/9deb1aa31a36b1aaf23c0d0b772cd2a4cdd198e0

Alesina, A., & Dollar, D. (2000). Who Gives Foreign Aid to Whom and Why? *Journal of Economic Growth*, *5*(1), 33–63. https://doi.org/10.1023/a:1009874203400

Allen, F., Qian, M., & Xie, J. (2019). Understanding Informal Financing. *Journal of Financial Intermediation, 39*(7), 19–33. https://doi.org/10.1016/j.jfi.2018.06.004

Altenburg, T., & Weikert, J. (2007). A Service of ZBW Trilateral Development Cooperation with "New Donors." https://www.econstor.eu/bitstream/10419/199612/1/die-bp-2007-05.pdf

Ambrose, J. (2017, July 3). Cost of Hinkley Point Nuclear Plant Climbs Another £1.5bn to Over £20bn, as Project Faces Further Delay. *The Telegraph*. https://www.telegraph.co.uk/business/2017/07/03/hinkley-nuclear-costs-climb-almost-20bn-start-delayed/

Ambrose, J. (2019a, July 27). Despite Hinkley, the New Plan for Nuclear is Hardly Better than the Old One. The Guardian. https://www.theguardian.com/business/2019/jul/27/despite-hinkley-new-plan-nuclear-hardly-better-than-old-one

Ambrose, J. (2019b, August 13). Hinkley Point C: Rising Costs and Long Delays at Vast New Power Station. The Guardian. https://www.theguardian.com/uk-news/2019/aug/13/hinkley-point-c-rising-costs-long-delays-power-station

Ambrose, J. (2019c, September 25). Hinkley Point Nuclear Plant Building Costs Rise by up to £2.9bn. The Guardian. https://www.theguardian.com/uk-news/2019/sep/25/hinkley-point-nuclear-plant-to-run-29m-over-budget

Ambrose, J. (2020, July 31). Hinkley Point C: French Watchdog Fines EDF €5m for False Claims on Cost. *The Guardian*. https://www.theguardian.com/uk-news/2020/jul/31/hinkley-point-c-french-watchdog-fines-edf-5m-for-false-claims-on-cost

Ambrose, J. (2021, October 27). Government Pledges £1.7bn of Public Money to New Nuclear Plant. *The Guardian*. https://www.theguardian.com/environment/2021/oct/27/government-pledges-17bn-of-public-money to new nuclear plant

Amihud, Y., Mendelson, H., & Pedersen, L. (2005). Liquidity and Asset Prices. *Foundations and Trends R in Finance, 1*(4), 269–364. https://pages.stern.nyu.edu/~lpederse/papers/LiquidityAssetPricing.pdf

Amit, R., & Schoemaker, P. J. H. (1993). Strategic Assets and Organizational Rent. *Strategic Management Journal, 14*(1), 33–46.

An, B., & Zhang, Y. (2019). PetroChina and Myanmar Ministry of Energy Sign Rights and Obligations Agreement for China Myanmar Crude Oil Pipeline. https://www.gov.cn/jrzg/2009-12/21/content_1492737.htm

Anaf, S., Drummond, C., & Sheppard, L. A. (2007). Combining Case Study Research and Systems Theory as a Heuristic Model. *Qualitative Health Research, 17*(10), 1309–1315. https://doi.org/10.1177/1049732307308946

Angeldonis, E. F. D. (2010). Access Regulation for Naturally Monopolistic Port Terminals. https://repub.eur.nl/pub/19881/EPS2010204LIS9789058922458.pdf

Anthony, L. (2021, October 1). NEWSTell Our People Real Reason Investors Withdrew from Ibom Deep Seaport Project—NKpubre to Gov Emmanuel. *Daily Post.* https://dailypost.ng/2021/10/01/tell-our-people-real-reason-investors-withdrew-from-ibom-deep-seaport-project-nkpubre-to-gov-emmanuel/

Anumihe, I. (2018, February 12). Lekki Deep Seaport: NPA Paid Only $23m Out of $110m Equity Share. *The Sun.* https://sunnewsonline.com/lekki-deep-seaport-npa-paid-only-23m-out-of-110m-equity-share/?expand_article=1

Apodaca, C. (2017). Foreign Aid as Foreign Policy Tool. In *Oxford Research Encyclopedia of Politics.* Oxford University Press. https://doi.org/10.1093/acrefore/9780190228637.013.332

Apostolopoulou, E. (2022). *China's Belt and Road Initiative Sustainability in the New Silk Road.* University of Cambridge Institute for Sustainability Leadership. https://www.cisl.cam.ac.uk/files/chinas_belt_and_road_initiative090622_en.pdf

Araujo, A. (2015, August 2). Nueva empresa interesada en la Refinería del Pacífico. *El Comercio.* https://www.elcomercio.com/actualidad/empresa-refineria-pacifico-petroleo-china.html

Araújo, S., & Sutherland, D. (2010). Public-Private Partnerships and Investment in Infrastructure. OECD Economics Department Working Papers. https://doi.org/10.1787/5km7jf6q8f0t-en

Arezki, R., Bolton, P., Peters, S., Samama, F., & Stiglitz, J. (2017). From Global Savings Glut to Financing Infrastructure. *Economic Policy, 32*(90), 221–261. https://doi.org/10.1093/epolic/eix005

Ashoff, G. (2010). Triangular Cooperation. *Development Outreach, 12*(2), 22–24. https://doi.org/10.1596/1020-797x_12_2_22

Atalawei, M. (2016, February). Kribi Deepwater Port in Cameroon. *Constructionreview.* https://constructionreviewonline.com/news/phase-2-construction-of-deep-sea-port-in-cameroon-approved/

Austin, G. (2010). African Economic Development and Colonial Legacies. *Revue Internationale de Politique de Développement, 1*(1), 11–32. https://doi.org/10.4000/poldev.78

Ayres, L., Kavanaugh, K., & Knafl, K. A. (2003). Within-Case and Across-Case Approaches to Qualitative Data Analysis. *Qualitative Health Research, 13*(6), 871–883. https://doi.org/10.1177/1049732303013006008

Baaz, M. (2005). *The Paternalism of Partnership: A Postcolonial Reading of Identity in Development Aid.* Zed Books.

Babic, M. (2021). State Capital in a Geoeconomic World: Mapping state-Led Foreign Investment in the Global Political Economy. *Review of International Political Economy, 30*(1), 1–28. https://doi.org/10.1080/09692290.2021.1993301

Babic, M., Fichtner, J., & Heemskerk, E. M. (2017). States Versus Corporations: Rethinking the Power of Business in International Politics. *The International Spectator, 52*(4), 20–43. https://doi.org/10.1080/03932729.2017.1389151

Babic, M., Garcia-Bernardo, J., & Heemskerk, E. M. (2019). The Rise of Transnational State Capital: State-Led Foreign Investment in the 21st Century. *Review of International Political Economy, 27*(3), 433–475. https://doi.org/10.1080/09692290.2019.1665084

Bai, B. (2021, December 15). Three Gorges Group and Portuguese Electric Power Company Sign a New Strategic Agreement: Launching Renewable Energy Cooperation. *Beijing Daily.* https://ie.bjd.com.cn/a/202112/15/AP61b9b618e4b0d5b7f3634cd0.html

Bance, P. (2003). Opening up Public Services to Competition by Putting Them Out to Tender: An Evaluation. *Annals of Public and Cooperative Economics, 74*(1), 33–61. https://doi.org/10.1111/1467-8292.00214

Banga, A. (2021, March 2). Remaking International Cooperation Post-COVID-19: The Role of Private Companies and Countries. *PIIE.* https://www.piie.com/events/remaking-international-cooperation-post-covid-19-role-private-companies-and-countries

BankTrack. (2010, September 17). Chinese Loan Underwrites Gibe 3 dam Destruction. https://www.banktrack.org/news/chinese_loan_underwrites_gibe_3_dam_destruction

Baroncelli, A., & Landoni, M. (2018). Chinese State-Owned Enterprises in the Market for Corporate Control. Evidences and Rationalities of Acquisition in Western Countries. In A. Vecchi (Ed.), *Chinese Acquisitions in Developed Countries* (pp. 17–36). Springer Cham. https://doi.org/10.1007/978-3-030-04251-6_2

Bartlett, C. A., & Ghoshal, S. G. (1987). Managing Across Borders: New Strategic Requirements. *MIT Sloan Management Review, 28*(4), 7–17. https://sloanreview.mit.edu/article/managing-across-borders-new-strategic-requirements/

Barzel, Y. (1985). Transaction Costs: Are They Just Costs? *Zeitschrift Für Die Gesamte Staatswissenschaft / Journal of Institutional and Theoretical Economics, 141*(1), 4–16. https://www.jstor.org/stable/40750776

Baumann, M.-O. (2017). Forever North–South? The Political Challenges of Reforming the UN Development System. *Third World Quarterly, 39*(4), 626–641. https://doi.org/10.1080/01436597.2017.1408405

Baumol, W. J., Bailey, E. E., & Willig, R. D. (1977). Weak Invisible Hand Theorems on the Sustainability of Multiproduct Natural Monopoly. *The American Economic Review, 67*(3), 350–365. https://www.jstor.org/stable/1831405

Baumol, W. J., Panzar, J. C., & Willig, R. D. (1982). *Contestable Markets and the Theory of Industry Structure.* Harcourt Brace Jovanovich.

BBC. (2013, February 4). Centrica Pulls Out of New UK Nuclear Projects. *BBC News.* https://www.bbc.com/news/business-21319031

BBC. (2022, May 20). Hinkley Point C Delayed by a Year as Cost Goes up by £3bn. *BBC News.* https://www.bbc.co.uk/news/uk-england-somerset-61519609

Beach, D., & Pedersen, R. B. (2016). *Causal Case Study Methods: Foundations and Guidelines for Comparing, Matching and Tracing.* University Of Michigan Press.

Beach, D., & Pedersen, R. B. (2019). *Process-Tracing Methods: Foundations and Guidelines.* University Of Michigan Press.

Beamish, P. W., & Killing, J. P. (1997). *Cooperative Strategies: Asian Pacific Perspectives.* New Lexington Press.

Begu, L., Vasilescu, M., Stanila, L., & Clodnitchi, R. (2018). China-Angola Investment Model. *Sustainability, 10*(8), 2936. https://doi.org/10.3390/su10082936

Benito, G. R. G. (2015). Why and how Motives (still) Matter. *Multinational Business Review, 23*(1), 15–24. https://doi.org/10.1108/mbr-02-2015-0005

Bennett, A. (2009). Process Tracing: A Bayesian Perspective. In J. M. Box-Steffensmeier, H. E. Brady, & D. Collier (Eds.), *Oxford Handbooks Online.* Oxford University Press. https://doi.org/10.1093/oxfordhb/9780199286546.003.0030

Bennett, A., & Checkel, J. T. (2015). *Process Tracing: From Metaphor to Analytic Tool.* Cambridge University Press.

Bergsen, P., Froggatt, A., Nouwens, V., & Pantucci, R. (2022). Briefing Paper Europe Programme Environment and Society Programme China and the Transatlantic Relationship Obstacles to Deeper European-US cooperation. https://www.chathamhouse.org/sites/default/files/2022-06/2022-06-16-china-transatlantic-relationship-bergsen-et-al_0.pdf

Bertucci, S., & Locatelli, M. (2020, February 4). Advancing EU-China-Africa Trilateral Partnerships: The Role of Joint Business Ventures in Promoting Sustainability, Innovation and Institutional Synergies. *EIAS.* https://eias.org/briefing-paper/advancing-eu-china-africa-trilateral-partnerships-the-role-of-joint-business-ventures-in-promoting-sustainability-innovation-and-institutional-synergies/

Besharati, N. A. (2013). South African Development Partnership Agency (SADPA): Strategic Aid or Development Packages for Africa? SAIIA. https://saiia.org.za/research/south-african-development-partnership-agency-sadpa-strategic-aid-or-development-packages-for-africa/

Blackridge. (2024, June 25). Final Investment Decision: Meaning, Definition, and Complete Guide. Www.blackridgeresearch.com. https://www.blackridgeresearch.com/blog/what-is-fid-final-investment-decision#feed

Blomkvist, K., & Drogendijk, R. (2016). Chinese Outward Foreign Direct Investments in Europe. *European J. Of International Management, 10*(3), 343. https://doi.org/10.1504/ejim.2016.076242

BMZ. (2022). Triangular Cooperation in German Development Cooperation. Federal Ministry for Economic Cooperation and Development; BMZ Strategy Paper 1. https://www.bmz.de/en/news/publications/triangular-cooperation-105782

Bollore. (2021). Two Mobile Port Cranes for the Port of Tincan in Nigeria. https://www.bollore-ports.com/en/media/press-releases/pour-cacher-les-ccp/two-mobile-port-cranes-for-the-port-of-tincan-in-nigeria

Bollore. (n.d.). Bollore Transport Logistics in Africa Press Kit. Retrieved February 7, 2024, from https://www.bollore-transport-logistics.com/fileadmin/user_upload/Dossier_Presse_Afrique_EN.pdf

Bolloré Logistics. (2023, July 11). Signing of the Share Purchase Agreement for the Sale of Bolloré Logistics to CMA CGM. https://www.bollore-logistics.com/en/news/signing-of-the-share-purchase-agreement-for-the-sale-of-bollore-logistics-to-cma-cgm/

Bone, R. M. (2021). China's Role in Cameroon's Risk of Debt Distress. Thediplomat.com. https://thediplomat.com/2021/06/chinas-role-in-cameroons-risk-of-debt-distress/

Bourne, L. (2019). *Stakeholder Relationship Management: A Maturity Model for Organisational Implementation.* London Routledge Ann Arbor, Michigan Proquest.

BP. (2015). BP and Sinopec Set Up Joint Venture Marine Bunkering Business. BP Global. https://www.bp.com/en/global/corporate/news-and-insights/press-releases/bp-and-sinopec-set-up-joint-venture-marine-bunkering-business.html

Branigan, T. (2016, August 8). Britain has Struck Out for a Special Relationship with China. If Only we Knew the Way. *The Guardian.* https://www.theguardian.com/commentisfree/2016/aug/08/britain-trading-relationship-china-hinkley-point

Bräutigam, D. (2009). China, Africa and the Global Aid Architecture. SSRN Electronic Journal. https://doi.org/10.2139/ssrn.1525934

Bräutigam, D. (2011). Aid "With Chinese Characteristics": Chinese Foreign Aid and Development Finance Meet the OECD-DAC Aid Regime. *Journal of International Development, 23*(5), 752–764. https://doi.org/10.1002/jid.1798

Brautigam, D. (2019). A critical Look at Chinese “Debt-Trap Diplomacy”: The Rise of a Meme. *Area Development and Policy, 5*(1), 1–14. https://doi.org/10.1080/23792949.2019.1689828

Brett, D. (2023, April 3). Bolloré Africa Logistics Rebrands Following Takeover. *Air Cargo News*. https://www.aircargonews.net/business/acquisitions/bollore-africa-logistics-rebrands-following-takeover/

Brewer, T., Young, S., & Guisinger, S. (2003). *The New Economic Analysis of Multinationals*. Edward Elgar Publishing. https://doi.org/10.4337/9781843766995

BRICS Policy Center. (2017). Paths for Developing South-South Cooperation Monitoring and Evaluation Systems. Brq. https://bricspolicycenter.org/en/publications-/paths-for-developing-south-south-cooperation-monitoring-and-evaluation-systems/

Broadbent, J., & Laughlin, R. (1999). The Private Finance Initiative: Clarification of a Future Research Agenda. *Financial Accountability & Management, 15*(2), 95–114. https://doi.org/10.1111/1468-0408.00076

Brooks, M. R., Van der Lugt, L., McCalla, R. J., & Pallis, A. (2010). Strategic Cooperation in Peripheral Ports: The Case of Atlantic Canada's Ports. *Canadian Journal of Transportation, 4*(1), 29–42. https://www.academia.edu/15269842/Strategic_Cooperation_in_Peripheral_Ports_The_Case_of_Atlantic_Canada_s_Ports

Brooks, M., McCalla, R., Palla, A. A., & Lugt, L. V. D. (2011, March 24). Strategic Cooperation in Peripheral Ports: The Case of Atlantic Canada's Ports. *Semantic Scholar*. https://www.semanticscholar.org/paper/Strategic-Cooperation-in-Peripheral-Ports%3A-The-Case-Brooks-McCalla/a6bf8113d7a313b7d0798575a3c4da02d6acea53

Bros, A., & Mitrova, T. A. (2016). *Yamal LNG: an Economic Project Under Political Pressure*. Foundation for Strategic Research. https://www.frstrategie.org/en/publications/notes/yamal-lng-economic-project-under-political-pressure-2016

Bryman, A. (2016). *Social Research Methods* (5th ed.). Oxford University Press.

Bryson, J. M. (2004). What to do when Stakeholders Matter. *Public Management Review, 6*(1), 21–53. https://doi.org/10.1080/14719030410001675722

Buckley, P. J., & Casson, M. (1976). *Future of the Multinational Enterprise*. Palgrave Macmillan London.

Buckley, P. J., Doh, J. P., & Benischke, M. H. (2017). Towards a Renaissance in International Business Research? Big Questions, Grand Challenges, and the Future of IB Scholarship. *Journal of International Business Studies, 48*(9), 1045–1064. https://doi.org/10.1057/s41267-017-0102-z

Burghart, S. (2017). Ownership in East-Asian Aid Discourses. *Forum for Development Studies, 44*(3), 401–427. https://doi.org/10.1080/08039410.2017.1372517

Burroughs, D. (2021, September 29). Construction of Etihad Rail Phase 2A completed. *International Railway Journal*. https://www.railjournal.com/infrastructure/construction-of-etihad-rail-phase-2a-completed/

Cai, F. (2011, April 28). Absolute and Relative Gains in the Real World. *E-International Relations*. https://www.e-ir.info/2011/04/28/absolute-and-relative-gains-in-the-real-world/

Cai, P. (2017). Understanding China's Belt and Road Initiative. Www.lowyinstitute.org; Lowy Institute. https://www.lowyinstitute.org/publications/understanding-china-s-belt-road-initiative

Calingaert, M. (1993). Government-Business Relations in the European Community. *California Management Review, 35*(2), 118–133. https://doi.org/10.2307/41166725

Carbone, M. (2011a). The European Union and China's Rise in Africa: Competing Visions, External Coherence and Trilateral Cooperation. *Journal of Contemporary African Studies, 29*(2), 203–221. https://doi.org/10.1080/02589001.2011.555195

Carbone, M. (2011b). *The European Union and International Development: The Politics of Foreign Aid*. Routledge.

Carbone, M. (2014). Much ado about Nothing? The European Union and the Global Politics of Untying Aid. *Contemporary Politics, 20*(1), 103–117. https://doi.org/10.1080/13569775.2014.882572

Carmody, P. (2020). Dependence not Debt-Trap Diplomacy. *Area Development and Policy, 5*(1), 23–31. https://doi.org/10.1080/23792949.2019.1702471

Carothers, T. (2008). Democracy Assistance: Political vs. Developmental? *Journal of Democracy, 20*(1), 5–19. https://doi.org/10.1353/jod.0.0047

Carpenter, G. S., & Nakamoto, K. (1989). Consumer Preference Formation and Pioneering Advantage. *Journal of Marketing Research, 26*(3), 285. https://doi.org/10.2307/3172901

Car-Pušić, D. (2014). PPP Model Opportunities, Limitations and Risks in Croatian Public Project Financing. *Procedia - Social and Behavioral Sciences, 119*, 663–671. https://doi.org/10.1016/j.sbspro.2014.03.074

Carrington, D. (2016, March 18). Hinkley Point C Nuclear Deal Contains £22bn "Poison Pill" for Taxpayer. *The Guardian*. https://www.theguardian.com/uk-news/2016/mar/18/hinkley-point-c-nuclear-deal-22bn-poison-pill-taxpayer

Casson, M. (1979). *Alternatives to the Multinational Enterprise*. Macmillan.

CCCC. (2012, May 18). China Communications Group Signed EPC Project for Nigeria's Lekki Deepwater Port. *China Communications Construction Group Corporation Limited*. http://www.sasac.gov.cn/n2588025/n2588124/c3853314/content.html

CCIEE. (2018, November 26). Spain will Lead the Third-Party Market Cooperation of the "The BELT and Road" Between China and Europe. *China Center for International Economic Exchange*. https://www.cciee.org.cn/Detail.aspx?newsId=15849&TId=231

CDB. (2023, February 10). CDB Assisted the Opening and Operation of Lekki Port in Nigeria. *China Development Bank*. https://www.cdb.com.cn/English/xwzx_715/khdt/202304/t20230410_10744.html

CGGT. (2016). CTG Seals the 30-year Operation Deal of Jupiá and Ilha Solteira Hydroelectric Power Plants in Brazil. *CGGT*. http://www.cggthinktank.com/2016-01-14/100075060.html

CGGT. (2016, January 14). CTG Seals the 30-year Operation Deal of Jupiá and Ilha Solteira Hydroelectric Power Plants in Brazil. *China Going Global Thinktank*. http://www.cggthinktank.com/2016-01-14/100075060.html

CGN. (2014, August 22). Independent Gen-III Hualong-1 Reactor Technology Passes National Review. *CGN Power Co*. http://en.cgnp.com.cn/encgnp/c100866/2014-08/22/content_551015cef0fc4461a2172b2fc3d11d4d.shtml

Chahoud, T. (2008). Financing for Development Series: Southern Non-DAC Actors in Development Cooperation. Www.die-Gdi.de. https://www.die-gdi.de/en/briefing-paper/article/financing-for-development-series-southern-non-dac-actors-in-development-cooperation/

Chaturvedi, S., Sidiropoulos, E., & Fues, T. (2012). *Development Cooperation and Emerging Powers: New Partners or Old Patterns?* Zed Books.

Checkel, J. T. (2001). Why Comply? Social Learning and European Identity Change. *International Organization, 55*(3), 553–588. https://doi.org/10.1162/00208180152507551

Che-Ghani, N. Z., Myeda, N. E., & Ali, A. S. (2023). Efficient Operation and Maintenance (O&M) Framework in Managing Stratified Residential Properties. *Journal of Facilities Management, 21*(4), 609–634. https://doi.org/10.1108/jfm-10-2021-0124

Chen, C., & Orr, R. J. (2009). Chinese Contractors in Africa: Home Government Support, Coordination Mechanisms, and Market Entry Strategies. *Journal of Construction Engineering and Management, 135*(11), 1201–1210. https://doi.org/10.1061/(asce)co.1943-7862.0000082

Chen, H., & Wu, B. (2020). Basic Conditions, Challenges and Countermeasures of China-Germany Third-Party Market Cooperation in Africa. *Intertrade, 11*, 45–53. https://doi.org/10.14114/j.cnki.itrade.2020.11.007

Chen, X. (2017, June 30). Exploring the Mystery of Restarting the China Myanmar Pipeline that has been on Hold for 2 years. https://www.china5e.com/news/news-993536-1.html

Chen, Y. (2019, April 28). Bridge of Dreams Brings Two Halves Together. Www.chinadaily.com.cn. https://www.chinadaily.com.cn/a/201904/28/WS5cc4ec06a3104842260b8cd8.html

Chen, Y., Zhai, R., & Zhang, K. H. (2020). Natural Resources and Foreign Direct Investment in Africa: Evidence from Chinese Firms. *Sustainability, 12*(22), 9616. https://doi.org/10.3390/su12229616

Cheru, F., Modi, R., & Afrikainstitutet, N. (2013). *Agricultural Development and Food Security in Africa: the Impact of Chinese, Indian & Brazilian Investments*. Zed Books.

Child, J., & Rodrigues, S. B. (2005). The Internationalisation of Chinese Firms: A Case for Theoretical Extension? *Management and Organization Review, 1*(3), 381–410. https://doi.org/10.1111/j.1740-8784.2005.0020a.x

Chin, G. T., & Gallagher, K. P. (2019). Coordinated Credit Spaces: The Globalisation of Chinese Development Finance. *Development and Change, 50*(1), 245–274. https://doi.org/10.1111/dech.12470

China Harbour. (2020, April 3). The Equity Delivery of the China Harbour for Nigeria Lekki Port Project has been Officially Completed. *China Harbour Engineering Company Ltd*. https://www.investgo.cn/article/yw/alfx/202004/482463.html

China International Development Cooperation Agency. (2011, April). China's Foreign Aid White Paper. *Information Office of the State Council the People's Republic of China*. http://www.scio.gov.cn/zfbps/ndhf/2011n/202207/t20220704_130061.html

Chittoor, R. (2009). Internationalisation of Emerging Economy Firms—Need for New Theorizing. *Indian Journal of Industrial Relations, 45*(1), 27–40. https://www.jstor.org/stable/27768252

Chrisafis, A. (2016, August 31). EDF Representatives File Legal Challenge in France over Hinkley Point. *The Guardian*. https://www.theguardian.com/uk-news/2016/aug/31/edf-representatives-file-legal-challenge-in-france-over-hinkley-point

Chu, Z., & Zhuang, H. (Eds.). (2018). Analyzing the New Model of International Oil and Gas Cooperation from the Successful Operation of the Yamal Project. http://energy.people.com.cn/n1/2018/0227/c71661-29836790.html

Clark, R. (2016, May 11). England Couldn't Cope with a Nuclear Accident at Hinkley Point. *The Spectator*. https://www.spectator.co.uk/article/england-couldn-t-cope-with-a-nuclear-accident-at-hinkley-point/

Clarkson, M. B. E. (1995). A Stakeholder Framework for Analyzing and Evaluating Corporate Social Performance. *The Academy of Management Review, 20*(1), 92–117. https://doi.org/10.2307/258888

Clercq, G. D. (2015, June 18). Portugal's EDP Springboard for China Three Gorges Investment Abroad. Reuters. https://www.reuters.com/article/us-edp-china-three-gorges-idUSKBN0OY1HU20150618

Clive, H. (2003). Private Participation in Infrastructure in Developing Countries. In World Bank Working Papers. The World Bank. https://doi.org/10.1596/0-8213-5512-0

Clò, S., Fiorio, C. V., & Florio, M. (2017). The Targets of State Capitalism: Evidence from M&A Deals. *European Journal of Political Economy, 47*(2), 61–74. https://doi.org/10.1016/j.ejpoleco.2016.12.005

Club of Mozambique. (2018, May 4). Portugal: EDP Enters Colombian Market and Studies Projects in Mozambique. https://clubofmozambique.com/news/portugal-edp-enters-colombian-market-and-studies-projects-in-mozambique/

CMA CGM. (2015). CMA CGM, Bolloré and CHEC obtain the Kribi Container Terminal concession for a period of 25 years. Cmacgm-Group. https://www.cmacgm-group.com/en/news-medias/cma-cgm-bollore-and-chec-obtain-the-kribi-container-terminal-concession-for-a-period-of-25-years

CMA CGM. (2018, April 16). The CMA CGM Group and Lekki Port LFTZ Enterprise sign a Memorandum of Agreement to Operate Lekki Port's future Container Terminal (Nigeria). https://www.cma-cgm.com/local/nigeria/news/35/the-cma-cgm-group-and-lekki-port-lftz-enterprise-sign-a-memorandum-of-agreement-to-operate-lekki-port-s-future-container-terminal-nigeria-

CMPG. (2024). China Merchants Port Group Co., Ltd. Annual Report 2023. https://file.finance.sina.com.cn/211.154.219.97:9494/MRGG/CNSESZ_STOCK/2024/2024-4/2024-04-02/9936539.PDF

CNNC. (2023, September 1). More Funding for Sizewell C Preparations: New Nuclear—World Nuclear News. *China National Nuclear Corporation*. https://en.cnnc.com.cn/2023-09/01/c_916378.htm

Coalición Regional. (2016, March 1). Chinese Dam Builder Eyeing Major Amazon Mega-Dam Contract. https://www.coalicionregional.net/chinese-dam-builder-eyeing-major-amazon-mega-dam-contract/

Coase, R. H. (1937). The Nature of the Firm. *Economica, 4*(16), 386–405. https://doi.org/10.1111/j.1468-0335.1937.tb00002.x

Coase, R. H. (1960). The Problem of Social Cost. *The Journal of Law & Economics, 3*, 1–44. https://www.jstor.org/stable/724810

Coase, R. H. (1972). Industrial Organization: A Proposal for Research. In V. R. Fuchs (Ed.), *Policy Issues and Research Opportunities in Industrial Organization* (pp. 59–73). National Bureau of Economic Research. https://chicagounbound.uchicago.edu/book_chapters/633/

Coase, R. H. (1992). The Institutional Structure of Production. *The American Economic Review, 82*(4), 713–719. https://www.jstor.org/stable/2117340

Coase, R. H. (1998). The New Institutional Economics. *The American Economic Review, 88*(2), 72–74. https://www.jstor.org/stable/116895

Coelho, M., Ratnoo, V., & Dellepiane, S. (2014). The Political Economy of Infrastructure in the UK. In ESRC. https://www.instituteforgovernment.org.uk/sites/default/files/publications/Political%20economy%20of%20infrastructure%20in%20the%20UK%20final%20v1.pdf

Coen, D., Grant, W., & Wilson, G. (2010). Political Science. In *The Oxford Handbook of Business and Government* (pp. 9–34). Oxford University Press. https://doi.org/10.1093/oxfordhb/9780199214273.003.0002

Consumer Scotland. (2024, March 14). Public Information note on Nuclear RAB and Sizewell C. *Consumer Scotland*. https://consumer.scot/publications/public-information-note-on-nuclear-rab-and-sizewell-c-html/#contents

CREG. (2017, May 5). China Railway Engineering Equipment Group Co—CREG Gripper TBM LEA First Breakthrough in Lebanon. *China Railway Engineering Equipment Group*. http://en.crectbm.com/detail/6238.html

Cruz, C. O., & Marques, R. C. (2011). Contribution to the Study of PPP Arrangements in Airport Development, Management and Operation. *Transport Policy, 18*(2), 392–400. https://doi.org/10.1016/j.tranpol.2010.12.001

CSCEC. (2019, April 3). How can China Construction Corporation Transform and Upgrade from the EPC General Contracting to a 30-year Franchise of Highway No.1. *China State Construction Engineering Corporation Ltd*. https://www.sohu.com/a/305902435_354905

CSCEC. (2020, May 30). The National Road No. 1 of the Republic of the Congo Franchising Project. *China State Construction Engineering Corporation Ltd*. https://csci.cscec.com/en/yyfw/tzyfz/202005/3108283.html

CSP Focus. (2019, November 12). Chinese EPC Consortium of Greece MINOS 50MW CSP Project Look for Partners and Vendors. http://www.cspfocus.cn/en/project/detail_183.htm

Cuervo-Cazurra, A. (2018). State-Owned Multinationals. In *JIBS Special Collections*. Springer International Publishing. https://doi.org/10.1007/978-3-319-51715-5

Cuervo-Cazurra, A., & Genc, M. (2008). Transforming Disadvantages into Advantages: Developing-Country MNEs in the Least Developed Countries. *Journal of International Business Studies, 39*(6), 957–979. https://doi.org/10.1057/palgrave.jibs.8400390

Cui, C., Liu, Y., Hope, A., & Wang, J. (2018). Review of Studies on the Public–private Partnerships (PPP) for Infrastructure Projects. *International Journal of Project Management, 36*(5), 773–794. https://doi.org/10.1016/j.ijproman.2018.03.004

Cui, L., Meyer, K. E., & Hu, H. W. (2014). What Drives Firms' Intent to Seek Strategic Assets by Foreign Direct Investment? A Study of Emerging Economy Firms. *Journal of World Business, 49*(4), 488–501. https://doi.org/10.1016/j.jwb.2013.12.003

Datti, Y. U., Zawawi, N. A. W. A., Umar, A. A., Sutanto, M. H., & Danyaro, K. U. (2022). Challenges of Maturity Models in Public-Private Partnerships (PPPs) in the Post-COVID-19 Era. *Journal of Engineering, Project, and Production Management, 12*(2), 149–165. https://doi.org/10.32738/jeppm-2022-0014

Davies, M., Naidu, S., Edinger, H., & Tay, N. (2008). How China Delivers Development Assistance to Africa. In *Stellenbosch, South Africa: Center for Chinese Studies*. University of Stellenbosch.

Davies, P. (2010). the Roles and Activities of New Development Partners. [Review of the Roles and Activities of New Development Partners]. World Bank. CFP Working Paper Series No. 4.

Davies, R. (2016a, April 24). Hinkley Point C Nuclear Power Plant Decision Delayed again by EDF. The Guardian. https://www.theguardian.com/business/2016/apr/24/hinkley-point-c-nuclear-power-plant-decision-delayed-again-by-edf

Davies, R. (2016b, August 8). EDF Decision on Hinkley Point should be Declared Void, Say French Unions. The Guardian. https://www.theguardian.com/uk-news/2016/aug/08/edf-decision-hinkley-point-should-be-declared-void-french-unions-government-approval-nuclear

Davies, R. (2016c, August 9). China-UK Investment: Key Questions Following Hinkley Point C Delay. The Guardian. https://www.theguardian.com/business/2016/aug/09/china-uk-investment-key-questions-following-hinkley-point-c-delay

Davies, R. (2017, September 21). Hinkley Point C: Fresh Strike Threat Over Pay Dispute. *The Guardian*. https://www.theguardian.com/uk-news/2017/sep/21/hinkley-point-c-fresh-strike-threat-over-pay-dispute-delays

Davis, L. E., & North, D. C. (1971). *Institutional Change and American Economic Growth*. Cambridge University Press. https://doi.org/10.1017/cbo9780511561078

De Beule, F., Elia, S., & Piscitello, L. (2014). Entry and Access to Competencies Abroad: Emerging Market Firms Versus Advanced Market Firms. *Journal of International Management, 20*(2), 137–152. https://doi.org/10.1016/j.intman.2013.05.002

de Graaff, N., & van Apeldoorn, B. (2017). US Elite Power and the Rise of "Statist" Chinese Elites in Global Markets. *International Politics, 54*(3), 338–355. https://doi.org/10.1057/s41311-017-0031-2

Defilippi, E. (2004). Intra-Port Competition, Regulatory Challenges and the Concession of Callao Port. *Maritime Economics & Logistics, 6*(4), 279–311. https://doi.org/10.1057/palgrave.mel.9100114

DeJonckheere, M., & Vaughn, L. M. (2019). Semistructured Interviewing in Primary Care Research: A Balance of Relationship and Rigour. *Family Medicine and Community Health, 7*(2), e000057. https://doi.org/10.1136/fmch-2018-000057

Del Biondo, K. (2016). The EU, the United States and Partnership in Development Cooperation: Bridging the Gap? *The Journal of Development Studies, 53*(8), 1238–1252. https://doi.org/10.1080/00220388.2016.1234037

Della Croce, R., & Yermo, J. (2013). Institutional Investors and Infrastructure Financing. Insurance and Private Pensions, 36. https://www.oecd.org/daf/fin/private-pensions/WP_36_InstitutionalInvestorsAndInfrastructureFinancing.pdf

Delmon, J. (2010). Understanding Options for Public-Private Partnerships in Infrastructure: Sorting Out the Forest from the Trees: Bot, Dbfo, Dcmf, Concession, Lease...World Bank Policy Research Working Paper, 5173. https://ssrn.com/abstract=1536986

Delmon, J. (2012). *Public-Private Partnership Projects in Infrastructure.* Cambridge University Press. https://doi.org/10.1017/cbo9780511974403

Demirbag, M., Tatoglu, E., & Glaister, K. W. (2008). Factors Affecting Perceptions of the Choice Between Acquisition and Greenfield Entry: The Case of Western FDI in an Emerging Market. *Management International Review, 48*(1), 5–38. https://doi.org/10.1007/s11575-008-0002-3

Demirel, H. Ç., Leendertse, W., Volker, L., & Hertogh, M. (2016). Flexibility in PPP Contracts—Dealing with Potential Change in the Pre-Contract Phase of a Construction Project. *Construction Management and Economics, 35*(4), 196–206. https://doi.org/10.1080/01446193.2016.1241414

Demsetz, H. (1968). The Cost of Transacting. *The Quarterly Journal of Economics, 82*(1), 33. https://doi.org/10.2307/1882244

Denekamp, J. G. (1995). Intangible Assets, Internalisation and Foreign Direct Investment in Manufacturing. *Journal of International Business Studies, 26*(3), 493–504. https://www.jstor.org/stable/155558

Deng, P. (2007). Investing for Strategic Resources and its Rationale: The Case of Outward FDI from Chinese Companies. *Business Horizons, 50*(1), 71–81. https://doi.org/10.1016/j.bushor.2006.07.001

Deng, P. (2013). Chinese Outward Direct Investment Research: Theoretical Integration and Recommendations. *Management and Organization Review, 9*(03), 513–539. https://doi.org/10.1111/more.12030

Deng, P., Liu, Y., Gallagher, V. C., & Wu, X. (2018). International Strategies of Emerging Market Multinationals: A Dynamic Capabilities Perspective. *Journal of Management & Organization, 26*(4), 1–18. https://doi.org/10.1017/jmo.2017.76

Deng, Q., & Gui, T. (2016, September 30). China, Britain, and France Sign the Final Agreement for the Hinckley Point Nuclear Power Project. *Xinhua News Agency.* https://www.gov.cn/xinwen/2016-09/30/content_5113771.htm

Department for Business, Energy and Industrial Strategy. (2017). The Government's Review of the National Security Implications of Foreign Ownership or Control. https://assets.publishing.service.gov.uk/media/5a82b1f3e5274a2e87dc281b/2017_10_16_NSII_Green_Paper_final.pdf

Department of Trade and Industry of the UK. (2006). The Energy Challenge Energy Review Report 2006. https://assets.publishing.service.gov.uk/government/uploads/system/uploads/attachment_data/file/272376/6887.pdf

Derviş, K. (2020). Multilateralism: What policy options to strengthen international cooperation? Brookings. https://www.brookings.edu/research/multilateralism-what-policy-options-to-strengthen-international-cooperation/

Devetak, R., Burke, A., & George, J. (2011). *An Introduction to International Relations*. Cambridge University Press.

Dhingra, T., & Sharma, S. (2022). Rail Infrastructure—Journey Since Indian Independence and Beyond. In *Studies in Infrastructure and Control* (pp. 53–87). Springer Nature. https://doi.org/10.1007/978-981-16-8837-9_4

Ding, Y. (2023). China Drives Transition of Construction Industry with Technological Innovation—People's Daily Online. People.cn. http://en.people.cn/n3/2023/0227/c90000-10213432.html

Divine, N. (2015, July 31). Kribi port's promises on hold. *African Business*. https://african.business/2015/07/trade-investment/kribi-ports-promises-on-hold/

Dixit, A. (1979). A Model of Duopoly Suggesting a Theory of Entry Barriers. *The Bell Journal of Economics, 10*(1), 20. https://doi.org/10.2307/3003317

Doloi, H. (2012). Understanding Impacts of Time and Cost Related Construction Risks On Operational Performance Of PPP Projects. *International Journal of Strategic Property Management, 16*(3), 316–337. https://doi.org/10.3846/1648715x.2012.688774

Donaldson, T., & Preston, L. E. (1995). The Stakeholder Theory of the Corporation: Concepts, Evidence, and Implications. *The Academy of Management Review, 20*(1), 65–91. https://doi.org/10.2307/258887

Donnelly, J. (2000). *Realism and International Relations*. Cambridge University Press.

Dooms, M. (2010). *Crafting the Integrative Value Proposition for Large Scale Transport Infrastructure Hubs*. ASP / VUBPRESS / UPA.

Dornan, M., & Brant, P. (2014). Chinese Assistance in the Pacific: Agency, Effectiveness and the Role of Pacific Island Governments. *Asia & the Pacific Policy Studies, 1*(2), 349–363. https://doi.org/10.1002/app5.35

Dowsett, K. (2019). Clifford Chance Advises on Colombia's First Private Investment Made by a Chinese Construction Company in a 4G Toll Road Project. Clifford Chance. https://www.cliffordchance.com/news/news/2019/08/clifford-chance-advises-on-colombia-s-first-private-investment-m.html

Doz, Y. L., & Hamel, G. (1998). *Alliance Advantage: The Art of Creating Value Through Partnering*. Harvard Business School Press.

Doz, Y. L., Santos, J., & Williamson, P. (2001). *From global to Metanational: How Companies Win in the Knowledge Economy*. Harvard Business School Press.

Drezner, D. W., & University of Cambridge (Gran Bretaña). (1999). *The Sanctions Paradox: Economic Statecraft and International Relations*. Cambridge University Press.

Druzin, B. H. (2016). Why does Soft Law have any Power Anyway? *Asian Journal of International Law, 7*, 1–18. https://doi.org/10.1017/S2044251316000229

Duchâtel, M. (2019). Triple Win? China and Third-Market Cooperation. https://www.institutmontaigne.org/en/expressions/triple-win-china-and-third-market-cooperation

Dudman, J. (2017, May 19). Why Size Matters: Measuring Success in the World of Megaprojects. *The Guardian*. https://www.theguardian.com/public-leaders-network/2017/may/19/crossrail-hs2-hinkley-point-infrastructure-measuring-success-megaprojects

Duffield, M. (2013). *Development, Security and Unending War Governing the World of Peoples*. Cambridge Polity Press.

Dunning, J. H. (1979). Explaining Changing Patterns of International Production: In Defence of the Eclectic Theory. *Oxford Bulletin of Economics and Statistics, 41*(4), 269–295. https://doi.org/10.1111/j.1468-0084.1979.mp41004003.x

Dunning, J. H. (1980). Toward an Eclectic Theory of International Production: Some Empirical Tests. *Journal of International Business Studies, 11*(1), 9–31. https://www.jstor.org/stable/154142

Dunning, J. H. (1988). The Eclectic Paradigm of International Production: A Restatement and Some Possible Extensions. *Journal of International Business Studies, 19*(1), 1–31. JSTOR. https://www.jstor.org/stable/154984

Dunning, J. H. (2001). The Eclectic (OLI) Paradigm of International Production: Past, Present and Future. *International Journal of the Economics of Business, 8*(2), 173–190. Tandfonline. https://doi.org/10.1080/13571510110051441

Dunning, J. H. (2003). Location and the Multinational Enterprise: A Neglected Factor? In S. Young & S. E. Guisinger (Eds.), *The New Economic Analysis of Multinationals*. Edward Elgar Publishing Limited. https://doi.org/10.4337/9781843766995.00011

Dunning, J. H. (2016). *Explaining International Production*. Routledge.

Dunning, J. H., & Lundan, S. M. (2008). *Multinational Enterprises and the Global Economy* (2nd Ed.). Edward Elgar.

Dunning, J. H., & Narula, R. (1996). *Foreign Direct Investment and Governments: Catalysts for Economic Restructuring*. Routledge.

Dussauge, P., Garrette, B., & Mitchell, W. (2000). Learning from Competing Partners: Outcomes and Durations of Scale and Link Alliances in Europe, North America and Asia. *Strategic Management Journal, 21*(2), 99–126. https://doi.org/10.1002/(SICI)1097-0266(200002)21:2<99::AID-SMJ80>3.0.CO;2 G

Dyer, J. H. (1997). Effective Interim Collaboration: How Firms Minimize Transaction Costs and Maximise Transaction Value. *Strategic Management Journal, 18*(7), 535–556. https://doi.org/10.1002/(SICI)1097-0266(199708)18:7<535::AID-SMJ885>3.0.CO;2-Z

Ebosele, M. (2016, May 4). NPA Votes N14.3b for Lekki Deep Seaport Project, Eyes N201.31b Revenue. *The Guardian Nigeria News*. https://guardian.ng/news/npa-votes-n14-3b-for-lekki-deep-seaport-project-eyes-n201-31b-revenue/

EBRD. (2021). Atyrau Refinery Modernisation Project, Atyrau Region, Kazakhstan. In European Bank for Reconstruction and Development. https://www.ebrd.com/what-we-do/project-information/environment-social-info-documents/1395298775167/Atyrau_Refinery_NTS_(English).pdf?blobnocache=true

Economic Times. (2023, May 19). Like its Apps in India, China has Turned World's Loan Mafia. *The Economic Times*. https://economictimes.indiatimes.com/news/international/world-news/like-its-apps-in-india-china-has-turned-worlds-loan-mafia/articleshow/100361672.cms?from=mdr

EDF. (2024, March 15). Presentation Powering China's Low-Carbon Energy Transition and High-Quality Development. *EDF in China*. https://china.edf.com/en/presentation

EDF 2023 Annual Results. (2024, February 16). Consolidated Financial Statements for 2023 as of December 31, 2023. https://www.edf.fr/sites/groupe/files/2024-02/annual-results-2023-consolidated-financial-statements-2024-02-16.pdf

EDF Energy. (2022). Annual Report and Financial Statements. In EDF ENERGY HOLDINGS LIMITED. https://www.edfenergy.com/sites/default/files/edf_energy_holdings_limited_fy22_signed_complete_set.pdf

EDP. (2011, December 22). EDP and China Three Gorges Establish Strategic Partnership | EDP Renováveis. Energias de Portugal, S.A. https://www.edpr.com/es/edp-and-china-three-gorges-establish-strategic-partnership

EDP. (2014, February 7). CTG Group Enters Partnership with EDP Brasil for Construction of Hydro Power Plant São Manoel. *Energias de Portugal, S.A.* https://www.edp.com/en/ctg-group-enters-partnership-edp-brasil-construction-hydro-power-plant-sao-manoel

EDP. (2022, July 29). Sell of 50% Stake in Hydro Global to CTG. Energias de Portugal, S.A. https://www.edp.com/en/news/2022/07/29/sell-50-stake-hydro-global-ctg

EDF. (n.d.). Nuclear Power Stations in the UK. Accessed July 24, 2024, https://www.edfenergy.com/about/nuclear/power-stations

EFE. (2015, November 25). Brazil Awards Rights to Operate 29 Hydro Plants, Raises $4.6 bn. *ElEconomista.es; elEconomista*. https://www.eleconomista.es/energia-eAm/noticias/7175046/11/15/Brazil-awards-rights-to-operate-29-hydro-plants-raises-46-bn.html

Ehlers, T. (2014). Understanding the Challenges for Infrastructure Finance Monetary and Economic Department. https://www.bis.org/publ/work454.pdf

Eka, I. (2021, February 9). A'Ibom Govt. Ready to Collaborate with U.S. to Develop Ibom Deep Seaport Project. *News.band*. https://news.band/aibom-govt-seeks-collaboration-with-u-s-to-develop-ibom-deep-seaport-project/

Ekapija. (2020, October 5). BG Subway to be Jointly Built by Alstom and POWERCHINA—French Company in Charge of Electromechanics, *Chinese Company to do Construction Works.* https://www.ekapija.com/en/news/3027706/bg-subway-to-be-jointly-built-by-alstom-and-powerchina-french-company

Ekholm, K., Forslid, R., & Markusen, J. R. (2003). *Export-Platform Foreign Direct Investment.* Nber.

Elias, A. A. (2017). Systems Thinking and Modelling for Stakeholder Management. *IIM Kozhikode Society & Management Review, 6*(2), 123–131. https://doi.org/10.1177/2277975216681105

Enderwick, P., & Buckley, P. J. (2021). The Role of Springboarding in Economic Catch-up: A Theoretical Perspective. *Journal of International Management, 27*(3), 100832. https://doi.org/10.1016/j.intman.2021.100832

ENEL. (2016, January 20). Enel Signs Framework Agreement with Bank of China and Sinosure. https://www.enel.com/media/explore/search-press-releases/press/2016/01/enel-signs-framework-agreement-with-bank-of-china-and-sinosure

NS Energy. (2017). Coral South FLNG Project. https://www.nsenergybusiness.com/projects/coral-south-flng-project-mozambique/

Eni. (2013, March 14). Eni Sells a 20% Share of Area 4 in Mozambique to CNPC and Signs a Joint Study Agreement for Cooperation for the Development of the Rongchang Shale Gas Block in China. https://www.eni.com/en-IT/media/press-release/2013/03/eni-sells-a-20-share-of-area-4-in-mozambique-to-cnpc-and-signs-a-joint-study-agreement-for-cooperation-for-the-development-of-the-rongchang-shale-gas-block-in-china.html

ENR. (2019, September 25). Award of Merit, Airport/Port: Maputo Bridge and Link Roads Project. *Engineering News-Record.* https://www.enr.com/articles/47608-award-of-merit-airportport-maputo-bridge-and-link-roads-project

Estache, A., Foster, V., & Wodon, Q. (2002). *Accounting for Poverty in Infrastructure Reform: Learning from Latin America's Experience.* World Bank.

EU. (2023). African Union: The African Political Integration Process and its Impact on EU-AU Relations in the Field of Foreign and Security Policy. STUDY Requested by the AFET Committee. https://www.europarl.europa.eu/RegData/etudes/STUD/2023/702587/EXPO_STU(2023)702587_EN.pdf

European Commission. (2008). Report on the Public Consultation on the Communication of the European Commission on The EU, Africa and China: Towards Trilateral Dialogue and Cooperation on Peace, Stability and Sustainable Development. http://ec.europa.eu/development/icenter/repository/afrique_chine_UE_public_consultation_report_final.pdf%2036

European Commission. (2011). Increasing the Impact of EU Development Policy: An Agenda for Change. https://www.europarl.europa.eu/meetdocs/2009_2014/documents/acp/dv/communication_/communication_en.pdf

European Commission. (2016). Concession Contracts. Single-Market-Economy. ec.europa.eu. https://single-market-economy.ec.europa.eu/single-market/public-procurement/legal-rules-and-implementation/concession-contracts_en

European Commission. (2019). EU-China—A Strategic Outlook. https://ec.europa.eu/info/sites/default/files/communication-eu-china-a-strategic-outlook.pdf

Evans, D. S., & Heckman, J. J. (1984). A Test for Subadditivity of the Cost Function with an Application to the Bell System. *The American Economic Review, 74*(4), 615–623. https://www.jstor.org/stable/1805127

EXPO. (2016, March 1). Construction of Hydroelectric Power Stations to Begin in GABON. *EXPO Group.* https://www.expogr.com/tanzania/powerenergy/detail_news.php?newsid=2770&pageid=2

Export-Import Bank of China. (2011, January 12). Preferential Buyer Credit Loan Agreement on Cameroon Kribi Deep Sea Port Project. https://www.documentcloud.org/documents/20485594-cmr_2011_171.3

Faeth, I. (2009). Determinants of Foreign Direct Investment—A Tale of Nine Theoretical Models. *Journal of Economic Surveys, 23*(1), 165–196. https://doi.org/10.1111/j.1467-6419.2008.00560.x

Fairfield, T., & Charman, A. (2015, June 5). Formal Bayesian Process Tracing: Guidelines, Opportunities, and Caveats. Www.lse.ac.uk. http://eprints.lse.ac.uk/62368/

Fairfield, T., & Charman, A. (2017). Explicit Bayesian Analysis for Process Tracing: Guidelines, Opportunities, and Caveats. *Political Analysis, 25*(3), 363–380. https://doi.org/10.1017/pan.2017.14

Fan, J., Zhao, J., Hu, H., & Zhang, P. (2016). Research on Strategic Shipping Development in China. *Journal of Shipping and Ocean Engineering, 6*(4), 255–260. https://doi.org/10.17265/2159-5879/2016.04.007

Farrell, S. (2016a, May 12). EDF Sets Aside Extra £2.7bn to Cover Hinkley Point Construction Costs. The Guardian. https://www.theguardian.com/business/2016/may/12/edf-extra-27bn-cover-hinkley-point-construction-costs

Farrell, S. (2016b, September 4). Peers Must Press New Chancellor on Policies. The Guardian. https://www.theguardian.com/business/2016/sep/04/peers-must-press-new-chancellor-on-economic-growth-plans

Fearon, J. D. (1998). Bargaining, Enforcement, and International Cooperation. *International Organization, 52*(2), 269–305. https://doi.org/10.1162/002081898753162820

Fearon, J. D., & Laitin, D. D. (2009). Integrating Qualitative and Quantitative Methods. In J. M. Box-Steffensmeier, H. E. Brady, & D. Collier (Eds.), *Oxford Handbooks Online*. Oxford University Press. https://doi.org/10.1093/oxfordhb/9780199286546.003.0033

Feng, Q. (2019). Vigorously Expanding Third-Party Market Cooperation. https://www.gov.cn/zhengce/2019-04/03/content_5379223.htm

Fernandes, C., Oliveira Cruz, C., & Moura, F. (2019). Ex Post Evaluation of PPP Government-led Renegotiations: Impacts on the Financing of Road Infrastructure. *The Engineering Economist, 64*(2), 116–141. https://doi.org/10.1080/0013791x.2018.1559384

Ferrari, M., Giovannini, A., & Pompei, M. (2016). The Challenge of Infrastructure Financing. *Oxford Review of Economic Policy, 32*(3), 446–474. https://doi.org/10.1093/oxrep/grw017

Fingermann, N. (2015). A Study of Brazilian Trilateral Development Cooperation in Mozambique: the Case of ProSAVANA and ProALIMENTOS | Eldis. Www.eldis.org. https://www.eldis.org/document/A72522

Finnemore, M. (1996). *National Interests in International Society*. Cornell University Press.

Fitzgerald, R., & Rui, H. (2016). Whose Fall and Whose Rise? Lessons of Japanese MNCs for Chinese and Emerging Economy MNCs. *Asia Pacific Business Review, 22*(4), 534–566. https://doi.org/10.1080/13602381.2016.1168624

Fordelone, T. Y. (2009). Triangular Co-operation and Aid Effectiveness, Paper prepared for the Policy Dialogue on Development Co-operation. http://www.oecd.org/dac/46387212.pdf

Fordelone, T. Y. (2011). Triangular Co-operation and Aid Effectiveness. *OECD Journal: General Papers, 2010*(1), 47–67. https://doi.org/10.1787/gen_papers-2010-5kgc6cl31rnx

Fourie, J. (2006). ECONOMIC INFRASTRUCTURE: A REVIEW OF DEFINITIONS, THEORY AND EMPIRICS. *South African Journal of Economics, 74*(3), 530–556. https://doi.org/10.1111/j.1813-6982.2006.00086.x

Freeman, R. E. (1984). *Strategic Management: A Stakeholder Approach*. Pitman.

Freeman, R. E. (2010). *Strategic Management*. Cambridge University Press. https://doi.org/10.1017/cbo9781139192675

Freeman, R. E., & Reed, D. L. (1983). Stockholders and Stakeholders: A New Perspective on Corporate Governance. *California Management Review, 25*(3), 88–106. https://doi.org/10.2307/41165018

Freeman, R. E., Wicks, A. C., & Parmar, B. (2004). Stakeholder Theory and "The Corporate Objective Revisited". *Organization Science, 15*(3), 364–369. https://doi.org/10.1287/orsc.1040.0066

Freitas, M. (2023, August 2). The Impact of Chinese Investments in Africa: Neocolonialism or Cooperation? *Policy Center*. https://www.policycenter.ma/publications/impact-chinese-investments-africa-neocolonialism-or-cooperation

French Government. (2020, July 21). China-France Joint Fact Sheet on the 7th High Level Economic and Financial Dialogue. https://www.economie.gouv.fr/files/files/2020/communique-conjoint-dialogue-franc-chinois.pdf

Friedman, A. L., & Miles, S. (2006). *Stakeholders: Theory and Practice*. Oxford University Press.

Gabriel, C. O., & Ajayi, F. (2023, May 15). The Impact of The Lekki Deep Sea Port On The Nigerian Maritime Industry—Marine/ Shipping - Nigeria. https://www.mondaq.com/nigeria/marine-shipping/1315344/the-impact-of-the-lekki-deep-sea-port-on-the-nigerian-maritime-industry

Gaitán, M. G. (2021). Licensing as a Central Structure of Technology Transfer Agreements. Joint Venture and Franchising Agreements. *GRUR International, 70*(5), 427–439. https://doi.org/10.1093/grurint/ikab032

Galp Energia. (2011, November 11). Galp Energia Announces a Partnership with Sinopec to Jointly Develop its Brazilian Upstream Portfolio, *Valued at $12.5 Billion*. https://www.galp.com/corp/en/investors/publications-and-announcements/investor-announcements/investor-announcement/id/259/

Gao, Q. (2018, December 14). The Disappearance of Thailand's High-Speed Rail Project in China Japan Third Country Cooperation. *NIKKEI*. https://cn.nikkei.com/columnviewpoint/column/33518-2018-12-14-02-54-16.html

Gao, X. (2018). New Model: The "Winning Alliance" of the Three Nations and Four Parties. http://www.rmhb.com.cn/zt/ydyl/201808/t20180831_800139852.html

García-Herrero, A., & Ng, G. (2021). China's State-Owned Enterprises and Competitive Neutrality. Policy Contribution. https://www.bruegel.org/sites/default/files/wp-content/uploads/2021/02/PC-05-2021.pdf

García-Herrero, A., & Xu, J. (2017). How to Handle State-Owned Enterprises in EU-China Investment Talks. https://www.bruegel.org/sites/default/files/wp-content/uploads/2017/06/PC-18-2017_2.pdf

GAUFF Engineering. (n.d.). Basic Planning and Construction Management for Grand Poubara Hydropower Station in south-Ea+*st Gabon. GAUFF Engineering. Retrieved July 23, 2024, from https://www.gauff.net/en/referenzen/gabon/grand-poubara.html

Gayle, D. (2016, August 10). Hinkley Point: Mandelson urges government to support China-backed project. *The Guardian*. https://www.theguardian.com/uk-news/2016/aug/10/hinkley-point-c-mandelson-government-china-backed-project

GCR. (2017, June 14). Consortiums Bidding for Huge Inga 3 dam Asked to Merge. *Global Construction Review*. https://www.globalconstructionreview.com/consortiums-bidding-huge-i7ga-3-da7m-as7ked/

GCR. (2018, June 14). Work on Congo's $14bn Inga 3 Dam "to Start this year." *Global Construction Review*. https://www.globalconstructionreview.com/work-congos-14bn-inga-3-dam-start-year/

GE. (2018, November 14). Five Years on—Belt and Road Breaks New Ground, Forges New Partnerships. *General Electric*. https://www.ge.com/news/reports/five-years-belt-road-breaks-new-ground-forges-new-partnerships

Ge, W. (2018, August 24). French Experts are Optimistic about the Beijing Summit of the Forum on China-Africa Cooperation of the Forum on China Africa Cooperation and the Trilateral Cooperation Between China, France and. *The 2018 Beijing Summit of the Forum on China-Africa Cooperation*. http://focacsummit.mfa.gov.cn/zpfh/201808/t20180824_5862886.htm

George, A. L., & Bennett, A. (2005). *Case Studies and Theory Development in the Social Sciences*. MIT Press.

German Foreign Office. (2023, September 22). German development cooperation with South Africa. *Auswärtiges Amt*. https://southafrica.diplo.de/sa-en/04_News/-/2220644

Gerring, J. (2009). Case Selection for Case-Study Analysis: Qualitative and Quantitative Techniques. In J. M. Box-Steffensmeier, H. E. Brady, & D. Collier (Eds.), *Oxford Handbooks Online*. Oxford University Press. https://doi.org/10.1093/oxfordhb/9780199286546.003.0028

Ghiretti, F., Gunter, J., & Sebastian, G. (2023). Chinese Investments in European Maritime Infrastructure Policy Department for Structural and Cohesion Policies Directorate-General for Internal Policies PE. https://www.europarl.europa.eu/RegData/etudes/STUD/2023/747278/IPOL_STU(2023)747278_EN.pdf

Gill, P. S. (2023, November 23). Thailand's High-Speed Railway: On the Fast Track to Ties with China, But at What Cost? Thediplomat.com. https://thediplomat.com/2023/11/thailands-high-speed-railway-on-the-fast-track-to-ties-with-china-but-at-what-cost/

Gilpatric, S. M., & Li, Y. (2020). Endogenous Price Leadership and Product Positioning. *Review of Industrial Organization, 58*(2), 287–302. https://doi.org/10.1007/s11151-020-09752-4

Gilpin, R. (1981). *War and Change in World Politics*. Cambridge University Press.

Gilpin, S. I. (2021). China, Africa and the International Aid System: A Challenge to (the Norms Underpinning) the Neoliberal World Order? *Journal of Asian and African Studies, 58*(3), 277–297. https://doi.org/10.1177/00219096211063804

Ginige, K., Amaratunga, D., & Haigh, R. (2018). Mapping Stakeholders Associated with Societal Challenges: A Methodological Framework. *Procedia Engineering, 212*, 1195–1202. researchgate. https://doi.org/10.1016/j.proeng.2018.01.154

Glaser, B. G., & Strauss, A. L. (1967). *The Discovery of Grounded Theory: Strategies for Qualitative Research*. Routledge.

Gleick, P. H. (2012). China Dams. In *The World's Water Volume 7 the Biennial Report on Freshwater Resources* (pp. 127–142). Island Press. https://doi.org/10.5822/978-1-59726-228-6_6

GMB Union. (2021, May 25). 1700 New jobs at Hinkley "Something the UK can be Proud of." https://www.gmb.org.uk/news/1700-new-jobs-hinkley-something-uk-can-be-proud

Goldhar, J. D., & Jelinek, M. (1983, November 1). Plan for Economies of Scope. *Harvard Business Review*. https://hbr.org/1983/11/plan-for-economies-of-scope

Goodley, S. (2016, April 17). France Gives go Ahead to Hinkley Point, French Minister Says. *The Guardian*. https://www.theguardian.com/uk-news/2016/apr/17/france-go-ahead-hinkley-point-macron-andrew-marr-show

Goodman, M. (2021). The G7's New Global Infrastructure Initiative. The Center for Strategic and International Studies. https://www.csis.org/analysis/g7s-new-global-infrastructure-initiative

Gordon, J. (2023, September 10). What is a Consortium? The Business Professor, LLC. https://thebusinessprofessor.com/en_US/business-management-amp-operations-strategy-entrepreneurship-amp-innovation/consortium-definition

Gosden, E. (2017, December 23). Has Nuclear Been Stuffed by Hinkley Turkey? *The Times*. https://www.thetimes.co.uk/article/has-nuclear-been-stuffed-by-hinkley-turkey-fzl7nxdkw

Goss, R. O. (1990). Economic Policies and Seaports: Are Port Authorities Necessary? *Maritime Policy & Management, 17*(4), 257–271. https://doi.org/10.1080/03088839000000032

GPI. (2019a). Triangular Co-operation in the Era of the 2030 Agenda, Global Partnership for Effective Development Co-operation. Www.effectivecooperation.org. https://www.effectivecooperation.org/content/triangular-co-operation-era-2030-agenda

GPI. (2019b). Voluntary Guidelines for Effective Triangular Co-Operation, Global Partnership for Effective Development Co-operation. https://www.effectivecooperation.org/content/voluntary-guidelines-effective-triangular-co-operation

Grauls, S., & Stahl, A. (2010). European Development Policy Towards Sub-Saharan Africa: Challenges of the Growing Chinese Presence. *Emulations—Revue De Sciences Sociales, 7*, 71–84. https://www.semanticscholar.org/paper/European-development-policy-towards-sub-Saharan-%3A-Grauls-Stahl/bf58c48ecf41bd3d78c9694cd56c933e31b1be6b

Greve, C. (2010). Public–Private Partnerships in Business and Government. In The Oxford Handbook of Business and Government (p. 585–599). https://doi.org/10.1093/oxfordhb/9780199214273.003.0026

Griffiths, J. (2013). *Global Financial Flows, Aid and Development.* Eurodad for Concord Aid Watch.

Grimm, S. (2008). Africa-China-Europe trilateral co-operation: is Europe naïve? Www.die-Gdi.de. https://www.die-gdi.de/en/others-publications/article/africa-china-europe-trilateral-co-operation-is-europe-naive/

Grimm, S. (2011). Engaging with China in Africa—Trilateral Cooperation as an Option? EDC2020. https://www.asienhaus.de/upload/pdf/materialien/grimm_2011_engaging_with_china_in_africa.pdf

Grimsey, D., & Lewis, M. (2017). *Global Developments in Public Infrastructure Procurement.* Edward Elgar Publishing.

Grosse, R. (Ed.). (2005). *International Business and Government Relations in the 21stCentury.* Cambridge University Press. https://doi.org/10.1017/cbo9780511488597

Grossman, G. M., & Helpman, E. (2002). Integration Versus Outsourcing in Industry Equilibrium. *The Quarterly Journal of Economics, 117*(1), 85–120. https://doi.org/10.1162/003355302753399454

Grubaugh, S. G. (1987). Determinants of Direct Foreign Investment. *The Review of Economics and Statistics, 69*(1), 149. https://doi.org/10.2307/1937913

Guasch, J. L. (2004). *Granting and Renegotiating Infrastructure Concessions: Doing it Right.* In openknowledge.worldbank.org. World Bank. http://hdl.handle.net/10986/15024

Guasch, J. L., Laffont, J.-J., & Straub, S. (2008). Renegotiation of Concession Contracts in Latin America. *International Journal of Industrial Organization, 26*(2), 421–442. https://doi.org/10.1016/j.ijindorg.2007.05.003

Guasch, J. L., & Straub, S. (2006). Renegotiation of Infrastructure Concessions: An Overview. *Annals of Public and Cooperative Economics, 77*(4), 479–493. https://doi.org/10.1111/j.1467-8292.2006.00316.x

Gubbi, S. R., Aulakh, P. S., Ray, S., Sarkar, M. B., & Chittoor, R. (2009). Do International Acquisitions by Emerging-Economy Firms Create Shareholder value? The Case of Indian Firms. *Journal of International Business Studies, 41*(3), 397–418. https://doi.org/10.1057/jibs.2009.47

Gugler, P. (2017). Emerging Countries' Country-Specific Advantages (CSAs) and Competitiveness of Emerging Market Multinational Enterprises (EMNEs). *Competitiveness Review, 27*(3), 194–207. https://doi.org/10.1108/cr-02-2016-0016

Gugler, P., & Vanoli, L. (2015). Technology-Sourcing Investment Abroad as an Enhancer of Chinese MNEs' Innovative Capabilities. *International Journal of Emerging Markets, 10*(2), 243–271. https://doi.org/10.1108/ijoem-12-2014-0217

Gulati, R. (1995). Social Structure and Alliance Formation Patterns: A Longitudinal Analysis. *Administrative Science Quarterly, 40*(4), 619–652. https://doi.org/10.2307/2393756

Guo, F., Chang-Richards, Y., Wilkinson, S., & Li, T. C. (2014). Effects of Project Governance Structures on the Management of Risks in Major Infrastructure Projects: A Comparative Analysis. *International Journal of Project Management, 32*(5), 815–826. https://doi.org/10.1016/j.ijproman.2013.10.001

Haaparanta, P. (1996). Competition for Foreign Direct Investments. *Journal of Public Economics, 63*(1), 141–153. https://doi.org/10.1016/0047-2727(95)01567-1

Haberly, D., & Wójcik, D. (2016). Earth Incorporated: Centralisation and Variegation in the Global Company Network. *Economic Geography, 93*(3), 241–266. https://doi.org/10.1080/00130095.2016.1267561

Haggard, S., & Simmons, B. A. (1987). Theories of International Regimes. *International Organization, 41*(3), 491–517. https://doi.org/10.1017/s0020818300027569

Hai Phong Thermal Power Station. (2021). Global Energy Monitor. https://www.gem.wiki/Hai_Phong_Thermal_Power_Station

Halper, S. A. (2010). *The Beijing Consensus: How China's Authoritarian Model will Dominate the Twenty-First Century*. Basic Books.

Hamada, Y. (2007). The Impact of the Traditional Business–Government Relationship on the Europeanization of Japanese Firms. *Journal of European Public Policy, 14*(3), 404–421. https://doi.org/10.1080/13501760701243780

Hamada, Y. (2010). Japanese Business–Government Relations. In *Oxford Handbooks Online*. Oxford University Press. https://doi.org/10.1093/oxfordhb/9780199214273.003.0015

Hamdi, H., & Sbia, R. (2013). Dynamic Relationships Between Oil Revenues, Government Spending and Economic Growth in an Oil-Dependent Economy. *Economic Modelling, 35*, 118–125. https://doi.org/10.1016/j.econmod.2013.06.043

Hammersley, M. (2013). *The Myth of Research-Based Policy and Practice*. SAGE.

Hampton, G., Baldwin, A. N., & Holt, G. (2012). Project Delays and Cost: Stakeholder Perceptions of Traditional v. PPP Procurement. *Journal of Financial Management of Property and Construction, 17*(1), 73–91. https://doi.org/10.1108/13664381211211055

Handoyo, S., Suharman, H., Ghani, E. K., & Soedarsono, S. (2023). A Business Strategy, Operational Efficiency, Ownership Structure, and Manufacturing Performance: The Moderating Role of Market Uncertainty and Competition Intensity and its Implication on Open Innovation. *Journal of Open Innovation: Technology, Market, and Complexity, 9*(2), 100039. https://doi.org/10.1016/j.joitmc.2023.100039

Hands, G., & Kwarteng, K. (2021, October 26). New Finance Model to Cut Cost of New Nuclear Power Stations. *GOV.UK*. https://www.gov.uk/government/news/new-finance-model-to-cut-cost-of-new-nuclear-power-stations

Haralambides, H. E. (2002). Competition, Excess Capacity, and the Pricing of Port Infrastructure. *International Journal of Maritime Economics, 4*(4), 323–347. https://doi.org/10.1057/palgrave.ijme.9100053

Harper, J. (2022, February 7). China France Cooperation Promotes Infrastructure Projects in Asia, Africa, and Eastern Europe. *Deutsche Welle*. https://p.dw.com/p/47bRZ

Harrar, J. (2019, November 5). Autopista al Mar 2's $658 Million Financing - Lawyer Monthly. *Lawyer-Monthly*. https://www.lawyer-monthly.com/2019/11/autopista-al-mar-2s-658-million-financing/

Hart, O., & Moore, J. (1990). Property Rights and the Nature of the Firm. *Journal of Political Economy, 98*(6), 1119–1158. https://doi.org/10.1086/261729

Hasenclever, A., Mayer, P., & Rittberger, V. (2000). Integrating Theories of International Regimes. *Review of International Studies, 26*(1), 3–33. https://doi.org/10.1017/s0260210500000036

Hasenclever, A., Mayer, P., & Rittberger, V. (1997). *Theories of International Regimes*. Cambridge University Press.

Hashai, N., & Buckley, P. J. (2014). Is Competitive Advantage a Necessary Condition for the Emergence of the Multinational Enterprise? *Global Strategy Journal, 4*(1), 35–48. https://doi.org/10.1111/j.2042-5805.2013.01069.x

Hashimzade, N., & Myles, G. D. (2010). GROWTH AND PUBLIC INFRASTRUCTURE. *Macroeconomic Dynamics, 14*(S2), 258–274. https://doi.org/10.1017/s1365100510000374

Hass, K. B. (2009). *Managing Complex Projects: A New Model*. Management Concepts.

Hathaway, T. (2010, August 27). Gibe 3: African Development Bank and European Investment Bank out. *Who's in? Banktrack*. https://www.banktrack.org/news/gibe_3_african_development_bank_and_european_investment_bank_out_who_s_in_

Hauck, V. (2011). Triangular Cooperation: Towards Horizontal Partnerships, But How? Bali Workshop Report, 27 February–1 March. Paris: OECD Task Team on South–South Cooperation. https://europa.eu/capacity4dev/public-cd-tc/discussions/triangular-cooperation-towards-horizontal-partnerships-how

He, L. (2023, January 23). Lekki Port and the Free Trade Zone Work in Resonance, and China Africa "the Belt and Road" Cooperation has Yielded Fruitful Results. *Southern Finance Omnimedia Group*. https://m.21jingji.com/article/20230113/herald/b553aa96462c1d3c3f8ab378c540616e.html

He, P., & Yan, Y. (2021). Japan's Third Party Market Cooperation in Africa: Models, Characteristics, and Inspirations. *Fudan Public Administration Review, 02*, 1–25. http://www.jsc.fudan.edu.cn/view.php?id=1596

Hennart, J.-F. (1988). A Transaction Costs Theory of Equity Joint Ventures. *Strategic Management Journal, 9*(4), 361–374. https://doi.org/10.1002/smj.4250090406

Hernandez, A. (2024a, April 26). TotalEnergies Chief Calls Potential EU Sanctions on Russian LNG a Financial Boon. Reuters. https://www.reuters.com/business/energy/totalenergies-chief-calls-potential-eu-sanctions-russian-lng-financial-boon-2024-04-26/

Hernandez, A. (2024b, June 19). French Senate Urges Government to Buy "Golden Share" in TotalEnergies. Reuters. https://www.reuters.com/world/europe/french-senate-urges-government-buy-golden-share-totalenergies-2024-06-19/

Herrendorf, B., & Teixeira, A. (2011). BARRIERS TO ENTRY AND DEVELOPMENT. *International Economic Review, 52*(2), 573–602. https://doi.org/10.1111/j.1468-2354.2011.00639.x

Hinkley Point C. (2015). EDF Energy. https://www.edfenergy.com/energy/nuclear-new-build-projects/hinkley-point-c

Hitachi. (2019, January 17). Horizon Suspends UK Nuclear New Build Activities. *Hitachi in Europe*. https://www.hitachi.eu/en/press/horizon-suspends-uk-nuclear-new-build-activities/

Hitchcock, W. I., & Moravcsik, A. (1999). The Choice for Europe: Social Purpose and State Power from Messina to Maastricht. *The American Historical Review, 104*(5), 1742. https://doi.org/10.2307/2649481

Hitt, M. A., Bierman, L., Uhlenbruck, K., & Shimizu, K. (2006). The Importance of Resources in the Internationalisation of Professional Service Firms: The Good, the Bad, and the Ugly. *Academy of Management Journal, 49*(6), 1137–1157. https://doi.org/10.5465/amj.2006.23478217

HKTDC. (n.d.). Arup—Advising the Construction of Bangladesh's First Underwater Tunnel. Hong Kong Trade Development Council. Retrieved February 8, 2024, from https://portal.hktdc.com/ires/en/s/ArupUnderwaterTunnel

Hollands, C. (2020, August 14). German Investors Interested in Funding DRC's Inga III Dam. *Energy Capital Power*. https://energycapitalpower.com/german-investors-interested-in-funding-drcs-inga-iii-dam/

Holtbrügge, D. (2004). Management of International Strategic Business Cooperation: Situational Conditions, Performance Criteria, and Success Factors. *Thunderbird International Business Review, 46*(3), 255–274. https://doi.org/10.1002/tie.20008

Honda, S. (2014). Japan's Triangular Cooperation Mechanism: With a Focus on JICA's Activities. JICA Ogata Research Institute. https://www.jica.go.jp/english/jica_ri/publication/booksandreports/pans_triangular_cooperation_mechanism_with_a_focus_on_jicas_activities.html

Honda, S., Kato, H., & Shimoda, Y. (2013). South-South and Triangular Cooperation for Sub-Saharan Africa's Development—With Special Emphasis on Knowledge Exchange and Co-creation. In *For Inclusive and Dynamic Development in Sub-Saharan*. JICA Research Institute.

Hong, E., Lee, I. H. (Ian), & Makino, S. (2019). Outbound Foreign Direct Investment (FDI) Motivation and Domestic Employment by Multinational Enterprises (MNEs). Journal of International Management, 25(2), 100657. https://doi.org/10.1016/j.intman.2018.11.003

Hooijmaaijers, B. (2018). China's Rise in Africa and the Response of the EU: A Theoretical Analysis of the EU-China-Africa Trilateral Cooperation Policy Initiative. *Journal of European Integration, 40*(4), 443–460. https://doi.org/10.1080/07036337.2018.1465418

Hook, S. W. (1995). *National Interest and Foreign Aid*. Rienner.

Hook, S. W., & Rumsey, J. G. (2016). The Development Aid Regime at Fifty: Policy Challenges Inside and Out. *International Studies Perspectives, 17*(1), 55–74. https://www.jstor.org/stable/44218891?sid=primo%3Fsid%3Dprimo&seq=4

Horn, S., Reinhart, C. M., & Trebesch, C. (2021). China's Overseas Lending. *Journal of International Economics, 133*, 103539. https://doi.org/10.1016/j.jinteco.2021.103539

Hoskisson, R. E., Eden, L., Lau, C. M., & Wright, M. (2000). Strategy in Emerging Economies. *Academy of Management Journal, 43*(3), 249–267. https://doi.org/10.5465/1556394

Hua, J., Xu, W., & Khalip, A. (2011, November 11). Sinopec to Pay Galp $3.5 Billion for Brazilian Oil Stake. Reuters. https://www.reuters.com/article/us-sinopec-galp-assets-f-idUSTRE7AA2R920111111

Huang, F., Chen, J., Sun, L., Zhang, Y., & Yao, S. (2019). Value-Based Contract for Smart Operation and Maintenance Service Based on Equitable Entropy. *International Journal of Production Research, 58*(4), 1271–1284. https://doi.org/10.1080/00207543.2019.1617450

Huang, L., Lasserre, F., Pic, P., & Chiu, Y.-Y. (2020). Opening up the Chinese Shipping Market 1988–2018: The Perspective of Chinese Shipping Companies Facing Foreign Competition. *Asian Transport Studies, 6*, 100004. https://doi.org/10.1016/j.eastsj.2020.100004

Huang, X. (2022, February 16). List of Demonstration Projects for the Fourth Round of Third-Party Market Cooperation Signed Between China and France. *Xinhua Silk Road*. https://www.imsilkroad.com/news/p/476922.html

Huang, Y. (2018). Solve the Problem or Escape Responsibility? The Politics of Chinese Privatization Reform. *Chinese Political Science Review, 4*(1), 1–27. https://doi.org/10.1007/s41111-018-0110-6

Huang, Y., & Li, Y. (2015). Sino French Cooperation in Operating the Kribi Deepsea Port in Cameroon. Finance China. https://finance.china.com.cn/roll/20150901/3321582.shtml

Hughes, J. S., Logue, D. E., & Sweeney, R. J. (1975). Corporate International Diversification and Market Assigned Measures of Risk and Diversification. *The Journal of Financial and Quantitative Analysis, 10*(4), 627–637. https://doi.org/10.2307/2330611

Hughes, K., & Oughton, C. (1992). Foreign and Domestic Multinational Presence in the UK. *Applied Economics, 24*(7), 745–749. https://doi.org/10.1080/00036849200000044

Hui, X., & Han, W. (2021). Third Party Market Cooperation Between China and Japan: Opportunities, Challenges, and Response Strategies. *India Ocean Economic and Political Review, 45*(3), 38–58, 152–153.

Huld, A. (2022, February 11). China Infrastructure Investment in 2022 - Spurring Economic Growth. China Briefing News. https://www.china-briefing.com/news/china-infratsructure-investment-in-2022-spurring-economic-growth/

Hydro Review. (2010, May 17). Ethiopia, China Sign Agreement for Gibe III Hydro Project Construction. https://www.hydroreview.com/world-regions/ethiopia-china-sign/#gref

Hydrocarbons Technology. (n.d.). Atyrau Refinery Modernisation Project. Retrieved February 8, 2024, from https://www.hydrocarbons-technology.com/projects/atyrau-refinery-modernisation-project/

Hymer, S. (1976). *The International Operations of National Firms: A Study of Direct Foreign Investment.* Mit Press.

ICDC. (2015, November 3). China and South Korea Sign a Memorandum of Cooperation to Jointly Promote the Cooperation of the Manufacturing. Industrial Culture Development Center of MIIT. https://www.miit-icdc.org/info/1013/3347.htm

ICE. (2017, April 24). The Changing Price of Wholesale UK Electricity Over more than a Decade. *ICE Group.* https://www.ice.org.uk/engineering-resources/briefing-sheets/the-changing-price-of-wholesale-uk-electricity-over-more-than-a-decade

Ichiro, F., Joo, H. S., Steinberg, J., & Friedhoff, K. (2021). *Cooperating, Competing, Confronting: US-Japan-South Korea Trilateral Cooperation as China Rises.* JSTOR. https://www.jstor.org/stable/resrep33467

ICMPD. (2013). Enhancing Diaspora Engagement: Operational Guidelines for South-South and Triangular Cooperation. In International Centre for Migration Policy Development. https://www.icmpd.org/file/download/48184/file/Promoting%2520Diaspora%2520Engagement_%2520What%2520Have%2520We%2520Learnt_EN.pdf

ICRC. (2014). Ibom Deep Sea Port and Free Trade Zone Outline Business Case Final. https://pp.icrc.gov.ng/media/291

IDS. (2014). Policy Briefing. https://assets.publishing.service.gov.uk/media/57a089c4ed915d3cfd000404/AD_ID151_PB75_China_online.pdf

InfraCredit. (2021, September 16). Issuance of the First Senior Guaranteed Fixed Rate Infrastructure Bonds. InfraCredit. https://infracredit.ng/infracredit-guarantee-supports-lagos-free-zone-companys-lfzc-issuance-of-n10-5billion-aaa-rated-20-year-senior-guaranteed-fixed-rate-series-1-infrastructure-bonds-due-2041/

InfraPPP. (2018, November 16). French-Chinese Consortium Selected to Develop US$4.2 Billion Port PPP in Nigeria. *InfraPPP.* https://www.infrapppworld.com/news/megaproject-1365-french-chinese-consortium-selected-to-develop-us-4-2-billion-port-ppp-in-nigeria

Inman, P. (2018, November 9). Toshiba's Failure Shows Business can't Deliver a Nuclear Future. *The Guardian.* https://www.theguardian.com/business/2018/nov/08/toshibas-failure-shows-business-cant-deliver-a-nuclear-future

International Labour Organisation. (2019). How-to-Guide on South-South and Triangular Cooperation design for Decent Work. South-South Galaxy. https://www.southsouth-galaxy.org/publications/how-to-guide-on-south-south-and-triangular-cooperation-design-for-decent-work-ilo-2019/

Irvine, A., Drew, P., & Sainsbury, R. (2013). "Am I not Answering your Questions Properly?" Clarification, Adequacy and Responsiveness in Semi-Structured Telephone and Face-to-Face Interviews. *Qualitative Research, 13*(1), 87–106.

Islam, A. K. (2009). Co-Operation Under Anarchy Neo-Liberal Institutional Explanations. *The Indian Journal of Political Science, 70*(3), 861–872. https://www.jstor.org/stable/42742767

ITOCHU. (2016, December 20). ITOCHU Announces Its Participation in One of the Largest Offshore Wind Power Generation Projects in Germany | Press Releases. *ITOCHU Corporation.* https://www.itochu.co.jp/en/news/press/2016/161220.html

Jack, S. (2018, June 4). Government U-turn on Nuclear Deal. BBC News. https://www.bbc.co.uk/news/business-44363366

Janus, H., Klingebiel, S., & Paulo, S. (2014). Beyond Aid: A Conceptual Perspective on the Transformation of Development Cooperation. *Journal of International Development, 27*(2), 155–169. https://doi.org/10.1002/jid.3045

Jedwab, R., & Moradi, A. (2016). The Permanent Effects of Transportation Revolutions in Poor Countries: Evidence from Africa. *Review of Economics and Statistics, 98*(2), 268–284. https://doi.org/10.1162/rest_a_00540

Jenkins, S. (2020, September 18). Hitachi Failed its Nuclear Test. If only it had the Vanity of HS2. *The Guardian.* https://www.theguardian.com/commentisfree/2020/sep/18/hitachi-nuclear-test-hs2-huge-projects-politicians-wasteful

Jensen, N. M. (2008). *Nation-States and the Multinational Corporation: A Political Economy of Foreign Direct Investment*. Princeton University Press.. https://doi.org/10.1515/9781400837373

Jepson, N. (2021). Hidden in Plain Sight: Chinese Development Finance in Central and Eastern Europe. *Development and Change, 52*(5), 1222–1250. https://doi.org/10.1111/dech.12686

Jervis, R. (1988). Realism, Game Theory, and Cooperation. *World Politics, 40*(3), 317–349. https://doi.org/10.2307/2010216

Jia, W., Chen, S., & Wu, S. (2019, November 20). Why is China's Insistence on Foreign Aid not Pretent Generous? http://politics.people.com.cn/n1/2019/1120/c429373-31465280.html

Jin, R. (2021). Research on the Superposition Effect of China-Japan Third-Party Market Cooperation in the New Era. *Japanese Studies, 06*, 67–88.

Jin, S. (2018). Triangular Cooperation in East Asia: Challenges and Opportunities for Japanese Official Development Assistance. *IDS Bulletin, 49*(3), 1–20. https://doi.org/10.19088/1968-2018.151

Jin, X., Xu, L., Xin, Y., & Adhikari, A. (2022). Political Governance in China's State-Owned Enterprises. *China Journal of Accounting Research, 15*(2), 100236. https://doi.org/10.1016/j.cjar.2022.100236

Jing, T. (2022). Third Party Market Cooperation: A Win-Win Model of 1+1+1>3. China Pictorial. http://www.rmhb.com.cn/zt/ydyl/202209/t20220920_800307171.html

Jinko Solar. (2017, January 3). JinkoSolar and Marubeni Corporation Enter Into Power Purchase Agreement for Sweihan Photovoltaic Independent Power Project in Abu Dhabi. https://ir.jinkosolar.com/news-releases/news-release-details/jinkosolar-and-marubeni-corporation-enter-power-purchase

Jobin, D. (2008). A Transaction Cost-Based Approach to Partnership Performance Evaluation. *Evaluation, 14*(4), 437–465. https://doi.org/10.1177/1356389008095487

Joe, T. C. (2022, June 20). Balancing Rivalry and Cooperation: Japan's Response to the BRI in Southeast Asia. *E-International Relations*. https://www.e-ir.info/2022/06/20/balancing-rivalry-and-cooperation-japans-response-to-the-bri-in-southeast-asia/

John de Sousa, S.-L. (2010). Brazil as an Emerging Actor in International Development Cooperation: A Good Partner for European Donors? Www.die-Gdi.de. https://www.die-gdi.de/en/briefing-paper/article/brazil-as-an-emerging-actor-in-international-development-cooperation-a-good-partner-for-european-donors/

Johnston, I. (2017, June 22). National Audit Office slams Government's "High Cost and Risky Deal" for Hinkley Point Nuclear Power Station. *The Independent*. https://www.independent.co.uk/climate-change/news/hinkley-point-nuclear-power-national-audit-office-slams-government-high-cost-risky-deal-a7803446.html

Jones, L., & Hameiri, S. (2020). Debunking the Myth of "Debt-trap Diplomacy." Chatham House—International Affairs Think Tank. https://www.chathamhouse.org/2020/08/debunking-myth-debt-trap-diplomacy

Joshi, Raghavi. (2018). Lekki Deep Sea Port, Lagos, Nigeria. *Ship Technology*. https://www.ship-technology.com/projects/lekki-deep-sea-port-lagosnigeria/.

Joskow, P. (2007). Regulation of Natural Monopoly. In *Handbook of Law and Economics* (pp. 1227–1348). Elsevier. https://econpapers.repec.org/bookchap/eeelawchp/2-16.htm

Joskow, P. L. (1985). Vertical Integration and Long-term Contracts: The Case of Coal-burning Electric Generating Plants. *The Journal of Law, Economics, and Organization, 1*(1), 33–81. https://doi.org/10.1093/oxfordjournals.jleo.a036889

Joskow, P. L. (1988). Asset Specificity and the Structure of Vertical Relationships: Empirical Evidence. *Journal of Law, Economics, & Organization, 4*(1), 95–117. https://www.jstor.org/stable/765016

Joskow, P. L. (1990). The Performance of Long-Term Contracts: Further Evidence from Coal Markets. *The RAND Journal of Economics, 21*(2), 251. https://doi.org/10.2307/2555423

Joubin-Bret, A., & Knoerich, J. (2010). Investor-State Disputes: Prevention and Alternatives to Arbitration. UNCTAD Series on International Investment Policies for Development. https://unctad.org/system/files/official-document/diaeia200911_en.pdf

Judd, C. M., Smith, E. R., & Kidder, L. H. (1991). *Research Methods in Social Relations*. Holt, Rinehart, and Winston.

Juhel, M. H. (2001). Globalisation, Privatisation and Restructuring of Ports. *International Journal of Maritime Economics, 3*(2), 139–174. https://doi.org/10.1057/palgrave.ijme.9100012

Kamal, M. A., Ullah, A., Zheng, J., Zheng, B., & Xia, H. (2019). Natural Resource or Market Seeking Motive of China's FDI in Asia? New Evidence at Income and Sub-regional Level. *Economic Research-Ekonomska Istraživanja, 32*(1), 3869–3894. https://doi.org/10.1080/1331677x.2019.1674679

Kamwengo, C. (2020). Beneficiary Country Ownership and the Politics of Partnership in Trilateral Development Cooperation: A Case Study of Zambia. Etheses.dur.ac.uk. http://etheses.dur.ac.uk/13696/

Kaplan, M., Busemann, D., & Wirtgen, K. (2020). Trilateral Cooperation in German Development Cooperation. German Institute for Development Evaluation (DEval), Bonn. https://www.deval.org/en/publications/trilateral-cooperation-in-german-development-cooperation

Kapsali, M., Roehrich, J. K., & Akhtar, P. (2019). Effective Contracting for High Operational Performance in Projects. *International Journal of Operations & Production Management, 39*(2), 294–325. https://doi.org/10.1108/ijopm-10-2017-0604

Kardaś, S. (2021, May 17). Great Ambitions: Russia Expands on the LNG Market. OSW Centre for Eastern Studies. https://www.osw.waw.pl/en/publikacje/osw-commentary/2021-05-17/great-ambitions-russia-expands-lng-market

Kato, H. (2012). *Scaling Up South-South and Triangular Cooperation*. JICA Research Institute.

Kaul, I., Grunberg, I., & Stern, M. A. (1999). *Global Public Goods: International Cooperation in the 21st Century*. Oxford University Press.

Kedia, B., Gaffney, N., & Clampit, J. (2012). EMNEs and Knowledge-seeking FDI. *Management International Review, 52*(2), 155–173. https://doi.org/10.1007/s11575-012-0132-5

Kell, N. P., van der Weijde, A. H., Li, L., Santibanez-Borda, E., & Pillai, A. C. (2023). Simulating Offshore Wind Contract for Difference Auctions to Prepare bid Strategies. *Applied Energy, 334*, 120645. https://doi.org/10.1016/j.apenergy.2023.120645

Kenton, W. (2021). Why Consortiums Matter. Investopedia. https://www.investopedia.com/terms/c/consortium.asp

Keohane, R. O. (1984). *After Hegemony: Cooperation and Discord in the Political Economy*. Princeton University Press.

Keohane, R. O. (1986). Reciprocity in International Relations. *International Organization, 40*(1), 1–27. https://doi.org/10.1017/s0020818300004458

Keohane, R. O. (1990). Multilateralism: An Agenda for Research. *International Journal, 45*(4), 731–764. https://doi.org/10.2307/40202705

Kerr, T. M. (1995). Supplying Water Infrastructure to Developing Countries Via Private Sector Project Financing. *Georgetown International Environmental Law Review, 8*(1), 91–108.

Khalili, L. (2020). Sinews of War and Trade: Shipping and Capitalism in the Arabian Peninsula. In *Shipping and Capitalism in The Arabian Peninsula*. Verso.

Kharas, H. J., Jung, W., & Makino, K. (2011). *Catalyzing Development: A New Vision for Aid*. Brookings Institution Press.

Khomami, N. (2016, September 3). Theresa May to Tell G20 UK is "Open for Business" Despite Brexit Vote. *The Guardian*. https://www.theguardian.com/politics/2016/sep/03/theresa-may-g20-uk-brexit-china-hinkley-point-c

Kim, S., & Lightfoot, S. (2011). Does "DAC-Ability" Really Matter? The emergence of non-DAC Donors: Introduction to Policy Arena. *Journal of International Development, 23*(5), 711–721. https://doi.org/10.1002/jid.1795

King, G., Keohane, R. O., & Verba, S. (1994). *Designing Social Inquiry: Scientific Inference in Qualitative Research*. Princeton University Press.

Kjøllesdal, K. A., & Welle-Strand, A. (2010). Foreign Aid Strategies: China Taking Over? Asian. *Social Science, 6*(10). https://doi.org/10.5539/ass.v6n10p3

Klein, P. G. (1999). New Institutional Economics. Mospace.umsystem.edu; Edward Elgar. https://mospace.umsystem.edu/xmlui/handle/10355/161

Knodt, M., & Piefer, N. (2012). Why Not Cooperate in a Triangle? Explaining Different Motivations in Triangular Cooperatio. In J. Langendorf et al. (Eds.), *Triangular Cooperation: A Guideline for Working in Practice*. Baden-Baden.

Knoerich, J. (2016). Has Outward Foreign Direct Investment Contributed to the Development of the Chinese Economy? *Transnational Corporations, 23*(2), 1–48. https://doi.org/10.18356/898d556e-en

Knoerich, J. (2017). How does Outward Foreign Direct Investment Contribute to Economic Development in Less Advanced Home Countries? *Oxford Development Studies, 45*(4), 443–459. https://doi.org/10.1080/13600818.2017.1283009

Knoerich, J. (2019). Re-orienting the Paradigm: Path Dependence in FDI Theory and the Emerging Multinationals. *International Journal of Emerging Markets, 14*(1), 51–69. https://doi.org/10.1108/ijoem-04-2017-0123

Koesalamwardi, A. B., Rostiyanti, S. F., & Reksapernata, R. T. (2020). Value Capture Instruments as an Infrastructure Project Financing Alternative For Rail-Based Mass Transportation: Qualitative Study from The Government Perspective. *CSID Journal of Infrastructure Development, 3*(2), 214. https://doi.org/10.32783/csid-jid.v3i2.151

Kong, X., & Han, W. (2021). China-Japan Third-party Market Cooperation:Opportunities,Challenges and Strategy. *Indian Ocean Economic and Political Review, 03*, 38–58+152153. https://doi.org/10.16717/j.cnki.53-1227/f.2021.03.003

Kogut, B., & Zander, U. (1993). Knowledge of the Firm and the Evolutionary Theory of the Multinational Corporation. *Journal of International Business Studies, 24*(4), 625–645. https://doi.org/10.1057/palgrave.jibs.8490248

Koopmans, T. C., & Beckmann, M. (1957). Assignment Problems and the Location of Economic Activities. *Econometrica, 25*(1), 53. https://doi.org/10.2307/1907742

Koopmans, T. C. (1991). *Three Essays on the State of Economic Science*. McGraw-Hill Book Company.

Kopel, M., & Löffler, C. (2008). Commitment, First-mover, and Second-mover Advantage. *Journal of Economics, 94*(2), 143–166. https://doi.org/10.1007/s00712-008-0004-4

Krasner, S. D. (1982a). Regimes and the Limits of Realism: Regimes as Autonomous Variables. *International Organization, 36*(2), 497–510. https://doi.org/10.1017/s0020818300019032

Krasner, S. D. (1982b). Structural Causes and Regime Consequences: Regimes as Intervening Variables. *International Organization, 36*(2), 185–205. https://doi.org/10.1017/s0020818300018920

Krasner, S. D. (1985). *International Regimes*. Cornell University Press.

Kratz, A., Zenglein, M., & Sebastian, G. (2021). Chinese FDI in Europe 2020 Update Investment Falls to 10-Year Low in an Economically and Politically Challenging Year. https://rhg.com/wp-content/uploads/2021/06/MERICSRhodium-GroupCOFDIUpdate2021.pdf

Kreps, D. M. (1990). Corporate Culture and Economic Theory. In E. J. Alt & K. A. Shepsle (Eds.), *Perspectives on Positive Political Economy*. Cambridge University Press.

Krikorian, S. (2019, September 4). France's Efficiency in the Nuclear Fuel Cycle: What Can "Oui" Learn? Www.iaea.org. https://www.iaea.org/newscenter/news/frances-efficiency-in-the-nuclear-fuel-cycle-what-can-oui-learn

Kuehberger, A. (2015). *Handbook of Process Tracing Methods for Decision Research: A Critical Review and Users Guide*. Psychology Press UK.

Kuemmerle, W. (1997). Building Effective R&D Capabilities Abroad. Harvard Business Review, March–April 1997. https://hbr.org/1997/03/building-effective-rd-capabilities-abroad

Kuemmerle, W. (1999). The Drivers of Foreign Direct Investment into Research and Development: An Empirical Investigation. *Journal of International Business Studies, 30*(1), 1–24. https://doi.org/10.1057/palgrave.jibs.8490058

Kumar, N. (2008). South-South and Triangular Cooperation in Asia-Pacific: Towards a New Paradigm in Development Cooperation 1 South-South and Triangular Cooperation in Asia-Pacific: Towards a New Paradigm in Development Cooperation. https://www.un.org/ecosoc/sites/www.un.org.ecosoc/files/publications/background_study_final.pdf

Kumaraswamy, M. M., & Zhang, X. Q. (2001). Governmental Role in BOT-led Infrastructure Development. *International Journal of Project Management, 19*(4), 195–205. https://doi.org/10.1016/s0263-7863(99)00069-1

Kurlantzick, J. (2006). Beijing's Safari: China's Move into Africa and its Implications for Aid, Development, and Governance. CARNEGIE ENDOWMENT for INTERNATIONAL PEACE. https://carnegieendowment.org/files/kurlantzick_outlook_africa.pdf

Kurlantzick, J. (2016). *State Capitalism: How the Return of Statism is Transforming the World*. OUP USA.

Lafarge. (2017, June 12). Hima Cement and CCCC sign MOU for Supply of Cement. https://www.lafarge.co.ug/hima_cement_and_cccc_sign_mou_for_supply_of_cement

Lam, K. C., Wang, D., Lee, P. T. K., & Tsang, Y. T. (2007). Modelling Risk Allocation Decision in Construction Contracts. *International Journal of Project Management, 25*(5), 485–493. https://doi.org/10.1016/j.ijproman.2006.11.005

Lancaster, C. (2007). *The Chinese Aid System*. Center for Global Development. https://www.cgdev.org/sites/default/files/13953_file_Chinese_aid.pdf

Lancaster, C. (2008). *Foreign Aid: Diplomacy, Development, Domestic Politics.* University Of Chicago Press.

Lancaster, C. (2009). Sixty Years of Foreign Aid. *International Journal: Canada's Journal of Global Policy Analysis, 64*(3), 799–810. https://doi.org/10.1177/002070200906400312

Langendorf, J., Piefer, N., Knodt, M., Müller, U., & Lázaro, L. (2012). *Triangular Cooperation A Guideline for Working in Practice. Deutsche Gesellschaft für Internationale Zusammenarbeit.* Nomos Verlagsgesellschaft Mbh & Co. Kg.

Lawer, E. T. (2019). Examining Stakeholder Participation and Conflicts Associated with Large Scale Infrastructure Projects: The Case of Tema Port Expansion Project. *Ghana. Maritime Policy & Management, 46*(6), 735–756. https://doi.org/10.1080/03088839.2019.1627013

Lawson, A. (2009). *Evaluating the Transaction Costs of Implementing the Paris Declaration.* OECD. https://www.oecd.org/dac/evaluation/dcdndep/44135805.pdf

Lawson, A. (2022, May 20). Boss of Hinkley Point C Blames Pandemic Disruption for £3bn Delay. *The Guardian.* https://www.theguardian.com/uk-news/2022/may/20/hinkley-point-c-nuclear-power-station-edf-delayed-covid-costs-rise

Lee, S. J., Liu, L. Q., & Stebunovs, V. (2017). Risk Taking and Interest Rates: Evidence from Decades in the Global Syndicated Loan Market. IMF. https://www.imf.org/en/Publications/WP/Issues/2017/01/27/Risk-Taking-and-Interest-Rates-Evidence-from-Decades-in-the-Global-Syndicated-Loan-Market-44595

Legro, J. (1995). *Cooperation Under Fire: Anglo-German Restraint During World War II.* Cornell University Press.

Leheny, D., & Warren, K. (2009). *Japanese Aid and the Construction of Global Development.* Routledge.

Leigland, J., & Palsson, G. (2007). Port reform in Nigeria Upstream policy reforms. https://pp.worldbank.org/public-private-partnership/sites/pp.worldbank.org/files/2022-06/397980Gridlines017NigPortRef01PUBLIC1.pdf

Lengfelder, C. S. (2015). Why Triangular Development Cooperation? Germany and the Emerging Powers. *German Politics, 25*(1), 1–24. https://doi.org/10.1080/09644008.2015.1024239

Lennane, A. (2023, September 4). Jobs safe in CMA CGM Takeover, Says Bolloré, but We may Lose our Brand. *The Loadstar.* https://theloadstar.com/jobs-safe-in-cma-cgm-takeover-says-bollore-but-we-may-lose-our-brand/

Li, K. X., Zhang, W., Chen, P. S. L., & Huo, W. (2019). International Port Investment of Chinese Port-related Companies. *International Journal of Shipping and Transport Logistics, 11*(5), 430. https://doi.org/10.1504/ijstl.2019.10022864

Li, L. (2014, July 12). Terminal opens doors for Chinese company. China Daily. http://global.chinadaily.com.cn/a/201407/21/WS5a2fd357a3108bc8c672a69f.html

Li, Q., Han, Y., Li, Z., Wei, D., & Zhang, F. (2020). The Influence of Cultural Exchange on International Trade: An Empirical Test of Confucius Institutes Based on China and the "Belt and Road" Areas. *Economic Research-Ekonomska Istraživanja, 34*(1), 1033–1059. https://doi.org/10.1080/1331677x.2020.1819849

Li, R. (2007). Correct Understanding of Debt Sustainability of Developing Countries. *World Economics and Politics, 4*, 7–13.

Li, X., & Bonschab, T. (2012). Nine Challenges of Triangular Cooperation. In J. Langendorf et al. (Eds.), *Triangular Cooperation: A Guideline for Working in Practice*. Nomos.

Li, T. G. (2021). The Third-party Market Cooperation Between China and Japan in Vietnam Under the Belt and Road Framework——A Comparative Study Based on Trade Relations. *Contemporary Economic Management, 43*(2), 40–47.

Li, Y. (2010). China Myanmar Oil and Gas Energy Cooperation Still Needs to be Deepened. Chinanews. https://www.chinanews.com.cn/ny/news/2010/06-23/2357550.shtml

Liang, H., & Cao, X. (2019, April 19). Third Party Market Cooperation is a "Timely Rain". People.com. http://opinion.people.com.cn/n1/2019/0409/c1003-31018678.html

Liao, J. C., & Katada, S. N. (2020). Geoeconomics, Easy Money, and Political Opportunism: The Perils Under China and Japan's High-Speed Rail Competition. *Contemporary Politics, 27*(1), 1–22. https://doi.org/10.1080/13569775.2020.1816626

Lieberman, M. B., & Montgomery, D. B. (1998). First-mover (dis)Advantages: Retrospective and Link with the Resource-Based View. *Strategic Management Journal, 19*(12), 1111–1125. https://www.anderson.ucla.edu/faculty/marvin.lieberman/publications/FMA2-SMH1998.pdf

Lin, C. (2011). China's New Silk Road to the Mediterranean: The Eurasian Land Bridge and Return of Admiral Zheng He. ISPSW Strategy Series. https://www.files.ethz.ch/isn/133405/165_Lin.pdf

Liu, B., Abe, M., Xie, F., & Subhanij, T. (2020). Asset-Backed Securitization of PPP Projects: The Case of China. *The Chinese Economy, 54*(4), 1–13. https://doi.org/10.1080/10971475.2020.1857058

Liu, X. (2016, August 8). Hinkley Point is a Test of Mutual Trust Between UK and China. *Financial Times*. https://www.ft.com/content/b8bc62dc-5d74-11e6-bb77-a121aa8abd95#axzz4GkigtUWR

Liu, Y., Li, X., Zhu, X., Lee, M.-K., & Lai, P.-L. (2023). The Theoretical Systems of OFDI Location Determinants in Global North and Global South Economies. *Humanities and Social Sciences Communications, 10*(1), 1–13. https://doi.org/10.1057/s41599-023-01597-y

Lool, H. (2016). How has China Moved-up the Global Value Chains? Blogs. worldbank.org. https://blogs.worldbank.org/developmenttalk/how-has-china-moved-global-value-chains

Loomis, P. (2015, August 25). Nigeria's Evolving Concession and PPP Architecture. *The Guardian Nigeria News*. https://guardian.ng/business-services/nigerias-evolving-concession-and-ppp-architecture/

Loree, D. W., & Guisinger, S. E. (1995). Policy and Non-Policy Determinants of U.S. Equity Foreign Direct Investment. *Journal of International Business Studies, 26*(2), 281–299. https://doi.org/10.1057/palgrave.jibs.8490174

Lough, R. (2019, January 17). Explainer: Why Siemens-Alstom rail Merger is Creating European Tensions. *Reuters*. https://www.reuters.com/article/us-alstom-m-a-siemens-politics-idUSKCN1PB216

LPLEL. (2020a, April 1). Lekki Port Receives $221 Million China Harbour's Equity Infusion. Lekki Port LFTZ Enterprise Limited. https://lekkiport.com/lekki-port-receives-221-million-china-harbours-equity-infusion/

LPLEL. (2020b, November 22). Amaechi Tasks Lekki Port Promoters on Commencement of Commercial Activity by 2022. Lekki Port LFTZ Enterprise Limited. https://lekkiport.com/amaechi-tasks-lekki-port-promoters-on-commencement-of-commercial-activity-by-2022/

LPLEL. (2021, March 8). Lekki Port Signs US$629m Facility Agreements with China Development Bank. *Lekki Port LFTZ Enterprise Limited*. https://lekkiport.com/lekki-port-signs-us629m-facility-agreements-with-china-development-bank/

LPLEL. (2023, January 24). Lekki Port and CMA CGM Group to Facilitate Trade Volume Growth, Increase GDP. *Lekki Port LFTZ Enterprise Limited*. https://lekkiport.com/lekki-port-and-cma-cgm-group-to-facilitate-trade-volume-growth-increase-gdp/

LUA. (2018, November 30). Bollore Ports, PowerChina win Deep-sea Port Contract in Nigeria. *Logistics Update Africa*. https://www.logupdateafrica.com/bollore-ports-powerchina-win-deepsea-port-contract-in-nigeria-logistics-shipping

Lubin, D. (2023). Collapsing Foreign Direct Investment Might not be all Bad for China's Economy. Chathamhouse. https://www.chathamhouse.org/2023/12/collapsing-foreign-direct-investment-might-not-be-all-bad-chinas-economy

Ludlow, P., & European Strategy Forum (Ponte De Lima, Portugal). (2007). The EU and China. European Strategy Forum.

Lum, T. G., & Library of Congress. Congressional Research Service. (2009). China's Foreign aid Activities in Africa, Latin America, and Southeast Asia. Congressional Research Service, Library of Congress.

Luo, Y., & Chen, Z. (2021). Challenges and Countermeasures of Chinese Engineering Contracting Enterprises Participating in Third-party Market Cooperation. *International Project Contracting & Labour, 12*, 54–56.

Luo, Y., & Park, S. H. (2004). Multiparty Cooperation and Performance in International Equity Joint Ventures. *Journal of International Business Studies, 35*(2), 142–160. https://doi.org/10.1057/palgrave.jibs.8400072

Luo, Y., & Rui, H. (2009). An Ambidexterity Perspective Toward Multinational Enterprises From Emerging Economies. *Academy of Management Perspectives, 23*(4), 49–70. https://doi.org/10.5465/amp.23.4.49

Luo, Y., Rui, H., & Maksimov, V. (2013). Tales of Rivals: Inter-Chinese Attacks in International Competition. *Organizational Dynamics, 42*(2), 156–166. https://doi.org/10.1016/j.orgdyn.2013.03.009

Luo, Y., & Tung, R. L. (2007). International Expansion of Emerging Market Enterprises: A Springboard Perspective. *Journal of International Business Studies, 38*(4), 481–498. https://doi.org/10.1057/palgrave.jibs.8400275

Luo, Y., & Tung, R. L. (2018). A General Theory of Springboard MNEs. *Journal of International Business Studies, 49*(2), 129–152. https://doi.org/10.1057/s41267-017-0114-8

Luo, Y., Zhang, H., & Bu, J. (2019). Developed Country MNEs Investing in Developing Economies: Progress and Prospect. *Journal of International Business Studies, 50*(4), 633–667. https://doi.org/10.1057/s41267-019-00230-y

Luo, Z., Ji, T., JIng, Z., & He, A. (2019). Design and Application of Contract for Difference in Electricity Market. *Power System Technology, 43*(8), 1–9. https://doi.org/10.13335/j.1000-3673.pst.2019.0538

Luttwak, E. N. (1990). From Geopolitics to Geo-Economics: Logic of Conflict, Grammar of Commerce. *The National Interest, 20*, 17–23. https://www.jstor.org/stable/42894676

Lynch, D. (2013, February 6). Centrica writes off £200M stake in Hinkley Point C project. *New Civil Engineer*. https://www.newcivilengineer.com/archive/centrica-writes-off-200m-stake-in-hinkley-point-c-project-06-02-2013/

Lynch, L., Andersen, S., & Zhu, T. (2020, July 9). China's Foreign Aid: A Primer for Recipient Countries, Donors, and Aid Providers. *Center for Global Development*. https://www.cgdev.org/publication/chinas-foreign-aid-primer-recipient-countries-donors-and-aid-providers

Lyons, K. (2016, August 28). Hinkley Point: EDF boss calls on Government to Look at "Bigger Picture." *The Guardian*. https://www.theguardian.com/uk-news/2016/aug/28/hinkley-point-c-edf-boss-vincent-de-rivaz-government-approve-plans-nuclear

M'Bida, A., & Maussion, E. (2020, January 24). DRC's Giant Inga III Dam: Spanish firm ACS Throws in the Towel. *The Africa Report*. https://www.theafricareport.com/22572/drcs-giant-inga-iii-dam-spanish-firm-acs-throws-in-the-towel/

Ma, X. (2017, August 7). China Myanmar Oil and Gas Pipeline (Part 2) a "Going Global" Project that Combines Strategic and Exemplary Significance. *China Pictorial*. http://www.rmhb.com.cn/zt/ydyl/201708/t20170807_800101870.html

Macalister, T. (2016a, April 3). Hinkley Point: China Incorporates Seven London-Based Firms. The Guardian. https://www.theguardian.com/uk-news/2016/apr/03/hinkley-point-china-incorporates-seven-london-based-firms
Macalister, T. (2016b, July 1). Hinkley Point C critics try to Derail it Amid Brexit Vote Turmoil. The Guardian. https://www.theguardian.com/uk-news/2016/jul/01/hinkley-point-c-critics-try-to-derail-it-amid-brexit-vote-turmoil
Macalister, T. (2016c, July 22). Hinkley Point C Nuclear Project Expected to Get Go-ahead Next Week. The Guardian. https://www.theguardian.com/uk-news/2016/jul/22/hinkley-point-c-nuclear-project
Macalister, T. (2016d, August 11). May Urged to Pull Plug Immediately on Hinkley C Over Spying Allegations. The Guardian. https://www.theguardian.com/uk-news/2016/aug/11/may-urged-to-pull-plug-immediately-on-hinkley-c-over-spying-allegations
Macalister, T. (2016e, September 3). Hinkley Point C: No Easy Solution to THERESA May's Chinese Puzzle. The Guardian. https://www.theguardian.com/uk-news/2016/sep/03/hinkley-point-c-theresa-may-china-g20-summit
MacDonald, F. (2011, June 28). Kuwait May Tap Private Investors for $14.5 Billion Refinery. *Bloomberg*. https://www.bloomberg.com/news/articles/2011-06-28/kuwait-council-approves-14-5-billion-refinery-project-oil-minister-says
Macneil, I. R. (1974). *The Many Futures of Contracts*. Gould School of Law, the Law Center University of Southern California.
Mahoney, J. (2012). The Logic of Process Tracing Tests in the Social Sciences. *Sociological Methods & Research, 41*(4), 570–597. https://doi.org/10.1177/0049124112437709
Mamatzakis, E., & Tsionas, M. (2018). Revisiting the Returns of Public Infrastructure in Mexico: A Limited Information Local Likelihood Estimation. *Economic Modelling, 75*, 132–141. https://doi.org/10.1016/j.econmod.2018.06.013
Mangano, G. (2014). Risks in Project Finance Initiatives: Current Trends and Future Directions. PhD Thesis. https://doi.org/10.6092/polito/porto/2572574
Marbot, M. (2020). Analysis of EU-Japan Business Cooperation in Third Countries. EU-Japan Centre for Industrial Cooperation. https://www.eu-japan.eu/publications/analysis-eu-japan-business-cooperation-third-countries
Martin, L. L. (1999). The Political Economy of International Cooperation. In I. Kaul (Ed.), *Global Public Goods: International Cooperation in the 21st Century Global Public Goods: International Cooperation in the 21st Century* (pp. 51–64). Oxford University Press. https://doi.org/10.1093/0195130529.003.0003
Marubeni. (2022, January 24). Issuance of Green Project Bond for Sweihan Photovoltaic Independent Power Project. https://www.marubeni.com/en/news/2022/release/00010.html

Mason, J. (2002). *Qualitative researching*. Sage.

Mason, R. (2016, September 29). Hinkley Point: Ministers Sign Go-ahead for Nuclear Power Plant. *The Guardian*. https://www.theguardian.com/uk-news/2016/sep/29/hinkley-point-ministers-sign-go-ahead-for-nuclear-power-plant

Mason, R., & Goodley, S. (2016, September 15). Hinkley Point C Nuclear Power Station Gets Government Green Light. *The Guardian*. https://www.theguardian.com/uk-news/2016/sep/15/hinkley-point-c-nuclear-power-station-gets-go-ahead

Masters, L. (2014). Building Bridges? South African Foreign Policy and Trilateral Development Cooperation. *South African Journal of International Affairs, 21*(2), 177–191. https://doi.org/10.1080/10220461.2014.942206

Mathews, J. A. (2006). Dragon Multinationals: New Players in 21st Century Globalisation. *Asia Pacific Journal of Management, 23*(1), 5–27. https://doi.org/10.1007/s10490-006-6113-0

Mattlin, M., & Nojonen, M. (2015). Conditionality and Path Dependence in Chinese Lending. *Journal of Contemporary China, 24*(94), 701–720. https://doi.org/10.1080/10670564.2014.978154

Mawdsley, E. (2011). The Changing Geographies of Foreign Aid and Development Cooperation: Contributions from Gift Theory. *Transactions of the Institute of British Geographers, 37*(2), 256–272. https://doi.org/10.1111/j.1475-5661.2011.00467.x

Mawdsley, E. (2012). The changing geographies of foreign aid and development cooperation: contributions from gift theory. *Transactions of the Institute of British Geographers, 37*(2), 256–272. https://doi.org/10.1111/j.1475-5661.2011.00467.x

Mawdsley, E. (2021). *From recipients to donors emerging powers and the changing development landscape*. Zed Books.

Mawdsley, E., Savage, L., & Kim, S.-M. (2013). A "Post-Aid World"? Paradigm Shift in Foreign Aid and Development Cooperation at the 2011 Busan High Level Forum. *The Geographical Journal, 180*(1), 27–38. https://doi.org/10.1111/j.1475-4959.2012.00490.x

Mbodiam, B. R. (2018). Cameroon: Kribi deepwater Port has Finally Been Commissioned. Business in Cameroon. https://www.businessincameroon.com/transport/0503-7843-cameroon-kribi-deepwater-port-has-finally-been-commissioned

McEwan, C., & Mawdsley, E. (2012). Trilateral Development Cooperation: Power and Politics in Emerging Aid Relationships. *Development and Change, 43*(6), 1185–1209. https://doi.org/10.1111/j.1467-7660.2012.01805.x

McFarland, K., Linn, E. C., & Hughes, E. S. (2022, May 17). Strategic Corruption Exemplified (Part 2): China, the New Kid on the Block. Medium;

The Diplomatic Pouch. https://medium.com/the-diplomatic-pouch/analysis-strategic-corruption-exemplified-part-2-china-the-new-kid-on-the-block-afa566d65305

Mearsheimer, J. J. (2001). *The Tragedy of Great Power Politics*. W.W. Norton & Company.

Megginson, W. L., & Mueller, P. C. (2022). Natural Monopoly Privatization: Minimizing Regulatory Trade-Offs Between Rent Extraction and Innovation. *Academy of Management Perspectives, 36*(1), 111–124. https://doi.org/10.5465/amp.2019.0170

Mehta, P. S., & Nanda, N. (2005). Trilateral Development Cooperation: An Emerging Trend Background. In Briefing Paper No. 1/2005, Centre for International Trade, Economics and Environment (CUTS). http://www.cuts-international.org/pdf/BP1-2005.pdf

Meng, H., & Yu, Q. (2020). Third Party Market Cooperation: Theoretical Construction, Historical Evolution, and China's Path. *Contemporary Asia Pacific, 6*(4–40), 153–154. 门洪华, 俞钦文. 第三方市场合作:理论建构、历史演进与中国路径[J]. 当代亚太, 2020(06):4-40+153-154.

Menard, C., & Shirley, M. M. (2014). The Future of New Institutional Economics: From Early Intuitions to a New Paradigm? *Journal of Institutional Economics, 10*(4), 541–565. https://doi.org/10.1017/s174413741400006x

Meyer, K. E. (2015). What is "Strategic Asset Seeking FDI"? *Multinational Business Review, 23*(1), 57–66. https://doi.org/10.1108/mbr-02-2015-0007

Meyer, K. E., Estrin, S., Bhaumik, S. K., & Peng, M. W. (2009). Institutions, Resources, and Entry Strategies in Emerging Economies. *Strategic Management Journal, 30*(1), 61–80. https://doi.org/10.1002/smj.720

MFA. (2024). The Hypocritical Nature and Factual Truth of US Foreign Aid. https://www.mfa.gov.cn/wjbxw_new/202404/t20240419_11284707.shtml

Michel, A., & Shaked, I. (1986). Multinational Corporations vs. Domestic Corporations: Financial Performance and Characteristics. *Journal of International Business Studies, 17*(3), 89–100. https://doi.org/10.1057/palgrave.jibs.8490435

Mikecz, R. (2012). Interviewing Elites: Addressing Methodological Issues. *Qualitative Inquiry, 18*(6), 482–493. https://doi.org/10.1177/1077800412442818

Miller, J. C., & Pras, B. (1980). The Effects of Multinational and Export Diversification on the Profit Stability of US. Corporations. *Southern Economic Journal, 46*(3), 792. https://doi.org/10.2307/1057148

Millington, A. I., & Bayliss, B. T. (1995). Transnational Joint Ventures between UK and EU Manufacturing Companies and the Structure of Competition. *Journal of International Business Studies, 26*(2), 239–254. https://www.jstor.org/stable/pdf/155539.pdf

Mills, G., & Nwokolo, M.-N. (2022). Africa's External Relations: Reinventing and Pursuing New Partnerships. Brookings. https://www.brookings.edu/articles/africas-external-relations-reinventing-and-pursuing-new-partnerships/

Milner, C., & Pentecost, E. (1996). Locational Advantage and US Foreign Direct Investment in UK Manufacturing. *Applied Economics, 28*(5), 605–615. https://doi.org/10.1080/000368496000000040

Milner, H. (1992). International Theories of Cooperation Among Nations: Strengths and Weaknesses. *World Politics, 44*(3), 466–496. https://doi.org/10.2307/2010546

Ministry of Foreign Affairs of Japan. (1974). Ministry of Foreign Affairs of Japan Bluebook in 1974—Chapter 3.1.4 Promotion of Relations with Other Countries. https://www.mofa.go.jp/policy/other/bluebook/1974/1974-3-1.htm

Ministry of Foreign Affairs of Japan. (2023, April 23). Free and Open Indo-Pacific. *Ministry of Foreign Affairs of Japan*. https://www.mofa.go.jp/policy/page25e_000278.html

Mitchell, R. K., Agle, B. R., & Wood, D. J. (1997). Toward a Theory of Stakeholder Identification and salience: Defining the Principle of who and what Really Counts. *The Academy of Management Review, 22*(4), 853–886. https://doi.org/10.2307/259247

MOC. (2019, October 25). The Financing Agreement for Nigeria's Lekki Deepwater Port Project has been Officially Signed in Lagos. *Ministry of Commerce of the People's Republic of China*. http://www.mofcom.gov.cn/article/i/jyjl/k/201910/20191002907649.shtml

Mody, A., & Rebucci, A. (2006). Overview in: IMF-Supported Programs. https://www.elibrary.imf.org/view/book/9781589063617/pr001.xml

Moghaddam, K., Sethi, D., Weber, T., & Wu, J. (2014). The Smirk of Emerging Market Firms: A Modification of the Dunning's Typology of Internationalisation Motivations. *Journal of International Management, 20*(3), 359–374. https://doi.org/10.1016/j.intman.2014.01.002

Monteiro, R., Rial, I., & Tandberg, E. (2020). Chapter 11 Fiscal Risks in Infrastructure. In G. Schwartz, M. Fouad, T. S. Hansen, & G. Verdier (Eds.), *Governance can End Waste in Public Investment*. International Monetary Fund. https://www.elibrary.imf.org/display/book/9781513511818/ch011.xml

Moran, T. H. (1975). *Multinational Corporations and the Politics of Dependence: Copper in Chile*. Princeton University Press.

Moravcsik, A. (1993). Preferences and Power in the European Community: A Liberal Intergovernmentalist Approach. *Journal of Common Market Studies, 31*(4), 473–524. https://doi.org/10.1111/j.1468-5965.1993.tb00477.x

Moravcsik, A. (1999). A New Statecraft? Supranational Entrepreneurs and International Cooperation. *International Organization, 53*(2), 267–306. https://doi.org/10.1162/002081899550887

Moreno, C. (2015). *O Brasil Made in China: Para pensar as reconfigurações do capitalismo contemporâneo*. Fundação Rosa Luxemburgo.

Morgenthau, H. J. (2006). *Politics Among Nations: The Struggle for Power and Peace* (7th ed.). Random House.

Morrow, J. D. (1994). Modeling the Forms of International Cooperation: Distribution Versus Information. *International Organization, 48*(3), 387–423. https://doi.org/10.1017/s0020818300028241

Morschett, D., Schramm-Klein, H., & Zentes, J. (2015). Motives for Internationalisation. In *Strategic International Management* (pp. 75–98). Springer. https://doi.org/10.1007/978-3-658-07884-3_4

Morvaridi, B., & Hughes, C. (2018). South-South Cooperation and Neoliberal Hegemony in a Post-aid World. *Development and Change, 49*(3), 867–892. https://doi.org/10.1111/dech.12405

Moszynski, P. (2011, March 7). Ethiopia's Controversial Dam Project. *The Guardian*. https://www.theguardian.com/global-development/poverty-matters/2011/mar/07/ethiopia-controversial-dam-criticism-communities

Motiar Rahman, M., & Kumaraswamy, M. M. (2002). Risk Management Trends in the Construction Industry: Moving Towards Joint Risk Management. *Engineering, Construction and Architectural Management, 9*(2), 131–151. https://doi.org/10.1108/eb021210

Mureithi, C. (2022, March 3). Is Uganda's Entebbe airport at risk of seizure by China? *QUARTZ*. https://qz.com/africa/2136934/will-china-take-over-ugandas-entebbe-airport/

Murray, S., Grantham, K., & Damle, S. (2011). Development of a Generic Risk Matrix to Manage Project Risks. *Journal of Industrial and Systems Engineering, 5*(1), 35–51. https://www.jise.ir/article_4040_b99470f366e-c6a2ff0658df670d86ca0.pdf

Murthy, K. R. S. (1990). MOU: More Memorandum than Understanding. *Economic and Political Weekly, 25*(21), M59–M66. https://www.jstor.org/stable/4396316

Musacchio, A., & Lazzarini, S. G. (2014). *Reinventing State Capitalism Leviathan in Business*. Harvard University Press.

Musso, E., Ferrari, C., & Benacchio, M. (2006). Port Investment: Profitability, Economic Impact and Financing. *Research in Transportation Economics, 16*, 171–218. https://doi.org/10.1016/s0739-8859(06)16008-4

NDRC. (2019). Third-Party Market Cooperation Guidelines and Cases. National Development and Reform Commision, P.R. China. http://images.mofcom.gov.cn/mz/201909/20190912093710956.pdf

NDRC. (2024). The National Development and Reform Commission Holds a Roundtable on Third Party Market Cooperation between China and France in Beijing. Ndrc.gov.cn. https://www.ndrc.gov.cn/fzggw/jgsj/wzs/sjjdt/202405/t20240501_1366304.html

NDRCC. (2018, May 10). The National Development and Reform Commission Signed a Memorandum of Understanding on Third-Party Market Cooperation Between China and Japan. *The National Development and Reform Commission*. https://www.ndrc.gov.cn/fzggw/jgsj/wzs/sjjdt/201805/t20180510_1037725.html

NDRCC. (2022, February 4). The Fourth Round China-France Third-Party Market Cooperation Pilot Project List Signed. *Department of Foreign Capital and Overseas Investment of China*. https://en.ndrc.gov.cn/news/pressreleases/202202/t20220214_1315538.html

Nederveen Pieterse, J. (2011). *Globalisation and Emerging Societies: Development and Inequality*. Palgrave Macmillan.

Nelson, R. R., & Winter, S. G. (1982). *An Evolutionary Theory of Economic Change*. Harvard University Press.

New Era Live. (2018, May 2). N$180 Million Wind Farm Commissioned at Lüderitz. https://neweralive.na/posts/n180-million-wind-farm-commissioned-at-luderitz

Newbery, D. M. (1997). Privatisation and Liberalisation of Network Utilities. *European Economic Review, 41*(3–5), 357–383. https://doi.org/10.1016/s0014-2921(97)00010-x

Nie, Z. (2022, August 8). Multi-Party Cooperation Supports the "Bridge of Dreams". *Xinhua Agency*. http://lw.news.cn/2022-08/08/c_1310650563.htm

Nigerian Investement Promotion Commission. (2016, December 14). FG Grants 50-year Concessions to Deep Seaport Projects. https://www.nipc.gov.ng/2016/12/14/fg-grants-50-year-concessions-deep-seaport-projects/

Nkot, F., & Amougou, G. (2021, June 3). Cameroon's Kribi Deep Seaport Construction Project: Between State Ownership and Tendencies of Extraversion. *Brill.com; Brill*. https://brill.com/downloadpdf/book/9789004465275/BP000017.xml

Norris, W. J. (2016). *CHINESE ECONOMIC STATECRAFT: Commercial Actors, Grand Strategy, and State Control*. Cornell University Press.

North, D. C. (1981). *Structure and Change in Economic History*. W.W. Norton.

North, D. C. (1991). Institutions. *Journal of Economic Perspectives, 5*(1), 97–112. https://doi.org/10.1257/jep.5.1.97

North, D. C., & Thomas, R. P. (1973). *The Rise of the Western World: A New Economic History*. Cambridge University Press.

Notteboom, T., Pallis, A., & Rodrigue, J.-P. (2022). *Port Economics, Management and Policy* (1st ed.). Routledge. https://doi.org/10.4324/9780429318184

NOVATEK. (2013, June 21). NOVATEK Concludes Framework Agreement on CNPC's Entrance into Yamal LNG. https://www.novatek.ru/en/investors/events/?id_4=756

NOVATEK. (2015, September 3). NOVATEK and the Silk Road Fund Conclude Framework Agreement on Acquisition of Stake in Yamal LNG. https://www.novatek.ru/en/investors/events/?id_4=984

NOVATEK. (2017, November 1). NOVATEK Signed MOU with China Development Bank. https://www.novatek.ru/en/investors/events/?id_4=1950

NPA. (2006, May). Project Summary of Tincan Island Container Terminal Limited A Public Private Partnership Between Nigerian Ports Authority And Tincan Island Container Terminal Limited. Nigerian Ports Authority. https://pp.icrc.gov.ng/media/146

NPA. (2016). Home. Nigerian Ports Authority. https://nigerianports.gov.ng/

Nyabiage, J. (2023, March 3). Why Chinese Players are Taking Private Stakes in Africa's New Megaprojects. *South China Morning Post*. https://www.scmp.com/news/china/diplomacy/article/3212071/new-megaprojects-africa-show-chinese-finance-skews-commercial-market-amid-beijings-lending-slowdown

Nye, J. S., & Keohane, R. O. (1977). *Power and Interdependence*. Harpercollins, Cop.

O'Neill, P. M. (2013). The Financialisation of Infrastructure: The Role of Categorisation and Property Relations. *Cambridge Journal of Regions, Economy and Society, 6*(3), 441–454. https://doi.org/10.1093/cjres/rst017

Odey, P. (2021, November 29). Akwa Ibom Dispatches Delegation to South Korea Over Deep Seaport. *PUNCH*. https://www.vanguardngr.com/2021/12/ibom-deep-seaport-will-transform-akwa-ibom-to-a-transhipment-city-gov-emmanuel/

OECD. (2005). Paris Declaration and Accra Agenda for Action. https://www.oecd.org/dac/effectiveness/parisdeclarationandaccraagendaforaction.htm

OECD. (2008). *Accra Agenda for Action*. OECD Publishing, Paris. https://doi.org/10.1787/9789264098107-en

OECD. (2009). The Paris Declaration on Aid Effectiveness and the Accra Agenda for Action. https://www.oecd.org/dac/effectiveness/34428351.pdf

OECD. (2012a). OECD Principles for Public Governance of Public-Private Partnerships - OECD. Www.oecd.org. https://www.oecd.org/gov/budgeting/oecd-principles-for-public-governance-of-public-private-partnerships.htm

OECD. (2012b). Triangular Co-operation: Emerging Policy Messages and Interim Findings from Analytical Work. https://www.oecd.org/dac/dac-global-relations/DAC%20HLM%20Technical%20document%20Triangular%20Co-operation.pdf

OECD. (2013). TRIANGULAR CO-OPERATION: What's the Literature Telling us? DAC Global Relations The Development Assistance Committee: Enabling Effective Development. https://www.oecd.org/dac/dac-global-relations/OECD%20Triangluar%20Co-operation%20Literature%20Review%20June%202013.pdf

OECD. (2014a). Active with the Peoples Republic of China. https://www.oecd.org/china/active-with-china.pdf

OECD. (2014b). Task Team on South-South Co-operation. https://www.oecd.org/dac/effectiveness/taskteamonsouth-southco-operation.htm

OECD (2016). Development Co-operation Report 2016: The Sustainable Development Goals as Business Opportunities, OECD Publishing, Paris, https://doi.org/10.1787/dcr-2016-en.

OECD. (2017). Dispelling the Myths of Triangular Co-operation—Evidence from the 2015 OECD survey. https://www.oecd.org/dac/dac-global-relations/2015-oecd-survey-report-on-triangular-co-operation.htm

OECD. (2018, September 20). OECD Development Co-operation Peer Reviews: France 2018. *OECD ILibrary*. https://www.oecd-ilibrary.org/sites/9789264302679-7-en/index.html?itemId=/content/component/9789264302679-7-en

OECD. (2018a). China's Belt and Road Initiative in the Global Trade, Investment and Finance Landscape. In OECD. https://www.oecd.org/finance/Chinas-Belt-and-Road-Initiative-in-the-global-trade-investment-and-finance-landscape.pdf

OECD. (2018b). International Workshop: Perspectives on triangular cooperation in the G20. https://www.adelante-i.eu/en/international-workshop-perspectives-triangular-cooperation-g20

OECD. (2018c). Triangular Co-operation: Why Does It Matter. https://www.oecd.org/dac/dac-global-relations/_Triangular%20Booklet%20A5%20pages.pdf

OECD. (2019a). Enabling Effective Triangular Co-operation. OECD Development Policy Papers. https://doi.org/10.1787/5fc4501e-en

OECD. (2019b). Toolkit for Identifying, Monitoring and Evaluating the Value Added of Triangular Co-operation. https://www.oecd.org/dac/triangular-co-operation/TOOLKIT%20-%20version%20August%202018.pdf

OECD. (2021). Official Development Assistance (ODA) WHAT IS ODA? https://www.oecd.org/dac/financing-sustainable-development/development-finance-standards/What-is-ODA.pdf

OECD. (2022). Triangular co-operation with Africa. https://triangular-cooperation.org/wp-content/uploads/2022/10/OECD_Triangular-co-operation-with-Africa.pdf

OECD. (2023, August 31). Development Co-operation Profiles—Japan. *OECD ILibrary*. https://www.oecd-ilibrary.org/sites/b8cf3944-en/index.html?itemId=/content/component/b8cf3944-en

OECD. (n.d.). Official Development Assistance—Definition and Coverage. OECD Development Assistance Committee. Retrieved February 8, 2024, from https://www.oecd.org/dac/financing-sustainable-development/development-finance-standards/officialdevelopmentassistancedefinitionandcoverage.htm

Ogbolu, C. (2023, January 22). First Vessel Berths at Lekki Deep Seaport. *News Agency of Nigeria*. https://nannews.ng/2023/01/22/64035/

Ogunlesi, T. (2023, January 22). Lekki Deep Sea Port: Buhari breaks another jinx. *PM News*. https://pmnewsnigeria.com/2023/01/22/lekki-deep-sea-port-buharibreaks-another-jinx/

Oladipo, O. (2023, November 6). Lekki Port: Innovating Nigeria's Approach to Trade for Modern Future. *Businessday NG*. https://businessday.ng/features/article/lekki-port-innovating-nigerias-approach-to-trade-for-modern-future/

ONS. (2022). Construction Statistics, Great Britain—Office for National Statistics. Office for National Statistics. https://www.ons.gov.uk/businessindustryandtrade/constructionindustry/articles/constructionstatistics/2021

Onyenucheya, A. (2022a, January 26). Amaechi Lauds Work at Lekki Deep Seaport. The Guardian Nigeria News. https://guardian.ng/business-services/maritime/amaechi-lauds-work-at-lekki-deep-seaport/

Onyenucheya, A. (2022b, March 10). Lekki Seaport to Begin Operations this year, Reaches 85 Per Cent Completion. The Guardian Nigeria News. https://guardian.ng/business-services/maritime/lekki-seaport-to-begin-operations-this-year-reaches-85-per-cent-completion/

Onyenucheya, A. (2022c, May 13). Lekki Deep Seaport: FG's Quest to Regain Transshipment Hub Status. The Guardian Nigeria News. https://guardian.ng/business-services/lekki-deep-seaport-fgs-quest-to-regain-transshipment-hub-status/

Onyenucheya, A. (2022d, August 3). Lekki Port Reaches 95% Completion, to be Ready in September. The Guardian Nigeria News. https://guardian.ng/business-services/maritime/lekki-port-reaches-95-completion-to-be-ready-in-september/

Onyenucheya, A. (2024, May 2). Tin Can Port Access Gate Automated to Enhance Efficiency. *The Guardian Nigeria News—Nigeria and World News*. https://guardian.ng/business-services/tin-can-port-access-gate-automated-to-enhance-efficiency/

Oritse, G. (2016, December 13). FG Grants 50-year Concessions to Deep Seaport Projects. *Vangard*. https://www.vanguardngr.com/2016/12/fg-grants-50-year-concessions-deep-seaport-projects/

Oritse, G. (2021, October 13). Controversy Hits Ibaka Deep Seaport Project. *Vanguard*. https://www.vanguardngr.com/2021/10/controversy-hits-ibaka-deep-seaport-project/

Oshodi, A.-G. T. (2022, August 18). Nigeria Sees China as a Steady Partner and its Largest Lender. *Merics*. https://merics.org/en/nigeria-sees-china-steady-partner-and-its-largest-lender

Osipova, E., & Eriksson, P. E. (2013). Balancing Control and Flexibility in Joint Risk Management: Lessons Learned from Two Construction Projects. *International Journal of Project Management, 31*(3), 391–399. https://doi.org/10.1016/j.ijproman.2012.09.007

Otero-Iglesias, M., & Vermeiren, M. (2015). China's State-Permeated Market Economy and Its Constraints to the Internationalisation of the Renminbi. *International Politics, 52*(6), 684–703. https://doi.org/10.1057/ip.2015.14

Owusu-Manu, D.-G., Edwards, D., Ghansah, F. A., Asiedu, R. O., Tagoe, D. S. N., & Birch, T. (2021). Assessing the Policy Provisions and Institutional Behavioral Factors Influencing Rail Infrastructure Financing in Developing Countries. *Journal of Infrastructure Systems, 27*(2), 05021004. https://doi.org/10.1061/(asce)is.1943-555x.0000610

Oye, K. A. (1985). Explaining Cooperation Under Anarchy: Hypotheses and Strategies. *World Politics, 38*(1), 1–24. https://doi.org/10.2307/2010349

Oye, K. A. (1986). *Cooperation Under Anarchy*. Princeton University Press.

Palat, R. A. (2008). A new Bandung? *Futures, 40*(8), 721–734. https://doi.org/10.1016/j.futures.2008.02.004

Pallis, A. A., & De, P. W. (2006). Analysis of the Benefits of Intra-Port Competition. *International Journal of Transport Economics, 33*(1), 1000–1017. https://doi.org/10.1400/16960

Pallis, A. A., Notteboom, T. E., & De Langen, P. W. (2008). Concession Agreements and Market Entry in the Container Terminal Industry. *Maritime Economics & Logistics, 10*(3), 209–228. https://doi.org/10.1057/mel.2008.1

Pamilih, J. (2022). Briefing: China's Involvement in UK Nuclear. China Research Group. https://chinaresearchgroup.org/research/briefing-chinas-involvement-in-uk-nuclear-power

Pan, C., Wei, W. X., Muralidharan, E., Liao, J., & Andreosso-O'Callaghan, B. (2020). Does China's Outward Direct Investment Improve the Institutional Quality of the Belt and Road Countries? *Sustainability, 12*(1), 415. https://doi.org/10.3390/su12010415

Pang, J. (2021). "Yi Dai Yi Lu" shiyu xia si san fang shichang hezuo de jizhixing jianshe yanjiu (Research on the mechanism construction of third-party market cooperation under the vision of the "the Belt and Road"). *Study and Exprolation, 12*, 43–47. https://www.cnki.com.cn/Article/CJFDTotal-GJGC202104002.htm

Pankaj, A. K. (2005). Revisiting Foreign Aid Theories. *International Studies, 42*(2), 103–121. https://doi.org/10.1177/002088170404200201

Pantoja, E. (2009). *Triangular Cooperation: New Paths to Development*. OECD. https://www.oecd.org/dac/dac-global-relations/43705278.pdf

Park, S. H., & Russo, M. V. (1996). When Competition Eclipses Cooperation: An Event History Analysis of Joint Venture Failure. *Management Science, 42*(6), 875–890. https://doi.org/10.1287/mnsc.42.6.875

Pasimeni, F. (2021). The Origin of the Sharing Economy Meets the Legacy of Fractional Ownership. *Journal of Cleaner Production, 319*, 128614. https://doi.org/10.1016/j.jclepro.2021.128614

Patey, L., & Large, D. (2012). Cooperating with China in Africa, DIIS Policy Brief. Copenhagen: Danish Institute for International Studies (DIIS). https://www.diis.dk/en/research/cooperating-with-china-in-africa

Patrick, M. (2023, July 12). Lekki Multi-Purpose Deep Seaport, the deepest of its kind in Nigeria. *Construction Review*. https://constructionreviewonline.com/biggest-projects/lekki-multi-purpose-deep-seaport-project-in-lagos-nigeria/

Patton, M. Q. (2002). *Qualitative Research and Evaluation Methods* (3rd ed.). Sage Publications.

Paul, E., & Vandeninden, F. (2012). Foreign Aid Transaction Costs: What Are They and When Are They Minimised? *Development Policy Review, 30*(3), 283–304. https://doi.org/10.1111/j.1467-7679.2012.00577.x

Paul Hastings LLP. (2019, August 1). Autopista al Mar 2 Secures $652 Million, Dual-Tranche, Dual Currency Project Financing. https://www.paulhastings.com/news/news-autopista-al-mar-2-secures-652-million-dual-tranche-dual-currency-project-financing

Paulo, S., & Reisen, H. (2010). Eastern Donors and Western Soft Law: Towards a DAC Donor Peer Review of China and India? *Development Policy Review, 28*(5), 535–552. https://doi.org/10.1111/j.1467-7679.2010.00497.x

Peng, M. W., & Parente, R. C. (2012). Institution-Based Weaknesses Behind Emerging Multinationals. *Revista de Administração de Empresas, 52*(3), 360–364. https://doi.org/10.1590/s0034-75902012000300007

Perkins, S. E. (2014). When Does Prior Experience Pay? Institutional Experience and the Multinational Corporation. *Administrative Science Quarterly, 59*(1), 145–181. https://doi.org/10.1177/0001839214523603

Péron, A. (2019, November 1). Willkie Advises CMA Terminals in Subconcession of Container Terminal Operations of Lekki Deep Sea Port in Nigeria. Willkie Farr & Gallagher LLP. https://www.willkie.com/news/2019/11/willkie-advises-cma

Pessoa, A. (2008). Public–Private Partnerships in Developing Countries: Are Infrastructures Responding to the new ODA Strategy? *Journal of International Development, 20*(3), 311–325. https://doi.org/10.1002/jid.1416

Pham, J. P. (2017). Germany's "Marshall Plan" for Africa. New Atlanticist. https://www.atlanticcouncil.org/blogs/new-atlanticist/germany-s-marshall-plan-for-africa/

Pheng, L. S., & Hou, L. S. (2019). The Economy and the Construction Industry. In *Construction Quality and the Economy* (pp. 21–54). Ncbi. https://doi.org/10.1007/978-981-13-5847-0_2

Phillips, T. (2016, September 16). UK's "China-Phobia" Spells Trouble Despite Hinkley Decision—Chinese Media. *The Guardian*. https://www.theguardian.com/uk-news/2016/sep/16/uks-china-phobia-spells-trouble-despite-hinkley-decision-chinese-media

Pickard, J., Parker, G., & White, S. (2024a, January 31). Paris Seeks UK Loan Guarantee after Hinkley Point Nuclear Plant Costs Soar. *Financial Times*. https://www.ft.com/content/c1e3bd19-763b-4ea1-b188-d2872cc36bb8

Pickard, J., Parker, G., & White, S. (2024b, January 31). Paris Seeks UK Loan Guarantee after Hinkley Point Nuclear Plant Costs Soar. *Financail Times*. https://www.ft.com/content/c1e3bd19-763b-4ea1-b188-d2872cc36bb8?emailId=2866caaf-e0ad-4386-994f-f0fc5bbebdf1&segmentId=22011ee7-8%E2%80%A6

PPIAF. (2007). *National program for Public Private Partnership*. https://www.ppiaf.org/sites/default/files/documents/2007-01/Quarterly_Booklet_English.pdf

Pickard, J., & Thomas, N. (2021, July 25). UK Looks to Remove China's CGN from Nuclear Power Projects. *Financial Times*. https://www.ft.com/content/c4a3fe02-8535-45a4-aacf-0c4fbce8409d

Pinto, M. J. (2017). What is Project Finance? *Investment Management and Financial Innovations, 14*(1), 200–210. https://doi.org/10.21511/imfi.14(1-1).2017.06

Pisano, G. P., Russo, M., & Teece, D. (1988). Joint Ventures and Collaborative Arrangements in the Telecommunications Equipment Industry. In D. Mowery (Ed.), *International Collaborative Ventures in U.S. Manufacturing*. Ballinger Publishing Company.

Portugese MFA. (2013). Policy Dialogue on Triangular Cooperation: Summary of Discussion. Portugese Ministry of Foreign Affairs.DAC Global Relations—OECD. https://www.oecd.org/dac/dac-global-relations/

Power, M., Mohan, G., & Tan-Mullins, M. (2012). *China's Resource Diplomacy in Africa: Powering Development?* Palgrave Macmillan.

Power Technology. (2020, August 17). Al Dhafra Solar Project, Abu Dhabi, UAE. https://www.power-technology.com/projects/al-dhafra-solar-project-abu-dhabi/

PowerChina. (2013). Gabonese Hydropower Project Began Operation. PowerChina. https://www.chinadaily.com.cn/m/powerchina/2013-08/28/content_16925790.htm

PPI. (2020). Annual Report Private Participation in Infrastructure (PPI) . https://ppi.worldbank.org/content/dam/PPI/documents/PPI_2020_AnnualReport.pdf

Prashad, V. (2007). *The Darker Nations: A People's History of the Third World*. New York The New Press.

Pratley, N. (2017, June 23). Hinkley Point C: Watchdog Confirms Fears of Political Vanity Project. *The Guardian*. https://www.theguardian.com/uk-news/nils-pratley-on-finance/2017/jun/23/hinkley-point-c-nuclear-energy-risky-expensive-national-audit-office

Pratley, N. (2020, July 7). No Business Need at all now for a Chinese Nuclear Plant in the UK. *The Guardian*. https://www.theguardian.com/business/nils-pratley-on-finance/2020/jul/07/no-business-need-at-all-now-for-a-chinese-nuclear-plant-in-the-uk

PT. (2020a). Al Dhafra Solar Project, Abu Dhabi, UAE. Power Technology. https://www.power-technology.com/projects/al-dhafra-solar-project-abu-dhabi/

PT. (2020b, May 1). Sweihan Photovoltaic Independent Power Project, Abu Dhabi. Power Technology | Energy News and Market Analysis. https://www.power-technology.com/projects/sweihan-photovoltaic-independent-power-project-abu-dhabi/

Punch, K. F. (2014). *Introduction to Social Research: Quantitative and Qualitative Approaches* (3rd ed.). Sage.
Punton, M., & Welle, K. (2015). Straws-in-the-wind, Hoops and Smoking Guns: What can Process Tracing Offer to Impact Evaluation? Institute of Development Studies. https://www.ids.ac.uk/publications/straws-in-the-wind-hoops-and-smoking-guns-what-can-process-tracing-offer-to-impact-evaluation/
Purnamasari, D. (2015). The Effect of Changes in Return on Assets, Return on Equity, and Economic Value Added to the Stock Price Changes and Its Impact on Earnings Per Share. *Research Journal of Finance and Accounting Www.iiste.org ISSN, 6*(6), 2222–2847. https://core.ac.uk/download/pdf/234630582.pdf
Qi, H., & Yang, M. (2017). Record of PetroChina's Participation in the Construction of the China Myanmar Oil and Gas Pipeline Project. http://www.ce.cn/xwzx/gnsz/gdxw/201706/06/t20170606_23445750.shtml
Qian, Z. (2021, December 3). The Prospect of Cooperation in the Third-Party Market Between China and Japan is Broad. *China Internet Information Center.* http://home.china.com.cn/txt/2021-12/03/content_41811360.htm
Qu, J. (2017, May 3). The China Myanmar Oil and Gas Pipeline Benefits "Four Countries and Six Parties". *Sciencenet.* https://news.sciencenet.cn/htmlnews/2017/5/375219.shtm
Quer, D., Claver, E., & Rienda, L. (2015). Chinese Outward Foreign Direct Investment: A Review of Empirical Research. *Frontiers of Business Research in China, 9*(3), 326–370. https://doi.org/10.3868/s070-004-015-0014-6
Quinn, B. (2016, August 8). China Warns UK Relations are at "Historical Juncture" Over Hinkley Point. *The Guardian.* https://www.theguardian.com/uk-news/2016/aug/08/china-warns-uk-relations-historical-juncture-hinkley-point-liu-xiaoming
Raisbeck, P., Duffield, C., & Xu, M. (2010). Comparative Performance of PPPs and Traditional Procurement in Australia. *Construction Management and Economics, 28*(4), 345–359. https://doi.org/10.1080/01446190903582731
Rakic, S. (2020, October 6). Chinese and French Companies to Build Belgrade Subway. *Serbian Monitor.* https://www.serbianmonitor.com/en/chinese-and-french-companies-to-build-belgrade-subway/
Ralston, J. (2021, October 18). China and UK Nuclear Power. *Energy & Climate Intelligence Unit.* https://eciu.net/analysis/briefings/uk-energy-policies-and-prices/china-and-uk-nuclear-power
Ramamurti, R. (2012). What is Really Different About Emerging Market Multinationals? *Global Strategy Journal, 2*(1), 41–47. https://doi.org/10.1002/gsj.1025
Ramamurti, R., & Williamson, P. J. (2019). Rivalry Between Emerging-Market MNEs and Developed-Country MNEs: Capability Holes and the Race to the Future. *Business Horizons, 62*(2), 157–169. https://doi.org/10.1016/j.bushor.2018.11.001

Rampa, F., & Bilal, S. (2011). Emerging Economies in Africa and the Development Effectiveness Debate. https://ecdpm.org/wp-content/uploads/2013/11/DP-107-Emerging-Economies-Africa-Development-Effectiveness-Debate-2011.pdf

Rangan, S., & Drummond, A. (2004). Explaining Outcomes in Competition Among Foreign Multinationals in a Focal Host Market. *Strategic Management Journal, 25*(3), 285–293. https://doi.org/10.1002/smj.375

Rankin, J. (2016, July 27). Flamanville: France's Beleaguered Forerunner to Hinkley Point C. *The Guardian*. https://www.theguardian.com/environment/2016/jul/27/flamanville-france-edf-nuclear-reactor-hinkley-point-c

Rawnsley, A. (2016, July 31). Hinkley Offers a Useful Guide to May's Plans for Cameron's Legacy. *The Observer*. https://www.theguardian.com/commentisfree/2016/jul/31/hinkley-offers-useful-guide-to-mays-plans-cameron-legacy

Regan, J., & Irish, J. (2016, March 7). EDF CEO Regrets CFO Departure, Sees Hinkley Point Decision Soon. *Reuters*. https://www.reuters.com/article/edf-britain-nuclear-idUKFWN16E003/

RENEWS. (2019, January 17). CGN Acquires 540MW Brazil Bounty from Enel. *RENEWS.BIZ*. https://renews.biz/51026/cgn-acquires-540mw-brazil-bounty-from-enel/

Reus-Smit, C., & Snidal, D. (2010). *The Oxford Handbook of International Relations*. OUP Oxford.

Rihoux, B. (2009). Case-Oriented Configura-Tional Research: Qualitative Comparative Analysis (Qca), Fuzzy Sets, and Related Techniques. In J. M. Box-Steffensmeier, H. E. Brady, & D. Collier (Eds.), *Oxford Handbooks Online*. Oxford University Press. https://doi.org/10.1093/oxfordhb/9780199286546.003.0028

Riordan, M. H., & Williamson, O. E. (1985). Asset Specificity and Economic Organization. *International Journal of Industrial Organization, 3*(4), 365–378. https://doi.org/10.1016/0167-7187(85)90030-x

Ritchie, J., Lewis, J., McNaughton Nicholls, C., & Ormston, R. (2014). *Qualitative Research Practice: a Guide for Social Science Students and Researchers*. SAGE.

Rittberger, V., & Mayer, P. (1993). *Regime Theory and International Relations*. Clarendon Press.

Robinson, H. J. (1961). *The Motivation and Flow of Private Foreign Investment*. International Development Center, Stanford Research Institute.

Rogers, D. (2016, May 9). Chinese Bidder Praised for Speed in DR Congo's Massive Dam Contest. *Global Construction Review*. https://www.globalconstructionreview.com/chinese-bidder-praised-speed-d7r-co7ngos-mas7sive/

Rose, M., & Hummel, T. (2022, July 6). France Plans Full Nationalisation of Power Utility EDF. Reuters. https://www.reuters.com/world/europe/frances-edf-be-fully-nationalised-borne-2022-07-06/

Rosseel, P., De Corte, E., Blommaert, J., & Verniers, E. (2009). Approaches to North-South, South-South and North-South-South collaboration. A policy document.

Rotberg, R. I. (2008). *China into Africa Trade, Aid, and Influence*. Dc Brookings Institution Press.

Rottig, D. (2016). Institutions and Emerging Markets: Effects and Implications for Multinational Corporations. *International Journal of Emerging Markets, 11*(1), 2–17. https://doi.org/10.1108/ijoem-12-2015-0248

Roy, A., Paul, P., Roy, M., & Mukhopadhyay, K. (2018). Mapping Confucian Values in the Context of Ethical Dimensions. *Business and Professional Ethics Journal, 37*(2), 181–212. https://doi.org/10.5840/bpej201841769

RT. (2019). High-Speed Rail Linked 3 Airport Project, Thailand. Railway Technology. https://www.railway-technology.com/projects/high-speed-rail-linked-3-airport-project-thailand/

Ruben, D.-H., & Little, D. (1993). Varieties of Social Explanation: An Introduction to the Philosophy of Social Science. *The Philosophical Review, 102*(1), 120. https://doi.org/10.2307/2185667

Ruddick, G. (2016, July 28). Resignation of EDF Director Paves Way for Hinkley Point go-ahead. *The Guardian*. https://www.theguardian.com/uk-news/2016/jul/28/resignation-edf-director-hinkley-point-gerard-magnin

Ruddick, G., Asthana, A., & Willsher, K. (2016, July 29). EDF Boss confident Hinkley Point C Nuclear Plant will be Built. *The Guardian*. https://www.theguardian.com/uk-news/2016/jul/29/edf-boss-confident-hinkley-point-c-nuclear-plant-will-be-built

Ruddick, G., & Grierson, J. (2016, July 29). Hinkley Point C in doubt after British government delays approval. *The Guardian*. https://www.theguardian.com/business/2016/jul/28/hinkley-point-c-to-go-ahead-after-edf-board-approves-project

Ruddick, G., & Phillips, T. (2016, September 16). China Must Wait Four Years for Decision on Bradwell Nuclear Plant. *The Guardian*. https://www.theguardian.com/uk-news/2016/sep/16/china-must-wait-four-years-for-decision-on-bradwell-nuclear-plant

Rugman, A. M. (1981). *Inside the Multinationals*. Croom Helm.

Rugman, A. M. (1985). Internalisation is Still a General Theory of Foreign Direct Investment. *Weltwirtschaftliches Archiv, 121*(3), 570–575. https://www.jstor.org/stable/40439351

Rugman, A. M. (2010). Reconciling Internalisation Theory and the Eclectic Paradigm. *Multinational Business Review, 18*(2), 1–12. https://doi.org/10.1108/1525383x201000007

Rui, H. (2010). Developing Country FDI and Development: The Case of Chinese FDI in the Sudan. *Transnational Corporations, 19*(3), 49–80. https://doi.org/10.18356/08e89398-en

Rui, H., & Bruyaka, O. (2021). Strategic Network Orchestration in Emerging Markets: China's Catch-up in the High-Speed Train Industry. *British Journal of Management, 32*(1), 97–123. https://doi.org/10.1111/1467-8551.12457

Rui, H., Cuervo-Cazurra, A., & Annique Un, C. (2016). Learning-by-Doing in Emerging Market Multinationals: Integration, Trial and Error, Repetition, and Extension. *Journal of World Business, 51*(5), 686–699. https://doi.org/10.1016/j.jwb.2016.07.007

Rui, H., & Yip, G. S. (2008). Foreign Acquisitions by Chinese firms: A Strategic Intent Perspective. *Journal of World Business, 43*(2), 213–226.

Rui, H., Zhang, M., & Shipman, A. (2016). Relevant Knowledge and Recipient Ownership: Chinese MNCS' Knowledge Transfer in Africa. *Journal of World Business, 51*(5), 713–728. https://doi.org/10.1016/j.jwb.2016.07.009

Rui, H., Zhang, M., & Shipman, A. (2017). Chinese Expatriate Management in Emerging Markets: A Competitive Advantage Perspective. *Journal of International Management, 23*(2), 124–138. https://doi.org/10.1016/j.intman.2017.01.002

Rumelt, R. P. (1984). Towards a Strategic Theory of the Firm. In R. B. Lamb (Ed.), *Competitive Strategic Management* (pp. 566–570). Englewood Cliffs.

Saglam, I. (2016). Regulating a Manager-Controlled Natural Monopoly with Unknown Costs. *Managerial and Decision Economics, 38*(6), 792–805. https://doi.org/10.1002/mde.2817

Saidi, M. D., & Wolf, C. (2011). Recalibrating Development Co-operation: How Can African Countries Benefit from Emerging Partners? OECD-Ilibrary, 302. https://doi.org/10.1787/5kg83kvgnz0v-en

Salau, S. (2018, March 30). Government earmarks N90b for special Economic Zones, to earn $200b from Lekki Deep Seaport. *The Guardian* Nigeria News. https://guardian.ng/news/government-earmarks-n90b-for-special-economic-zones-to-earn-200b-from-lekki-deep-seaport/

Samb, S., Miridzhanian, A., & Christensen, S. (2023). Work Set to Resume at Simandou after Guinea, Shareholders Agree on Terms. Reuters. https://www.mining.com/web/work-set-to-resume-at-simandou-project-after-guinea-shareholders-agree-terms/

Samy, Y. (2010). China's Aid Policies in Africa: Opportunities and Challenges. *The Round Table, 99*(406), 75–90. https://doi.org/10.1080/00358530903513756

Sánchez, P. C. (2000). A subadditivity Test for the Cost Function of the Principal European Railways. *Transport Reviews, 20*(3), 275–290. https://doi.org/10.1080/014416400412814

SASAC. (2005, July 26). Dongfang Electric Group Signed a General Contracting Project for the Vietnam Haiphong Thermal Power Station Project. *State-Owned Assets Supervision and Administration Commission of the State Council.* http://www.sasac.gov.cn/n2588025/n2588124/c3843801/content.html

SASAC. (2017, July 10). China Three Gorges Group and Germany Voith Sign Deepening Cooperation Agreement. *State-Owned Assets Supervision and Administration Commission of the State Council*. http://www.sasac.gov.cn/n2588025/n2588124/c7345892/content.html

SASAC. (2023, December 28). The opening and operation of West Africa's largest deep-water port. State Owned Assets Supervision and Administration Commission of the State Council. http://www.sasac.gov.cn/n4470048/n26915116/n29670038/n29670102/c29681289/content.html

SaudiGulf Projects. (2020, April 28). EDF Consortium Submits Lowest bid for 2GW Al-Dhafra Solar PV project. https://www.saudigulfprojects.com/2020/04/edf-consortium-submits-lowest-bid-for-abu-dhabis-2gw-al-dhafra-solar-pv-project/

Sawamura, N. (2004). Japan's Philosophy of Self-Help Efforts in International Development Cooperation: Does It Work in Africa? *Journal of International Cooperation in Education, 7*(1), 27–40. https://cice.hiroshima-u.ac.jp/wp-content/uploads/publications/Journal7-1/7-1-4.pdf

Schmitter, P. C. (2008). The Design of Social and Political Research. In *Approaches and Methodologies in the Social Sciences* (pp. 263–295). Cambridge University Press. https://doi.org/10.1017/cbo9780511801938.015

Schneider, M., Froggatt, A. P., & Thomas, S. (2014, August 21). The saga of Hinkley Point C: Europe's Key Nuclear Decision. *Energy Post*. https://energy-post.eu/saga-hinkley-point-c-europes-key-nuclear-decision/

Scholz, I. (2020). Beyond Vested Interests: Reforming International Cooperation Post Covid-19. OECD Development Matters. https://devinit.org/blog/beyond-vested-interests-reforming-international-cooperation-post-covid-19/

Schreier, M. (2012). *Qualitative Content Analysis in Practice*. Sage.

Schroder, N. (1977). America's Economic Stake in Taiwan. *The International Trade Law Journal, 3*(1) https://digitalcommons.law.umaryland.edu/cgi/viewcontent.cgi?article=1372&context=mjil

Schulz, N-S. (2010). Boosting South-South Cooperation in the Context of Aid Effectiveness Telling the Story of Partners Involved in more than 110 Cases of South-South and Triangular Cooperation. https://www.oecd.org/dac/effectiveness/46080462.pdf

Schuman, M., & Shullman, D. O. (2022, July 28). Cooperation with China: Challenges and Opportunities. *Atlantic Council*. https://www.atlanticcouncil.org/in-depth-research-reports/report/cooperation-with-china-challenges-and-opportunities/

Seaman, J., Huotari, M., & Otero-Iglesias, M. (2017). Chinese Investment in Europe A Country-Level Approach A Report by the European Think-tank Network on China (ETNC). https://www.ifri.org/sites/default/files/atoms/files/etnc_reports_2017_final_20dec2017.pdf

Seawright, J., & Gerring, J. (2008). Options Case Selection Techniques in Case Study Research: A Menu of Qualitative and Quantitative. *Political Research Quarterly, 61*(294), 294–308.
Sebenius, J. K. (1992). Challenging Conventional Explanations of International Cooperation: Negotiation Analysis and the Case of Epistemic Communities. *International Organization, 46*(1), 323–365. https://doi.org/10.1017/s0020818300001521
Sergejeff, K. (2020). Will European Public Opinion on International Cooperation Change in the Face of COVID-19? ECDPM. https://ecdpm.org/talking-points/european-public-opinion-international-cooperation-change-covid-19/
Severino, J.-M., & Ray, O. (2009). The End of ODA: Death and Rebirth of a Global Public Policy. *SSRN Electronic Journal, 19*(1), 5–44. https://doi.org/10.2139/ssrn.1392460
Shaked, A., & Sutton, J. (1983). Natural Oligopolies. *Econometrica, 51*(5), 1469–1483. https://www.tcd.ie/Economics/staff/ppwalsh/papers/sutton.pdf
Shaked, A., & Sutton, J. (1987). Product Differentiation and Industrial Structure. *The Journal of Industrial Economics, 36*(2), 131. https://doi.org/10.2307/2098408
Shang, K. (2024). Sino French Economic and Trade Cooperation for Mutual Benefit and Win-Win Results. Paper.people.com.cn. http://paper.people.com.cn/rmrb/html/2024-01/29/nw.D110000renmrb_20240129_1-03.htm
Shanghai Electric. (2018, November 29). Leaders from Both China and the West Witnessed Shanghai Electric and Abengoa Sign a Cooperation Agreement for the Dubai Solar Thermal Power Project. http://www.cnste.org/html/xiangmu/2018/1129/4143.html
Sharafi, A., Sadegh Amalnick, M., & Allah Taleizadeh, A. (2021). Outcome of Financial Conflicts in the Operation Phase of Public–Private Partnership Contracts. Journal of Construction Engineering and Management, 147(6). https://doi.org/10.1061/(asce)co.1943-7862.0002011
Sharkey, W. W. (1982). *The Theory of Natural Monopoly*. In The Economic Journal. Oxford University Press. https://doi.org/10.1017/cbo9780511571817
Shelton, G., & Paruk, F. (2008). The Forum on China- Africa Cooperation A Strategic Opportunity. https://www.files.ethz.ch/isn/103618/mono156full.pdf
Shiga, H. (2016). No.130 Normative Framing of Development Cooperation: Japanese Bilateral Aid between the DAC and Southern Donors. https://www.jica.go.jp/jica-ri/publication/workingpaper/wp_130.html
Sidiropoulos, E. (2012). Rising Powers, South–South Co-operation and Africa. Policy Brief 47, Global Powers and Africa Programme, SAIIA. https://saiia.org.za/research/rising-powers-south-south-co-operation-and-africa/

Siemens. (2019, March 26). Siemens and the National Development and Reform Commission of China Strengthen the Cooperation of "the Belt and Road". *Siemens*. https://w1.siemens.com.cn/news/news_articles/7971.aspx

Sim, A. B., & Ali, Y. (1998). Performance of International Joint Ventures from Developing and Developed Countries: An Empirical Study in a Developing Country Context. *Journal of World Business, 33*(4), 357–377. https://doi.org/10.1016/s1090-9516(99)80080-7

Simon, H. A. (1984). On the Behavioral and Rational Foundations of Economic Dynamics. *Journal of Economic Behavior & Organization, 5*(1), 35–55. https://doi.org/10.1016/0167-2681(84)90025-8

Singh, A. (2020). The Myth of "Debt-Trap Diplomacy" and Realities of Chinese Development Finance. *Third World Quarterly, 42*(2), 239–253.

Sinkkonen, E. (2019). The More the Merrier? Sino-Japanese Security Relations in the Context of Complex Interstate Rivalry in the Asia-Pacific Region. *The Pacific Review, 32*(5), 748–777. https://doi.org/10.1080/09512748.2019.1569113

Siu, S. (2010). Sovereign-Commercial Hybrid: Chinese Minerals for Infrastructure Financing in the Democratic Republic of the Congo. *Columbia Journal of Transnational Law, 48*(3), 599–654.

Six, C. (2009). The Rise of Postcolonial States as Donors: A Challenge to the Development Paradigm? *Third World Quarterly, 30*(6), 1103–1121. https://doi.org/10.1080/01436590903037366

Skupien, S. (2019). Searching for Macro-Meso-Micro-Level Links in Studies of North-South Research Collaborations. *Learning and Policy, 57*(3), 391–410. https://doi.org/10.1007/s11024-019-09371-8

Slack, B., & Fremont, A. (2005). Transformation of Port Terminal Operations: From the Local to the Global. *Transport Reviews, 25*(1), 117–130. https://doi.org/10.1080/0144164042000206051

SMD. (2015, October 22). Comment: The Hinkley Point C project is a Great Opportunity for Chinese Nuclear Power Enterprises to Forge Ahead. Southern Metropolis Daily. https://finance.sina.cn/china/cjpl/2015-10-22/detail-ifxizwti6864635.d.html?vt=4&sid=165302

Smith, M., Browne, P., & Dube, N. (2006). High Level Forum on the Harmonization for Aid Effectiveness in South Africa Final Report. https://citeseerx.ist.psu.edu/document?repid=rep1&type=pdf&doi=4d8583eee1d088b4d75c3fd2c1041d47d4225457

Smith, T., & Ikenberry, G. J. (2001). After Victory: Institutions, Strategic Restraint, and the Rebuilding of Order after Major Wars. *Foreign Affairs, 80*(2), 170. https://doi.org/10.2307/20050090

Smyth, S., & Whitfield, D. (2017). Maintaining Market Principles: Government Auditors, PPP Equity Sales and Hegemony. *Accounting Forum, 41*(1), 44–56. https://doi.org/10.1016/j.accfor.2016.06.003

Solís, M. (2021, January 22). Japan's Democratic Renewal and the Survival of the Liberal Order. Brookings. https://www.brookings.edu/articles/japans-democratic-renewal-and-the-survival-of-the-liberal-order/

South African Government. (2011). White Paper on South African Foreign Policy—Building a Better World: The Diplomacy of Ubuntu. https://www.gov.za/documents/white-papers/white-paper-south-african-foreign-policy-building-better-world-diplomacy

Spencer, R., McCormack, M. J., Drew, A. L., Gowdy, G., & Keller, T. E. (2021). (Not) Minding the Gap: A Qualitative Interview Study of how Social Class Bias can Influence Youth Mentoring Relationships. *Journal of Community Psychology., 50*(3), 1579–1596. https://doi.org/10.1002/jcop.22737

Spulber, D. F. (1989). *Regulation and Markets*. MIT Press.

Staalesen, A. (2015, January 5). Russian crisis money for Yamal. Barentsobserver. https://barentsobserver.com/en/energy/2015/01/russian-crisis-money-yamal-05-01

Stahl, A. (2016). Chinas Relations with Sub-Saharan Africa. (IAI Working Paper No. 16). Rome: Istituto Affairi Internazionali. https://www.iai.it/sites/default/files/iaiwp1622.pdf

Stahl, A. K. (2012). *Trilateral Development Cooperation Between the European Union, China and Africa: What Prospects for South Africa?* Centre for Chinese Studies, Stellenbosch University. https://scholar.sun.ac.za/handle/10019.1/70766

Stahl, A. K. (2018). *EU-China-Africa Trilateral Relations in a Multipolar World: Hic sunt dracones*. Palgrave Macmillan.

Stallings, B., & Szkely, G. (1993). *Japan, the United States, and Latin America: Toward a Trilateral Relationship in the Western Hemisphere?* Palgrave Macmillan London.

State Council. (2021). China's International Development Cooperation in the New Era. https://english.www.gov.cn/archive/whitepaper/202101/10/content_WS5ffa6bbbc6d0f72576943922.html

Stefanini, S. (2016a, July 28). Hinkley Nuclear Plant Faces UK Delay. POLITICO. https://www.politico.eu/article/france-approves-hinkley-nuclear-plant-for-the-uk-despite-brexit-worries-edf/

Stefanini, S. (2016b, September 15). Theresa May Gives Hinkley the Green Light. POLITICO. https://www.politico.eu/article/uk-has-approved-hinkley-with-conditions-report/

Steurer, R. (2005). Mapping Stakeholder Theory Anew: From the "Stakeholder Theory of the Firm" to Three Perspectives on Business-Society Relations. *Business Strategy and the Environment, 15*(1), 55–69. https://doi.org/10.1002/bse.467

Stewart, H. (2016, September 14). Theresa May Set to Give Go-Ahead for Hinkley Point C Nuclear Plant. *The Guardian*. https://www.theguardian.com/uk-news/2016/sep/14/theresa-may-conditional-approval-hinkley-point-c-nuclear-power-station

Stewart, H., Mason, R., & Ruddick, G. (2016, September 15). Theresa May Accused of Avoiding Security and Cost Issues of Hinkley. *The Guardian*. https://www.theguardian.com/uk-news/2016/sep/15/theresa-may-accused-backing-down-hinkley-point-c-deal

Stewart, H., & Quinn, B. (2016, August 9). Theresa May Seeks Close Ties with China Despite Hinkley Point delay. *The Guardian*. https://www.theguardian.com/uk-news/2016/aug/09/government-says-links-with-china-are-vital-after-hinkley-point-warning

Stojkovic, M. (2021, January 14). Implementation of Belgrade Metro Project. *Stojković Attorneys*. https://statt.rs/implementation-of-belgrade-metro-project/

Stone, R. W., Wang, Y., & Yu, S. (2021). Chinese Power and the State-Owned Enterprise. *International Organization, 76*(1), 1–22. https://doi.org/10.1017/s0020818321000308

Story, J., & Lawton, T. (2010). Business Studies: The Global Dynamics of Business–State Relations. In *The Oxford Handbook of Business and Government* (pp. 89–120). Oxford University Press. https://doi.org/10.1093/oxfordhb/9780199214273.003.0005

Sudžuka, E., & Osmanović, I. (2021). Concession contract in Bosnia and Herzegovina: Introducing the World Commerce & Contracting Principles in the concession contract. *Journal of Strategic Contracting and Negotiation, 5*(4), 235–246. https://doi.org/10.1177/20555636221090207

Suleiman, F. (2024, January 24). British Taxpayers Wont Bear Cost of Hinkley Point C Overruns. *Reuters*. https://www.reuters.com/world/uk/british-taxpayers-wont-bear-cost-hinkley-point-c-overruns-uk-government-2024-01-23/

Sunday, O., Salau, S., & Ojo, Y. A. (2018, March 29). Buhari Visits Lagos, Kicks off $1.5b Deep Seaport Today. *The Guardian Nigeria News*. https://guardian.ng/news/buhari-visits-lagos-kicks-off-1-5b-deep-seaport-today/

Suri, G. (2016). China's 21 Century Maritime Silk Road Old String with New Pearls? Vivekananda International Foundation 3, San Martin Marg, Chanakyapuri, New Delhi—110021. https://www.vifindia.org/sites/default/files/china-s-21st-century-maritime-silk-road-old-string-with-new-pearls.pdf

Tan, J., & Zhao, J. Z. (2019). The Rise of Public–Private Partnerships in China: An Effective Financing Approach for Infrastructure Investment? *Public Administration Review, 79*(4), 514–518. https://doi.org/10.1111/puar.13046

Tang, W., Duffield, C. F., & Young, D. M. (2006). Partnering Mechanism in Construction: An Empirical Study on the Chinese Construction Industry.

Journal of Construction Engineering and Management, 132(3), 217–229. https://doi.org/10.1061/(asce)0733-9364(2006)132:3(217)
Tang, Y. (2022, April 19). Triple-Win Model. *China Daily*. https://www.chinadaily.com.cn/a/202204/19/WS625e0b63a310fd2b29e57b51.html
Tang, Y., Chen, Y., Hua, Y., & Fu, Y. (2020). Impacts of Risk Allocation on Conflict Negotiation Costs in Construction Projects: Does Managerial Control Matter? *International Journal of Project Management, 38*(3), 188–199. https://doi.org/10.1016/j.ijproman.2020.03.002
Tan-Mullins, M., Mohan, G., & Power, M. (2010). Redefining "Aid" in the China-Africa Context. *Development and Change, 41*(5), 857–881. https://doi.org/10.1111/j.1467-7660.2010.01662.x
Tarzi, S. M. (2003). International Regimes and International Relations Theory: Search for Synthesis. *International Studies, 40*(1), 23–39. https://doi.org/10.1177/002088170304000102
Teece, D. J. (1981). The Market for Know-How and the Efficient International Transfer of Technology. *The ANNALS of the American Academy of Political and Social Science, 458*(1), 81–96. https://doi.org/10.1177/000271628145800107
Teece, D. J. (1986). Transactions Cost Economics and the Multinational Enterprise An Assessment. *Journal of Economic Behavior & Organization, 7*(1), 21–45. https://doi.org/10.1016/0167-2681(86)90020-x
Teece, D. J. (2008). The Multinational Enterprise: Market Failure and Market Power Considerations. In *The Transfer and Licensing of Know-How and Intellectual Property* (pp. 405–419). World Scientific Publishing. https://doi.org/10.1142/9789812833181_0018
The Belt and Road Portal. (2019, November 2). Why is the Deep-Water Port Project in Nigeria so Important, with Financing from Chinese Companies and Participation from French Companies?. https://www.investgo.cn/article/yw/tzyj/201911/467566.html
The European Commission. (2017, May 19). Mergers: The Commission Clears the Takeover of the Areva Group's Nuclear Reactors Business by EDF. https://ec.europa.eu/commission/presscorner/detail/en/IP_17_1466
The Guardian. (2019). TICT Invests N70bn in Ports Infrastructure. The Guardian Nigeria News. https://guardian.ng/business-services/maritime/tict-invests-n70bn-in-ports-infrastructure/
The Morning. (2020, October 25). Debt Trap: Made in China or Made in Sri Lanka? Latest in the News Sphere; Liberty Publishers. https://www.themorning.lk/articles/102539
The Nation. (2018, August 7). Corporate Giants Jockey to form Alliances for High-Speed Rail Bid. https://www.nationthailand.com/Corporate/30351673

The Russian Government. (2021). The Long-Term Plan for the Development of Liquefied Natural Gas Production in the Russian Federation. http://static.government.ru/media/files/l6DePkb3cDKTgzxbb6sdFc2npEPAd7SE.pdf

The World Bank. (2017, June 16). Container Terminals Concessions—Making the Most of Ports in West Africa. https://documents1.worldbank.org/curated/en/919071469608006706/pdf/Container-Terminals-Concessions-Making-the-Most-of-Ports-in-West-Africa.pdf

Theys, C., Notteboom, T. E., Pallis, A. A., & De Langen, P. W. (2010). The Economics Behind the Awarding of Terminals in Seaports: Towards a Research Agenda. *Research in Transportation Economics, 27*(1), 37–50. https://doi.org/10.1016/j.retrec.2009.12.006

ThisDay. (2016). Lekki Deep Seaport Promoters Jittery over FG Disinvestment Plans. THISDAYLIVE. https://www.thisdaylive.com/index.php/2016/12/31/lekki-deep-seaport-promoters-jittery-over-fg-disinvestment-plans/

Thomas, E. (2023, April 3). Workers Protest as MSC Group Completes Acquisition of Bollore Africa Logistics—Starconnect Media. Starconnect Media. https://starconnectmedia.com/2023/04/workers-protest-as-msc-group-completes-acquisition-of-bollore-africa-logistics/

Thomas, N., & White, S. (2023, February 17). EDF Faces Shouldering More of Soaring Bill for Hinkley Point. *Financial Times*. https://www.ft.com/content/ae5fb399-08ce-4045-bb70-45a6531ac5f2

Thompson, G. (Ed.). (1991). *Markets, Hierarchies, and Networks: The Coordination of Social Life*. Sage Publications.

Thompson, R. S. (1985). Risk Reduction and International Diversification: An Analysis of Large UK Multinational Companies. *Applied Economics, 17*(3), 529–541. https://doi.org/10.1080/00036848500000055

Thomson, A. (2016, March 17). French Government Pledges Support to EDF "If Needed." *Financial Times*. https://www.ft.com/content/cde46a9f-40c0-3334-92ea-d56cf882e567

Tian, A. (2016, April 29). Visit Yamal LNG Project: The two Heaviest Core Modules of the Project have been Successfully. *China Daily*. http://caijing.chinadaily.com.cn/2016-04/29/content_24965623.htm

Tinsley, R. (2014). *Advanced Project Financing: Structuring Risk*. Euromoney Books

Tjønneland, E. (2008). Norwegian Aid and Triangular South-South Cooperation—Mapping, analysis and implications for Norwegian knowledge transfer. Oslo: Norad (Discussion Paper, Norad Report). https://www.norad.no/en/toolspublications/publications/2019/norwegian-aid-and-triangular-south-south-cooperation/

Tomotaka, S. (2020). "Belt and Road" vs. "Free and Open Indo-Pacific": Competition over Regional Order and ASEAN's Responses*. *NIDS Journal* *of Defense and Security, 22*(2) https://www.nids.mod.go.jp/english/publication/security/pdf/2021/01/04.pdf

Topping, A. (2016, September 15). Your Guide to Hinkley Point C—the UK's First New Nuclear Plant for 20 years. *The Guardian.* https://www.theguardian.com/uk-news/2016/sep/15/hinkley-point-c-guide-uk-first-new-nuclear-plant-for-20-years

Torres, L. (2016, July 28). Hinkley Point C Timeline: All the Key Moments. *The Guardian.* https://www.theguardian.com/environment/2016/jul/28/hinkley-point-c-timeline-all-the-key-moments

TotalEnergies. (2022a, August 24). No, TotalEnergies Does Not Produce Kerosene for the Russian Army. TotalEnergies.com. https://totalenergies.com/media/news/press-releases/no-totalenergies-does-not-produce-kerosene-russian-army

TotalEnergies. (2022b, September 12). Russia: TotalEnergies Decides to Withdraw its Directors from Novatek and will no Longer Equity Account for its Stake in Novatek and Record a 3.7 b$ Impairment in Q4. TotalEnergies.com. https://totalenergies.com/media/news/press-releases/russia-totalenergies-decides-withdraw-its-directors-novatek-and-will-no

Toyne, B. (1989). International Exchange: A Foundation for Theory Building in International Business. *Journal of International Business Studies, 20*(1), 1–17. https://doi.org/10.1057/palgrave.jibs.8490348

Trivedi, P. (1990). Lack of Understanding on Memorandum of Understanding. *Economic and Political Weekly, 25*(47), M175–M182. https://www.jstor.org/stable/4397025

Tseng, H.-K., & Krog, R. (2016). No Strings Attached: Chinese Foreign Aid and Regime Stability in Resource-Rich Recipient Countries. https://api.semanticscholar.org/CorpusID:53312

Tsurumi, Y. (1976). *The Japanese are Coming.* Ballinger Publishing Company.

Tull, D. (2023). France's Africa policy under president Macron: Good intentions, partial reform and the fiasco in the Sahel. SWP Comments; Stiftung Wissenschaft und Politik (SWP), German Institute for International and Security Affairs. https://ideas.repec.org/p/zbw/swpcom/279945.html

UK GOV. (2016). Hinkley Point C: Value for Money Assessment. Department for Energy Security and Net Zero and Department for Business, Energy & Industrial Strategy. https://assets.publishing.service.gov.uk/media/5a8226f8ed915d74e6236106/Detailed_value_for_money_assessment.pdf

UK government. (2022, November 29). UK Government Takes Major Steps Forward to Secure Britain's Energy Independence. *GOV.UK.* https://www.gov.uk/government/news/uk-government-takes-major-steps-forward-to-secure-britains-energy-independence

Umirdinov, A. (2019). Generating a Reform of the BRI from the Inside: Japan's Contribution via Soft Law Diplomacy. Discussion Papers, Research Institute

of Economy, Trade and Industry, 19076. https://ideas.repec.org/p/eti/dpaper/19076.html
UN. (2019, April 8). Buenos Aires Outcome Document of the 2nd High-Level United Nations Conference on South-South Cooperation. https://digitallibrary.un.org/record/3799433
UNCTAD. (1998). Guidelines for Port Authorities and Governments on the Privatization of Port Facilities. https://unctad.org/system/files/official-document/posdtetibd1.pdf
UNDP. (2009). Enhancing South–South and Triangular Cooperation. Study of the Current Situation and Existing Good Practices in Policy, Institutions, and Operation of South–South and Triangular Cooperation. https://www.cbd.int/financial/southsouth/undp-casebook.pdf
UNDP. (2017a). South-South Cooperation in Sub-Saharan Africa: Strategies for UNDP Engagement. UNDP. https://www.africa.undp.org/content/rba/en/home/library/reports/south-south-cooperation-in-sub-saharan-africa0.html
UNDP. (2017b). Trilateral Cooperation with China: Discussion Paper Sharing China's Development Experience Through Innovative Partnerships. https://www.undp.org/china/publications/trilateral-cooperation-china
UNECE. (2012). Can public-private Partnerships Improve Infrastructure and Deliver Better Public Services? United Nations Economic Commission for Europe. https://unece.org/DAM/ceci/images/ICoE/Introductionpp.pdf
UNECOSOC. (2008). Background Study for the Development Cooperation Forum: Trends in South-South and Triangular Development Cooperation. United Nations Economic and Social Council. https://www.iukdpf.com/background-study-for-the-development-cooperation-forum-trends-in-south-south-and-triangular-development-cooperation/
United Nation. (2009). Nairobi Outcome Document of the High-level United Nations Conference on South-South Cooperation. Undocs.org. https://undocs.org/A/RES/64/222
United Nation. (2018). Role of South-South Cooperation and the Implementation of the 2030 Agenda for Sustainable Development: Challenges and opportunities—Report of the Secretary-General. http://www.un.org/ga/search/view_doc.asp?symbol=A/73/383
United Nation. (2019). Buenos Aires outcome Document of the Second High-level United Nations Conference on South-South Cooperation. https://undocs.org/en/A/73/L.80
United Nations. (2003, March 17). Revised Guidelines for the Review of Policies and Procedures Concerning Technical Cooperation Among Developing Countries. *United Nations Office of South-South and Triangular Cooperation.* https://documents.un.org/doc/undoc/gen/n03/285/18/pdf/n0328518.pdf?token=ZUgSPGo5xkYDD8mNkc&fe=true

United Nations. (2015). Closing the Infrastructure Gap. Developmentfinance.un.org. https://developmentfinance.un.org/closing-the-infrastructure-gap

Van Evera, S. (1997). *Guide to Methods for Students of Political Science*. Cornell University Press.

Van Niekerk, H. C. (2005). Port Reform and Concessioning in Developing Countries. *Maritime Economics & Logistics*, *7*(2), 141–155. https://doi.org/10.1057/palgrave.mel.9100129

Vanelslander, T. (2005). The Economics Behind Co-operation and Competition in Sea-port Container Handling. In www.proquest.com. https://www.proquest.com/docview/305351367?pq-origsite=gscholar&fromopenview=true&sourcetype=Dissertations%20&%20Theses

Vanguard. (2022, July 29). Lekki Deep Sea Port: NPA Gets Approval for Designation as Customs Port, approved Wharf. https://www.vanguardngr.com/2022/07/lekki-deep-sea-port-npa-gets-approval-for-designation-as-customs-port-approved-wharf/

Vaughan, A. (2017a, January 27). Brexit will Delay New British Nuclear Power Stations, Warn Experts. The Guardian. https://www.theguardian.com/business/2017/jan/27/uk-exit-eu-atomic-treaty-brexit-euratom-hinkley-point-c

Vaughan, A. (2017b, March 25). Foreign Companies Flock to Build Nuclear Plants in the UK. The Observer. https://www.theguardian.com/business/2017/mar/25/foreign-firms-flock-to-build-nuclear-plants-in-uk

Vaughan, A. (2017c, June 22). Spending Watchdog Condemns "Risky and Expensive" Hinkley Point. The Guardian. https://www.theguardian.com/uk-news/2017/jun/23/spending-watchdog-condemns-risky-expensive-hinkley-point-c-nuclear

Vaughan, A. (2017d, July 3). Hinkley Point C is £1.5bn Over Budget and a Year Behind Schedule, EDF Admits. The Guardian. https://www.theguardian.com/uk-news/2017/jul/03/hinkley-point-c-is-22bn-over-budget-and-a-year-behind-schedule-edf-admits

Vaughan, A. (2018a, March 25). Nuclear Watchdog Raises Hinkley Point C Concerns. The Guardian. https://www.theguardian.com/uk-news/2018/mar/25/nuclear-watchdog-raises-hinkley-point-c-concerns

Vaughan, A. (2018b, November 8). UK Nuclear Power Station Plans Scrapped as Toshiba Pulls Out. The Guardian. https://www.theguardian.com/environment/2018/nov/08/toshiba-uk-nuclear-power-plant-project-nu-gen-cumbria

Vaughan, A., & Kuo, L. (2018, July 26). China's Long Game to Dominate Nuclear Power Relies on the UK. *The Guardian*. https://www.theguardian.com/environment/2018/jul/26/chinas-long-game-to-dominate-nuclear-power-relies-on-the-uk

Verbeke, A., & Kano, L. (2015). The New Internalisation Theory and Multinational Enterprises from Emerging Economies: A Business History Perspective. *Business History Review, 89*(03), 415–445. https://doi.org/10.1017/s0007680515000689

Verhoeven, P. (2010). A Review of Port Authority Functions: Towards a Renaissance? *Maritime Policy & Management, 37*(3), 247–270. https://doi.org/10.1080/03088831003700645

Vetschera, R. (2009). Learning about Preferences in Electronic Negotiations—A Volume-Based Measurement Method. *European Journal of Operational Research, 194*(2), 452–463. https://doi.org/10.1016/j.ejor.2007.12.016

Visión 360. (2017, September 4). Refinería en polvo [Video]. YouTube. https://www.youtube.com/watch?v=I15PLiHJ28c&ab_channel=Vision360

Waitzman, E. (2023, October 3). UK: Long-term Strategic Challenges Posed by China. UK Parliament, House of Lords Library. https://lordslibrary.parliament.uk/uk-long-term-strategic-challenges-posed-by-china/

Walker, P. (2016, July 28). EDF Set to Give Green Light to Hinkley Point Nuclear Project. *The Guardian*. https://www.theguardian.com/uk-news/2016/jul/28/edf-to-give-green-light-to-hinkley-point-project

Wall, A., & Connolly, C. (2009). The Private Finance Initiative. *Public Management Review, 11*(5), 707–724. https://doi.org/10.1080/14719030902798172

Wallace, C. (2019). Japan's Strategic Contrast: Continuing Influence Despite Relative Power Decline in Southeast Asia. *The Pacific Review, 32*(5), 1–35. https://doi.org/10.1080/09512748.2019.1569115

Walt, S. M. (1987). *The Origins of Alliances.* Cornell University Press.

Waltz, K. (1979). *Theory of International Politics.* Addison-Wesley Publishing Company.

Wan, J., & Wang, Y. (2020). *Tripartite Cooperation and Triple Win.* Chinese Foreign Currency.

Wan, J., & Wang, Y. (2021). Progress, Challenges, and Countermeasures of Third Party Market Cooperation. HKTDC Research. https://research.hktdc.com/sc/article/NzMyNzE1NjAw

Wang, H., Sexton, M., & Lu, S.-L. (2016). Investment by Chinese Construction firms in the UK Infrastructure Sector: Volumes, Patterns and Trends. Centaur.reading.ac.uk. http://centaur.reading.ac.uk/67075/

Wang, H., Xiong, W., Wu, G., & Zhu, D. (2017). Public–Private Partnership in Public Administration Discipline: A Literature Review. *Public Management Review, 20*(2), 293–316. https://doi.org/10.1080/14719037.2017.1313445

Wang, J., Mirsardin, I., Sun, Y., & Yang, X. (2021). The Internationalisation of Chinese Multinational Enterprises Under the Belt-and-Road Initiative. *Strategic Change, 30*(6), 509–515. https://doi.org/10.1002/jsc.2467

Wang, J., & Sampson, M. (2021). Development Finance: A New Model? Chatham House—International Affairs Think Tank. https://www.chathamhouse.org/2021/12/chinas-approach-global-economic-governance/development-finance-new-model

Wang, S. L., Luo, Y., Lu, X., Sun, J., & Maksimov, V. (2013). Autonomy Delegation to Foreign Subsidiaries: An Enabling Mechanism for Emerging-Market Multinationals. *Journal of International Business Studies, 45*(2), 111–130. https://doi.org/10.1057/jibs.2013.40

Wang, X., Wang, S., & Gao, Y. (2023). Optimal Equity Structure of PPP Projects when Private-Sector Shareholders' "Investor-Contractor" Dual Roles is Considered. *Construction Management & Economics, 41*(11–12), 910–925. https://doi.org/10.1080/01446193.2023.2216319

Wang, Y. (2015). The Rise of the "Shareholding State": Financialisation of Economic Management in China. *Socio-Economic Review, 13*(3), 603–625. https://doi.org/10.1093/ser/mwv016

Wang, Y. (2019, September 20). Port Portal for Sino-African pragmatic cooperation. *China Daily*. https://www.chinadaily.com.cn/global/2019-09/20/content_37511188.htm

Wang, Y. (2020). Financialisation and State Transformations. In P. Mader, D. Mertens, & N. van der Zwan (Eds.), *The Routledge International handbook of Financialisation* (pp. 188–199). Taylor & Francis. https://doi.org/10.4324/9781315142876

Ward, A., Pickard, J., & Stothard, M. (2016, September 15). UK Gives Go-ahead for "Revised" £18bn Hinkley Point Plant. *Financial Times*. https://www.ft.com/content/466704e6-7a4b-11e6-b837-eb4b4333ee43

Washington State Development. (2019). WA-State Contract Management Manual. https://des.wa.gov/sites/default/files/2022-06/CMmanual.pdf

Waterson, M. (1987). Recent Developments in the Theory of Natural Monopoly. *Journal of Economic Surveys, 1*(1–2), 59–80. https://doi.org/10.1111/j.1467-6419.1987.tb00024.x

Watt, H. (2017, December 21). Hinkley Point: the "Dreadful Deal" Behind the World's Most Expensive Power plant. *The Guardian*. https://www.theguardian.com/news/2017/dec/21/hinkley-point-c-dreadful-deal-behind-worlds-most-expensive-power-plant

Wei, Y. (2007). Factors Influencing the Success of Virtual Cooperation within Dutch-Chinese Strategic Alliances. [PhD Thesis - Research UT, graduation UT, University of Twente]. University of Twente. https://doi.org/10.3990/1.9789036521628

Wei, T., Clegg, J., & Ma, L. (2015). The Conscious and Unconscious Facilitating Role of the Chinese Government in Shaping the Internationalisation of Chinese MNCs. *International Business Review, 24*(2), 331–343. https://doi.org/10.1016/j.ibusrev.2014.08.008

Wendt, A. (1992). Anarchy is what States Make of it: The Social Construction of Power Politics. *International Organization, 46*(02), 391–425.
Wendt, A. (1999). *Social Theory of International Politics.* Cambridge University Press.
Wernerfelt, B. (1984). A Resource-Based View of the Firm. *Strategic Management Journal, 5*(2), 171–180. https://www.jstor.org/stable/2486175
Wesson, T. (2009). A Model of Asset-Seeking Foreign Direct Investment Driven by Demand Conditions. *Canadian Journal of Administrative Sciences / Revue Canadienne Des Sciences de L'Administration, 16*(1), 1–10. https://doi.org/10.1111/j.1936-4490.1999.tb00183.x
White, S. (2024, February 16). EDF Confident of UK Compromise as it Reveals €12.9bn Hinkley Point Hit. *Financial Times.* https://www.ft.com/content/ca24da3e-6db8-40ca-b99a-a1e7f190cc1a
Whitfield, D., & Smyth, S. (2019). Infrastructure Investment—The Emergent PPP Equity Market. *Annals of Public and Cooperative Economics, 90*(2), 291–309. https://doi.org/10.1111/apce.12234
Wild, P. (2017). Determining Commercially Viable two-way and One-way "Contract-for-Difference" Strike Prices and Revenue Receipts. *Energy Policy, 110*, 191–201. https://doi.org/10.1016/j.enpol.2017.08.020
Wilkinson, B. W., & Kindleberger, C. P. (1969). American Business Abroad: Six Lectures on Direct Investment. *The Canadian Journal of Economics, 2*(4), 630. https://doi.org/10.2307/133853
Williamson, O. E. (1971). The Vertical Integration of Production: Market Failure Considerations. *The American Economic Review, 61*(2), 112–123. https://www.jstor.org/stable/1816983
Williamson, O. E. (1975). *Markets and Hierarchies: Analysis and Antitrust Implications.* Free Press.
Williamson, O. E. (1976). Franchise Bidding for Natural Monopolies—in General and with Respect to CATV. *Bell Journal of Economics, 7*(1), 73–104. https://econpapers.repec.org/article/rjebellje/v_3a7_3ay_3a1976_3ai_3aspring_3ap_3a73-104.htm
Williamson, O. E. (1983). Credible Commitments: Using Hostages to Support Exchange. *The American Economic Review, 73*(4), 519–540. https://www.jstor.org/stable/1816557
Williamson, O. E. (1986). *Economic Organization.* New York University Press.
Williamson, O. E. (1992). Markets, Hierarchies, and the Modern Corporation. *Journal of Economic Behavior & Organization, 17*(3), 335–352. https://doi.org/10.1016/s0167-2681(95)90012-8
Williamson, O. E. (1995). Hierarchies, Markets and Power in the Economy: An Economic Perspective. *Industrial and Corporate Change, 4*(1), 21–49. https://doi.org/10.1093/icc/4.1.21
Williamson, O. E. (1996). *The Mechanisms of governance.* Oxford University Press.

Williamson, O. E. (2008). Transaction Cost Economics: The Precursors. *Economic Affairs, 28*(3), 7–14. https://doi.org/10.1111/j.1468-0270.2008.00838.x

Williamson, O. E., & Winter, S. G. (Eds.). (1993). *The Nature of the Firm: Origins, Evolution and Development.* Oxford University Press.

Winning International Group. (2018, June 26). The Messenger of Hope for the "Land of Red Soil"—A Documentary of Winning Alliance's Guinea Bauxite Project Development. https://www.winninggroup.com.sg/cn/1364.html

Wintour, P. (2013, October 21). David Cameron Hails Nuclear Power Plant Deal as Big Day for Britain. *The Guardian.* https://www.theguardian.com/environment/2013/oct/21/britain-nuclear-power-station-hinkley-edf

Woetzel, J., Garemo, N., Mischke, J., Kamra, P., & Palter, R. (2017). Bridging Infrastructure Gaps: Has the World Made Progress? Www.mckinsey.com. https://www.mckinsey.com/capabilities/operations/our-insights/bridging-infrastructure-gaps-has-the-world-made-progress

Woods, N. (2008). Whose Aid? Whose Influence? China, Emerging Donors and the Silent Revolution in Development Assistance. *International Affairs (Royal Institute of International Affairs 1944-), 84*(6), 1205–1221. https://www.jstor.org/stable/25144989

Workshop on Triangular Cooperation: Opportunity for Shared Responsibility in Africa. (2009). Heiligendamm Process. https://paperzz.com/doc/7128750/win-win-win-situation

World Bank. (2007). PUBLIC-PRIVATE-PARTNERSHIP LEGAL RESOURCE CENTER. https://pp.worldbank.org/public-private-partnership/library/power-purchase-agreement-ppa-emergency-power-mobile-plant

World Bank. (2012). Public-Private Partnerships: Reference Guide Version 1.0. https://openknowledge.worldbank.org/handle/10986/16055

World Bank. (2017). Bank Policy Development Policy Financing. https://thedocs.worldbank.org/en/doc/b07a01de330e0775384b66b21e54b103-0290012023/original/Bank-Policy-Development-pol-fin.pdf

World Population Review. (2021). Afghanistan Population 2020 (Demographics, Maps, Graphs). Worldpopulationreview.com. https://worldpopulationreview.com/countries/afghanistan-population

Wu, B., & Ding, M. (2020). Third Party Market Cooperation Between China and South Korea: Progress, Resistance, and Countermeasures. *Northeast Asia Forum, 29*(3), 75–89+128. https://doi.org/10.13654/j.cnki.naf.2020.03.006

Wu, C., Xu, L., & Xin, Y. (2023). The State Capital Investing and Operating Company Pilot Reform and SOE Bailouts. *China Journal of Accounting Research, 16*(2), 100302. https://doi.org/10.1016/j.cjar.2023.100302

Wu, J., & Chen, X. (2014). Home Country Institutional Environments and Foreign Expansion of Emerging Market Firms. *International Business Review, 23*(5), 862–872. https://doi.org/10.1016/j.ibusrev.2014.01.004

Xan, R. (2010, May 6). Ethiopia's Push for Mega-Dams. *China Dialogue*. https://chinadialogue.net/en/energy/3602-ethiopia-s-push-for-mega-dams/

Xie, W. (2016, November 1). Revealing the Entire Process of Signing a Nuclear Power Project Agreement Between China, Britain, and France: Over 3000 Pages of Text. *China Economic Weekly*. https://news.sina.cn/gn/2016-11-01/detail-ifxxfuff7411509.d.html?from=wap

Xinhua News. (2015, December 11). Coopération sino-française sur l'exploitation de l'énergie propre en Afrique_French.news.cn. http://french.xinhuanet.com/2015-12/11/c_134906950.htm

Xinhua News Agency. (2020). China to Boost Construction of New Infrastructure, Advance Industrial and Consumption Upgrade. Xinhua News Agency—CEIS. https://www.proquest.com/wire-feeds/china-boost-construction-new-infrastructure/docview/2395234857/se-2

Xiong, L. (2022). Third Party Market Cooperation Under the "the Belt and Road" Initiative. *Frontiers, 21*, 56–65+75. https://doi.org/10.16619/j.cnki.rmltxsqy.2022.21.007

Xu, D., & Meyer, K. E. (2012). Linking Theory and Context: "Strategy Research in Emerging Economies" after Wright et al. (2005). *Journal of Management Studies, 50*(7), 1322–1346. https://doi.org/10.1111/j.1467-6486.2012.01051.x

Xu, J., Ru, X., & Song, P. (2021). Can a New Model of Infrastructure Financing Mitigate Credit Rationing in Poorly Governed Countries? *Economic Modelling, 95*, 111–120. https://doi.org/10.1016/j.econmod.2020.12.001

Xu, Y., Yeung, J. F. Y., Chan, A. P. C., Chan, D. W. M., Wang, S. Q., & Ke, Y. (2010). Developing a Risk Assessment Model for PPP Projects in China—A Fuzzy Synthetic Evaluation Approach. *Automation in Construction, 19*(7), 929–943. https://doi.org/10.1016/j.autcon.2010.06.006

Yamal LNG. (2014a, March 6). Intergovernmental Agreement Regarding Cooperation on The Yamal LNG Project Enacted. http://yamallng.ru/en/press/news/207/

Yamal LNG. (2014b, May 20). Memorandum on Project Financing for the Yamal LNG project. http://yamallng.ru/en/press/news/281/

Yamal LNG. (2021). About the Project. http://yamallng.ru/en/

Yan, D., & Warner, M. (2001). Research Papers In Management Studies "Sino-Foreign Joint Ventures" Versus "Wholly Foreign Owned Enterprises" In The People's Republic Of China. https://www.jbs.cam.ac.uk/wp-content/uploads/2020/08/wp0111-1.pdf

Yang, H. (2020, February 6). "Three Party Win-win" in Third-party Market Cooperation. *China Investment*. https://m.thepaper.cn/newsDetail_forward_5833859

Yang, J. Y., Li, J., & Delios, A. (2015). Will a Second Mouse Get the Cheese? Learning from Early Entrants' Failures in a Foreign Market. *Organization Science, 26*(3), 908–922. https://doi.org/10.1287/orsc.2015.0967

Yang, X. (2018, April 14). Exclusive Interview: "The Belt and Road" Cooperation Enables China, France and Britain to Achieve "Three wins"—Interview with Zheng Dongshan, General Manager of CGN UK. *Xinhua News Agency*. http://www.xinhuanet.com/world/2019-04/24/c_1124409411.htm

Yang, X., & Stoltenberg, D. C. (2014). A Review of Institutional Influences on the Rise of Made-in-China Multinationals. *International Journal of Emerging Markets, 9*(2), 162–180. https://doi.org/10.1108/ijoem-09-2012-0095

Yang, Y., & An, R. (2019, March 26). Deepening third-Party Market Cooperation and Opening up New Space for Sino French Cooperation. *China Development Institution*. http://www.cdi.com.cn/Article/Detail?Id=13249

Yin, R. K. (2018). *Case Study Research and Applications: Design and Methods* (6th ed.). Sage Publications.

Yoshimatsu, H. (1998). Japan's Keidanren and Political Influence on Market Liberalisation. *Asian Survey, 38*(3), 328–345. https://doi.org/10.2307/2645431

Youngs, R. (2008). Trends in Democracy Assistance: What Has Europe Been Doing? *Journal of Democracy, 19*(2), 160–169. https://www.journalofdemocracy.org/articles/trends-in-democracy-assistance-what-has-europe-been-doing/

Yu, P. (2021, March 31). Myanmar–China Oil and Gas Pipelines. *The People's Map of Global China*. https://thepeoplesmap.net/project/myanmar-china-oil-and-gas-pipelines/

Yu, R. (2023, December 10). "Five Links+Cooperation in New Fields" Becomes a Key Field of Jointly Building the *"The Belt and Road" in the Next Decade*. https://www.yidaiyilu.gov.cn/p/0JR970E1.html

Zajac, E., & Olsen, C. P. (1993). From Transaction Cost to Transactional Value Analysis: Implications for the Study of Interorganizational Strategies. *Journal of Management Studies, 30*(1), 131–145. https://doi.org/10.1111/J.1467-6486.1993.TB00298.X

Zelikow, D., & Savas, F. (2022). Mind the Gap: Time to Rethink Infrastructure Finance. Blogs.worldbank.org. https://blogs.worldbank.org/ppps/mind-gap-time-rethink-infrastructure-finance

Zeng, M., & Williamson, P. J. (2007). *Dragons at your Door: How Chinese Cost Innovation is Disrupting Global Competition*. Harvard Business School Press.

Zhang, D. (2017a). *A Promising New Trend? Factors Driving Chinas Growing Trilateral Aid Cooperation [Doctoral Dissertation]*. Australian National University (ANU) Press.

Zhang, D. (2017b). Why Cooperate with Others? Demystifying China's Trilateral aid Cooperation. *The Pacific Review, 30*(5), 750–768. https://doi.org/10.1080/09512748.2017.1296886

Zhang, D. (2018). A Tango by two Superpowers: China-US Cooperation in Trilateral Aid and Implications for Their Bilateral Relations. *Asian Journal of Political Science, 26*(2), 181–200. https://doi.org/10.1080/02185377.2018.1462218

Zhang, D. (2022, November 23). China, France Launches First Third-Party Market Cooperation on Sewage Treatment in Senegal. ECNS. https://www.ecns.cn/cns-wire/2022-11-23/detail-ihchchpu5657009.shtml

Zhang, D., & Smith, G. (2017). China's Foreign Aid System: Structure, Agencies, and Identities. *Third World Quarterly, 38*(10), 2330–2346. https://doi.org/10.1080/01436597.2017.1333419

Zhang, F., & Li, H. (2020). Third Party Market Cooperation: A new Model of International Cooperation Under the "The Belt and Road" Initiative—based on the Analysis of the Third Party Market Cooperation Between China and France. *International Economic Cooperation, 02*, 26–33.

Zhang, H. (2023). From Contractors to Investors? Evolving Engagement of Chinese State Capital in Global Infrastructure Development and the case of Lekki Port in Nigeria. https://www.econstor.eu/bitstream/10419/268858/1/1837167907.pdf

Zhang, H., & Wang, J. (2021). Entry Mode Choices and Overseas Business Performance: Evidence from the Chinese Multinational Enterprises. *Strategic Change, 30*(6), 517–525. https://doi.org/10.1002/jsc.2473

Zhang, J., Liu, G., & Gao, R. (2019, May 15). Inspiration from the Successful Operation of Yamal Natural Gas Project. *China National Petroleum Corporation*. https://news.cnpc.com.cn/system/2019/05/14/001729899.shtml

Zhang, S., Chan, A. P. C., Feng, Y., Duan, H., & Ke, Y. (2016). Critical Review on PPP Research—A Search from the Chinese and International Journals. *International Journal of Project Management, 34*(4), 597–612. https://doi.org/10.1016/j.ijproman.2016.02.008

Zhang, Y. (2020). Third-Party Market Cooperation Under the Belt and Road Initiative: Progress, Challenges, and Recommendations. *China International Strategy Review, 1*, 310–329. https://doi.org/10.1007/s42533-019-00026-7

Zhao, J., & Jing, Y. (2019). The Governance of China's Foreign Aid System: Evolution and Path Dependence. *Public Administration and Development, 39*(4–5), 182–192. https://doi.org/10.1002/pad.1870

Zhao, X. (2014, July 21). Former Chairman of China South Locomotive&Rolling Stock Corporation (CSR) Stated in Person about the Cooperation with Siemens. *China's Electromechanical Industry*. http://finance.sina.com.cn/zl/energy/20140721/145719772488.shtml

Zheng, C. (2020). *Zhong Ou Di San Fang Shi Chang He Zuo Mian Lin De Ji Yu He Tiao Zhan (Opportunities and Chanlleages in China-Europe Tripartite Cooperation)*. World Knowledge.

Zhou, M. (2020). Third Party Market Cooperation: The Three Optimal Choices after Resource Collaboration and Integration. *International Project Monitor, 16*, 4–10. https://www.chinca.org/CICA/info/20102609570411

Zhou, S. (2019, April 16). Win Cooperation and Borderless Construction of the "The Belt and Road". https://www.ey.com/zh_cn/china-overseas-investment-network/borderless-win-win-cooperation-in-building-the-belt-and-road

Zhu, Y. (2020). Third Party Market Cooperation: Differences in Understanding Between China and Japan and Their Impact. *China International Strategy Review, 2*(1), 110–119. http://www.iiss.pku.edu.cn/fj/PDF/ciss_cn/upload/docs/2020-09-25/doc_7981601047297.pdf

Zimmermann, A. J., & Jauer, N. (2021). Possible Indirect Legal Effects under International Law of Non-Legally Binding Instruments. KFG Working Paper Series, 48. https://papers.ssrn.com/sol3/papers.cfm?abstract_id=3840767

FSC
www.fsc.org
MIX
Papier | Fördert
gute Waldnutzung
FSC® C083411

Kolibri 360 GmbH
Ferdinand-Jühlke-Straße 7
99095 Erfurt, Deutschland
produktsicherheit@kolibri360.de